The UCAS Guide to getting into

ENGINEERING AND
MATHEMATICS

For entry to university and college in 2013

Published by: UCAS Rosehill New Barn Lane Cheltenham GL52 3LZ

Produced in conjunction with GTI Media Ltd

© UCAS 2012

UCAS, a company limited by guarantee, is registered in England and Wales number: 2839815
Registered charity number: 1024741 (England and Wales) and SC038598 (Scotland)

UCAS reference number: PU033013
Publication reference: 12_044
ISBN: 978-1-908077-18-9
Price £15.99

Further copies available from UCAS (p&p charges apply):

contact Publication Services PO Box 130 Cheltenham GL52 3ZF

email: publicationservices@ucas.ac.uk or fax: 01242 544806.

For further information about the UCAS application process go to www.ucas.com.

If you need to contact us, details can be found at www.ucas.com/about_us/contact_us.

UCAS QUALITY AWARDS

CONTENTS

Foreword

**THINKING ABOUT ENGINEERING
OR MATHEMATICS?**

Finding the course that's right for you at the right university or college can take time and it's important that you use all the resources available to you in making this key decision. We at UCAS have teamed up with TARGETjobs.co.uk to provide you with the *UCAS Guide to getting into Engineering and Mathematics* to show you how you can progress from being a student to careers in engineering and mathematics. You will find information on what the subject includes, entry routes and real-life case studies showing how it worked out for others.

Once you know which subject area you might be interested in, you can use the listings of all the full-time higher education courses in engineering and mathematics to see where you can study your subject. The course entry requirements are listed so you can check if getting in would be achievable for you. There's also advice on applying through UCAS, telling you what you need to know at each stage of the application process in just six easy steps to starting university or college.

We hope you find this publication helps you to choose and make your application to a course and university or college that is right for you.

On behalf of UCAS and TARGETjobs.co.uk, I wish you every success in your research.

Mary Curnock Cook, Chief Executive, UCAS

At TARGETjobs we champion paid work experience for UK university students. Find internships and placements across all sectors, plus take part in the TARGETjobs Undergraduate of the Year awards.

TARGETjobs.co.uk

the best possible start to your career

Introducing
engineering

It could be you...

... designing cutting-edge gadgets — engineering design

... creating cleaner, sustainable power — energy conservation

... designing the cities of the future — civil engineering

... creating new and better cars — mechanical engineering

... designing sports kit and technology — sports engineering

... designing forestry machinery — agricultural engineering

... an engineering degree could give you the know-how to create special effects for blockbuster movies (CGI scripting), make high-quality sound recordings for the entertainment industry (sound engineering) and maintain communications networks (satellite technician).

A CAREER IN ENGINEERING?

In 2010–2011*:

- Engineering or industrial jobs were predicted to make up over 6.0% of graduate jobs by sector among AGR (Association of Graduate Recruiters) employers.
- For every graduate vacancy in the engineering and industrial sector, 46 applications were received.
- The median predicted starting salary for graduates in engineering or industrial companies was £24,500 for 2010–2011 – a rise of 2.0% over the previous year.
- The median predicted starting salary for graduates employed in manufacturing engineering roles was £26,500.

*Source: *The AGR Graduate Recruitment Survey 2011, Summer Review*

ENGINEERING IN CONTEXT

A career in engineering is one with almost limitless possibilities. Just about everything that wasn't made by nature was created by engineers: the car you drive, the house you live in, the aircraft that takes you on holiday or the airport that you land at when you arrive, they were all designed, created and maintained by engineers. Most of the world's problems, from global warming through to natural disasters, will be solved or dealt with by engineers.

This is the age of opportunity for engineers in the UK. Never before have there been as many openings offered by new technologies, or the amount of need created by the challenges we face. The need for clean energy and environmentally sustainable manufacturing, travel and housing present the biggest issues facing us in the 21st century, and they're not going to go away without the creative problem-solving skills of engineers.

YOUR PART IN ENGINEERING

Are you good at problem solving? Are you analytical? Are you good at working in groups? Great. How about turning these skills to something really important, groundbreaking and challenging? How about designing the next generation of mobile phones, or the next generation of car? How about finding out new ways to harness energy to power our lives cleanly? Still on board? Welcome to your world of engineering.

Inside this guide you'll find help and guidance to choose the course that's right for you in the institution that suits you best. You'll find examples of the great jobs you can do in engineering, and the people doing them. You'll also find information on how much you can expect to be paid and some of the companies that employ engineers.

Your career starts here, so go on – engineer your future.

Why engineering?

Choose a career that is...

Well paid

According to the Engineering UK 2011 report, while graduates can expect to earn around an extra £160,000 during their working life than people who went into work after A levels, for engineering graduates that figure rises to £243,730. In terms of where engineers currently start off, engineering organisations typically offer graduates between £21,000 and £27,000, comparing favourably with the Association of Graduate Recruiters (AGR) predicted median graduate salary figure of £25,500 for 2010–2011.

Important

The main challenges that we face globally – including clean water, clean energy and sustainable transport – are challenges that engineers can answer.

Cutting edge

Engineering has produced more medical advances than any other discipline, even medical science and healthcare. This includes devices such as pacemakers, electronic stethoscopes and joint replacements. A similar story extends to disciplines such as transport, construction and utilities.

Open to flexible entry

Through flexible entry routes, engineers can enter the profession in many ways. Apprenticeships, for example, offer engineers the opportunity to combine degree-level study with work.

Creative

Many engineers work on projects that need creative thinking both in terms of problem solving and aesthetic design. Think of the London Eye or the 'Gherkin' skyscraper in London.

Open to travel

With so many large-scale international projects needing engineers, a well-qualified engineer has the opportunity to travel the world. You could have a taste of life in other countries with permanent positions abroad, overseas projects or short work trips.

Constantly evolving

Despite the fact that engineering already offers an incredibly diverse career path, this is ever expanding. We're now looking at the beginning of technologies such as biometrics and nanotechnology, and can only imagine what the future might hold.

Cross-sectoral

There are so many options to pursue in engineering that it's almost mind-blowing. The ability to move between these ensures that you will always have new challenges if you want them.

WHAT DO ENGINEERS SAY?

'I find the projects the most interesting and exciting part of my role; they are always different and can require skills never used before. I learn a lot as I go along. The sense of achievement in these situations is why I enjoy it.'
Cheryl Bosworth, project engineer, page 40

'I've always had a keen interest in biology and understanding how things work. I wanted to study something that I felt would allow me to help people in some way and to make a contribution towards something meaningful. The combination of biological and engineering principles within biomedical engineering makes it a practical and interesting degree choice.'
Shaunagh McCurdy, final year biomedical engineering student, page 48

Connect with us...

 www.facebook.com/ucasonline

 www.twitter.com/ucas_online

 www.youtube.com/ucasonline

Introducing
mathematics

$$A_v = \frac{R_1 + R_f}{R_1}$$

$$\frac{10k + 100k\Omega}{10k\Omega} =$$

V_0

It could be you...

... cracking the code in a top-secret lab	– GCHQ
... investing assets worth millions of pounds	– investment banking
... modelling climate change and flood risk	– environmental science
... advising a minister with vital figures for Parliament	– Office for National Statistics (ONS)
... grabbing the headlines with the latest statistical findings	– government statistician
... auditing a high-profile multinational company	– accountancy
... modelling the outbreak of major diseases	– epidemiology

... and lots more besides. Could a degree in mathematics be for you? The aim of this guide is to help you decide.

Why mathematics?

WHY MATHS?

If you've got a flair for logical thought and precision, and are prepared to rise to the mental challenge of understanding problems that have baffled science for hundreds of years, then a degree in mathematics could be for you. Just ask yourself how many job descriptions *don't* mention problem solving?

Mathematicians don't work only in mathematical jobs: any profession that asks you to analyse, assimilate and present information of any sort will welcome mathematicians. Employers include research firms, financial organisations such as banks, insurance, actuarial and accountancy firms, the government, and education institutions.

DEMAND FOR MATHS GRADUATES

A report in 2010 by the Confederation of British Industry (CBI) said that in spite of the recession, 45 percent of employers are having a tough time recruiting staff with STEM skills (science, technology, engineering and maths), and that 59 per cent of employers predict difficulties in finding STEM-skilled employees in the next three years.

Richard Lambert, the CBI's Director-General, said: 'In the future, people with qualifications in science and maths will be particularly sought after.'

WHAT IS MATHEMATICS?

Applied

Mathematics can be used to describe almost everything, and applied mathematics can show you how to model anything from birdsong to bird flu. Anything you can see (and just as many things you can't) has been described mathematically at some time or other.

Pure

Pure mathematics, or 'maths for maths' sake', is the concept of exploring the more abstract topics of mathematics. Advances in cryptography, for example, would not have been made without generations of mathematicians pondering over prime numbers – simply because they were curious about what they might find.

Statistics

Statistics is the area of mathematics that deals with uncertainty and variability and, as the whole world is uncertain and variable, statistics and statisticians are everywhere. Statistics helps us to understand how tall the next Thames Barrier might need to be, work out the likelihood that two DNA samples from a crime scene would match, or help build better and more reliable cars.

If you're interested in learning more about a subject that will give you more options, more valuable skills and more potential earnings then this guide can help you. Read on to discover:

- the degree subject that's right for you
- how to make your application stand out
- the variety of careers that mathematicians follow
- how a mathematical degree can work for you.

THE INSIDE VIEW

'At the end of my second year I spent 12 months with a pharmaceutical company in their statistics department. Not only did I learn what it was like to work in an office, but I also used statistics to investigate how genetic data could be used to treat lung disease.'
Peter Broad, assistant statistician

'Languages and linguistics always interested me at school, and it was a tough choice picking between that area and mathematics. Luckily while studying at university I found a cross-over area in speech and language processing.'
Matt Henderson, PhD student

'It is a pleasure to impart your knowledge to the students, and it is most satisfying to watch students develop an understanding of concepts that they originally had difficulties with.'
Vanessa Styles, senior lecturer, mathematics

WHERE CAN YOU WORK WITH A MATHS DEGREE?

Mathematicians work in a huge number of sectors, including:

Accountancy – eg Grant Thornton, ACCA

Aerospace and defence – eg BAE Systems, QinetiQ, Thales

Automotive – eg Rolls-Royce, Ford

Chemical industry – eg Air Products Europe, Proctor & Gamble

Construction industry – eg Balfour Beatty, Skanska

Consulting – eg Arup Group, ORC International

Education – eg schools, FE colleges, universities, academic research

Engineering – eg Ove Arup, British Energy

Environment sector – eg AEA Technology, Wildfowl and Wetlands Trust (Consulting) Ltd

Financial services – eg Royal Bank of Scotland, Towers Watson

Food and drink – eg Marks & Spencer, Sainsbury

Government – eg Royal Navy, Government Statistical Service

Healthcare – eg Aviva, BUPA

Insurance – eg Legal & General, Pearl Assurance

IT and computing – eg Oracle Corporation, IBM, Fujitsu

Manufacturing – eg Unilever, Siemens

Market research – eg Ipsos MORI

Metals and minerals – eg Corus, Anglo American

Pharmaceuticals – eg Glaxosmithkline, Pfizer

Professional services – eg Towers Watson, PricewaterhouseCooper

Science – eg Johnson Matthey, National Oceanography Centre

Telecoms – eg BT Group, Vodafone

Transport – eg London Underground, Network Rail

Utilities – eg Exxon Mobil Corporation, BP

FOR MORE INFORMATION:

The Institute of Mathematics and its Applications – **www.ima.org.uk**

The Royal Statistical Society – **www.rss.org.uk**

Maths Careers – **www.mathscareers.org.uk**

The London Mathematical Society – **www.lms.ac.uk**

WHAT NEXT?

- A mathematics degree can help you achieve your ambitions. Find out which course is for you on page 67.
- Already convinced? Head straight to page 84 for top tips on **How to apply through UCAS**.
- Find out what graduate mathematicians do in our **Case studies** on page 39.

Focus your career with the TARGETjobs Careers Report. Using biographical data, information about your interests and insightful psychometric testing, the Careers Report gives you a clear picture of jobs that match your skills and personality.

TARGETjobs.co.uk

the best possible start to your career

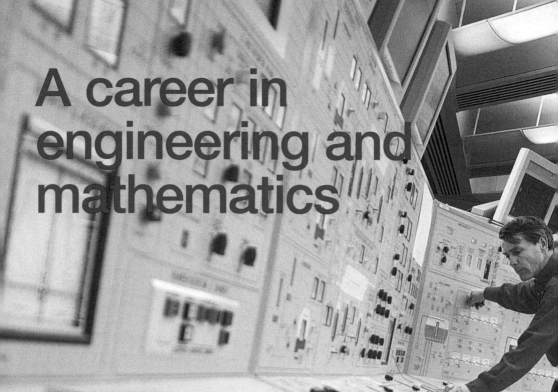

A career in engineering and mathematics

A career in engineering

According to a 2011 report by Engineering UK, the engineering sector makes up nearly a fifth of the UK economy (19.6% of GDP), is nearly three times larger than the financial services sector, and employs more than 4.5 million people in nearly half a million different enterprises. This means that our engineers will be vital to our economic revival over the next few years.

As an engineer you could be anything from an energy conservation officer making sure we use the cleanest energy in the most efficient way, to an automotive engineer who designs cars for Formula 1. You could also be a structural engineer making sure that new buildings are structurally sound, or a satellite technician making sure that communications satellites are functioning properly. Look around you: everything you see will have been made, designed or developed by an engineer. It's that varied.

The salaries in engineering are generally very good. According to EngineeringUK, many people don't know about these excellent salaries: 'Analysis of the Annual Survey of Hours and Earnings (ASHE) shows that pay for professional engineers and technicians/craft level engineers is comparable to many other STEM (Science, Technology, Engineering and Mathematics) professions. The highest paid in the STEM sector are health professionals, with a mean annual salary of £71,422. Managers in mining and energy come second, with a mean annual salary of £67,153. At £26,291 the mean annual salary for engineering technicians and craftsmen compares favourably with the approximate mean salary for all non-engineering occupations (£22,320) and is higher than the national median salary of £25,800'.

The work environments in engineering are incredibly diverse. You could find yourself in a laboratory, on a test track, in a production plant or out at sea on an oil rig. Depending on the discipline you choose, and the industry sector, the possibilities are endless.

Employers include everyone from Ford UK and Rolls-Royce to Mars and GlaxoSmithKline. As well as these big names, other major employers include companies in the construction, energy and food industries. Most manufacturing companies are large employers of engineers, too.

Engineering is an equal opportunities sector but more women are needed! Engineering UK's 2011 report quotes findings by McKinsey that the best performing engineering and industrial companies are those with the highest number of women in top management positions.

Which area?

Where do your interests lie? Cars? Aeroplanes? Buildings? Design? Take your pick.

AERONAUTICAL ENGINEER

The work

Aeronautical engineers work with civil and military aircraft, as well as satellites, space vehicles and weapons systems. Largely concerned with improving flight quality and safety, they work across many roles, and can specialise in areas such as instrumentation, aerodynamics or design.

The conditions

Firmly based around teamwork, aeronautical engineers spend most of their time in offices, labs or airport offices, but with frequent visits to sites. Due to ever-developing technologies in aeronautics, long career breaks are difficult.

AGRICULTURAL ENGINEER

The work

Agricultural engineers, also known as biological and agricultural engineers, work on agriculture and maximising our use of biological resources. This broad field includes the design of agricultural machinery and storage structures, water and soil conservation, and food and bioprocess engineering.

The conditions

Agricultural engineers tend to spend a lot of time travelling and working outdoors, as this area of work requires frequent visits to farms and other sites that rear animals or produce food. Good communication skills are essential, as frequent interaction with farmers and growers is required.

AUTOMOTIVE ENGINEER

The work

Automotive engineers are responsible for designing, developing and testing vehicles and vehicle components. This can stretch all the way through from early concept stage to finished vehicle, or even later on in responding to customer feedback. An incredibly varied role, automotive engineers can specialise in a number of fields, including motor sport, rapid prototyping, supply chain management, ergonomics, electronics, aerodynamics, safety and more. Opportunities also exist in research and development of alternative fuels.

The conditions

During the course of the job (work hours are generally 9am to 5pm) an automotive engineer will be heavily involved with testing. This will include real-life track testing as well as computer modelling the behaviour of vehicles under different conditions. As the work needs specialist machinery, it is generally based around one site. However, some areas require considerable travel, for example motor sport.

BIOCHEMICAL ENGINEER

The work

Biochemical engineers work with biological materials to refine and make new products. These could be anything from foods and cattle feed to vaccines and sweeteners. They are also involved in reducing pollution and treating waste products to make them safe and eco-friendly. Biochemical engineers are likely to find themselves working for pharmaceutical companies, environment agencies or the food industry.

The conditions

Biochemical engineering is one of the fastest-moving sectors, with new, breakthrough technologies being realised almost constantly. It is one of the most highly paid engineering sectors, and is largely lab-based with solid 9am to 5pm hours.

BIOMEDICAL ENGINEER

The work

Biomedical engineers apply their engineering skills to areas of healthcare and medicine. They may perform research to understand human physiology and disease, they may be involved in designing and maintaining new equipment to diagnose, monitor or treat patients or they may be involved in reverse engineering biological systems to develop novel solutions to non-medical problems. Biomedical engineers tend to work in multidisciplinary teams made up of people from other engineering backgrounds such as mechanical or electrical engineers, as well as clinicians and technicians in the healthcare industry.

The conditions

Working hours are variable as the variety of jobs is so great. Graduates entering a medical device maintenance company or the NHS as a trainee clinical radiographer, for example, are likely to have more regular hours than a graduate entering a research based small business.

CIVIL ENGINEER

The work

Civil engineers work across most engineering disciplines but tend to specialise in construction, structural engineering, transport and water. They have a full understanding of the construction process and will be involved at most stages. Civil engineers are vital to ensuring that projects are completed safely, with the appropriate resources and according to schedule. This often involves liaising with clients and taking on a project-management role.

The conditions

Though based in an office, civil engineers will make very frequent site visits and will occasionally have to work unsocial hours. Considering the level of involvement that civil engineers have with projects, it is a very responsible – and occasionally stressful – job.

ELECTRICAL ENGINEER

The work

Electrical engineers work in designing and maintaining electrical systems. As electrics are central to just about everything, electrical engineers tend to work closely in multidisciplinary teams, including people such as architects, technicians and engineers from other disciplines.

The conditions

Working hours vary a lot, depending on which sector you work in. The same also applies to where you work: it could be a factory, site, laboratory or workshop.

ENERGY CONSERVATION OFFICER

The work

Energy conservation officers make sure that commercial businesses, as well as domestic properties, are as efficient as possible in how they use energy. The job demands practical skill and strategic thinking in supplying energy-saving solutions. Following legislation (such as the Home Energy Conservation Act 1995) all local authorities now have an obligation to improve energy efficiency. Other, similar legislation now makes it compulsory for electricity and gas suppliers to improve energy efficiency, all of which creates demand for energy conservation staff.

The conditions

As much an advocate as a technician, the energy conservation officer will probably spend a reasonable amount of time travelling and making presentations to promote the energy conservation cause. He or she will be conversant with new energy-saving technologies and will have a thorough understanding of the business and domestic environment in which they may be used.

ENVIRONMENTAL ENGINEER

The work

Environmental engineers research and put into practice methods to protect the environment, for example by reducing pollution and protecting natural resources. Activities include cleaning up our water systems (oceans, rivers and drinking water) and designing better recycling systems and ways of disposing of toxic materials.

The conditions

Environmental engineers will often travel to spend time with clients they are working with and, depending on the project, may spend significant amounts of time working outdoors. In this fast-changing field it's important to keep abreast of new regulations and technology and to be able to work calmly with those who may not agree with proposed changes.

GEOTECHNICAL ENGINEER

The work

Geotechnical engineers, also known as soil scientists, assess the impact of the local geology (the nature of the soil or rock) on proposed building methods and materials for a new construction site, in order to ensure that foundations, slopes and retaining structures are safely designed. Most geotechnical engineers train as civil engineers and go on to specialise through a combination of practical work and further study.

The conditions

Geotechnical engineers carry out their work both in the office and on site. Field studies include collecting data, carrying out tests and considering computer-generated analyses. In the office, geotechnical engineers research and write work proposals and run two- and three-dimensional computer simulations. Geotechnical engineers work alongside hydrogeologists, other engineers (eg construction and structural engineers) and clients, so good communication skills are vital.

MECHANICAL ENGINEER

The work

Largely working in manufacturing, mechanical engineers are involved with the development, design and production of products or machinery with mechanical properties. This can be anything from mechanical hearts to cars, to large-scale production plants.

The conditions

Mainly office based, but with visits to plants and sites, the job may include extra hours but rarely weekends. Deadlines are a frequent feature of mechanical engineering, especially when working as a consultant. Working internationally is a strong possibility, particularly with the emergence of new industries in Eastern Europe.

MINING ENGINEER

The work

Mining engineers are involved in a variety of processes required to extract mineral deposits from the earth, from assessing new ventures for commercial viability to filling in mine shafts safely. Responsibilities include the design of mines and mining equipment, the supervision of their construction and operation, and minimising any harmful environmental effects of the work.

The conditions

The nature of the work means that much of a mining engineer's time will be spent on site, for example to evaluate potential projects or to oversee work in progress, which could be above or below ground. Mining expertise is needed globally, so there are plenty of opportunities to work internationally.

PETROLEUM ENGINEER

The work

Petroleum engineers study the earth to locate new oil and gas reservoirs to meet our energy needs, evaluating and developing new sites, and extracting and transporting oil and gas safely. Research into new technologies to allow more effective extraction of oil and gas from each well is ongoing, to enable the financial and environmental costs to be kept as low as possible.

The conditions

Petroleum engineers may work in an office or on-site, depending on what aspect of this broad field they are involved in. Petroleum engineering is a global business, with the five major oil-producing regions being Saudi Arabia, Russia, China, Iran and the US, so international working is a strong possibility.

SOFTWARE ENGINEER

The work

Software engineers, also called software developers or computer programmers, design, build, test, implement and maintain software systems. Software is broken down into systems software (which looks at a computer's operating systems) and applications software (such as word processing and spreadsheets). Working in teams or alone they are at the front end of the ever-changing software and IT world. Software engineering is one of the most popular IT professions.

The conditions

IT is entirely integral to everything in business, so software engineers become heavily involved in project planning, sales and marketing, production and design. Hours will generally be 9am to 5pm, but some maintenance work will need to be done out of regular hours. Self-employment is an option with relevant experience.

Which mathematics degree?

There are many different undergraduate mathematics courses available at universities.

Most courses combine theory and practice-based study, and incorporate the use of specialist mathematical software. Vocational elements such as statistics, financial mathematics or operational research add to the breadth of study of your degree. It is also possible to combine mathematics with other subjects, from astrophysics to Welsh history, in a joint honours degree.

Competition for places varies. A few universities require an extremely good performance at A level or equivalent, perhaps in both mathematics and further mathematics. Elsewhere a good, if more modest, performance in the single subject of mathematics will enable you to join an honours degree programme.

Most students follow a 'single-subject' course of which there are many varieties but two basic forms. Firstly, there is the traditional three-year BA or BSc honours degree, which varies in content between universities. Some universities offer the opportunity to extend the three-year course with a year abroad or an industrial placement year.

Secondly, some mathematics students follow a four-year course, leading to what is often called an 'integrated masters' degree such as MMath. This offers a more in-depth study of mathematics, gives insight into current research topics and eases the transition from undergraduate study to research.

Any mathematics course will provide a foundation in both pure and applied mathematics and will allow you to choose which of these you would like to focus on in later years. Statistics degree courses give a vocational direction to your study, and some are professionally accredited to help start your career. See The Royal Statistical Society website **www.rss.org.uk** for more details.

Having a strong interest in another subject (for example, a language, business, computing, or one of the sciences) can be a good reason to study mathematics as part of a combined degree. The mathematics studied will be less extensive than in a single honours programme, but you will reach an equivalent level in suitably selected areas. At university or indeed for employment, mathematics can stand alone as a course; another subject is not essential, as is sometimes suggested. Nevertheless, opportunities to combine mathematics with other interests are extensive because many subjects have a mathematical basis. Studying a foreign language may allow you to spend a year abroad as part of your course.

So where does all this lead? Specialising in pure mathematics over applied by no means limits you to academia. The great strength of graduates in mathematical sciences is their ability to formulate and solve problems, and many employers appreciate this. Mathematics can be applied to many fields, including economics, finance, engineering, computing and the sciences. The Maths Careers website **www.mathscareers.org.uk** highlights possible career options.

Applied mathematics courses and dedicated subject degrees such as statistics are more obvious in their routes to employment, with modelling and statistical work of vital importance in many areas of industry and government. The Royal Statistical Society careers website **www.rss.org.uk/careers** specialises in statistical careers.

Many different postgraduate courses are also available to hone your qualifications once you have completed your first degree.

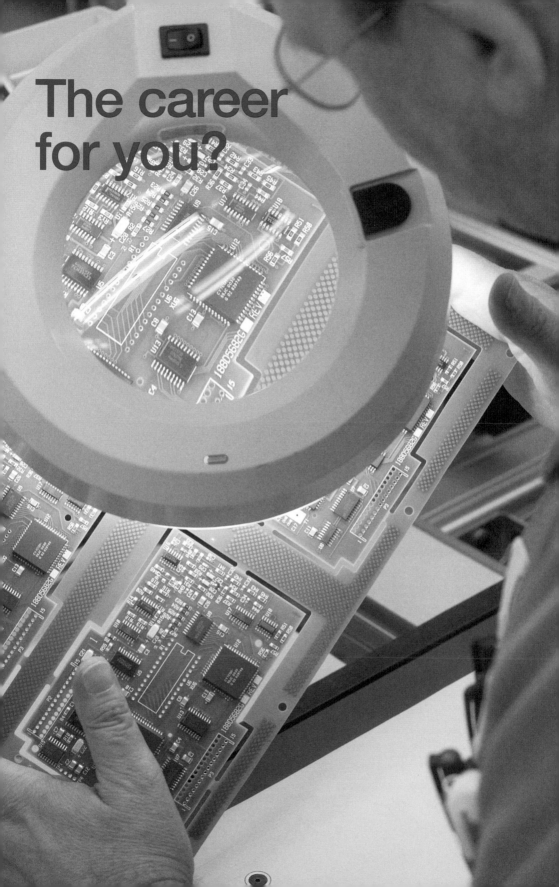

The career
for you?

Is engineering for you?

WHAT DO YOU WANT FROM WORK?

Engineers are known for their technical ability, but a successful engineer will have many more talents as well. They'll have good communication skills, creative flair, and a solid understanding of the businesses and markets surrounding the projects that they work on.

QUESTIONS TO ASK YOURSELF BEFORE CHOOSING A CAREER IN ENGINEERING

- What kind of an environment do you see yourself working in? An office, on site or in a lab?
- Do you want to have the opportunity to work for yourself?
- What kind of hobbies do you enjoy?
- What are your favourite subjects at school and why?
- What are your least favourite subjects and why?
- Are you a 'hands-on' kind of a person?
- What have you enjoyed most during any work experience that you've had?

WHAT DOES AN ENGINEERING COURSE TYPICALLY INVOLVE?

As engineering is based on applying practical knowledge grounded in maths, science and technology, you can expect these subjects to feature prominently on any engineering course. Also important to most engineering courses is an understanding of business, market and ethical factors. After all, engineers provide real-life (rather than abstract) solutions, so they have to be aware of the impact their work is likely to have. From the beginning, practical work is likely to feature prominently. For this reason many engineering departments develop close links with industry.

WHAT SKILLS DO EMPLOYERS LOOK FOR?

Engineering employers tend to look for a solid technical and analytical background backed by 'real-world' sensibilities. Being able to manage resources and time, use IT effectively and work in a multidisciplinary team are important. A willingness to be involved with lifelong learning is also necessary.

WHAT EMPLOYERS AND UNIVERSITIES WANT

'A career in engineering is varied and challenging. Beyond having the right qualifications, universities and employers are looking for people who can demonstrate that they understand the various applications of engineering and recognise its importance in the modern world. Young people can learn more about engineering and the application of science and mathematics by taking part in relevant activities at school, such as Tomorrow's Engineers or The Big Bang UK Young Scientists and Engineers Fair, and by finding out about engineering in a variety of work settings.'
Paul Jackson, Chief Executive, EngineeringUK

'Obviously academic achievements are important but it's also very important for students to be able to demonstrate soft skills such as team working and communication – all companies need staff to be able to communicate with each other as well as clients. Skills such as creative thinking and problem solving are also important. Look at a company website, ascertain what they are looking for and ensure you have some good examples of your previous experience before attending any interviews.'
Jillian Burton, Graduate Programme Manager, Lloyds Register

Alternative careers

One of the great things about a qualification in engineering is the range of options open to you.

CIVIL SERVICE

In addition to the more obvious jobs in the Civil Service (for example, an engineer in the Home Office or the Ministry of Defence), engineers are also sought after in other areas. The Civil Service Fast Stream is a training programme for talented graduates who have the potential to become future leaders. One of the Fast Stream options is Science and Engineering, and its graduates are used to fill positions at BIS (the Department for Business Innovation and Skills) and the MOD (Ministry of Defence). These jobs could range from procurement (defence or health, for example) to advising on policy.

CONSULTANCY

As well as working as engineering consultants, engineers are in demand as IT or strategic consultants. This kind of work involves a lot of analysis and problem solving, and is a close match to an engineer's key transferable skills.

EDUCATION

A career in teaching or lecturing is also a good option, especially as the education profession is short of people with a strong technological background. There are many routes in: you can train on the job or you could take a postgraduate certificate in education. There is also a scheme aimed at high-flyers called Teach First, which allows entry into investment management or management consultancy after two years of teaching. See the *UCAS Guide to getting into Teaching and Education* for further information.

INVESTMENT BANKING

Engineers often work for investment banks in operations (looking at the process of making deals), in technology departments (making sure that IT processes are kept running smoothly), or in trading. Because of its analytical nature and heavy reliance on maths, trading suits an engineer's skills. Most banking organisations run graduate schemes, but these are fiercely competitive. As such, many engineering graduates undertake further study before entering the profession. See the *UCAS Guide to getting into Economics, Finance and Accountancy* for further information.

TECHNICAL WRITING

All complex engineered products need a technical explanation and documentation, and this is where technical writers come in. Technical writing requires a thorough understanding of the product and its uses, and would cover user instructions, maintenance details and marketing copy. These jobs tend to be with large manufacturers.

LAW

Many engineers complete two years at law school to study to be a solicitor or a barrister. The first year covers the Graduate Diploma in Law (also known as the Common Professional Examination) and the second year, depending on the direction you want to take, could be either the Legal Practice Course (to become a solicitor) or the Bar Professional Training Course (to become a barrister). After this, another period of training takes place (a training contract for solicitors or a pupillage for barristers). See the *UCAS Guide to getting into Law* for further information.

Professional bodies

Professional bodies are responsible for overseeing a particular profession or career area, ensuring that people who work in the area are fully trained and meet ethical guidelines. Professional bodies may be known as institutions, societies and associations. They generally have regulatory roles: they make sure that members of the profession are able to work successfully in their jobs without endangering lives or abusing their position.

Professional bodies are often involved in training and career development, so courses and workplace training may have to follow the body's guidelines. In order to be fully qualified and licensed to work in your profession of choice, you will have to follow the professional training route. In many areas of work, completion of the professional training results in gaining chartered status – and the addition of some extra letters after your name. Other institutions may award other types of certification once certain criteria have been met. Chartered or certified members will usually need to take further courses and training to ensure their skills are kept up to date.

WHAT PROFESSIONAL BODIES ARE THERE?

Not all career areas have professional bodies. Those jobs that require extensive learning and training are likely to have bodies with a regulatory focus. This includes careers such as engineering, law, construction, health and finance. If you want to work in one of these areas, it's important to make sure your degree course is accredited by the professional body – otherwise you may have to undertake further study or training later on.

Other bodies may play more of a supportive role, looking after the interests of people who work in the sector. This includes journalism, management and arts-based careers. Professional bodies may also be learned bodies, providing opportunities for further learning and promoting the development of knowledge in the field.

CAN I JOIN AS A STUDENT?

Many professional bodies offer student membership – sometimes free or for reduced fees. Membership can be extremely valuable as a source of advice, information and resources. You'll have the opportunity to meet other students in the field, as well as experienced professionals. It will also look good on your CV when you come to apply for jobs.

See below for a list of professional bodies in the fields of engineering and mathematics.

ENGINEERING

British Institute of Facilities Management (BIFM)
www.bifm.org.uk

The Chartered Institute of Building (CIOB)
www.ciob.org.uk

The Chartered Institute of Building Services Engineers (CIBSE)
www.cibse.org

The Energy Institute (EI)
www.energyinst.org.uk

The Engineering Council
www.engc.org.uk

The Institution of Chemical Engineers (IChemE)
www.icheme.org

The Institution of Civil Engineers (ICE)
www.ice.org.uk

The Institution of Engineering and Technology (IET)
www.theiet.org

The Institution of Mechanical Engineers (IMechE)
www.imeche.org

The Institution of Structural Engineers (IStructE)
www.istructe.org

The Royal Academy of Engineering (RAEng)
www.raeng.org.uk

MATHEMATICS

The Institute of Mathematics and its Applications (IMA)
www.ima.org.uk

The London Mathematical Society (LMS)
www.lms.ac.uk

The Royal Statistical Society (RSS)
www.rss.org.uk

Graduate destinations

Engineering and mathematics
HESA Destination of Leavers of Higher Education

Each year, comprehensive statistics are collected on what graduates are doing six months after they complete their course. The survey is co-ordinated by the Higher Education Statistics Agency (HESA) and provides information about how many graduates move into employment (and what type of career) or further study and how many are believed to be unemployed.

The full results across all subject areas are published by the Higher Education Careers Service Unit (HECSU) and the Association of Graduate Careers Advisory Services (AGCAS) in *What Do Graduates Do?*, which is available from **www.ucasbooks.com**.

	Engineering and mathematics
In UK employment	56.1%
In overseas employment	1.8%
Working and studying	8.1%
Studying in the UK for a higher degree	11.5%
Studying in the UK for a teaching qualification	2.7%
Undertaking other further study or training in the UK	2.0%
Studying overseas	0.2%
Not available for employment, study or training	3.2%
Assumed to be unemployed	10.1%
Other	4.3%

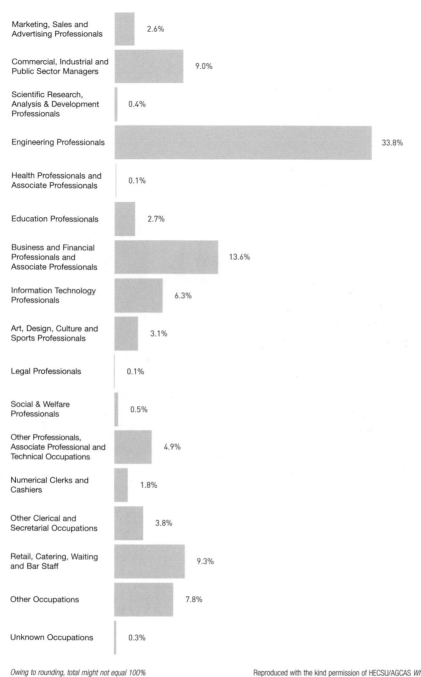

Marketing, Sales and Advertising Professionals	2.6%
Commercial, Industrial and Public Sector Managers	9.0%
Scientific Research, Analysis & Development Professionals	0.4%
Engineering Professionals	33.8%
Health Professionals and Associate Professionals	0.1%
Education Professionals	2.7%
Business and Financial Professionals and Associate Professionals	13.6%
Information Technology Professionals	6.3%
Art, Design, Culture and Sports Professionals	3.1%
Legal Professionals	0.1%
Social & Welfare Professionals	0.5%
Other Professionals, Associate Professional and Technical Occupations	4.9%
Numerical Clerks and Cashiers	1.8%
Other Clerical and Secretarial Occupations	3.8%
Retail, Catering, Waiting and Bar Staff	9.3%
Other Occupations	7.8%
Unknown Occupations	0.3%

Owing to rounding, total might not equal 100%

Reproduced with the kind permission of HECSU/AGCAS *What Do Graduates Do? 2011*. All data comes from the *HESA Destination of Leavers from Higher Education Survey 2009/10*.

Want to see UCAS in action?
Visit www.ucas.tv to watch

case studies
how-to guides

UCAS

Case studies

Project Engineer

Prysmian Cables & Systems

CHERYL BOSWORTH

Route into engineering:
BTEC National Diploma (2002); AS levels – physics, psychology, sociology (2003); BSc industrial design
(engineering), De Montfort University (2007)

WHY ENGINEERING?

I chose the design-based engineering route as I've
always had an interest in engineering, but found the
most enjoyable and challenging part to be in the field of
creativity and innovation. This I discovered from a
school work placement in a factory that designed and
manufactured cylinders for Rolls-Royce aircraft engines.
My degree allowed me to see the full product design
process starting with a specification or feasibility study,
working through concept generation, CAD design,
modelling, rendering and testing, all the way to final
product development.

HOW DID YOU GET WHERE YOU ARE TODAY?

I joined Prysmian Cables & Systems in 2005 as a
student CAD design and test engineer for a one-year
placement as part of my sandwich degree course. In
2007, I joined the company as a full-time graduate
engineer as part of their development programme for
engineers. There were three of us on the scheme,
which involved 18 months of placements in different
factories, within the development engineering role.
These placements included roles involved with material
approvals, testing, project management, 2D- and 3D-
CAD designs, and new product development. Alongside

this was an intensive training programme that included courses to help develop a full understanding across all business areas. These courses included project and people management, commercial awareness, presentation skills, supply chain and logistics, value engineering, metallurgy, Institute of Occupational Safety and Health (IOSH) health and safety, polymer science, business and finance, and contract law.

WHAT DOES YOUR JOB INVOLVE?

I work for a global company that manufactures energy and telecommunication cables and accessories. I work on the North Wales site where we manufacture energy cables for power distribution. My job is in the engineering development team and includes tasks such as material approvals, new product development, and value engineering. I also participate in projects to improve efficiencies within the factory. I manage some projects, and am a team member of others, which have to conform to required quality standards and provide the most cost-effective solutions.

I usually work from 8.30am to 5.00pm and am office based, but I also spend a lot of time in the factory, especially when completing trials or projects. Being in both the office and factory allows me to work with various types of people and departments. This has helped me to improve the communication and integration skills required to do well in project management.

WHAT HAS BEEN YOUR BIGGEST CHALLENGE?

Having had an education in design and engineering, linking engineering to a business scenario proved quite a challenge. However, with courses, the aid of my colleagues and the projects, I have managed to link both of these fields much better and continue to improve the association between engineering and the business part of the company.

AND THE BEST BITS?

I find the projects the most interesting and exciting part of my role; they are always different and can require skills never used before. I learn a lot as I go along. The sense of achievement in these situations is why I enjoy it.

CHERYL'S TOP TIPS

My top tip would be to try any opportunity you are given and, if you have a subject or a field you find most interesting, try to pursue a career in that. It is much easier to do a job you enjoy even if it has its difficult days.

Assistant statistician

Office for National Statistics, Civil Service

PETER BROAD

Route into statistics:

A levels – biology, chemistry, mathematics (2006); AS level – further mathematics (2006) and history (2005); BSc mathematics and statistics, University of Bath (2010); MSc statistics, University of Warwick (2012)

WHY STATISTICS?

There were a few of us in my class who enjoyed maths and wanted to take it further, but I think I was the only one who enjoyed statistics! Before that, I was interested in history and was also very close to applying for a chemistry degree. If it wasn't for my maths teacher encouraging me, I could be in a lab coat right now!

HOW DID YOU GET WHERE YOU ARE TODAY?

When applying to different universities, I was attracted to courses that offered an industrial placement. The course in Bath was perfect as at the end of my second year I spent 12 months with a pharmaceutical company in their statistics department. Not only did I learn what it was like to work in an office (my only previous job was working on the checkouts of a well-known supermarket!), but I also used statistics to investigate how genetic data could be used to treat lung disease.

A few friends spent their placements working in a government department and after finding out more from them I decided it was something I'd like to do. When I returned to Bath I applied for an MSc course in statistics at Warwick and during that applied for the Civil Service Fast Stream graduate programme.

WHAT DOES YOUR JOB INVOLVE?

I work for the Office for National Statistics (ONS), the largest producer of official statistics in the UK. Official statistics give parliament and the public a window on society and the economy, such as the weekly price of diesel or the rate of unemployment in the UK. The ONS is also responsible for the Census held every 10 years. We make sure that the data is collected in a fair, representative way and that it's brought together and analysed correctly.

Historically, ONS has always collected data in paper questionnaires, but I'm looking at the effects of collecting data online or using tax return data from Her Majesty's Revenue & Customs. Each project is different and requires different levels of team work. I work mainly on my own with the web data collection project, but there are about 10 of us working on the tax return data project. Those results feed into a European-wide initiative looking to use data from different sources.

The great thing about working for ONS is the flexible working hours. As long as I have my manager's permission, I can spread my 37 hours a week however I want.

WHAT HAS BEEN YOUR BIGGEST CHALLENGE?

I'm relatively new, so I'm still getting used to the acronyms and terminology as well as the normal day-to-day work. When you start a new job, you just have to keep asking questions.

AND THE BEST BITS?

I know this might sound sad, but I most enjoy producing pretty graphs or tables, presenting my results to other people and explaining the meaning behind the results. In the future I'd like to work in a different government department where I can see first-hand the impact my work has on government policy.

PETER'S TOP TIPS

Don't worry if you haven't done further maths – lots of people haven't and you can soon pick it up in the second year of sixth form if your school or college lets you. I was worried I'd get left behind in my first year at university, but I've found that universities like to get everyone to the same level in the first year.

Senior lecturer, mathematics

University of Sussex

VANESSA STYLES

Route into mathematics
A levels – chemistry, further mathematics, mathematics (1990); BSc mathematics, University of Sussex (1993); PhD applied mathematics, University of Sussex (1997)

WHY MATHEMATICS?

I chose to study for a degree in mathematics as it was always my favourite subject at school and college. The more I learnt about it the more interesting I found it and then the more I wanted to learn. I was very excited by the thought of studying mathematics at degree level as I had been told that it was more to do with proving and understanding mathematical results rather than performing routine calculations.

HOW DID YOU GET WHERE YOU ARE TODAY?

The main factor, with the exception of the mathematics itself, that led me to decide that I wanted to be a university lecturer, was the enthusiasm and passion for the subject that was displayed by my lecturers at university. During the final year of my degree I realised that I wished to study mathematics at a higher level and so embarked upon a PhD in applied mathematics. This gave me an insight into how interesting and fulfilling mathematical research is. As a result, I decided that I would like to stay in academia and hopefully become a university lecturer in mathematics. To this end, I held three postgraduate research fellowships that lasted in total seven years: the first was at Oxford Brookes University, the second at the University of Sussex and the third was at the University of Regensburg in Germany. I then applied for my current post as a lecturer at the University of Sussex.

WHAT DOES YOUR JOB INVOLVE?

I am a senior lecturer at the University of Sussex. My job has two main parts – lecturing and research – and my time is pretty much divided equally between them. Part of my time involves direct interaction with students, which can take the form of giving lectures or tutorials, or it can involve talking to students on a one-to-one basis. I also spend time writing exam papers or updating existing lecture notes and problem sheets. The remainder of my time is spent doing research, which involves writing papers for publication in journals, writing presentations to give at conferences and writing proposals for grants. My main research areas are concerned with mathematical modelling in superconductivity and grain boundary motion.

WHAT HAS BEEN YOUR BIGGEST CHALLENGE?

I found that the biggest challenge I faced in my career was getting my PhD. This involved learning how to do novel research in mathematics, rather than being taught known mathematical results. It was a skill that took quite some time to master during which I was given invaluable guidance by my PhD supervisor.

AND THE BEST BITS?

I find doing mathematical research exceptionally interesting; it really grabs hold of you and time simply disappears when you are doing it. The teaching aspects of my job are very enjoyable – it is a pleasure to impart your knowledge to the students, and it is most satisfying to watch students develop an understanding of concepts that they originally had difficulties with.

VANESSA'S TOP TIPS

I would advise anybody considering my career path to think very carefully when they choose their PhD topic and supervisor as these play a large part in determining the direction that your research takes.

PhD student

University of Cambridge

MATT HENDERSON

Route into language processing:
Scottish Highers – English, French, Latin, mathematics, physics (2006); Advanced Highers – applied mathematics (mechanics), physics, pure mathematics (2007); BA mathematics, University of Cambridge (2010); MSc speech and language processing, University of Edinburgh (2011)

WHY MATHEMATICS?

Languages and linguistics always interested me at school, and it was a tough choice picking between that area and mathematics. Luckily while studying at university I found a cross-over area in speech and language processing. This includes automatic translation, speech recognition, text-to-speech, and computers you can talk to. All of these problems are best tackled using the approach of a reasoned mathematician, modelling the processes with a rigorous and well-motivated mathematical model. For example, you could decide to invent a new mathematical model which takes as input a French sentence, and outputs

one in English. What would happen in the middle? A university course on mathematics will give you lots of interesting mathematical objects and methods which you can try out.

HOW DID YOU GET WHERE YOU ARE TODAY?

Studying mathematics at university prepares you for attacking a wide range of problems in a reasoned and efficient manner. It's not just about getting the answer right, or proving a theorem successfully, but doing so in a succinct and elegant manner. These skills are attractive to employers, and are perfect for starting a career in research as I have done.

WHAT DOES YOUR JOB INVOLVE?

My research lab, the Dialogue Systems Group in the University of Cambridge's Engineering Department, is particularly interested in modelling every part of spoken conversations using statistical models. Our demo application is an automated tourist information system, which can help you find restaurants, cafés and bars in your town.

As a PhD student, you are given a lot of freedom to pursue your own ideas. At the moment I am working on a mobile application, a new method of converting speech into meaning, and also helping out my colleagues running an experiment. There is a good atmosphere working in a small research group (mine has seven people) with good discussions, and we try to help each other out.

You also have freedom in planning out your schedule. There is no set time when you need to be at your desk, and though your colleagues might worry if you go missing for a month, I've found it pretty relaxed!

WHAT HAS BEEN YOUR BIGGEST CHALLENGE?

It is rewarding and exciting to take a project from a fledgling idea into a final system. It can be quite a challenge to turn what seems like a good idea into something that actually works in practice. Though many of your ideas might turn out to not work, and the number of possible routes to take can be overwhelming, the sense of accomplishment when your idea finally does just work makes it worthwhile.

AND THE BEST BITS?

You can learn about all sorts of different things other than language when doing this kind of research. My supervisor at Edinburgh was working on a robot bartender and a system to help people with depression. I got to learn about the sculpture of Paolozzi in my master's project when I made a robot tour guide.

MATT'S TOP TIPS

I would highly recommend talking to people who are researching areas that interest you. Get in touch by email and I am sure they will be happy to tell you more about what they do. This is what I did during my undergraduate course. It was invaluable in helping me pick a master's course, which then helped make me an attractive PhD candidate.

Final year biomedical engineering student

University of Ulster

SHAUNAGH MCCURDY

Route into biomedical engineering:

A levels – biology, chemistry, English literature, geography (2008); BSc biomedical engineering, University of Ulster (graduating 2012)

WHY BIOMEDICAL ENGINEERING?

I've always had a keen interest in biology and understanding how things work. I wanted to study something that I felt would allow me to help people in some way and to make a contribution towards something meaningful. The combination of biological and engineering principles within biomedical engineering makes it a practical and interesting degree choice.

WHAT HAS YOUR DEGREE INVOLVED SO FAR?

The degree is broadly based with mathematics, mechanical and electrical engineering, anatomy, chemistry, nanotechnology, cell biology, and tissue engineering. This is fantastic as the field is so vast and the modules covered really give you a feel for what is out there and the areas you can work in.

TELL US ABOUT YOUR WORK PLACEMENT

I spent 14 months at Boston Scientific in Galway working in research and development. I had a wide range of tasks ranging from writing protocols and technical reports to conducting feasibility testing and statistical analysis of results using Minitab and Excel. I was involved with six legacy products going through periodic review and one acquisition product. I also guided an employee who joined my team on different tasks for three months.

I worked a 39-hour week, generally from 9am to 5.30pm. I had the option to attend a selection of different courses during the placement, ranging from measurement systems analysis to design control and cardiovascular impacts. It was also an opportunity to meet different people from other groups in the company and hear about the work they do. There were opportunities to represent the company at university and school events to help others understand what the company did and why. The staff were very supportive and giving of their time. The placement was a learning experience that I'll never forget and now, looking towards employment, I feel that it has prepared me well and set me apart from other graduates.

WHAT WAS THE TOUGHEST CHALLENGE?

Taking the leap from a university to working environment. I had to apply my skills and trust my knowledge, but knew I could ask colleagues if I was unsure about anything. The broad range of tasks I undertook on a day-to-day basis has made me more driven and improved my organisation skills.

AND THE BEST BITS?

I had the opportunity to attend a hospital procedure to see how the products I was working with were used by clinicians. The procedure allowed me to appreciate how our work impacts people's lives every day. Most of all, the work experience has made me appreciate the dedication put in to achieve everyday goals and understand what it takes to have the drive to overcome and succeed in particularly challenging tasks. Sometimes the workload was tough or a task was demanding, but when completed the feeling that something had been accomplished made everything worthwhile. Enjoying and being challenged by what you do creates a great working environment. The report writing, analysis and practical skills gained through placement have made me more prepared for my final year of university.

SHAUNAGH'S TOP TIPS

Biomedical engineering has something for everyone. The course prepares you well for the working world and placements are a great opportunity. For a placement, just apply to everything you're interested in and talk to your careers advisers about preparing your CV and for interview.

The
UCAS Guide
to getting into
University
and College

The UCAS Guide
to getting into
University
and College

First Edition

UCAS

What would 650,000 potential students like to know about UCAS? Everything!

- With rising costs and high competition for places, thorough research and preparation have never been more crucial for future students.

- Relevant throughout the whole year.

- Published by UCAS, a well-known and respected brand with direct access to the most up-to-date information.

- Written in a friendly, step-by-step format, with myth busters, checklists and helpful tips from students and experts at universities and colleges.

'...the most comprehensive guide... completely impartial... offers fabulous tips and advice...'
David Fullerton, Head of Careers

'Absolutely brilliant!'
Debbie Verdino,
Post-16 Manager

Order your copy now...

t +44 (0)1242 544 610

f +44(0)1242 544 806

e publicationservices@ucas.ac.uk

Price: £11.99

Entry routes

Routes to qualification

There are many 'levels' of engineer in the UK, with even more educational routes in to the profession. In addition to degree courses, there is a range of apprenticeships (see page 54 for more details), vocational qualifications and diplomas at foundation, higher and advanced levels, and they all offer progression to a rewarding engineering career. Whatever route you take, make sure the educational course you choose is accredited by a professional institution. Visit the Engineering Council website **www.engc.org.uk** to find out more about professional registration.

ENGINEERING EMPLOYMENT LEVELS

Engineering is one of the few careers where you can work at any level, and work – with the right training and experience – from the bottom all the way to the top. Here are some of the levels you might experience.

Engineering operators
Operators work in a range of activities, including car manufacturing and electronics assembly. Many will be involved in production line duties.

Craft level engineers

Craft level engineers create and maintain things by machining, fitting, welding and fabricating. They are generally very hands-on and can interpret complex instructions.

Technicians (EngTech)

Technicians are currently in huge demand and are employed in areas such as estimating, technical sales, production planning, maintenance and quality assurance.

Incorporated engineers (IEng)

Incorporated engineers manage current and developing technology, and may be involved with engineering design, development, manufacture or operations, as well as technical and commercial management.

Chartered engineers (CEng)

These are the most qualified engineers, and are responsible for introducing new and more efficient production techniques and construction concepts. They also pioneer new engineering services and management methods.

DEGREE LEVELS

BEng (Hons) degree

A BEng (Hons) degree focuses on the practical application of technology and understanding to solve problems. This is underpinned by scientific and mathematical knowledge and can be focused on multidisciplinary or specialised environments.

BEng (Hons) degrees are usually available as three-year full-time courses or as four-year sandwich courses. The three-year course will typically be delivered within universities, although there is the possibility of an industrial placement.

MEng degree

MEng degrees have a greater range and depth of specialist knowledge. As well as developing specific skills, they are designed to provide both a foundation for leadership and a wider appreciation of the economic, social and environmental context of engineering.

An MEng degree is an integrated masters programme in engineering, so it should not be perceived as simply an 'add-on' year to a bachelors degree.

MASTER'S DEGREES

Some graduates choose to take conversion or specialist master's degrees in engineering. To research and apply for a range of postgradute courses at different higher education institutions, go to **www.ukpass.ac.uk**.

To find out more, visit:
www.engc.org.uk

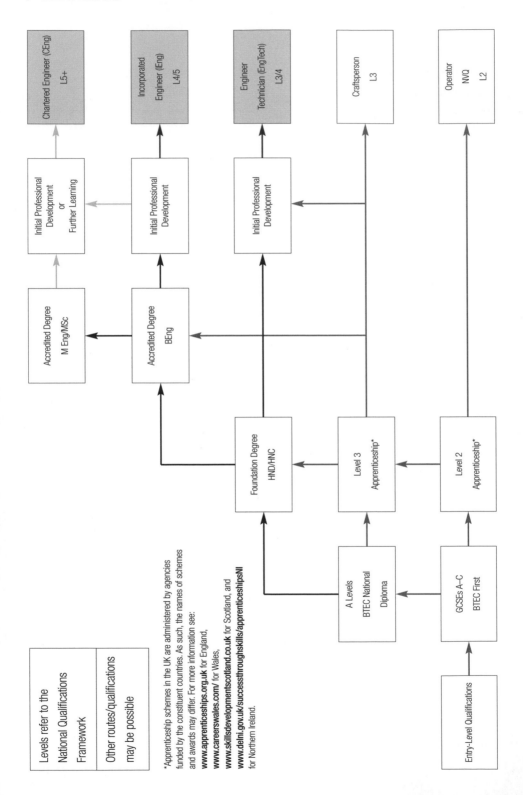

Chartered Engineer (CEng)
L5+

Incorporated Engineer (IEng)
L4/5

Engineer Technician (EngTech)
L3/4

Craftsperson
L3

Operator
NVQ
L2

Initial Professional Development or Further Learning

Initial Professional Development

Initial Professional Development

Accredited Degree
M Eng/MSc

Accredited Degree
BEng

Foundation Degree
HND/HNC

Level 3
Apprenticeship*

Level 2
Apprenticeship*

A Levels
BTEC National Diploma

GCSEs A–C
BTEC First

Entry-Level Qualifications

Levels refer to the National Qualifications Framework

Other routes/qualifications may be possible

*Apprenticeship schemes in the UK are administered by agencies funded by the constituent countries. As such, the names of schemes and awards may differ. For more information see:
www.apprenticeships.org.uk for England,
www.careerswales.com/ for Wales,
www.skillsdevelopmentscotland.co.uk for Scotland, and
www.delni.gov.uk/successthroughskills/apprenticeshipsNI for Northern Ireland.

What others say...

What others say...

These are extracts from case studies in previous editions of this book. They give some insights into the experiences and thoughts of people who were once in the same position as you.

NICKY REDFERN – FINAL YEAR STUDENT, ENGINEERING

'I always enjoyed studying maths and technology and when thinking about what degree to do, I knew that I didn't want to do pure design or pure engineering. My course (BSc technology and enterprise management) combines aspects of both, so it seemed to be a really good compromise.

'During my third year I did a paid placement at 3M. I was placed in the manufacturing technology team, which is responsible for enabling the production of new lines. I was mainly working on products related to abrasive technology. I spent my first week on the shop floor, learning how everything worked, and attending senior management meetings to get a feel for the business at the higher level.

'My workload was varied, ranging from rewriting process standard manuals for operators and producing new health and safety notices, to carrying out life cycle analyses and working on other projects. I was looked after by the team manager, who made sure that I was working on appropriate projects and that I could access the help I needed.

'The most challenging thing was discovering how to use what I had learned at university – in other words, applying it to real-world situations. I started to realise that what I had studied at university was not necessarily as straightforward as it had appeared to be in lectures.'

MAX LITTLE – POSTDOCTORAL RESEARCH FELLOW AND LECTURER

Max did a part-time mathematics degree with the Open University then a PhD in mathematics and engineering. He then went on to do a three-year postdoctoral research fellowship and also works as an associate lecturer.

'If you want to pursue an academic career you have to make a name for and establish yourself as a research leader in your own right, while distinguishing yourself from collaborators. This can be difficult as, to an extent, you have to follow funding rules, which are often directed at relatively short-term projects, because these are what pay you. This in turn can make it hard to maintain a consistent direction in your research. Essentially you have to be idealistic as well as practical.

'Studying maths is difficult, but if you master the basics and work hard you will get results. Mathematical research allows plenty of room for creativity and different perspectives.'

PAUL JEFFERYS – EQUITY TRADER

Paul studied BA mathematics and MMath. He was sponsored through university and did a summer internship in the vacation after the second year of his degree. At the end of the internship he was offered a graduate job, which he took up two years later and worked towards a professional qualification as a chartered financial analyst. Paul says, 'Doing an internship is the best way to figure out if you're willing to commit to a particular field of work. Before any interviews, make sure you're up to date with what is going on in the world around you by dipping into relevant publications such as The Economist.

'My current job is varied, ranging from designing client algorithms to enable clients to trade automatically to pricing up risk portfolios for clients. I work within a team of ten, with different colleagues having different priorities. I talk a lot with my colleagues about different approaches to solving problems, which is very collegial, but there are some things that you have to just do yourself; you can't allocate risk management to a committee because then no one will do it.

'It is a very diverse area to work in. I like the fact that if I have had an idea that I think may push the business forward, by helping clients to make money or manage risk better, it is possible for me to spend time researching it. I feel I can make a real contribution to the business.'

REBECCA WHEWAY – GRADUATE ENGINEER

Rebecca did an MEng in civil engineering and says, 'There is financial help available to those wanting to study engineering degrees, so try to secure sponsorship before you begin university. Work experience is extremely helpful to making an informed decision about what area of the industry is right for you.

'Before I started my degree I was awarded a QUEST Scholarship from the Institution of Civil Engineers. This entitled me to a bursary each year towards my studies, as well as the chance to gain paid work experience with an engineering company while studying. I was partnered with an engineering contractor, and worked on building and rail projects in different locations in the UK during my summer vacations. The placements made me realise that I wanted to pursue a more office-based, design and consultancy role as opposed to a predominantly on-site position.

'I am working towards becoming chartered, which takes four years on average after graduation. Chartership is granted by the Institution of Civil Engineers, but my employer provides support via mentoring and enabling me to gain the right range of experience, while I monitor and write reports on my professional development, attend lectures and get involved with events to promote the profession.

'When you start working there is a lot to learn that you may not have covered in your degree. Obtaining the requisite knowledge involves a combination of gaining more project experience, attending training courses and asking for help and advice from colleagues.'

SAMUAL SMITH – SUSTAINABILITY CONSULTANT

Samual studied for a BEng in medical engineering before taking a masters in sustainable energy and the environment. He says:

'After my undergraduate degree I wrote to my current employer to see if they could offer me any work experience. I hoped this would improve my chances of being accepted onto the masters. Fortunately, I was offered a placement for two months, which I spent working on a pioneering recycling project as well as on a sustainability strategy for the Olympics.

'When I was considering what to do for my masters dissertation, I wrote to Bioregional again to see if they had any research needs. The result was a feasibility study on using food waste from businesses in central London to generate energy via anaerobic digestion.

'While studying, I made it clear to Bioregional that I would be very interested in working for them in the future. A vacancy for a sustainability consultant came up around the time when I was finishing my course. I applied for it and got the job.

'To be a good consultant I have to keep up to date with current research and legislation so I can advise my clients on how to maximise their energy savings. For example, there may be funds they can access to help make their buildings more efficient. I also work on improving carbon footprinting methodologies so my engineering and maths skills are very useful!'

Samual's top tip: 'Even if you don't end up as an engineer, a degree in the field will give you skills that are applicable and transferable to many different sectors. Also, an engineering degree is highly respected by employers.'

ANDREW LANGSTONE – MATHEMATICS TEACHER

Andrew studied for a BSC before completing a PGCE, both in mathematics. He explains how he got where he is today.

'While at university I was not sure what I wanted to do when I left, but teaching had always been in the back of my mind. I enjoyed my time at school and sharing my passion for mathematics with others sounded like something I would enjoy. I went back to my secondary school and helped out for two weeks and this confirmed my love for teaching and maths.

'I applied to do a PGCE in mathematics early on in my third year of university. The PGCE was a tough year, but well worth it. The course gave me enough experience to be confident in teaching full-time, while letting me reflect on what I was experiencing and giving me the tools to improve.'

WILLIAM ROBERTS – BUDGET AND PERFORMANCE ADVISER

William gained a BSC in mathematics and then completed an ACA.

'My job relates to everyday life in London. The Greater London Assembly scrutinises the Mayor of London's decisions and helps develop policy for services that the Mayor has control over: the Metropolitan Police, Transport for London, London Fire and Emergency Services, and the London Development Agency. I use my analytical skills and accountancy knowledge to assess the performance of these services.

'I love that my work relates to the city I work in and the things I experience around me. My job is also really varied and involves working with lots of people and situations. I am in a position to influence the areas I work on and enjoy a high level of autonomy.'

JAMES PRENTICE – GRADUATE TRAINEE

James did a MEng in aerospace engineering; he gives an account of his experience.

'In my fourth year at university we had to find an industrial placement. I was lucky enough to get a placement with Flight Refuelling Ltd (now Cobham Mission Equipment). I worked in the manufacturing engineering department, which predominantly makes air-to-air refuelling equipment and weapons carriage and release systems. At the end of the placement I was offered sponsorship through the final six months of my course if I came back onto the graduate development programme, which I accepted.

'I enjoy being set difficult challenges at work that I can get my teeth into as these are always the most rewarding. It used to be daunting being thrown into a new department, possibly in a new company, every six months, but I have learnt to relish it. That is truly when you learn the most, with a great support network around you.'

VICTORIA HAMILTON – FINAL YEAR STUDENT, MECHANICAL ENGINEERING

Victoria told us what her MEng at Brunel University involves:

'My four-year course is made up of several modules each year, including solid body mechanics, thermofluids, analytical methods, modelling and design. I have worked on a number of design projects: one of which involved designing and constructing a miniature bridge out of wood. I have also used computer packages for design projects, such as redesigning a gear box and a fruit juicer. The last two years involve two major projects: one individual and one group. My final year includes more group assignments in preparation for a career in engineering.'

ROBERT MILNE – ELECTRICAL ENGINEER

Robert completed a MEng in electrical engineering, he tells us about this job.

'I work as an on-site commissioning engineer for a company that specialises in the design and commissioning of electrical power systems. I work on worldwide projects so I spend a lot of time travelling. I test electrical plant, coordinate with engineers and management on-site, and do preparatory work to enable a power system or an item of electrical plant to be energised. This includes ensuring the item I am working on is safe and fit for purpose. Often I am the sole representative of my company on-site and have the final say on whether to energise expensive equipment or not, and ensure it will not be damaged or cause harm to people.'

Applicant journey

SIX EASY STEPS TO UNIVERSITY AND COLLEGE

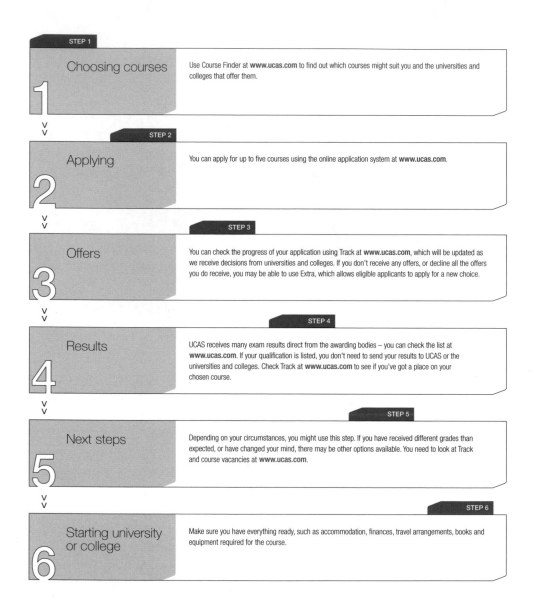

STEP 1

Choosing courses

Use Course Finder at **www.ucas.com** to find out which courses might suit you and the universities and colleges that offer them.

1

STEP 2

Applying

You can apply for up to five courses using the online application system at **www.ucas.com**.

2

STEP 3

Offers

You can check the progress of your application using Track at **www.ucas.com**, which will be updated as we receive decisions from universities and colleges. If you don't receive any offers, or decline all the offers you do receive, you may be able to use Extra, which allows eligible applicants to apply for a new choice.

3

STEP 4

Results

UCAS receives many exam results direct from the awarding bodies – you can check the list at **www.ucas.com**. If your qualification is listed, you don't need to send your results to UCAS or the universities and colleges. Check Track at **www.ucas.com** to see if you've got a place on your chosen course.

4

STEP 5

Next steps

Depending on your circumstances, you might use this step. If you have received different grades than expected, or have changed your mind, there may be other options available. You need to look at Track and course vacancies at **www.ucas.com**.

5

STEP 6

Starting university or college

Make sure you have everything ready, such as accommodation, finances, travel arrangements, books and equipment required for the course.

6

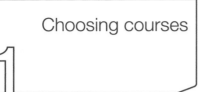

Choosing courses

1

Step 1 – Planning your application for engineering

Are you wondering how to get into engineering, and what kind of course might be best for you? Sometimes all the decisions you have to make can seem daunting, but help is at hand.

PICK YOUR ROUTE

Engineering is one of the few areas where experience and training, as opposed to just academic qualifications, can take you right to the top. With the right background – usually involving science, maths and technology – the engineering world is your oyster.

For example, four or more GCSEs at Grades C–E could lead to on-the-job training and an apprenticeship (level 2), which in turn could lead to a job as an engineering operator.

Four or five GCSEs (grade C minimum and including English, mathematics and science) could also lead to an Advanced Apprenticeship (level 3–4) and a career as an engineering technician. Further study could lead to level 4–5 training and sponsorship for a Foundation degree, an HND or a degree course.

Degrees, with further professional training, can lead to chartered or incorporated status. For more information about the routes into engineering, see the diagram on page 54 and visit **www.tomorrowsengineers.co.uk**, which also has individual route maps for England, Wales and Scotland (**www.tomorrowsengineers.co.uk/resources.cfm**).

WHAT ARE YOUR CHANCES?

At the moment there aren't enough engineers in the UK
to meet demand, so your chances could be pretty good.
In short, the time is now. If you're the right person with
the right level of dedication, creativity and application
there will be no stopping you.

HOW DO I FIND THE BEST COURSE FOR ME?

For courses on offer, see Course Finder at **www.ucas.com**.

Applicants are advised to use various sources of information in order to make their choices for higher education.
League tables might be a component of this research, but applicants should bear in mind that these tables attempt
to rank institutions in an overall order, which reflects the interests, preoccupations and decisions of those who have
produced and edited them. The ways in which they are compiled vary greatly and you need to look closely at the
criteria that have been used. See page 72 for more information about league tables.

TOP TIP

Make a list of the things that matter to you – entry requirements, campus facilities, accredited courses, industrial
placements, year abroad options, choice of modules – and ask the same questions at each open day to make your
comparison.

Choosing courses

1

Planning your application for mathematics

At least one mathematics A level (or equivalent) is essential for all courses in mathematical science. Further mathematics is very useful too, though two AS level mathematics qualifications may be considered. Many courses are designed so that applicants who didn't get the chance to study further mathematics at A level will still find the course accessible, but in every case studying more mathematics will help you succeed. Generally, by the end of the first year, all students should have been brought up to a similar level irrespective of their previous qualifications.

Some courses provide the possibility of including a year working for an employer in industry, business or commerce. This gives an opportunity to see how applied mathematics courses such as statistics are implemented in real-life work situations.

Topics in applied mathematics link well with subjects such as physics, but mathematics forms the basis of so many sciences that an A level in almost any science-based subject is a bonus. Common joint honours courses include physics, computing, philosophy, business, finance or a language – if you're considering this then previous study will help but is not always essential. Interest in other subjects can be nurtured in the final year at some institutions; ask for details when you visit.

In general, the more pure mathematics you study at A level standard the better. A solid understanding at this level will smooth the pathway to all areas of mathematics, including applied mathematics and statistics courses.

Most courses will contain some work involving mathematical computing software, and the university's facilities for this should be considered whether you plan to focus on this area or not.

Some universities will make you an offer based on the UCAS Tariff, but most are more interested in your specific mathematics grades and an offer is more likely to be conditional on these.

There are three professional societies in the mathematical sciences, each of which can give help and guidance: the Institute of Mathematics and its Applications (IMA, **www.ima.org.uk**), the London Mathematical Society (LMS, **www.lms.ac.uk**) and the Royal Statistical Society (RSS, **www.rss.org.uk**). They all run lively scientific meetings and publish journals. The IMA and the RSS each offer chartered status to members with appropriate qualifications and experience, and the LMS is particularly active in supporting mathematicians in research.

HOW DO I FIND THE BEST COURSE FOR ME?

For courses on offer, see Course Finder at **www.ucas.com**.

Applicants are advised to use various sources of information in order to make their choices for higher education. League tables might be a component of this research, but applicants should bear in mind that these tables attempt to rank institutions in an overall order, which reflects the interests, preoccupations and decisions of those who have produced and edited them. The ways in which they are compiled vary greatly and you need to look closely at the criteria that have been used. See page 72 for more information about league tables.

TOP TIP

Make a list of the things that matter to you – entry requirements, campus facilities, accredited courses, industrial placements, year abroad options, choice of modules – and ask the same questions at each open day to make your comparison.

Choosing courses

1

Choosing courses

Start thinking about what you want to study and where you want to go. This section will help you, and see what courses are available where in the listings (starting on page 127). Check that the entry requirements required for each course meet your academic expectations.

Use the UCAS website – www.ucas.com has lots of advice on how to find a course. Go to the students' section of the website for the best advice or go straight to Course Finder to see all the courses available through UCAS. Our map of the UK at **www.ucas.com/students/choosingcourses/choosinguni/map/** shows you where all the universities and colleges are located.

Watch UCAStv – at **www.ucas.tv** there are videos on *How to choose your course, Attending events, and Open days* as well as case studies from students talking about their experience of finding a course at university or college.

Attend UCAS conventions – UCAS conventions are held throughout the country. Universities and colleges have exhibition stands where their staff offer information about their courses and institutions. Details of when the conventions are happening, and a convention planner to help you prepare, are at **www.ucas.com/conventions**.

Look at university and college websites and prospectuses – Universities and colleges have prospectuses and course-specific leaflets on their undergraduate courses. Your school or college library may have copies or go to the university's website to download a copy, or ask them to send one to you.

Go to university and college open days – most institutions offer open days to anyone who wants to attend. See the list of universities and colleges on **www.ucas.com** and the UCAS *Open Days* publication (see the Essential Reading chapter) for information on when they are taking place. Aim to visit all of the universities and colleges you are interested in before you apply. It will help with your expectations of university life and make sure the course is the right one for you.

League tables – these can be helpful but bear in mind that they attempt to rank institutions in an overall order reflecting the views of those that produce them. They may not reflect your views and needs. Examples can be found at **www.thecompleteuniversityguide.co.uk**, **www.guardian.co.uk/education/universityguide**, **www.thetimes.co.uk** (subscription service) and **www.thesundaytimes.co.uk** (subscription service). See page 72 for more information about league tables.

Do your research – speak and refer to as many trusted sources as you can find. Talk to someone already doing the job you have in mind. The section on 'Which area?' on page 22 will help you identify the different areas of engineering you might want to enter.

UCAS CARD

At its simplest, the UCAS Card scheme is the start of your UCAS journey. It can save you a packet on the high street with exclusive offers to UCAS Card holders, as well as providing you with hints and tips about finding the best course at the right university or college. If that's not enough you'll also receive these benefits:

- frequent expert help from UCAS, with all the essential information you need on the application process
- free monthly newsletters providing advice, hints, tips and exclusive discounts
- tailored information on the universities and courses you're interested in
- and much more.

If you're in Year 12, S5 or equivalent and thinking about higher education for autumn 2013, sign up for your FREE UCAS Card today to receive all these benefits at **www.ucas.com/ucascard**.

DECIDING ON YOUR COURSE CHOICES

Through UCAS you can initially apply for up to five courses. How do you find out more information to make an informed decision?

Remember you don't have to make five course choices. Only apply for a course if you're completely happy with both the course and the university or college and you would definitely be prepared to accept a place.

How do you narrow down your course choices? First of all, look up course details in this book or on Course Finder at **www.ucas.com**. This will give you an idea of the full range of courses and topics on offer. You may want to study engineering or maths as single subjects, but there are also many courses which also include

additional options, such as a modern language (check out the degree subjects studied by our case studies). You'll quickly be able to eliminate institutions that don't offer the right course, or you can choose a 'hit list' of institutions first, and then see what they have to offer.

Once you've made a short(er) list, look at university or college websites, and generally find out as much as you can about the course, department and institution. Don't be afraid to contact them to ask for more information, request their prospectus or arrange an open day visit.

1 Choosing courses

Choosing
your institution

Different people look for different things from their university or college course, but the checklist on the next page sets out the kinds of factors all prospective students should consider when choosing their university. Keep this list in mind on open days, when talking to friends about their experiences at various universities and colleges, or while reading prospectuses and websites.

HOW WILL THEY CHOOSE YOU?

Most engineering and maths admissions departments will have different entry criteria, so make sure that you check prospectuses, websites and all other materials thoroughly before you apply. Even better, why not give them a call and discuss it with them directly? Not only will it leave you better prepared to submit a targeted application, but it will also demonstrate that you're self-motivated.

Unlike some other subjects, it's unlikely that you'll have to sit an entry test. This means that if there is an interview (and in many cases there will be) it is particularly important.

THE INTERVIEW

Talk to someone who has been – or is currently – on the course that you are applying for. What was their interview like? What kinds of questions were they asked? Be prepared and if possible do a mock interview with a friend before you go for the real thing.

DEMONSTRATE YOUR PASSION

University admissions tutors need to know that you're genuinely interested in the subject you've chosen to study for three or four years and that it's the right one for you. You, too, need to know exactly why you've applied for a specific course and be able to explain your motivation. It might be that a particular event in your life sparked your interest: this could be a course you took at school, a trip to a museum, a hobby, someone you know who works in the field, time spent in a related work environment, and so on. The first place to convince tutors about your interest will be in the personal statement you send through UCAS – for information and help on personal statements, go to page 87.

THINGS TO CONSIDER WHEN CHOOSING YOUR INSTITUTION	
Location	Do you want to stay close to home? Would you prefer to study at a city or campus university or college?
Grades required	Use the Course Finder facility on the UCAS website, **www.ucas.com**, to view entry requirements for courses you are interested in. Also, check out the university or college website or call up the admissions office. Some institutions specify grades required, eg AAB, while others specify points required, eg 340. If they ask for points, it means they're using the UCAS Tariff system, which awards points to different types and levels of qualification. For example, an A grade at A level = 120 points; a B grade at A level = 100 points. The full Tariff tables are available on pages 98-105 and at **www.ucas.com**.
Employer links	Ask the course tutor or department about links with employers, especially for placements or work experience.
Graduate prospects	Ask the careers office for their list of graduate destinations.
Cost	Some institutions offer more financial assistance than others. Make sure you know the list of options before you commit.
Coursework and structure	How much time are you likely to spend in lectures? How much time will be spent in tutorials?
Instinct	After you've weighed up all the pros and cons, what does your heart tell you?
'Fit'	Even if all the above criteria stack up, this one relies on gut feel – go and visit the institution if you can and see if it's 'you'.

> Choosing courses

1

League tables

The information that follows has been provided by Dr Bernard Kingston of *The Complete University Guide*.

League tables are worth consulting early in your research and perhaps for confirmation later on. But never rely on them in isolation – always use them alongside other information sources available to you. Universities typically report that over a third of prospective students view league tables as important or very important in making their university choices. They give an insight into quality and are mainly based on data from the universities themselves. Somewhat confusingly, tables published in, say, 2012 are referred to as the 2013 tables because they are aimed at applicants going to university in that following year. The well known ones - *The Complete University Guide*, *The Guardian*, *The Times*, and *The Sunday Times* - rank the institutions and the subjects they teach using input measures (eg entry standards), throughput measures (eg student : staff ratios) and output measures (eg graduate prospects). Some tables are free to access whilst others are behind pay walls. All are interactive and enable users to create their own tables based on the measures important to them.

The universities are provided with their raw data for checking and are regularly consulted on methodology. But ultimately it is the compilers who decide what measures to use and what weights to put on them. They are competitors and rarely consult amongst themselves. So, for example, *The Times* tables differ significantly from *The Sunday Times* ones even though both newspapers belong to the same media proprietor.

Whilst the main university rankings tend to get the headlines, we would stress that the individual subject tables are as least as important, if not more so, when deciding where to study. All universities, regardless of their overall ranking, have some academic departments that rank highly in their subjects. Beware also giving much weight to an institution being a few places higher or lower in the tables – this is likely to be of little significance. This is particularly true in the lower half of the main table where overall scores show considerable bunching.

Most of the measures used to define quality come from hard factual data provided by the Higher Education Statistics Agency (HESA) but some, like student satisfaction and peer assessment, are derived from surveys of subjective impressions where you might wish to query sample size. We give a brief overview of the common measures here but please go to the individual websites for full details.

- **Student satisfaction** is derived from the annual National Student Survey (NSS) and is heavily used by *The Guardian* and *The Sunday Times.*
- **Research assessment** comes from a 2008 exercise (RAE) aimed at defining the quality of a university's research (excluded by *The Guardian*).
- **Entry standards** are based on the full UCAS Tariff scores obtained by new students.
- **Student : staff ratio** gives the number of students per member of academic staff.
- **Expenditure figures** show the costs of academic and student services.
- **Good honours** lists the proportion of graduates gaining a first or upper second honours degree.
- **Completion** indicates the proportion of students who successfully complete their studies.

- **Graduate prospects** usually reports the proportion of graduates who obtain a graduate job – not any job – or continue studying within six months of leaving.
- **Peer assessment** is used only by *The Sunday Times* which asks academics to rate other universities in their subjects.
- **Value added** is used only by *The Guardian* and compares entry standards with good honours.

All four main publishers of UK league tables (see Table 1) also publish university subject tables. *The Complete University Guide* and *The Times* are based on four measures: student satisfaction, research quality, entry standards and graduate destinations. *The Sunday Times* uses student satisfaction, entry standards, graduate destinations, graduate unemployment, good degrees and drop-out rate, while *The Guardian* uses student satisfaction (as three separate measures), entry standards, graduate destinations, student-staff ratio, spend per student and value added. This use of different measures is one reason why the different tables can yield different results (sometimes very different, especially in the case of *The Guardian* which has least in common with the other tables).

League tables compiled by *The Complete University Guide* (**www.thecompleteuniversityguide.co.uk**) and *The Guardian* (**www.guardian.co.uk**) are available in spring, those by *The Times* (**www.thetimes.co.uk**) and *The Sunday Times* (**www.thesundaytimes.co.uk**) in the summer.

Table 1 – measures used by the main publishers of UK league tables

	Universities	Measures	Subjects	Measures
The Complete University Guide	116	9	62	4
The Guardian	119	8	46	8
The Sunday Times	122	8	39	6
The Times	116	8	62	4

THINGS TO WATCH OUT FOR WHEN READING SUBJECT LEAGUE TABLES

- Some subject tables may combine two or more of the engineering subject disciplines (eg civil engineering and chemical engineering in *The Sunday Times*).
- The tables make no distinction between universities which offer courses that are accredited by the Engineering Council and those which do not.
- Many universities offer engineering courses with a foundation year – an additional year at the start of the course for students who do not qualify for direct entry to year one. The qualifications of these students are usually omitted from the Tariff score.

WHO PUBLISHES ENGINEERING AND MATHEMATICS LEAGUE TABLES?

The Complete University Guide	Aeronautical and manufacturing engineering Chemical engineering Civil engineering Electrical and electronic engineering General engineering Materials technology Mathematics Mechanical engineering
The Guardian	Engineering: chemical Engineering: civil Engineering: electrical and electronic Engineering: materials and mineral Mathematics Engineering: mechanical
The Sunday Times	Civil, chemical and other engineering Electronic and electrical engineering Mathematical sciences Mechanical engineering
The Times	Aeronautical and manufacturing engineering Chemical engineering Civil engineering Electrical and electronic engineering General engineering Materials technology Mathematics Mechanical engineering

wondering how much higher education costs?

need information about student finance?

Visit www.ucas.com/students/studentfinance and find sources for all the information on student money matters you need.

With access to up-to-date information on bursaries, scholarships and variable fees, plus our online budget calculator. Visit us today and get the full picture.

www.ucas.com/students/studentfinance

Choosing courses

1

The cost of higher education

The information in this section was up-to-date when this book was published. You should visit the websites mentioned in this section for the very latest information.

The cost of studying in the UK

As a student, you will usually have to pay for two things: tuition fees for your course, which for most students do not need to be paid for up front, and living costs such as rent, food, books, transport and entertainment. Fees charged vary between courses, between universities and colleges and also according to your normal country of residence, so it's important to check these before you apply. Course fee information is supplied to UCAS by the universities and is displayed in Course Finder at **www.ucas.com**.

Student loans

The purpose of student loans from the Government is to help cover the costs of your tuition fees and basic living costs (rent, bills, food and so on). Two types are available: a tuition fee loan to cover the tuition charges and a maintenance loan to help with accommodation and other living costs. Both types of student loan are available to all students who meet the basic eligibility requirements. Interest will be charged at inflation plus a fixed percentage while you are studying. In addition, many other commercial loans are available to students studying at university or college but the interest rate can vary considerably. Loans to help with living costs will be available for all eligible students, irrespective of family income.

Find out more information from the relevant sites below:

England: Student Finance England –
www.direct.gov.uk/studentfinance
Northern Ireland: Student Finance Northern Ireland –
www.studentfinanceni.co.uk
Scotland: Student Awards Agency for Scotland –
www.saas.gov.uk
Wales: Student Finance Wales –
www.studentfinancewales.co.uk or
www.cyllidmyfyrwyrcymru.co.uk

Bursaries and scholarships

- The National Scholarships Programme gives financial help to students studying in England. The scheme is designed to help students whose families have lower incomes.
- Students from families with lower incomes will be entitled to a non-repayable maintenance grant to help with living costs.
- Many universities and colleges also offer non-repayable scholarships and bursaries to help students cover tuition and living costs whilst studying.
- All eligible part-time undergraduates who study for at least 25% of their time will be able to apply for a loan to cover the costs of their tuition, which means they no longer have to pay up front.

There will be extra support for disabled students and students with child or adult dependants. For more information, visit the country-specific websites listed above.

Choosing courses

1

International students

APPLYING TO STUDY IN THE UK

Deciding to go to university or college in the UK is very exciting. You need to think about what course to do, where to study, and how much it will cost. The decisions you make can have a huge effect on your future but UCAS is here to help.

How to apply

Whatever your age or qualifications, if you want to apply for any of over 35,000 courses listed at 300 universities and colleges on the UCAS website, you must apply through UCAS at **www.ucas.com**. If you are unsure, your school, college, adviser, or local British Council office will be able to help. Further advice and a video guide for international students can be found on the non-UK students' section of the UCAS website at **www.ucas.com/international**.

Students may apply on their own or through their school, college, adviser, or local British Council if this is registered with UCAS to use Apply. If you choose to use an education agent's services, check with the British Council to see if they hold a list of certificated or registered agents in your country. Check also on any charges you may need to pay. UCAS charges only the application fee (see below) but agents may charge for additional services.

How much will my application cost?

If you choose to apply to more than one course, university or college you need to pay UCAS £23 GBP when you apply. If you only apply to one course at one university or college, you pay UCAS £12 GBP.

WHAT LEVEL OF ENGLISH?

UCAS provides a list of English language qualifications and grades that are acceptable to most UK universities and colleges, however you are advised to contact the institutions directly as each have their own entry requirement in English. For more information go to **www.ucas.com/students/wheretostart/nonukstude nts/englangprof**.

INTERNATIONAL STUDENT FEES

If you study in the UK, your fee status (whether you pay full-cost fees or a subsidised fee rate) will be decided by the UK university or college you plan to attend. Before you decide which university or college to attend, you need to be absolutely certain that you can pay the full cost of:

- your tuition fees (the amount is set by universities and colleges, so contact them for more information – visit their websites where many list their fees. Fee details will also be included on Course Finder at **www.ucas.com**
- the everyday living expenses for you (and your family) for the whole time that you are in the UK, including accommodation, food, gas and electricity bills, clothes, travel and leisure activities
- books and equipment for your course
- travel to and from your country.

You must include everything when you work out how much it will cost. You can get information to help you do this accurately from the international offices at universities and colleges, UKCISA (UK Council for International Student Affairs) and the British Council. There is a useful website tool to help you manage your money at university – **www.studentcalculator.org.uk**.

Scholarships and bursaries are offered at some universities and colleges and you should contact them for more information. In addition, you should check with your local British Council for additional scholarships available to students from your country who want to study in the UK.

LEGAL DOCUMENTS YOU WILL NEED

As you prepare to study in the UK, it is very important to think about the legal documents you will need to enter the country.

Everyone who comes to study in the UK needs a valid passport, details of which will be collected either in your UCAS application or later through Track. If you do not yet have a passport, you should apply for one as soon as possible. People from certain countries also need visas before they come into the UK. They are known as 'visa nationals'. You can check if you require a visa to travel to the UK by visiting the UK Border Agency website and selecting 'Studying in the UK', so please check the UK Border Agency website at **www.ukba.homeoffice.gov.uk** for the most up-to-date guidance and information about the United Kingdom's visa requirements.

When you apply for your visa you need to make sure you have the following documents.

- A confirmation of acceptance for studies (CAS) number from the university or college where you are going to study. The university or college must be on the UKBA Register of Sponsors in order to accept international students.
- A valid passport.

- Evidence that you have enough money to pay for your course and living costs.
- Certificates for all qualifications you have that are relevant to the course you have been accepted for and for any English language qualifications.

You will also have to give your biometric data.

Do check for further information from your local British Embassy or High Commission. Guidance information for international students is also available from UKCISA and from UKBA.

ADDITIONAL RESOURCES

There are a number of organisations that can provide further guidance and information to you as you prepare to study in the UK:

- British Council
  www.britishcouncil.org
- Education UK (British Council website dealing with educational matters)
  www.educationuk.org
- English UK (British Council accredited website listing English language courses in the UK)
  www.englishuk.com
- UK Border Agency (provides information on visa requirements and applications)
  www.ukba.homeoffice.gov.uk
- UKCISA (UK Council for International Student Affairs)
  www.ukcisa.org.uk
- Directgov (the official UK government website)
  www.direct.gov.uk
- Prepare for Success
  www.prepareforsuccess.org.uk

www.ucas.com

at the heart of connecting people to higher education

Applying

2

Step 2 – Applying

You apply through UCAS using the online application system, called Apply, at **www.ucas.com**. You can apply for a maximum of five choices, but you don't have to use them all if you don't want to. If you apply for fewer than five choices, you can add more at a later date if you want to. But be aware of the course application deadlines (you can find these in Course Finder at **www.ucas.com**).

APPLICANT JOURNEY <

IMPORTANT DATES FOR 2012 ENTRY	
Early June 2012	UCAS Apply opens for 2013 entry registration.
Mid-September 2012	Applications can be sent to UCAS.
15 October 2012	Application deadline for the receipt at UCAS of applications for all medicine, dentistry, veterinary medicine and veterinary science courses and for all courses at the universities of Oxford and Cambridge.
15 January 2013	Application deadline for the receipt at UCAS of applications for all courses except those listed above with a 15 October deadline, and some art and design courses with a 24 March deadline.
25 February 2013	Extra starts (see page 94 for more information about Extra).
24 March 2013	Application deadline for the receipt at UCAS of applications for art and design courses except those listed on Course Finder at **www.ucas.com** with a 15 January deadline.
31 March 2013	If you apply by 15 January, the universities and colleges should aim to have sent their decisions by this date (but they can take longer).
9 May 2013	If you apply by 15 January, universities and colleges need to send their decisions by this date. If they don't, UCAS will make any outstanding choices unsuccessful on their behalf.
30 June 2013	If you send your application to us by this date, we will send it to your chosen universities and colleges. Applications received after this date are entered into Clearing (see page 108 for more information about Clearing).
3 July 2013	Last date to apply through Extra.
August 2013 (date to be confirmed)	Scottish Qualifications Authority (SQA) results are published.
15 August 2013	GCE and Advanced Diploma results are published (often known as 'A level results day'). Adjustment opens for registration (see page 109 for more information about Adjustment).

DON'T FORGET...

Universities and colleges guarantee to consider your application only if we receive it by the appropriate deadline. Check application deadlines for your courses on Course Finder at **www.ucas.com**.

If you send it to UCAS after the deadline but before 30 June 2013, universities and colleges will consider your application only if they still have places available.

Applying

2

How to apply

You apply online at **www.ucas.com** through Apply – a secure, web-based application service that is designed for all our applicants, whether they are applying through a UCAS-registered centre or as an individual, anywhere in the world. Apply is:

- easy to access – all you need is an internet connection
- easy to use – you don't have to complete your application all in one go: you can save the sections as you complete them and come back to it later
- easy to monitor – once you've applied, you can use Track to check the progress of your application, including any decisions from universities or colleges. You can also reply to your offers using Track.

Watch the UCAStv guide to applying through UCAS at **www.ucas.tv.**

APPLICATION FEE

For 2013 entry the fee for applying through UCAS is £23 for two or more choices and £12 for one choice.

You can submit only one UCAS application in each year's application cycle.

DEFERRED ENTRY

If you want to apply for deferred entry in 2014, perhaps because you want to take a year out between school or college and higher education, you should check that the university or college will accept a deferred entry application. Occasionally, tutors are not happy to accept students who take a gap year, because it interrupts the flow of their learning. If you apply for deferred entry, you must meet the conditions of any offers by 31 August 2013 unless otherwise agreed by the university or college. If you accept a place for 2014 entry and then change your mind, you cannot reapply through us in the 2014 entry cycle unless you withdraw your original application.

1 GET SCHOOL OR COLLEGE 'BUZZWORD'

Ask your UCAS application coordinator (may be your sixth form tutor) for your school or college UCAS 'buzzword'. This is a password for the school or college.

2 REGISTER

Go to **www.ucas.com/students/apply** and click on **Register/Log in to use Apply** and then **register**. After you have entered your registration details, the online system will automatically generate a username for you, but you'll have to come up with a password and answers to security questions.

3 COMPLETE SEVEN SECTIONS

Complete all the sections of the application. To access any section, click on the section name at the left of the screen and follow the instructions. The sections are:

Personal details – contact details, residential status, disability status

Additional information – only UK applicants need to complete this section

Student finance – UK students can share some of their application details with their student finance company. Finance information is provided for other EU and international applicants.

Choices – which courses you'd like to apply for

Education – your education and qualifications

Employment – eg work experience, holiday jobs

Statement – see page 87 for personal statement advice.

Before you can send your application you need to go to the **View all details** screen and tick the **section completed** box.

4 PASS TO REFEREE

Once you've completed all the sections, send your application electronically to your referee (normally your form tutor). They'll check it, approve it and add their reference to it, and will then send it to UCAS on your behalf.

- Important details like date of birth and course codes will be checked by Apply. It will alert you if they are not valid.
- We strongly recommend that the personal statement and reference are written in a word-processing package and pasted in to Apply.
- If you want to, you can enter European characters into certain areas of Apply.
- You can change your application at any time before it is completed and sent to UCAS.
- You can print and preview your application at any time. Before you send it you need to go to the **View all details** screen and tick the **section completed** box.
- Your school, college or centre can choose different payment methods. For example, they may want us to bill them, or you may be able to pay online by debit or credit card.

NOT APPLYING THROUGH A SCHOOL OR COLLEGE

If you're not currently studying, you'll probably be applying as an independent applicant rather than through a school, college or other UCAS-registered centre. In this case you won't be able to provide a 'buzzword', but we'll ask you a few extra questions to check you are eligible to apply.

If you're not applying through a UCAS-registered centre, the procedure you use for obtaining a reference will depend on whether or not you want your reference to be provided through a registered centre. For information on the procedures for providing references, visit **www.ucas.com/students/applying/howtoapply/reference**.

INVISIBILITY OF CHOICES

Universities and colleges cannot see details of the other choices on your application until you reply to any offers or you are unsuccessful at all your choices.

You can submit only one UCAS application in each year's application cycle.

APPLICATION CHECKLIST

We want this to run smoothly for you and we also want to process your application as quickly as possible. You can help us to do this by remembering to do the following:

✓ check the closing dates for applications – see page 83
✓ check the student finance information at **www.ucas.com/students/studentfinance/** and course fees information in Course Finder at **www.ucas.com**
✓ start early and allow plenty of time for completing your application – including enough time for your referee to complete the reference section
✓ read the online instructions carefully before you start
✓ consider what each question is actually asking for – use the 'help'
✓ pay special attention to your personal statement (see page 87) and start drafting it early
✓ ask a teacher, parent, friend or careers adviser to review your draft application – particularly the personal statement
✓ if you get stuck, watch our videos on YouTube where we answer your frequently asked questions on completing a UCAS application at **www.youtube.com/ucasonline**
✓ if you have extra information that will not fit on your application, send it direct to your chosen universities or colleges after we have sent you your Welcome letter with your Personal ID – don't send it to us
✓ print a copy of the final version of your application, in case you are asked questions on it at an interview.

Applying

2

The personal statement

Next to choosing your courses, this section of your application will be the most time-consuming. It is of immense importance as many universities and colleges make their selection relying solely on the information in the UCAS application, rather than interviews and admissions tests. The personal statement can be the deciding factor in whether or not they offer you a place. If it is an institution that interviews, your statement could be the deciding factor in whether you get invited for interview.

Keep a copy of your personal statement – if you are called for interview, you will almost certainly be asked questions based on it.

Tutors will look carefully at your exam results, actual and predicted, your reference and your personal statement. Remember, they are looking for reasons to offer you a place – try to give them every opportunity to do so!

A SALES DOCUMENT

The personal statement is your opportunity to sell yourself, so do so. The university or college admissions tutor wants to get a rounded picture of you to decide whether you will make an interesting member of the university or college both academically and socially. They want to know more about you than the subjects you are studying at school.

HOW TO START

At **www.ucas.com** you'll find several tools to help you write a good personal statement.

- Personal statement timeline, to help you do all your research and plan your statement over several drafts and checks.
- Personal statement mind map, which gives you reminders and hints on preparation, content and presentation, with extra hints for mature and international applicants.
- Personal statement worksheet, which gets you to start writing by asking relevant questions so that you include everything you need. You can also check your work against a list of dos and don'ts .

WHAT TO INCLUDE

As well as putting across your enthusiasm for the subject in general, explain why you are applying for the specific course: what interests you about it and why? Try to show what has sparked your appetite for this area and how you have followed it up, for example with further reading or other activities. Talk about what aspects of engineering or mathematics you have most enjoyed studying so far. If you can, say something about your goals and career plans. You may not know exactly what you would like to do in the future but show that you have done a little research into the possibilities.

For maths courses include any participation in maths-related activities such as competitions or maths and science-related enrichment programmes organised by your school or other bodies.

For engineering courses include any experiences of extra-curricular applications of engineering that have demonstrated your analytical skills and practical

engagement with engineering to solve problems in the real world.

Try to use real examples to show you have the skills to successfully study at a higher level, for example time management skills (maybe you have juggled study with regular part-time work or extra-curricular interests?), commitment and maturity.

Your interests and hobbies also have a place: tutors want to know that you will be an interesting person to have around the department!

WORK EXPERIENCE

Work experience, voluntary or paid, that has some relevance to the subject you want to study is of course very helpful! For would-be engineers, this could be some time spent working in your uncle's garage, in a local bike shop or in a computer shop. For mathematicians, a work experience placement in a bank or financial services firm is useful material to show your understanding of the importance of mathematics in the real world.

If you are a school leaver, admissions tutors will be aware that it may not always have been possible to find 'relevant' work experience, so don't worry unduly if you fall into this category. Admissions tutors recognise the value of the skills developed from other kinds of experience too: any work experience, from a paper round to a stint helping out in an old people's home, can be a great way of building transferable skills, such as good communication, teamwork and problem solving (very important attributes for engineers), and showing that you are a reliable and hardworking individual. So think about what you learned and discovered about your skills during any work experience you have had, and use it in your personal statement.

Visit **www.ucas.tv** to view our video to help guide you through the process and address the most common fears and concerns about writing a personal statement.

WHAT ADMISSIONS TUTORS LOOK FOR

- Your reasons for wanting to take this subject in general and this particular course.
- Your communication skills – not only what you say but how you say it. Your grammar and spelling must be perfect.
- Relevant experience – practical things you've done that are related to your choice of course.
- Evidence of your teamworking ability, leadership capability, independence.
- Evidence of your skills, for example: IT skills, empathy and people skills, debating and public speaking, research and analysis.
- Other activities that show your dedication and ability to apply yourself and maintain your motivation.

WHAT TO TELL THEM

- Why you want to do this subject – how you know it is the subject for you.
- What experience you already have in this field – for example work experience, school projects, hobbies, voluntary work.
- The skills and qualities you have as a person that would make you a good student, for example anything that shows your dedication, communication ability, academic achievement, initiative.
- Examples that show you can knuckle down and apply yourself, for example running a marathon or your Extended Project.
- If you're taking a gap year, why you've chosen this and (if possible) what you're going to do during it.
- About your other interests and activities away from studying – to show you're a rounded person. (But remember that it is mainly your suitability for the particular course that they're looking to judge.)

Save with UCAS Card

If you're in Year 12, S5 or equivalent and thinking about higher education, sign up for the **FREE** UCAS Card to receive all these benefits:

- information about courses and unis
- expert advice from UCAS
- exclusive discounts for card holders

UCAS

Register today at
www.ucas.com/ucascard

find us on
Facebook

Offers

3

Step 3 – Offers

Once we have sent your application to your chosen universities and colleges, they will each consider it independently and tell us whether or not they can offer you a place. Some universities and colleges will take longer to make decisions than others. You may be asked to attend an interview, sit an additional test or provide a piece of work, such as an essay, before a decision can be made.

INTERVIEWS

Many universities (particularly the more popular ones, running competitive courses) use interviews as part of their selection process. Universities will want to find out why you want to study your chosen course at their institution, and they want to judge whether the course is suitable for you and your future career plans. Interviews also give you an opportunity to visit the university and ask any questions you may have about the course or their institution.

If you are called for interview, the key areas they are likely to cover will be:

- evidence of your academic ability
- your capacity to study hard
- your commitment to an engineering or maths career, best shown by work experience
- your awareness of current issues in the news that may have an impact on your chosen field of study
- your logic and reasoning ability.

A lot of the interview will be based on information on your application, especially your personal statement. See pages 87-89 for tips about the personal statement.

Whenever a university or college makes a decision about your application, we record it and let you know. You can check the progress of your application using Track at **www.ucas.com**. This is our secure online service which gives you access to your application, using the same username and password you used when you applied. You use it to find out if you have been invited for an interview or need to provide an additional piece of work, and you can check to see if you have received any offers. Whenever there is any change in your application status, we email you to advise you to check Track.

TYPES OF OFFER

Universities can make two types of offer: conditional or unconditional.

Conditional offer

A conditional offer means the university or college will offer you a place if you meet certain conditions – usually based on exam results. The conditions may be based on Tariff points (for example, 300 points from three A levels), or specify certain grades in named subjects (for example, A in economics, B in accounting, C in business studies).

Unconditional offer

If you've met all the academic requirements for the course and the university or college wants to accept you, they will make you an unconditional offer. If you accept this you'll have a definite place. However, there might be other requirements, such as medical or financial conditions, that you need to meet before you can start your course.

REPLYING TO OFFERS

When you have received decisions for all your choices, you must decide which offers you want to accept. You will be given a deadline in Track by which you have to make your replies. Before replying, get advice from family, friends or advisers, but remember that you're the one taking the course so it's your decision.

Firm acceptance

- Your firm acceptance is your first choice - this is your preferred choice out of all the offers you have received. You can only have one firm acceptance.
- If you accept an unconditional offer, you are entering a contract that you will attend the course, so you must decline any other offers.
- If you accept a conditional offer, you are agreeing that you will attend the course at that university or college if you meet the conditions of the offer. You can accept another offer as an insurance choice.

Insurance acceptance

- If your firm acceptance is a conditional offer, you can accept another offer as an insurance choice. Your insurance choice can be conditional or unconditional and acts as a back-up, so if you don't meet the conditions for your firm choice but meet the conditions for your insurance, you will be committed to the insurance choice. You can only have one insurance choice.
- The conditions for your insurance choice would usually be lower than your firm choice.
- You don't have to accept an insurance choice if you don't want one; you need to be certain that it's an offer you would be happy to accept.

For more information watch our video guides *How to use Track, Making sense of your offers,* and *How to reply to your offers* at **www.ucas.tv**.

WHAT IF YOU HAVE NO OFFERS?

If you have used all five choices on your application and either received no offers, or decided to turn down any offers you have received, you may be eligible to apply for another choice through Extra. Find out more about Extra on page 94.

If you are not eligible for Extra, in the summer you can contact universities and colleges with vacancies in Clearing. See page 108 for more information.

> 3   Offers

Extra

Extra allows you to make additional choices, one at a time, without having to wait for Clearing in July. It is completely optional and free, and is designed to encourage you to continue researching and choosing courses if you are holding no offers. You can search for courses available through Extra on Course Finder, at **www.ucas.com**. The Extra service is available to eligible applicants from 25 February to early July 2013 through Track at **www.ucas.com**.

WHO IS ELIGIBLE?

You will be eligible for Extra if you have already made five choices and:

- you have had unsuccessful or withdrawal decisions from all five of your choices, or
- you have cancelled your outstanding choices and hold no offers, or
- you have received decisions from all five choices and have declined all offers made to you.

HOW DOES IT WORK?

We contact you and explain what to do if you are eligible for Extra. If you are eligible a special Extra button will be available on your Track screen. If you want to use Extra you should:

- tick the 'Available in extra' box in the study options section when looking for courses on Course Finder
- choose a course that you would like to apply for and enter the details on your Track screen.

When you have chosen a course, the university or college will be able to view your application and consider you for a place.

WHAT HAPPENS NEXT?

We give universities and colleges a maximum of 21 days to consider your Extra application. During this time, you cannot be considered by another university or college. If you have not heard after 21 days you can apply to a different university or college if you wish, but it is a good idea to ring the one currently considering you before doing so. If you are made an offer, you can choose whether or not to
accept it.

If you accept any offer, conditional or unconditional, you will not be able to take any further part in Extra.

If you are currently studying for examinations, any offer that you receive is likely to be an offer conditional on exam grades. If you already have your examination results, it is possible that a university or college may make an unconditional offer. If you accept an unconditional offer, you will be placed. If you decide to decline the offer, or the university or college decides they cannot make you an offer, you will be given another opportunity to use Extra, time permitting. Your Extra button on Track will be reactivated.

Once you have accepted an offer in Extra, you are committed to it in the same way as you would be with an offer through the main UCAS system. Conditional offers made through Extra will be treated in the same way as other conditional offers, when your examination results become available.

If your results do not meet the conditions and the university or college decides that they cannot confirm your Extra offer, you will automatically become eligible for Clearing if it is too late for you to be considered by another university or college in Extra.

If you are unsuccessful, decline an offer, or do not receive an offer, or 21 days have elapsed since choosing a course through Extra, you can use Extra to apply for another course, time permitting.

ADVICE

Do some careful research and seek guidance on your Extra choice of university or college and course as you did for your initial choices. If you applied to high-demand courses and institutions in your original application and were unsuccessful, you could consider related or alternative subjects or perhaps apply for the subject you want in combination with another. Your teachers or careers advisers or the universities and colleges themselves can provide useful guidance. Course Finder at **www.ucas.com** is another important source of information. Be flexible, that is the key to success. But you are the only one who knows how flexible you are prepared to be.

Visit **www.ucas.tv** to watch the video guide on how to use Extra.

Offers

3

The Tariff

Finding out what qualifications are needed for different higher education courses can be very confusing.

The UCAS Tariff is the system for allocating points to qualifications used for entry to higher education. Universities and colleges can use the UCAS Tariff to make comparisons between applicants with different qualifications. Tariff points are often used in entry requirements, although other factors are often taken into account. Information on Course Finder at **www.ucas.com** provides a fuller picture of what admissions tutors are seeking.

The tables on the following pages show the qualifications covered by the UCAS Tariff. There may have been changes to these tables since this book was printed. You should visit **www.ucas.com** to view the most up-to-date tables.

FURTHER INFORMATION?

Although Tariff points can be accumulated in a variety of ways, not all of these will necessarily be acceptable for entry to a particular higher education course. The achievement of a points score therefore does not give an automatic entitlement to entry, and many other factors are taken into account in the admissions process.

The Course Finder facility at **www.ucas.com** is the best source of reference to find out what qualifications are acceptable for entry to specific courses. Updates to the Tariff, including details on how new qualifications are added, can be found at **www.ucas.com/students/ucas_tariff/.**

HOW DOES THE TARIFF WORK?

- Students can collect Tariff points from a range of different qualifications, eg GCE A level with BTEC Nationals.
- There is no ceiling to the number of points that can be accumulated.
- There is no double counting. Certain qualifications within the Tariff build on qualifications in the same subject. In these cases only the qualification with the higher Tariff score will be counted. This principle applies to:
    - GCE Advanced Subsidiary level and GCE Advanced level
    - Scottish Highers and Advanced Highers
    - Speech, drama and music awards at grades 6, 7 and 8.
- Tariff points for the Advanced Diploma come from the Progression Diploma score plus the relevant Additional and Specialist Learning (ASL) Tariff points. Please see the appropriate qualification in the Tariff tables to calculate the ASL score.
- The Extended Project Tariff points are included within the Tariff points for Progression and Advanced Diplomas. Extended Project points represented in the Tariff only count when the qualification is taken outside of these Diplomas.
- Where the Tariff tables refer to specific awarding organisations, only qualifications from these awarding organisations attract Tariff points. Qualifications with a similar title, but from a different qualification awarding organisation do not attract Tariff points.

HOW DO UNIVERSITIES AND COLLEGES USE THE TARIFF?

The Tariff provides a facility to help universities and colleges when expressing entrance requirements and when making conditional offers. Entry requirements and conditional offers expressed as Tariff points will often require a minimum level of achievement in a specified subject (for example, '300 points to include grade A at A level chemistry', or '260 points including SQA Higher grade B in mathematics').

Use of the Tariff may also vary from department to department at any one institution, and may in some cases be dependent on the programme being offered.

In July 2010, UCAS announced plans to review the qualifications information provided to universities and colleges. You can read more about the review at **www.ucas.com/qireview**.

WHAT QUALIFICATIONS ARE INCLUDED IN THE TARIFF?

The following qualifications are included in the UCAS Tariff. See the number on the qualification title to find the relevant section of the Tariff table.

1   AAT NVQ Level 3 in Accounting
2   AAT Level 3 Diploma in Accounting (QCF)
3   Advanced Diploma
4   Advanced Extension Awards
5   Advanced Placement Programme (US and Canada)
6   Arts Award (Gold)
7   ASDAN Community Volunteering qualification
8   Asset Languages Advanced Stage
9   British Horse Society (Stage 3 Horse Knowledge & Care, Stage 3 Riding and Preliminary Teacher's Certificate)
10   BTEC Awards (NQF)
11   BTEC Certificates and Extended Certificates (NQF)
12   BTEC Diplomas (NQF)
13   BTEC National in Early Years (NQF)
14   BTEC Nationals (NQF)
15   BTEC QCF Qualifications (Suite known as Nationals)
16   BTEC Specialist Qualifications (QCF)
17   CACHE Award, Certificate and Diploma in Child Care and Education
18   CACHE Level 3 Extended Diploma for the Children and Young People's Workforce (QCF)
19   Cambridge ESOL Examinations
20   Cambridge Pre-U
21   Certificate of Personal Effectiveness (COPE)
22   CISI Introduction to Securities and Investment
23   City & Guilds Land Based Services Level 3 Qualifications
24   Graded Dance and Vocational Graded Dance
25   Diploma in Fashion Retail
26   Diploma in Foundation Studies (Art & Design; Art, Design & Media)
27   EDI Level 3 Certificate in Accounting, Certificate in Accounting (IAS)
28   Essential Skills (Northern Ireland)
29   Essential Skills Wales
30   Extended Project (stand alone)
31   Free-standing Mathematics
32   Functional skills
33   GCE (AS, AS Double Award, A level, A level Double Award and A level (with additional AS))
34   Hong Kong Diploma of Secondary Education (from 2012 entry onwards)
35   ifs School of Finance (Certificate and Diploma in Financial Studies)
36   iMedia (OCR level Certificate/Diploma for iMedia Professionals)
37   International Baccalaureate (IB) Diploma
38   International Baccalaureate (IB) Certificate
39   Irish Leaving Certificate (Higher and Ordinary levels)
40   IT Professionals (iPRO) (Certificate and Diploma)
41   Key Skills (Levels 2, 3 and 4)
42   Music examinations (grades 6, 7 and 8)
43   OCR Level 3 Certificate in Mathematics for Engineering
44   OCR Level 3 Certificate for Young Enterprise
45   OCR Nationals (National Certificate, National Diploma and National Extended Diploma)
46   Principal Learning Wales
47   Progression Diploma
48   Rockschool Music Practitioners Qualifications
49   Scottish Qualifications
50   Speech and Drama examinations (grades 6, 7 and 8 and Performance Studies)
51   Sports Leaders UK
52   Welsh Baccalaureate Advanced Diploma (Core)

Updates on the Tariff, including details on the incorporation of any new qualifications, are posted on **www.ucas.com**.

UCAS TARIFF TABLES

1

AAT NVQ LEVEL 3 IN ACCOUNTING

GRADE	TARIFF POINTS
PASS	160

2

AAT LEVEL 3 DIPLOMA IN ACCOUNTING

GRADE	TARIFF POINTS
PASS	160

3

ADVANCED DIPLOMA

Advanced Diploma = Progression Diploma plus Additional & Specialist Learning (ASL). Please see the appropriate qualification to calculate the ASL score. Please see the Progression Diploma (Table 47) for Tariff scores

4

ADVANCED EXTENSION AWARDS

GRADE	TARIFF POINTS
DISTINCTION	40
MERIT	20

Points for Advanced Extension Awards are over and above those gained from the A level grade

5

ADVANCED PLACEMENT PROGRAMME (US & CANADA)

GRADE	TARIFF POINTS
Group A	
5	120
4	90
3	60
Group B	
5	50
4	35
3	20

Details of the subjects covered by each group can be found at www.ucas.com/students/ucas_tariff/tarifftables

6

ARTS AWARD (GOLD)

GRADE	TARIFF POINTS
PASS	35

7

ASDAN COMMUNITY VOLUNTEERING QUALIFICATION

GRADE	TARIFF POINTS
CERTIFICATE	50
AWARD	30

8

ASSET LANGUAGES ADVANCED STAGE

GRADE	TARIFF POINTS	GRADE	TARIFF POINTS
Speaking		Listening	
GRADE 12	28	GRADE 12	25
GRADE 11	20	GRADE 11	18
GRADE 10	12	GRADE 10	11
Reading		Writing	
GRADE 12	25	GRADE 12	25
GRADE 11	18	GRADE 11	18
GRADE 10	11	GRADE 10	11

9

BRITISH HORSE SOCIETY

GRADE	TARIFF POINTS
Stage 3 Horse Knowledge & Care	
PASS	35
Stage 3 Riding	
PASS	35
Preliminary Teacher's Certificate	
PASS	35

Awarded by Equestrian Qualifications (GB) Ltd (EQL)

10

BTEC AWARDS (NQF) (EXCLUDING BTEC NATIONAL QUALIFICATIONS)

GRADE	TARIFF POINTS		
	Group A	Group B	Group C
DISTINCTION	20	30	40
MERIT	13	20	26
PASS	7	10	13

Details of the subjects covered by each group can be found at www.ucas.com/students/ucas_tariff/tarifftables

11

BTEC CERTIFICATES AND EXTENDED CERTIFICATES (NQF) (EXCLUDING BTEC NATIONAL QUALIFICATIONS)

GRADE	TARIFF POINTS				
	Group A	Group B	Group C	Group D	Extended Certificates
DISTINCTION	40	60	80	100	60
MERIT	26	40	52	65	40
PASS	13	20	26	35	20

Details of the subjects covered by each group can be found at www.ucas.com/students/ucas_tariff/tarifftables

12

BTEC DIPLOMAS (NQF) (EXCLUDING BTEC NATIONAL QUALIFICATIONS)

GRADE	TARIFF POINTS		
	Group A	Group B	Group C
DISTINCTION	80	100	120
MERIT	52	65	80
PASS	26	35	40

Details of the subjects covered by each group can be found at www.ucas.com/students/ucas_tariff/tarifftables

UCAS TARIFF TABLES

13

BTEC NATIONAL IN EARLY YEARS (NQF)

GRADE	TARIFF POINTS	GRADE	TARIFF POINTS	GRADE	TARIFF POINTS
Theory				Practical	
Diploma		Certificate		D	120
DDD	320	DD	200	M	80
DDM	280	DM	160	P	40
DMM	240	MM	120		
MMM	220	MP	80		
MMP	160	PP	40		
MPP	120				
PPP	80				

Points apply to the following qualifications only: BTEC National Diploma in Early Years (100/1279/5); BTEC National Certificate in Early Years (100/1280/1)

14

BTEC NATIONALS (NQF)

GRADE	TARIFF POINTS	GRADE	TARIFF POINTS	GRADE	TARIFF POINTS
Diploma		Certificate		Award	
DDD	360	DD	240	D	120
DDM	320	DM	200	M	80
DMM	280	MM	160	P	40
MMM	240	MP	120		
MMP	200	PP	80		
MPP	160				
PPP	120				

15

BTEC QUALIFICATIONS (QCF)
(SUITE OF QUALIFICATIONS KNOWN AS NATIONALS)

EXTENDED DIPLOMA	DIPLOMA	90 CREDIT DIPLOMA	SUBSIDIARY DIPLOMA	CERTIFICATE	TARIFF POINTS
D*D*D*					420
D*D*D					400
D*DD					380
DDD					360
DDM					320
DMM	D*D*				280
	D*D				260
MMM	DD				240
		D*D*			210
MMP	DM	D*D			200
		DD			180
MPP	MM	DM			160
			D*		140
PPP	MP	MM	D		120
		MP			100
	PP		M		80
				D*	70
		PP		D	60
			P	M	40
				P	20

16

BTEC SPECIALIST (QCF)

GRADE	TARIFF POINTS		
	Diploma	Certificate	Award
DISTINCTION	120	60	20
MERIT	80	40	13
PASS	40	20	7

UCAS TARIFF TABLES

17

CACHE LEVEL 3 AWARD, CERTIFICATE AND DIPLOMA IN CHILD CARE & EDUCATION					
AWARD		CERTIFICATE		DIPLOMA	
GRADE	TARIFF POINTS	GRADE	TARIFF POINTS	GRADE	TARIFF POINTS
A	30	A	110	A	360
B	25	B	90	B	300
C	20	C	70	C	240
D	15	D	55	D	180
E	10	E	35	E	120

18

CACHE LEVEL 3 EXTENDED DIPLOMA FOR THE CHILDREN AND YOUNG PEOPLE'S WORKFORCE (QCF)	
GRADE	TARIFF POINTS
A*	420
A	340
B	290
C	240
D	140
E	80

19

CAMBRIDGE ESOL EXAMINATIONS	
GRADE	TARIFF POINTS
Certificate of Proficiency in English	
A	140
B	110
C	70
Certificate in Advanced English	
A	70

20

CAMBRIDGE PRE-U							
GRADE	TARIFF POINTS	GRADE	TARIFF POINTS	GRADE	TARIFF POINTS	GRADE	TARIFF POINTS
Principal Subject		Global Perspectives and Research		Short Course			
D1	TBC	D1	TBC	D1	TBC		
D2	145	D2	140	D2	TBC		
D3	130	D3	126	D3	60		
M1	115	M1	112	M1	53		
M2	101	M2	98	M2	46		
M3	87	M3	84	M3	39		
P1	73	P1	70	P1	32		
P2	59	P2	56	P2	26		
P3	46	P3	42	P3	20		

21

CERTIFICATE OF PERSONAL EFFECTIVENESS (COPE)	
GRADE	TARIFF POINTS
PASS	70

Points are awarded for the Certificate of Personal Effectiveness (CoPE) awarded by ASDAN and CCEA

22

CISI INTRODUCTION TO SECURITIES AND INVESTMENT	
GRADE	TARIFF POINTS
PASS WITH DISTINCTION	60
PASS WITH MERIT	40
PASS	20

23

CITY AND GUILDS LAND BASED SERVICES LEVEL 3 QUALIFICATIONS				
GRADE	TARIFF POINTS			
	EXTENDED DIPLOMA	DIPLOMA	SUBSIDIARY DIPLOMA	CERTIFICATE
DISTINCTION*	420	280	140	70
DISTINCTION	360	240	120	60
MERIT	240	160	80	40
PASS	120	80	40	20

24

GRADED DANCE AND VOCATIONAL GRADED DANCE					
GRADE	TARIFF POINTS	GRADE	TARIFF POINTS	GRADE	TARIFF POINTS
Graded Dance					
Grade 8		Grade 7		Grade 6	
DISTINCTION	65	DISTINCTION	55	DISTINCTION	40
MERIT	55	MERIT	45	MERIT	35
PASS	45	PASS	35	PASS	30
Vocational Graded Dance					
Advanced Foundation		Intermediate			
DISTINCTION	70	DISTINCTION	65		
MERIT	55	MERIT	50		
PASS	45	PASS	40		

25

DIPLOMA IN FASHION RETAIL	
GRADE	TARIFF POINTS
DISTINCTION	160
MERIT	120
PASS	80

Applies to the NQF and QCF versions of the qualifications awarded by ABC Awards

26

DIPLOMA IN FOUNDATION STUDIES (ART & DESIGN AND ART, DESIGN & MEDIA)	
GRADE	TARIFF POINTS
DISTINCTION	285
MERIT	225
PASS	165

Awarded by ABC, Edexcel, UAL and WJEC

27

EDI LEVEL 3 CERTIFICATE IN ACCOUNTING, CERTIFICATE IN ACCOUNTING (IAS)	
GRADE	TARIFF POINTS
DISTINCTION	120
MERIT	90
PASS	70

28

ESSENTIAL SKILLS (NORTHERN IRELAND)	
GRADE	TARIFF POINTS
LEVEL 2	10

Only allocated at level 2 if studied as part of a wider composite qualification such as 14-19 Diploma or Welsh Baccalaureate

29

ESSENTIAL SKILLS WALES	
GRADE	TARIFF POINTS
LEVEL 4	30
LEVEL 3	20
LEVEL 2	10

Only allocated at level 2 if studied as part of a wider composite qualification such as 14-19 Diploma or Welsh Baccalaureate

30

EXTENDED PROJECT (STAND ALONE)	
GRADE	TARIFF POINTS
A*	70
A	60
B	50
C	40
D	30
E	20

Points for the Extended Project cannot be counted if taken as part of Progression/Advanced Diploma

31

FREE-STANDING MATHEMATICS	
GRADE	TARIFF POINTS
A	20
B	17
C	13
D	10
E	7

Covers free-standing Mathematics - Additional Maths, Using and Applying Statistics, Working with Algebraic and Graphical Techniques, Modelling with Calculus

32

FUNCTIONAL SKILLS	
GRADE	TARIFF POINTS
LEVEL 2	10

Only allocated if studied as part of a wider composite qualification such as 14-19 Diploma or Welsh Baccalaureate

33

GCE AND VCE									
GRADE	TARIFF POINTS	GRADE	TARIFF POINTS	GRADE	TARIFF POINTS	GRADE	TARIFF POINTS	GRADE	TARIFF POINTS
GCE & AVCE Double Award		GCE A level with additional AS (9 units)		GCE A level & AVCE		GCE AS Double Award		GCE AS & AS VCE	
A*A*	280	A*A	200	A*	140	AA	120	A	60
A*A	260	AA	180	A	120	AB	110	B	50
AA	240	AB	170	B	100	BB	100	C	40
AB	220	BB	150	C	80	BC	90	D	30
BB	200	BC	140	D	60	CC	80	E	20
BC	180	CC	120	E	40	CD	70		
CC	160	CD	110			DD	60		
CD	140	DD	90			DE	50		
DD	120	DE	80			EE	40		
DE	100	EE	60						
EE	80								

34

HONG KONG DIPLOMA OF SECONDARY EDUCATION					
GRADE	TARIFF POINTS	GRADE	TARIFF POINTS	GRADE	TARIFF POINTS
All subjects except mathematics		Mathematics compulsory component		Mathematics optional components	
5**	No value	5**	No value	5**	No value
5*	130	5*	60	5*	70
5	120	5	45	5	60
4	80	4	35	4	50
3	40	3	25	3	40

No value for 5** pending receipt of candidate evidence (post 2012)

UCAS TARIFF TABLES

35

IFS SCHOOL OF FINANCE (NQF & QCF)			
GRADE	TARIFF POINTS	GRADE	TARIFF POINTS
Certificate in Financial Studies (CeFS)		Diploma in Financial Studies (DipFS)	
A	60	A	120
B	50	B	100
C	40	C	80
D	30	D	60
E	20	E	40

Applicants with the ifs Diploma cannot also count points allocated to the ifs Certificate. Completion of both qualifications will result in a maximum of 120 UCAS Tariff points

36

LEVEL 3 CERTIFICATE / DIPLOMA FOR iMEDIA USERS (iMEDIA)	
GRADE	TARIFF POINTS
DIPLOMA	66
CERTIFICATE	40

Awarded by OCR

37

INTERNATIONAL BACCALAUREATE (IB) DIPLOMA			
GRADE	TARIFF POINTS	GRADE	TARIFF POINTS
45	720	34	479
44	698	33	457
43	676	32	435
42	654	31	413
41	632	30	392
40	611	29	370
39	589	28	348
38	567	27	326
37	545	26	304
36	523	25	282
35	501	24	260

38

INTERNATIONAL BACCALAUREATE (IB) CERTIFICATE					
GRADE	TARIFF POINTS	GRADE	TARIFF POINTS	GRADE	TARIFF POINTS
Higher Level		Standard Level		Core	
7	130	7	70	3	120
6	110	6	59	2	80
5	80	5	43	1	40
4	50	4	27	0	10
3	20	3	11		

39

IRISH LEAVING CERTIFICATE			
GRADE	TARIFF POINTS	GRADE	TARIFF POINTS
Higher		Ordinary	
A1	90	A1	39
A2	77	A2	26
B1	71	B1	20
B2	64	B2	14
B3	58	B3	7
C1	52		
C2	45		
C3	39		
D1	33		
D2	26		
D3	20		

40

IT PROFESSIONALS (iPRO)	
GRADE	TARIFF POINTS
DIPLOMA	100
CERTIFICATE	80

Awarded by OCR

41

KEY SKILLS	
GRADE	TARIFF POINTS
LEVEL 4	30
LEVEL 3	20
LEVEL 2	10

Only allocated at level 2 if studied as part of a wider composite qualification such as 14-19 Diploma or Welsh Baccalaureate

UCAS TARIFF TABLES

42

MUSIC EXAMINATIONS					
GRADE	TARIFF POINTS	GRADE	TARIFF POINTS	GRADE	TARIFF POINTS
Practical					
Grade 8		Grade 7		Grade 6	
DISTINCTION	75	DISTINCTION	60	DISTINCTION	45
MERIT	70	MERIT	55	MERIT	40
PASS	55	PASS	40	PASS	25
Theory					
Grade 8		Grade 7		Grade 6	
DISTINCTION	30	DISTINCTION	20	DISTINCTION	15
MERIT	25	MERIT	15	MERIT	10
PASS	20	PASS	10	PASS	5

Points shown are for the ABRSM, LCMM/University of West London, Rockschool and Trinity Guildhall/Trinity College London Advanced Level music examinations

43

OCR LEVEL 3 CERTIFICATE IN MATHEMATICS FOR ENGINEERING	
GRADE	TARIFF POINTS
A*	TBC
A	90
B	75
C	60
D	45
E	30

44

OCR LEVEL 3 CERTIFICATE FOR YOUNG ENTERPRISE	
GRADE	TARIFF POINTS
DISTINCTION	40
MERIT	30
PASS	20

45

OCR NATIONALS							
GRADE	TARIFF POINTS	GRADE	TARIFF POINTS	GRADE	TARIFF POINTS		
National Extended Diploma		National Diploma		National Certificate			
D1	360	D	240	D	120		
D2/M1	320	M1	200	M	80		
M2	280	M2/P1	160	P	40		
M3	240	P2	120				
P1	200	P3	80				
P2	160						
P3	120						

46

PRINCIPAL LEARNING WALES	
GRADE	TARIFF POINTS
A*	210
A	180
B	150
C	120
D	90
E	60

47

PROGRESSION DIPLOMA	
GRADE	TARIFF POINTS
A*	350
A	300
B	250
C	200
D	150
E	100

Advanced Diploma = Progression Diploma plus Additional & Specialist Learning (ASL). Please see the appropriate qualification to calculate the ASL score

UCAS TARIFF TABLES

48

	TARIFF POINTS				
GRADE	Extended Diploma	Diploma	Subsidiary Diploma	Extended Certificate	Certificate
DISTINCTION	240	180	120	60	30
MERIT	160	120	80	40	20
PASS	80	60	40	20	10

ROCKSCHOOL MUSIC PRACTITIONERS QUALIFICATIONS

49

SCOTTISH QUALIFICATIONS

GRADE	TARIFF POINTS	GRADE	TARIFF POINTS	GRADE	TARIFF POINTS	GROUP	TARIFF POINTS
Advanced Higher		Higher		Scottish Interdisciplinary Project		Scottish National Certificates	
A	130	A	80	A	65	C	125
B	110	B	65	B	55	B	100
C	90	C	50	C	45	A	75
D	72	D	36				
Ungraded Higher		NPA PC Passport					
PASS	45	PASS	45				
		Core Skills					
		HIGHER	20				

Details of the subjects covered by each Scottish National Certificate can be found at www.ucas.com/students/ucas_tariff/tarifftables

50

SPEECH AND DRAMA EXAMINATIONS

GRADE	TARIFF POINTS	GRADE	TARIFF POINTS	GRADE	TARIFF POINTS	GRADE	TARIFF POINTS
PCertLAM		Grade 8		Grade 7		Grade 6	
DISTINCTION	90	DISTINCTION	65	DISTINCTION	55	DISTINCTION	40
MERIT	80	MERIT	60	MERIT	50	MERIT	35
PASS	60	PASS	45	PASS	35	PASS	20

Details of the Speech and Drama Qualifications covered by the Tariff can be found at www.ucas.com/students/ucas_tariff/tarifftables

51

SPORTS LEADERS UK	
GRADE	TARIFF POINTS
PASS	30

These points are awarded to Higher Sports Leader Award and Level 3 Certificate in Higher Sports Leadership (QCF)

52

WELSH BACCALAUREATE ADVANCED DIPLOMA (CORE)	
GRADE	TARIFF POINTS
PASS	120

These points are awarded only when a candidate achieves the Welsh Baccalaureate Advanced Diploma

Results

4

Step 4 – Results

You should arrange your holidays so that you are at home when your exam results are published because, if there are any issues to discuss, admissions tutors will want to speak to you in person.

We receive many exam results direct from the exam boards – check the list at **www.ucas.com**. If your qualification is listed, we send your results to the universities and colleges that you have accepted as your firm and insurance choices. If your qualification is not listed, you must send your exam results to the universities and colleges where you are holding offers.

After you have received your exam results check Track to find out if you have a place on your chosen course.

If you have met all the conditions for your firm choice, the university or college will confirm that you have a place. Occasionally, they may still confirm you have a place even if you have not quite met all the offer conditions; or they may offer you a place on a similar course.

If you have not met the conditions of your firm choice and the university or college has not confirmed your place, but you have met all the conditions of your insurance offer, your insurance university or college will confirm that you have a place.

When a university or college tells us that you have a place, we send you confirmation by letter.

RE-MARKED EXAMS

If you ask for any of your exams to be re-marked, you must tell the universities and colleges where you're holding offers. If a university or college cannot confirm your place based on the initial results, you should ask them if they would be able to reconsider their decision after the re-mark. They are under no obligation to reconsider their position even if your re-mark results in higher grades. Don't forget that re-marks may also result in lower grades.

The exam boards tell us about any re-marks that result in grade changes. We then send the revised grades to the universities and colleges where you're holding offers. As soon as you know about any grade changes, you should also tell these universities and colleges.

'CASHING IN' A LEVEL RESULTS

If you have taken A levels, your school or college must certificate or 'cash in' all your unit scores before the exam board can award final grades. If when you collect your A level results you have to add up your unit scores to find out your final grades, this means your school or college has not 'cashed in' your results.

We only receive cashed in results from the exam boards, so if your school or college has not cashed in your results, you must ask them to send a 'cash in' request to the exam board. You also need to tell the universities and colleges where you're holding offers that there'll be a delay in receiving your results and call our Customer Service Unit to find out when your results have been received.

When we receive your 'cashed in' results from the exam board we send them straight away to the universities and colleges where you're holding offers.

WHAT IF YOU DON'T HAVE A PLACE?

If you have not met the conditions of either your firm or insurance choice, and your chosen universities or colleges have not confirmed your place, you are eligible for Clearing. In Clearing you can apply for any courses that still have vacancies (but remember that admissions tutors will stil be reading your original personal statement). Clearing operates from mid-July to late September 2013 (page 108).

BETTER RESULTS THAN EXPECTED?

If you obtain exam results that meet and exceed the conditions of the offer for your firm choice, you can for a short period use a process called Adjustment to look for an alternative place, whilst still keeping your original firm choice. See page 109 for information about Adjustment.

Next steps

5

Step 5 – Next steps

You might find yourself with different exam results than you were expecting, or you may change your mind about what you want to do. If so, there may be other options open to you.

CLEARING

Clearing is a service that helps people without a place find suitable course vacancies. It runs from mid-July until the end of September, but most people use it after the exam results are published in August.

You could consider related or alternative subjects or perhaps combining your original choice of subject with another. Your teachers or careers adviser, or the universities and colleges themselves, can provide useful guidance.

Course vacancies are listed at **www.ucas.com** and in the national media following the publication of exam results in August. **Once you have your exam results**, if you're in Clearing you need to look at the vacancy listings and then contact any university or college you are interested in.

Talk to the institutions; don't be afraid to call them. Make sure you have your Personal ID and Clearing Number ready and prepare notes on what you will say to them about:

- why you want to study the course
- why you want to study at their university or college
- any relevant employment or activities you have done that relate to the course
- your grades.

Accepting an offer - you can contact as many universities and colleges as you like through Clearing, and you may informally be offered more than one place. If this happens, you will need to decide which offer you want to accept. If you're offered a place you want to be formally considered for, you enter the course details in Track, and the university or college will then let you know if they're accepting you.

ADJUSTMENT

If you receive better results than expected, and meet and exceed the conditions of your conditional firm choice, you have the opportunity to reconsider what and where you want to study. This process is called Adjustment.

Adjustment runs from A level results day on 15 August 2013 until the end of August. Your individual Adjustment period starts on A level results day or when your conditional firm choice changes to unconditional firm, whichever is the later. You then have a maximum of five calendar days to register and secure an alternative course, if you decide you want to do this. If you want to try to find an alternative course you must register in Track to use Adjustment, so universities and colleges can view your application.

There are no vacancy listings for Adjustment, so you'll need to talk to the institutions. When you contact a university or college make it clear that you are applying through Adjustment, not Clearing. If they want to consider you they will ask for your Personal ID, so they can view your application.

If you don't find an alternative place then you remain accepted at your original firm choice.

Adjustment is entirely optional; remember that nothing really beats the careful research you carried out to find the right courses before you made your UCAS application. Talk to a careers adviser at your school, college or local careers office, as they can help you decide if registering to use Adjustment is right for you.

More information about Adjustment and Clearing is available at **www.ucas.com**. You can also view UCAStv video guides on how to use Adjustment and Clearing at **www.ucas.tv**.

IF YOU ARE STILL WITHOUT A PLACE TO STUDY:

If you haven't found a suitable place, or changed your mind about what you want to do, there are lots of other options. Ask for advice from your school, college or careers office. Here are some suggestions you might want to consider:

- studying a part-time course (there's a part-time course search at **www.ucas.com** from July until September)
- studying a foundation degree
- re-sit your exams
- getting some work experience
- studying in another country

- reapplying next year to university or college through UCAS
- taking a gap year
- doing an apprenticeship (you'll find a vacancy search on the National Apprenticeship Service (NAS) website at **www.apprenticeships.org.uk**)
- finding a job
- starting a business.

More advice and links to other organisations can be found on the UCAS website at **www.ucas.com/students/nextsteps/advice**.

UCAS

Confused about courses?

Indecisive about institutions?

Stressed about student life?

Unsure about UCAS?

Frowning over finance?

Help is available at
www.ucasbooks.com

Starting university or college

Step 6 – Starting university or college

Congratulations! Now that you have confirmed your place at university or college you will need to finalise your plans on how to get there, where to live and how to finance it. Make lists of things to do with deadlines, and start contacting people whose help you can call on. Will you travel independently or can your parents or relatives help with transport? If you are keeping a car at uni, have you checked out parking facilities and told your insurance company?

Make sure you have everything organised, including travel arrangements, essential documents and paperwork, books and equipment required for the course. The university will send you joining information – contact the Admissions Office or the Students' Union if you have questions about anything to do with starting your course.

Freshers week will help you settle in and make friends, but don't forget you are there to study. You may find the teaching methods rather alien at first, but remember there are plenty of sources of help, including your tutors, other students or student mentors, and the Students' Union.

Where to live - unless you are planning to live at home, your university or college will usually provide you with guidance on how to find somewhere to live. The earlier you contact them the better your chance of finding a suitable range of options, from hall to private landlords. Find out what facilities are available at the different types of accommodation, and check whether it fits within your budget. Check also what you need to bring with you and what is supplied. Don't leave it all to the last minute – especially things like arranging a bank

account, checking what proof of identity you might
need, gathering together a few essentials like a mug
and supplies of coffee, insurance cover, TV licence etc.

Student finance - you will need to budget for living
costs, accommodation, travel and books (and tuition
fees if you are paying them up front). Learn about
budgeting by visiting **www.ucas.com** where you will
find further links to useful resources to help you
manage your money. Remember that if you do get into
financial difficulties the welfare office at the university
will help you change tack and manage better in future,
but it is always better to live within your means from the
outset. If you need help, find it before the situation gets
too stressful.

www.ucas.com

at the heart of connecting people to higher education

Useful contacts

CONNECTING WITH UCAS

You can follow UCAS on Twitter at
www.twitter.com/ucas_online, and ask a question or
see what others are asking on Facebook at
www.facebook.com/ucasonline. You can also watch
videos of UCAS advisers answering frequently asked
questions on YouTube at
www.youtube.com/ucasonline.

There are many UCAStv video guides to help with your
journey into higher education, such as *How to choose
your courses, Attending events, Open days,* and
How to apply. These can all be viewed at
www.ucas.tv or in the relevant section of
www.ucas.com.

If you need to speak to UCAS, please contact the
Customer Service Unit on 0871 468 0 468 or 0044
871 468 0 468 from outside the UK. Calls from BT
landlines within the UK will cost no more than 9p per
minute. The cost of calls from mobiles and other
networks may vary.

If you have hearing difficulties, you can call the Text
Relay service on 18001 0871 468 0 468 (outside the
UK 0044 151 494 1260). Calls are charged at normal
rates.

CAREERS ADVICE

The Directgov Careers Helpline for Young People is for you if you live in England, are aged 13 to 19 and want advice on getting to where you want to be in life.

Careers advisers can give you information, advice and practical help with all sorts of things, like choosing subjects at school or mapping out your future career options. They can help you with anything that might be affecting you at school, college, work or in your personal or family life.

Contact a careers adviser at
www.direct.gov.uk/en/youngpeople/index.htm.

Skills Development Scotland provides a starting point for anyone looking for careers information, advice or guidance.
www.myworldofwork.co.uk.

Careers Wales – Wales' national all-age careers guidance service.
www.careerswales.com or **www.gyrfacymru.com**.

Northern Ireland Careers Service website for the new, all-age careers guidance service in Northern Ireland.
www.nidirect.gov.uk/careers.

If you're not sure what job you want or you need help to decide which course to do, give learndirect a call on 0800 101 901 or visit
www.learndirect.co.uk.

GENERAL HIGHER EDUCATION ADVICE

National Union of Students (NUS) is the national voice of students, helping them to campaign, get cheap student discounts and provide advice on living student life to the full - **www.nus.org.uk**.

STUDENTS WITH DISABILITIES

If you have a disability or specific learning difficulty, you are strongly encouraged to make early direct contact with individual institutions before submitting your application. Most universities and colleges have disability coordinators or advisers. You can find their contact details and further advice on the Disability Rights UK website - **www.disabilityalliance.org**.

There is financial help for students with disabilities, known as Disabled Students' Allowances (DSAs). More information is available on the Directgov website at **www.direct.gov.uk/disabledstudents**.

YEAR OUT

For useful information on taking a year out, see **www.gap-year.com**.

The Year Out Group website is packed with information and guidance for young people and their parents and advisers. **www.yearoutgroup.org**.

Essential reading

UCAS has brought together the best books and resources you need to make the important decisions regarding entry to higher education. With guidance on choosing courses, finding the right institution, information about student finance, admissions tests, gap years and lots more, you can find the most trusted guides at **www.ucasbooks.com**.

The publications listed on the following pages and many others are available through **www.ucasbooks.com** or from UCAS Publication Services unless otherwise stated.

UCAS PUBLICATION SERVICES

UCAS Publication Services
PO Box 130, Cheltenham, Gloucestershire GL52 3ZF

f: 01242 544 806
e: publicationservices@ucas.ac.uk
// **www.ucasbooks.com**

ENTIRE RESEARCH AND APPLICATION PROCESS EXPLAINED

The UCAS Guide to getting into University and College

This guide contains advice and up-to-date information about the entire research and application process, and brings together the expertise of UCAS staff, along with insights and tips from well known universities including Oxford and Cambridge, and students who are involved with or have experienced the process first-hand.

The book clearly sets out the information you need in an easy-to-read format, with myth busters, tips from students, checklists and much more; this book will be a companion for applicants throughout their entire journey into higher education.
Published by UCAS
Price £11.99
Publication date January 2011

NEED HELP COMPLETING YOUR APPLICATION?

How to Complete your UCAS Application 2013
A must for anyone applying through UCAS. Contains advice on the preparation needed, a step-by-step guide to filling out the UCAS application, information on the UCAS process and useful tips for completing the personal statement.
Published by Trotman
Price £12.99
Publication date May 2012

Insider's Guide to Applying to University
Full of honest insights, this is a thorough guide to the application process. It reveals advice from careers advisers and current students, guidance on making sense of university information and choosing courses. Also includes tips for the personal statement, interviews, admissions tests, UCAS Extra and Clearing.
Published by Trotman
Price £12.99
Publication date June 2011

How to Write a Winning UCAS Personal Statement
The personal statement is your chance to stand out from the crowd. Based on information from admissions tutors, this book will help you sell yourself. It includes specific guidance for over 30 popular subjects, common mistakes to avoid, information on what admissions tutors look for, and much more.
Published by Trotman
Price £12.99
Publication date March 2010

CHOOSING COURSES

Progression Series 2013 entry
The 'UCAS Guide to getting into…' titles are designed to help you access good quality, useful information on some of the most competitive subject areas. The books cover advice on applying through UCAS, routes to qualifications, course details, job prospects, case studies and career advice.

New for 2013: information on the pros and cons of league tables and how to read them.

The UCAS Guide to getting into…
Art and Design
Economics, Finance and Accountancy
Engineering and Mathematics
Journalism, Broadcasting, Media Production and
  Performing Arts
Law
Medicine, Dentistry and Optometry
Nursing, Healthcare and Social Work
Psychology
Sports Science and Physiotherapy
Teaching and Education
Published by UCAS
Price £15.99 each
Publication date June 2012

UCAS Parent Guide
Free of charge.
Order online at **www.ucas.com/parents**.
Publication date February 2012

Open Days 2012

Attending open days, taster courses and higher education conventions is an important part of the application process. This publication makes planning attendance at these events quick and easy.
Published annually by UCAS.
Price £3.50
Publication date January 2012

Heap 2013: University Degree Course Offers

An independent, reliable guide to selecting university degree courses in the UK.

The guide lists degree courses available at universities and colleges throughout the UK and the grades, UCAS points or equivalent that you need to achieve to get on to each course listed.
Published by Trotman
Price £32.99
Publication date May 2012

ESSENTIAL READING

Choosing Your Degree Course & University

With so many universities and courses to choose from, it is not an easy decision for students embarking on their journey to higher education. This guide will offer expert guidance on the questions students need to ask when considering the opportunities available.
Published by Trotman
Price £24.99
Publication date April 2012

Degree Course Descriptions

Providing details of the nature of degree courses, the descriptions in this book are written by heads of departments and senior lecturers at major universities. Each description contains an overview of the course area, details of course structures, career opportunities and more.
Published by COA
Price £12.99
Publication date September 2011

CHOOSING WHERE TO STUDY

The Virgin Guide to British Universities

An insider's guide to choosing a university or college. Written by students and using independent statistics, this guide evaluates what you get from a higher education institution.
Published by Virgin
Price £15.99
Publication date May 2011

Times Good University Guide 2013

How do you find the best university for the subject you wish to study? You need a guide that evaluates the quality of what is available, giving facts, figures and comparative assessments of universities. The rankings provide hard data, analysed, interpreted and presented by a team of experts.
Published by Harper Collins
Price £16.99
Publication date June 2012

A Parent's Guide to Graduate Jobs

A must-have guide for any parent who is worried about their child's job prospects when they graduate.
In this guide, the graduate careers guru, Paul Redmond, advises parents how to help their son or daughter:

- increase their employability
- boost their earning potential
- acquire essential work skills
- use their own contacts to get them ahead
- gain the right work experience.

Published by Trotman
Price £12.99
Publication date January 2012

Which Uni?

One person's perfect uni might be hell for someone else. Picking the right one will give you the best chance of future happiness, academic success and brighter job prospects. This guide is packed with tables from a variety of sources, rating universities on everything from the quality of teaching to the make-up of the student population and much more.
Published by Trotman
Price £14.99
Publication date September 2011

Getting into the UK's Best Universities and Courses

This book is for those who set their goals high and dream of studying on a highly regarded course at a good university. It provides information on selecting the best courses for a subject, the application and personal statement, interviews, results day, timescales for applications and much more.
Published by Trotman
Price £12.99
Publication date June 2011

FINANCIAL INFORMATION

Student Finance - e-book

All students need to know about tuition fees, loans, grants, bursaries and much more. Covering all forms of income and expenditure, this comprehensive guide is produced in association with UCAS and offers great value for money.
Published by Constable Robinson
Price £4.99
Publication date May 2012

CAREERS PLANNING

A-Z of Careers and Jobs

It is vital to be well informed about career decisions and this guide will help you make the right choice. It provides full details of the wide range of opportunities on the market, the personal qualities and skills needed for each job, entry qualifications and training, realistic salary expectations and useful contact details.
Published by Kogan Page
Price £16.99
Publication date March 2012

The Careers Directory

An indispensable resource for anyone seeking careers information, covering over 350 careers. It presents up-to-date information in an innovative double-page format. Ideal for students in years 10 to 13 who are considering their futures and for other careers professionals.
Published by COA
Price £14.99
Publication date September 2011

Careers with a Science Degree

Over 100 jobs and areas of work for graduates of biological, chemical and physical sciences are described in this guide.

Whether you have yet to choose your degree subject and want to know where the various choices could lead, or are struggling for ideas about what to do with your science degree, this book will guide and inspire you. The title includes: nature of the work and potential employers, qualifications required for entry, including personal qualities and skills; training routes and opportunities for career development and postgraduate study options.
Published by Lifetime Publishing
Price £12.99
Publication date September 2010

Careers with an Arts and Humanities Degree

Covers careers and graduate opportunities related to these degrees.

The book describes over 100 jobs and areas of work suitable for graduates from a range of disciplines including: English and modern languages, history and geography, music and the fine arts. The guide highlights: graduate opportunities, training routes, postgraduate study options and entry requirements.
Published by Lifetime Publishing
Price £12.99
Publication date September 2010

'Getting into...' guides

Clear and concise guides to help applicants secure places. They include qualifications required, advice on applying, tests, interviews and case studies. The guides give an honest view and discuss current issues and careers.

Getting into Oxford and Cambridge
Publication date April 2011
Getting into Veterinary School
Publication date February 2011
Published by Trotman
Price £12.99 each

DEFERRING ENTRY

Gap Years: The Essential Guide

The essential book for all young people planning a gap year before continuing with their education. This up-to-date guide provides essential information on specialist gap year programmes, as well as the vast range of jobs and voluntary opportunities available to young people around the world.
Published by Crimson Publishing
Price £9.99
Publication date April 2012

Gap Year Guidebook 2012

This thorough and easy-to-use guide contains everything you need to know before taking a gap year. It includes real-life traveller tips, hundreds of contact details, realistic advice on everything from preparing, learning and working abroad, coping with coming home and much more.
Published by John Catt Education
Price £14.99
Publication date November 2011

Summer Jobs Worldwide 2012

This unique and specialist guide contains over
40,000 jobs for all ages. No other book includes
such a variety and wealth of summer work
opportunities in Britain and aboard. Anything from
horse trainer in Iceland, to a guide for nature walks
in Peru, to a yoga centre helper in Greece, to an
animal keeper for London Zoo, can be found.
Published by Crimson Publishing
Price £14.99
Publication date November 2011

Please note all publications incur a postage and packing
charge. All information was correct at the time of
printing.

For a full list of publications, please visit
www.ucasbooks.com.

UCAS HIGHER EDUCATION CONVENTIONS

Meet face-to-face with over 100 UK university representatives, attend seminars on How to Apply through UCAS and Financing yourself through university.

For further details visit
www.ucas.com/conventions

Courses

Courses

Keen to get started on your engineering or mathematics career? This section contains details of the various degree courses available at UK institutions.

EXPLAINING THE LIST OF COURSES

The list of courses has been divided into subject categories (see over for list of subjects). We list the universities and colleges by their UCAS institution codes. Within each institution, courses are listed first by award type (such as BA, BSc, FdA, HND, MA and many others), then alphabetically by course title.

You might find some courses showing an award type '(Mod)', which indicates a combined degree that might be modular in design. A small number of courses have

award type '(FYr)'. This indicates a 12-month foundation course, after which students can choose to apply for a degree course. In either case, you should contact the university or college for further details.

Generally speaking, when a course comprises two or more subjects, the word used to connect the subjects indicates the make-up of the award: 'Subject A and Subject B' is a joint award, where both subjects carry equal weight; 'Subject A with Subject B' is a major/minor award, where Subject A accounts for at least 60% of your study. If the title shows 'Subject A/Subject B', it may indicate that students can decide on the weighting of the subjects at the end of the first year. You should check with the university or college for full details.

Each entry shows the UCAS course code and the duration of the course. Where known, the entry contains details of the minimum qualification requirements for the course, as supplied to UCAS by the universities and colleges. Bear in mind that possessing the minimum qualifications does not guarantee acceptance to the course: there may be far more applicants than places. You may be asked to attend an interview, present a portfolio or sit an admissions test.

Courses with entry requirements that require applicants to disclose information about spent and unspent convictions and may require a Criminal Records Bureau (CRB) check, are marked '**CRB Check:** Required'.

Before applying for any course, you are advised to contact the university or college to check any changes in entry requirements and to see if any new courses have come on stream since the lists were approved for publication. To make this easy, each institution's entry starts with their address, email, phone and fax details, as well as their website address.

LIST OF SUBJECT CATEGORIES

The list of courses in this section has been divided into the following subject categories.

BIOMEDICAL ENGINEERING

A80 ASTON UNIVERSITY, BIRMINGHAM
ASTON TRIANGLE
BIRMINGHAM B4 7ET
t: 0121 204 4444 f: 0121 204 3696
e: admissions@aston.ac.uk (automatic response)
// www.aston.ac.uk/prospective-students/ug

C900 BSc Biomedical Science
Duration: 3FT/4SW Hon   CRB Check: Required
Entry Requirements: *GCE:* ABB-BBB. *SQAH:* BBBBB. *SQAAH:* BBB.
IB: 33.

B56 THE UNIVERSITY OF BRADFORD
RICHMOND ROAD
BRADFORD
WEST YORKSHIRE BD7 1DP
t: 0800 073 1225 f: 01274 235585
e: course-enquiries@bradford.ac.uk
// www.bradford.ac.uk

H1B1 BEng Medical Engineering
Duration: 3FT Hon
Entry Requirements: *GCE:* 240. *IB:* 24.

H1BC BEng Medical Engineering (4 years)
Duration: 4SW Hon
Entry Requirements: *GCE:* 240. *IB:* 24.

HB11 MEng Medical Engineering
Duration: 4FT Hon
Entry Requirements: *GCE:* 300. *IB:* 26.

HB1C MEng Medical Engineering
Duration: 5SW Hon
Entry Requirements: *GCE:* 300. *IB:* 26.

C15 CARDIFF UNIVERSITY
PO BOX 927
30-36 NEWPORT ROAD
CARDIFF CF24 0DE
t: 029 2087 9999 f: 029 2087 6138
e: admissions@cardiff.ac.uk
// www.cardiff.ac.uk

H1B8 BEng Medical Engineering
Duration: 3FT Hon
Entry Requirements: *GCE:* AAB. *IB:* 32.

BH99 BEng Medical Engineering (Year in Industry)
Duration: 4SW Hon
Entry Requirements: *GCE:* AAB. *IB:* 32.

B120 BSc Biomedical Sciences (Physiology) with Preliminary and Professional Training Year
Duration: 5FT Hon
Entry Requirements: *GCE:* AAB-ABB. *SQAAH:* AAB-ABB. *IB:* 34.

H1BV MEng Medical Engineering
Duration: 4FT Hon
Entry Requirements: *GCE:* AAB. *SQAAH:* AAB.

HB99 MEng Medical Engineering (Year in Industry)
Duration: 5SW Hon
Entry Requirements: *GCE:* AAB. *SQAAH:* AAB. Interview required. Admissions Test required.

C60 CITY UNIVERSITY
NORTHAMPTON SQUARE
LONDON EC1V 0HB
t: 020 7040 5060 f: 020 7040 8995
e: ugadmissions@city.ac.uk
// www.city.ac.uk

BH81 BEng Biomedical Engineering
Duration: 3FT Hon
Entry Requirements: *GCE:* 340. *IB:* 30.

BHV1 BEng Biomedical Engineering
Duration: 4SW Hon
Entry Requirements: *GCE:* 340. *IB:* 30.

H72 THE UNIVERSITY OF HULL
THE UNIVERSITY OF HULL
COTTINGHAM ROAD
HULL HU6 7RX
t: 01482 466100 f: 01482 442290
e: admissions@hull.ac.uk
// www.hull.ac.uk

HB38 BEng Mechanical and Medical Engineering
Duration: 3FT Hon
Entry Requirements: *GCE:* 280. *IB:* 27. *BTEC ExtDip:* DMM.

H390 BSc Medical Product Design
Duration: 3FT Hon
Entry Requirements: *GCE:* 260. *IB:* 26. *BTEC ExtDip:* MMM.

HBH8 MEng Mechanical and Medical Engineering
Duration: 4FT Hon
Entry Requirements: *GCE:* 320. *IB:* 30. *BTEC ExtDip:* DDD.

H73 HULL COLLEGE
QUEEN'S GARDENS
HULL HU1 3DG
t: 01482 329943 f: 01482 598733
e: info@hull-college.ac.uk
// www.hull-college.ac.uk/higher-education

CF00 FdSc Biomedical and Applied Science
Duration: 2FT Fdg
Entry Requirements: *GCE:* 160. Interview required. Admissions Test required.

I50 IMPERIAL COLLEGE LONDON
REGISTRY
SOUTH KENSINGTON CAMPUS
IMPERIAL COLLEGE LONDON
LONDON SW7 2AZ
t: 020 7589 5111 f: 020 7594 8004
// www.imperial.ac.uk

BH81 BEng Biomedical Engineering
Duration: 3FT Hon
Entry Requirements: *GCE:* AAA. *SQAAH:* AAA. *IB:* 38.

BH9C MEng Biomedical Engineering
Duration: 4FT Hon
Entry Requirements: *GCE:* AAA. *SQAAH:* AAA. *IB:* 38.

K60 KING'S COLLEGE LONDON (UNIVERSITY OF LONDON)
STRAND
LONDON WC2R 2LS
t: 020 7836 5454 f: 020 7848 7171
e: prospective@kcl.ac.uk
// www.kcl.ac.uk/prospectus

H160 BEng Biomedical Engineering
Duration: 3FT Hon
Entry Requirements: Contact the institution for details.

L23 UNIVERSITY OF LEEDS
THE UNIVERSITY OF LEEDS
WOODHOUSE LANE
LEEDS LS2 9JT
t: 0113 343 3999
e: admissions@leeds.ac.uk
// www.leeds.ac.uk

HHH6 MEng/BEng Medical Engineering
Duration: 3FT/4FT Hon
Entry Requirements: *GCE:* AAA. *SQAAH:* AAA. *IB:* 38.

L41 THE UNIVERSITY OF LIVERPOOL
THE FOUNDATION BUILDING
BROWNLOW HILL
LIVERPOOL L69 7ZX
t: 0151 794 2000 f: 0151 708 6502
e: ugrecruitment@liv.ac.uk
// www.liv.ac.uk

H673 BEng Medical Electronics and Instrumentation
Duration: 3FT Hon
Entry Requirements: *GCE:* ABB. *SQAAH:* ABB. *IB:* 33.

H675 MEng Medical Electronics and Instrumentation (4 years)
Duration: 4FT Hon
Entry Requirements: *GCE:* ABB. *SQAAH:* ABB. *IB:* 33.

O33 OXFORD UNIVERSITY
UNDERGRADUATE ADMISSIONS OFFICE
UNIVERSITY OF OXFORD
WELLINGTON SQUARE
OXFORD OX1 2JD
t: 01865 288000 f: 01865 270212
e: undergraduate.admissions@admin.ox.ac.uk
// www.admissions.ox.ac.uk

H811 MEng Biomedical Engineering
Duration: 4FT Hon
Entry Requirements: *GCE:* A*AA. *SQAH:* AAAAA-AAAAB. *SQAAH:* AAB. Interview required. Admissions Test required.

Q50 QUEEN MARY, UNIVERSITY OF LONDON
QUEEN MARY, UNIVERSITY OF LONDON
MILE END ROAD
LONDON E1 4NS
t: 020 7882 5555 f: 020 7882 5500
e: admissions@qmul.ac.uk
// www.qmul.ac.uk

HBC8 BEng Medical Engineering
Duration: 3FT Hon
Entry Requirements: *GCE:* 300. *IB:* 32.

HBD8 BEng Medical Engineering with Industrial Experience
Duration: 4FT Hon
Entry Requirements: *GCE:* 300. *IB:* 32.

HB18 MEng Medical Engineering
Duration: 4FT Hon
Entry Requirements: *GCE:* 360. *IB:* 36.

HB1V MEng Medical Engineering with Industrial Experience
Duration: 5FT Hon
Entry Requirements: *GCE:* 360. *IB:* 36.

S49 ST GEORGE'S, UNIVERSITY OF LONDON
CRANMER TERRACE
LONDON SW17 0RE
t: +44 (0)20 8725 2333 f: +44 (0)20 8725 0841
e: enquiries@sgul.ac.uk
// www.sgul.ac.uk

J750 BSc Biomedical Science (International)
Duration: 3FT Hon
Entry Requirements: *GCE:* ABB. *IB:* 27.

S85 UNIVERSITY OF SURREY
STAG HILL
GUILDFORD
SURREY GU2 7XH
t: +44(0)1483 689305 f: +44(0)1483 689388
e: ugteam@surrey.ac.uk
// www.surrey.ac.uk

HBJ8 BEng Medical Engineering (4 years)
Duration: 4SW Hon
Entry Requirements: *GCE:* ABB. *SQAH:* BBBB. Interview required.

HB38 MEng Medical Engineering (3 years)
Duration: 3FT Hon
Entry Requirements: *GCE:* ABB. *SQAH:* BBBB. Interview required.

HB3V MEng Medical Engineering (4 years)
Duration: 4FT Hon
Entry Requirements: *GCE:* AAA. Interview required.

HBH8 MEng Medical Engineering (5 years)
Duration: 5SW Hon
Entry Requirements: *GCE:* AAA. Interview required.

S93 SWANSEA UNIVERSITY
SINGLETON PARK
SWANSEA SA2 8PP
t: 01792 295111 f: 01792 295110
e: admissions@swansea.ac.uk
// www.swansea.ac.uk

HB18 BEng Medical Engineering
Duration: 3FT Hon
Entry Requirements: *GCE:* BBB. *IB:* 32.

HB1V MEng Medical Engineering
Duration: 4FT Hon
Entry Requirements: *GCE:* AAB. *IB:* 32.

U20 UNIVERSITY OF ULSTER
COLERAINE
CO. LONDONDERRY
NORTHERN IRELAND BT52 1SA
t: 028 7012 4221 f: 028 7012 4908
e: online@ulster.ac.uk
// www.ulster.ac.uk

BH81 BSc Biomedical Engineering
Duration: 4SW Hon
Entry Requirements: *GCE:* 280. *IB:* 24. Interview required.
Admissions Test required.

AVIATION AND AEROSPACE ENGINEERING

B16 UNIVERSITY OF BATH
CLAVERTON DOWN
BATH BA2 7AY
t: 01225 383019 f: 01225 386366
e: admissions@bath.ac.uk
// www.bath.ac.uk

H6H4 BEng Electronic Engineering with Space Science Technology
Duration: 3FT/4SW Hon
Entry Requirements: *GCE:* ABB. *SQAAH:* BBB. *IB:* 34.

H400 MEng Aerospace Engineering
Duration: 4FT Hon
Entry Requirements: *GCE:* A*AA. *SQAAH:* AAA. *IB:* 36.

H423 MEng Aerospace Engineering (Sandwich)
Duration: 5SW Hon
Entry Requirements: *GCE:* A*AA. *SQAAH:* AAA. *IB:* 36.

H6HK MEng Electronic Engineering with Space Science Technology
Duration: 4FT/5SW Hon
Entry Requirements: *GCE:* AAB. *SQAAH:* AAB. *IB:* 36.

B41 BLACKPOOL AND THE FYLDE COLLEGE AN ASSOCIATE COLLEGE OF LANCASTER UNIVERSITY
ASHFIELD ROAD
BISPHAM
BLACKPOOL
LANCS FY2 0HB
t: 01253 504346 f: 01253 504198
e: admissions@blackpool.ac.uk
// www.blackpool.ac.uk

H410 HNC Aeronautical Engineering
Duration: 1FT HNC
Entry Requirements: *GCE:* 120-360. *IB:* 24.

B72 UNIVERSITY OF BRIGHTON
MITHRAS HOUSE 211
LEWES ROAD
BRIGHTON BN2 4AT
t: 01273 644644 f: 01273 642607
e: admissions@brighton.ac.uk
// www.brighton.ac.uk

H410 BEng Aeronautical Engineering
Duration: 3FT/4SW Hon
Entry Requirements: *GCE:* BBB. *IB:* 32.

H415 BEng Aeronautical Engineering (with integrated Foundation Year)
Duration: 4FT Hon
Entry Requirements: *GCE:* BBC. *IB:* 30.

H414 BSc Aeronautical Engineering (Top-Up)
Duration: 1FT Hon
Entry Requirements: HND required.

H416 MEng Aeronautical Engineering
Duration: 4FT/5SW Hon
Entry Requirements: *GCE:* ABB. *IB:* 34.

B77 BRISTOL, CITY OF BRISTOL COLLEGE
SOUTH BRISTOL SKILLS ACADEMY
CITY OF BRISTOL COLLEGE
PO BOX 2887 BS2 2BB
t: 0117 312 5000
e: HEAdmissions@cityofbristol.ac.uk
// www.cityofbristol.ac.uk

014H HND Aeronautical Engineering
Duration: 2FT HND
Entry Requirements: *GCE:* 140. Interview required.

B78 UNIVERSITY OF BRISTOL
UNDERGRADUATE ADMISSIONS OFFICE
SENATE HOUSE
TYNDALL AVENUE
BRISTOL BS8 1TH
t: 0117 928 9000 f: 0117 331 7391
e: ug-admissions@bristol.ac.uk
// www.bristol.ac.uk

H410 MEng Aerospace Engineering
Duration: 4FT Hon
Entry Requirements: *GCE:* A*AA-AAB. *SQAH:* AAAAA-AAABB.
SQAAH: AA.

H401 MEng Aerospace Engineering with Study in Continental Europe
Duration: 4FT Hon
Entry Requirements: *GCE:* A*AA-AAB. *SQAH:* AAAAA-AAABB.
SQAAH: AA.

B80 UNIVERSITY OF THE WEST OF ENGLAND, BRISTOL
FRENCHAY CAMPUS
COLDHARBOUR LANE
BRISTOL BS16 1QY
t: +44 (0)117 32 83333 f: +44 (0)117 32 82810
e: admissions@uwe.ac.uk
// www.uwe.ac.uk

H403 BEng (Hons Aerospace Engineering
Duration: 3FT/4SW Hon
Entry Requirements: *GCE:* 280.

H402 FdSc Aerospace Engineering Manufacturing
Duration: 2FT Fdg
Entry Requirements: *GCE:* 120.

H404 MEng Aerospace Engineering
Duration: 4FT/5SW Hon
Entry Requirements: *GCE:* 300.

B84 BRUNEL UNIVERSITY
UXBRIDGE
MIDDLESEX UB8 3PH
t: 01895 265265 f: 01895 269790
e: admissions@brunel.ac.uk
// www.brunel.ac.uk

H402 BEng Aerospace Engineering
Duration: 3FT Hon
Entry Requirements: *GCE:* ABB. *SQAAH:* ABB. *IB:* 33. *BTEC SubDip:* D*. *BTEC Dip:* D*D. *BTEC ExtDip:* D*DD. *OCR ND:* D

H401 BEng Aerospace Engineering (4 year Thick SW)
Duration: 4SW Hon
Entry Requirements: *GCE:* ABB. *SQAAH:* ABB. *IB:* 33. *BTEC SubDip:* D*. *BTEC Dip:* D*D. *BTEC ExtDip:* D*DD. *OCR ND:* D

HH4C BEng Aviation Engineering
Duration: 3FT Hon
Entry Requirements: *GCE:* ABB. *SQAAH:* ABB. *IB:* 33. *BTEC SubDip:* D*. *BTEC Dip:* D*D. *BTEC ExtDip:* D*DD. *OCR ND:* D

HHC4 BEng Aviation Engineering (4 year Thick SW)
Duration: 4SW Hon
Entry Requirements: *GCE:* ABB. *SQAAH:* ABB. *IB:* 33. *BTEC SubDip:* D*. *BTEC Dip:* D*D. *BTEC ExtDip:* D*DD. *OCR ND:* D

H1HK BEng Aviation Engineering with Pilot Studies
Duration: 3FT Hon
Entry Requirements: *GCE:* ABB. *SQAAH:* ABB. *IB:* 33. *BTEC SubDip:* D*. *BTEC Dip:* D*D. *BTEC ExtDip:* D*DD. *OCR ND:* D

H4H1 BEng Aviation Engineering with Pilot Studies (4 year Thick SW)
Duration: 4SW Hon
Entry Requirements: *GCE:* ABB. *SQAAH:* ABB. *IB:* 33. *BTEC SubDip:* D*. *BTEC Dip:* D*D. *BTEC ExtDip:* D*DD. *OCR ND:* D

H3HL BEng Mechanical Engineering with Aeronautics
Duration: 3FT Hon
Entry Requirements: *GCE:* ABB. *SQAAH:* ABB. *IB:* 33. *BTEC SubDip:* D*. *BTEC Dip:* D*D. *BTEC ExtDip:* D*DD. *OCR ND:* D

H3HK BEng Mechanical Engineering with Aeronautics (4 year Thick SW)
Duration: 4SW Hon
Entry Requirements: *GCE:* ABB. *SQAAH:* ABB. *IB:* 33. *BTEC SubDip:* D*. *BTEC Dip:* D*D. *BTEC ExtDip:* D*DD. *OCR ND:* D

H400 MEng Aerospace Engineering (4 years)
Duration: 4FT Hon
Entry Requirements: *GCE:* AAA-AAB. *SQAAH:* AAA-AAB. *IB:* 37. *BTEC ExtDip:* D*D*D*.

H403 MEng Aerospace Engineering (5 year Thick SW)
Duration: 5SW Hon
Entry Requirements: *GCE:* AAA-AAB. *SQAAH:* AAA-AAB. *IB:* 37.
BTEC ExtDip: D*D*D*.

HH41 MEng Aviation Engineering (4 years)
Duration: 4FT Hon
Entry Requirements: *GCE:* AAA-AAB. *SQAAH:* AAA-AAB. *IB:* 37.
BTEC ExtDip: D*D*D*.

HH14 MEng Aviation Engineering (5 year Thick SW)
Duration: 5SW Hon
Entry Requirements: *GCE:* AAA-AAB. *SQAAH:* AAA-AAB. *IB:* 37.
BTEC ExtDip: D*D*D*.

H1H4 MEng Aviation Engineering with Pilot Studies (4 years)
Duration: 4FT Hon
Entry Requirements: *GCE:* AAA-AAB. *SQAAH:* AAA-AAB. *IB:* 37.
BTEC ExtDip: D*D*D*.

H1HL MEng Aviation Engineering with Pilot Studies (5 year Thick SW)
Duration: 5SW Hon
Entry Requirements: *GCE:* AAA-AAB. *SQAAH:* AAA-AAB. *IB:* 37.
BTEC ExtDip: D*D*D*.

HH34 MEng Mechanical Engineering with Aeronautics (4 years)
Duration: 4FT Hon
Entry Requirements: *GCE:* AAA-AAB. *SQAAH:* AAA-AAB. *IB:* 37.
BTEC ExtDip: D*D*D*.

HHH4 MEng Mechanical Engineering with Aeronautics (5 year Thick SW)
Duration: 5SW Hon
Entry Requirements: *GCE:* AAA-AAB. *SQAAH:* AAA-AAB. *IB:* 37.
BTEC ExtDip: D*D*D*.

B94 BUCKINGHAMSHIRE NEW UNIVERSITY
QUEEN ALEXANDRA ROAD
HIGH WYCOMBE
BUCKINGHAMSHIRE HP11 2JZ
t: 0800 0565 660 f: 01494 605 023
e: admissions@bucks.ac.uk
// bucks.ac.uk

N8H4 BA Air Transport with Commercial Pilot Training
Duration: 3FT Hon
Entry Requirements: *GCE:* 240-280. *IB:* 25. *OCR ND:* D *OCR NED:* M2

H490 BA Air Transport with Pilot Training
Duration: 3FT Hon
Entry Requirements: *GCE:* 240-280. *IB:* 25. *OCR ND:* D *OCR NED:* M2

C60 CITY UNIVERSITY
NORTHAMPTON SQUARE
LONDON EC1V 0HB
t: 020 7040 5060 f: 020 7040 8995
e: ugadmissions@city.ac.uk
// www.city.ac.uk

H401 BEng Aeronautical Engineering (4 year SW) (a)
Duration: 4SW Hon
Entry Requirements: *GCE:* 340. *IB:* 30.

H410 BEng Aeronautical Engineering (a)
Duration: 3FT Hon
Entry Requirements: *GCE:* 340. *IB:* 30.

H400 BEng Air Transport Engineering (4 year SW) (b)
Duration: 4SW Hon
Entry Requirements: *GCE:* 340. *IB:* 30.

H402 BEng Air Transport Engineering (4 years including Foundation Year) (b)
Duration: 4FT Hon
Entry Requirements: *GCE:* DD-DE. *SQAH:* BC.

H422 BEng Air Transport Engineering (b)
Duration: 3FT Hon
Entry Requirements: *GCE:* 340. *IB:* 28.

H4N1 BSc Air Transport Operations with ATPL
Duration: 3FT Hon
Entry Requirements: *GCE:* 340. *SQAH:* BBBBC. *IB:* 30.

H403 MEng Aeronautical Engineering (4 years) (a)
Duration: 4FT Hon
Entry Requirements: *GCE:* 360. *IB:* 32.

H405 MEng Aeronautical Engineering (5 year SW) (a)
Duration: 5SW Hon
Entry Requirements: *GCE:* 360. *IB:* 32.

H424 MEng Air Transport Engineering (4 years) (b)
Duration: 4FT Hon
Entry Requirements: *GCE:* 360. *IB:* 30.

H423 MEng Air Transport Engineering (5 year SW) (b)
Duration: 5SW Hon
Entry Requirements: *GCE:* 360. *IB:* 32.

C85 COVENTRY UNIVERSITY
THE STUDENT CENTRE
COVENTRY UNIVERSITY
1 GULSON RD
COVENTRY CV1 2JH
t: 024 7615 2222 f: 024 7615 2223
e: studentenquiries@coventry.ac.uk
// www.coventry.ac.uk

HH46 BEng Aerospace Electronics
Duration: 3FT/4SW Hon
Entry Requirements: *GCE:* CCC. *SQAH:* CCCCC. *IB:* 27. *BTEC ExtDip:* MMM. *OCR NED:* M3

H410 BEng Aerospace Systems Engineering
Duration: 3FT/4SW Hon
Entry Requirements: *GCE:* BCC. *SQAH:* BCCCC. *IB:* 28. *BTEC ExtDip:* DMM. *OCR NED:* M2

H402 BEng Aerospace Technology
Duration: 3FT/4SW Hon
Entry Requirements: *GCE:* CCC. *SQAH:* CCCCC. *IB:* 27. *BTEC ExtDip:* MMM. *OCR NED:* M3

HG67 BSc Aviation Management
Duration: 3FT/4SW Hon
Entry Requirements: *GCE:* BCC. *SQAH:* BCCCC. *IB:* 28. *BTEC ExtDip:* DMM. *OCR NED:* M2

D86 DURHAM UNIVERSITY
DURHAM UNIVERSITY
UNIVERSITY OFFICE
DURHAM DH1 3HP
t: 0191 334 2000 f: 0191 334 6055
e: admissions@durham.ac.uk
// www.durham.ac.uk

H420 MEng Aeronautics
Duration: 4FT Hon
Entry Requirements: *GCE:* AAA. *SQAH:* AAAAB. *SQAAH:* AAA. *IB:* 37.

F66 FARNBOROUGH COLLEGE OF TECHNOLOGY
BOUNDARY ROAD
FARNBOROUGH
HAMPSHIRE GU14 6SB
t: 01252 407028 f: 01252 407041
e: admissions@farn-ct.ac.uk
// www.farn-ct.ac.uk

H411 BEng Aeronautical Engineering
Duration: 3FT Hon
Entry Requirements: Contact the institution for details.

H414 BEng Aeronautical Engineering (Top-Up)
Duration: 1FT Hon
Entry Requirements: Admissions Test required.

H401 FdEng Aeronautical Engineering
Duration: 2FT Fdg
Entry Requirements: *GCE:* 160-200.

G14 UNIVERSITY OF GLAMORGAN, CARDIFF AND PONTYPRIDD
ENQUIRIES AND ADMISSIONS UNIT
PONTYPRIDD CF37 1DL
t: 08456 434030 f: 01443 654050
e: enquiries@glam.ac.uk
// www.glam.ac.uk

H410 BEng Aeronautical Engineering
Duration: 3FT Hon
Entry Requirements: *GCE:* BBB. *IB:* 26. *BTEC SubDip:* M. *BTEC Dip:* D*D*. *BTEC ExtDip:* DDM. Interview required.

HK10 BEng Aeronautical Engineering
Duration: 4SW Hon
Entry Requirements: *GCE:* BBB. *IB:* 26. *BTEC SubDip:* M. *BTEC Dip:* D*D*. *BTEC ExtDip:* DMM. Interview required.

H490 BEng Aeronautical Systems Engineering with Avionics
Duration: 3FT Hon
Entry Requirements: *GCE:* BBB. *IB:* 26. *BTEC SubDip:* M. *BTEC Dip:* D*D. *BTEC ExtDip:* DMM.

H402 BSc Aircraft Maintenance Engineering
Duration: 3FT Hon
Entry Requirements: *GCE:* 240. *BTEC SubDip:* M. *BTEC Dip:* D*D*. *BTEC ExtDip:* DMM.

H403 FYr Aeronautical Engineering
Duration: 1FT FYr
Entry Requirements: *GCE:* 40. *BTEC SubDip:* M. *BTEC Dip:* PP. *BTEC ExtDip:* PPP. Interview required.

G28 UNIVERSITY OF GLASGOW
71 SOUTHPARK AVENUE
UNIVERSITY OF GLASGOW
GLASGOW G12 8QQ
t: 0141 330 6062 f: 0141 330 2961
e: student.recruitment@glasgow.ac.uk
// www.glasgow.ac.uk

H415 BEng Aeronautical Engineering
Duration: 4FT Hon
Entry Requirements: *GCE:* ABB. *SQAH:* AAAB-BBB. *IB:* 32.

H402 BEng Aerospace Systems
Duration: 4FT Hon
Entry Requirements: *GCE:* ABB. *SQAH:* AAAB-BBB. *IB:* 32.

H3H4 BEng Mechanical Engineering with Aeronautics
Duration: 4FT Hon
Entry Requirements: *GCE:* ABB. *SQAH:* AAAB-BBB. *IB:* 32.

H410 MEng Aeronautical Engineering
Duration: 5FT Hon
Entry Requirements: *GCE:* AAB. *SQAH:* AAAA-AAABB. *IB:* 34.

H414 MEng Aeronautical Engineering (Faster Route)
Duration: 4FT Hon
Entry Requirements: *GCE:* AAA. *SQAH:* AB. *SQAAH:* AA. *IB:* 38.

H401 MEng Aerospace Systems
Duration: 5FT Hon
Entry Requirements: *GCE:* AAB. *SQAH:* AAAA-AAABB. *IB:* 34.

H430 MEng Aerospace Systems (Faster Route)
Duration: 4FT Hon
Entry Requirements: *GCE:* AAA. *SQAH:* AB. *SQAAH:* AA. *IB:* 38.

H3HK MEng Mechanical Engineering with Aeronautics
Duration: 5FT Hon
Entry Requirements: *GCE:* AAB. *SQAH:* AAAA-AAABB. *IB:* 34.

H3HL MEng Mechanical Engineering with Aeronautics (Faster Route)
Duration: 4FT Hon
Entry Requirements: *GCE:* ABB. *SQAH:* AAAB-BBB. *IB:* 32.

G53 GLYNDWR UNIVERSITY
PLAS COCH
MOLD ROAD
WREXHAM LL11 2AW
t: 01978 293439 f: 01978 290008
e: sid@glyndwr.ac.uk
// www.glyndwr.ac.uk

HH34 BEng Aeronautical and Mechanical Engineering
Duration: 3FT Hon
Entry Requirements: *GCE:* 240.

H431 BEng Performance Car Technology
Duration: 3FT Hon
Entry Requirements: *GCE:* 240.

H36 UNIVERSITY OF HERTFORDSHIRE
UNIVERSITY ADMISSIONS SERVICE
COLLEGE LANE
HATFIELD
HERTS AL10 9AB
t: 01707 284800
// www.herts.ac.uk

H410 BEng Aerospace Engineering
Duration: 3FT/4SW Hon
Entry Requirements: *GCE:* 260.

H408 BEng Aerospace Engineering (Extended)
Duration: 4FT/5SW Hon
Entry Requirements: *GCE:* 80.

H400 BEng Aerospace Engineering with Space Technology
Duration: 3FT/4SW Hon
Entry Requirements: Contact the institution for details.

H430 BEng Aerospace Systems Engineering
Duration: 3FT/4SW Hon
Entry Requirements: *GCE:* 260.

H438 BEng Aerospace Systems Engineering (Extended)
Duration: 4FT/5SW Hon
Entry Requirements: *GCE:* 80.

H492 BEng Aerospace Systems Engineering with Pilot Studies
Duration: 3FT/4SW Hon
Entry Requirements: *GCE:* 260.

H493 BEng Aerospace Systems Engineering with Pilot Studies (Extended)
Duration: 4FT/5SW Hon
Entry Requirements: *GCE:* 80.

H422 BSc Aerospace Technology with Management
Duration: 3FT/4SW Hon
Entry Requirements: *GCE:* 240.

H4N2 BSc Aerospace Technology with Management (Extended)
Duration: 4FT/5SW Hon
Entry Requirements: *GCE:* 80.

H490 BSc Aerospace Technology with Pilot Studies
Duration: 3FT/4SW Hon
Entry Requirements: *GCE:* 240.

H494 BSc Aerospace Technology with Pilot Studies (Extended)
Duration: 4FT/5SW Hon
Entry Requirements: *GCE:* 80.

H401 MEng Aerospace Engineering
Duration: 4FT Hon
Entry Requirements: *GCE:* 320. *IB:* 30.

H402 MEng Aerospace Engineering with Space Technology
Duration: 4FT/5SW Hon
Entry Requirements: Contact the institution for details.

H431 MEng Aerospace Systems Engineering
Duration: 4FT Hon
Entry Requirements: *GCE:* 320. *IB:* 30.

H491 MEng Aerospace Systems Engineering with Pilot Studies
Duration: 4FT/5SW Hon
Entry Requirements: *GCE:* 320.

H49 UNIVERSITY OF THE HIGHLANDS AND ISLANDS
UHI EXECUTIVE OFFICE
NESS WALK
INVERNESS
SCOTLAND IV3 5SQ
t: 01463 279000 f: 01463 279001
e: info@uhi.ac.uk
// www.uhi.ac.uk

H414 BEng Aircraft Engineering
Duration: 3FT Hon
Entry Requirements: HND required.

014H HNC Aircraft Engineering
Duration: 1FT HNC
Entry Requirements: *GCE:* D. *SQAH:* C.

I50 IMPERIAL COLLEGE LONDON
REGISTRY
SOUTH KENSINGTON CAMPUS
IMPERIAL COLLEGE LONDON
LONDON SW7 2AZ
t: 020 7589 5111 f: 020 7594 8004
// www.imperial.ac.uk

H401 MEng Aeronautical Engineering
Duration: 4FT Hon
Entry Requirements: *GCE:* A*A*A. *SQAAH:* AAA. *IB:* 40. Interview required.

H410 MEng Aeronautical Engineering with a Year Abroad
Duration: 4FT Hon
Entry Requirements: *GCE:* A*A*A. *IB:* 40.

HJ45 MEng Aerospace Materials
Duration: 4FT Hon
Entry Requirements: *GCE:* AAA. *SQAAH:* AAA. *IB:* 37.

K84 KINGSTON UNIVERSITY
STUDENT INFORMATION & ADVICE CENTRE
COOPER HOUSE
40-46 SURBITON ROAD
KINGSTON UPON THAMES KT1 2HX
t: 0844 8552177 f: 020 8547 7080
e: aps@kingston.ac.uk
// www.kingston.ac.uk

H421 BEng Aerospace Engineering
Duration: 3FT Hon
Entry Requirements: *GCE:* 240. *IB:* 26.

H422 BEng Aerospace Engineering (4-year SW)
Duration: 4SW Hon
Entry Requirements: *GCE:* 240. *IB:* 26.

H408 BEng Aerospace Engineering (Foundation)
Duration: 4FT/5SW Hon
Entry Requirements: *GCE:* 120. *IB:* 22.

H430 BEng Aerospace Engineering, Astronautics and Space Technology
Duration: 3FT Hon
Entry Requirements: *GCE:* 240. *IB:* 26.

H427 BEng Aerospace Engineering, Astronautics and Space Technology (4-year SW)
Duration: 4SW Hon
Entry Requirements: *GCE:* 240. *IB:* 26.

H400 BSc Aerospace Engineering
Duration: 3FT Hon
Entry Requirements: *GCE:* 160. *IB:* 24.

H401 BSc Aerospace Engineering (4-year SW)
Duration: 4SW Hon
Entry Requirements: *GCE:* 160. *IB:* 24.

H416 BSc Aircraft Engineering (top-up)
Duration: 1FT Hon
Entry Requirements: Contact the institution for details.

H403 FYr Aircraft Engineering Introductory Year 0
Duration: 1FT FYr
Entry Requirements: *GCE:* 80. *IB:* 20.

H410 FdEng Aircraft Engineering
Duration: 2FT Fdg
Entry Requirements: *GCE:* 160. *IB:* 24. Admissions Test required.

H418 FdEng Aircraft Engineering (Norwich) - June intake
Duration: 2FT Fdg
Entry Requirements: *GCE:* 160. *IB:* 24. Admissions Test required.

H411 FdEng Aircraft Maintenance Repair and Overhaul
Duration: 2FT Fdg
Entry Requirements: *GCE:* 160. *IB:* 24. Interview required. Admissions Test required.

H460 FdEng Aviation Studies for Commercial Pilot Training
Duration: 2FT Fdg
Entry Requirements: *GCE:* 200. *IB:* 24. Interview required.

H415 FdSc Aircraft Engineering including Foundation (Year 0)
Duration: 3FT Fdg
Entry Requirements: *GCE:* 80. *IB:* 20.

H425 MEng Aerospace Engineering
Duration: 4FT Hon
Entry Requirements: *GCE:* 300. *IB:* 30.

H426 MEng Aerospace Engineering (5-year SW)
Duration: 5SW Hon
Entry Requirements: *GCE:* 300. *IB:* 30.

H428 MEng Aerospace Engineering, Astronautics and Space Technology
Duration: 4FT Hon
Entry Requirements: *GCE:* 300. *IB:* 30.

H429 MEng Aerospace Engineering, Astronautics and Space Technology (5-year SW)
Duration: 5SW Hon
Entry Requirements: *GCE:* 300. *IB:* 30.

L23 UNIVERSITY OF LEEDS
THE UNIVERSITY OF LEEDS
WOODHOUSE LANE
LEEDS LS2 9JT
t: 0113 343 3999
e: admissions@leeds.ac.uk
// www.leeds.ac.uk

HN42 BSc Aviation Technology and Management
Duration: 3FT Hon
Entry Requirements: *GCE:* AAA. *SQAAH:* AAA. *IB:* 38.

H460 BSc Aviation Technology with Pilot Studies
Duration: 3FT Hon
Entry Requirements: *GCE:* AAA. *SQAAH:* AAA. *IB:* 38.

H410 MEng/BEng Aeronautical and Aerospace Engineering
Duration: 3FT/4FT Hon
Entry Requirements: *GCE:* AAA. *SQAAH:* AAA. *IB:* 38.

L34 UNIVERSITY OF LEICESTER
UNIVERSITY ROAD
LEICESTER LE1 7RH
t: 0116 252 5281 f: 0116 252 2447
e: admissions@le.ac.uk
// www.le.ac.uk

H400 BEng Aerospace Engineering
Duration: 3FT Hon
Entry Requirements: *GCE:* BBB-BBC. *SQAH:* BBBBB-BBBCC. *SQAAH:* BBB-BBC.

H404 BEng Aerospace Engineering (with a Year in Industry)
Duration: 4FT Hon
Entry Requirements: *GCE:* BBB-BBC. *SQAH:* BBBBB-BBBCC. *SQAAH:* BBB-BBC.

H403 BEng Aerospace Engineering (with a year abroad)
Duration: 3FT Hon
Entry Requirements: *GCE:* BBB-BBC. *SQAH:* BBBBB-BBBCC. *SQAAH:* BBB-BBC.

H401 MEng Aerospace Engineering
Duration: 4FT Hon
Entry Requirements: *GCE:* AAB-ABB. *SQAH:* AAABB-AABBB. *SQAAH:* AAB-ABB.

H402 MEng Aerospace Engineering (With a Year Abroad, USA)
Duration: 4FT Hon
Entry Requirements: *GCE:* AAB-ABB. *SQAH:* AAABB-AABBB. *SQAAH:* AAB-ABB.

H405 MEng Aerospace Engineering (with a Year in Industry)
Duration: 5FT Hon
Entry Requirements: *GCE:* AAB-ABB. *SQAH:* AAABB-AABBB. *SQAAH:* AAB-ABB.

L41 THE UNIVERSITY OF LIVERPOOL
THE FOUNDATION BUILDING
BROWNLOW HILL
LIVERPOOL L69 7ZX
t: 0151 794 2000 f: 0151 708 6502
e: ugrecruitment@liv.ac.uk
// www.liv.ac.uk

H425 BEng Aerospace Engineering
Duration: 3FT Hon
Entry Requirements: *GCE:* ABB. *SQAAH:* ABB. *IB:* 33. Interview required.

H401 BEng Aerospace Engineering with Pilot Studies
Duration: 3FT Hon
Entry Requirements: *GCE:* ABB. *SQAAH:* ABB. *IB:* 33. Interview required.

H430 BEng Avionic Systems
Duration: 3FT Hon
Entry Requirements: *GCE:* ABB. *SQAAH:* ABB. *IB:* 33.

H490 BEng Avionic Systems with Pilot Studies
Duration: 3FT Hon
Entry Requirements: *GCE:* ABB. *SQAAH:* ABB. *IB:* 33.

H492 BEng Avionic Systems with Pilot Studies with a Year in Industry
Duration: 4FT Hon
Entry Requirements: *GCE:* ABB. *SQAAH:* ABB. *IB:* 33.

H432 BEng Avionic Systems with a Year in Industry
Duration: 4FT Hon
Entry Requirements: *GCE:* ABB. *SQAAH:* ABB. *IB:* 33.

H421 MEng Aerospace Engineering (4 years)
Duration: 4FT Hon
Entry Requirements: *GCE:* AAB. *SQAAH:* AAB. *IB:* 35. Interview required.

H402 MEng Aerospace Engineering with Pilot Studies (4 years)
Duration: 4FT Hon
Entry Requirements: *GCE:* AAB. *SQAAH:* AAB. *IB:* 35. Interview required.

H431 MEng Avionic Systems (4 years)
Duration: 4FT Hon
Entry Requirements: *GCE:* ABB. *SQAAH:* ABB. *IB:* 33.

H491 MEng Avionic Systems with Pilot Studies (4 years)
Duration: 4FT Hon
Entry Requirements: *GCE:* ABB. *SQAAH:* ABB. *IB:* 33.

H493 MEng Avionic Systems with Pilot Studies with a Year in Industry
Duration: 5FT Hon
Entry Requirements: *GCE:* ABB. *SQAAH:* ABB. *IB:* 33.

H433 MEng Avionic Systems with a Year in Industry
Duration: 5FT Hon
Entry Requirements: *GCE:* ABB. *SQAAH:* ABB. *IB:* 33.

L68 LONDON METROPOLITAN UNIVERSITY
166-220 HOLLOWAY ROAD
LONDON N7 8DB
t: 020 7133 4200
e: admissions@londonmet.ac.uk
// www.londonmet.ac.uk

H490 BSc Aviation Management
Duration: 3FT Hon
Entry Requirements: *GCE:* 240. *IB:* 28.

HNK8 FdSc Airline Flight and Ground Operations (Flight Operations & Ground Operations)
Duration: 2FT Fdg
Entry Requirements: *GCE:* 100. *IB:* 28.

HNL8 FdSc Airline Flight and Ground Operations (Pilot Pathway)
Duration: 2FT Fdg
Entry Requirements: *GCE:* 100. *IB:* 28. Interview required.

L79 LOUGHBOROUGH UNIVERSITY
LOUGHBOROUGH
LEICESTERSHIRE LE11 3TU
t: 01509 223522 f: 01509 223905
e: admissions@lboro.ac.uk
// www.lboro.ac.uk

H401 BEng Aeronautical Engineering
Duration: 4SW Hon
Entry Requirements: *GCE:* AAA-AAB. *SQAH:* AB. *SQAAH:* AA. *IB:* 34.

H410 BEng Aeronautical Engineering
Duration: 3FT Hon
Entry Requirements: *GCE:* AAA-AAB. *SQAH:* AB. *SQAAH:* AA. *IB:* 34.

HN49 BSc Air Transport Management
Duration: 3FT Hon
Entry Requirements: *GCE:* 280. *SQAH:* BBBBB-BBBBC. *SQAAH:* BB. *IB:* 30. *BTEC ExtDip:* DMM.

HNK9 BSc Air Transport Management
Duration: 4SW Hon
Entry Requirements: *GCE:* 280. *SQAH:* BBBBB-BBBBC. *SQAAH:* BB. *IB:* 30. *BTEC ExtDip:* DMM.

H402 MEng Aeronautical Engineering
Duration: 5SW Hon
Entry Requirements: *GCE:* AAA. *SQAH:* AA. *SQAAH:* AA. *IB:* 36.

H403 MEng Aeronautical Engineering
Duration: 4FT Hon
Entry Requirements: *GCE:* AAA. *SQAH:* AA. *SQAAH:* AA. *IB:* 36.

M20 THE UNIVERSITY OF MANCHESTER
RUTHERFORD BUILDING
OXFORD ROAD
MANCHESTER M13 9PL
t: 0161 275 2077 f: 0161 275 2106
e: ug-admissions@manchester.ac.uk
// www.manchester.ac.uk

H400 BEng Aerospace Engineering
Duration: 3FT Hon
Entry Requirements: *GCE:* AAB. *SQAAH:* AAB. *IB:* 35. Interview required.

H402 MEng Aerospace Engineering
Duration: 4FT Hon
Entry Requirements: *GCE:* AAA. *SQAAH:* AAA. *IB:* 37. Interview required.

H406 MEng Aerospace Engineering with Industrial Experience (5 years)
Duration: 5FT Hon
Entry Requirements: *GCE:* AAA. *SQAAH:* AAA. *IB:* 37. Interview required.

H4ND MEng Aerospace Engineering with Management
Duration: 4FT Hon
Entry Requirements: *GCE:* AAA. *SQAAH:* AAA. *IB:* 37. Interview required.

Q50 QUEEN MARY, UNIVERSITY OF LONDON
QUEEN MARY, UNIVERSITY OF LONDON
MILE END ROAD
LONDON E1 4NS
t: 020 7882 5555 f: 020 7882 5500
e: admissions@qmul.ac.uk
// www.qmul.ac.uk

H421 BEng Aerospace Engineering
Duration: 3FT Hon
Entry Requirements: *GCE:* 300. *IB:* 32.

H401 BEng Aerospace Engineering with Industrial Experience
Duration: 4FT Hon
Entry Requirements: *GCE:* 300. *IB:* 32.

H400 MEng Aerospace Engineering
Duration: 4FT Hon
Entry Requirements: *GCE:* 360. *IB:* 36.

HK00 MEng Aerospace Engineering with Industrial Experience
Duration: 5FT Hon
Entry Requirements: *GCE:* 360. *IB:* 36.

Q75 QUEEN'S UNIVERSITY BELFAST
UNIVERSITY ROAD
BELFAST BT7 1NN
t: 028 9097 3838 f: 028 9097 5151
e: admissions@qub.ac.uk
// www.qub.ac.uk

H400 BEng Aerospace Engineering
Duration: 3FT Hon
Entry Requirements: *GCE:* BBC-BCC. *SQAH:* BBBBC-BBBCC. *SQAAH:* BBC-BCC.

H404 BEng Aerospace Engineering (with a Year in Industry)
Duration: 4SW Hon
Entry Requirements: *GCE:* BBC-BCC. *SQAH:* BBBBC-BBBCC. *SQAAH:* BBC-BCC.

H402 MEng Aerospace Engineering
Duration: 4FT Hon
Entry Requirements: *GCE:* ABB-BBB. *SQAH:* ABBBB-BBBBB. *SQAAH:* ABB-BBB.

H405 MEng Aerospace Engineering (with a Year in Industry)
Duration: 5SW Hon
Entry Requirements: *GCE:* ABB-BBB. *SQAH:* ABBBB-BBBBB. *SQAAH:* ABB-BBB.

S03 THE UNIVERSITY OF SALFORD
SALFORD M5 4WT
t: 0161 295 4545 f: 0161 295 4646
e: ug-admissions@salford.ac.uk
// www.salford.ac.uk

H410 BEng Aeronautical Engineering
Duration: 3FT Hon
Entry Requirements: *GCE:* 260. *IB:* 30.

H415 BEng Aeronautical Engineering with Foundation Year
Duration: 4FT Hon
Entry Requirements: Contact the institution for details.

H490 BEng Aircraft Engineering with Pilot Studies
Duration: 3FT/4SW Hon
Entry Requirements: *GCE:* 260. *IB:* 30.

H405 BSc Aeronautical Engineering with Foundation Year
Duration: 4FT Hon
Entry Requirements: *GCE:* 160. *IB:* 24.

H491 BSc Aviation Technology with Pilot Studies
Duration: 3FT/4SW Hon
Entry Requirements: *GCE:* 220. *IB:* 28.

H404 MEng Aeronautical Engineering
Duration: 4FT Hon
Entry Requirements: *GCE:* 300. *IB:* 35.

H492 MEng Aircraft Engineering with Pilot Studies
Duration: 4FT/5SW Hon
Entry Requirements: *GCE:* 300.

S18 THE UNIVERSITY OF SHEFFIELD
THE UNIVERSITY OF SHEFFIELD
LEVEL 2, ARTS TOWER
WESTERN BANK
SHEFFIELD S10 2TN
t: 0114 222 8030 f: 0114 222 8032
// www.sheffield.ac.uk

H402 BEng Aerospace Engineering (3 years)
Duration: 3FT Hon
Entry Requirements: *GCE:* AAB. *SQAH:* AAABB. *SQAAH:* AB. *IB:* 35. *BTEC ExtDip:* DDD.

H460 BEng Aerospace Engineering (Private Pilot Instruction)
Duration: 3FT Hon
Entry Requirements: *GCE:* AAB. *SQAH:* AAABB. *SQAAH:* AB. *IB:* 35. *BTEC ExtDip:* DDD.

H404 BEng Aerospace Engineering with a Year in Industry
Duration: 4FT Hon
Entry Requirements: *GCE:* AAB. *SQAH:* AAABB. *SQAAH:* AB. *IB:* 35. *BTEC ExtDip:* DDD.

H401 BEng Aerospace Materials
Duration: 3FT Hon
Entry Requirements: *GCE:* ABC-BBB. *SQAH:* BBBBB. *SQAAH:* BB. *IB:* 32. *BTEC Dip:* DD. *BTEC ExtDip:* DDM. Interview required.

H400 MEng Aerospace Engineering (4 years)
Duration: 4FT Hon
Entry Requirements: *GCE:* AAA. *SQAH:* AAAAB. *SQAAH:* AA. *IB:* 37. *BTEC ExtDip:* DDD.

H490 MEng Aerospace Engineering (Private Pilot Instruction)
Duration: 4FT Hon
Entry Requirements: *GCE:* AAA. *SQAH:* AAAAB. *SQAAH:* AA. *IB:* 37. *BTEC ExtDip:* DDD.

H407 MEng Aerospace Engineering with a Foundation Year
Duration: 5FT Hon
Entry Requirements: *GCE:* ABB. *SQAH:* AABBB. *SQAAH:* AB. *IB:* 33. *BTEC ExtDip:* DDD. Interview required.

H405 MEng Aerospace Engineering with a Year in Industry
Duration: 5FT Hon
Entry Requirements: *GCE:* AAA. *SQAH:* AAAAB. *SQAAH:* AA. *IB:* 37. *BTEC ExtDip:* DDD.

H406 MEng Aerospace Engineering with a Year in North America
Duration: 4FT Hon
Entry Requirements: *GCE:* AAA. *SQAH:* AAAAB. *SQAAH:* AA. *IB:* 37. *BTEC ExtDip:* DDD.

H403 MEng Aerospace Materials
Duration: 4FT Hon
Entry Requirements: *GCE:* AAB. *SQAH:* AAABB. *SQAAH:* AB. *IB:* 35. *BTEC Dip:* DD. *BTEC ExtDip:* DDD. Interview required.

S21 SHEFFIELD HALLAM UNIVERSITY
CITY CAMPUS
HOWARD STREET
SHEFFIELD S1 1WB
t: 0114 225 5555 f: 0114 225 2167
e: admissions@shu.ac.uk
// www.shu.ac.uk

H415 BEng Aerospace Engineering
Duration: 3FT/4SW Hon
Entry Requirements: *GCE:* 240.

H410 BSc Aeronautical Engineering
Duration: 3FT/4SW Hon
Entry Requirements: *GCE:* 200.

H401 BSc Aerospace Technology
Duration: 3FT/4SW Hon
Entry Requirements: *GCE:* 240.

H414 MEng Aerospace Engineering
Duration: 4FT/5SW Hon
Entry Requirements: *GCE:* 300.

S26 SOLIHULL COLLEGE
BLOSSOMFIELD ROAD
SOLIHULL
WEST MIDLANDS B91 1SB
t: 0121 678 7006 f: 0121 678 7200
e: enquiries@solihull.ac.uk
// www.solihull.ac.uk

004H HND Aerospace Engineering
Duration: 2FT HND
Entry Requirements: *GCE:* A-E. *IB:* 24. *BTEC Dip:* MM. *BTEC ExtDip:* MMM. *OCR ND:* M2 *OCR NED:* M3 Interview required. Portfolio required.

S27 UNIVERSITY OF SOUTHAMPTON
HIGHFIELD
SOUTHAMPTON SO17 1BJ
t: 023 8059 4732 f: 023 8059 3037
e: admissions@soton.ac.uk
// www.southampton.ac.uk

H422 BEng Aeronautics & Astronautics (3 years)
Duration: 3FT Hon
Entry Requirements: *GCE:* AAA. *SQAAH:* AAA. *IB:* 34.

H401 MEng Aeronautics & Astronautics (4 years)
Duration: 4FT Hon
Entry Requirements: *GCE:* AAA. *SQAAH:* AAA. *IB:* 34.

HJ45 MEng Aeronautics & Astronautics/Advanced Materials
Duration: 4FT Hon
Entry Requirements: *GCE:* AAA. *SQAAH:* AAA. *IB:* 34.

H490 MEng Aeronautics & Astronautics/Aerodynamics
Duration: 4FT Hon
Entry Requirements: *GCE:* AAA. *SQAAH:* AAA. *IB:* 34.

H491 MEng Aeronautics & Astronautics/Airvehicle Systems Design
Duration: 4FT Hon
Entry Requirements: *GCE:* AAA. *SQAAH:* AAA. *IB:* 34.

HN42 MEng Aeronautics & Astronautics/Engineering Management
Duration: 4FT Hon
Entry Requirements: *GCE:* AAA. *SQAAH:* AAA. *IB:* 34.

H425 MEng Aeronautics & Astronautics/European Studies (4 years)
Duration: 4FT Hon
Entry Requirements: *GCE:* AAA. *SQAAH:* AAB. *IB:* 34.

H493 MEng Aeronautics & Astronautics/Spacecraft Engineering
Duration: 4FT Hon
Entry Requirements: *GCE:* AAA. *SQAAH:* AAA. *IB:* 34.

H492 MEng Aeronautics & Astronautics/Structural Design
Duration: 4FT Hon
Entry Requirements: *GCE:* AAA. *SQAAH:* AAA. *IB:* 34.

HH34 MEng Mechanical Engineering/Aerospace
Duration: 4FT Hon
Entry Requirements: *GCE:* AAA. *SQAAH:* AAA. *IB:* 34.

H400 MEng Space Systems Engineering
Duration: 4FT Hon
Entry Requirements: *GCE:* AAA. *SQAAH:* AAA. *IB:* 34.

S72 STAFFORDSHIRE UNIVERSITY
COLLEGE ROAD
STOKE ON TRENT ST4 2DE
t: 01782 292753 f: 01782 292740
e: admissions@staffs.ac.uk
// www.staffs.ac.uk

H410 BSc Aeronautical Technology
Duration: 3FT/4SW Hon
Entry Requirements: *GCE:* 200-240. *IB:* 24.

S76 STOCKPORT COLLEGE
WELLINGTON ROAD SOUTH
STOCKPORT SK1 3UQ
t: 0161 958 3143 f: 0161 958 3663
e: susan.kelly@stockport.ac.uk
// www.stockport.ac.uk

004H HND Aeronautical Engineering
Duration: 2FT HND
Entry Requirements: *GCE:* 80. Interview required.

S78 THE UNIVERSITY OF STRATHCLYDE
GLASGOW G1 1XQ
t: 0141 552 4400 f: 0141 552 0775
// www.strath.ac.uk

H420 BEng Aero-Mechanical Engineering
Duration: 4FT Hon
Entry Requirements: *GCE:* A*AA-AAB. *SQAH:* AAAAB-AAAB. *IB:* 32. Interview required.

H421 MEng Aero-Mechanical Engineering
Duration: 5FT Deg
Entry Requirements: *GCE:* A*A*A-AAA. *SQAH:* AAAAAB-AAAAB. *IB:* 36. Interview required.

H3H4 MEng Mechanical Engineering with Aeronautics (d)
Duration: 5FT Hon
Entry Requirements: *GCE:* A*A*A-AAA. *SQAH:* AAAAAB-AAAAB. *IB:* 36. Interview required.

S85 UNIVERSITY OF SURREY
STAG HILL
GUILDFORD
SURREY GU2 7XH
t: +44(0)1483 689305 f: +44(0)1483 689388
e: ugteam@surrey.ac.uk
// www.surrey.ac.uk

H400 BEng Aerospace Engineering (3 years)
Duration: 3FT Hon
Entry Requirements: *GCE:* AAB. *SQAH:* ABBBB. *IB:* 35. Interview required.

H401 BEng Aerospace Engineering (4 years)
Duration: 4SW Hon
Entry Requirements: *GCE:* ABB. *SQAH:* ABBBB. *IB:* 34. Interview required.

H409 MEng Aerospace Engineering (4 years)
Duration: 4FT Hon
Entry Requirements: *GCE:* AAA. *SQAH:* AAAA. *IB:* 37. Interview required.

H402 MEng Aerospace Engineering (5 years)
Duration: 5SW Hon
Entry Requirements: *GCE:* AAA. *SQAH:* AAAA. *IB:* 36. Interview required.

S93 SWANSEA UNIVERSITY
SINGLETON PARK
SWANSEA SA2 8PP
t: 01792 295111 f: 01792 295110
e: admissions@swansea.ac.uk
// www.swansea.ac.uk

H400 BEng Aerospace Engineering
Duration: 3FT Hon
Entry Requirements: *GCE:* BBB. *IB:* 32.

H402 BEng Aerospace Engineering (with a Year in Industry)
Duration: 4FT Hon
Entry Requirements: *GCE:* ABB. *IB:* 33.

H4N2 BEng Aerospace Engineering with Management
Duration: 3FT Hon
Entry Requirements: *GCE:* 260-300.

H4J5 BEng Aerospace Engineering with Materials
Duration: 3FT Hon
Entry Requirements: *GCE:* 260-300.

H4JM BEng Aerospace Engineering with Materials (with a year in Industry) (4 years)
Duration: 4FT Hon
Entry Requirements: *GCE:* 260-300.

H4H6 BEng Aerospace Engineering with Power Electronics
Duration: 3FT Hon
Entry Requirements: *GCE:* 260-300.

H4HP BEng Aerospace Engineering with Power Electronics (with a Year in Industry) (4 years)
Duration: 4FT Hon
Entry Requirements: *GCE:* 260-300.

H450 BEng Aerospace Engineering with Propulsion
Duration: 3FT Hon
Entry Requirements: *GCE:* BBB.

H452 BEng Aerospace Engineering with Propulsion (with a year in Industry) (4 years)
Duration: 4FT Hon
Entry Requirements: *GCE:* ABB.

H403 MEng Aerospace Engineering
Duration: 4FT Hon
Entry Requirements: *GCE:* AAB. *IB:* 34.

H404 MEng Aerospace Engineering (with a Year in Industry)
Duration: 5FT Hon
Entry Requirements: *GCE:* AAA. *IB:* 36.

H4NF MEng Aerospace Engineering with Management
Duration: 4FT Hon
Entry Requirements: *GCE:* 320-380.

H4JL MEng Aerospace Engineering with Materials
Duration: 4FT Hon
Entry Requirements: *GCE:* 320-380.

H4JN MEng Aerospace Engineering with Materials (with a year in Industry) (5 years)
Duration: 5FT Hon
Entry Requirements: *GCE:* 320-380.

H453 MEng Aerospace Engineering with Propulsion
Duration: 4FT Hon
Entry Requirements: *GCE:* AAB.

H454 MEng Aerospace Engineering with Propulsion (with a year in Industry) (5 years)
Duration: 5FT Hon
Entry Requirements: *GCE:* AAA.

T20 TEESSIDE UNIVERSITY
MIDDLESBROUGH TS1 3BA
t: 01642 218121 f: 01642 384201
e: registry@tees.ac.uk
// www.tees.ac.uk

H400 BEng Aerospace Engineering
Duration: 3FT/4SW Hon
Entry Requirements: *GCE:* 280. *IB:* 30. *BTEC Dip:* D*D*. *BTEC ExtDip:* DMM. *OCR ND:* M2 *OCR NED:* M2 Interview required.

N846 FdA Tourism and Aviation
Duration: 2FT Fdg
Entry Requirements: *GCE:* 120. Interview required.

H410 HND Aeronautical Engineering
Duration: 2FT HND
Entry Requirements: *GCE:* 120-200. *BTEC SubDip:* M. *BTEC Dip:* MP. *BTEC ExtDip:* PPP. *OCR ND:* P2 *OCR NED:* P3 Interview required.

H401 MEng Aerospace Engineering
Duration: 4FT/5SW Hon/Ord
Entry Requirements: *GCE:* 300. *IB:* 30. *BTEC Dip:* D*D*. *BTEC ExtDip:* DDM. *OCR ND:* M2 *OCR NED:* M2 Interview required.

U40 UNIVERSITY OF THE WEST OF SCOTLAND
PAISLEY
RENFREWSHIRE
SCOTLAND PA1 2BE
t: 0141 848 3727 f: 0141 848 3623
e: admissions@uws.ac.uk
// www.uws.ac.uk

H410 BEng Aircraft Engineering
Duration: 2FT Hon
Entry Requirements: HND required.

CHEMICAL, PROCESS AND ENERGY ENGINEERING

A20 THE UNIVERSITY OF ABERDEEN
UNIVERSITY OFFICE
KING'S COLLEGE
ABERDEEN AB24 3FX
t: +44 (0) 1224 273504 f: +44 (0) 1224 272034
e: sras@abdn.ac.uk
// www.abdn.ac.uk/sras

H813 BEng Chemical Engineering
Duration: 4FT Hon
Entry Requirements: *GCE:* BBB. *SQAH:* BBBC. *IB:* 28.

H3H8 BEng Engineering (Mechanical with Oil and Gas Studies)
Duration: 4FT Hon
Entry Requirements: *GCE:* BBB. *SQAH:* BBBC. *IB:* 28.

H851 BEng Petroleum Engineering
Duration: 4FT Hon
Entry Requirements: *GCE:* BBB. *SQAH:* BBBC. *IB:* 28.

H810 MEng Chemical Engineering
Duration: 5FT Hon
Entry Requirements: *GCE:* BBB. *SQAH:* BBBB. *IB:* 30.

H850 MEng Petroleum Engineering
Duration: 5FT Hon
Entry Requirements: *GCE:* BBB. *SQAH:* BBBB. *IB:* 30.

A80 ASTON UNIVERSITY, BIRMINGHAM
ASTON TRIANGLE
BIRMINGHAM B4 7ET
t: 0121 204 4444 f: 0121 204 3696
e: admissions@aston.ac.uk (automatic response)
// www.aston.ac.uk/prospective-students/ug

H803 BEng Chemical Engineering
Duration: 3FT/4SW Hon
Entry Requirements: *GCE:* 300-320. *IB:* 32.

H804 MEng Chemical Engineering
Duration: 4FT/5SW Hon
Entry Requirements: *GCE:* 340-360. *IB:* 34.

B16 UNIVERSITY OF BATH
CLAVERTON DOWN
BATH BA2 7AY
t: 01225 383019 f: 01225 386366
e: admissions@bath.ac.uk
// www.bath.ac.uk

H813 BEng Chemical Engineering
Duration: 3FT Hon
Entry Requirements: *GCE:* AAB. *SQAAH:* AAB. *IB:* 36.

H814 BEng Chemical Engineering
Duration: 4SW Hon
Entry Requirements: *GCE:* AAB. *SQAAH:* AAB. *IB:* 36.

H831 BEng Chemical and Bioprocess Engineering
Duration: 3FT Hon
Entry Requirements: *GCE:* AAB. *SQAAH:* AAB. *IB:* 36.

H832 BEng Chemical and Bioprocess Engineering
Duration: 4SW Hon
Entry Requirements: *GCE:* AAB. *SQAAH:* AAB. *IB:* 36.

H811 MEng Biochemical Engineering
Duration: 4FT Hon
Entry Requirements: *GCE:* AAB. *SQAAH:* AAB. *IB:* 36.

H871 MEng Biochemical Engineering
Duration: 5SW Hon
Entry Requirements: *GCE:* AAB. *SQAAH:* AAB. *IB:* 36.

H803 MEng Chemical Engineering
Duration: 4FT Hon
Entry Requirements: *GCE:* AAB. *SQAAH:* AAB. *IB:* 36.

H804 MEng Chemical Engineering
Duration: 5SW Hon
Entry Requirements: *GCE:* AAB. *SQAAH:* AAB. *IB:* 36.

B32 THE UNIVERSITY OF BIRMINGHAM
EDGBASTON
BIRMINGHAM B15 2TT
t: 0121 415 8900 f: 0121 414 7159
e: admissions@bham.ac.uk
// www.birmingham.ac.uk

H800 BEng Chemical Engineering
Duration: 3FT Hon
Entry Requirements: *GCE:* AAA-AAB. *SQAH:* AAAAB-AABBB. *SQAAH:* AA.

H8ND BEng Chemical Engineering with Business Management
Duration: 3FT Hon
Entry Requirements: *GCE:* AAA-AAB. *SQAH:* AAAAB-AABBB. *SQAAH:* AA.

HV10 BEng Chemical Engineering with Industrial Study
Duration: 4FT Hon
Entry Requirements: *GCE:* AAA-AAB. *SQAH:* AAAAB-AABBB. *SQAAH:* AA.

H803 BEng Chemical and Energy Engineering
Duration: 3FT Hon
Entry Requirements: *GCE:* AAA-AAB. *SQAH:* AAAAB-AABBB. *SQAAH:* AA.

H890 BEng Chemical and Energy Engineering with Industrial Study
Duration: 4FT Hon
Entry Requirements: *GCE:* AAA-AAB. *SQAH:* AAAAB-AABBB. *SQAAH:* AA.

HH28 BEng Civil and Energy Engineering
Duration: 3FT Hon
Entry Requirements: *GCE:* AAA-AAB. *SQAH:* AAAAB-AABBB. *SQAAH:* AA.

HH68 BEng Electrical and Energy Engineering
Duration: 3FT Hon
Entry Requirements: *GCE:* AAB. *SQAH:* AAABB-AABBB. *SQAAH:* AA.

HH6W BEng Electrical and Energy Engineering (with an Industrial Year)
Duration: 4FT Hon
Entry Requirements: Contact the institution for details.

H892 BEng/MEng Chemical Engineering with Foundation Year
Duration: 4FT Hon
Entry Requirements: Contact the institution for details.

JH58 BEng/MEng Materials Science and Energy Engineering
Duration: 3FT Hon
Entry Requirements: *GCE:* AAB. *SQAH:* AAABB-AABBB. *SQAAH:* AA.

H821 BSc Nuclear Science and Materials
Duration: 3FT Hon
Entry Requirements: *GCE:* ABB. *SQAH:* AABBB-ABBBB. *SQAAH:* AB.

H810 MEng Chemical Engineering
Duration: 4FT Hon
Entry Requirements: *GCE:* AAA. *SQAH:* AAAAB-AAABB. *SQAAH:* AA.

H802 MEng Chemical Engineering (Industrial Experience) (5 years)
Duration: 5FT Hon
Entry Requirements: *GCE:* AAA. *SQAH:* AAAAB-AAABB. *SQAAH:* AA.

H801 MEng Chemical Engineering (International Study) (4 years)
Duration: 4FT Hon
Entry Requirements: *GCE:* AAA. *SQAH:* AAAAB-AAABB. *SQAAH:* AA.

H8N2 MEng Chemical Engineering with Business Management
Duration: 4FT Hon
Entry Requirements: *GCE:* AAA. *SQAH:* AAAAB-AAABB. *SQAAH:* AA.

HW10 MEng Chemical Engineering with International and Industrial Study
Duration: 5FT Hon
Entry Requirements: *GCE:* AAA. *SQAH:* AAAAB-AAABB. *SQAAH:* AA.

HH81 MEng Chemical and Energy Engineering
Duration: 4FT Hon
Entry Requirements: *GCE:* AAA. *SQAH:* AAAAB-AAABB. *SQAAH:* AA.

H891 MEng Chemical and Energy Engineering with Industrial Study
Duration: 5FT Hon
Entry Requirements: *GCE:* AAA. *SQAH:* AAAAB-AAABB. *SQAAH:* AA.

H2H8 MEng Civil and Energy Engineering
Duration: 4FT Hon
Entry Requirements: *GCE:* AAA-AAB. *SQAH:* AAAAB-AABBB. *SQAAH:* AA.

HH6V MEng Electrical and Energy Engineering
Duration: 4FT Hon
Entry Requirements: *GCE:* AAA. *SQAH:* AAAAB-AAABB. *SQAAH:* AA.

HH86 MEng Electrical and Energy Engineering with an Industrial Year
Duration: 5FT Hon
Entry Requirements: Contact the institution for details.

FH28 MEng Materials Science and Energy Engineering
Duration: 4FT Hon
Entry Requirements: *GCE:* AAA. *SQAH:* AAAAB-AAABB. *SQAAH:* AA.

H822 MEng Nuclear Engineering
Duration: 4FT Hon
Entry Requirements: *GCE:* AAB. *SQAH:* AAABB-AABBB. *SQAAH:* AA.

B56 THE UNIVERSITY OF BRADFORD
RICHMOND ROAD
BRADFORD
WEST YORKSHIRE BD7 1DP
t: 0800 073 1225 f: 01274 235585
e: course-enquiries@bradford.ac.uk
// www.bradford.ac.uk

H810 BEng Chemical Engineering
Duration: 4SW Hon
Entry Requirements: *GCE:* 260. *IB:* 24.

H8D0 BEng Chemical Engineering
Duration: 3FT Hon
Entry Requirements: *GCE:* 260. *IB:* 24.

H8C0 MEng Chemical Engineering
Duration: 5SW Hon
Entry Requirements: *GCE:* 300. *IB:* 26.

H8X0 MEng Chemical Engineering
Duration: 4FT Hon
Entry Requirements: *GCE:* 300. *IB:* 26.

C05 UNIVERSITY OF CAMBRIDGE
CAMBRIDGE ADMISSIONS OFFICE
FITZWILLIAM HOUSE
32 TRUMPINGTON STREET
CAMBRIDGE CB2 1QY
t: 01223 333 308 f: 01223 746 868
e: admissions@cam.ac.uk
// www.study.cam.ac.uk/undergraduate/

H810 MEng Chemical Engineering (via Engineering)
Duration: 4FT Hon
Entry Requirements: *GCE:* A*AA. *SQAAH:* AAA-AAB. Interview required.

H813 MEng Chemical Engineering (via Natural Sciences)
Duration: 4FT Hon
Entry Requirements: *GCE:* A*AA. *SQAAH:* AAA-AAB. Interview required.

C30 UNIVERSITY OF CENTRAL LANCASHIRE
PRESTON
LANCS PR1 2HE
t: 01772 201201 f: 01772 894954
e: uadmissions@uclan.ac.uk
// www.uclan.ac.uk

H862 BEng Fire Engineering
Duration: 3FT Hon
Entry Requirements: *GCE:* 260. *SQAH:* BBCCC. *IB:* 28. *OCR NED:* M2

C85 COVENTRY UNIVERSITY
THE STUDENT CENTRE
COVENTRY UNIVERSITY
1 GULSON RD
COVENTRY CV1 2JH
t: 024 7615 2222 f: 024 7615 2223
e: studentenquiries@coventry.ac.uk
// www.coventry.ac.uk

NH82 BSc Oil, Gas and Energy Management
Duration: 3FT/4SW Hon
Entry Requirements: *GCE:* BBB-BBC. *SQAH:* BBBBC-BBCCC. *BTEC ExtDip:* DDM. *OCR NED:* M1

E56 THE UNIVERSITY OF EDINBURGH
STUDENT RECRUITMENT & ADMISSIONS
57 GEORGE SQUARE
EDINBURGH EH8 9JU
t: 0131 650 4360 f: 0131 651 1236
e: sra.enquiries@ed.ac.uk
// www.ed.ac.uk/studying/undergraduate/

H800 BEng Chemical Engineering
Duration: 4FT Hon
Entry Requirements: *GCE:* AAA-ABB. *SQAH:* AAAA-ABBB.

H8N2 BEng Chemical Engineering with Management
Duration: 4FT Hon
Entry Requirements: *GCE:* AAA-ABB. *SQAH:* AAAA-ABBB.

H804 MEng Chemical Engineering
Duration: 5FT Hon
Entry Requirements: *GCE:* AAA-ABB. *SQAH:* AAAA-ABBB.

H8NF MEng Chemical Engineering with Management
Duration: 5FT Hon
Entry Requirements: *GCE:* AAA-ABB. *SQAH:* AAAA-ABBB.

G74 GREENWICH SCHOOL OF MANAGEMENT
MERIDIAN HOUSE
ROYAL HILL
GREENWICH
LONDON SE10 8RD
t: +44(0)20 8516 7800 f: +44(0)20 8516 7801
e: admissions@greenwich-college.ac.uk
// www.greenwich-college.ac.uk/
?utm_source=UCAS&utm_medium=Profil

H893 BSc Oil and Gas Management
Duration: 3FT Hon
Entry Requirements: *GCE:* 80-120. *SQAH:* A-B. *IB:* 24. *OCR ND:* P3 *OCR NED:* P3 Interview required.

H891 BSc Oil and Gas Management (Accelerated with Foundation Year)
Duration: 3FT Hon
Entry Requirements: *OCR ND:* P3 Interview required.

H890 BSc Oil and Gas Management (Accelerated)
Duration: 2FT Hon
Entry Requirements: *GCE:* 80-120. *SQAH:* A-B. *IB:* 24. *OCR ND:* P3 *OCR NED:* P3 Interview required.

H892 BSc Oil and Gas Management (with Foundation Year)
Duration: 4FT Hon
Entry Requirements: *OCR ND:* P3 Interview required.

H24 HERIOT-WATT UNIVERSITY, EDINBURGH
EDINBURGH CAMPUS
EDINBURGH EH14 4AS
t: 0131 449 5111 f: 0131 451 3630
e: ugadmissions@hw.ac.uk
// www.hw.ac.uk

H800 BEng Chemical Engineering
Duration: 4FT Hon
Entry Requirements: *GCE:* BBB. *SQAH:* AABB-BBBBC. *SQAAH:* BB. *IB:* 29.

H802 BEng Chemical Engineering with Diploma in Industrial Training
Duration: 5FT Hon
Entry Requirements: *GCE:* BBB. *SQAH:* AABB-BBBBC. *SQAAH:* BB. *IB:* 29.

HH3V BEng Mechanical and Energy Engineering
Duration: 4FT Hon
Entry Requirements: *GCE:* BBB. *SQAH:* AABB-BBBBC. *SQAAH:* BB. *IB:* 29.

H801 MEng Chemical Engineering
Duration: 5FT Hon
Entry Requirements: *GCE:* BBB. *SQAH:* AABB-BBBBC. *SQAAH:* BB.
IB: 29.

H803 MEng Chemical Engineering with Diploma in Industrial Training
Duration: 6FT Hon
Entry Requirements: *GCE:* BBB. *SQAH:* AABB-BBBBC. *SQAAH:* BB.
IB: 29.

H8H2 MEng Chemical Engineering with Energy Engineering
Duration: 5FT Hon
Entry Requirements: *GCE:* BBB. *SQAH:* AABB-BBBBC. *SQAAH:* BB.
IB: 29.

H8HF MEng Chemical Engineering with Energy Engineering with Diploma in Industrial Training
Duration: 6FT Hon
Entry Requirements: *GCE:* BBB. *SQAH:* AABB-BBBBC. *SQAAH:* BB.
IB: 29.

H890 MEng Chemical Engineering with Oil & Gas Technology
Duration: 5FT Hon
Entry Requirements: *GCE:* BBB. *SQAH:* AABB-BBBBC. *SQAAH:* BB.
IB: 29.

H891 MEng Chemical Engineering with Oil & Gas Technology with Diploma in Ind Training
Duration: 6FT Hon
Entry Requirements: *GCE:* BBB. *SQAH:* AABB-BBBBC. *SQAAH:* BB.
IB: 29.

H8FC MEng Chemical Engineering with Pharmaceutical Chemistry
Duration: 5FT Hon
Entry Requirements: *GCE:* BBB. *SQAH:* AABB-BBBBC. *SQAAH:* BB.
IB: 29.

H8F1 MEng Chemical Engineering with Pharmaceutical Chemistry w. Dip in Industrial Training
Duration: 6FT Hon
Entry Requirements: *GCE:* BBB. *SQAH:* AABB-BBBBC. *SQAAH:* BB.
IB: 29.

H810 MEng Industrial Engineering (Chemical)
Duration: 5FT Hon
Entry Requirements: *GCE:* BBB. *SQAH:* AABB-BBBBC. *SQAAH:* BB.
IB: 29.

HH38 MEng Mechanical and Energy Engineering
Duration: 5FT Hon
Entry Requirements: *GCE:* BBC. *SQAH:* AABB. *SQAAH:* AB. *IB:* 34.

H49 UNIVERSITY OF THE HIGHLANDS AND ISLANDS
UHI EXECUTIVE OFFICE
NESS WALK
INVERNESS
SCOTLAND IV3 5SQ
t: 01463 279000 f: 01463 279001
e: info@uhi.ac.uk
// www.uhi.ac.uk

HH68 BEng Hons Electrical and Energy Engineering
Duration: 1FT Hon
Entry Requirements: Contact the institution for details.

HH38 BEng Hons Mechanical and Energy Engineering
Duration: 1FT Hon
Entry Requirements: Contact the institution for details.

H60 THE UNIVERSITY OF HUDDERSFIELD
QUEENSGATE
HUDDERSFIELD HD1 3DH
t: 01484 473969 f: 01484 472765
e: admissionsandrecords@hud.ac.uk
// www.hud.ac.uk

HF81 BSc Chemical Engineering and Chemistry
Duration: 3FT/4SW Ord
Entry Requirements: *GCE:* 240.

F1H8 BSc Chemistry with Chemical Engineering
Duration: 3FT Hon
Entry Requirements: *GCE:* 240. *SQAH:* BBB.

H72 THE UNIVERSITY OF HULL
THE UNIVERSITY OF HULL
COTTINGHAM ROAD
HULL HU6 7RX
t: 01482 466100 f: 01482 442290
e: admissions@hull.ac.uk
// www.hull.ac.uk

H810 BEng Chemical Engineering
Duration: 3FT Hon
Entry Requirements: *GCE:* 300. *IB:* 30. *BTEC ExtDip:* DDD.

H811 MEng Chemical Engineering
Duration: 4FT Hon
Entry Requirements: *GCE:* 340. *IB:* 30. *BTEC ExtDip:* DDD.

I50 IMPERIAL COLLEGE LONDON
REGISTRY
SOUTH KENSINGTON CAMPUS
IMPERIAL COLLEGE LONDON
LONDON SW7 2AZ
t: 020 7589 5111 f: 020 7594 8004
// www.imperial.ac.uk

H801 MEng Chemical Engineering
Duration: 4FT Hon
Entry Requirements: *GCE:* A*AA. *SQAAH:* AAA. *IB:* 39.

H802 MEng Chemical Engineering with a Year Abroad
Duration: 4FT Hon
Entry Requirements: *GCE:* A*AA. *SQAAH:* AAA. *IB:* 39.

H890 MEng Chemical with Nuclear Engineering
Duration: 4FT Hon
Entry Requirements: *GCE:* A*AA. *SQAAH:* AAA. *IB:* 39.

J5H8 MEng Materials with Nuclear Engineering
Duration: 4FT Hon
Entry Requirements: *GCE:* AAA. *SQAAH:* AAA. *IB:* 37.

L14 LANCASTER UNIVERSITY
THE UNIVERSITY
LANCASTER
LANCASHIRE LA1 4YW
t: 01524 592029 f: 01524 846243
e: ugadmissions@lancaster.ac.uk
// www.lancs.ac.uk

H800 BEng Chemical Engineering
Duration: 3FT Hon
Entry Requirements: *GCE:* ABB. *SQAH:* BBBBB. *SQAAH:* BBB. *IB:* 32.

H811 MEng Chemical Engineering
Duration: 4FT Hon
Entry Requirements: *GCE:* AAB. *SQAH:* ABBBB. *SQAAH:* AAB. *IB:* 35.

H821 MEng Nuclear Engineering
Duration: 4FT Hon
Entry Requirements: *GCE:* AAA. *SQAH:* AAABB. *SQAAH:* AAA. *IB:* 36.

L23 UNIVERSITY OF LEEDS
THE UNIVERSITY OF LEEDS
WOODHOUSE LANE
LEEDS LS2 9JT
t: 0113 343 3999
e: admissions@leeds.ac.uk
// www.leeds.ac.uk

HF69 BSc Nanotechnology (Chemical)
Duration: 3FT Hon
Entry Requirements: *GCE:* AAB. *SQAAH:* AAB. *IB:* 35.

H891 MEng Chemical and Nuclear Engineering
Duration: 4FT Hon
Entry Requirements: *GCE:* AAA. *SQAAH:* AAA. *IB:* 38.

H3H8 MEng Mechanical with Nuclear Engineering
Duration: 4FT Hon
Entry Requirements: *GCE:* AAA. *SQAAH:* AAA. *IB:* 38.

H851 MEng Petroleum Engineering
Duration: 4FT Hon
Entry Requirements: *GCE:* AAA. *SQAAH:* AAA. *IB:* 38.

H800 MEng/BEng Chemical Engineering
Duration: 3FT/4FT Hon
Entry Requirements: *GCE:* AAA. *SQAAH:* AAA. *IB:* 38.

H801 MEng/BEng Chemical and Energy Engineering
Duration: 3FT/4FT Hon
Entry Requirements: *GCE:* AAA. *SQAAH:* AAA. *IB:* 38.

HJ85 MEng/BEng Chemical and Materials Engineering
Duration: 3FT/4FT Hon
Entry Requirements: *GCE:* AAA. *SQAAH:* AAA. *IB:* 38.

H890 MEng/BEng Chemical and Pharmaceutical Engineering
Duration: 3FT/4FT Hon
Entry Requirements: *GCE:* AAA. *SQAAH:* AAA. *IB:* 38.

L53 COLEG LLANDRILLO CYMRU
LLANDUDNO ROAD
RHOS-ON-SEA
COLWYN BAY
NORTH WALES LL28 4HZ
t: 01492 542338/339 f: 01492 543052
e: degrees@llandrillo.ac.uk
// www.llandrillo.ac.uk

8565 FdEng Energy and Power Technologies
Duration: 2FT Fdg
Entry Requirements: *GCE:* 120. Interview required.

L75 LONDON SOUTH BANK UNIVERSITY
ADMISSIONS AND RECRUITMENT CENTRE
90 LONDON ROAD
LONDON SE1 6LN
t: 0800 923 8888 f: 020 7815 8273
e: course.enquiry@lsbu.ac.uk
// www.lsbu.ac.uk

H801 BEng Chemical & Process Engineering
Duration: 3FT/4SW Hon
Entry Requirements: *GCE:* 240. *IB:* 24.

H850 BEng Petroleum Engineering
Duration: 3FT/4SW Hon
Entry Requirements: *GCE:* 240. *IB:* 24.

008H HND Chemical Engineering
Duration: 2FT HND
Entry Requirements: *GCE:* 40. *IB:* 24.

L79 LOUGHBOROUGH UNIVERSITY
LOUGHBOROUGH
LEICESTERSHIRE LE11 3TU
t: 01509 223522 f: 01509 223905
e: admissions@lboro.ac.uk
// www.lboro.ac.uk

H805 BEng Chemical Engineering
Duration: 3FT Hon
Entry Requirements: *GCE:* AAB. *SQAH:* AAB. *SQAAH:* AB. *IB:* 36.
BTEC ExtDip: DDD.

H806 BEng Chemical Engineering
Duration: 4SW Hon
Entry Requirements: *GCE:* AAB. *SQAH:* AAB. *SQAAH:* AB. *IB:* 36.
BTEC ExtDip: DDD.

H80A BEng Chemical Engineering with Foundation Year
Duration: 4FT Hon
Entry Requirements: *GCE:* AAB. *IB:* 36.

H802 MEng Chemical Engineering
Duration: 5SW Hon
Entry Requirements: *GCE:* AAB. *SQAH:* AAB. *SQAAH:* AB. *IB:* 36.

H803 MEng Chemical Engineering
Duration: 4FT Hon
Entry Requirements: *GCE:* AAB. *SQAH:* AAB. *SQAAH:* AB. *IB:* 36.
BTEC ExtDip: DDD.

H8N2 MEng Chemical Engineering with Management
Duration: 4FT Hon
Entry Requirements: *GCE:* AAB. *SQAH:* AAB. *SQAAH:* AB. *IB:* 36.
BTEC ExtDip: DDD.

H8NF MEng Chemical Engineering with Management
Duration: 5SW Hon
Entry Requirements: *GCE:* AAB. *SQAH:* AAB. *SQAAH:* AB. *IB:* 36.
BTEC ExtDip: DDD.

M20 THE UNIVERSITY OF MANCHESTER
RUTHERFORD BUILDING
OXFORD ROAD
MANCHESTER M13 9PL
t: 0161 275 2077 f: 0161 275 2106
e: ug-admissions@manchester.ac.uk
// www.manchester.ac.uk

H800 BEng Chemical Engineering
Duration: 3FT Hon
Entry Requirements: *GCE:* AAA. *SQAAH:* AAA. *IB:* 37. Interview required.

H3H8 BEng Mechanical Engineering with Nuclear Engineering
Duration: 3FT Hon
Entry Requirements: *GCE:* AAB. *SQAAH:* AAB. *IB:* 35. Interview required.

H850 BEng Petroleum Engineering
Duration: 3FT Hon
Entry Requirements: *GCE:* AAB. *SQAAH:* AAB. Interview required.

H801 MEng Chemical Engineering
Duration: 4FT Hon
Entry Requirements: *GCE:* AAA. *SQAAH:* AAA. *IB:* 37. Interview required.

HN82 MEng Chemical Engineering (Business Management)
Duration: 4FT Hon
Entry Requirements: *GCE:* AAA. *SQAAH:* AAA. *IB:* 37. Interview required.

H8F4 MEng Chemical Engineering (Energy and the Environment)
Duration: 4FT Hon
Entry Requirements: *GCE:* AAA. *SQAAH:* AAA. *IB:* 37.

H8C5 MEng Chemical Engineering with Biotechnology
Duration: 4FT Hon
Entry Requirements: *GCE:* AAA. *SQAAH:* AAA. *IB:* 37. Interview required.

H8F1 MEng Chemical Engineering with Chemistry
Duration: 4FT Hon
Entry Requirements: *GCE:* AAA. *SQAAH:* AAA. *IB:* 37. Interview required.

H8F8 MEng Chemical Engineering with Environmental Technology
Duration: 4FT Hon
Entry Requirements: *GCE:* AAA. *SQAAH:* AAA. *IB:* 37. Interview required.

H803 MEng Chemical Engineering with Industrial Experience
Duration: 4SW Hon
Entry Requirements: *GCE:* AAA. *SQAAH:* AAA. *IB:* 37. Interview required.

H810 MEng Chemical Engineering with Study in Europe
Duration: 4FT Hon
Entry Requirements: *GCE:* AAA. *SQAAH:* AAA. *IB:* 37. Interview required.

H3HV MEng Mechanical Engineering with Nuclear Engineering
Duration: 4FT Hon
Entry Requirements: *GCE:* AAA. *SQAAH:* AAA. *IB:* 37. Interview required.

H851 MEng Petroleum Engineering
Duration: 4FT Hon
Entry Requirements: *GCE:* AAB. *SQAAH:* AAB. *IB:* 35. Interview required.

N21 NEWCASTLE UNIVERSITY
KING'S GATE
NEWCASTLE UPON TYNE NE1 7RU
t: 01912083333
// www.ncl.ac.uk

H810 BEng Chemical Engineering
Duration: 3FT Hon
Entry Requirements: *GCE:* AAB-ABB. *SQAAH:* AB.

H814 BEng Chemical Engineering (4 years)
Duration: 4FT Hon
Entry Requirements: *GCE:* AAB-ABB. *SQAAH:* AB.

H813 MEng Chemical Engineering
Duration: 4FT Hon
Entry Requirements: *GCE:* AAB. *SQAAH:* AA-AB. *IB:* 36.

H816 MEng Chemical Engineering (5 years)
Duration: 5FT Hon
Entry Requirements: *GCE:* AAB. *SQAAH:* AA-AB. *IB:* 36. *BTEC ExtDip:* DDD.

H815 MEng Chemical Engineering (Industry)
Duration: 4FT Hon
Entry Requirements: *GCE:* AAB. *SQAAH:* AA-AB. *IB:* 36.

H831 MEng Chemical Engineering with Honours in Bioprocess Engineering
Duration: 4FT Hon
Entry Requirements: *GCE:* AAB. *SQAAH:* AA-AB. *IB:* 36.

H833 MEng Chemical Engineering with Honours in Intensified Processing
Duration: 4FT Hon
Entry Requirements: *GCE:* AAB. *SQAAH:* AA-AB. *IB:* 36.

H830 MEng Chemical Engineering with Honours in Process Control
Duration: 4FT Hon
Entry Requirements: *GCE:* AAB. *SQAAH:* AA-AB. *IB:* 36.

HH82 MEng Chemical Engineering with Honours in Sustainable Engineering
Duration: 4FT Hon
Entry Requirements: *GCE:* AAB. *SQAAH:* AA-AB. *IB:* 36.

H3H8 MEng Mechanical Engineering with Bioengineering
Duration: 4FT Hon
Entry Requirements: *GCE:* AAA-AAB. *SQAAH:* AAA-AAB. *IB:* 37. Interview required.

N84 THE UNIVERSITY OF NOTTINGHAM
THE ADMISSIONS OFFICE
THE UNIVERSITY OF NOTTINGHAM
UNIVERSITY PARK
NOTTINGHAM NG7 2RD
t: 0115 951 5151 f: 0115 951 4668
// www.nottingham.ac.uk

HVH2 BEng Chemical Eng with Environmental Eng with a Year in Industry
Duration: 3FT Hon
Entry Requirements: *GCE:* AAA-AAB. *SQAAH:* AAA-AAB. *IB:* 36. *BTEC ExtDip:* DDD.

H810 BEng Chemical Engineering
Duration: 3FT Hon
Entry Requirements: *GCE:* AAA-AAB. *SQAAH:* AAA-AAB. *IB:* 36. *BTEC ExtDip:* DDD.

H8HF BEng Chemical Engineering with Environmental Engineering
Duration: 3FT Hon
Entry Requirements: *GCE:* AAA-AAB. *SQAAH:* AAA-AAB. *IB:* 36. *BTEC ExtDip:* DDD.

H81B BEng Chemical Engineering with a Year in Industry
Duration: 3FT Hon
Entry Requirements: *GCE:* AAA-AAB. *SQAAH:* AAA-AAB. *IB:* 36. *BTEC ExtDip:* DDD.

H800 MEng Chemical Engineering
Duration: 4FT Hon
Entry Requirements: *GCE:* AAA-AAB. *SQAAH:* AAA-AAB. *IB:* 36. *BTEC ExtDip:* DDD.

H81A MEng Chemical Engineering w a Year in Industry
Duration: 4FT Hon
Entry Requirements: *GCE:* AAA-AAB. *SQAAH:* AAA-AAB. *IB:* 36. *BTEC ExtDip:* DDD.

H8HG MEng Chemical Engineering with Environmental Eng with a Yr in Industry
Duration: 4FT Hon
Entry Requirements: *GCE:* AAA-AAB. *SQAAH:* AAA-AAB. *IB:* 36.
BTEC ExtDip: DDD.

H8H2 MEng Chemical Engineering with Environmental Engineering
Duration: 4FT Hon
Entry Requirements: *GCE:* AAA-AAB. *SQAAH:* AAA-AAB. *IB:* 36.
BTEC ExtDip: DDD.

O33 OXFORD UNIVERSITY
UNDERGRADUATE ADMISSIONS OFFICE
UNIVERSITY OF OXFORD
WELLINGTON SQUARE
OXFORD OX1 2JD
t: 01865 288000 f: 01865 270212
e: undergraduate.admissions@admin.ox.ac.uk
// www.admissions.ox.ac.uk

H800 MEng Chemical Engineering (4 years)
Duration: 4FT Hon
Entry Requirements: *GCE:* A*AA. *SQAH:* AAAAA-AAAAB. *SQAAH:* AAB. Interview required. Admissions Test required.

P80 UNIVERSITY OF PORTSMOUTH
ACADEMIC REGISTRY
UNIVERSITY HOUSE
WINSTON CHURCHILL AVENUE
PORTSMOUTH PO1 2UP
t: 023 9284 8484 f: 023 9284 3082
e: admissions@port.ac.uk
// www.port.ac.uk

H850 BEng Petroleum Engineering
Duration: 3FT/4SW Hon
Entry Requirements: *GCE:* 240-280. *IB:* 26. *BTEC SubDip:* P. *BTEC Dip:* PP. *BTEC ExtDip:* DMM.

Q75 QUEEN'S UNIVERSITY BELFAST
UNIVERSITY ROAD
BELFAST BT7 1NN
t: 028 9097 3838 f: 028 9097 5151
e: admissions@qub.ac.uk
// www.qub.ac.uk

H800 BEng Chemical Engineering
Duration: 3FT Hon
Entry Requirements: *GCE:* BBC-BCCb. *SQAAH:* BBC. *IB:* 30.

H804 BEng Chemical Engineering (with a Year in Industry)
Duration: 4SW Hon
Entry Requirements: *GCE:* BBC-BCCb. *SQAAH:* BBC. *IB:* 30.

H802 MEng Chemical Engineering
Duration: 4FT Hon
Entry Requirements: *GCE:* ABB-BBBb. *SQAAH:* ABB. *IB:* 33.

H805 MEng Chemical Engineering (with a Year in Industry)
Duration: 5SW Hon
Entry Requirements: *GCE:* ABB-BBBb. *SQAAH:* ABB. *IB:* 33.

S03 THE UNIVERSITY OF SALFORD
SALFORD M5 4WT
t: 0161 295 4545 f: 0161 295 4646
e: ug-admissions@salford.ac.uk
// www.salford.ac.uk

H8H3 BEng Petroleum and Mechanical Engineering
Duration: 3FT/4SW Hon
Entry Requirements: *IB:* 30. *OCR NED:* M3

S18 THE UNIVERSITY OF SHEFFIELD
THE UNIVERSITY OF SHEFFIELD
LEVEL 2, ARTS TOWER
WESTERN BANK
SHEFFIELD S10 2TN
t: 0114 222 8030 f: 0114 222 8032
// www.sheffield.ac.uk

H810 BEng Chemical Engineering (3 years)
Duration: 3FT Hon
Entry Requirements: *GCE:* AAB. *SQAH:* AAABB. *SQAAH:* AB. *IB:* 35. *BTEC ExtDip:* DDD.

H800 MEng Chemical Engineering (4 years)
Duration: 4FT Hon
Entry Requirements: *GCE:* AAB. *SQAH:* AAABB. *SQAAH:* AB. *IB:* 35. *BTEC ExtDip:* DDD.

H8J7 MEng Chemical Engineering with Biotechnology
Duration: 4FT Hon
Entry Requirements: *GCE:* AAB. *SQAH:* AAABB. *SQAAH:* AB. *IB:* 35. *BTEC ExtDip:* DDD.

H8F1 MEng Chemical Engineering with Chemistry
Duration: 4FT Hon
Entry Requirements: *GCE:* AAB. *SQAH:* AAABB. *SQAAH:* AB. *IB:* 35. *BTEC ExtDip:* DDD.

H840 MEng Chemical Engineering with Energy
Duration: 4FT Hon
Entry Requirements: *GCE:* AAB. *SQAH:* AAABB. *SQAAH:* AB. *IB:* 35. *BTEC ExtDip:* DDD.

H990 MEng Chemical Engineering with Nuclear Technology
Duration: 4FT Hon
Entry Requirements: *GCE:* AAB. *SQAH:* AAABB. *SQAAH:* AB. *IB:* 35. *BTEC ExtDip:* DDD.

H8T9 MEng Chemical Engineering with a Modern Language (4 years)
Duration: 4FT Hon
Entry Requirements: *GCE:* AAB. *SQAH:* AAABB. *SQAAH:* AB. *IB:* 35. *BTEC ExtDip:* DDD.

H801 MEng Chemical and Biological Engineering (foundation year)
Duration: 5FT Hon
Entry Requirements: *GCE:* ABB. *SQAH:* AAABB. *SQAAH:* AB. *IB:* 33. *BTEC ExtDip:* DDD.

F2H8 MEng Materials Science with Nuclear Engineering
Duration: 4FT Hon
Entry Requirements: *GCE:* AAB. *SQAH:* BBBBB. *SQAAH:* BB. *IB:* 35. *BTEC ExtDip:* DDD. Interview required.

H3H8 MEng Mechanical Engineering with Nuclear Technology
Duration: 4FT Hon
Entry Requirements: *GCE:* AAA. *SQAH:* AAAAB. *SQAAH:* AA. *IB:* 37. *BTEC ExtDip:* DDD. Interview required.

S27 UNIVERSITY OF SOUTHAMPTON
HIGHFIELD
SOUTHAMPTON SO17 1BJ
t: 023 8059 4732 f: 023 8059 3037
e: admissions@soton.ac.uk
// www.southampton.ac.uk

HH38 MEng Mechanical Engineering/Bioengineering
Duration: 4FT Hon
Entry Requirements: *GCE:* AAA. *SQAAH:* AAA. *IB:* 34.

S78 THE UNIVERSITY OF STRATHCLYDE
GLASGOW G1 1XQ
t: 0141 552 4400 f: 0141 552 0775
// www.strath.ac.uk

H800 BEng Chemical Engineering
Duration: 4FT Hon
Entry Requirements: *GCE:* A*A*A-AAA. *SQAH:* AAAABB-AAAAB. *IB:* 36.

H801 MEng Chemical Engineering
Duration: 5FT Hon
Entry Requirements: *GCE:* A*A*A-AAA. *SQAH:* AAAABB-AAAAB. *IB:* 36.

FH18 MSci Applied Chemistry and Chemical Engineering
Duration: 5FT Hon
Entry Requirements: *GCE:* ABB. *SQAH:* AAAC-AABB. *IB:* 34.

S85 UNIVERSITY OF SURREY
STAG HILL
GUILDFORD
SURREY GU2 7XH
t: +44(0)1483 689305 f: +44(0)1483 689388
e: ugteam@surrey.ac.uk
// www.surrey.ac.uk

H802 BEng Chemical Engineering (3 years)
Duration: 3FT Hon
Entry Requirements: *GCE:* ABB. *SQAH:* AABBB. *IB:* 34. Interview required.

H800 BEng Chemical Engineering (4 years)
Duration: 4SW Hon
Entry Requirements: *GCE:* ABB. *SQAH:* AABBB. *IB:* 34. Interview required.

H8CD BEng Chemical and Bio-Systems Engineering (3 years)
Duration: 3FT Hon
Entry Requirements: *GCE:* ABB. *SQAH:* AABBB. *IB:* 34. Interview required.

H8CA BEng Chemical and Bio-Systems Engineering (4 years)
Duration: 4SW Hon
Entry Requirements: *GCE:* ABB. *SQAH:* AABBB. *IB:* 34. Interview required.

H803 MEng Chemical Engineering (4 years)
Duration: 4FT Hon
Entry Requirements: *GCE:* AAB-ABB. *SQAH:* AAABB-AABBB. Interview required.

H801 MEng Chemical Engineering (5 years)
Duration: 5SW Hon
Entry Requirements: *GCE:* AAB-ABB. *SQAH:* AAABB-AABBB. Interview required.

H8C1 MEng Chemical and Bio-Systems Engineering (4 years)
Duration: 4FT Hon
Entry Requirements: *GCE:* AAB-ABB. *SQAH:* AAABB-AABBB. Interview required.

H8CC MEng Chemical and Bio-Systems Engineering (5 years)
Duration: 5SW Hon
Entry Requirements: *GCE:* AAB-ABB. *SQAH:* AAABB-AABBB. Interview required.

S93 SWANSEA UNIVERSITY
SINGLETON PARK
SWANSEA SA2 8PP
t: 01792 295111 f: 01792 295110
e: admissions@swansea.ac.uk
// www.swansea.ac.uk

H831 BEng Chemical Engineering
Duration: 3FT Hon
Entry Requirements: ***GCE:*** BBB. ***IB:*** 32.

H832 BEng Chemical Engineering (with a Year in Industry)
Duration: 4FT Hon
Entry Requirements: ***GCE:*** ABB. ***IB:*** 33.

H834 BEng Environmental Engineering
Duration: 3FT Hon
Entry Requirements: ***GCE:*** BBB. ***IB:*** 32.

H801 MEng Chemical Engineering
Duration: 4FT Hon
Entry Requirements: ***GCE:*** AAB. ***IB:*** 34.

H890 MEng Chemical Engineering (with a Year in Industry)
Duration: 5FT Hon
Entry Requirements: ***GCE:*** AAA. ***IB:*** 34.

H836 MEng Environmental Engineering
Duration: 4FT Hon
Entry Requirements: ***GCE:*** AAB. ***IB:*** 34.

T20 TEESSIDE UNIVERSITY
MIDDLESBROUGH TS1 3BA
t: 01642 218121 f: 01642 384201
e: registry@tees.ac.uk
// www.tees.ac.uk

H813 BEng Chemical Engineering
Duration: 3FT/4SW Hon
Entry Requirements: ***GCE:*** 280. ***IB:*** 30. ***BTEC SubDip:*** M. ***BTEC Dip:*** D*D*. ***BTEC ExtDip:*** DMM. ***OCR ND:*** M2 ***OCR NED:*** M2 Interview required.

H814 BEng Chemical Engineering (Extended)
Duration: 4FT/5SW Hon
Entry Requirements: ***GCE:*** 120-200. ***BTEC SubDip:*** D. ***BTEC Dip:*** MP. ***BTEC ExtDip:*** PPP. ***OCR ND:*** P2 ***OCR NED:*** P3 Interview required.

H850 BEng Tech Petroleum Engineering
Duration: 1FT Hon
Entry Requirements: HND required.

008H HND Chemical Engineering
Duration: 2FT HND
Entry Requirements: ***GCE:*** 120-200. ***BTEC SubDip:*** D. ***BTEC Dip:*** MP. ***BTEC ExtDip:*** PPP. ***OCR ND:*** P2 ***OCR NED:*** P3 Interview required.

H810 MEng Chemical Engineering
Duration: 4FT/5SW Hon
Entry Requirements: ***GCE:*** 280-300. ***IB:*** 30. ***BTEC SubDip:*** M. ***BTEC Dip:*** MM. ***BTEC ExtDip:*** DDM. ***OCR ND:*** M2 ***OCR NED:*** D2 Interview required.

U40 UNIVERSITY OF THE WEST OF SCOTLAND
PAISLEY
RENFREWSHIRE
SCOTLAND PA1 2BE
t: 0141 848 3727 f: 0141 848 3623
e: admissions@uws.ac.uk
// www.uws.ac.uk

H810 BEng Hons Chemical Engineering
Duration: 3FT/4FT Ord/Hon
Entry Requirements: ***GCE:*** CD. ***SQAH:*** BBB.

H813 BSc Chemical Engineering
Duration: 3FT/4FT Ord/Hon
Entry Requirements: ***GCE:*** CD. ***SQAH:*** BBC.

U80 UNIVERSITY COLLEGE LONDON (UNIVERSITY OF LONDON)
GOWER STREET
LONDON WC1E 6BT
t: 020 7679 3000 f: 020 7679 3001
// www.ucl.ac.uk

H811 BEng Biochemical Engineering
Duration: 3FT Hon
Entry Requirements: ***GCE:*** AAAe-AABe. ***SQAAH:*** AAA-AAB. ***BTEC ExtDip:*** DDD. Interview required.

H800 BEng Chemical Engineering
Duration: 3FT Hon
Entry Requirements: ***GCE:*** A*AAe-AABe. ***SQAAH:*** AAA-AAB. Interview required.

H813 MEng Biochemical Engineering
Duration: 4FT Hon
Entry Requirements: ***GCE:*** AAAe-AABe. ***SQAAH:*** AAA-AAB. ***BTEC ExtDip:*** DDD. Interview required.

H814 MEng Biochemical Engineering (with Study Abroad)
Duration: 4FT Hon
Entry Requirements: ***GCE:*** AAAe-AABe. ***SQAAH:*** AAA-AAB. ***BTEC ExtDip:*** DDD. Interview required.

H817 MEng Biochemical Engineering with Bioprocess Management
Duration: 4FT Hon
Entry Requirements: ***GCE:*** AAAe-AABe. ***SQAAH:*** AAA-AAB. ***BTEC ExtDip:*** DDD. Interview required.

H815 MEng Biochemical with Chemical Engineering
Duration: 4FT Hon
Entry Requirements: *GCE:* AAAe-AABe. *SQAAH:* AAA-AAB. *BTEC ExtDip:* DDD. Interview required.

H801 MEng Chemical Engineering
Duration: 4FT Hon
Entry Requirements: *GCE:* A*AAe-AABe. *SQAAH:* AAA-AAB. Interview required.

H802 MEng Chemical Engineering (with Study Abroad)
Duration: 4FT Hon
Entry Requirements: *GCE:* A*AAe-AABe. *SQAAH:* AAA-AAB. Interview required.

H816 MEng Chemical with Biochemical Engineering
Duration: 4FT Hon
Entry Requirements: *GCE:* A*AAe-AABe. *SQAAH:* AAA-AAB. Interview required.

W50 UNIVERSITY OF WESTMINSTER
2ND FLOOR, CAVENDISH HOUSE
101 NEW CAVENDISH STREET,
LONDON W1W 6XH
t: 020 7915 5511
e: course-enquiries@westminster.ac.uk
// www.westminster.ac.uk

H811 BEng Biochemical Engineering
Duration: 3FT Hon
Entry Requirements: *IB:* 32.

H813 MEng Biochemical Engineering
Duration: 4FT Hon
Entry Requirements: *IB:* 32.

CIVIL ENGINEERING

A20 THE UNIVERSITY OF ABERDEEN
UNIVERSITY OFFICE
KING'S COLLEGE
ABERDEEN AB24 3FX
t: +44 (0) 1224 273504 f: +44 (0) 1224 272034
e: sras@abdn.ac.uk
// www.abdn.ac.uk/sras

H220 BEng Engineering (Civil and Environmental)
Duration: 4FT Hon
Entry Requirements: *GCE:* BBB. *SQAH:* BBBC. *IB:* 28.

H221 BEng Engineering (Civil and Structural)
Duration: 4FT Hon
Entry Requirements: *GCE:* BBB. *SQAH:* BBBC. *IB:* 28.

H202 BEng Engineering (Civil with European Studies)
Duration: 4FT Hon
Entry Requirements: *GCE:* BBB. *SQAH:* BBBC. *IB:* 28.

H200 BEng Engineering (Civil)
Duration: 4FT Hon
Entry Requirements: *GCE:* BBB. *SQAH:* BBBC. *IB:* 28.

H201 BScEng Engineering (Civil)
Duration: 3FT/4FT Ord
Entry Requirements: Contact the institution for details.

H205 MEng Civil Engineering
Duration: 5FT Hon
Entry Requirements: *GCE:* BBB. *SQAH:* BBBB. *IB:* 30.

H255 MEng Civil and Environmental Engineering
Duration: 5FT Hon
Entry Requirements: *GCE:* BBB. *SQAH:* BBBB. *IB:* 30.

H256 MEng Civil and Environmental Engineering with European Studies
Duration: 5FT Hon
Entry Requirements: *GCE:* BBB. *SQAH:* BBBB. *IB:* 30.

H225 MEng Civil and Structural Engineering
Duration: 5FT Hon
Entry Requirements: *GCE:* BBB. *SQAH:* BBBB. *IB:* 30.

H226 MEng Civil and Structural Engineering with European Studies
Duration: 5FT Hon
Entry Requirements: *GCE:* BBB. *SQAH:* BBBB. *IB:* 30.

A30 UNIVERSITY OF ABERTAY DUNDEE
BELL STREET
DUNDEE DD1 1HG
t: 01382 308080 f: 01382 308081
e: sro@abertay.ac.uk
// www.abertay.ac.uk

H202 BSc Civil Engineering
Duration: 4FT Hon
Entry Requirements: *GCE:* CDD. *SQAH:* BBC. *IB:* 26.

A60 ANGLIA RUSKIN UNIVERSITY
BISHOP HALL LANE
CHELMSFORD
ESSEX CM1 1SQ
t: 0845 271 3333 f: 01245 251789
e: answers@anglia.ac.uk
// www.anglia.ac.uk

H202 BEng Civil Engineering
Duration: 3FT Hon
Entry Requirements: *GCE:* 225.

H200 BSc Civil Engineering
Duration: 3FT Hon
Entry Requirements: *GCE:* 200. *IB:* 26.

H201 FdSc Civil Engineering
Duration: 2FT Fdg
Entry Requirements: *GCE:* 120. *IB:* 24.

H20A FdSc Construction
Duration: 2FT Fdg
Entry Requirements: Contact the institution for details.

B16 UNIVERSITY OF BATH
CLAVERTON DOWN
BATH BA2 7AY
t: 01225 383019 f: 01225 386366
e: admissions@bath.ac.uk
// www.bath.ac.uk

H204 BEng Civil Engineering
Duration: 3FT Hon
Entry Requirements: *GCE:* A*AA. *SQAH:* AAABB. *SQAAH:* AAB. *IB:* 36. Interview required.

H201 BEng Civil Engineering (Sandwich)
Duration: 4SW Hon
Entry Requirements: *GCE:* A*AA. *SQAH:* AAABB. *SQAAH:* AAB. *IB:* 36. Interview required.

H200 MEng Civil Engineering
Duration: 4FT Hon
Entry Requirements: *GCE:* A*AA. *SQAH:* AAABB. *SQAAH:* AAB. *IB:* 36. Interview required.

H205 MEng Civil Engineering
Duration: 5SW Hon
Entry Requirements: *GCE:* A*AA. *SQAH:* AAABB. *SQAAH:* AAB. *IB:* 36. Interview required.

H202 MEng Civil and Architectural Engineering
Duration: 4FT Hon
Entry Requirements: *GCE:* A*AA. *SQAH:* AAABB. *SQAAH:* AAB. *IB:* 36. Interview required.

H203 MEng Civil and Architectural Engineering (Sandwich)
Duration: 5SW Hon
Entry Requirements: *GCE:* A*AA. *SQAH:* AAABB. *SQAAH:* AAB. *IB:* 36. Interview required.

B32 THE UNIVERSITY OF BIRMINGHAM
EDGBASTON
BIRMINGHAM B15 2TT
t: 0121 415 8900 f: 0121 414 7159
e: admissions@bham.ac.uk
// www.birmingham.ac.uk

H200 BEng Civil Engineering
Duration: 3FT Hon
Entry Requirements: *GCE:* AAA-AAB. *SQAH:* AAAAB-AABBB. *SQAAH:* AA.

H2NC BEng Civil Engineering with Business Management
Duration: 3FT Hon
Entry Requirements: *GCE:* AAA-AAB. *SQAH:* AAAAB-AABBB. *SQAAH:* AA.

H294 BEng/MEng Civil Engineering with Foundation Year
Duration: 4FT Hon
Entry Requirements: Contact the institution for details.

H201 MEng Civil Engineering
Duration: 4FT Hon
Entry Requirements: *GCE:* AAA-AAB. *SQAH:* AAAAB-AABBB. *SQAAH:* AA.

H203 MEng Civil Engineering (International Study) (4 years)
Duration: 4FT Hon
Entry Requirements: *GCE:* AAA-AAB. *SQAH:* AAAAB-AABBB. *SQAAH:* AA.

H2N2 MEng Civil Engineering with Business Management
Duration: 4FT Hon
Entry Requirements: *GCE:* AAA-AAB. *SQAH:* AAAAB-AABBB. *SQAAH:* AA.

H202 MEng Civil Engineering with Industrial Experience (4 years)
Duration: 4FT Hon
Entry Requirements: *GCE:* AAA-AAB. *SQAH:* AAAAB-AABBB. *SQAAH:* AA.

B44 UNIVERSITY OF BOLTON
DEANE ROAD
BOLTON BL3 5AB
t: 01204 903903 f: 01204 399074
e: enquiries@bolton.ac.uk
// www.bolton.ac.uk

H206 BEng Civil Engineering
Duration: 3FT Hon
Entry Requirements: *GCE:* 260. *IB:* 24. Interview required.

H207 BEng Civil Engineering (with foundation year)
Duration: 4FT Hon
Entry Requirements: *GCE:* 80. Interview required.

B56 THE UNIVERSITY OF BRADFORD
RICHMOND ROAD
BRADFORD
WEST YORKSHIRE BD7 1DP
t: 0800 073 1225 f: 01274 235585
e: course-enquiries@bradford.ac.uk
// www.bradford.ac.uk

H220 BEng Civil and Structural Engineering
Duration: 3FT Hon
Entry Requirements: *GCE:* 240. *IB:* 24.

H221 BEng Civil and Structural Engineering
Duration: 4SW Hon
Entry Requirements: *GCE:* 240. *IB:* 24.

H290 MEng Civil and Structural Engineering
Duration: 4FT Hon
Entry Requirements: *GCE:* 300. *IB:* 26.

H291 MEng Civil and Structural Engineering
Duration: 5SW Hon
Entry Requirements: *GCE:* 300. *IB:* 26.

B60 BRADFORD COLLEGE: AN ASSOCIATE COLLEGE OF LEEDS METROPOLITAN UNIVERSITY
GREAT HORTON ROAD
BRADFORD
WEST YORKSHIRE BD7 1AY
t: 01274 433008 f: 01274 431652
e: heregistry@bradfordcollege.ac.uk
// www.bradfordcollege.ac.uk/
university-centre

H201 HND Civil Engineering
Duration: 2FT HND
Entry Requirements: Contact the institution for details.

B72 UNIVERSITY OF BRIGHTON
MITHRAS HOUSE 211
LEWES ROAD
BRIGHTON BN2 4AT
t: 01273 644644 f: 01273 642607
e: admissions@brighton.ac.uk
// www.brighton.ac.uk

H201 BEng Civil Engineering (BEng)
Duration: 3FT Hon
Entry Requirements: *GCE:* BBB. *IB:* 32.

H202 BEng Civil Engineering (with integrated Foundation Year)
Duration: 4FT Hon
Entry Requirements: *GCE:* BBC. *IB:* 28.

H290 BEng Civil with Environmental Engineering
Duration: 3FT/4SW Hon
Entry Requirements: *GCE:* BBB. *IB:* 32.

H200 MEng Civil Engineering (MEng)
Duration: 4FT Hon
Entry Requirements: *GCE:* ABB. *IB:* 32.

B78 UNIVERSITY OF BRISTOL
UNDERGRADUATE ADMISSIONS OFFICE
SENATE HOUSE
TYNDALL AVENUE
BRISTOL BS8 1TH
t: 0117 928 9000 f: 0117 331 7391
e: ug-admissions@bristol.ac.uk
// www.bristol.ac.uk

H205 BEng Civil Engineering
Duration: 3FT Hon
Entry Requirements: *GCE:* A*AA-AAA. *SQAH:* AAAAA. *SQAAH:* AA.

H200 MEng Civil Engineering
Duration: 4FT Hon
Entry Requirements: *GCE:* A*AA-AAA. *SQAH:* AAAAA. *SQAAH:* AA.

H201 MEng Civil Engineering with Study in Continental Europe
Duration: 4FT Hon
Entry Requirements: *GCE:* A*AA-AAA. *SQAH:* AAAAA. *SQAAH:* AA.

B80 UNIVERSITY OF THE WEST OF ENGLAND, BRISTOL
FRENCHAY CAMPUS
COLDHARBOUR LANE
BRISTOL BS16 1QY
t: +44 (0)117 32 83333 f: +44 (0)117 32 82810
e: admissions@uwe.ac.uk
// www.uwe.ac.uk

KH12 BEng Architecture and Environmental Engineering
Duration: 4FT Hon
Entry Requirements: *GCE:* 320.

H290 BEng Civil and Environmental Engineering
Duration: 3FT/4SW Hon
Entry Requirements: *GCE:* 280.

H200 BSc Civil Engineering
Duration: 3FT/4SW Hon
Entry Requirements: *GCE:* 280.

B84 BRUNEL UNIVERSITY
UXBRIDGE
MIDDLESEX UB8 3PH
t: 01895 265265 f: 01895 269790
e: admissions@brunel.ac.uk
// www.brunel.ac.uk

H204 BEng Civil Engineering
Duration: 3FT Hon
Entry Requirements: *GCE:* ABB. *SQAAH:* ABB. *IB:* 33. *BTEC SubDip:* D*. *BTEC Dip:* D*D. *BTEC ExtDip:* D*DD. *OCR NED:* D1

H206 BEng Civil Engineering with Professional Development
Duration: 4SW Hon
Entry Requirements: *GCE:* ABB. *SQAAH:* ABB. *IB:* 33. *BTEC SubDip:* D*. *BTEC Dip:* D*D. *BTEC ExtDip:* D*DD. *OCR NED:* D1

H200 BEng Civil Engineering with Sustainability
Duration: 3FT Hon
Entry Requirements: *GCE:* ABB. *SQAAH:* ABB. *IB:* 33. *BTEC SubDip:* D*. *BTEC Dip:* D*D. *BTEC ExtDip:* D*DD. *OCR NED:* D1

H201 BEng Civil Engineering with Sustainability (4 year Thick SW)
Duration: 4SW Hon
Entry Requirements: *GCE:* ABB. *SQAAH:* ABB. *IB:* 33. *BTEC SubDip:* D*. *BTEC Dip:* D*D. *BTEC ExtDip:* D*DD. *OCR NED:* D1

H205 MEng Civil Engineering
Duration: 4FT Hon
Entry Requirements: *GCE:* AAA-AAB. *SQAAH:* AAA-AAB. *IB:* 37. *BTEC ExtDip:* D*D*D*. Interview required.

H207 MEng Civil Engineering with Professional Development
Duration: 5SW Hon
Entry Requirements: *GCE:* AAA-AAB. *SQAAH:* AAA-AAB. *IB:* 37. *BTEC ExtDip:* D*D*D*. Interview required.

H202 MEng Civil Engineering with Sustainability (MEng 4yrs)
Duration: 4FT Hon
Entry Requirements: *GCE:* AAA-AAB. *SQAAH:* AAA-AAB. *IB:* 37. *BTEC ExtDip:* D*D*D*. Interview required.

H203 MEng Civil Engineering with Sustainability (MEng 5yrs)
Duration: 5SW Hon
Entry Requirements: *GCE:* AAA-AAB. *SQAAH:* AAA-AAB. *IB:* 37. *BTEC ExtDip:* D*D*D*. Interview required.

H6H2 MEng Electrical Engineering with Renewable Energy Systems
Duration: 4FT Deg
Entry Requirements: *GCE:* AAB. *SQAAH:* AAB. *IB:* 35. *BTEC ExtDip:* D*D*D. Interview required.

H6HF MEng Electrical Engineering with Renewable Energy Systems 5 year Thick Sandwich
Duration: 5SW Hon
Entry Requirements: *GCE:* AAB. *SQAAH:* AAB. *IB:* 35. *BTEC ExtDip:* D*D*D. Interview required.

HK22 MEng Mechanical Engineering with Building Services (4 years)
Duration: 4FT Hon
Entry Requirements: *GCE:* AAA-AAB. *SQAAH:* AAA-AAB. *IB:* 37. *BTEC ExtDip:* D*D*D*.

HKF2 MEng Mechanical Engineering with Building Services (5 year Thick SW)
Duration: 5SW Hon
Entry Requirements: *GCE:* AAA-AAB. *SQAAH:* AAA-AAB. *IB:* 37. *BTEC ExtDip:* D*D*D*.

C15 CARDIFF UNIVERSITY
PO BOX 927
30-36 NEWPORT ROAD
CARDIFF CF24 0DE
t: 029 2087 9999 f: 029 2087 6138
e: admissions@cardiff.ac.uk
// www.cardiff.ac.uk

H292 BEng Architectural Engineering
Duration: 3FT Hon
Entry Requirements: *GCE:* AAB. *SQAAH:* AAB. *IB:* 32. Interview required. Admissions Test required.

H293 BEng Architectural Engineering (Year in Industry)
Duration: 4SW Hon
Entry Requirements: *GCE:* AAB. *SQAAH:* AAB. *IB:* 32. Interview required. Admissions Test required.

H200 BEng Civil Engineering
Duration: 3FT Hon
Entry Requirements: *GCE:* AAB. *SQAAH:* AAB. *IB:* 32. Interview required. Admissions Test required.

H201 BEng Civil Engineering (Year in Industry)
Duration: 4SW Hon
Entry Requirements: *GCE:* AAB. *SQAAH:* AAB. *IB:* 32. Interview required. Admissions Test required.

H221 BEng Civil and Environmental Engineering
Duration: 3FT Hon
Entry Requirements: *GCE:* AAB. *SQAAH:* AAB. *IB:* 32. Interview required. Admissions Test required.

H222 BEng Civil and Environmental Engineering (Year in Industry)
Duration: 4SW Hon
Entry Requirements: *GCE:* AAB. *SQAAH:* AAB. *IB:* 32. Interview required. Admissions Test required.

www.ucas.com

at the heart of connecting people to higher education

H294 MEng Architectural Engineering
Duration: 4FT Hon
Entry Requirements: *GCE:* AAB. *SQAAH:* AAB. *IB:* 32. Interview required. Admissions Test required.

H295 MEng Architectural Engineering (Year in Industry)
Duration: 5SW Hon
Entry Requirements: *GCE:* AAB. *SQAAH:* AAB. *IB:* 32. Interview required. Admissions Test required.

H291 MEng Architectural Engineering with Year in Europe (France)
Duration: 5SW Hon
Entry Requirements: *GCE:* AAB. *SQAAH:* AAB. *IB:* 32. Interview required. Admissions Test required.

H207 MEng Civil Engineering
Duration: 4FT Hon
Entry Requirements: *GCE:* AAB. *SQAAH:* AAB. *IB:* 32. Interview required. Admissions Test required.

H208 MEng Civil Engineering (Year in Industry)
Duration: 5SW Hon
Entry Requirements: *GCE:* AAB. *SQAAH:* AAB. *IB:* 32. Interview required. Admissions Test required.

H209 MEng Civil Engineering with Year in Europe (France)
Duration: 5SW Hon
Entry Requirements: *GCE:* AAB. *SQAAH:* AAB. *IB:* 32. Interview required. Admissions Test required.

H203 MEng Civil Engineering with Year in Europe (Germany)
Duration: 5SW Hon
Entry Requirements: *GCE:* AAB. *SQAAH:* AAB. *IB:* 32. Interview required. Admissions Test required.

H204 MEng Civil Engineering with Year in Europe (Spain)
Duration: 5SW Hon
Entry Requirements: *GCE:* AAB. *SQAAH:* AAB. *IB:* 32. Interview required. Admissions Test required.

H226 MEng Civil and Environmental Engineering
Duration: 4FT/4SW Hon
Entry Requirements: *GCE:* AAB. *SQAAH:* AAB. *IB:* 32. Interview required. Admissions Test required.

H224 MEng Civil and Environmental Engineering (Year in Industry)
Duration: 5SW Hon
Entry Requirements: *GCE:* AAB. *SQAAH:* AAB. *IB:* 32. Interview required. Admissions Test required.

H225 MEng Civil and Environmental Engineering Year in Europe (France)
Duration: 5SW Hon
Entry Requirements: *GCE:* AAB. *SQAAH:* AAB. *IB:* 32. Interview required. Admissions Test required.

H296 MEng Civil and Environmental Engineering with Year in Europe (Germany)
Duration: 5SW Hon
Entry Requirements: *GCE:* AAB. *SQAAH:* AAB. *IB:* 32. Interview required. Admissions Test required.

H297 MEng Civil and Environmental Engineering with Year in Europe (Spain)
Duration: 5SW Hon
Entry Requirements: *GCE:* AAB. *SQAAH:* AAB. *IB:* 32. Interview required. Admissions Test required.

C30 UNIVERSITY OF CENTRAL LANCASHIRE
PRESTON
LANCS PR1 2HE
t: 01772 201201 f: 01772 894954
e: uadmissions@uclan.ac.uk
// www.uclan.ac.uk

KH22 BEng Building Services and Sustainable Engineering
Duration: 3FT/4SW Hon
Entry Requirements: *GCE:* 240. *SQAH:* CCCCC. *IB:* 24. *OCR ND:* D *OCR NED:* M3

H225 BSc Sustainable Energy Management
Duration: 3FT Hon
Entry Requirements: *GCE:* 240. *SQAH:* CCCCC. *IB:* 24.

C60 CITY UNIVERSITY
NORTHAMPTON SQUARE
LONDON EC1V 0HB
t: 020 7040 5060 f: 020 7040 8995
e: ugadmissions@city.ac.uk
// www.city.ac.uk

H201 BEng Civil Engineering (4 year SW) (e)
Duration: 4SW Hon
Entry Requirements: *GCE:* 340. *SQAH:* BBCCC. *IB:* 30.

H202 BEng Civil Engineering (4 years including Foundation Year) (e)
Duration: 4FT Hon
Entry Requirements: *GCE:* 130. *SQAH:* BC.

H200 BEng Civil Engineering (e)
Duration: 3FT Hon
Entry Requirements: *GCE:* 340. *SQAH:* BBCCC. *IB:* 30.

H2K1 BEng Civil Engineering with Architecture (e)
Duration: 3FT Hon
Entry Requirements: *GCE:* 340. *SQAH:* BBCCC. *IB:* 30.

H2KD BEng Civil Engineering with Architecture (e)
Duration: 4SW Hon
Entry Requirements: *GCE:* 340. *SQAH:* BBCCC. *IB:* 30.

H207 BEng Civil Engineering with Surveying (4 year SW) (e)
Duration: 4SW Hon
Entry Requirements: *GCE:* 340. *SQAH:* BBCCC. *IB:* 30.

H206 BEng Civil Engineering with Surveying (e)
Duration: 3FT Hon
Entry Requirements: *GCE:* 340. *SQAH:* BBCCC. *IB:* 30.

HJ39 BEng Energy Engineering (h)
Duration: 3FT Hon
Entry Requirements: *GCE:* 340. *IB:* 30.

H204 MEng Civil Engineering (4 years) (e)
Duration: 4FT Hon
Entry Requirements: *GCE:* 360. *SQAH:* ABBB. *IB:* 32.

H205 MEng Civil Engineering (5 year SW) (e)
Duration: 5SW Hon
Entry Requirements: *GCE:* 360. *SQAH:* ABBB. *IB:* 32.

H2KA MEng Civil Engineering with Architecture (e)
Duration: 5SW Hon
Entry Requirements: *GCE:* 360. *SQAH:* ABBB. *IB:* 32.

H2KC MEng Civil Engineering with Architecture (e)
Duration: 4FT Hon
Entry Requirements: *GCE:* 360. *SQAH:* ABBB. *IB:* 32.

H208 MEng Civil Engineering with Surveying (4 years) (e)
Duration: 4FT Hon
Entry Requirements: *GCE:* 360. *SQAH:* ABBB. *IB:* 32.

H209 MEng Civil Engineering with Surveying (5 year SW) (e)
Duration: 5SW Hon
Entry Requirements: *GCE:* 360. *SQAH:* ABBB. *IB:* 32.

JH93 MEng Energy Engineering (h)
Duration: 4FT Hon
Entry Requirements: *GCE:* 360. *IB:* 32.

C85 COVENTRY UNIVERSITY
THE STUDENT CENTRE
COVENTRY UNIVERSITY
1 GULSON RD
COVENTRY CV1 2JH
t: 024 7615 2222 f: 024 7615 2223
e: studentenquiries@coventry.ac.uk
// www.coventry.ac.uk

WH22 BA Transport Design
Duration: 3FT/4SW Hon
Entry Requirements: *Foundation:* Merit. *GCE:* BCC. *SQAH:* BCCCC. *IB:* 27. *BTEC ExtDip:* MMM. *OCR NED:* M3 Interview required. Portfolio required.

H290 BEng Building Services Engineering
Duration: 3FT/4SW Hon
Entry Requirements: *GCE:* BCC. *SQAH:* BCCCC. *IB:* 28. *BTEC ExtDip:* DMM. *OCR NED:* M2

H200 BEng Civil Engineering
Duration: 3FT/4SW Hon
Entry Requirements: *GCE:* BCC. *SQAH:* BCCCC. *IB:* 28. *BTEC ExtDip:* DMM. *OCR NED:* M2

H221 BEng Civil and Structural Engineering
Duration: 3FT/4SW Hon
Entry Requirements: *GCE:* BCC. *SQAH:* BCCCC. *IB:* 28. *BTEC ExtDip:* DMM. *OCR NED:* M2

HK22 BEng Construction Engineering
Duration: 1FT Hon
Entry Requirements: Contact the institution for details.

H203 BSc Civil Engineering
Duration: 3FT/4SW Hon
Entry Requirements: *GCE:* CCC. *SQAH:* CCCCC. *IB:* 27. *BTEC ExtDip:* MMM. *OCR NED:* M3

NH22 BSc Disaster Management
Duration: 3FT/4SW Hon
Entry Requirements: *GCE:* BBC-BCC. *SQAH:* BBCCC-BCCCC. Interview required.

FH82 BSc Geography and Natural Hazards
Duration: 3FT/4SW Hon
Entry Requirements: *GCE:* BBC. *SQAH:* BBCCC. *IB:* 29. *BTEC ExtDip:* DDM. *OCR NED:* M1

H202 MEng Civil Engineering
Duration: 4FT/5SW Hon
Entry Requirements: *GCE:* ABB. *SQAH:* BBBBC. *IB:* 30. *BTEC ExtDip:* DDM. *OCR NED:* M1

C99 UNIVERSITY OF CUMBRIA
FUSEHILL STREET
CARLISLE
CUMBRIA CA1 2HH
t: 01228 616234 f: 01228 616235
// www.cumbria.ac.uk

H224 BEng Sustainable Energy Technologies
Duration: 3FT Hon
Entry Requirements: *GCE:* 200.

D39 UNIVERSITY OF DERBY
KEDLESTON ROAD
DERBY DE22 1GB
t: 01332 591167 f: 01332 597724
e: askadmissions@derby.ac.uk
// www.derby.ac.uk

H291 BEng Civil and Infrastructure Engineering
Duration: 3FT Hon
Entry Requirements: *Foundation:* Distinction. *GCE:* 260. *IB:* 28. *BTEC Dip:* D*D*. *BTEC ExtDip:* DMM. *OCR NED:* M2

H202 BSc Civil Engineering
Duration: 3FT Hon
Entry Requirements: *Foundation:* Merit. *GCE:* 220. *IB:* 26. *BTEC Dip:* D*D*. *BTEC ExtDip:* DMM. *OCR ND:* D *OCR NED:* M3

H204 FYr Civil Engineering Foundation
Duration: 1FT FYr
Entry Requirements: *Foundation:* Pass. *GCE:* 160. *IB:* 24. *BTEC Dip:* D*D*. *BTEC ExtDip:* DMM. *OCR ND:* M2 *OCR NED:* P2

H292 FYr Civil and Infrastructure Engineering Foundation
Duration: 1FT FYr
Entry Requirements: *Foundation:* Pass. *GCE:* 160. *IB:* 24. *BTEC Dip:* D*D*. *BTEC ExtDip:* DMM. *OCR ND:* M2 *OCR NED:* P2

H201 FdEng Civil Engineering
Duration: 2FT Fdg
Entry Requirements: *Foundation:* Pass. *GCE:* 160. *IB:* 26. *BTEC Dip:* D*D*. *BTEC ExtDip:* DMM. *OCR ND:* M2 *OCR NED:* P2

D52 DONCASTER COLLEGE
THE HUB
CHAPPELL DRIVE
SOUTH YORKSHIRE DN1 2RF
t: 01302 553610
e: he@don.ac.uk
// www.don.ac.uk

HH26 FdEng Building Services Engineering
Duration: 2FT Fdg
Entry Requirements: Contact the institution for details.

D65 UNIVERSITY OF DUNDEE
NETHERGATE
DUNDEE DD1 4HN
t: 01382 383838 f: 01382 388150
e: contactus@dundee.ac.uk
// www.dundee.ac.uk/admissions/undergraduate/

H200 BEng Civil Engineering
Duration: 4FT Hon
Entry Requirements: *GCE:* BCC. *SQAH:* ABBB. *IB:* 30.

HN22 BEng Civil Engineering and Management
Duration: 4FT Hon
Entry Requirements: *GCE:* BCC. *SQAH:* ABBB. *IB:* 30.

H221 BSc Renewable Energy
Duration: 4FT Hon
Entry Requirements: *GCE:* BCC. *SQAH:* ABBB. *IB:* 30.

H201 MEng Civil Engineering Design and Management
Duration: 5FT Hon
Entry Requirements: *GCE:* BBB. *SQAH:* AABB. *IB:* 32.

H224 MSci Renewable Energy
Duration: 5FT Hon
Entry Requirements: *GCE:* BBB. *SQAH:* AABB. *IB:* 32.

D86 DURHAM UNIVERSITY
DURHAM UNIVERSITY
UNIVERSITY OFFICE
DURHAM DH1 3HP
t: 0191 334 2000 f: 0191 334 6055
e: admissions@durham.ac.uk
// www.durham.ac.uk

H200 MEng Civil Engineering
Duration: 4FT Hon
Entry Requirements: *GCE:* AAA. *SQAH:* AAAAB. *SQAAH:* AAA. *IB:* 37.

H221 MEng New and Renewable Energy
Duration: 4FT Hon
Entry Requirements: *GCE:* AAA. *SQAH:* AAAAB. *SQAAH:* AAA. *IB:* 37.

E14 UNIVERSITY OF EAST ANGLIA
NORWICH NR4 7TJ
t: 01603 591515 f: 01603 591523
e: admissions@uea.ac.uk
// www.uea.ac.uk

H221 BEng Energy Engineering with Environmental Management
Duration: 3FT Hon   CRB Check: Required
Entry Requirements: *GCE:* AAB. *SQAH:* AAABB. *SQAAH:* AAB. *IB:* 33. *BTEC ExtDip:* DDD.

H22A BEng Energy Engineering with Environmental Management with a Year in Industry
Duration: 4FT Hon   CRB Check: Required
Entry Requirements: *GCE:* AAA. *SQAH:* AAAAA. *SQAAH:* AAA. *IB:* 34. *BTEC ExtDip:* DDD.

H220 MEng Energy Engineering with Environmental Management
Duration: 4FT Hon   CRB Check: Required
Entry Requirements: *GCE:* AAA. *SQAH:* AAAAA. *SQAAH:* AAA. *IB:* 34. *BTEC ExtDip:* DDD.

E28 UNIVERSITY OF EAST LONDON
DOCKLANDS CAMPUS
UNIVERSITY WAY
LONDON E16 2RD
t: 020 8223 3333 f: 020 8223 2978
e: study@uel.ac.uk
// www.uel.ac.uk

H208 BEng Civil Engineering (Extended)
Duration: 4FT/5SW Hon
Entry Requirements: *GCE:* 120.

H200 BEng Civil Engineering (Honours)
Duration: 3FT/4SW Hon
Entry Requirements: *GCE:* 240. *IB:* 26.

H205 BSc Civil Engineering
Duration: 3FT Hon
Entry Requirements: *GCE:* 240.

H206 BSc Civil Engineering Surveying and Mapping Sciences
Duration: 3FT Hon
Entry Requirements: Contact the institution for details.

H243 FdSc Civil Engineering Surveying
Duration: 2FT Fdg
Entry Requirements: *GCE:* 120.

HK22 FdSc Civil Engineering and Construction Management
Duration: 2FT Fdg
Entry Requirements: Contact the institution for details.

E30 EASTON COLLEGE
EASTON
NORWICH
NORFOLK NR9 5DX
t: 01603 731232 f: 01603 741438
e: info@easton.ac.uk
// www.easton.ac.uk

H220 FdSc Engineering (Pathways in Agricultural or Mechanical Engineering)
Duration: 2FT Fdg
Entry Requirements: Interview required.

E56 THE UNIVERSITY OF EDINBURGH
STUDENT RECRUITMENT & ADMISSIONS
57 GEORGE SQUARE
EDINBURGH EH8 9JU
t: 0131 650 4360 f: 0131 651 1236
e: sra.enquiries@ed.ac.uk
// www.ed.ac.uk/studying/undergraduate/

H200 BEng Civil Engineering
Duration: 4FT Hon
Entry Requirements: *GCE:* AAA-ABB. *SQAH:* AAAA-ABBB.

H6H2 BEng Electrical Engineering with Renewable Energy
Duration: 4FT Hon
Entry Requirements: *GCE:* AAA-ABB. *SQAH:* AAAA-ABBB.

H224 BEng Engineering for Sustainable Energy
Duration: 4FT Hon
Entry Requirements: *GCE:* AAA-ABB. *SQAH:* AAAA-ABBB.

H2K1 BEng Structural Engineering with Architecture
Duration: 4FT Hon
Entry Requirements: *GCE:* AAA-ABB. *SQAH:* AAAA-ABBB.

HH21 BEng Structural and Fire Safety Engineering
Duration: 4FT Hon
Entry Requirements: *GCE:* AAA-ABB. *SQAH:* AAAA-ABBB.

HL23 MA Sustainable Development
Duration: 4FT Hon
Entry Requirements: *GCE:* AAA-BBB. *SQAH:* AABB-BBBB. *IB:* 34.

H203 MEng Civil Engineering
Duration: 5FT Hon
Entry Requirements: *GCE:* AAA-ABB. *SQAH:* AAAA-ABBB.

H6HF MEng Electrical Engineering with Renewable Energy
Duration: 5FT Hon
Entry Requirements: *GCE:* AAA-ABB. *SQAH:* AAAA-ABBB.

H225 MEng Engineering for Sustainable Energy
Duration: 5FT Hon
Entry Requirements: *GCE:* AAA-ABB. *SQAH:* AAAA-ABBB.

H2KC MEng Structural Engineering with Architecture
Duration: 5FT Hon
Entry Requirements: *GCE:* AAA-ABB. *SQAH:* AAAA-ABBB.

HHF1 MEng Structural and Fire Safety Engineering
Duration: 5FT Hon
Entry Requirements: *GCE:* AAA-ABB. *SQAH:* AAAA-ABBB.

E59 EDINBURGH NAPIER UNIVERSITY
CRAIGLOCKHART CAMPUS
EDINBURGH EH14 1DJ
t: +44 (0)8452 60 60 40 f: 0131 455 6464
e: info@napier.ac.uk
// www.napier.ac.uk

H203 BEng Civil Engineering
Duration: 3FT/4FT Ord/Hon
Entry Requirements: *GCE:* 245.

HH23 BEng Civil and Transportation Engineering
Duration: 3FT/4FT Ord/Hon
Entry Requirements: *GCE:* 245.

H200 BSc Civil Engineering
Duration: 3FT/4FT Ord/Hon
Entry Requirements: *GCE:* 215.

H201 BSc Civil and Timber Engineering
Duration: 3FT/4FT Ord/Hon
Entry Requirements: *GCE:* 215.

H290 MEng Civil & Transportation Engineering
Duration: 5FT Hon
Entry Requirements: *GCE:* 260.

H202 MEng Civil Engineering
Duration: 5FT Hon
Entry Requirements: *GCE:* 260.

E84 UNIVERSITY OF EXETER
LAVER BUILDING
NORTH PARK ROAD
EXETER
DEVON EX4 4QE
t: 01392 723044 f: 01392 722479
e: admissions@exeter.ac.uk
// www.exeter.ac.uk

H200 BEng Civil Engineering
Duration: 3FT Hon
Entry Requirements: *GCE:* AAB-ABB. *SQAH:* AAABB-AABBB. *SQAAH:* ABB-BBB.

H203 BEng Civil Engineering with Industrial Experience
Duration: 3FT Hon
Entry Requirements: *GCE:* AAB-ABB. *SQAH:* AAABB-AABBB. *SQAAH:* ABB-BBB.

H205 BEng Civil Engineering with International Study
Duration: 3FT Hon
Entry Requirements: *GCE:* AAB-ABB. *SQAH:* AAABB-AABBB. *SQAAH:* ABB-BBB.

H202 MEng Civil Engineering
Duration: 4FT Hon
Entry Requirements: *GCE:* AAA-AAB. *SQAH:* AAAAB-AAABB. *SQAAH:* AAB-ABB. *BTEC ExtDip:* DDM.

H291 MEng Civil Engineering and Environmental Engineering with Industrial Experience
Duration: 4FT Hon
Entry Requirements: *GCE:* AAA-AAB. *SQAH:* AAAAB-AAABB. *SQAAH:* AAB-ABB. *BTEC ExtDip:* DDM.

H201 MEng Civil Engineering with Industrial Experience
Duration: 4FT Hon
Entry Requirements: *GCE:* AAA-AAB. *SQAH:* AAAAB-AAABB. *SQAAH:* AAB-ABB. *BTEC ExtDip:* DDM.

H207 MEng Civil Engineering with International Study (4 years)
Duration: 4FT Hon
Entry Requirements: *GCE:* AAA-AAB. *SQAH:* AAAAB-AAABB. *SQAAH:* AAB-ABB. *BTEC ExtDip:* DDM.

H290 MEng Civil and Environmental Engineering
Duration: 4FT Hon
Entry Requirements: *GCE:* AAA-AAB. *SQAH:* AAAAB-AAABB. *SQAAH:* AAB-ABB. *BTEC ExtDip:* DDM.

H292 MEng Civil and Environmental Engineering with International Study
Duration: 4FT Hon
Entry Requirements: *GCE:* AAA-AAB. *SQAH:* AAAAB-AAABB. *SQAAH:* AAB-ABB. *BTEC ExtDip:* DDM.

H221 MEng Renewable Energy (4 years) (Cornwall Campus)
Duration: 4FT Hon
Entry Requirements: *GCE:* AAB-ABB. *SQAH:* AAABB-AABBB. *SQAAH:* ABB-BBB.

G14 UNIVERSITY OF GLAMORGAN, CARDIFF AND PONTYPRIDD
ENQUIRIES AND ADMISSIONS UNIT
PONTYPRIDD CF37 1DL
t: 08456 434030 f: 01443 654050
e: enquiries@glam.ac.uk
// www.glam.ac.uk

H200 BEng Civil Engineering
Duration: 3FT Hon
Entry Requirements: *GCE:* BBB. *IB:* 26. *BTEC SubDip:* M. *BTEC Dip:* DD. *BTEC ExtDip:* DMM. Interview required.

HG00 BEng Civil Engineering
Duration: 4SW Hon
Entry Requirements: *GCE:* BBB. *IB:* 26. *BTEC SubDip:* M. *BTEC Dip:* D*D*. *BTEC ExtDip:* DMM. Interview required.

H201 BSc Civil Engineering
Duration: 3FT Hon
Entry Requirements: *GCE:* CCC. *IB:* 24. *BTEC SubDip:* M. *BTEC Dip:* DD. *BTEC ExtDip:* MMM. Interview required.

HF00 BSc Civil Engineering
Duration: 4SW Hon
Entry Requirements: *GCE:* CCC. *IB:* 24. *BTEC SubDip:* M. *BTEC Dip:* DD. *BTEC ExtDip:* MMM. Interview required.

H206 BSc Civil Engineering (Post Diploma)
Duration: 1FT Hon
Entry Requirements: Contact the institution for details.

H631 BSc Renewable Energy Systems
Duration: 3FT Hon
Entry Requirements: *GCE:* BBC. *BTEC SubDip:* M. *BTEC Dip:* D*D. *BTEC ExtDip:* DMM. Interview required.

H208 FYr Civil Engineering Foundation Year
Duration: 1FT FYr
Entry Requirements: *BTEC SubDip:* M. *BTEC Dip:* PP. *BTEC ExtDip:* PPP. Interview required.

002H HND Civil Engineering
Duration: 2FT HND
Entry Requirements: *GCE:* 80-120. *BTEC SubDip:* M. *BTEC Dip:* MP. *BTEC ExtDip:* PPP.

G28 UNIVERSITY OF GLASGOW
71 SOUTHPARK AVENUE
UNIVERSITY OF GLASGOW
GLASGOW G12 8QQ
t: 0141 330 6062 f: 0141 330 2961
e: student.recruitment@glasgow.ac.uk
// www.glasgow.ac.uk

H202 BEng Civil Engineering
Duration: 4FT Hon
Entry Requirements: *GCE:* ABB. *SQAH:* AAAB-BBB. *IB:* 32.

H2KC BEng Civil Engineering with Architecture
Duration: 4FT Hon
Entry Requirements: *GCE:* ABB. *SQAH:* AAAB-BBB. *IB:* 32.

H200 MEng Civil Engineering
Duration: 5FT Hon
Entry Requirements: *GCE:* AAB. *SQAH:* AAAA-AAABB. *IB:* 34.

H201 MEng Civil Engineering (Faster Route)
Duration: 4FT Hon
Entry Requirements: *GCE:* AAA. *SQAH:* AB. *SQAAH:* AA. *IB:* 38.

H2K1 MEng Civil Engineering with Architecture
Duration: 5FT Hon
Entry Requirements: *GCE:* AAB. *SQAH:* AAAA-AAABB. *IB:* 34.

G42 GLASGOW CALEDONIAN UNIVERSITY
STUDENT RECRUITMENT & ADMISSIONS SERVICE
CITY CAMPUS
COWCADDENS ROAD
GLASGOW G4 0BA
t: 0141 331 3000 f: 0141 331 8676
e: undergraduate@gcu.ac.uk
// www.gcu.ac.uk

HH32 BEng Mechanical and Power Plant Systems
Duration: 4FT/5SW Hon
Entry Requirements: Contact the institution for details.

H220 BSc Environmental Civil Engineering
Duration: 4FT Hon
Entry Requirements: Contact the institution for details.

G70 UNIVERSITY OF GREENWICH
GREENWICH CAMPUS
OLD ROYAL NAVAL COLLEGE
PARK ROW
LONDON SE10 9LS
t: 020 8331 9000 f: 020 8331 8145
e: courseinfo@gre.ac.uk
// www.gre.ac.uk

H200 BEng Civil Engineering
Duration: 3FT Hon
Entry Requirements: *GCE:* 260-300. *IB:* 24.

H208 BEng Civil Engineering (incl Foundation)
Duration: 4FT Hon
Entry Requirements: *GCE:* 160. *IB:* 24.

H2N2 BEng Civil Engineering with Project Management
Duration: 3FT Hon
Entry Requirements: *GCE:* 260-300. *IB:* 24.

H2F9 BEng Civil Engineering with Water & Environmental Management
Duration: 3FT Hon
Entry Requirements: *GCE:* 260-300. *IB:* 24.

H202 BSc Civil Engineering
Duration: 3FT Hon
Entry Requirements: *GCE:* 220-240. *IB:* 24.

002H HND Civil Engineering Studies
Duration: 2FT HND
Entry Requirements: *GCE:* 160.

H203 MEng Civil Engineering
Duration: 4FT Hon
Entry Requirements: *GCE:* 320-360.

H12 HARPER ADAMS UNIVERSITY COLLEGE
NEWPORT
SHROPSHIRE TF10 8NB
t: 01952 820280 f: 01952 813210
e: admissions@harper-adams.ac.uk
// www.harper-adams.ac.uk

H220 BSc Agricultural Engineering (Top-Up)
Duration: 1.5FT Hon
Entry Requirements: Contact the institution for details.

H24 HERIOT-WATT UNIVERSITY, EDINBURGH
EDINBURGH CAMPUS
EDINBURGH EH14 4AS
t: 0131 449 5111 f: 0131 451 3630
e: ugadmissions@hw.ac.uk
// www.hw.ac.uk

H200 BEng Civil Engineering
Duration: 4FT Hon
Entry Requirements: GCE: BBB. SQAH: AAAB-BBBBC. SQAAH: BB. IB: 31.

H210 BEng Structural Engineering
Duration: 4FT Hon
Entry Requirements: GCE: BBB. SQAH: AAAB-BBBBC. SQAAH: BB. IB: 31.

H2K1 BEng Structural Engineering with Architectural Design
Duration: 4FT Hon
Entry Requirements: GCE: BBB. SQAH: AAAB-BBBBC. SQAAH: BB. IB: 31.

H201 MEng Civil Engineering
Duration: 5FT Hon
Entry Requirements: GCE: BBB. SQAH: AAAB. SQAAH: BB. IB: 33.

H2L2 MEng Civil Engineering with International Studies
Duration: 5FT Hon
Entry Requirements: GCE: BBB. SQAH: AAAB. SQAAH: BB. IB: 33.

H241 MEng Structural Engineering
Duration: 5FT Hon
Entry Requirements: GCE: BBB. SQAH: AAAB. SQAAH: BB. IB: 33.

H2KC MEng Structural Engineering with Architectural Design
Duration: 5FT Hon
Entry Requirements: GCE: BBB. SQAH: AAAB. SQAAH: BB. IB: 33.

H211 MEng Structural Engineering with International Studies
Duration: 5FT Hon
Entry Requirements: GCE: BBB. SQAH: AAAB. SQAAH: BB. IB: 33.

H49 UNIVERSITY OF THE HIGHLANDS AND ISLANDS
UHI EXECUTIVE OFFICE
NESS WALK
INVERNESS
SCOTLAND IV3 5SQ
t: 01463 279000 f: 01463 279001
e: info@uhi.ac.uk
// www.uhi.ac.uk

H220 BEng Energy Engineering
Duration: 1FT Ord
Entry Requirements: HND required.

H221 BEng Hons Energy Engineering
Duration: 1FT Hon
Entry Requirements: Contact the institution for details.

102H HNC Civil Engineering
Duration: 1FT HNC
Entry Requirements: GCE: D. SQAH: C.

H60 THE UNIVERSITY OF HUDDERSFIELD
QUEENSGATE
HUDDERSFIELD HD1 3DH
t: 01484 473969 f: 01484 472765
e: admissionsandrecords@hud.ac.uk
// www.hud.ac.uk

H224 BEng Energy Engineering
Duration: 3FT/4SW Hon
Entry Requirements: GCE: 300.

H221 MEng Energy Engineering
Duration: 3FT/4SW Hon
Entry Requirements: GCE: 340.

I50 IMPERIAL COLLEGE LONDON
REGISTRY
SOUTH KENSINGTON CAMPUS
IMPERIAL COLLEGE LONDON
LONDON SW7 2AZ
t: 020 7589 5111 f: 020 7594 8004
// www.imperial.ac.uk

H201 MEng Civil Engineering
Duration: 4FT Hon
Entry Requirements: GCE: A*A*A. SQAAH: AAA. IB: 38.

H202 MEng Civil Engineering with a Year Abroad
Duration: 4FT Hon
Entry Requirements: GCE: A*A*A. SQAAH: AAA. IB: 38.

K24 THE UNIVERSITY OF KENT
RECRUITMENT & ADMISSIONS OFFICE
REGISTRY
UNIVERSITY OF KENT
CANTERBURY, KENT CT2 7NZ
t: 01227 827272 f: 01227 827077
e: information@kent.ac.uk
// www.kent.ac.uk

H200 FdEng Civil Engineering
Duration: 2FT Fdg
Entry Requirements: *OCR NED:* M2

K84 KINGSTON UNIVERSITY
STUDENT INFORMATION & ADVICE CENTRE
COOPER HOUSE
40-46 SURBITON ROAD
KINGSTON UPON THAMES KT1 2HX
t: 0844 8552177 f: 020 8547 7080
e: aps@kingston.ac.uk
// www.kingston.ac.uk

H200 BEng Civil Engineering
Duration: 3FT Hon
Entry Requirements: *GCE:* 280. *IB:* 26.

H201 BEng Civil Engineering (4-year SW)
Duration: 4SW Hon
Entry Requirements: *GCE:* 280. *IB:* 26.

H208 BEng Civil Engineering (Foundation)
Duration: 4FT/5SW Hon
Entry Requirements: *GCE:* 120. *IB:* 22.

H202 BSc Civil Engineering
Duration: 3FT Hon
Entry Requirements: *GCE:* 240. *IB:* 24.

H205 BSc Civil Engineering (4-year SW)
Duration: 4SW Hon
Entry Requirements: *GCE:* 240. *IB:* 24.

H220 BSc Sustainable Development (including year 0)
Duration: 4FT Hon
Entry Requirements: *GCE:* 60.

L05 LAKES COLLEGE - WEST CUMBRIA
HALLWOOD ROAD
LILLYHALL
WORKINGTON CA14 4JN
t: 01946 839300 f: 01946 839302
e: student.services@lcwc.ac.uk
// www.lcwc.ac.uk

H200 HNC Construction & The Built Environment
Duration: 2FT HNC
Entry Requirements: Contact the institution for details.

L14 LANCASTER UNIVERSITY
THE UNIVERSITY
LANCASTER
LANCASHIRE LA1 4YW
t: 01524 592029 f: 01524 846243
e: ugadmissions@lancaster.ac.uk
// www.lancs.ac.uk

H220 BEng Sustainable Engineering
Duration: 3FT Hon
Entry Requirements: *GCE:* AAB. *SQAH:* ABBBB. *SQAAH:* AAB. *IB:* 35.

H224 MEng Sustainable Engineering
Duration: 4FT Hon
Entry Requirements: *GCE:* AAA. *SQAH:* AAABB. *SQAAH:* AAA. *IB:* 36.

L23 UNIVERSITY OF LEEDS
THE UNIVERSITY OF LEEDS
WOODHOUSE LANE
LEEDS LS2 9JT
t: 0113 343 3999
e: admissions@leeds.ac.uk
// www.leeds.ac.uk

H2KC MEng Architectural Engineering (International)
Duration: 4FT Hon
Entry Requirements: *GCE:* AAA. *SQAAH:* AAA. *IB:* 38.

H2N2 MEng Civil Engineering with Project Management
Duration: 4FT Hon
Entry Requirements: *GCE:* AAA. *SQAAH:* AAA. *IB:* 38.

N2H2 MEng Civil Engineering with Project Management (International)
Duration: 4FT Hon
Entry Requirements: *GCE:* AAA. *SQAAH:* AAA. *IB:* 38.

H291 MEng Civil and Environmental Engineering
Duration: 3FT/4FT Hon
Entry Requirements: *GCE:* AAA. *SQAAH:* AAA. *IB:* 38.

H22H MEng Civil and Environmental Engineering (International)
Duration: 4FT Hon
Entry Requirements: *GCE:* AAA. *SQAAH:* AAA. *IB:* 38.

H290 MEng Civil and Structural Engineering (Europe)
Duration: 4FT Hon
Entry Requirements: *GCE:* AAA. *SQAAH:* AAA. *IB:* 38.

H292 MEng Civil and Structural Engineering (International)
Duration: 4FT Hon
Entry Requirements: *GCE:* AAA. *SQAAH:* AAA. *IB:* 38.

HK21 MEng/BEng Architectural Engineering
Duration: 3FT/4FT Hon
Entry Requirements: *GCE:* AAA. *SQAAH:* AAA. *IB:* 38.

H200 MEng/BEng Civil and Structural Engineering
Duration: 3FT/4FT Hon
Entry Requirements: *GCE:* AAA. *SQAAH:* AAA. *IB:* 38.

H220 MEng/BEng Energy Engineering
Duration: 3FT/4FT Hon
Entry Requirements: *GCE:* AAA. *SQAAH:* AAA. *IB:* 38.

L27 LEEDS METROPOLITAN UNIVERSITY
COURSE ENQUIRIES OFFICE
CITY CAMPUS
LEEDS LS1 3HE
t: 0113 81 23113 f: 0113 81 23129
// www.leedsmet.ac.uk

H200 BSc Civil Engineering
Duration: 3FT Hon
Entry Requirements: *GCE:* 200. *IB:* 24.

H262 BSc Civil Engineering Commercial Management
Duration: 1FT/2SW Hon
Entry Requirements: HND required.

H220 BSc Environmental Design and Engineering
Duration: 3FT Hon
Entry Requirements: Contact the institution for details.

L41 THE UNIVERSITY OF LIVERPOOL
THE FOUNDATION BUILDING
BROWNLOW HILL
LIVERPOOL L69 7ZX
t: 0151 794 2000 f: 0151 708 6502
e: ugrecruitment@liv.ac.uk
// www.liv.ac.uk

H200 BEng Civil Engineering
Duration: 3FT Hon
Entry Requirements: *GCE:* ABB. *SQAAH:* ABB. *IB:* 33. Interview required.

H202 MEng Civil Engineering
Duration: 4FT Hon
Entry Requirements: *GCE:* AAB. *SQAAH:* AAB. *IB:* 35. Interview required.

H220 MEng Civil and Structural Engineering (4 years)
Duration: 4FT Hon
Entry Requirements: *GCE:* AAB. *SQAAH:* AAB. *IB:* 35. Interview required.

L42 LINCOLN COLLEGE
MONKS ROAD
LINCOLN LN2 5HQ
t: 01522 876000 f: 01522 876200
e: enquiries@lincolncollege.ac.uk
// www.lincolncollege.ac.uk

002H HND Civil Engineering
Duration: 2FT HND
Entry Requirements: Contact the institution for details.

H210 HND Construction
Duration: 2FT HND
Entry Requirements: Contact the institution for details.

L51 LIVERPOOL JOHN MOORES UNIVERSITY
KINGSWAY HOUSE
HATTON GARDEN
LIVERPOOL L3 2AJ
t: 0151 231 5090 f: 0151 904 6368
e: courses@ljmu.ac.uk
// www.ljmu.ac.uk

H200 BEng Civil Engineering
Duration: 3FT/4SW Hon
Entry Requirements: *GCE:* 270.

002H HND Civil Engineering Studies
Duration: 2FT HND
Entry Requirements: *GCE:* 180.

H202 MEng Civil Engineering
Duration: 4FT Hon
Entry Requirements: *GCE:* 320.

L53 COLEG LLANDRILLO CYMRU
LLANDUDNO ROAD
RHOS-ON-SEA
COLWYN BAY
NORTH WALES LL28 4HZ
t: 01492 542338/339 f: 01492 543052
e: degrees@llandrillo.ac.uk
// www.llandrillo.ac.uk

H200 FdEng Civil Engineering
Duration: 2FT Fdg
Entry Requirements: Contact the institution for details.

H221 FdSc Renewable Energy Technology
Duration: 2FT Fdg
Entry Requirements: Contact the institution for details.

L62 THE LONDON COLLEGE, UCK
VICTORIA GARDENS
NOTTING HILL GATE
LONDON W11 3PE
t: 020 7243 4000 f: 020 7243 1484
e: admissions@lcuck.ac.uk
// www.lcuck.ac.uk

202H HNC Construction and Built Environment (Civil Engineering)
Duration: 1FT HNC
Entry Requirements: Contact the institution for details.

22KH HNC Construction and the Built Environment
Duration: 1FT HNC
Entry Requirements: Contact the institution for details.

193H HNC General Engineering
Duration: 1FT HNC
Entry Requirements: Contact the institution for details.

302H HND Construction and Built Environment (Civil Engineering)
Duration: 2FT HND
Entry Requirements: Contact the institution for details.

22HK HND Construction and the Built Environment
Duration: 2FT HND
Entry Requirements: Contact the institution for details.

093H HND General Engineering
Duration: 2FT HND
Entry Requirements: Contact the institution for details.

L75 LONDON SOUTH BANK UNIVERSITY
ADMISSIONS AND RECRUITMENT CENTRE
90 LONDON ROAD
LONDON SE1 6LN
t: 0800 923 8888 f: 020 7815 8273
e: course.enquiry@lsbu.ac.uk
// www.lsbu.ac.uk

H200 BEng Civil Engineering (3/4 years)
Duration: 3FT/4SW Hon
Entry Requirements: *GCE:* 240. *IB:* 24.

H201 BSc Civil Engineering
Duration: 3FT/4SW Hon
Entry Requirements: *GCE:* 200. *IB:* 24.

L79 LOUGHBOROUGH UNIVERSITY
LOUGHBOROUGH
LEICESTERSHIRE LE11 3TU
t: 01509 223522 f: 01509 223905
e: admissions@lboro.ac.uk
// www.lboro.ac.uk

H200 BEng Civil Engineering
Duration: 3FT Hon
Entry Requirements: *GCE:* ABB. *SQAH:* AAABB. *SQAAH:* AB. *IB:* 34. *BTEC ExtDip:* DDD.

H201 BEng Civil Engineering
Duration: 4SW Hon
Entry Requirements: *GCE:* ABB. *SQAH:* AAABB. *SQAAH:* AB. *IB:* 34. *BTEC ExtDip:* DDD.

HK22 BSc Commercial Management and Quantity Surveying
Duration: 4SW Hon
Entry Requirements: *GCE:* 300. *SQAH:* BBBBB. *SQAAH:* BB. *IB:* 32. *BTEC ExtDip:* DDM.

H202 MEng Civil Engineering
Duration: 5SW Hon
Entry Requirements: *GCE:* AAB. *SQAH:* AAAAB. *SQAAH:* AB. *IB:* 36. *BTEC ExtDip:* DDD.

H203 MEng Civil Engineering
Duration: 4FT Hon
Entry Requirements: *GCE:* AAB. *SQAH:* AAAAB. *SQAAH:* AB. *IB:* 36. *BTEC ExtDip:* DDD.

M20 THE UNIVERSITY OF MANCHESTER
RUTHERFORD BUILDING
OXFORD ROAD
MANCHESTER M13 9PL
t: 0161 275 2077 f: 0161 275 2106
e: ug-admissions@manchester.ac.uk
// www.manchester.ac.uk

H200 BEng Civil Engineering
Duration: 3FT Hon
Entry Requirements: *GCE:* AAB. *SQAAH:* AAB. *IB:* 35. Interview required.

H201 MEng Civil Engineering
Duration: 4FT Hon
Entry Requirements: *GCE:* AAA. *SQAAH:* AAA. *IB:* 37. Interview required.

H204 MEng Civil Engineering (Enterprise)
Duration: 4FT Hon
Entry Requirements: *GCE:* AAA. *SQAAH:* AAA. *IB:* 37. Interview required.

H207 MEng Civil Engineering with Industrial Experience
Duration: 5FT Hon
Entry Requirements: *GCE:* AAA. *SQAAH:* AAA. *IB:* 37. Interview required.

H2T7 MEng Civil Engineering with Study in North America
Duration: 4FT Hon
Entry Requirements: *GCE:* AAA. *SQAAH:* AAA. *IB:* 37. Interview required.

H220 MEng Civil and Structural Engineering
Duration: 4FT Hon
Entry Requirements: *GCE:* AAA. *SQAAH:* AAA. *IB:* 37. Interview required.

M99 MYERSCOUGH COLLEGE
MYERSCOUGH HALL
BILSBORROW
PRESTON PR3 0RY
t: 01995 642222 f: 01995 642333
e: enquiries@myerscough.ac.uk
// www.myerscough.ac.uk

HJ29 FdSc Heavy Plant Machinery Management and Logistics
Duration: 2FT Fdg
Entry Requirements: Interview required.

N21 NEWCASTLE UNIVERSITY
KING'S GATE
NEWCASTLE UPON TYNE NE1 7RU
t: 01912083333
// www.ncl.ac.uk

H200 BEng Civil Engineering
Duration: 3FT Hon
Entry Requirements: *GCE:* AAB-ABB. *SQAAH:* AAB. *IB:* 35. Interview required.

H201 BEng Civil Engineering (4 years)
Duration: 4FT Hon
Entry Requirements: *GCE:* AAB-ABB. *SQAAH:* AAB. *IB:* 35. Interview required.

H210 BEng Civil and Structural Engineering
Duration: 3FT Hon
Entry Requirements: *GCE:* AAB-ABB. *SQAAH:* AAB. *IB:* 35. Interview required.

FH82 BSc Physical Geography
Duration: 3FT Hon
Entry Requirements: *GCE:* ABB-BBB. *SQAH:* AAAAB. *SQAAH:* AB. *IB:* 32. Interview required.

H244 BSc Surveying and Mapping Science
Duration: 3FT Hon
Entry Requirements: *GCE:* AAB-BBB. *SQAH:* AAABB-AABB. *IB:* 35. Interview required.

H290 MEng Civil Engineering
Duration: 4FT Hon
Entry Requirements: *GCE:* AAA. *SQAAH:* AAA. *IB:* 37. Interview required.

H291 MEng Civil Engineering (5 years)
Duration: 5FT Hon
Entry Requirements: *GCE:* AAA. *SQAAH:* AAA. *IB:* 37. *BTEC ExtDip:* DDD.

H242 MEng Civil and Structural Engineering
Duration: 4FT Hon
Entry Requirements: *GCE:* AAA. *SQAAH:* AAA. *IB:* 37. Interview required.

N23 NEWCASTLE COLLEGE
STUDENT SERVICES
RYE HILL CAMPUS
SCOTSWOOD ROAD
NEWCASTLE UPON TYNE NE4 7SA
t: 0191 200 4110 f: 0191 200 4349
e: enquiries@ncl-coll.ac.uk
// www.newcastlecollege.co.uk

H202 BSc Civil Engineering (Top-up)
Duration: 1FT Hon   CRB Check: Required
Entry Requirements: Contact the institution for details.

H200 FdSc Civil Engineering
Duration: 2FT Fdg
Entry Requirements: *GCE:* 160-200. *OCR ND:* P2 *OCR NED:* P3 Interview required.

H201 FdSc Management of Construction Technologies
Duration: 2FT Fdg
Entry Requirements: *GCE:* 160-200. *OCR ND:* P2 *OCR NED:* P3 Interview required.

H221 FdSc Renewable Energy Technologies
Duration: 2FT Fdg
Entry Requirements: *GCE:* 160-200. *OCR ND:* P2 *OCR NED:* P3 Interview required.

N30 NEW COLLEGE NOTTINGHAM
ADAMS BUILDING
STONEY STREET
THE LACE MARKET
NOTTINGHAM NG1 1NG
t: 0115 910 0100 f: 0115 953 4349
e: he.team@ncn.ac.uk
// www.ncn.ac.uk

002H HNC Construction and the Built Environment (Civil Engineering)
Duration: 1FT HNC
Entry Requirements: Contact the institution for details.

N37 UNIVERSITY OF WALES, NEWPORT
ADMISSIONS
LODGE ROAD
CAERLEON
NEWPORT NP18 3QT
t: 01633 432030 f: 01633 432850
e: admissions@newport.ac.uk
// www.newport.ac.uk

HK22 BSc Civil and Construction Engineering
Duration: 3FT Hon
Entry Requirements: *GCE:* 240. *IB:* 24.

002H HND Civil and Construction Engineering
Duration: 2FT HND
Entry Requirements: *GCE:* 80. *IB:* 24.

N38 UNIVERSITY OF NORTHAMPTON
PARK CAMPUS
BOUGHTON GREEN ROAD
NORTHAMPTON NN2 7AL
t: 0800 358 2232 f: 01604 722083
e: admissions@northampton.ac.uk
// www.northampton.ac.uk

H200 BSc Civil Engineering (top-up)
Duration: 1FT Hon
Entry Requirements: Contact the institution for details.

H201 FdSc Civil Engineering
Duration: 2FT Fdg
Entry Requirements: *GCE:* 140-160. *SQAH:* BC-CCC. *IB:* 24.
BTEC Dip: MP. *BTEC ExtDip:* MPP. *OCR ND:* P1 *OCR NED:* P2

N84 THE UNIVERSITY OF NOTTINGHAM
THE ADMISSIONS OFFICE
THE UNIVERSITY OF NOTTINGHAM
UNIVERSITY PARK
NOTTINGHAM NG7 2RD
t: 0115 951 5151 f: 0115 951 4668
// www.nottingham.ac.uk

H201 BEng Civil Engineering
Duration: 3FT Hon
Entry Requirements: *GCE:* AAA. *SQAAH:* AAA. *IB:* 36.

H2RC BEng Civil Engineering with French
Duration: 3FT Hon
Entry Requirements: *GCE:* ABB. *SQAAH:* ABB. *IB:* 34.

H2RF BEng Civil Engineering with German
Duration: 3FT Hon
Entry Requirements: *GCE:* ABB. *SQAAH:* ABB. *IB:* 34.

H294 BEng Civil and Environmental Engineering
Duration: 3FT Hon
Entry Requirements: *GCE:* AAA. *SQAAH:* ABB. *IB:* 34.

HH6F BEng Electrical Engineering and Renewable Energy Systems
Duration: 3FT Hon
Entry Requirements: *GCE:* AAB-BBB. *SQAAH:* AAB-BBB. Interview required.

H227 BEng Environmental Engineering
Duration: 3FT Hon
Entry Requirements: *GCE:* AAA-AAB. *SQAAH:* AAA-AAB. *IB:* 36.
BTEC ExtDip: DDD.

H22B BEng Environmental Engineering with a Year in Industry
Duration: 3FT Hon
Entry Requirements: *GCE:* AAA-AAB. *SQAAH:* AAA-AAB. *IB:* 36.
BTEC ExtDip: DDD.

H200 MEng Civil Engineering
Duration: 4FT Hon
Entry Requirements: *GCE:* AAA. *SQAAH:* AAA. *IB:* 36.

H2R1 MEng Civil Engineering with French
Duration: 4FT Hon
Entry Requirements: *GCE:* AAA. *SQAAH:* AAA. *IB:* 38.

H2R2 MEng Civil Engineering with German
Duration: 4FT Hon
Entry Requirements: *GCE:* AAA. *SQAAH:* AAA. *IB:* 38.

H295 MEng Civil and Environmental Engineering
Duration: 4FT Hon
Entry Requirements: *GCE:* AAA. *SQAAH:* AAA. *IB:* 38.

HH62 MEng Electrical Engineering and Renewable Energy Systems
Duration: 4FT Hon
Entry Requirements: *GCE:* AAB-BBB. *SQAAH:* AAB-BBB. Interview required.

H220 MEng Environmental Engineering
Duration: 4FT Hon
Entry Requirements: *GCE:* AAA-AAB. *SQAAH:* AAA-AAB. *IB:* 36.
BTEC ExtDip: DDD.

H22A MEng Environmental Engineering with a Year in Industry
Duration: 4FT Hon
Entry Requirements: *GCE:* AAA-AAB. *SQAAH:* AAA-AAB. *IB:* 36.
BTEC ExtDip: DDD.

N91 NOTTINGHAM TRENT UNIVERSITY
DRYDEN BUILDING
BURTON STREET
NOTTINGHAM NG1 4BU
t: +44 (0) 115 848 4200 f: +44 (0) 115 848 8869
e: applications@ntu.ac.uk
// www.ntu.ac.uk

H200 BEng Civil Engineering
Duration: 3FT/4SW Hon
Entry Requirements: *GCE:* 280. *BTEC ExtDip:* DMM. *OCR NED:* M2

H202 BSc Civil Engineering
Duration: 3FT/4SW Hon
Entry Requirements: *GCE:* 220. *BTEC Dip:* DD. *BTEC ExtDip:* MMM. *OCR NED:* M3

O33 OXFORD UNIVERSITY
UNDERGRADUATE ADMISSIONS OFFICE
UNIVERSITY OF OXFORD
WELLINGTON SQUARE
OXFORD OX1 2JD
t: 01865 288000 f: 01865 270212
e: undergraduate.admissions@admin.ox.ac.uk
// www.admissions.ox.ac.uk

H200 MEng Civil Engineering (4 years)
Duration: 4FT Hon
Entry Requirements: *GCE:* A*AA. *SQAH:* AAAAA-AAAAB. *SQAAH:* AAB. Interview required. Admissions Test required.

P51 PETROC
OLD STICKLEPATH HILL
BARNSTAPLE
NORTH DEVON EX31 2BQ
t: 01271 852365 f: 01271 338121
e: he@petroc.ac.uk
// www.petroc.ac.uk

HD24 FdSc Sustainability and the Built Environment
Duration: 2FT Fdg
Entry Requirements: Contact the institution for details.

P56 UNIVERSITY CENTRE PETERBOROUGH
PARK CRESCENT
PETERBOROUGH PE1 4DZ
t: 0845 1965750 f: 01733 767986
e: UCPenquiries@anglia.ac.uk
// www.anglia.ac.uk/ucp

H200 FdA Civil Engineering
Duration: 2FT Fdg
Entry Requirements: *GCE:* 80.

P60 PLYMOUTH UNIVERSITY
DRAKE CIRCUS
PLYMOUTH PL4 8AA
t: 01752 585858 f: 01752 588055
e: admissions@plymouth.ac.uk
// www.plymouth.ac.uk

H200 BEng Civil Engineering
Duration: 3FT Hon
Entry Requirements: *GCE:* 280. *IB:* 28.

H203 BEng Civil Engineering with Foundation Year
Duration: 5SW Hon
Entry Requirements: *GCE:* 180. *IB:* 24.

H255 BEng Civil and Coastal Engineering
Duration: 3FT Hon
Entry Requirements: *GCE:* 280. *IB:* 28.

H201 BSc Civil Engineering
Duration: 3FT Hon
Entry Requirements: *GCE:* 220. *IB:* 26.

H256 BSc Civil and Coastal Engineering
Duration: 3FT Hon
Entry Requirements: *GCE:* 220. *IB:* 25.

H204 FdSc Civil Engineering
Duration: 2FT Fdg
Entry Requirements: *GCE:* 120-180. *IB:* 24.

HH62 FdSc Electrical Engineering & Renewable Energy
Duration: 2FT Fdg
Entry Requirements: *GCE:* 120-180. *IB:* 24.

H202 MEng Civil Engineering
Duration: 5SW Hon
Entry Requirements: *GCE:* 320. *IB:* 30.

H251 MEng Civil and Coastal Engineering
Duration: 5SW Hon
Entry Requirements: *GCE:* 320. *IB:* 30.

P80 UNIVERSITY OF PORTSMOUTH
ACADEMIC REGISTRY
UNIVERSITY HOUSE
WINSTON CHURCHILL AVENUE
PORTSMOUTH PO1 2UP
t: 023 9284 8484 f: 023 9284 3082
e: admissions@port.ac.uk
// www.port.ac.uk

H200 BEng Civil Engineering
Duration: 3FT/4SW Hon
Entry Requirements: *GCE:* 270-300. *IB:* 26. *BTEC SubDip:* P. *BTEC Dip:* PP. *BTEC ExtDip:* DMM.

H202 MEng Civil Engineering
Duration: 4FT/5SW Hon
Entry Requirements: *GCE:* 300-360. *IB:* 27. *BTEC SubDip:* M. *BTEC Dip:* MM. *BTEC ExtDip:* DDD.

Q50 QUEEN MARY, UNIVERSITY OF LONDON
QUEEN MARY, UNIVERSITY OF LONDON
MILE END ROAD
LONDON E1 4NS
t: 020 7882 5555 f: 020 7882 5500
e: admissions@qmul.ac.uk
// www.qmul.ac.uk

H221 BEng Sustainable Energy Engineering
Duration: 3FT Hon
Entry Requirements: *GCE:* 300. *IB:* 32.

HF21 BEng Sustainable Energy Engineering with Industrial Experience
Duration: 4FT Hon
Entry Requirements: *GCE:* 300. *IB:* 32.

H224 MEng Sustainable Energy Engineering
Duration: 4FT Hon
Entry Requirements: *GCE:* 360. *IB:* 36.

HG21 MEng Sustainable Energy Engineering with Industrial Experience
Duration: 5FT Hon
Entry Requirements: *GCE:* 360. *IB:* 36.

Q75 QUEEN'S UNIVERSITY BELFAST
UNIVERSITY ROAD
BELFAST BT7 1NN
t: 028 9097 3838 f: 028 9097 5151
e: admissions@qub.ac.uk
// www.qub.ac.uk

H200 BEng Civil Engineering
Duration: 3FT Hon
Entry Requirements: *GCE:* BBC-BCCb. *SQAH:* BBBBC. *SQAAH:* BBC. *IB:* 30.

H204 BEng Civil Engineering (with a Year in Industry)
Duration: 4SW Hon
Entry Requirements: *GCE:* BBC-BCCb. *SQAH:* BBBBC. *SQAAH:* BBC. *IB:* 30.

H202 MEng Civil Engineering
Duration: 4FT Hon
Entry Requirements: *GCE:* ABB-BBBb. *SQAH:* ABBBB. *SQAAH:* ABB.

H205 MEng Civil Engineering (with a Year in Industry)
Duration: 5SW Hon
Entry Requirements: *GCE:* ABB-BBBb. *SQAH:* ABBBB. *SQAAH:* ABB.

H252 MEng Environmental and Civil Engineering
Duration: 4FT Hon
Entry Requirements: *GCE:* ABB-BBBb. *SQAH:* ABBBB. *SQAAH:* ABB.

H255 MEng Environmental and Civil Engineering (with a Year in Industry)
Duration: 5SW Hon
Entry Requirements: *GCE:* ABB-BBBb. *SQAH:* ABBBB. *SQAAH:* ABB.

H2K1 MEng Structural Engineering with Architecture
Duration: 4FT Hon
Entry Requirements: *GCE:* ABB-BBBb. *SQAH:* ABBBB. *SQAAH:* ABB.

H2KC MEng Structural Engineering with Architecture (with a Year in Industry)
Duration: 5SW Hon
Entry Requirements: *GCE:* ABB-BBBb. *SQAH:* ABBBB. *SQAAH:* ABB.

S03 THE UNIVERSITY OF SALFORD
SALFORD M5 4WT
t: 0161 295 4545 f: 0161 295 4646
e: ug-admissions@salford.ac.uk
// www.salford.ac.uk

H200 BEng Civil Engineering
Duration: 3FT Hon
Entry Requirements: *GCE:* 260. *IB:* 30.

H201 BEng Civil Engineering with Foundation Year
Duration: 4FT/5SW Hon
Entry Requirements: *GCE:* 160. *IB:* 26.

HK2C BEng Civil and Architectural Engineering
Duration: 3FT/4SW Hon/Ord
Entry Requirements: *GCE:* 260. *IB:* 30.

H208 BSc Civil Engineering
Duration: 3FT Hon
Entry Requirements: *GCE:* 220. *IB:* 28.

H210 MEng Civil Engineering
Duration: 4FT/5SW Hon
Entry Requirements: *GCE:* 300. *IB:* 35.

HK21 MEng Civil and Architectural Engineering
Duration: 3FT/4SW Hon
Entry Requirements: *GCE:* 300. *IB:* 35.

S18 THE UNIVERSITY OF SHEFFIELD
THE UNIVERSITY OF SHEFFIELD
LEVEL 2, ARTS TOWER
WESTERN BANK
SHEFFIELD S10 2TN
t: 0114 222 8030 f: 0114 222 8032
// www.sheffield.ac.uk

H202 BEng Civil Engineering (3 years)
Duration: 3FT Hon
Entry Requirements: *GCE:* AAA. *SQAH:* AAAAB. *SQAAH:* AA. *IB:* 37. *BTEC ExtDip:* DDD.

HK2D MEng Architectural Engineering Design
Duration: 4FT Hon
Entry Requirements: *GCE:* AAA. *SQAH:* AAAAB. *SQAAH:* AA. *IB:* 37. *BTEC ExtDip:* DDD.

H200 MEng Civil Engineering (4 years)
Duration: 4FT Hon
Entry Requirements: *GCE:* AAA. *SQAH:* AAAAB. *SQAAH:* AA. *IB:* 37. *BTEC ExtDip:* DDD.

H201 MEng Civil Engineering with a Foundation Year (5 years)
Duration: 5FT Hon
Entry Requirements: *GCE:* ABB. *SQAH:* AABBB. *SQAAH:* AB. *IB:* 33. *BTEC ExtDip:* DDD.

H2T9 MEng Civil Engineering with a Modern Language (4 years)
Duration: 4FT Hon
Entry Requirements: *GCE:* AAA. *SQAH:* AAAAB. *SQAAH:* AA. *IB:* 37. *BTEC ExtDip:* DDD.

H210 MEng Civil and Structural Engineering (4 years)
Duration: 4FT Hon
Entry Requirements: *GCE:* AAA. *SQAH:* AAAAB. *SQAAH:* AA. *IB:* 37. *BTEC ExtDip:* DDD.

HK21 MEng Structural Engineering and Architecture (4 years)
Duration: 4FT Hon
Entry Requirements: *GCE:* AAA. *SQAH:* AAAAB. *SQAAH:* AA. *IB:* 37. *BTEC ExtDip:* DDD.

S21 SHEFFIELD HALLAM UNIVERSITY
CITY CAMPUS
HOWARD STREET
SHEFFIELD S1 1WB
t: 0114 225 5555 f: 0114 225 2167
e: admissions@shu.ac.uk
// www.shu.ac.uk

H22C BEng Energy Engineering
Duration: 3FT/4SW Hon
Entry Requirements: *GCE:* 220.

S22 SHEFFIELD COLLEGE
THE SHEFFIELD COLLEGE
HE UNIT
HILLSBOROUGH COLLEGE AT THE BARRACKS
SHEFFIELD S6 2LR
t: 0114 260 2597
e: heunit@sheffcol.ac.uk
// www.sheffcol.ac.uk

H200 HND Construction & the Built Environment - Civil Engineering
Duration: 2FT HND
Entry Requirements: Contact the institution for details.

S27 UNIVERSITY OF SOUTHAMPTON
HIGHFIELD
SOUTHAMPTON SO17 1BJ
t: 023 8059 4732 f: 023 8059 3037
e: admissions@soton.ac.uk
// www.southampton.ac.uk

H200 BEng Civil Engineering
Duration: 3FT Hon
Entry Requirements: *GCE:* AAA. *SQAH:* AAAA. *SQAAH:* AA. *IB:* 36.

H201 MEng Civil Engineering (4 years)
Duration: 4FT Hon
Entry Requirements: *GCE:* AAA. *SQAH:* AAAA. *SQAAH:* AA. *IB:* 36.

H202 MEng Civil Engineering (with a year in Industry)
Duration: 4FT Hon
Entry Requirements: *GCE:* AAA. *SQAH:* AAAA. *SQAAH:* AA. *IB:* 36.

HK21 MEng Civil Engineering and Architecture
Duration: 4FT Hon
Entry Requirements: *GCE:* AAA. *SQAH:* AAAA. *SQAAH:* AA. *IB:* 36.

H251 MEng Environmental Engineering (4 years)
Duration: 4FT Hon
Entry Requirements: *GCE:* AAA. *SQAH:* AAAA. *SQAAH:* AA. *IB:* 36.

HH32 MEng Mechanical Engineering/Sustainable Energy Systems
Duration: 4FT Hon
Entry Requirements: *GCE:* AAA. *SQAAH:* AAA. *IB:* 34.

S30 SOUTHAMPTON SOLENT UNIVERSITY
EAST PARK TERRACE
SOUTHAMPTON
HAMPSHIRE SO14 0RT
t: +44 (0) 23 8031 9039 f: + 44 (0)23 8022 2259
e: admissions@solent.ac.uk
// www.solent.ac.uk/

HH52 BEng Yacht Production and Surveying
Duration: 3FT Hon
Entry Requirements: *GCE:* 180.

HH5F BEng Yacht Production and Surveying (with foundation)
Duration: 4FT Hon
Entry Requirements: *GCE:* 40.

S78 THE UNIVERSITY OF STRATHCLYDE
GLASGOW G1 1XQ
t: 0141 552 4400 f: 0141 552 0775
// www.strath.ac.uk

H200 BEng Civil Engineering (e)
Duration: 4FT Hon
Entry Requirements: *GCE:* AAB. *SQAH:* AAAA-AAAB. *IB:* 32.

H291 BEng Civil and Environmental Engineering
Duration: 4FT Hon
Entry Requirements: *GCE:* AAB. *SQAH:* AAAA-AAAB. *IB:* 32.

H202 MEng Civil Engineering (e)
Duration: 5FT Hon
Entry Requirements: *GCE:* AAA. *SQAH:* AAABBB-AAABB. *IB:* 36.

H290 MEng Civil and Environmental Engineering
Duration: 5FT Hon
Entry Requirements: *GCE:* AAA. *SQAH:* AAAA-AAABB. *IB:* 36.

S84 UNIVERSITY OF SUNDERLAND
STUDENT HELPLINE
THE STUDENT GATEWAY
CHESTER ROAD
SUNDERLAND SR1 3SD
t: 0191 515 3000 f: 0191 515 3805
e: student.helpline@sunderland.ac.uk
// www.sunderland.ac.uk

H221 BEng Renewable Energy Engineering
Duration: 3FT/4SW Hon
Entry Requirements: *GCE:* 260. *IB:* 24. *OCR ND:* D *OCR NED:* M3

S85 UNIVERSITY OF SURREY
STAG HILL
GUILDFORD
SURREY GU2 7XH
t: +44(0)1483 689305 f: +44(0)1483 689388
e: ugteam@surrey.ac.uk
// www.surrey.ac.uk

H200 BEng Civil Engineering (3 years)
Duration: 3FT Hon
Entry Requirements: *GCE:* ABB. *SQAH:* BBBB. *IB:* 34. Interview required.

H201 BEng Civil Engineering (4 years)
Duration: 4SW Hon
Entry Requirements: *GCE:* ABB. *SQAH:* BBBB. *IB:* 34. Interview required.

H209 MEng Civil Engineering (4 years)
Duration: 4FT Hon
Entry Requirements: *GCE:* AAB-ABB. *IB:* 35. Interview required.

H210 MEng Civil Engineering (5 years)
Duration: 5SW Hon
Entry Requirements: *GCE:* AAB-ABB. *IB:* 35. Interview required.

S93 SWANSEA UNIVERSITY
SINGLETON PARK
SWANSEA SA2 8PP
t: 01792 295111 f: 01792 295110
e: admissions@swansea.ac.uk
// www.swansea.ac.uk

H200 BEng Civil Engineering
Duration: 3FT Hon
Entry Requirements: *GCE:* ABB. *IB:* 33.

H202 BEng Civil Engineering (with a Year in Industry)
Duration: 4FT Hon
Entry Requirements: *GCE:* AAB. *IB:* 34.

H2G0 BEng Environmental Engineering (with a year in industry)
Duration: 4FT Hon
Entry Requirements: Contact the institution for details.

H201 MEng Civil Engineering
Duration: 4FT Hon
Entry Requirements: *GCE:* AAB. *IB:* 34.

H204 MEng Civil Engineering (with a Year in Industry)
Duration: 5FT Hon
Entry Requirements: *GCE:* AAA. *IB:* 34.

H2F0 MEng Environmental Engineering (with a year in industry)
Duration: 5FT Hon
Entry Requirements: Contact the institution for details.

S96 SWANSEA METROPOLITAN UNIVERSITY
MOUNT PLEASANT CAMPUS
SWANSEA SA1 6ED
t: 01792 481000 f: 01792 481061
e: gemma.green@smu.ac.uk
// www.smu.ac.uk

HF29 BSc Civil Engineering and Environmental Management
Duration: 3FT Hon
Entry Requirements: *GCE:* 160-360. *IB:* 24. Interview required.

002H HND Civil Engineering Studies
Duration: 2FT HND
Entry Requirements: *GCE:* 80-360. *IB:* 24. Interview required.

S98 SWINDON COLLEGE
NORTH STAR AVENUE
SWINDON
WILTSHIRE SN2 1DY
t: 0800 731 2250 f: 01793 430503
e: headmissions@swindon-college.ac.uk
// www.swindon-college.ac.uk

002H HND Civil Engineering
Duration: 2FT HND
Entry Requirements: *GCE:* A-C. *IB:* 24. *BTEC ExtDip:* PPP. *OCR ND:* P2 *OCR NED:* P3 Interview required.

T20 TEESSIDE UNIVERSITY
MIDDLESBROUGH TS1 3BA
t: 01642 218121 f: 01642 384201
e: registry@tees.ac.uk
// www.tees.ac.uk

H200 BEng Civil Engineering
Duration: 3FT/4SW Hon
Entry Requirements: *GCE:* 280. *IB:* 30. *BTEC SubDip:* M. *BTEC Dip:* D*D*. *BTEC ExtDip:* DMM. *OCR ND:* M2 *OCR NED:* M2 Interview required.

H210 BEng Civil Engineering (Extended)
Duration: 4FT/5SW Hon
Entry Requirements: *GCE:* 120-200. *BTEC SubDip:* D. *BTEC Dip:* MP. *BTEC ExtDip:* PPP. *OCR ND:* P2 *OCR NED:* P3 Interview required.

H290 BEng Civil Engineering with Disaster Management
Duration: 3FT/4SW Hon
Entry Requirements: *GCE:* 280. *IB:* 30. Interview required.

H201 MEng Civil Engineering
Duration: 4FT/5SW Hon
Entry Requirements: *GCE:* 300. *IB:* 30. *BTEC SubDip:* M. *BTEC Dip:* MM. *BTEC ExtDip:* DDM. Interview required.

U20 UNIVERSITY OF ULSTER
COLERAINE
CO. LONDONDERRY
NORTHERN IRELAND BT52 1SA
t: 028 7012 4221 f: 028 7012 4908
e: online@ulster.ac.uk
// www.ulster.ac.uk

H200 BEng/MEng Civil Engineering
Duration: 4SW/5SW Hon
Entry Requirements: *GCE:* 270. *IB:* 24.

KH22 BEng/MEng Energy and Building Services Engineering
Duration: 4SW/5SW Hon
Entry Requirements: *GCE:* 260. *IB:* 24.

KH2F BSc Building Engineering and Materials
Duration: 3FT Hon
Entry Requirements: *GCE:* 260. *IB:* 24.

H202 BSc Civil Engineering (Geoinformatics)
Duration: 4SW Hon
Entry Requirements: *GCE:* 240. *IB:* 24.

U40 UNIVERSITY OF THE WEST OF SCOTLAND
PAISLEY
RENFREWSHIRE
SCOTLAND PA1 2BE
t: 0141 848 3727 f: 0141 848 3623
e: admissions@uws.ac.uk
// www.uws.ac.uk

H200 BEng Civil Engineering
Duration: 4SW Hon
Entry Requirements: *GCE:* CC. *SQAH:* BBB.

H201 BSc Civil Engineering
Duration: 3FT Ord
Entry Requirements: *GCE:* CD. *SQAH:* BCC.

U80 UNIVERSITY COLLEGE LONDON (UNIVERSITY OF LONDON)
GOWER STREET
LONDON WC1E 6BT
t: 020 7679 3000 f: 020 7679 3001
// www.ucl.ac.uk

H200 BEng Civil Engineering
Duration: 3FT Hon
Entry Requirements: *GCE:* A*AAe-AAAe. *SQAAH:* AAA. Interview required.

H220 BEng Environmental Engineering
Duration: 3FT Hon
Entry Requirements: *GCE:* A*AAe-AAAe. *SQAAH:* AAA. Interview required.

H202 MEng Civil Engineering
Duration: 4FT Hon
Entry Requirements: *GCE:* A*AAe-AAAe. *SQAAH:* AAA. Interview required.

H205 MEng Civil Engineering (International Programme)
Duration: 4FT Hon
Entry Requirements: *GCE:* A*AAe-AAAe. *SQAAH:* AAA. Interview required.

H224 MEng Environmental Engineering
Duration: 4FT Hon
Entry Requirements: *GCE:* A*AAe-AAAe. *SQAAH:* AAA. Interview required.

H225 MEng Environmental Engineering (International Programme)
Duration: 4FT Hon
Entry Requirements: *GCE:* A*AAe-AAAe. *SQAAH:* AAA. Interview required.

W05 THE UNIVERSITY OF WEST LONDON
ST MARY'S ROAD
EALING
LONDON W5 5RF
t: 0800 036 8888 f: 020 8566 1353
e: learning.advice@uwl.ac.uk
// www.uwl.ac.uk

H290 BEng Civil and Environmental Engineering
Duration: 3FT Hon
Entry Requirements: *GCE:* 240. Interview required.

W20 THE UNIVERSITY OF WARWICK
COVENTRY CV4 8UW
t: 024 7652 3723 f: 024 7652 4649
e: ugadmissions@warwick.ac.uk
// www.warwick.ac.uk

H200 BEng Civil Engineering
Duration: 3FT Hon
Entry Requirements: *GCE:* AAB. *SQAAH:* AA-AB. *IB:* 36.

H202 MEng Civil Engineering
Duration: 4FT Hon
Entry Requirements: *GCE:* AAB. *SQAAH:* AA-AB. *IB:* 36.

H202 MEng Civil Engineering option - Business Management
Duration: 4FT Hon
Entry Requirements: *GCE:* AAB-ABB. *SQAAH:* AA-AB. *IB:* 36.

H202 MEng Civil Engineering option - Sustainability
Duration: 4FT Hon
Entry Requirements: *GCE:* AAB-ABB. *SQAAH:* AA-AB. *IB:* 36.

W75 UNIVERSITY OF WOLVERHAMPTON
ADMISSIONS UNIT
MX207, CAMP STREET
WOLVERHAMPTON
WEST MIDLANDS WV1 1AD
t: 01902 321000 f: 01902 321896
e: admissions@wlv.ac.uk
// www.wlv.ac.uk

H200 BEng Civil Engineering
Duration: 3FT/4SW Hon
Entry Requirements: *GCE:* 160-220. *IB:* 26.

H290 BSc Civil and Environmental Engineering
Duration: 3FT/4SW Hon
Entry Requirements: *GCE:* 180.

H203 FdA Civil Engineering
Duration: 2FT Fdg
Entry Requirements: Contact the institution for details.

ELECTRONIC AND ELECTRICAL ENGINEERING

A20 THE UNIVERSITY OF ABERDEEN
UNIVERSITY OFFICE
KING'S COLLEGE
ABERDEEN AB24 3FX
t: +44 (0) 1224 273504 f: +44 (0) 1224 272034
e: sras@abdn.ac.uk
// www.abdn.ac.uk/sras

H602 BEng Engineering (Electrical & Electronic with European Studies)
Duration: 4FT Hon
Entry Requirements: *GCE:* BBB. *SQAH:* BBBC. *IB:* 28.

H620 BEng Engineering (Electrical & Electronic)
Duration: 4FT Hon
Entry Requirements: *GCE:* BBB. *SQAH:* BBBC. *IB:* 28.

HH36 BEng Engineering (Mechanical and Electrical)
Duration: 4FT Hon
Entry Requirements: *GCE:* BBB. *SQAH:* BBBC. *IB:* 28.

H601 BScEng Engineering (Electrical)
Duration: 3FT/4FT Ord
Entry Requirements: Contact the institution for details.

H604 BScEng Engineering (Electronic)
Duration: 3FT/4FT Ord
Entry Requirements: Contact the institution for details.

H606 MEng Electrical & Electronic Engineering with European Studies
Duration: 5FT Hon
Entry Requirements: *GCE:* BBB. *SQAH:* BBBB. *IB:* 30.

H605 MEng Electrical and Electronic Engineering
Duration: 5FT Hon
Entry Requirements: *GCE:* BBB. *SQAH:* BBBB. *IB:* 30.

HHH6 MEng Mechanical and Electrical Engineering
Duration: 5FT Hon
Entry Requirements: *GCE:* BBB. *SQAH:* BBBB. *IB:* 30.

A40 ABERYSTWYTH UNIVERSITY
ABERYSTWYTH UNIVERSITY, WELCOME CENTRE
PENGLAIS CAMPUS
ABERYSTWYTH
CEREDIGION SY23 3FB
t: 01970 622021 f: 01970 627410
e: ug-admissions@aber.ac.uk
// www.aber.ac.uk

GH76 BSc Artificial Intelligence and Robotics
Duration: 3FT Hon
Entry Requirements: *GCE:* 280. *IB:* 24.

GH7P BSc Artificial Intelligence and Robotics (incl indust & prof training)
Duration: 4SW Hon
Entry Requirements: *GCE:* 280. *IB:* 24.

FH56 BSc Space Science and Robotics
Duration: 3FT Hon
Entry Requirements: *GCE:* 280. *IB:* 27.

FH5P MPhys Space Science and Robotics
Duration: 4FT Hon
Entry Requirements: *GCE:* 300. *IB:* 27.

A60 ANGLIA RUSKIN UNIVERSITY
BISHOP HALL LANE
CHELMSFORD
ESSEX CM1 1SQ
t: 0845 271 3333 f: 01245 251789
e: answers@anglia.ac.uk
// www.anglia.ac.uk

H602 BEng Electronics
Duration: 3FT Hon
Entry Requirements: *GCE:* 150. *SQAH:* BBCC. *SQAAH:* BC. *IB:* 24.

A80 ASTON UNIVERSITY, BIRMINGHAM
ASTON TRIANGLE
BIRMINGHAM B4 7ET
t: 0121 204 4444 f: 0121 204 3696
e: admissions@aston.ac.uk (automatic response)
// www.aston.ac.uk/prospective-students/ug

H640 BEng Communications Engineering
Duration: 3FT/4SW Hon
Entry Requirements: *GCE:* 300-320. *IB:* 32.

H600 BEng Electrical and Electronic Engineering
Duration: 3FT/4SW Hon
Entry Requirements: *GCE:* 300-320. *IB:* 32. *OCR NED:* D1

HH36 BEng Electromechanical Engineering
Duration: 3FT/4SW Hon
Entry Requirements: *GCE:* 300-320. *IB:* 32. *OCR NED:* D1

GH46 BEng Electronic Engineering and Computer Science
Duration: 3FT/4SW Hon
Entry Requirements: *GCE:* 300-320. *IB:* 32. *OCR NED:* D1

H601 MEng Electrical and Electronic Engineering
Duration: 4FT Hon
Entry Requirements: *GCE:* 340-360. *IB:* 34.

GH64 MEng Electronic Engineering and Computer Science
Duration: 4FT Hon
Entry Requirements: *GCE:* 340-360. *IB:* 34.

B06 BANGOR UNIVERSITY
BANGOR UNIVERSITY
BANGOR
GWYNEDD LL57 2DG
t: 01248 388484 f: 01248 370451
e: admissions@bangor.ac.uk
// www.bangor.ac.uk

JH9P BA Music Technology and Electronics
Duration: 3FT Hon
Entry Requirements: *GCE:* 280. *IB:* 28.

H610 BEng Electronic Engineering
Duration: 3FT Hon
Entry Requirements: *GCE:* 240-260. *IB:* 28.

H614 BSc Electronics (Hardware Systems)
Duration: 3FT Hon
Entry Requirements: *GCE:* 220-260. *IB:* 28.

HG66 BSc Electronics (Software Programming)
Duration: 3FT Hon
Entry Requirements: *GCE:* 220-260. *IB:* 28.

JH96 BSc Music Technology and Electronics
Duration: 3FT Hon
Entry Requirements: *GCE:* 280. *IB:* 28.

H661 MEng Control and Instrumentation Engineering
Duration: 4FT Hon
Entry Requirements: Contact the institution for details.

H660 MEng Critical Safety Engineering
Duration: 4FT Hon
Entry Requirements: Contact the institution for details.

H601 MEng Electronic Engineering
Duration: 4FT Hon
Entry Requirements: *GCE:* 300-320. *IB:* 28.

B16 UNIVERSITY OF BATH
CLAVERTON DOWN
BATH BA2 7AY
t: 01225 383019 f: 01225 386366
e: admissions@bath.ac.uk
// www.bath.ac.uk

GH46 BEng Computer Systems Engineering
Duration: 3FT Hon
Entry Requirements: *GCE:* ABB. *SQAAH:* BBB. *IB:* 34.

GHK6 BEng Computer Systems Engineering (Sandwich)
Duration: 4SW Hon
Entry Requirements: *GCE:* ABB. *SQAAH:* BBB. *IB:* 34.

H630 BEng Electrical Power Engineering
Duration: 3FT Hon
Entry Requirements: *GCE:* ABB. *SQAAH:* BBB. *IB:* 34.

H631 BEng Electrical Power Engineering
Duration: 4SW Hon
Entry Requirements: *GCE:* ABB. *SQAAH:* BBB. *IB:* 34.

H603 BEng Electrical and Electronic Engineering
Duration: 3FT Hon
Entry Requirements: *GCE:* ABB. *SQAAH:* BBB. *IB:* 34.

H604 BEng Electrical and Electronic Engineering (Sandwich)
Duration: 4SW Hon
Entry Requirements: *GCE:* BBB. *SQAAH:* BBB. *IB:* 34.

H640 BEng Electronic and Communication Engineering
Duration: 3FT Hon
Entry Requirements: *GCE:* ABB. *SQAAH:* BBB. *IB:* 34.

H641 BEng Electronic and Communication Engineering (Sandwich)
Duration: 4SW Hon
Entry Requirements: *GCE:* ABB. *SQAAH:* BBB. *IB:* 34.

HH36 BEng Integrated Mechanical and Electrical Engineering
Duration: 3FT Hon
Entry Requirements: *GCE:* AAA. *SQAAH:* AAA. *IB:* 36.

HH3P BEng Integrated Mechanical and Electrical Engineering
Duration: 4FT Hon
Entry Requirements: *GCE:* AAA. *SQAAH:* AAA. *IB:* 36.

HG64 MEng Computer Systems Engineering
Duration: 4FT Hon
Entry Requirements: *GCE:* AAB. *SQAAH:* AAB. *IB:* 36.

HGP4 MEng Computer Systems Engineering
Duration: 5SW Hon
Entry Requirements: *GCE:* AAB. *SQAAH:* AAB. *IB:* 36.

H632 MEng Electrical Power Engineering
Duration: 4FT Hon
Entry Requirements: *GCE:* AAB. *SQAAH:* AAB. *IB:* 36.

H633 MEng Electrical Power Engineering
Duration: 5SW Hon
Entry Requirements: *GCE:* AAB. *SQAAH:* AAB. *IB:* 36.

H600 MEng Electrical and Electronic Engineering
Duration: 4FT Hon
Entry Requirements: *GCE:* AAB. *SQAAH:* AAB. *IB:* 36.

H601 MEng Electrical and Electronic Engineering (Sandwich)
Duration: 5SW Hon
Entry Requirements: *GCE:* AAB. *SQAAH:* AAB. *IB:* 36.

H622 MEng Electronic and Communication Engineering
Duration: 4FT Hon
Entry Requirements: *GCE:* AAB. *SQAAH:* AAB. *IB:* 36.

H623 MEng Electronic and Communication Engineering (Sandwich)
Duration: 5SW Hon
Entry Requirements: *GCE:* AAB. *SQAAH:* AAB. *IB:* 36.

HH3Q MEng Integrated Mechanical and Electrical Engineering
Duration: 5SW Hon
Entry Requirements: *GCE:* AAA. *SQAAH:* AAA. *IB:* 36.

HHJ6 MEng Integrated Mechanical and Electrical Engineering
Duration: 4FT Hon
Entry Requirements: *GCE:* AAA. *SQAAH:* AAA. *IB:* 36.

B22 UNIVERSITY OF BEDFORDSHIRE
PARK SQUARE
LUTON
BEDS LU1 3JU
t: 0844 8482234 f: 01582 489323
e: admissions@beds.ac.uk
// www.beds.ac.uk

H650 BEng Computer Systems Engineering
Duration: 3FT Hon
Entry Requirements: *GCE:* 200.

H610 BEng Electronic Engineering
Duration: 3FT Hon
Entry Requirements: Contact the institution for details.

H641 BEng Telecommunications and Network Engineering
Duration: 3FT Hon
Entry Requirements: *GCE:* 200.

GH76 BSc Artificial Intelligence and Robotics
Duration: 3FT Hon
Entry Requirements: *Foundation:* Pass. *GCE:* 200. *SQAH:* BCC. *SQAAH:* BCC. *IB:* 24. *OCR ND:* M1 *OCR NED:* P1

GH46 BSc Computer Science and Robotics
Duration: 3FT Hon
Entry Requirements: *Foundation:* Pass. *GCE:* 200. *SQAH:* BCC. *SQAAH:* BCC. *IB:* 24. *OCR ND:* M1 *OCR NED:* P1

B23 BEDFORD COLLEGE
CAULDWELL STREET
BEDFORD MK42 9AH
t: 01234 291000 f: 01234 342674
e: info@bedford.ac.uk
// www.bedford.ac.uk

006H HND Electrical/Electronic Engineering
Duration: 2FT HND
Entry Requirements: *GCE:* 120-160. Interview required.

B25 BIRMINGHAM CITY UNIVERSITY
PERRY BARR
BIRMINGHAM B42 2SU
t: 0121 331 5595 f: 0121 331 7994
// www.bcu.ac.uk

H610 BEng Electronic Engineering
Duration: 3FT/4SW Hon
Entry Requirements: *GCE:* 300. *IB:* 30.

H609 BEng Electronic Engineering with Foundation Year
Duration: 4FT/5SW Hon
Entry Requirements: *GCE:* 160. *IB:* 24.

H641 BEng Telecommunication and Networks with Foundation Year
Duration: 4FT/5SW Hon
Entry Requirements: *GCE:* 200. *IB:* 24.

H643 BEng Telecommunications and Networks
Duration: 3FT/4SW Hon
Entry Requirements: Contact the institution for details.

HW66 BSc Television Technology and Production
Duration: 3FT/4SW Hon
Entry Requirements: *GCE:* 280. *IB:* 30.

B32 THE UNIVERSITY OF BIRMINGHAM
EDGBASTON
BIRMINGHAM B15 2TT
t: 0121 415 8900 f: 0121 414 7159
e: admissions@bham.ac.uk
// www.birmingham.ac.uk

H6N0 BEng Computer Systems Engineering (with an Industrial Year)
Duration: 4FT Hon
Entry Requirements: Contact the institution for details.

H6ND BEng Computer Systems Engineering with Business Management (with an Industrial Year)
Duration: 4FT Hon
Entry Requirements: Contact the institution for details.

HN61 BEng Electronic Engineering with Business Management
Duration: 3FT Hon
Entry Requirements: *GCE:* AAB. *SQAH:* AAABB-AABBB. *SQAAH:* AA.

HPN1 BEng Electronic Engineering with Business Management (with an Industrial Year)
Duration: 4FT Hon
Entry Requirements: Contact the institution for details.

H606 BEng Electronic and Electrical Engineering (with an Industrial Year)
Duration: 4FT Hon
Entry Requirements: Contact the institution for details.

H602 BEng/MEng Computer Systems Engineering
Duration: 3FT Hon
Entry Requirements: *GCE:* AAB. *SQAH:* AAABB-AABBB. *SQAAH:* AA.

H600 BEng/MEng Electronic and Electrical Engineering
Duration: 3FT Hon
Entry Requirements: *GCE:* AAB. *SQAH:* AAABB-AABBB. *SQAAH:* AA.

H608 BEng/MEng Electronic and Electrical Engineering with Foundation Year
Duration: 4FT Hon
Entry Requirements: Contact the institution for details.

H604 MEng Computer Systems Engineering
Duration: 4FT Hon
Entry Requirements: *GCE:* AAA. *SQAH:* AAAAB-AAABB. *SQAAH:* AA.

HP50 MEng Computer Systems Engineering (with an Industrial Year)
Duration: 5FT Hon
Entry Requirements: Contact the institution for details.

H6NF MEng Computer Systems Engineering with Business Management
Duration: 4FT Hon
Entry Requirements: *GCE:* AAA. *SQAH:* AAAAB-AAABB. *SQAAH:* AA.

H6N1 MEng Computer Systems Engineering with Business Management (with an Industrial Year)
Duration: 5FT Hon
Entry Requirements: Contact the institution for details.

H6NG MEng Electronic Engineering with Business Management
Duration: 4FT Hon
Entry Requirements: *GCE:* AAA. *SQAH:* AAAAB-AAABB. *SQAAH:* AA.

H6NC MEng Electronic Engineering with Business Management (with an Industrial Year)
Duration: 5FT Hon
Entry Requirements: Contact the institution for details.

H605 MEng Electronic and Electrical Engineering
Duration: 4FT Hon
Entry Requirements: *GCE:* AAA. *SQAH:* AAAAB-AAABB. *SQAAH:* AA.

H607 MEng Electronic and Electrical Engineering (with an Industrial Year)
Duration: 5FT Hon
Entry Requirements: Contact the institution for details.

B40 BLACKBURN COLLEGE
FEILDEN STREET
BLACKBURN BB2 1LH
t: 01254 292594 f: 01254 679647
e: he-admissions@blackburn.ac.uk
// www.blackburn.ac.uk

H622 BEng Electrical Engineering
Duration: 3FT Hon
Entry Requirements: *GCE:* 160.

H621 BEng Electrical Engineering (Top-Up)
Duration: 1FT/2FT Ord/Hon
Entry Requirements: Contact the institution for details.

006H HND Electrical/Electronic Engineering
Duration: 2FT HND
Entry Requirements: *GCE:* 120.

B41 BLACKPOOL AND THE FYLDE COLLEGE AN ASSOCIATE COLLEGE OF LANCASTER UNIVERSITY
ASHFIELD ROAD
BISPHAM
BLACKPOOL
LANCS FY2 0HB
t: 01253 504346 f: 01253 504198
e: admissions@blackpool.ac.uk
// www.blackpool.ac.uk

HH3P FdA Autosport Engineering and Technology
Duration: 2FT Fdg
Entry Requirements: *GCE:* 120-360. *IB:* 24. *OCR ND:* P *OCR NED:* P

GH46 FdSc Network Engineering Security and Systems Administration (NESSA)
Duration: 2FT Fdg
Entry Requirements: *GCE:* 120-360. *IB:* 24. Interview required.

H600 HNC Electrical and Electronic Engineering
Duration: 1FT HNC
Entry Requirements: *GCE:* 120-360. *IB:* 24.

H601 HNC Mechanical Engineering
Duration: 1FT HNC
Entry Requirements: *GCE:* 120-360. *IB:* 24.

006H HND Electrical / Electronic Engineering
Duration: 2FT HND
Entry Requirements: *GCE:* 120-360. *IB:* 24.

B44 UNIVERSITY OF BOLTON
DEANE ROAD
BOLTON BL3 5AB
t: 01204 903903 f: 01204 399074
e: enquiries@bolton.ac.uk
// www.bolton.ac.uk

GH46 BA Games Art
Duration: 3FT Hon
Entry Requirements: *GCE:* 260. Interview required.

H600 BSc Computing Technology
Duration: 3FT Hon
Entry Requirements: *GCE:* 240. Interview required.

HH36 BSc Mechatronics
Duration: 1FT Hon
Entry Requirements: Contact the institution for details.

B56 THE UNIVERSITY OF BRADFORD
RICHMOND ROAD
BRADFORD
WEST YORKSHIRE BD7 1DP
t: 0800 073 1225 f: 01274 235585
e: course-enquiries@bradford.ac.uk
// www.bradford.ac.uk

H606 BEng Electrical and Electronic Engineering
Duration: 3FT Hon
Entry Requirements: *GCE:* 240. *IB:* 24.

H604 BEng Electrical and Electronic Engineering (4 years)
Duration: 4SW Hon
Entry Requirements: *GCE:* 240. *IB:* 24.

H695 BEng Electronic, Telecommunications and Internet Engineering
Duration: 3FT Hon
Entry Requirements: *GCE:* 240. *IB:* 24.

H690 BEng Electronic, Telecommunications and Internet Engineering (4 years)
Duration: 4SW Hon
Entry Requirements: *GCE:* 240. *IB:* 24.

GH76 BSc Intelligent Systems and Robotics
Duration: 3FT Hon
Entry Requirements: *GCE:* 240. *IB:* 24.

GH7P BSc Intelligent Systems and Robotics
Duration: 4SW Hon
Entry Requirements: *GCE:* 240. *IB:* 24.

HP63 BSc Media Technology and Production
Duration: 3FT Hon
Entry Requirements: *GCE:* 260. *IB:* 24. Interview required.

H693 MEng Electrical and Electronic Engineering
Duration: 5FT Hon
Entry Requirements: *GCE:* 300.

H691 MEng Electrical and Electronic Engineering (4 years)
Duration: 4FT Hon
Entry Requirements: *GCE:* 300. *IB:* 26.

H694 MEng Electronic, Telecommunications and Internet Engineering
Duration: 5SW Hon
Entry Requirements: *GCE:* 300.

H692 MEng Electronic, Telecommunications and Internet Engineering (4 years)
Duration: 4FT Hon
Entry Requirements: *GCE:* 300. *IB:* 26.

B60 BRADFORD COLLEGE: AN ASSOCIATE COLLEGE OF LEEDS METROPOLITAN UNIVERSITY
GREAT HORTON ROAD
BRADFORD
WEST YORKSHIRE BD7 1AY
t: 01274 433008 f: 01274 431652
e: heregistry@bradfordcollege.ac.uk
// www.bradfordcollege.ac.uk/university-centre

H620 HND Electrical Engineering
Duration: 2FT HND
Entry Requirements: Contact the institution for details.

B72 UNIVERSITY OF BRIGHTON
MITHRAS HOUSE 211
LEWES ROAD
BRIGHTON BN2 4AT
t: 01273 644644 f: 01273 642607
e: admissions@brighton.ac.uk
// www.brighton.ac.uk

HG64 BEng Digital Electronics, Computing and Communications
Duration: 3FT/4SW Hon
Entry Requirements: *GCE:* BBB. *IB:* 32.

H605 BEng Electrical and Electronic Engineering
Duration: 3FT/4SW Hon
Entry Requirements: *GCE:* BBB. *IB:* 32.

H606 BEng Electrical and Electronic Engineering (with integrated Foundation Year)
Duration: 4FT Hon
Entry Requirements: *GCE:* BBC. *IB:* 30.

HI61 BEng(Hons) Digital Electronics, Computing & Communications (with integrated foundation yr)
Duration: 4FT Hon
Entry Requirements: Contact the institution for details.

H611 BSc Electronic Engineering
Duration: 3SW Hon
Entry Requirements: Contact the institution for details.

H610 BSc Electronic Engineering (Top-Up)
Duration: 1FT Hon
Entry Requirements: HND required.

H600 FdEng Electrical and Electronic Engineering
Duration: 2FT Fdg
Entry Requirements: *GCE:* 120. *IB:* 24.

HG6K MEng Digital Electronics, Computing and Communications
Duration: 4FT/5SW Hon
Entry Requirements: *GCE:* ABB. *IB:* 34.

H601 MEng Electrical and Electronic Engineering
Duration: 5FT/6SW Hon
Entry Requirements: Contact the institution for details.

H607 MEng Electrical and Electronic Engineering
Duration: 4FT/5SW Hon
Entry Requirements: *GCE:* ABB. *IB:* 34.

B78 UNIVERSITY OF BRISTOL
UNDERGRADUATE ADMISSIONS OFFICE
SENATE HOUSE
TYNDALL AVENUE
BRISTOL BS8 1TH
t: 0117 928 9000 f: 0117 331 7391
e: ug-admissions@bristol.ac.uk
// www.bristol.ac.uk

H600 BEng Electrical and Electronic Engineering
Duration: 3FT Hon
Entry Requirements: *GCE:* A*AB-AAA. *SQAH:* AAAAA. *SQAAH:* AAA. *IB:* 37.

H640 BEng Electronic and Communications Engineering
Duration: 3FT Hon
Entry Requirements: *GCE:* A*AB-AAA. *SQAH:* AAAAA. *SQAAH:* AAA. *IB:* 37.

GH46 MEng Computer Science and Electronics
Duration: 4FT Hon
Entry Requirements: *GCE:* A*AA-AAA. *SQAH:* AAAAA. *SQAAH:* AAA.

GH4P MEng Computer Science and Electronics with Study Abroad
Duration: 4FT Hon
Entry Requirements: *GCE:* A*AA-AAA. *SQAH:* AAAAA. *SQAAH:* AAA.

H606 MEng Electrical and Electronic Engineering
Duration: 4FT Hon
Entry Requirements: *GCE:* A*AB-AAA. *SQAH:* AAAAA. *SQAAH:* AAA. *IB:* 37.

H605 MEng Electrical and Electronic Engineering with Study in Continental Europe
Duration: 4FT Hon
Entry Requirements: *GCE:* A*AB-AAA. *SQAH:* AAAAA. *SQAAH:* AAA. *IB:* 37.

H623 MEng Electronic and Communications Engineering
Duration: 4FT Hon
Entry Requirements: *GCE:* A*AB-AAA. *SQAH:* AAAAA. *SQAAH:* AAA. *IB:* 37.

B80 UNIVERSITY OF THE WEST OF ENGLAND, BRISTOL
FRENCHAY CAMPUS
COLDHARBOUR LANE
BRISTOL BS16 1QY
t: +44 (0)117 32 83333 f: +44 (0)117 32 82810
e: admissions@uwe.ac.uk
// www.uwe.ac.uk

H606 BEng Electrical and Electronic Engineering
Duration: 3FT/4SW Hon
Entry Requirements: *GCE:* 280.

HH36 BEng (Hons Building Services Engineering
Duration: 3FT Hon
Entry Requirements: *GCE:* 280.

H640 BEng (Hons Electronics and Communications
Duration: 1FT Hon
Entry Requirements: HND required.

H671 BSc Robotics
Duration: 3FT/4SW Hon
Entry Requirements: *GCE:* 300.

H605 MEng Electrical and Electronic Engineering
Duration: 4FT/5SW Hon
Entry Requirements: *GCE:* 300.

B84 BRUNEL UNIVERSITY
UXBRIDGE
MIDDLESEX UB8 3PH
t: 01895 265265 f: 01895 269790
e: admissions@brunel.ac.uk
// www.brunel.ac.uk

GH56 BEng Computer Systems Engineering
Duration: 3FT Hon
Entry Requirements: *GCE:* BBB. *SQAAH:* BBB. *IB:* 32. *BTEC SubDip:* D. *BTEC Dip:* DD. *BTEC ExtDip:* DDD. *OCR ND:* D *OCR NED:* D2 Interview required.

GH5P BEng Computer Systems Engineering (4 year Thick SW)
Duration: 4SW Hon
Entry Requirements: *GCE:* BBB. *SQAAH:* BBB. *IB:* 32. *BTEC SubDip:* D. *BTEC Dip:* DD. *BTEC ExtDip:* DDD. *OCR ND:* D *OCR NED:* D2 Interview required.

G603 BEng Computer Systems Engineering (Software)
Duration: 3FT Hon
Entry Requirements: *GCE:* BBB. *SQAAH:* BBB. *IB:* 32. *BTEC SubDip:* D. *BTEC Dip:* DD. *BTEC ExtDip:* DDD. *OCR ND:* D *OCR NED:* D2 Interview required.

H690 BEng Electronic & Communications Engineering with Prof Dev
Duration: 4FT Hon
Entry Requirements: *GCE:* BBB. *SQAAH:* BBB. *IB:* 32. *BTEC SubDip:* D. *BTEC Dip:* DD. *BTEC ExtDip:* DDD. *OCR ND:* D *OCR NED:* D2 Interview required.

H693 BEng Electronic and Communications Engineering
Duration: 3FT Hon
Entry Requirements: *GCE:* BBB. *SQAAH:* BBB. *IB:* 32. *BTEC SubDip:* D. *BTEC Dip:* DD. *BTEC ExtDip:* DDD. *OCR ND:* D *OCR NED:* D2 Interview required.

H604 BEng Electronic and Computer Engineering
Duration: 3FT Hon
Entry Requirements: *GCE:* BBB. *SQAAH:* BBB. *IB:* 32. *BTEC SubDip:* D. *BTEC Dip:* DD. *BTEC ExtDip:* DDD. *OCR ND:* D *OCR NED:* D2 Interview required.

H6N6 BEng Electronic and Computer Engineering with Professional Development
Duration: 4FT Hon
Entry Requirements: *GCE:* BBB. *SQAAH:* BBB. *IB:* 32. *BTEC SubDip:* D. *BTEC Dip:* DD. *BTEC ExtDip:* DDD. *OCR ND:* D *OCR NED:* D2 Interview required.

H600 BEng Electronic and Electrical Engineering
Duration: 3FT Hon
Entry Requirements: *GCE:* BBB. *SQAAH:* BBB. *IB:* 32. *BTEC SubDip:* D. *BTEC Dip:* DD. *BTEC ExtDip:* DDD. *OCR ND:* D *OCR NED:* D2 Interview required.

H602 BEng Electronic and Electrical Engineering (4 year Thick SW)
Duration: 4SW Hon
Entry Requirements: *GCE:* BBB. *SQAAH:* BBB. *IB:* 32. *BTEC SubDip:* D. *BTEC Dip:* DD. *BTEC ExtDip:* DDD. *OCR ND:* D *OCR NED:* D2 Interview required.

HW62 BSc Broadcast Media (Design & Technology)
Duration: 3FT Hon
Entry Requirements: *GCE:* BBB. *SQAAH:* BBB. *IB:* 32. *BTEC SubDip:* D. *BTEC Dip:* DD. *BTEC ExtDip:* DDD. Interview required.

HW6F BSc Broadcast Media (Design & Technology) (4 year Thick SW)
Duration: 4SW Hon
Entry Requirements: *GCE:* BBB. *SQAAH:* BBB. *IB:* 32. *BTEC SubDip:* D. *BTEC Dip:* DD. *BTEC ExtDip:* DDD. Interview required.

GH5Q MEng Computer Systems Engineering (5 year Thick SW)
Duration: 5FT Hon
Entry Requirements: *GCE:* AAB. *SQAAH:* AAB. *IB:* 35. *BTEC ExtDip:* D*D*D. Interview required.

H691 MEng Electronic & Communications Engineering with Prof Dev
Duration: 5FT Hon
Entry Requirements: *GCE:* AAB. *SQAAH:* AAB. *IB:* 35. *BTEC ExtDip:* D*D*D. Interview required.

H692 MEng Electronic and Communications Engineering
Duration: 4FT Hon
Entry Requirements: *GCE:* AAB. *SQAAH:* AAB. *IB:* 35. *BTEC ExtDip:* D*D*D. Interview required.

HGP4 MEng Electronic and Computer Engineering
Duration: 4FT Hon
Entry Requirements: *GCE:* AAB. *SQAAH:* AAB. *IB:* 35. *BTEC ExtDip:* D*D*D. Interview required.

HG6L MEng Electronic and Computer Engineering (5 year Thick SW)
Duration: 5SW Hon
Entry Requirements: *GCE:* AAB. *SQAAH:* AAB. *IB:* 35. *BTEC ExtDip:* D*D*D. Interview required.

H601 MEng Electronic and Electrical Engineering (4 years)
Duration: 4FT Hon
Entry Requirements: *GCE:* AAB. *SQAAH:* AAB. *IB:* 35. *BTEC ExtDip:* D*D*D. Interview required.

H603 MEng Electronic and Electrical Engineering (5 year Thick SW)
Duration: 5SW Hon
Entry Requirements: *GCE:* AAB. *SQAAH:* AAB. *IB:* 35. *BTEC ExtDip:* D*D*D. Interview required.

C15 CARDIFF UNIVERSITY
PO BOX 927
30-36 NEWPORT ROAD
CARDIFF CF24 0DE
t: 029 2087 9999 f: 029 2087 6138
e: admissions@cardiff.ac.uk
// www.cardiff.ac.uk

HG66 BEng Computer Systems Engineering
Duration: 3FT Hon
Entry Requirements: *GCE:* ABB. *IB:* 32. Interview required.

HGQ6 BEng Computer Systems Engineering (Year in Industry)
Duration: 4SW Hon
Entry Requirements: *GCE:* ABB. *IB:* 32. Interview required.

H605 BEng Electrical and Electronic Engineering
Duration: 3FT Hon
Entry Requirements: *GCE:* ABB. *SQAAH:* ABB. *IB:* 32. Interview required. Admissions Test required.

H606 BEng Electrical and Electronic Engineering (Year in Industry)
Duration: 4SW Hon
Entry Requirements: *GCE:* ABB. *SQAAH:* ABB. *IB:* 32. Interview required. Admissions Test required.

H610 BEng Electronic and Communication Engineering
Duration: 3FT Hon
Entry Requirements: *GCE:* ABB. *SQAAH:* ABB. *IB:* 32. Interview required. Admissions Test required.

H604 BEng Electronic and Communication Engineering(Year in Industry)
Duration: 4SW Hon
Entry Requirements: *GCE:* ABB. *SQAAH:* ABB. *IB:* 32. Interview required. Admissions Test required.

GH46 BSc Computer Systems Engineering
Duration: 3FT Hon
Entry Requirements: *GCE:* ABB. *SQAH:* AAABB. *SQAAH:* ABB. *IB:* 33. Interview required.

HG6K MEng Computer Systems Engineering
Duration: 4FT Hon
Entry Requirements: *GCE:* ABB. *IB:* 32.

HG6Q MEng Computer Systems Engineering (Year in Industry)
Duration: 5SW Hon
Entry Requirements: *GCE:* ABB. *IB:* 32.

H601 MEng Electrical and Electronic Engineering
Duration: 4FT Hon
Entry Requirements: *GCE:* ABB. *SQAAH:* ABB. *IB:* 32. Interview required. Admissions Test required.

H600 MEng Electrical and Electronic Engineering (Year in Industry)
Duration: 5SW Hon
Entry Requirements: *GCE:* ABB. *SQAAH:* ABB. *IB:* 32. Interview required. Admissions Test required.

H602 MEng Electronic and Communication Engineering
Duration: 4FT Hon
Entry Requirements: *GCE:* ABB. *SQAAH:* ABB. *IB:* 32. Interview required. Admissions Test required.

H603 MEng Electronic and Communication Engineering (Year in Industry)
Duration: 5SW Hon
Entry Requirements: *GCE:* ABB. *SQAAH:* ABB. *IB:* 32. Interview required. Admissions Test required.

C30 UNIVERSITY OF CENTRAL LANCASHIRE
PRESTON
LANCS PR1 2HE
t: 01772 201201 f: 01772 894954
e: uadmissions@uclan.ac.uk
// www.uclan.ac.uk

H610 BEng Electronic Engineering
Duration: 3FT/4SW Hon
Entry Requirements: *GCE:* 240-280. *IB:* 24.

H608 BEng Electronic Engineering (Foundation entry)
Duration: 4FT Hon
Entry Requirements: *GCE:* 100. *IB:* 24. *OCR ND:* P2 *OCR NED:* P3

HH36 BEng Robotics and Mechatronics
Duration: 3FT/4SW Hon
Entry Requirements: *GCE:* 240-280. *IB:* 24.

HP63 BSc Media Production & Technology
Duration: 3FT Hon
Entry Requirements: *GCE:* 300. *SQAH:* AAAB. *IB:* 30. *OCR ND:* D *OCR NED:* D2

C60 CITY UNIVERSITY
NORTHAMPTON SQUARE
LONDON EC1V 0HB
t: 020 7040 5060 f: 020 7040 8995
e: ugadmissions@city.ac.uk
// www.city.ac.uk

H601 BEng Computer Systems Engineering (4 year SW) (f)
Duration: 4SW Hon
Entry Requirements: *GCE:* 340. *SQAH:* BBBBB. *IB:* 30.

H608 BEng Computer Systems Engineering (4 years including Foundation Year) (f)
Duration: 4FT Hon
Entry Requirements: *GCE:* 160. *SQAH:* CCCC. *IB:* 20.

H600 BEng Computer Systems Engineering (f)
Duration: 3FT Hon
Entry Requirements: *GCE:* 340. *SQAH:* BBBBB. *IB:* 30.

H642 BEng Electrical and Electronic Engineering (4 year SW) (g)
Duration: 4SW Hon
Entry Requirements: *GCE:* 340. *SQAH:* BBBBB. *IB:* 30.

H606 BEng Electrical and Electronic Engineering (4 years including Foundation Year) (g)
Duration: 4FT Hon
Entry Requirements: *GCE:* 160. *SQAH:* CCCC. *IB:* 20.

H602 BEng Electrical and Electronic Engineering (g)
Duration: 3FT/4SW Hon/Deg
Entry Requirements: *GCE:* 340. *SQAH:* BBBBB. *IB:* 30.

H641 BEng Electrical and Electronic Engineering Specialisations (4 year SW) (g)
Duration: 4SW Hon
Entry Requirements: *GCE:* 340. *SQAH:* BBBBB. *IB:* 30.

H645 BEng Telecommunications (g)
Duration: 3FT Hon
Entry Requirements: *GCE:* 340. *IB:* 30.

H646 BEng Telecommunications (g)
Duration: 4SW Hon
Entry Requirements: *GCE:* 340. *IB:* 30.

H607 MEng Electrical and Electronic Engineering (g)
Duration: 4FT Hon
Entry Requirements: Contact the institution for details.

H609 MEng Electrical and Electronic Engineering (g)
Duration: 5SW Hon
Entry Requirements: Contact the institution for details.

C75 COLCHESTER INSTITUTE
SHEEPEN ROAD
COLCHESTER
ESSEX CO3 3LL
t: 01206 712777 f: 01206 712800
e: info@colchester.ac.uk
// www.colchester.ac.uk

H610 HNC Engineering (Electronics)
Duration: 1FT HNC
Entry Requirements: Contact the institution for details.

H620 HNC Engineering Electrical (Power)
Duration: 1FT HNC
Entry Requirements: Contact the institution for details.

016H HND Electronics Engineering
Duration: 2FT HND
Entry Requirements: Contact the institution for details.

C85 COVENTRY UNIVERSITY
THE STUDENT CENTRE
COVENTRY UNIVERSITY
1 GULSON RD
COVENTRY CV1 2JH
t: 024 7615 2222 f: 024 7615 2223
e: studentenquiries@coventry.ac.uk
// www.coventry.ac.uk

H641 BEng Communications Engineering
Duration: 3FT/4SW Hon
Entry Requirements: *GCE:* CCC. *SQAH:* CCCCC. *IB:* 27. *BTEC ExtDip:* MMM. *OCR NED:* M3

H621 BEng Computers, Networking and Communications Technology
Duration: 3FT/4SW Hon
Entry Requirements: *GCE:* CCC. *SQAH:* CCCCC. *IB:* 27. *BTEC ExtDip:* MMM. *OCR NED:* M3

H651 BEng Electrical Systems Engineering
Duration: 3FT/4SW Hon
Entry Requirements: *GCE:* CCC. *SQAH:* CCCCC. *IB:* 27. *BTEC ExtDip:* MMM. *OCR NED:* M3

H600 BEng Electrical and Electronic Engineering
Duration: 3FT/4SW Hon
Entry Requirements: *GCE:* BCC. *SQAH:* BCCCC. *IB:* 28. *BTEC ExtDip:* DMM. *OCR NED:* M2

H601 BEng Electronic Engineering
Duration: 3FT/4SW Hon
Entry Requirements: *GCE:* CCC. *SQAH:* CCCCC. *IB:* 27. *BTEC ExtDip:* MMM. *OCR NED:* M3

D26 DE MONTFORT UNIVERSITY
THE GATEWAY
LEICESTER LE1 9BH
t: 0116 255 1551 f: 0116 250 6204
e: enquiries@dmu.ac.uk
// www.dmu.ac.uk

H610 BEng Electronic Engineering
Duration: 3FT/4SW Hon
Entry Requirements: *IB:* 28. *BTEC ExtDip:* DDM. Interview required.

HH36 BEng Mechatronics
Duration: 3FT/4SW Hon
Entry Requirements: *GCE:* 300. *IB:* 28. *BTEC ExtDip:* DDM. *OCR NED:* M2 Interview required.

G7H6 BSc Artificial Intelligence with Robotics
Duration: 4SW Hon
Entry Requirements: *IB:* 28. *BTEC ExtDip:* DDM. *OCR NED:* M2 Interview required.

HG64 BSc Information and Communication Technology
Duration: 3FT/4SW Hon
Entry Requirements: *GCE:* 300. *IB:* 28. *BTEC ExtDip:* DDM. Interview required.

HP63 BSc Media Technology
Duration: 3FT/4SW Hon
Entry Requirements: *GCE:* 300. *IB:* 28. *BTEC ExtDip:* DDM. Interview required.

HW66 BSc Radio Production and Technology
Duration: 3FT/4SW Hon
Entry Requirements: *GCE:* 300. *IB:* 28. *BTEC ExtDip:* DDM. Interview required.

D39 UNIVERSITY OF DERBY
KEDLESTON ROAD
DERBY DE22 1GB
t: 01332 591167 f: 01332 597724
e: askadmissions@derby.ac.uk
// www.derby.ac.uk

H600 BEng Electrical and Electronic Engineering
Duration: 3FT Hon
Entry Requirements: *GCE:* 260. *IB:* 28. *BTEC Dip:* D*D*. *BTEC ExtDip:* DMM. *OCR ND:* D *OCR NED:* M3

H601 FYr Electrical and Electronic Engineering Foundation
Duration: 1FT FYr
Entry Requirements: *Foundation:* Pass. *GCE:* 160. *IB:* 24. *BTEC Dip:* D*D*. *BTEC ExtDip:* DMM. *OCR ND:* M2 *OCR NED:* P2

D52 DONCASTER COLLEGE
THE HUB
CHAPPELL DRIVE
SOUTH YORKSHIRE DN1 2RF
t: 01302 553610
e: he@don.ac.uk
// www.don.ac.uk

026H HND Electronic Engineering and Computing Technology
Duration: 2FT HND
Entry Requirements: *GCE:* 40.

D58 DUDLEY COLLEGE OF TECHNOLOGY
THE BROADWAY
DUDLEY DY1 4AS
t: 01384 363277/6 f: 01384 363311
e: admissions@dudleycol.ac.uk
// www.dudleycol.ac.uk

006H HND Engineering (Electrical/Electronics)
Duration: 2FT HND
Entry Requirements: *GCE:* 40-80.

D65 UNIVERSITY OF DUNDEE
NETHERGATE
DUNDEE DD1 4HN
t: 01382 383838 f: 01382 388150
e: contactus@dundee.ac.uk
// www.dundee.ac.uk/admissions/undergraduate/

HF63 BEng Electronic Engineering and Physics
Duration: 4FT Hon
Entry Requirements: *GCE:* BCC. *SQAH:* ABBB. *IB:* 30.

H600 BEng Electronic and Electrical Engineering
Duration: 4FT Hon
Entry Requirements: *GCE:* BCC. *SQAH:* ABBB. *IB:* 30.

FH3Q BSc Physics and Microelectronics
Duration: 4FT Hon
Entry Requirements: *GCE:* BCC. *SQAH:* ABBB. *IB:* 30.

FH36 MEng Electronic Engineering and Physics
Duration: 5FT Hon
Entry Requirements: *GCE:* BBB. *SQAH:* AABB. *IB:* 32.

H601 MEng Electronic and Electrical Engineering
Duration: 5FT Hon
Entry Requirements: *GCE:* BBB. *SQAH:* AABB. *IB:* 32.

D86 DURHAM UNIVERSITY
DURHAM UNIVERSITY
UNIVERSITY OFFICE
DURHAM DH1 3HP
t: 0191 334 2000 f: 0191 334 6055
e: admissions@durham.ac.uk
// www.durham.ac.uk

H640 MEng Communications Engineering
Duration: 4FT Hon
Entry Requirements: *GCE:* AAA. *SQAH:* AAAAB. *SQAAH:* AAA. *IB:* 37.

H610 MEng Electronic Engineering
Duration: 4FT Hon
Entry Requirements: *GCE:* AAA. *SQAH:* AAAAB. *SQAAH:* AAA. *IB:* 37.

E14 UNIVERSITY OF EAST ANGLIA
NORWICH NR4 7TJ
t: 01603 591515 f: 01603 591523
e: admissions@uea.ac.uk
// www.uea.ac.uk

HG65 BEng Computer Systems Engineering
Duration: 3FT Hon   CRB Check: Required
Entry Requirements: *GCE:* ABB. *SQAH:* AAABB. *SQAAH:* ABB. *IB:* 32.

HG6M BEng Computer Systems Engineering with a year in Industry
Duration: 4FT Hon   CRB Check: Required
Entry Requirements: *GCE:* ABB. *SQAH:* AAABB. *SQAAH:* ABB. *IB:* 32.

www.ucas.com
www.cukas.ac.uk

at the heart of connecting people to higher education

E28 UNIVERSITY OF EAST LONDON
DOCKLANDS CAMPUS
UNIVERSITY WAY
LONDON E16 2RD
t: 020 8223 3333 f: 020 8223 2978
e: study@uel.ac.uk
// www.uel.ac.uk

G456 BEng Digital and Embedded Systems Engineering
Duration: 3FT Hon
Entry Requirements: *GCE:* 240. *IB:* 24.

H600 BEng Electrical & Electronic Engineering
Duration: 3FT/4SW Hon
Entry Requirements: *GCE:* 240. *IB:* 26.

H608 BEng Electrical & Electronic Engineering (Extended)
Duration: 4FT Hon
Entry Requirements: *GCE:* 120.

H6P9 BEng Electrical & Electronic Engineering with Communication Studies
Duration: 3FT Hon
Entry Requirements: *GCE:* 240. *IB:* 26.

H6L6 BEng Electrical & Electronic Engineering with Cultural Studies
Duration: 3FT Hon
Entry Requirements: *GCE:* 240. *IB:* 26.

H6B9 BEng Electrical & Electronic Engineering with Health Promotion
Duration: 3FT Hon
Entry Requirements: *GCE:* 240. *IB:* 26.

H6N1 BEng Electrical & Electronic Engineering with International Business
Duration: 3FT Hon
Entry Requirements: *GCE:* 240. *IB:* 26.

H6GC BSc Electrical & Electronic Engineering with Mathematics
Duration: 3FT Hon
Entry Requirements: *GCE:* 240.

E56 THE UNIVERSITY OF EDINBURGH
STUDENT RECRUITMENT & ADMISSIONS
57 GEORGE SQUARE
EDINBURGH EH8 9JU
t: 0131 650 4360 f: 0131 651 1236
e: sra.enquiries@ed.ac.uk
// www.ed.ac.uk/studying/undergraduate/

GH46 BEng Computer Science and Electronics
Duration: 4FT Hon
Entry Requirements: *GCE:* AAA-ABB. *SQAH:* AAAA-ABBB.

HH36 BEng Electrical and Mechanical Engineering
Duration: 4FT Hon
Entry Requirements: *GCE:* AAA-ABB. *SQAH:* AAAA-ABBB.

H615 BEng Electronics
Duration: 4FT Hon
Entry Requirements: *GCE:* AAA-ABB. *SQAH:* AAAA-ABBB.

H600 BEng Electronics and Electrical Engineering
Duration: 4FT Hon
Entry Requirements: *GCE:* AAA-ABB. *SQAH:* AAAA-ABBB.

H640 BEng Electronics and Electrical Engineering (Communications)
Duration: 4FT Hon
Entry Requirements: *GCE:* AAA-ABB. *SQAH:* AAAA-ABBB.

H6N2 BEng Electronics and Electrical Engineering with Management
Duration: 4FT Hon
Entry Requirements: *GCE:* AAA-ABB. *SQAH:* AAAA-ABBB.

GH66 BEng Electronics and Software Engineering
Duration: 4FT Hon
Entry Requirements: *GCE:* AAA-ABB. *SQAH:* AAAA-ABBB.

H620 MEng Electrical Engineering
Duration: 5FT Hon
Entry Requirements: *GCE:* AAA-ABB. *SQAH:* AAAA-ABBB.

HHH6 MEng Electrical and Mechanical Engineering
Duration: 5FT Hon
Entry Requirements: *GCE:* AAA-ABB. *SQAH:* AAAA-ABBB.

H610 MEng Electronics
Duration: 5FT Hon
Entry Requirements: *GCE:* AAA-ABB. *SQAH:* AAAA-ABBB.

GHK6 MEng Electronics and Computer Science
Duration: 5FT Hon
Entry Requirements: *GCE:* AAA-ABB. *SQAH:* AAAA-ABBB.

H601 MEng Electronics and Electrical Engineering
Duration: 5FT Hon
Entry Requirements: *GCE:* AAA-ABB. *SQAH:* AAAA-ABBB.

H602 MEng Electronics and Electrical Engineering (Communications)
Duration: 4FT Hon
Entry Requirements: *GCE:* AAA-ABB. *SQAH:* AAAA-ABBB.

H6NF MEng Electronics and Electrical Engineering with Management
Duration: 5FT Hon
Entry Requirements: *GCE:* AAA-ABB. *SQAH:* AAAA-ABBB.

GHP6 MEng Electronics and Software Engineering
Duration: 5FT Hon
Entry Requirements: *GCE:* AAA-ABB. *SQAH:* AAAA-ABBB.

H690 MEng Electronics with Bioelectronics
Duration: 5FT Hon
Entry Requirements: *GCE:* AAA-ABB. *SQAH:* AAAA-ABBB.

E59 EDINBURGH NAPIER UNIVERSITY
CRAIGLOCKHART CAMPUS
EDINBURGH EH14 1DJ
t: +44 (0)8452 60 60 40 f: 0131 455 6464
e: info@napier.ac.uk
// www.napier.ac.uk

H602 BEng Computer Systems And Networks
Duration: 3FT/4FT/5SW Hon
Entry Requirements: *GCE:* 230.

H620 BEng Electrical Engineering
Duration: 3FT/4FT Ord/Hon
Entry Requirements: *GCE:* 245.

H610 BEng Electronic Engineering
Duration: 3FT/4FT Ord/Hon
Entry Requirements: Contact the institution for details.

H606 BEng Electronic and Electrical Engineering
Duration: 3FT/4FT Ord/Hon
Entry Requirements: *GCE:* 245.

HJ69 BEng Energy and Environmental Engineering
Duration: 3FT/4FT Ord/Hon
Entry Requirements: *GCE:* 245.

HH63 BEng Mechatronics
Duration: 3FT/4FT Hon/Ord
Entry Requirements: *GCE:* 245.

E70 THE UNIVERSITY OF ESSEX
WIVENHOE PARK
COLCHESTER
ESSEX CO4 3SQ
t: 01206 873666 f: 01206 874477
e: admit@essex.ac.uk
// www.essex.ac.uk

H650 BEng Computer Systems Engineering
Duration: 3FT Hon
Entry Requirements: *GCE:* BBB. *SQAH:* AABB. *IB:* 32. *OCR ND:* D

GH4P BEng Computers and Electronics
Duration: 3FT Hon
Entry Requirements: *GCE:* BBB. *SQAH:* AABB. *IB:* 32. *OCR ND:* D

GH4Q BEng Computers and Electronics (Including Year Abroad)
Duration: 4FT Hon
Entry Requirements: *GCE:* BBB. *SQAH:* AABB. *IB:* 32. *OCR ND:* D

GH46 BEng Computers and Electronics (including Foundation Year)
Duration: 4FT Hon
Entry Requirements: *GCE:* 180. *SQAH:* CCCD. *IB:* 24.

H610 BEng Electronic Engineering
Duration: 3FT Hon
Entry Requirements: *SQAH:* AABB. *IB:* 32. *OCR ND:* D

H611 BEng Electronic Engineering (Including Year Abroad)
Duration: 4FT Hon
Entry Requirements: *SQAH:* AABB. *IB:* 32. *OCR ND:* D

H641 BEng Telecommunication Engineering
Duration: 3FT Hon
Entry Requirements: *SQAH:* AABB. *IB:* 32. *OCR ND:* D

HP41 BEng Telecommunication Engineering (Including Foundation Year)
Duration: 4FT Hon
Entry Requirements: Contact the institution for details.

HQ41 BEng Telecommunication Engineering (Including Year Abroad)
Duration: 4FT Hon
Entry Requirements: *SQAH:* AABB. *IB:* 32. *OCR ND:* D

GH56 BSc Information and Communication Technology
Duration: 3FT Hon
Entry Requirements: *GCE:* BBB. *SQAH:* AABB. *IB:* 32. *OCR ND:* D

H613 MEng Electronic Engineering (four-year integrated masters)
Duration: 4FT Hon
Entry Requirements: *SQAH:* AAAA. *IB:* 36. *OCR ND:* D

E81 EXETER COLLEGE
HELE ROAD
EXETER
DEVON EX4 4JS
t: 0845 111 6000
e: info@exe-coll.ac.uk
// www.exe-coll.ac.uk/he

H620 FdSc Electrical Engineering
Duration: 2FT Fdg
Entry Requirements: *GCE:* 160.

H610 FdSc Electronic Engineering
Duration: 2FT Fdg
Entry Requirements: *GCE:* 160.

E84 UNIVERSITY OF EXETER
LAVER BUILDING
NORTH PARK ROAD
EXETER
DEVON EX4 4QE
t: 01392 723044 f: 01392 722479
e: admissions@exeter.ac.uk
// www.exeter.ac.uk

H610 BEng Electronic Engineering
Duration: 3FT Hon
Entry Requirements: *GCE:* AAB-ABB. *SQAH:* AAABB-AABBB. *SQAAH:* ABB-BBB.

HG6K BEng Electronic Engineering and Computer Science
Duration: 3FT Hon
Entry Requirements: *GCE:* AAB-ABB. *SQAH:* AAABB-AABBB. *SQAAH:* ABB-BBB.

HI61 BEng Electronic Engineering and Computer Science with Industrial Experience
Duration: 3FT Hon
Entry Requirements: *GCE:* AAB-ABB. *SQAH:* AAABB-AABBB. *SQAAH:* ABB-BBB.

HI16 BEng Electronic Engineering and Computer Science with International Study
Duration: 3FT Hon
Entry Requirements: *GCE:* AAB-ABB. *SQAH:* AAABB-AABBB. *SQAAH:* ABB-BBB.

HP10 BEng Electronic Engineering with Industrial Experience
Duration: 3FT Hon
Entry Requirements: *GCE:* AAB-ABB. *SQAH:* AAABB-AABBB. *SQAAH:* ABB-BBB.

HPC0 BEng Electronic Engineering with International Study
Duration: 3FT Hon
Entry Requirements: *GCE:* AAA-AAB. *SQAH:* AAAAB-AAABB. *SQAAH:* AAB-ABB.

H601 MEng Electronic Engineering
Duration: 4FT Hon
Entry Requirements: *GCE:* AAA-AAB. *SQAH:* AAAAB-AAABB. *SQAAH:* AAB-ABB. *BTEC ExtDip:* DDM.

HG64 MEng Electronic Engineering and Computer Science
Duration: 4FT Hon
Entry Requirements: *GCE:* AAA-AAB. *SQAH:* AAAAB-AAABB. *SQAAH:* AAB-ABB. *BTEC ExtDip:* DDM.

IH61 MEng Electronic Engineering and Computer Science with Industrial Experience (4 years)
Duration: 4FT Hon
Entry Requirements: *GCE:* AAA-AAB. *SQAH:* AAAAB-AAABB. *SQAAH:* AAB-ABB. *BTEC ExtDip:* DDM.

IH16 MEng Electronic Engineering and Computer Science with International Study (4 years)
Duration: 4FT Hon
Entry Requirements: *GCE:* AAA-AAB. *SQAH:* AAAAB-AAABB. *SQAAH:* AAB-ABB. *BTEC ExtDip:* DDM.

HPD0 MEng Electronic Engineering with Industrial Experience (4 years)
Duration: 4FT Hon
Entry Requirements: *GCE:* AAA-AAB. *SQAH:* AAAAB-AAABB. *SQAAH:* AAB-ABB. *BTEC ExtDip:* DDM.

H1C0 MEng Electronic Engineering with International Study (4 years)
Duration: 4FT Hon
Entry Requirements: *GCE:* AAB-ABB. *SQAH:* AAABB-AABBB. *SQAAH:* ABB-BBB. *BTEC ExtDip:* DDM.

F66 FARNBOROUGH COLLEGE OF TECHNOLOGY
BOUNDARY ROAD
FARNBOROUGH
HAMPSHIRE GU14 6SB
t: 01252 407028 f: 01252 407041
e: admissions@farn-ct.ac.uk
// www.farn-ct.ac.uk

HP63 BA Media Production
Duration: 3FT Hon
Entry Requirements: *GCE:* 180-200. *OCR ND:* M2 *OCR NED:* M3 Admissions Test required.

G14 UNIVERSITY OF GLAMORGAN, CARDIFF AND PONTYPRIDD
ENQUIRIES AND ADMISSIONS UNIT
PONTYPRIDD CF37 1DL
t: 08456 434030 f: 01443 654050
e: enquiries@glam.ac.uk
// www.glam.ac.uk

H602 BEng Computer Systems Engineering
Duration: 3FT Hon
Entry Requirements: *GCE:* BBC. *BTEC SubDip:* M. *BTEC Dip:* DD. *BTEC ExtDip:* DMM. Interview required.

HP00 BEng Computer Systems Engineering
Duration: 4SW Hon
Entry Requirements: *GCE:* BBC. *BTEC SubDip:* M. *BTEC Dip:* DD. *BTEC ExtDip:* DMM. Interview required.

H601 BEng Electrical & Electronic Engineering
Duration: 3FT Hon
Entry Requirements: *GCE:* BBC. *BTEC SubDip:* M. *BTEC Dip:* DD. *BTEC ExtDip:* DMM. Interview required.

HQ00 BEng Electrical and Electronic Engineering
Duration: 4SW Hon
Entry Requirements: *GCE:* BBC. *BTEC SubDip:* M. *BTEC Dip:* DD. *BTEC ExtDip:* DMM. Interview required.

H640 BEng Electronic & Communication Engineering
Duration: 3FT Hon
Entry Requirements: *GCE:* BBC. *BTEC SubDip:* M. *BTEC Dip:* DD. *BTEC ExtDip:* DMM. Interview required.

HP40 BEng Electronic and Communication Engineering
Duration: 4SW Hon
Entry Requirements: *BTEC SubDip:* M. *BTEC Dip:* DD. *BTEC ExtDip:* DMM.

H609 BSc Electrical and Electronic Engineering (Top-Up)
Duration: 1FT Ord
Entry Requirements: Contact the institution for details.

H605 FYr Electrical & Electronic Engineering Foundation Year
Duration: 1FT FYr
Entry Requirements: *GCE:* 40. *BTEC SubDip:* M. *BTEC Dip:* PP. *BTEC ExtDip:* PPP. Interview required.

006H HND Electrical & Electronic Engineering
Duration: 2FT/3SW HND
Entry Requirements: *GCE:* DD. *IB:* 24. *BTEC SubDip:* D. *BTEC Dip:* MP. *BTEC ExtDip:* PPP. *OCR ND:* M2

G28 UNIVERSITY OF GLASGOW
71 SOUTHPARK AVENUE
UNIVERSITY OF GLASGOW
GLASGOW G12 8QQ
t: 0141 330 6062 f: 0141 330 2961
e: student.recruitment@glasgow.ac.uk
// www.glasgow.ac.uk

H641 BEng Audio and Video Engineering
Duration: 4FT Hon
Entry Requirements: *GCE:* ABB. *SQAH:* AAAB-BBB. *IB:* 32.

GHP6 BEng Electronic and Software Engineering
Duration: 4FT Hon
Entry Requirements: *GCE:* ABB. *SQAH:* AAAB-BBB. *IB:* 32.

H600 BEng Electronics and Electrical Engineering
Duration: 4FT Hon
Entry Requirements: *GCE:* ABB. *SQAH:* AAAB-BBB. *IB:* 32.

H6W3 BEng Electronics with Music
Duration: 4FT Hon
Entry Requirements: *GCE:* ABB. *SQAH:* AAAB-BBB. *IB:* 32.

H613 BEng Microcomputer Systems Engineering
Duration: 4FT Hon
Entry Requirements: *GCE:* ABB. *SQAH:* AAAB-BBB. *IB:* 32.

GH66 BSc Electronic and Software Engineering
Duration: 4FT Hon
Entry Requirements: *GCE:* ABB. *SQAH:* AAAB-BBBB. *IB:* 32.

HJ69 MEng Audio and Video Engineering
Duration: 5FT Hon
Entry Requirements: *GCE:* AAB. *SQAH:* AAAA-AAABB. *IB:* 34.

H640 MEng Audio and Video Engineering (Faster Route)
Duration: 4FT Hon
Entry Requirements: *GCE:* AAA. *SQAH:* AB. *SQAAH:* AA. *IB:* 38.

HG66 MEng Electronic and Software Engineering
Duration: 5FT Hon
Entry Requirements: *GCE:* AAB. *SQAH:* AAAA-AAABB. *IB:* 34.

H601 MEng Electronics and Electrical Engineering
Duration: 5FT Hon
Entry Requirements: *GCE:* AAB. *SQAH:* AAAA-AAABB. *IB:* 34.

H603 MEng Electronics and Electrical Engineering (Faster Route)
Duration: 4FT Hon
Entry Requirements: *GCE:* AAA. *SQAH:* AB. *SQAAH:* AA. *IB:* 38.

H6WJ MEng Electronics with Music
Duration: 5FT Hon
Entry Requirements: *GCE:* AAB. *SQAH:* AAAA-AAABB. *IB:* 34.

H614 MEng Microcomputer Systems Engineering
Duration: 5FT Hon
Entry Requirements: *GCE:* AAB. *SQAH:* AAAA-AAABB. *IB:* 34.

H611 MEng Microcomputer Systems Engineering (Faster Route)
Duration: 4FT Deg
Entry Requirements: *GCE:* AAA. *SQAH:* AB. *SQAAH:* AA. *IB:* 38.

G42 GLASGOW CALEDONIAN UNIVERSITY
STUDENT RECRUITMENT & ADMISSIONS SERVICE
CITY CAMPUS
COWCADDENS ROAD
GLASGOW G4 0BA
t: 0141 331 3000 f: 0141 331 8676
e: undergraduate@gcu.ac.uk
// www.gcu.ac.uk

H630 BEng Electrical Power Engineering
Duration: 4FT/5SW Hon
Entry Requirements: *GCE:* BC. *SQAH:* BBBC.

H661 BEng Instrumentation Systems Engineering
Duration: 4FT/5SW Hon
Entry Requirements: Contact the institution for details.

GH46 BEng Network and Communications Engineering
Duration: 4FT/5SW Hon
Entry Requirements: Contact the institution for details.

H691 BEng Robotic and Mechatronic Systems Engineering
Duration: 4FT/5SW Hon
Entry Requirements: Contact the institution for details.

GH4P BSc Computer and Communications Systems Engineering
Duration: 4FT Hon
Entry Requirements: Contact the institution for details.

H692 BSc Instrumentation and Robotic Systems Engineering
Duration: 4FT Hon
Entry Requirements: Contact the institution for details.

HH36 MENG Mechanical Power Plant Systems
Duration: 5FT/6SW Hon
Entry Requirements: Contact the institution for details.

H631 MEng Electrical Power Engineering
Duration: 5FT/6SW Hon
Entry Requirements: Contact the institution for details.

G53 GLYNDWR UNIVERSITY
PLAS COCH
MOLD ROAD
WREXHAM LL11 2AW
t: 01978 293439 f: 01978 290008
e: sid@glyndwr.ac.uk
// www.glyndwr.ac.uk

HW66 BA Television Production and Technology
Duration: 3FT Hon
Entry Requirements: GCE: 240.

H600 BEng Electrical and Electronic Engineering
Duration: 3FT Hon
Entry Requirements: GCE: 240.

HH36 BEng Renewable Energy and Sustainable Technologies
Duration: 3FT Hon
Entry Requirements: GCE: 240.

HWP3 BSc Studio Recording and Performance Technology
Duration: 3FT Hon
Entry Requirements: GCE: 240.

G70 UNIVERSITY OF GREENWICH
GREENWICH CAMPUS
OLD ROYAL NAVAL COLLEGE
PARK ROW
LONDON SE10 9LS
t: 020 8331 9000 f: 020 8331 8145
e: courseinfo@gre.ac.uk
// www.gre.ac.uk

H640 BEng Communications Systems and Software Engineering
Duration: 3FT Hon
Entry Requirements: GCE: 260-300. IB: 24.

H6G6 BEng Computer Systems and Software Engineering
Duration: 3FT/4SW Hon
Entry Requirements: GCE: 260-300. IB: 24.

H6GP BEng Computer Systems with Software Engineering (incl Foundation)
Duration: 4FT Hon
Entry Requirements: GCE: 160. IB: 24.

H663 BEng Control and Instrumentation Engineering
Duration: 3FT Hon
Entry Requirements: GCE: 260-280. IB: 24.

H660 BEng Control and Instrumentation Engineering (incl Foundation)
Duration: 4FT Hon
Entry Requirements: GCE: 160. IB: 24.

H620 BEng Electrical Engineering
Duration: 3FT Hon
Entry Requirements: GCE: 260-280. IB: 24.

H600 BEng Electrical and Electronic Engineering
Duration: 3FT Hon
Entry Requirements: GCE: 260-280. IB: 24.

H609 BEng Electrical and Electronic Engineering (Extended)
Duration: 4FT Hon
Entry Requirements: GCE: 160. IB: 24.

H690 BEng Electrical and Electronic Engineering Technology
Duration: 3FT Hon
Entry Requirements: GCE: 200-220. IB: 24.

H610 BEng Electronic Engineering
Duration: 3FT Hon
Entry Requirements: GCE: 260-280. IB: 24.

H608 BEng Electronic Engineering (Extended)
Duration: 4FT Hon
Entry Requirements: Contact the institution for details.

HP41 BEng Telecommunications Systems Engineering
Duration: 3FT Hon
Entry Requirements: Contact the institution for details.

H641 BEng Wireless Mobile Communication Systems Engineering
Duration: 3FT Hon
Entry Requirements: *GCE:* 260-300. *IB:* 24.

H622 BEng(Hons) Sustainable Electrical Power Engineering
Duration: 3FT/4SW Hon
Entry Requirements: Contact the institution for details.

H602 FdEng Electrical and Electronic Engineering
Duration: 2FT Fdg
Entry Requirements: *GCE:* 160. *IB:* 24.

H603 MEng Electrical and Electronic Engineering
Duration: 4FT Hon
Entry Requirements: *GCE:* 320-360.

H645 MEng Wireless Mobile Communications Systems Engineering
Duration: 4FT Hon
Entry Requirements: *GCE:* 320-360. *IB:* 30.

G80 GRIMSBY INSTITUTE OF FURTHER AND HIGHER EDUCATION
NUNS CORNER
GRIMSBY
NE LINCOLNSHIRE DN34 5BQ
t: 0800 328 3631
e: headmissions@grimsby.ac.uk
// www.grimsby.ac.uk

006H HNC Engineering (Electrical/Electronic)
Duration: 1FT HNC
Entry Requirements: Contact the institution for details.

106H HND Engineering (Electrical/Electronic)
Duration: 2FT HND
Entry Requirements: Contact the institution for details.

H24 HERIOT-WATT UNIVERSITY, EDINBURGH
EDINBURGH CAMPUS
EDINBURGH EH14 4AS
t: 0131 449 5111 f: 0131 451 3630
e: ugadmissions@hw.ac.uk
// www.hw.ac.uk

GH46 BEng Computing and Electronics
Duration: 4FT Hon
Entry Requirements: *GCE:* BBB. *SQAH:* AABB-BBBBC. *SQAAH:* BB. *IB:* 29. Interview required.

HQ30 BEng Electrical Power and Energy
Duration: 4FT Hon
Entry Requirements: *GCE:* BBB. *SQAH:* AABB-BBBBC. *SQAAH:* BB. *IB:* 29. Interview required.

H600 BEng Electrical and Electronic Engineering
Duration: 4FT Hon
Entry Requirements: *GCE:* BBB. *SQAH:* AABB-BBBBC. *SQAAH:* BB. *IB:* 29. Interview required.

HP71 BEng Robotics, Autonomous and Interactive Systems
Duration: 4FT Hon
Entry Requirements: *GCE:* BBB. *SQAH:* AABB-BBBBC. *SQAAH:* BB. *IB:* 29. Interview required.

F3H6 BSc Physics with Electronic Engineering
Duration: 4FT Hon
Entry Requirements: *GCE:* BBB. *SQAH:* AABB-BBBBC. *SQAAH:* BB. *IB:* 29.

GHK6 MEng Computing and Electronics
Duration: 5FT Hon
Entry Requirements: *GCE:* BBB. *SQAH:* AABB-BBBBC. *SQAAH:* BB. *IB:* 29. Interview required.

HP32 MEng Electrical Power and Energy
Duration: 5FT Hon
Entry Requirements: *GCE:* BBB. *SQAH:* AABB-BBBBC. *SQAAH:* BB. *IB:* 29. Interview required.

H605 MEng Electrical and Electronic Engineering (5 years)
Duration: 5FT Hon
Entry Requirements: *GCE:* BBB. *SQAH:* AABB-BBBBC. *SQAAH:* BB. *IB:* 29. Interview required.

H601 MEng Industrial Engineering (Electrical and Electronic)
Duration: 5FT Hon
Entry Requirements: *GCE:* BBB. *SQAH:* AABB-BBBBC. *SQAAH:* BB. *IB:* 29. Interview required.

H671 MEng Robotics, Autonomous and Interactive Systems
Duration: 5FT Hon
Entry Requirements: *GCE:* BBB. *SQAH:* AABB-BBBBC. *SQAAH:* BB. *IB:* 29. Interview required.

F3HP MPhys Physics with Electronic Engineering
Duration: 5FT Hon
Entry Requirements: *GCE:* BBB. *SQAH:* AABB. *SQAAH:* BB. *IB:* 29.

H36 UNIVERSITY OF HERTFORDSHIRE
UNIVERSITY ADMISSIONS SERVICE
COLLEGE LANE
HATFIELD
HERTS AL10 9AB
t: 01707 284800
// www.herts.ac.uk

H641 BEng Digital Communications and Electronics
Duration: 3FT/4SW Hon
Entry Requirements: *GCE:* 260.

H645 BEng Digital Communications and Electronics (Extended)
Duration: 4FT/5SW Hon
Entry Requirements: *GCE:* 80.

H651 BEng Digital Systems and Computer Engineering
Duration: 3FT/4SW Hon
Entry Requirements: *GCE:* 260.

H653 BEng Digital Systems and Computer Engineering (Extended)
Duration: 4FT/5SW Hon
Entry Requirements: *GCE:* 80.

H600 BEng Electrical and Electronic Engineering
Duration: 3FT/4SW Hon
Entry Requirements: *GCE:* 260.

H606 BEng Electrical and Electronic Engineering (Extended)
Duration: 4FT/5SW Hon
Entry Requirements: *GCE:* 80.

WH66 BSc Digital Film and Television Technology
Duration: 3FT/4SW Hon
Entry Requirements: *GCE:* 240.

WH6P BSc Digital Rights Technology
Duration: 3FT/4SW Hon
Entry Requirements: *GCE:* 240.

HW66 BSc Film and TV Production
Duration: 3FT/4SW Hon
Entry Requirements: *GCE:* 240.

HG66 BSc Games and Graphics Hardware Technology
Duration: 3FT/4FT Hon
Entry Requirements: *GCE:* 240.

HG6P BSc Games and Graphics Hardware Technology (Extended)
Duration: 4FT/5SW Hon
Entry Requirements: Contact the institution for details.

H646 MEng Digital Communications and Electronics
Duration: 4FT/5SW Hon
Entry Requirements: *GCE:* 320.

H654 MEng Digital Systems and Computer Engineering
Duration: 4FT/5SW Hon
Entry Requirements: *GCE:* 320.

H49 UNIVERSITY OF THE HIGHLANDS AND ISLANDS
UHI EXECUTIVE OFFICE
NESS WALK
INVERNESS
SCOTLAND IV3 5SQ
t: 01463 279000 f: 01463 279001
e: info@uhi.ac.uk
// www.uhi.ac.uk

HH36 BEng Electrical and Mechanical Engineering
Duration: 1FT Ord
Entry Requirements: HND required.

H642 BSc Audio Engineering
Duration: 3FT Hon
Entry Requirements: Interview required.

H600 BSc Electrical and Electronic Engineering
Duration: 1FT Ord
Entry Requirements: HND required.

356H HNC Engineering Systems
Duration: 1FT HNC
Entry Requirements: *GCE:* D. *SQAH:* C.

056H HND Engineering Systems
Duration: 2FT HND
Entry Requirements: *GCE:* DD. *SQAH:* CC.

H54 HOPWOOD HALL COLLEGE
ROCHDALE ROAD
MIDDLETON
MANCHESTER M24 6XH
t: 0161 643 7560 f: 0161 643 2114
e: admissions@hopwood.ac.uk
// www.hopwood.ac.uk

006H HND Electrical Engineering
Duration: 2FT HND
Entry Requirements: *GCE:* 40. Interview required.

H60 THE UNIVERSITY OF HUDDERSFIELD
QUEENSGATE
HUDDERSFIELD HD1 3DH
t: 01484 473969 f: 01484 472765
e: admissionsandrecords@hud.ac.uk
// www.hud.ac.uk

HW63 BA Music Technology
Duration: 3FT/4SW Hon
Entry Requirements: *GCE:* 300.

H6G4 BEng Computer Systems Engineering
Duration: 3FT/4SW Hon
Entry Requirements: *GCE:* 280.

H610 BEng Electronic Engineering
Duration: 3FT Hon
Entry Requirements: *GCE:* 300.

GH46 BEng Electronic Engineering and Computer Systems
Duration: 3FT Hon
Entry Requirements: *GCE:* 300.

H640 BEng Electronic and Communication Engineering
Duration: 3FT Hon
Entry Requirements: *GCE:* 300.

H600 BEng Electronic and Electrical Engineering
Duration: 3FT Hon
Entry Requirements: *GCE:* 300.

H602 BEng Engineering with Technology Management (Electronic & Electrical)
Duration: 2SW/1FT Hon
Entry Requirements: HND required.

HJ6X BSc Electronics and Music Technology
Duration: 3FT/4SW Hon
Entry Requirements: *GCE:* 260. *SQAH:* BBBB. *IB:* 26.

H6W3 BSc Music Technology and Audio Systems
Duration: 3FT/4SW Hon
Entry Requirements: *GCE:* 300.

H612 MEng Electronic Engineering
Duration: 4FT Hon
Entry Requirements: *GCE:* 340.

H611 MEng Electronic and Electrical Engineering
Duration: 5SW Hon
Entry Requirements: *GCE:* 340.

H72 THE UNIVERSITY OF HULL
THE UNIVERSITY OF HULL
COTTINGHAM ROAD
HULL HU6 7RX
t: 01482 466100 f: 01482 442290
e: admissions@hull.ac.uk
// www.hull.ac.uk

H610 BEng Electronic Engineering
Duration: 3FT Hon
Entry Requirements: *GCE:* 280. *IB:* 27. *BTEC ExtDip:* DMM.

H603 BEng Electronic Engineering (with foundation year)
Duration: 4FT Hon
Entry Requirements: Contact the institution for details.

H600 BSc Computer Systems Engineering
Duration: 3FT Hon
Entry Requirements: *GCE:* 280-300. *IB:* 25. *BTEC ExtDip:* MMM.

H601 BSc Computer Systems Engineering (with foundation year)
Duration: 4FT Hon
Entry Requirements: Contact the institution for details.

H650 BSc Computer Systems Engineering with Industrial Experience
Duration: 4FT Hon
Entry Requirements: *GCE:* 280-300. *IB:* 25. *BTEC ExtDip:* MMM.

H606 MEng Computer Systems Engineering
Duration: 4FT Hon
Entry Requirements: Contact the institution for details.

H602 MEng Electronic Engineering
Duration: 4FT Hon
Entry Requirements: *GCE:* 320. *IB:* 30. *BTEC ExtDip:* DDD.

I50 IMPERIAL COLLEGE LONDON
REGISTRY
SOUTH KENSINGTON CAMPUS
IMPERIAL COLLEGE LONDON
LONDON SW7 2AZ
t: 020 7589 5111 f: 020 7594 8004
// www.imperial.ac.uk

H600 BEng Electrical & Electronic Engineering
Duration: 3FT Hon
Entry Requirements: *GCE:* A*AA. *SQAAH:* AAA. *IB:* 38.

HG65 BEng Electronic and Information Engineering
Duration: 3FT Hon
Entry Requirements: *GCE:* A*AA. *SQAAH:* AAA. *IB:* 38.

H604 MEng Electrical & Electronic Engineering
Duration: 4FT Hon
Entry Requirements: *GCE:* A*AA. *SQAAH:* AAA. *IB:* 38.

H6N2 MEng Electrical & Electronic Engineering with Management
Duration: 4FT Hon
Entry Requirements: *GCE:* A*AA. *SQAAH:* AAA. *IB:* 38.

H601 MEng Electrical & Electronic Engineering with a Year Abroad
Duration: 4FT Hon
Entry Requirements: *GCE:* A*AA. *SQAAH:* AAA. *IB:* 38.

GH56 MEng Electronic and Information Engineering
Duration: 4FT Hon
Entry Requirements: *GCE:* A*AA. *SQAAH:* AAA. *IB:* 38.

HG6M MEng Electronic and Information Engineering with a Year Abroad
Duration: 4FT Hon
Entry Requirements: *GCE:* A*AA. *SQAAH:* AAA. *IB:* 38.

K24 THE UNIVERSITY OF KENT
RECRUITMENT & ADMISSIONS OFFICE
REGISTRY
UNIVERSITY OF KENT
CANTERBURY, KENT CT2 7NZ
t: 01227 827272 f: 01227 827077
e: information@kent.ac.uk
// www.kent.ac.uk

H618 BEng Computer Systems Engineering
Duration: 3FT Hon
Entry Requirements: *GCE:* 300. *IB:* 33. *OCR ND:* M1 *OCR NED:* M1

H614 BEng Computer Systems Engineering including a foundation year (4 years)
Duration: 4FT Hon
Entry Requirements: *GCE:* 160. *IB:* 33.

H615 BEng Computer Systems Engineering with a year in Industry (4 years)
Duration: 4SW Hon
Entry Requirements: *GCE:* 300. *IB:* 33. *OCR ND:* M1 *OCR NED:* M1

H619 BEng Electronic and Communication Engineering
Duration: 3FT Hon
Entry Requirements: *GCE:* 300. *IB:* 33. *OCR ND:* M1 *OCR NED:* M1

H605 BEng Electronic and Communication Engineering including a foundation year (4 years)
Duration: 4FT Hon
Entry Requirements: *GCE:* 160. *IB:* 33.

H604 BEng Electronic and Communications Engineering with a year in Industry
Duration: 4SW Hon
Entry Requirements: *GCE:* 300. *IB:* 33. *OCR ND:* M1 *OCR NED:* M1

H691 BEng Electronic and Computer Systems (Top-up)
Duration: 1FT Hon
Entry Requirements: Contact the institution for details.

H609 FYr Electronic Engineering International Foundation Programme
Duration: 1FT FYr
Entry Requirements: Contact the institution for details.

H624 FdEng Engineering (Electrical Engineering)
Duration: 2FT Hon
Entry Requirements: *OCR NED:* M2

H610 FdEng Engineering (Electronic Engineering)
Duration: 2FT Hon
Entry Requirements: *OCR NED:* M2

H613 MEng Computer Systems Engineering
Duration: 4FT Hon
Entry Requirements: *GCE:* 320. *IB:* 33. *OCR ND:* D *OCR NED:* D2

H617 MEng Computer Systems Engineering with a Year in Industry
Duration: 5FT Hon
Entry Requirements: *GCE:* 320. *IB:* 33. *OCR ND:* D *OCR NED:* D2

H607 MEng Electronic and Communications Engineering
Duration: 4FT Hon
Entry Requirements: *GCE:* 320. *IB:* 33. *OCR ND:* D *OCR NED:* D2

H608 MEng Electronic and Communications Engineering with a Year in Industry
Duration: 5FT Hon
Entry Requirements: *GCE:* 320. *IB:* 33. *OCR ND:* D *OCR NED:* D2

K60 KING'S COLLEGE LONDON (UNIVERSITY OF LONDON)
STRAND
LONDON WC2R 2LS
t: 020 7836 5454 f: 020 7848 7171
e: prospective@kcl.ac.uk
// www.kcl.ac.uk/prospectus

G0H6 BSc Computer Science with Robotics
Duration: 3FT Hon
Entry Requirements: *GCE:* AAAc. *SQAH:* AAB. *SQAAH:* AA. *IB:* 38.

H6G0 MSci Robotics and Intelligent Systems
Duration: 4FT Hon
Entry Requirements: *GCE:* AAA. *IB:* 36.

K84 KINGSTON UNIVERSITY
STUDENT INFORMATION & ADVICE CENTRE
COOPER HOUSE
40-46 SURBITON ROAD
KINGSTON UPON THAMES KT1 2HX
t: 0844 8552177 f: 020 8547 7080
e: aps@kingston.ac.uk
// www.kingston.ac.uk

H625 BSc Communication Systems
Duration: 3FT Hon
Entry Requirements: *GCE:* 200-280. Interview required.

H640 BSc Communication Systems
Duration: 4SW Hon
Entry Requirements: *GCE:* 160-280. Interview required.

H628 BSc Communication Systems (Foundation)
Duration: 4FT Hon
Entry Requirements: *GCE:* 60.

GHLP BSc Computer Science (Computer Graphics & Digital Imaging) (including year 0)
Duration: 4FT Hon
Entry Requirements: *GCE:* 80.

GH4P BSc Computer Science (Computer Graphics and Digital Imaging)
Duration: 3FT Hon
Entry Requirements: *GCE:* 280. *IB:* 24.

GHL6 BSc Computer Science (Computer Graphics and Digital Imaging)
Duration: 4SW Hon
Entry Requirements: *GCE:* 280. *IB:* 24.

GHK6 BSc Computer Science (Network Communications)
Duration: 4SW Hon
Entry Requirements: *GCE:* 280. *IB:* 24.

HW66 BSc Television & Video Technology
Duration: 3FT Hon
Entry Requirements: *GCE:* 240-280.

HW6P BSc Television & Video Technology
Duration: 4SW Hon
Entry Requirements: *GCE:* 240-280.

L14 LANCASTER UNIVERSITY
THE UNIVERSITY
LANCASTER
LANCASHIRE LA1 4YW
t: 01524 592029 f: 01524 846243
e: ugadmissions@lancaster.ac.uk
// www.lancs.ac.uk

H647 BEng Communication Systems and Electronics
Duration: 3FT Hon
Entry Requirements: *GCE:* ABB. *SQAH:* BBBBB. *SQAAH:* BBB. *IB:* 32.

HH66 BEng Computer Systems Engineering
Duration: 3FT Hon
Entry Requirements: *GCE:* AAB. *SQAH:* ABBBB. *SQAAH:* AAB. *IB:* 35.

H607 BEng Electronic and Electrical Engineering
Duration: 3FT Hon
Entry Requirements: *GCE:* AAB. *SQAH:* ABBBB. *SQAAH:* AAB. *IB:* 35.

HH63 BEng Mechatronics
Duration: 3FT Hon
Entry Requirements: *GCE:* AAB. *SQAH:* ABBBB. *SQAAH:* AAB. *IB:* 35.

GH56 BSc Information Technology for Creative Industries
Duration: 3FT Hon
Entry Requirements: *GCE:* ABB. *SQAH:* BBBBB. *SQAAH:* BBB. *IB:* 32.

H648 MEng Communication Systems and Electronics (with Industrial Experience)
Duration: 4FT Hon
Entry Requirements: *GCE:* AAB. *SQAH:* ABBBB. *SQAAH:* AAB. *IB:* 35.

HHP6 MEng Computer Systems Engineering
Duration: 4FT Hon
Entry Requirements: *GCE:* AAA. *SQAH:* AAABB. *SQAAH:* AAA. *IB:* 36.

H606 MEng Electronic and Electrical Engineering
Duration: 4FT Hon
Entry Requirements: *GCE:* AAA. *SQAH:* AAABB. *SQAAH:* AAA. *IB:* 36.

HHH6 MEng Mechatronics
Duration: 4FT Hon
Entry Requirements: *GCE:* AAA. *SQAH:* AAABB. *SQAAH:* AAA. *IB:* 36.

GH5P MSci Information Technology for Creative Industries
Duration: 4FT Hon
Entry Requirements: *GCE:* AAB. *SQAH:* ABBBB. *SQAAH:* AAB. *IB:* 35.

L21 LEEDS CITY COLLEGE
TECHNOLOGY CAMPUS
COOKRIDGE STREET
LEEDS LS2 8BL
t: 0113 216 2406 f: 0113 216 2401
e: helen.middleton@leedscitycollege.ac.uk
// www.leedscitycollege.ac.uk

H600 BEng Electrical and Electronic Engineering
Duration: 1FT Hon
Entry Requirements: HND required.

H602 FdSc Electrical and Electronic Engineering
Duration: 2FT Fdg
Entry Requirements: *GCE:* 80.

L23 UNIVERSITY OF LEEDS
THE UNIVERSITY OF LEEDS
WOODHOUSE LANE
LEEDS LS2 9JT
t: 0113 343 3999
e: admissions@leeds.ac.uk
// www.leeds.ac.uk

HF6X BSc Nanotechnology (Physical)
Duration: 3FT Hon
Entry Requirements: *GCE:* AAB. *SQAAH:* AAB. *IB:* 35.

H610 MEng/BEng Electronic Engineering
Duration: 3FT/4FT Hon
Entry Requirements: *GCE:* AAA. *SQAAH:* AAA. *IB:* 38.

H640 MEng/BEng Electronic and Communications Engineering
Duration: 3FT/4FT Hon
Entry Requirements: *GCE:* AAA. *SQAAH:* AAA. *IB:* 38.

H600 MEng/BEng Electronic and Electrical Engineering
Duration: 3FT/4FT Hon
Entry Requirements: *GCE:* AAA. *SQAAH:* AAA. *IB:* 38.

HF63 MEng/BEng Electronics and Nanotechnology
Duration: 3FT/4FT Hon
Entry Requirements: *GCE:* AAA. *SQAAH:* AAA. *IB:* 38.

HH36 MEng/BEng Mechatronics and Robotics
Duration: 3FT/4FT Hon
Entry Requirements: *GCE:* AAA. *SQAAH:* AAA. *IB:* 38.

L27 LEEDS METROPOLITAN UNIVERSITY
COURSE ENQUIRIES OFFICE
CITY CAMPUS
LEEDS LS1 3HE
t: 0113 81 23113 f: 0113 81 23129
// www.leedsmet.ac.uk

HP63 BSc Broadcast Media Technologies
Duration: 3FT Hon
Entry Requirements: *GCE:* 200. *IB:* 24. Interview required.

L34 UNIVERSITY OF LEICESTER
UNIVERSITY ROAD
LEICESTER LE1 7RH
t: 0116 252 5281 f: 0116 252 2447
e: admissions@le.ac.uk
// www.le.ac.uk

H640 BEng Communications and Electronic Engineering
Duration: 3FT Hon
Entry Requirements: *GCE:* BBB-BBC. *SQAH:* BBBBB-BBBCC. *SQAAH:* BBB-BBC.

H641 BEng Communications and Electronic Engineering (with Year in Industry)
Duration: 4FT Hon
Entry Requirements: *GCE:* BBB-BBC. *SQAH:* BBBBB-BBBCC. *SQAAH:* BBB-BBC.

H690 BEng Communications and Electronic Engineering (with a Year Abroad)
Duration: 3FT Hon
Entry Requirements: *GCE:* BBB-BBC. *SQAH:* BBBBB-BBBCC. *SQAAH:* BBB-BBC. *IB:* 30.

H604 BEng Electrical and Electronic Engineering
Duration: 3FT Hon
Entry Requirements: *GCE:* BBB-BBC. *SQAH:* BBBBB-BBBCC. *SQAAH:* BBB-BBC.

H609 BEng Electrical and Electronic Engineering (with Year in Industry)
Duration: 4SW Hon
Entry Requirements: *GCE:* BBB-BBC. *SQAH:* BBBBB-BBBCC. *SQAAH:* BBB-BBC.

H600 BEng Electrical and Electronic Engineering (with a Year Abroad)
Duration: 3FT Hon
Entry Requirements: *GCE:* BBB-BBC. *SQAH:* BBBBB-BBBCC. *SQAAH:* BBB-BBC.

GH6Q BEng Software and Electronic Engineering
Duration: 3FT Hon
Entry Requirements: *GCE:* BBB-BBC. *SQAH:* BBBBB-BBBCC. *SQAAH:* BBB-BBC.

HGQQ BEng Software and Electronic Engineering (with Year in Industry)
Duration: 3FT Hon
Entry Requirements: *GCE:* BBB-BBC. *SQAH:* BBBBB-BBBCC. *SQAAH:* BBB-BBC.

GHQQ BEng Software and Electronic Engineering (with a Year Abroad)
Duration: 3FT Hon
Entry Requirements: *GCE:* BBB-BBC. *SQAH:* BBBBB-BBBCC. *SQAAH:* BBB-BBC.

H643 MEng Communications and Electronic Engineering
Duration: 4FT Hon
Entry Requirements: *GCE:* AAB-ABB. *SQAH:* AAABB-AABBB. *SQAAH:* AAB-ABB.

H644 MEng Communications and Electronic Engineering (with Year in Industry)
Duration: 5FT Hon
Entry Requirements: *GCE:* AAB-ABB. *SQAH:* AAABB-AABBB. *SQAAH:* AAB-ABB.

H691 MEng Communications and Electronic Engineering (with a year abroad)
Duration: 4FT Hon
Entry Requirements: *GCE:* AAB-ABB. *SQAH:* AAABB-AABBB. *SQAAH:* AAB-ABB.

H603 MEng Electrical & Electronic Engineering (with a year abroad)
Duration: 4FT Hon
Entry Requirements: *GCE:* AAB-ABB. *SQAH:* AAABB-AABBB. *SQAAH:* AAB-ABB.

H606 MEng Electrical and Electronic Engineering
Duration: 4FT Hon
Entry Requirements: *GCE:* AAB-ABB. *SQAH:* AAABB-AABBB. *SQAAH:* AAB-ABB.

H607 MEng Electrical and Electronic Engineering (with Year in Industry)
Duration: 5SW Hon
Entry Requirements: *GCE:* AAB-ABB. *SQAH:* AAABB-AABBB. *SQAAH:* AAB-ABB.

GHQP MEng Software and Electronic Engineering
Duration: 4FT Hon
Entry Requirements: *GCE:* AAB-ABB. *SQAH:* AAABB-AABBB. *SQAAH:* AAB-ABB.

HGQP MEng Software and Electronic Engineering (with Year in Industry)
Duration: 4FT Hon
Entry Requirements: *GCE:* AAB-ABB. *SQAH:* AAABB-AABBB. *SQAAH:* AAB-ABB.

HG6Q MEng Software and Electronic Engineering (with a year abroad)
Duration: 4FT Hon
Entry Requirements: *GCE:* AAB-ABB. *SQAH:* AAABB-AABBB. *SQAAH:* AAB-ABB.

L41 THE UNIVERSITY OF LIVERPOOL
THE FOUNDATION BUILDING
BROWNLOW HILL
LIVERPOOL L69 7ZX
t: 0151 794 2000 f: 0151 708 6502
e: ugrecruitment@liv.ac.uk
// www.liv.ac.uk

HH66 BEng Computer Science and Electronic Engineering
Duration: 3FT Hon
Entry Requirements: *GCE:* ABB. *SQAAH:* ABB. *IB:* 33.

HG6L BEng Computer Science and Electronic Engineering with a Year in Industry
Duration: 4FT Hon
Entry Requirements: *GCE:* ABB. *SQAAH:* ABB. *IB:* 33.

H620 BEng Electrical Engineering
Duration: 3FT Hon
Entry Requirements: *GCE:* ABB. *SQAAH:* ABB. *IB:* 33.

H603 BEng Electrical Engineering and Electronics
Duration: 3FT Hon
Entry Requirements: *GCE:* ABB. *SQAAH:* ABB. *IB:* 33.

H605 BEng Electrical Engineering and Electronics with a Year in Industry
Duration: 4FT Hon
Entry Requirements: *GCE:* ABB. *SQAAH:* ABB. *IB:* 33.

H624 BEng Electrical Engineering with a Year in Industry
Duration: 4FT Hon
Entry Requirements: *GCE:* ABB. *SQAAH:* ABB. *IB:* 33.

H621 BEng Electronic and Communication Engineering
Duration: 3FT Hon
Entry Requirements: *GCE:* ABB. *SQAAH:* ABB. *IB:* 33.

H622 BEng Electronic and Communications Engineering with a Year in Industry
Duration: 4FT Hon
Entry Requirements: *GCE:* ABB. *SQAAH:* ABB. *IB:* 33.

H610 BEng Electronics
Duration: 3FT Hon
Entry Requirements: *GCE:* ABB. *SQAAH:* ABB. *IB:* 33.

H613 BEng Electronics with a Year in Industry
Duration: 4FT Hon
Entry Requirements: *GCE:* ABB. *SQAAH:* ABB. *IB:* 33.

HH67 BEng Mechatronics and Robotic Systems
Duration: 3FT Hon
Entry Requirements: *GCE:* ABB. *SQAAH:* ABB. *IB:* 33.

HHP7 BEng Mechatronics and Robotic Systems with a Year in Industry
Duration: 4FT Hon
Entry Requirements: *GCE:* ABB. *SQAAH:* ABB. *IB:* 33.

GHK6 MEng Computer Science and Electronic Engineering (4 years)
Duration: 4FT Hon
Entry Requirements: *GCE:* ABB. *SQAAH:* ABB. *IB:* 33.

GHKP MEng Computer Science and Electronic Engineering with a Year in Industry
Duration: 5FT Hon
Entry Requirements: *GCE:* ABB. *SQAAH:* ABB. *IB:* 33.

H606 MEng Electrical Engineering and Electronics (4 years)
Duration: 4FT Hon
Entry Requirements: *GCE:* ABB. *SQAAH:* ABB. *IB:* 33.

H607 MEng Electrical Engineering and Electronics with a Year in Industry
Duration: 5FT Hon
Entry Requirements: *GCE:* ABB. *SQAAH:* ABB. *IB:* 33.

H646 MEng Electronic and Communication Engineering (4 years)
Duration: 4FT Hon
Entry Requirements: *GCE:* ABB. *SQAAH:* ABB. *IB:* 33.

H623 MEng Electronic and Communication Engineering with a Year in Industry
Duration: 5FT Hon
Entry Requirements: *GCE:* ABB. *SQAAH:* ABB. *IB:* 33.

H602 MEng Electronics (4 years)
Duration: 4FT Hon
Entry Requirements: *GCE:* ABB. *SQAAH:* ABB. *IB:* 33.

H614 MEng Electronics with a Year in Industry
Duration: 5FT Hon
Entry Requirements: *GCE:* ABB. *SQAAH:* ABB. *IB:* 33.

HH76 MEng Mechatronics and Robotic Systems (4 years)
Duration: 4FT Hon
Entry Requirements: *GCE:* ABB. *SQAAH:* ABB. *IB:* 33.

HHR6 MEng Mechatronics and Robotic Systems with a Year in Industry
Duration: 5FT Hon
Entry Requirements: *GCE:* ABB. *SQAAH:* ABB. *IB:* 33.

L42 LINCOLN COLLEGE
MONKS ROAD
LINCOLN LN2 5HQ
t: 01522 876000 f: 01522 876200
e: enquiries@lincolncollege.ac.uk
// www.lincolncollege.ac.uk

H600 HNC Electrical and Electronic Engineering
Duration: 1FT HNC
Entry Requirements: Contact the institution for details.

006H HND Electrical and Electronic Engineering
Duration: 2FT HND
Entry Requirements: *GCE:* 80. Interview required.

L43 LIVERPOOL COMMUNITY COLLEGE
LIVERPOOL COMMUNITY COLLEGE
CLARENCE STREET
LIVERPOOL L3 5TP
t: 0151 252 3352 f: 0151 252 3351
e: enquiry@liv-coll.ac.uk
// www.liv-coll.ac.uk

H600 HNC Electrical and Electronic Engineering
Duration: 1FT HNC
Entry Requirements: Contact the institution for details.

H601 HND Electrical and Electronic Engineering
Duration: 2FT HND
Entry Requirements: Contact the institution for details.

L48 THE LIVERPOOL INSTITUTE FOR PERFORMING ARTS
MOUNT STREET
LIVERPOOL L1 9HF
t: 0151 330 3000 f: 0151 330 3131
e: admissions@lipa.ac.uk
// www.lipa.ac.uk

HW63 BA Sound Technology
Duration: 3FT Hon
Entry Requirements: *GCE:* 280. Interview required.

L51 LIVERPOOL JOHN MOORES UNIVERSITY
KINGSWAY HOUSE
HATTON GARDEN
LIVERPOOL L3 2AJ
t: 0151 231 5090 f: 0151 904 6368
e: courses@ljmu.ac.uk
// www.ljmu.ac.uk

H600 BEng Electrical & Electronic Engineering
Duration: 3FT/4SW Hon
Entry Requirements: *GCE:* 260. Interview required. Admissions Test required.

HP63 BSc Broadcast and Media Production
Duration: 3FT/4SW Hon
Entry Requirements: *GCE:* 280. *OCR ND:* M2 *OCR NED:* M2 Interview required.

H610 BSc Computer Technology
Duration: 3FT/4SW Hon
Entry Requirements: *GCE:* 280. Interview required.

H602 MEng Electrical and Electronic Engineering
Duration: 4FT/5SW Hon
Entry Requirements: *GCE:* 280. Interview required. Admissions Test required.

L54 LONDON ELECTRONICS COLLEGE
LONDON ELECTRONICS COLLEGE
20 PENYWERN ROAD
KENSINGTON
LONDON SW5 9SU
t: 020 7373 8721 f: 020 7244 8733
e: contact@lec.org.uk
// www.lec.org.uk

116H HNC Electronics Engineering
Duration: 1FT HNC
Entry Requirements: Interview required. Admissions Test required.

016H HND Electronic Engineering
Duration: 2FT HND
Entry Requirements: Interview required. Admissions Test required.

L62 THE LONDON COLLEGE, UCK
VICTORIA GARDENS
NOTTING HILL GATE
LONDON W11 3PE
t: 020 7243 4000 f: 020 7243 1484
e: admissions@lcuck.ac.uk
// www.lcuck.ac.uk

306H HNC Electrical Engineering
Duration: 1FT HNC
Entry Requirements: Contact the institution for details.

106H HNC Electrical and Electronic Engineering
Duration: 1FT HNC
Entry Requirements: Contact the institution for details.

116H HNC Electronic Engineering
Duration: 1FT HNC
Entry Requirements: Contact the institution for details.

226H HND Electrical Engineering
Duration: 2FT HND
Entry Requirements: Contact the institution for details.

006H HND Electrical and Electronic Engineering
Duration: 2FT HND
Entry Requirements: Contact the institution for details.

216H HND Electronic Engineering
Duration: 2FT HND
Entry Requirements: Contact the institution for details.

L68 LONDON METROPOLITAN UNIVERSITY
166-220 HOLLOWAY ROAD
LONDON N7 8DB
t: 020 7133 4200
e: admissions@londonmet.ac.uk
// www.londonmet.ac.uk

HG65 BEng Computer Systems Engineering
Duration: 3FT Hon
Entry Requirements: *GCE:* 220. *IB:* 28.

H641 BEng Electronic and Communications Engineering
Duration: 3FT Hon
Entry Requirements: *GCE:* 220. *IB:* 28.

HG6K BEng Telecommunications and Network Engineering
Duration: 3FT Hon
Entry Requirements: *GCE:* 220. *IB:* 28.

L75 LONDON SOUTH BANK UNIVERSITY
ADMISSIONS AND RECRUITMENT CENTRE
90 LONDON ROAD
LONDON SE1 6LN
t: 0800 923 8888 f: 020 7815 8273
e: course.enquiry@lsbu.ac.uk
// www.lsbu.ac.uk

H650 BEng Computer Systems and Networks
Duration: 3FT/4SW Hon
Entry Requirements: *GCE:* 240. *IB:* 24.

H600 BEng Electrical and Electronic Engineering
Duration: 3FT/4SW Hon
Entry Requirements: *GCE:* 240. *IB:* 24.

HH36 BEng Mechatronics
Duration: 4SW Hon
Entry Requirements: *GCE:* 240. *IB:* 24.

H640 BEng Telecommunications and Computer Networks Engineering
Duration: 3FT/4SW Hon
Entry Requirements: *GCE:* 240. *IB:* 24.

GH56 BSc Computer Systems and Networks
Duration: 1.5FT Hon
Entry Requirements: HND required.

H601 BSc Electrical and Electronic Engineering
Duration: 1.5FT Hon
Entry Requirements: HND required.

H6H6 BSc Telecommunications and Computer Networks Engineering
Duration: 1.5FT Hon
Entry Requirements: HND required.

H630 FdEng Power Distribution
Duration: 2FT Fdg
Entry Requirements: *GCE:* 200. *IB:* 24.

006H HND Electrical and Electronic Engineering
Duration: 2FT HND
Entry Requirements: *GCE:* 200. *IB:* 24.

L77 LOUGHBOROUGH COLLEGE
RADMOOR ROAD
LOUGHBOROUGH LE11 3BT
t: 0845 166 2950 f: 0845 833 2840
e: info@loucoll.ac.uk
// www.loucoll.ac.uk

H601 BEng Electrical and Electronic Engineering (Top-Up)
Duration: 1FT Hon
Entry Requirements: Contact the institution for details.

H600 FdEng Electrical and Electronic Engineering
Duration: 2FT Fdg
Entry Requirements: *GCE:* 80. Interview required.

006H HND Electronics
Duration: 2FT HND
Entry Requirements: *GCE:* 80. Interview required.

L79 LOUGHBOROUGH UNIVERSITY
LOUGHBOROUGH
LEICESTERSHIRE LE11 3TU
t: 01509 223522 f: 01509 223905
e: admissions@lboro.ac.uk
// www.lboro.ac.uk

H611 BEng Electronic and Computer Systems Engineering
Duration: 3FT Hon
Entry Requirements: *GCE:* ABB. *SQAH:* AABBB. *SQAAH:* BB. *IB:* 32. *BTEC ExtDip:* DMM.

H614 BEng Electronic and Computer Systems Engineering
Duration: 4SW Hon
Entry Requirements: *GCE:* ABB. *SQAH:* AABBB. *SQAAH:* BB. *IB:* 32. *BTEC ExtDip:* DMM.

H600 BEng Electronic and Electrical Engineering
Duration: 3FT Hon
Entry Requirements: *GCE:* ABB. *SQAH:* AABBB. *SQAAH:* BB. *IB:* 32. *BTEC ExtDip:* DMM.

H604 BEng Electronic and Electrical Engineering
Duration: 4SW Hon
Entry Requirements: *GCE:* ABB. *SQAH:* AABBB. *SQAAH:* BB. *IB:* 32. *BTEC ExtDip:* DMM.

H650 BEng Systems Engineering
Duration: 4SW Hon
Entry Requirements: *GCE:* ABB. *SQAH:* AABBB. *SQAAH:* BB. *IB:* 32. *BTEC ExtDip:* DMM.

H652 BEng Systems Engineering
Duration: 3FT Hon
Entry Requirements: *GCE:* ABB. *SQAH:* AABBB. *SQAAH:* BB. *IB:* 32. *BTEC ExtDip:* DMM.

H612 MEng Electronic and Computer Systems Engineering
Duration: 5SW Hon
Entry Requirements: *GCE:* AAA-AAB. *SQAH:* AABBB. *SQAAH:* AB. *IB:* 34. *BTEC ExtDip:* DDM.

H613 MEng Electronic and Computer Systems Engineering
Duration: 4FT Hon
Entry Requirements: *GCE:* AAA-AAB. *SQAH:* AABBB. *SQAAH:* AB. *IB:* 34. *BTEC ExtDip:* DDM.

H601 MEng Electronic and Electrical Engineering
Duration: 4FT Hon
Entry Requirements: *GCE:* AAA-AAB. *SQAH:* AABBB. *SQAAH:* AB. *IB:* 34. *BTEC ExtDip:* DDM.

H605 MEng Electronic and Electrical Engineering
Duration: 5SW Hon
Entry Requirements: *GCE:* AAA-AAB. *SQAH:* AABBB. *SQAAH:* AB. *IB:* 34. *BTEC ExtDip:* DDM.

H641 MEng Systems Engineering
Duration: 5SW Hon
Entry Requirements: *GCE:* AAA-AAB. *SQAH:* AABBB. *SQAAH:* AB. *IB:* 34. *BTEC ExtDip:* DDM.

H660 MEng Systems Engineering
Duration: 4FT Hon
Entry Requirements: *GCE:* AAA-AAB. *SQAH:* AABBB. *SQAAH:* AB. *IB:* 34. *BTEC ExtDip:* DDM.

M10 THE MANCHESTER COLLEGE
OPENSHAW CAMPUS
ASHTON OLD ROAD
OPENSHAW
MANCHESTER M11 2WH
t: 0800 068 8585 f: 0161 920 4103
e: enquiries@themanchestercollege.ac.uk
// www.themanchestercollege.ac.uk

GH46 FdSc Computer System Support
Duration: 2FT Fdg
Entry Requirements: *GCE:* 160. *BTEC ExtDip:* MPP.

M20 THE UNIVERSITY OF MANCHESTER
RUTHERFORD BUILDING
OXFORD ROAD
MANCHESTER M13 9PL
t: 0161 275 2077 f: 0161 275 2106
e: ug-admissions@manchester.ac.uk
// www.manchester.ac.uk

HH66 BEng Computer Systems Engineering
Duration: 3FT Hon
Entry Requirements: *GCE:* AAB. *SQAH:* AAABB. *SQAAH:* AAB. *IB:* 35. *BTEC ExtDip:* DMM. Interview required.

HHQ6 BEng Computer Systems Engineering with Industrial Experience (4 years)
Duration: 4SW Hon
Entry Requirements: *GCE:* AAB. *SQAH:* AAABB. *SQAAH:* AAB. *IB:* 35. Interview required.

H600 BEng Electrical and Electronic Engineering
Duration: 3FT Hon
Entry Requirements: *GCE:* AAB. *SQAH:* AAABB. *SQAAH:* AAB. *IB:* 35. Interview required.

H606 BEng Electrical and Electronic Engineering with Industrial Experience (4 years)
Duration: 4FT Hon
Entry Requirements: *GCE:* AAB. *SQAH:* AAAAB. *SQAAH:* AAB. *IB:* 35. Interview required.

H610 BEng Electronic Engineering
Duration: 3FT Hon
Entry Requirements: *GCE:* AAB. *SQAH:* AAABB. *SQAAH:* AAB. *IB:* 35. Interview required.

H613 BEng Electronic Engineering (with Industrial Experience)
Duration: 4FT Hon
Entry Requirements: *GCE:* AAB. *SQAH:* AAAAB. *SQAAH:* AAB. *IB:* 35. Interview required.

HH36 BEng Mechatronic Engineering
Duration: 3FT Hon
Entry Requirements: *GCE:* AAB. *SQAH:* AAAAB. *SQAAH:* AAB. *IB:* 35. Interview required.

HH63 BEng Mechatronic Engineering with Industrial Experience (4 years)
Duration: 4FT Hon
Entry Requirements: *GCE:* AAB. *SQAH:* AAAAB. *SQAAH:* AAB. *IB:* 35. Interview required.

GH4P MEng Computer Systems Engineering
Duration: 4FT Hon
Entry Requirements: *GCE:* A*AA. *SQAH:* AAAAA. *SQAAH:* AAA. *IB:* 38. Interview required.

H605 MEng Electrical and Electronic Engineering
Duration: 4FT Hon
Entry Requirements: *GCE:* AAA. *SQAH:* AAAAA. *SQAAH:* AAA. *IB:* 37. Interview required.

H601 MEng Electrical and Electronic Engineering with Industrial Experience
Duration: 5FT Hon
Entry Requirements: *GCE:* AAA. *SQAH:* AAAAA. *SQAAH:* AAA. *IB:* 37. Interview required.

H614 MEng Electronic Engineering
Duration: 4FT Hon
Entry Requirements: *GCE:* AAA. *SQAH:* AAAAA. *SQAAH:* AAA. *IB:* 37. Interview required.

H615 MEng Electronic Engineering with Industrial Experience
Duration: 5FT Hon
Entry Requirements: *GCE:* AAA. *SQAH:* AAAAA. *SQAAH:* AAA. *IB:* 37. Interview required.

HHH6 MEng Mechatronic Engineering
Duration: 4FT Hon
Entry Requirements: *GCE:* AAA. *SQAH:* AAAAA. *SQAAH:* AAA. *IB:* 37. Interview required.

HHP3 MEng Mechatronic Engineering with Industrial Experience (5 years)
Duration: 5FT Hon
Entry Requirements: *GCE:* AAA. *SQAH:* AAAAA. *SQAAH:* AAA. *IB:* 37. Interview required.

M40 THE MANCHESTER METROPOLITAN UNIVERSITY
ADMISSIONS OFFICE
ALL SAINTS (GMS)
ALL SAINTS
MANCHESTER M15 6BH
t: 0161 247 2000
// www.mmu.ac.uk

HH36 BEng Automation and Control
Duration: 3FT/4SW Hon
Entry Requirements: *GCE:* 280. *IB:* 27.

HHH6 BEng Automation and Control (Foundation)
Duration: 4FT/5SW Hon
Entry Requirements: *GCE:* 160. *IB:* 24. *BTEC Dip:* MM. *BTEC ExtDip:* MPP.

HH16 BEng Computer and Communication Engineering
Duration: 3FT/4SW Hon
Entry Requirements: *GCE:* 280. *IB:* 27.

HHC6 BEng Computer and Communication Engineering (Foundation)
Duration: 4FT/5SW Hon
Entry Requirements: *GCE:* 160. *IB:* 24. *BTEC Dip:* MM. *BTEC ExtDip:* MPP.

H600 BEng Electrical and Electronic Engineering
Duration: 3FT/4SW Hon
Entry Requirements: *GCE:* 240-280. *IB:* 27.

H608 BEng Electrical and Electronic Engineering (Foundation)
Duration: 4FT/5SW Hon
Entry Requirements: *GCE:* 160. *IB:* 24. *BTEC Dip:* MM. *BTEC ExtDip:* MPP.

HP63 BSc Media Technology
Duration: 3FT/4SW Hon
Entry Requirements: *GCE:* 280. *IB:* 28.

HPP3 BSc Media Technology (Foundation)
Duration: 4FT/5SW Hon
Entry Requirements: *GCE:* 160. *IB:* 24. *BTEC Dip:* MM. *BTEC ExtDip:* MPP.

M77 MID CHESHIRE COLLEGE
HARTFORD CAMPUS
NORTHWICH
CHESHIRE CW8 1LJ
t: 01606 74444 f: 01606 720700
e: eandrews@midchesh.ac.uk
// www.midchesh.ac.uk

001H FdEng Engineering (Mechanical and Electrical)
Duration: 2FT Fdg
Entry Requirements: *GCE:* 100-120. Interview required.

M80 MIDDLESEX UNIVERSITY
MIDDLESEX UNIVERSITY
THE BURROUGHS
LONDON NW4 4BT
t: 020 8411 5555 f: 020 8411 5649
e: enquiries@mdx.ac.uk
// www.mdx.ac.uk

H641 BEng Design Engineering: Digital Systems
Duration: 3FT/4SW Hon
Entry Requirements: Contact the institution for details.

H611 BEng Design Engineering: Electronics
Duration: 3FT/4SW Hon
Entry Requirements: Contact the institution for details.

H650 BEng Design Engineering: Embedded Systems
Duration: 3FT/4SW Hon
Entry Requirements: Contact the institution for details.

H610 BSc Design Engineering (Top-Up)
Duration: 1FT Hon
Entry Requirements: Contact the institution for details.

N21 NEWCASTLE UNIVERSITY
KING'S GATE
NEWCASTLE UPON TYNE NE1 7RU
t: 01912083333
// www.ncl.ac.uk

H607 BEng Electrical and Electronic Engineering
Duration: 3FT Hon
Entry Requirements: *GCE:* AAB-ABB. *SQAAH:* BB. *IB:* 35. *BTEC ExtDip:* DDD.

H604 BEng Electrical and Electronic Engineering (4 years)
Duration: 4FT Hon
Entry Requirements: *GCE:* AAB-BBB. *SQAAH:* BB. *IB:* 35.

H640 BEng Electronic Communications
Duration: 3FT Hon
Entry Requirements: *GCE:* AAB-ABB. *SQAAH:* BB. *IB:* 35. *BTEC ExtDip:* DDD.

H610 BEng Electronic Engineering
Duration: 3FT Hon
Entry Requirements: *GCE:* AAB-ABB. *SQAAH:* BB. *IB:* 35. *BTEC ExtDip:* DDD.

H652 BEng Electronics and Computer Engineering
Duration: 3FT Hon
Entry Requirements: *GCE:* AAB-ABB. *SQAAH:* BB. *IB:* 35. *BTEC ExtDip:* DDD.

H606 MEng Electrical and Electronic Engineering (5 years)
Duration: 5FT Hon
Entry Requirements: *GCE:* AAB. *SQAAH:* AA-AB. *IB:* 37. *BTEC ExtDip:* DDD.

H605 MEng Electrical and Electronic Engineering (with Industrial Project)
Duration: 4FT Hon
Entry Requirements: *GCE:* AAB. *SQAAH:* AA-AB. *IB:* 36.

H621 MEng Electronic Communications (with Industrial Project)
Duration: 4FT Hon
Entry Requirements: *GCE:* AAB. *SQAAH:* AA-AB. *IB:* 36.

H602 MEng Electronic Engineering (with Industrial Project)
Duration: 4FT Hon
Entry Requirements: *GCE:* AAB. *SQAAH:* AA-AB. *IB:* 36.

H654 MEng Electronics and Computer Engineering (with Industrial Project)
Duration: 4FT Hon
Entry Requirements: *GCE:* AAB. *SQAAH:* AA-AB. *IB:* 36.

N23 NEWCASTLE COLLEGE
STUDENT SERVICES
RYE HILL CAMPUS
SCOTSWOOD ROAD
NEWCASTLE UPON TYNE NE4 7SA
t: 0191 200 4110 f: 0191 200 4349
e: enquiries@ncl-coll.ac.uk
// www.newcastlecollege.co.uk

H601 BSc Electrical Electronic Engineering (Top-up)
Duration: 1FT Hon
Entry Requirements: Contact the institution for details.

H600 FdSc Electrical and Electronic Engineering
Duration: 2FT Fdg
Entry Requirements: *GCE:* 160-200. *OCR ND:* P2 *OCR NED:* P3
Interview required.

HH36 FdSc Sub-Sea Engineering
Duration: 2FT Fdg
Entry Requirements: *GCE:* 160-200. *OCR ND:* P2 *OCR NED:* P3
Interview required.

N30 NEW COLLEGE NOTTINGHAM
ADAMS BUILDING
STONEY STREET
THE LACE MARKET
NOTTINGHAM NG1 1NG
t: 0115 910 0100 f: 0115 953 4349
e: he.team@ncn.ac.uk
// www.ncn.ac.uk

026H HNC Electrical Engineering
Duration: 1FT HNC
Entry Requirements: Contact the institution for details.

N37 UNIVERSITY OF WALES, NEWPORT
ADMISSIONS
LODGE ROAD
CAERLEON
NEWPORT NP18 3QT
t: 01633 432030 f: 01633 432850
e: admissions@newport.ac.uk
// www.newport.ac.uk

H620 BEng Electrical Engineering
Duration: 3FT Hon
Entry Requirements: *GCE:* 240. *IB:* 24.

H691 BEng Electronic and Communication Engineering
Duration: 3FT Hon
Entry Requirements: *GCE:* 240. *IB:* 24.

N64 NORTH LINDSEY COLLEGE
KINGSWAY
SCUNTHORPE
NORTH LINCS DN17 1AJ
t: 01724 294125 f: 01724 295378
e: he@northlindsey.ac.uk
// www.northlindsey.ac.uk

006H HND Electrical and Electronic Engineering
Duration: 2FT HND
Entry Requirements: Contact the institution for details.

N77 NORTHUMBRIA UNIVERSITY
TRINITY BUILDING
NORTHUMBERLAND ROAD
NEWCASTLE UPON TYNE NE1 8ST
t: 0191 243 7420 f: 0191 227 4561
e: er.admissions@northumbria.ac.uk
// www.northumbria.ac.uk

H600 BEng Electrical and Electronic Engineering
Duration: 3FT/4SW Hon
Entry Requirements: *GCE:* 280. *SQAH:* BBCCC. *SQAAH:* BCC. *IB:* 25.

H688 BEng Electrical and Electronic Engineering
Duration: 4FT/5SW Hon
Entry Requirements: *GCE:* 200. *SQAH:* CCCC. *IB:* 24. *BTEC Dip:* DM. *OCR ND:* M1 *OCR NED:* P1

H610 BEng Electronic Design Engineering
Duration: 1FT Hon
Entry Requirements: HND required.

H621 BSc Computer and Network Technology
Duration: 3FT/4SW Hon
Entry Requirements: *GCE:* 280. *SQAH:* BBCCC. *SQAAH:* BCC. *IB:* 25. *BTEC Dip:* D*D*. *BTEC ExtDip:* DMM. *OCR NED:* M2

H628 BSc Computer and Network Technology
Duration: 4FT/5SW Hon
Entry Requirements: *GCE:* 200. *SQAH:* CCCC. *IB:* 24. *BTEC Dip:* DM. *OCR ND:* M1 *OCR NED:* P1

H602 MEng Electrical and Electronic Engineering
Duration: 4FT/5SW Hon
Entry Requirements: Contact the institution for details.

N84 THE UNIVERSITY OF NOTTINGHAM
THE ADMISSIONS OFFICE
THE UNIVERSITY OF NOTTINGHAM
UNIVERSITY PARK
NOTTINGHAM NG7 2RD
t: 0115 951 5151 f: 0115 951 4668
// www.nottingham.ac.uk

H6NB BEng Electrical & Electronic Engineering with Management Studies
Duration: 3FT Hon
Entry Requirements: *GCE:* AAB-BBB. *SQAAH:* AAB-BBB. Interview required.

H6GC BEng Electrical & Electronic Engineering with Mathematics
Duration: 3FT Hon
Entry Requirements: *GCE:* AAB-BBB. *SQAAH:* AAB-BBB. Interview required.

H622 BEng Electrical Engineering
Duration: 3FT Hon
Entry Requirements: *GCE:* AAB-BBB. *SQAAH:* AAB-BBB. Interview required.

H603 BEng Electrical and Electronic Engineering
Duration: 3FT Hon
Entry Requirements: *GCE:* AAB-BBB. *SQAAH:* AAB-BBB. Interview required.

H606 BEng Electrical and Electronic Engineering with a Year Abroad
Duration: 3FT Hon
Entry Requirements: *GCE:* AAB-BBB. *SQAAH:* AAB-BBB. Interview required.

H612 BEng Electronic Engineering
Duration: 3FT Hon
Entry Requirements: *GCE:* AAB-BBB. *SQAAH:* AAB-BBB. Interview required.

H690 BEng Electronic and Communications Engineering
Duration: 3FT Hon
Entry Requirements: *GCE:* AAB-BBB. *SQAAH:* AAB-BBB. Interview required.

H613 BEng Electronic and Computer Engineering
Duration: 3FT Hon
Entry Requirements: *GCE:* AAB-BBB. *SQAAH:* AAB-BBB. Interview required.

H600 MEng Electrical & Electronic Engineering
Duration: 4FT Hon
Entry Requirements: *GCE:* AAB-BBB. *SQAAH:* AAB-BBB. Interview required.

H6NG MEng Electrical & Electronic Engineering with Management Studies
Duration: 4FT Hon
Entry Requirements: *GCE:* AAB-BBB. *SQAAH:* AAB-BBB. Interview required.

H6G1 MEng Electrical & Electronic Engineering with Mathematics
Duration: 4FT Hon
Entry Requirements: *GCE:* AAB-BBB. *SQAAH:* AAB-BBB. Interview required.

H601 MEng Electrical Engineering
Duration: 4FT Hon
Entry Requirements: *GCE:* AAB-BBB. *SQAAH:* AAB-BBB. Interview required.

H605 MEng Electrical and Electronic Engineering with a Year Abroad
Duration: 4FT Hon
Entry Requirements: *GCE:* AAB-BBB. *SQAAH:* AAB-BBB. Interview required.

H610 MEng Electronic Engineering
Duration: 4FT Hon
Entry Requirements: *GCE:* AAB-BBB. *SQAAH:* AAB-BBB. Interview required.

H640 MEng Electronic and Communications Engineering
Duration: 4FT Hon
Entry Requirements: *GCE:* AAB-BBB. *SQAAH:* AAB-BBB. Interview required.

H611 MEng Electronic and Computer Engineering
Duration: 4FT Hon
Entry Requirements: *GCE:* AAB-BBB. *SQAAH:* AAB-BBB. Interview required.

N91 NOTTINGHAM TRENT UNIVERSITY
DRYDEN BUILDING
BURTON STREET
NOTTINGHAM NG1 4BU
t: +44 (0) 115 848 4200 f: +44 (0) 115 848 8869
e: applications@ntu.ac.uk
// www.ntu.ac.uk

GH4P BSc Digital Media Technology
Duration: 3FT/4SW Hon
Entry Requirements: *GCE:* 240.

GH56 BSc Information and Communications Technology
Duration: 3FT/4SW Hon
Entry Requirements: *GCE:* 240.

O25 OXFORD & CHERWELL VALLEY COLLEGE
BANBURY CAMPUS
BROUGHTON ROAD
BANBURY
OXON OX16 9QA
t: 01865 551691 f: 01865 551777
e: uni@ocvc.ac.uk
// www.ocvc.ac.uk

006H HND Electrical and Electronic Engineering
Duration: 2FT HND
Entry Requirements: Contact the institution for details.

O33 OXFORD UNIVERSITY
UNDERGRADUATE ADMISSIONS OFFICE
UNIVERSITY OF OXFORD
WELLINGTON SQUARE
OXFORD OX1 2JD
t: 01865 288000 f: 01865 270212
e: undergraduate.admissions@admin.ox.ac.uk
// www.admissions.ox.ac.uk

H620 MEng Electrical Engineering (4 years)
Duration: 4FT Hon
Entry Requirements: *GCE:* A*AA. *SQAH:* AAAAA-AAAAB. *SQAAH:* AAB. Interview required. Admissions Test required.

H630 MEng Information Engineering (4 years)
Duration: 4FT Hon
Entry Requirements: *GCE:* A*AA. *SQAH:* AAAAA-AAAAB. *SQAAH:* AAB. Interview required. Admissions Test required.

O66 OXFORD BROOKES UNIVERSITY
ADMISSIONS OFFICE
HEADINGTON CAMPUS
GIPSY LANE
OXFORD OX3 0BP
t: 01865 483040 f: 01865 483983
e: admissions@brookes.ac.uk
// www.brookes.ac.uk

H690 FdSc Electrical and Electronic Engineering (Abingdon and Witney)
Duration: 2FT Fdg
Entry Requirements: Contact the institution for details.

P35 PEMBROKESHIRE COLLEGE (ACCREDITED COLLEGE OF UNIVERSITY OF GLAMORGAN)
HAVERFORDWEST
PEMBROKESHIRE SA61 1SZ
t: 01437 753000 f: 01437 753001
e: admissions@pembrokeshire.ac.uk
// www.pembrokeshire.ac.uk

H600 BSc Electrical and Electronic Engineering
Duration: 1FT Ord
Entry Requirements: Contact the institution for details.

006H HND Electrical/Electronic Engineering
Duration: 2FT HND
Entry Requirements: *GCE:* 80. *IB:* 26.

P51 PETROC
OLD STICKLEPATH HILL
BARNSTAPLE
NORTH DEVON EX31 2BQ
t: 01271 852365 f: 01271 338121
e: he@petroc.ac.uk
// www.petroc.ac.uk

H610 FdSc Digital Technology
Duration: 2FT Fdg
Entry Requirements: Contact the institution for details.

P60 PLYMOUTH UNIVERSITY
DRAKE CIRCUS
PLYMOUTH PL4 8AA
t: 01752 585858 f: 01752 588055
e: admissions@plymouth.ac.uk
// www.plymouth.ac.uk

H604 BEng Electrical and Electronic Engineering
Duration: 3FT/4SW Hon
Entry Requirements: *GCE:* 300. *IB:* 28.

H609 BEng Electrical and Electronic Engineering with Foundation Year
Duration: 5SW Hon
Entry Requirements: *GCE:* 180. *IB:* 24.

H675 BEng Robotics
Duration: 3FT/4SW Hon
Entry Requirements: *GCE:* 300. *IB:* 28.

H677 BEng Robotics with Foundation Year
Duration: 5SW Hon
Entry Requirements: *GCE:* 180. *IB:* 24.

H622 BSc Electrical and Electronic Engineering
Duration: 4SW Hon
Entry Requirements: *GCE:* 280. *IB:* 27.

H671 BSc Robotics
Duration: 3FT/4SW Hon
Entry Requirements: *GCE:* 280. *IB:* 27.

H602 FdSc Electrical and Electronic Engineering
Duration: 2FT Fdg
Entry Requirements: *GCE:* 80. *IB:* 24. *OCR ND:* P *OCR NED:* P

H608 MEng Electrical and Electronic Engineering
Duration: 4FT Hon
Entry Requirements: *GCE:* 320. *IB:* 30.

H676 MEng Robotics
Duration: 4FT Hon
Entry Requirements: *GCE:* 320. *IB:* 30.

P80 UNIVERSITY OF PORTSMOUTH
ACADEMIC REGISTRY
UNIVERSITY HOUSE
WINSTON CHURCHILL AVENUE
PORTSMOUTH PO1 2UP
t: 023 9284 8484 f: 023 9284 3082
e: admissions@port.ac.uk
// www.port.ac.uk

H645 BEng Communication Systems
Duration: 3FT/4SW Hon
Entry Requirements: *GCE:* 260-300. *IB:* 26. *BTEC SubDip:* M.
BTEC Dip: MM. *BTEC ExtDip:* DMM.

H601 BEng Computer Engineering
Duration: 3FT/4SW Hon
Entry Requirements: *GCE:* 260-300. *IB:* 26. *BTEC SubDip:* M.
BTEC Dip: MM. *BTEC ExtDip:* DMM.

H610 BEng Electronic Engineering
Duration: 3FT/4SW Hon
Entry Requirements: *GCE:* 260-300. *IB:* 26. *BTEC SubDip:* M.
BTEC Dip: MM. *BTEC ExtDip:* DMM.

GH46 BSc Entertainment Technology
Duration: 3FT/4SW Hon
Entry Requirements: *GCE:* 240-300. *IB:* 28. *BTEC SubDip:* P.
BTEC Dip: DD. *BTEC ExtDip:* DMM.

H646 MEng Communication Systems
Duration: 4FT/5SW Hon
Entry Requirements: *GCE:* 300-340. *IB:* 27. *BTEC SubDip:* M.
BTEC Dip: MM. *BTEC ExtDip:* DDM.

H603 MEng Computer Engineering
Duration: 4FT/5SW Hon
Entry Requirements: *GCE:* 300-340. *IB:* 27. *BTEC SubDip:* M.
BTEC Dip: MM. *BTEC ExtDip:* DDM.

H613 MEng Electronic Engineering
Duration: 4FT/5SW Hon
Entry Requirements: *GCE:* 300-340. *IB:* 27. *BTEC SubDip:* M.
BTEC Dip: MM. *BTEC ExtDip:* DDM.

Q50 QUEEN MARY, UNIVERSITY OF LONDON
QUEEN MARY, UNIVERSITY OF LONDON
MILE END ROAD
LONDON E1 4NS
t: 020 7882 5555 f: 020 7882 5500
e: admissions@qmul.ac.uk
// www.qmul.ac.uk

H657 BEng Audio Systems Engineering
Duration: 3FT Hon
Entry Requirements: *GCE:* 300-340. *IB:* 32.

H600 BEng Electrical and Electronic Engineering
Duration: 3FT Hon
Entry Requirements: *GCE:* 300-340. *IB:* 32.

H610 BEng Electronic Engineering
Duration: 3FT Hon
Entry Requirements: *GCE:* 300-340. *IB:* 32.

H691 BEng Electronic Engineering & Telecommunications
Duration: 3FT Hon
Entry Requirements: *GCE:* 300-340. *IB:* 32.

H692 BEng Electronic Engineering & Telecommunications with Industrial Experience
Duration: 4FT Hon
Entry Requirements: *GCE:* 300-340. *IB:* 32.

HI61 BEng Electronic Engineering and Computing
Duration: 3FT Hon
Entry Requirements: *GCE:* 300-340. *IB:* 32.

H611 BEng Electronic Engineering with Industrial Experience
Duration: 4FT Hon
Entry Requirements: *GCE:* 300-340. *IB:* 32.

HHX6 BEng Science & Engineering Foundation Programme (Electronic Engineering 4 Year)
Duration: 4FT Hon
Entry Requirements: *GCE:* 260.

H642 MEng Audio Systems Engineering
Duration: 4FT Hon
Entry Requirements: *GCE:* 340. *IB:* 34.

H690 MEng Electronic Engineering & Telecommunications
Duration: 4FT Hon
Entry Requirements: *GCE:* 340. *IB:* 34.

HI6C MEng Electronic Engineering and Computing
Duration: 4FT Hon
Entry Requirements: *GCE:* 340. *IB:* 34.

HHY6 MEng Science & Engineering Foundation Programme (Electronic Engineering 5 Year)
Duration: 5FT Hon
Entry Requirements: *GCE:* 260.

Q75 QUEEN'S UNIVERSITY BELFAST
UNIVERSITY ROAD
BELFAST BT7 1NN
t: 028 9097 3838 f: 028 9097 5151
e: admissions@qub.ac.uk
// www.qub.ac.uk

H600 BEng Electrical and Electronic Engineering
Duration: 3FT Hon
Entry Requirements: *GCE:* BBC-BCC. *SQAH:* BBBBC-BBBCC. *SQAAH:* BBC-BCC.

H604 BEng Electrical and Electronic Engineering (with a Year in Industry)
Duration: 4SW Hon
Entry Requirements: *GCE:* BBC-BCC. *SQAH:* BBBBC-BBBCC. *SQAAH:* BBC-BCC.

GH6P BEng Software and Electronic Systems Engineering
Duration: 3FT Hon
Entry Requirements: Contact the institution for details.

GH67 BEng Software and Electronic Systems Engineering (with Year in Industry)
Duration: 4SW Hon
Entry Requirements: Contact the institution for details.

H602 MEng Electrical and Electronic Engineering
Duration: 4FT Hon
Entry Requirements: *GCE:* ABB-BBB. *SQAH:* ABBBB-BBBBB. *SQAAH:* ABB-BBB.

H605 MEng Electrical and Electronic Engineering (with a Year in Industry)
Duration: 5SW Hon
Entry Requirements: *GCE:* ABB-BBB. *SQAH:* ABBBB-BBBBB. *SQAAH:* ABB-BBB.

GH6Q MEng Software and Electronic Systems Engineering
Duration: 4FT Hon
Entry Requirements: Contact the institution for details.

GH68 MEng Software and Electronic Systems Engineering (with Year in Industry)
Duration: 5SW Hon
Entry Requirements: Contact the institution for details.

R06 RAVENSBOURNE
6 PENROSE WAY
GREENWICH PENINSULA
LONDON SE10 0EW
t: 020 3040 3998
e: info@rave.ac.uk
// www.rave.ac.uk

H646 BA Editing and Post Production (Top-Up)
Duration: 1FT Hon
Entry Requirements: Interview required. Portfolio required.

HP63 BA Production (Top-Up)
Duration: 1FT Hon
Entry Requirements: Interview required. Portfolio required.

HP42 BSc Broadcast Audio Technology
Duration: 3FT Hon
Entry Requirements: Contact the institution for details.

HQ42 BSc Broadcast Information Technology
Duration: 3FT/2FT Hon
Entry Requirements: Contact the institution for details.

HJ6X BSc Broadcast Technology (Audio) Top-Up
Duration: 1FT Hon
Entry Requirements: Interview required. Portfolio required.

HG6M BSc Broadcast Technology (Computing) Top-Up
Duration: 1FT Hon
Entry Requirements: Interview required. Portfolio required.

H648 BSc Broadcast Technology (Outside Broadcast) Top-Up
Duration: 1FT Hon
Entry Requirements: Interview required. Portfolio required.

H645 BSc Broadcast Technology (Systems) Top-Up
Duration: 1FT Hon
Entry Requirements: Interview required. Portfolio required.

H649 BSc Broadcast Technology (with Foundation Year)
Duration: 4FT Hon
Entry Requirements: *Foundation:* Pass. *GCE:* A-E. *IB:* 28. Interview required. Admissions Test required.

H6L2 BSc Outside Broadcast Technology
Duration: 3FT Hon
Entry Requirements: Contact the institution for details.

HPL2 BSc Outside Broadcast Technology (Fast-Track)
Duration: 2FT Hon
Entry Requirements: Contact the institution for details.

H64F FdA Editing and Post Production: (Industry Practice with Foundation Year)
Duration: 3FT Hon
Entry Requirements: Contact the institution for details.

H6K2 FdA Editing and Post Production: Industry Practice
Duration: 2FT Fdg
Entry Requirements: Contact the institution for details.

R12 THE UNIVERSITY OF READING
THE UNIVERSITY OF READING
PO BOX 217
READING RG6 6AH
t: 0118 378 8619 f: 0118 378 8924
e: student.recruitment@reading.ac.uk
// www.reading.ac.uk

H610 BEng Electronic Engineering
Duration: 3FT Hon
Entry Requirements: *GCE:* BBC. *SQAH:* BBCCC. *SQAAH:* BBC.

H615 BEng Electronic Engineering with Industrial Year
Duration: 4SW Hon
Entry Requirements: *GCE:* BBC. *SQAH:* BBCCC. *SQAAH:* BBC.

GH76 BSc Artificial Intelligence
Duration: 3FT Hon
Entry Requirements: *GCE:* BBC. *SQAH:* BBCCC. *SQAAH:* BBC.

HG67 BSc Artificial Intelligence with Industrial Year
Duration: 4SW Hon
Entry Requirements: *GCE:* BBC. *SQAH:* BBCCC. *SQAAH:* BBC.

H651 BSc Cybernetics
Duration: 3FT Hon
Entry Requirements: *GCE:* BBC. *SQAH:* BBCCC. *SQAAH:* BBC.

H690 BSc Cybernetics with Industrial Year
Duration: 4FT Hon
Entry Requirements: *GCE:* BBC. *SQAH:* BBCCC. *SQAAH:* BBC.

H671 BSc Robotics
Duration: 3FT Hon
Entry Requirements: *GCE:* BBC. *SQAH:* BBCCC. *SQAAH:* BBC.

H67D BSc Robotics with Industrial Year
Duration: 4SW Hon
Entry Requirements: *GCE:* BBC. *SQAH:* BBCCC. *SQAAH:* BBC.

GH7P MEng Artificial Intelligence
Duration: 4FT Hon
Entry Requirements: *GCE:* ABB. *SQAH:* ABBBB. *SQAAH:* ABB.

H654 MEng Cybernetics (MEng) (4 years)
Duration: 4FT Hon
Entry Requirements: *GCE:* ABB. *SQAH:* ABBBB. *SQAAH:* ABB.

H603 MEng Electronic Engineering (MEng) (4 years)
Duration: 4FT Hon
Entry Requirements: *GCE:* ABB. *SQAH:* ABBBB. *SQAAH:* ABB.

H675 MEng Robotics
Duration: 4FT Hon
Entry Requirements: *GCE:* ABB. *SQAH:* ABBBB. *SQAAH:* ABB.

R36 ROBERT GORDON UNIVERSITY
ROBERT GORDON UNIVERSITY
SCHOOLHILL
ABERDEEN
SCOTLAND AB10 1FR
t: 01224 26 27 28 f: 01224 26 21 47
e: UGOffice@rgu.ac.uk
// www.rgu.ac.uk

H606 BEng Electronic and Electrical Engineering
Duration: 4FT Hon
Entry Requirements: *GCE:* BCC. *SQAH:* BBBC. *SQAAH:* BCC. *IB:* 27.

HH36 BEng Mechanical and Electrical Engineering
Duration: 4FT Hon
Entry Requirements: *GCE:* BCC. *SQAH:* BBBC. *SQAAH:* BCC. *IB:* 27.

H620 BSc Computer Network Management and Design
Duration: 2FT Hon
Entry Requirements: HND required.

H600 MEng Electronic and Electrical Engineering
Duration: 4.5FT Hon
Entry Requirements: *GCE:* BBC. *SQAH:* ABBB-ABBCC. *SQAAH:* BBB. *IB:* 28.

S03 THE UNIVERSITY OF SALFORD
SALFORD M5 4WT
t: 0161 295 4545 f: 0161 295 4646
e: ug-admissions@salford.ac.uk
// www.salford.ac.uk

HW64 BSc Media Technology
Duration: 3FT Hon
Entry Requirements: *GCE:* 240. *IB:* 28. *OCR ND:* D *OCR NED:* M3
Interview required.

H620 BSc Multimedia and Internet Technology
Duration: 3FT Hon
Entry Requirements: *GCE:* 260. *IB:* 28.

H649 BSc Professional Sound and Video Technology
Duration: 3FT Hon
Entry Requirements: *GCE:* 240. *IB:* 28.

S18 THE UNIVERSITY OF SHEFFIELD
THE UNIVERSITY OF SHEFFIELD
LEVEL 2, ARTS TOWER
WESTERN BANK
SHEFFIELD S10 2TN
t: 0114 222 8030 f: 0114 222 8032
// www.sheffield.ac.uk

H620 BEng Electrical Engineering (3 years)
Duration: 3FT Hon
Entry Requirements: *GCE:* ABB. *SQAH:* AAABB. *IB:* 33. *BTEC ExtDip:* DDM. Interview required.

H610 BEng Electronic Engineering (3 years)
Duration: 3FT Hon
Entry Requirements: *GCE:* ABB. *SQAH:* AAABB. *IB:* 33. *BTEC ExtDip:* DDM. Interview required.

H647 BEng Electronic and Communications Engineering (3 years)
Duration: 3FT Hon
Entry Requirements: *GCE:* ABB. *SQAH:* AAABB. *IB:* 33. *BTEC ExtDip:* DDM. Interview required.

H653 BEng Systems Engineering with a Foundation Year (4 years)
Duration: 4FT Hon
Entry Requirements: *GCE:* ABB. *SQAH:* AABBB. *SQAAH:* AB. *IB:* 33. *BTEC ExtDip:* DDM.

H690 BEng Systems and Control Engineering (3 years)
Duration: 3FT Hon
Entry Requirements: *GCE:* ABB. *SQAH:* AABBB. *SQAAH:* AB. *IB:* 33. *BTEC ExtDip:* DDM.

HN62 BEng Systems and Control Engineering (Engineering Management)
Duration: 3FT Hon
Entry Requirements: *GCE:* ABB. *SQAH:* AABBB. *SQAAH:* AB. *IB:* 33. *BTEC ExtDip:* DDM.

H651 MEng Digital Electronics
Duration: 4FT Hon
Entry Requirements: *GCE:* AAB. *SQAH:* AAAAB. *IB:* 35. *BTEC ExtDip:* DDD. Interview required.

H621 MEng Electrical Engineering (4 years)
Duration: 4FT Hon
Entry Requirements: *GCE:* AAB. *SQAH:* AAAAB. *IB:* 35. *BTEC ExtDip:* DDD. Interview required.

H603 MEng Electrical Engineering with a Foundation Year (4 or 5 years)
Duration: 4FT Hon
Entry Requirements: *GCE:* BBC. *SQAH:* BBBBB. *IB:* 30. *BTEC ExtDip:* DMM. Interview required.

H613 MEng Electronic Engineering (4 years)
Duration: 4FT Hon
Entry Requirements: *GCE:* AAB. *SQAH:* AAAAB. *IB:* 35. *BTEC ExtDip:* DDD. Interview required.

H602 MEng Electronic Engineering with a Foundation Year (4 or 5 years)
Duration: 4FT Hon
Entry Requirements: *GCE:* BBC. *SQAH:* BBBBB. *IB:* 30. *BTEC ExtDip:* DMM. Interview required.

H645 MEng Electronic and Communications Engineering (4 years)
Duration: 4FT Hon
Entry Requirements: *GCE:* AAB. *SQAH:* AAAAB. *IB:* 35. *BTEC ExtDip:* DDD. Interview required.

H6T9 MEng Electronic and Electrical Engineering with a Modern Language
Duration: 4FT Hon
Entry Requirements: *GCE:* AAB. *SQAH:* AAAAB. *IB:* 35. *BTEC ExtDip:* DDD. Interview required.

H614 MEng Microelectronics (4 years)
Duration: 4FT Hon
Entry Requirements: *GCE:* AAB. *SQAH:* AAAAB. *IB:* 35. *BTEC ExtDip:* DDD. Interview required.

H659 MEng Systems Engineering with a Foundation Year (5 years)
Duration: 5FT Hon
Entry Requirements: *GCE:* ABB. *SQAH:* AABBB. *SQAAH:* AB. *IB:* 33. *BTEC ExtDip:* DDM.

H660 MEng Systems and Control Engineering (4 years)
Duration: 4FT Hon
Entry Requirements: *GCE:* AAB. *SQAH:* AAABB. *SQAAH:* AB. *IB:* 35. *BTEC ExtDip:* DDD.

H1NF MEng Systems and Control Engineering (Engineering Management)
Duration: 4FT Hon
Entry Requirements: *GCE:* AAB. *SQAH:* AAABB. *SQAAH:* AB. *IB:* 35. *BTEC ExtDip:* DDD.

S21 SHEFFIELD HALLAM UNIVERSITY
CITY CAMPUS
HOWARD STREET
SHEFFIELD S1 1WB
t: 0114 225 5555 f: 0114 225 2167
e: admissions@shu.ac.uk
// www.shu.ac.uk

HG66 BEng Computer and Network Engineering
Duration: 3FT/4SW Hon
Entry Requirements: *GCE:* 240.

H620 BEng Electrical Engineering Top-up
Duration: 1FT Hon
Entry Requirements: Contact the institution for details.

H606 BEng Electrical and Electronic Engineering
Duration: 3FT/4SW Hon
Entry Requirements: *GCE:* 240.

H610 BEng Electronic Engineering
Duration: 3FT/4SW Hon
Entry Requirements: *GCE:* 200.

H690 BEng Telecommunication and Electronic Systems
Duration: 1FT Hon
Entry Requirements: HND required.

H600 MEng Electrical and Electronic Engineering
Duration: 4FT/5SW Hon
Entry Requirements: *GCE:* 300.

S26 SOLIHULL COLLEGE
BLOSSOMFIELD ROAD
SOLIHULL
WEST MIDLANDS B91 1SB
t: 0121 678 7006 f: 0121 678 7200
e: enquiries@solihull.ac.uk
// www.solihull.ac.uk

006H HND Electrical and Electronic Engineering
Duration: 2FT HND
Entry Requirements: *GCE:* A-E. *IB:* 24. *BTEC Dip:* MM. *BTEC ExtDip:* MMM. *OCR ND:* M2 *OCR NED:* M3 Interview required. Portfolio required.

S27 UNIVERSITY OF SOUTHAMPTON
HIGHFIELD
SOUTHAMPTON SO17 1BJ
t: 023 8059 4732 f: 023 8059 3037
e: admissions@soton.ac.uk
// www.southampton.ac.uk

H620 BEng Electrical Engineering
Duration: 3FT Hon
Entry Requirements: *GCE:* AAB. *IB:* 34.

HH36 BEng Electromechanical Engineering
Duration: 3FT Hon
Entry Requirements: *GCE:* AAB. *IB:* 34.

H610 BEng Electronic Engineering
Duration: 3FT Hon
Entry Requirements: *GCE:* AAA. *IB:* 36.

H601 MEng Electrical Engineering (4 years)
Duration: 4FT Hon
Entry Requirements: *GCE:* AAB. *IB:* 34.

HHH6 MEng Electromechanical Engineering (4 years)
Duration: 4FT Hon
Entry Requirements: *GCE:* AAB. *IB:* 34.

H603 MEng Electronic Engineering (4 years)
Duration: 4FT Hon
Entry Requirements: *GCE:* AAA. *IB:* 36.

H6G7 MEng Electronic Engineering with Artificial Intelligence
Duration: 4FT Hon
Entry Requirements: *GCE:* AAA. *IB:* 36.

H6G4 MEng Electronic Engineering with Computer Systems
Duration: 4FT Hon
Entry Requirements: *GCE:* AAA. *IB:* 36.

H691 MEng Electronic Engineering with Mobile & Secure Systems
Duration: 4FT Hon
Entry Requirements: *GCE:* AAA. *IB:* 36.

H611 MEng Electronic Engineering with Nanotechnology
Duration: 4FT Hon
Entry Requirements: *GCE:* AAA. *IB:* 36.

H680 MEng Electronic Engineering with Optical Communications
Duration: 4FT Hon
Entry Requirements: *GCE:* AAA. *IB:* 36.

H690 MEng Electronic Engineering with Power Systems
Duration: 4FT Hon
Entry Requirements: *GCE:* AAA. *IB:* 36.

H641 MEng Electronic Engineering with Wireless Communications
Duration: 4FT Hon
Entry Requirements: *GCE:* AAA. *IB:* 36.

S28 SOMERSET COLLEGE OF ARTS AND TECHNOLOGY
WELLINGTON ROAD
TAUNTON
SOMERSET TA1 5AX
t: 01823 366331 f: 01823 366418
e: enquiries@somerset.ac.uk
// www.somerset.ac.uk/student-area/considering-a-degree.html

H620 FdA Engineering Electrical Systems
Duration: 2FT Fdg
Entry Requirements: Contact the institution for details.

S30 SOUTHAMPTON SOLENT UNIVERSITY
EAST PARK TERRACE
SOUTHAMPTON
HAMPSHIRE SO14 0RT
t: +44 (0) 23 8031 9039 f: + 44 (0)23 8022 2259
e: admissions@solent.ac.uk
// www.solent.ac.uk/

H610 BEng Electronic Engineering
Duration: 3FT Hon
Entry Requirements: *GCE:* 120.

H608 BEng Electronic Engineering (with foundation)
Duration: 4FT Hon
Entry Requirements: *GCE:* 40.

H612 BEng Electronic Engineering with IFY (International Only - Jan)
Duration: 4FT Hon
Entry Requirements: Contact the institution for details.

H6QH BEng Electronic Engineering with IFY (Intl only, Sept)
Duration: 4FT Hon
Entry Requirements: Contact the institution for details.

H6N1 BEng Engineering with Business with IFY (International Only - Jan)
Duration: 4FT Hon
Entry Requirements: Contact the institution for details.

WH36 BSc Audio Technology
Duration: 3FT Hon
Entry Requirements: *GCE:* 160.

WHH6 BSc Audio Technology (with foundation)
Duration: 4FT Hon
Entry Requirements: *GCE:* 40.

H601 BSc Computer Network Management
Duration: 3FT Hon
Entry Requirements: *GCE:* 160.

H609 BSc Computer Network Management (with foundation)
Duration: 4FT Hon
Entry Requirements: *GCE:* 40.

H603 BSc Computer Systems and Networks
Duration: 3FT Hon
Entry Requirements: *GCE:* 160.

H613 BSc Electronic Engineering
Duration: 3FT Hon
Entry Requirements: *GCE:* 180.

H611 BSc Electronic Engineering (with foundation)
Duration: 4FT Hon
Entry Requirements: *GCE:* 40.

GH56 BSc Information and Communication Technology
Duration: 3FT Hon
Entry Requirements: *GCE:* 160.

GHN6 BSc Information and Communication Technology
Duration: 4SW Hon
Entry Requirements: *GCE:* 160.

GH5P BSc Information and Communication Technology (with foundation)
Duration: 5SW Hon
Entry Requirements: *GCE:* 40.

GHM6 BSc Information and Communication Technology (with foundation)
Duration: 4FT Hon
Entry Requirements: *GCE:* 40.

HP63 BSc Media Technology
Duration: 3FT Hon
Entry Requirements: *GCE:* 160.

HP6H BSc Media Technology (with foundation)
Duration: 4FT Hon
Entry Requirements: *GCE:* 40.

H6QJ BSc Media Technology with IFY (Intl only, Sept)
Duration: 4FT Hon
Entry Requirements: *GCE:* 160.

H646 BSc Sound for Film, Television and Games
Duration: 3FT Hon
Entry Requirements: *GCE:* 160.

H641 BSc Sound for Film, Television and Games (with Foundation)
Duration: 4FT Hon
Entry Requirements: *GCE:* 40.

006H HND Electronic Engineering
Duration: 2FT HND
Entry Requirements: *GCE:* 40.

S35 SOUTHPORT COLLEGE
MORNINGTON ROAD
SOUTHPORT
MERSEYSIDE PR9 0TT
t: 08450066236 f: 01704 392610
e: guidance@southport-college.ac.uk
// www.southport-college.ac.uk

H641 HND e-Commerce and Mobile App Development
Duration: 2FT HND
Entry Requirements: Contact the institution for details.

S41 SOUTH CHESHIRE COLLEGE
DANE BANK AVENUE
CREWE CW2 8AB
t: 01270 654654 f: 01270 651515
e: admissions@s-cheshire.ac.uk
// www.s-cheshire.ac.uk

H600 FdEng Electrical/Electronic Engineering
Duration: 2FT Fdg
Entry Requirements: Contact the institution for details.

S46 SOUTH NOTTINGHAM COLLEGE
WEST BRIDGFORD CENTRE
GREYTHORN DRIVE
WEST BRIDGFORD
NOTTINGHAM NG2 7GA
t: 0115 914 6400 f: 0115 914 6444
e: enquiries@snc.ac.uk
// www.snc.ac.uk

006H HND Electrical/Electronic Engineering (Electrical)
Duration: 2FT HND
Entry Requirements: Contact the institution for details.

S51 ST HELENS COLLEGE
WATER STREET
ST HELENS
MERSEYSIDE WA10 1PP
t: 01744 733766 f: 01744 623400
e: enquiries@sthelens.ac.uk
// www.sthelens.ac.uk

HW63 FdA Music Production and Sound Design
Duration: 2FT Fdg
Entry Requirements: *GCE:* 40-80. *IB:* 18. Interview required. Admissions Test required.

S69 STEPHENSON COLLEGE COALVILLE
THORNBOROUGH ROAD
COALVILLE
LEICESTERSHIRE LE67 3TN
t: 01530 836136 f: 01530 814253
e: highereducation@stephensoncoll.ac.uk
// www.stephensoncoll.ac.uk

026H HND Electrical Engineering
Duration: 2FT HND
Entry Requirements: Interview required.

S72 STAFFORDSHIRE UNIVERSITY
COLLEGE ROAD
STOKE ON TRENT ST4 2DE
t: 01782 292753 f: 01782 292740
e: admissions@staffs.ac.uk
// www.staffs.ac.uk

H620 BEng Electrical Engineering
Duration: 3FT/4SW Hon
Entry Requirements: *GCE:* 200-240. *IB:* 24.

H610 BEng Electronic Engineering
Duration: 3FT/4SW Hon
Entry Requirements: *GCE:* 200-240. *IB:* 24.

HH36 BEng Mechatronics
Duration: 3FT/4SW Hon
Entry Requirements: *GCE:* 200-240. *IB:* 24.

H602 BSc (Hons) Electrical and Electronic Technology (Top-Up)
Duration: 1FT Hon
Entry Requirements: Contact the institution for details.

S76 STOCKPORT COLLEGE
WELLINGTON ROAD SOUTH
STOCKPORT SK1 3UQ
t: 0161 958 3143 f: 0161 958 3663
e: susan.kelly@stockport.ac.uk
// www.stockport.ac.uk

006H HND Electrical & Electronic Engineering
Duration: 2FT HND
Entry Requirements: GCE: 80. Interview required. Admissions Test required.

S78 THE UNIVERSITY OF STRATHCLYDE
GLASGOW G1 1XQ
t: 0141 552 4400 f: 0141 552 0775
// www.strath.ac.uk

GH46 BEng Computer and Electronic Systems
Duration: 4FT Hon
Entry Requirements: GCE: AAA-AAB. SQAH: AAAAB-AAAAB. IB: 32. Interview required.

HH63 BEng Electrical and Mechanical Engineering
Duration: 4FT Hon
Entry Requirements: GCE: AAA-AAB. SQAH: AAAAB-AAAAB. IB: 32. Interview required.

H600 BEng Electronic and Electrical Engineering (h)
Duration: 4FT Hon
Entry Requirements: GCE: AAA-AAB. SQAH: AAAAB-AAAAB. IB: 32. Interview required.

GHK6 MEng Computer and Electronic Systems
Duration: 5FT Hon
Entry Requirements: GCE: A*AA-AAA. SQAH: AAAABB-AAAAB. IB: 36. Interview required.

H630 MEng Electrical Energy Systems(h)
Duration: 5FT Deg
Entry Requirements: GCE: A*AA-AAA. SQAH: AAAABB-AAAAB. IB: 36. Interview required.

HH6H MEng Electrical and Mechanical Engineering
Duration: 5FT Hon
Entry Requirements: GCE: A*AA-AAA. SQAH: AAAABB-AAAAB. IB: 36. Interview required.

H3H6 MEng Electrical and Mechanical Engineering with International Study
Duration: 5FT Hon
Entry Requirements: GCE: A*AA-AAA. SQAH: AAAABB-AAAAB. IB: 36. Interview required.

H690 MEng Electronic & Digital Systems (h)
Duration: 5FT Deg
Entry Requirements: GCE: A*AA-AAA. SQAH: AAAABB-AAAAB. IB: 36. Interview required.

H601 MEng Electronic & Electrical Engineering (h)
Duration: 5FT Hon
Entry Requirements: GCE: A*AA-AAA. SQAH: AAAABB-AAAAB. IB: 36. Interview required.

H6N1 MEng Electronic and Electrical Engineering with Business Studies
Duration: 5FT Hon
Entry Requirements: GCE: A*AA-AAA. SQAH: AAAABB-AAAAB. IB: 36. Interview required.

H6L2 MEng Electronic and Electrical Engineering with International Studies
Duration: 5FT Hon
Entry Requirements: GCE: A*AA-AAA. SQAH: AAAABB-AAAAB. IB: 36. Interview required.

S82 UNIVERSITY CAMPUS SUFFOLK (UCS)
WATERFRONT BUILDING
NEPTUNE QUAY
IPSWICH
SUFFOLK IP4 1QJ
t: 01473 338833 f: 01473 339900
e: info@ucs.ac.uk
// www.ucs.ac.uk

H620 FdSc Electrical Engineering
Duration: 2FT Fdg
Entry Requirements: Contact the institution for details.

H610 FdSc Electronic Engineering
Duration: 2FT Fdg
Entry Requirements: Contact the institution for details.

S84 UNIVERSITY OF SUNDERLAND
STUDENT HELPLINE
THE STUDENT GATEWAY
CHESTER ROAD
SUNDERLAND SR1 3SD
t: 0191 515 3000 f: 0191 515 3805
e: student.helpline@sunderland.ac.uk
// www.sunderland.ac.uk

HP63 BA Media Production (Television and Radio)
Duration: 3FT Hon
Entry Requirements: GCE: 260-360. IB: 30. Interview required.

PH36 BA Media Production (Video and New Media)
Duration: 3FT Hon
Entry Requirements: GCE: 260-360. IB: 30. Interview required.

H601 BEng Electronic and Electrical Engineering
Duration: 3FT/4SW Hon
Entry Requirements: GCE: 260. IB: 24. OCR ND: D OCR NED: M3

www.ucas.com

at the heart of connecting people to higher education

H600 BEng Electronic and Electrical Engineering (Top-up)
Duration: 1FT Hon
Entry Requirements: HND required.

GH46 BSc Network Systems (Top-up)
Duration: 1FT Hon
Entry Requirements: HND required.

S85 UNIVERSITY OF SURREY
STAG HILL
GUILDFORD
SURREY GU2 7XH
t: +44(0)1483 689305 f: +44(0)1483 689388
e: ugteam@surrey.ac.uk
// www.surrey.ac.uk

H606 BEng Electronic Engineering (3 years)
Duration: 3FT Hon
Entry Requirements: GCE: AAB. IB: 35. Interview required.

H604 BEng Electronic Engineering (4 years)
Duration: 4SW Hon
Entry Requirements: GCE: AAB. IB: 35. Interview required.

H640 BEng Electronic Engineering with Audio-Visual Systems (3/4 years)
Duration: 3FT/4SW Hon
Entry Requirements: GCE: AAB. IB: 35. Interview required.

H647 BEng Electronic Engineering with Communications (3 Years)
Duration: 3FT Hon
Entry Requirements: GCE: 320. IB: 32. Interview required.

H646 BEng Electronic Engineering with Communications (4 years)
Duration: 4SW Hon
Entry Requirements: GCE: 320. IB: 32. Interview required.

H632 BEng Electronic Engineering with Computer Systems (3 years)
Duration: 3FT Hon
Entry Requirements: GCE: AAB. IB: 35. Interview required.

H630 BEng Electronic Engineering with Computer Systems (4 years)
Duration: 4SW Hon
Entry Requirements: GCE: AAB. IB: 35. Interview required.

H614 MEng Electronic Engineering (4 years)
Duration: 4FT Hon
Entry Requirements: GCE: AAA. IB: 36. Interview required.

H615 MEng Electronic Engineering (5 years)
Duration: 5SW Hon
Entry Requirements: GCE: AAA. IB: 36. Interview required.

H645 MEng Electronic Engineering with Audio-Visual Systems (4/5 Years)
Duration: 4FT/5SW Hon
Entry Requirements: GCE: AAA. IB: 36. Interview required.

H641 MEng Electronic Engineering with Communications (4 Years)
Duration: 4FT Hon
Entry Requirements: GCE: 340. IB: 35. Interview required.

H636 MEng Electronic Engineering with Communications (5 Years)
Duration: 5SW Hon
Entry Requirements: GCE: 340. IB: 35. Interview required.

H633 MEng Electronic Engineering with Computer Systems (4 Years)
Duration: 4FT Hon
Entry Requirements: GCE: AAA. IB: 36. Interview required.

H631 MEng Electronic Engineering with Computer Systems (5 years)
Duration: 5SW Hon
Entry Requirements: GCE: AAA. IB: 36. Interview required.

H621 MEng Electronic Engineering with Space Systems (4 years)
Duration: 4FT Hon
Entry Requirements: GCE: AAA. IB: 36. Interview required.

H627 MEng Electronic Engineering with Space Systems (5 Years)
Duration: 5SW Hon
Entry Requirements: GCE: AAA. IB: 36. Interview required.

S90 UNIVERSITY OF SUSSEX
UNDERGRADUATE ADMISSIONS
SUSSEX HOUSE
UNIVERSITY OF SUSSEX
BRIGHTON BN1 9RH
t: 01273 678416 f: 01273 678545
e: ug.applicants@sussex.ac.uk
// www.sussex.ac.uk

HG66 BEng Computer Engineering
Duration: 3FT Hon
Entry Requirements: GCE: ABB. SQAH: AABBB. SQAAH: ABB. IB: 34. BTEC SubDip: D. BTEC Dip: DD. BTEC ExtDip: DDD. OCR ND: D OCR NED: D2

H606 BEng Electrical and Electronic Engineering
Duration: 3FT Hon
Entry Requirements: GCE: ABB. SQAH: AABBB. SQAAH: ABB. IB: 34. BTEC SubDip: D. BTEC Dip: DD. BTEC ExtDip: DDD. OCR ND: D OCR NED: D2

H610 BEng Electronic Engineering
Duration: 3FT Hon
Entry Requirements: GCE: ABB. SQAH: AABBB. SQAAH: ABB. IB: 34. BTEC SubDip: D. BTEC Dip: DD. BTEC ExtDip: DDD. OCR ND: D OCR NED: D2

GH4P MEng Computer Engineering
Duration: 4FT Hon
Entry Requirements: *GCE:* ABB. *SQAH:* AABBB. *SQAAH:* ABB. *IB:*
34. *BTEC SubDip:* D. *BTEC Dip:* DD. *BTEC ExtDip:* DDD. *OCR*
ND: D *OCR NED:* D2

H600 MEng Electrical and Electronic Engineering
Duration: 4FT Hon
Entry Requirements: *GCE:* ABB. *SQAH:* AABBB. *SQAAH:* ABB. *IB:*
34. *BTEC SubDip:* D. *BTEC Dip:* DD. *BTEC ExtDip:* DDD. *OCR*
ND: D *OCR NED:* D2

H613 MEng Electronic Engineering
Duration: 4FT Hon
Entry Requirements: *GCE:* ABB. *SQAH:* AABBB. *SQAAH:* ABB. *IB:*
34. *BTEC SubDip:* D. *BTEC Dip:* DD. *BTEC ExtDip:* DDD. *OCR*
ND: D *OCR NED:* D2

S93 SWANSEA UNIVERSITY
SINGLETON PARK
SWANSEA SA2 8PP
t: 01792 295111 f: 01792 295110
e: admissions@swansea.ac.uk
// www.swansea.ac.uk

H613 BEng Electonic Engineering with Nanoelectronics
Duration: 3FT Hon
Entry Requirements: *GCE:* BBB. *IB:* 32. Interview required.

H615 BEng Electronic Engineering with Nanoelectrics
Duration: 4FT Hon
Entry Requirements: Contact the institution for details.

H602 BEng Electronic and Electrical Engineering
Duration: 3FT Hon
Entry Requirements: *GCE:* BBB. *IB:* 32. Interview required.

H603 BEng Electronic and Electrical Engineering (Europe, Australia, N America or Industry)
Duration: 4FT Hon
Entry Requirements: *GCE:* ABB. *IB:* 33. Interview required.

HG64 BEng Electronics with Computer Science (Europe, Australia, N America or Industry)
Duration: 4FT Hon
Entry Requirements: *GCE:* ABB. *IB:* 33. Interview required.

H6G4 BEng Electronics with Computing Science
Duration: 3FT Hon
Entry Requirements: *GCE:* BBB. *IB:* 32. Interview required.

H640 BEng Telecommunications Engineering
Duration: 3FT Hon
Entry Requirements: *GCE:* BBB. Interview required.

H622 BEng Telecommunications Engineering (with a Year Abroad or Industry)
Duration: 4FT Hon
Entry Requirements: *GCE:* ABB. *IB:* 33. Interview required.

H614 MEng Electonic Engineering with Nanoelectronics
Duration: 4FT Hon
Entry Requirements: *GCE:* AAB. *IB:* 34. Interview required.

H606 MEng Electronic and Electrical Engineering
Duration: 4FT Hon
Entry Requirements: *GCE:* ABB. *IB:* 33. Interview required.

H600 MEng Electronic and Electrical Engineering (Europe, Australia, N America or Industry)
Duration: 5FT Hon
Entry Requirements: *GCE:* AAB. *IB:* 34. Interview required.

H6GL MEng Electronics with Computing Sci (Europe, Australia, N America or Industry)
Duration: 5FT Hon
Entry Requirements: *GCE:* AAB. *IB:* 34. Interview required.

H6GK MEng Electronics with Computing Science
Duration: 4FT Hon
Entry Requirements: *GCE:* ABB. *IB:* 33. Interview required.

H621 MEng Telecommunications Engineering
Duration: 4FT Hon
Entry Requirements: *GCE:* ABB. *IB:* 33. Interview required.

H623 MEng Telecommunications Engineering (with a Year Abroad or Industry)
Duration: 5FT Hon
Entry Requirements: *GCE:* AAB. *IB:* 34. Interview required.

S96 SWANSEA METROPOLITAN UNIVERSITY
MOUNT PLEASANT CAMPUS
SWANSEA SA1 6ED
t: 01792 481000 f: 01792 481061
e: gemma.green@smu.ac.uk
// www.smu.ac.uk

H610 BEng Computer Systems and Electronics
Duration: 3FT Hon
Entry Requirements: *GCE:* 160-360. *IB:* 24. Interview required.

H608 BEng Computer Systems and Electronics (4-year programme)
Duration: 4FT Hon
Entry Requirements: *GCE:* 80-360. *IB:* 24. Interview required.

H674 BSc Computer Games Development
Duration: 3FT Hon
Entry Requirements: *GCE:* 160-360. *IB:* 24. Interview required.

H611 BSc Computer Networks
Duration: 3FT Hon
Entry Requirements: *GCE:* 160-360. *IB:* 24. Interview required.

016H HND Computer Networks
Duration: 2FT HND
Entry Requirements: *GCE:* 80-360. *IB:* 24. Interview required.

116H HND Electronic Engineering
Duration: 2FT HND
Entry Requirements: *GCE:* 80-360. *IB:* 24. Interview required.

T10 TAMESIDE COLLEGE
ASHTON CENTRE
BEAUFORT ROAD
ASHTON-UNDER-LYNE
LANCS OL6 6NX
t: 0161 908 6789 f: 0161 908 6611
e: info@tameside.ac.uk
// www.tameside.ac.uk

006H HND Electrical & Electronic Engineering
Duration: 2FT HND
Entry Requirements: *GCE:* 80-100. *IB:* 24.

T20 TEESSIDE UNIVERSITY
MIDDLESBROUGH TS1 3BA
t: 01642 218121 f: 01642 384201
e: registry@tees.ac.uk
// www.tees.ac.uk

H601 BEng Electrical and Electronic Engineering
Duration: 3FT/4SW Hon
Entry Requirements: *GCE:* 280. *IB:* 30. *BTEC SubDip:* M. *BTEC Dip:* D*D*. *BTEC ExtDip:* DMM. *OCR ND:* M2 *OCR NED:* M2 Interview required.

H690 BEng Electrical and Electronic Engineering (Extended)
Duration: 4FT/5SW Hon
Entry Requirements: *GCE:* 120-200. *BTEC SubDip:* D. *BTEC Dip:* MP. *BTEC ExtDip:* PPP. *OCR ND:* P2 *OCR NED:* P3 Interview required.

H660 BEng Instrumentation and Control Engineering
Duration: 3FT/4SW Hon
Entry Requirements: *GCE:* 280. *IB:* 30. *BTEC SubDip:* M. *BTEC Dip:* D*D*. *BTEC ExtDip:* DMM. *OCR ND:* M2 *OCR NED:* M2 Interview required.

H603 BEng Tech Electrical and Electronic Engineering
Duration: 1FT Hon
Entry Requirements: HND required.

H602 MEng Electrical and Electronic Engineering
Duration: 4FT/5SW Hon
Entry Requirements: *GCE:* 280-300. *IB:* 30. Interview required.

H661 MEng Instrumentation and Control Engineering
Duration: 4FT/5SW Hon
Entry Requirements: *GCE:* 280-300. *IB:* 30. *BTEC SubDip:* M. *BTEC Dip:* D*D*. *BTEC ExtDip:* DDM. *OCR ND:* M1 *OCR NED:* M2 Interview required.

T85 TRURO AND PENWITH COLLEGE
TRURO COLLEGE
COLLEGE ROAD
TRURO
CORNWALL TR1 3XX
t: 01872 267122 f: 01872 267526
e: heinfo@trurocollege.ac.uk
// www.truro-penwith.ac.uk

086H HND Sound Engineering and Multimedia Integration
Duration: 2FT HND
Entry Requirements: *GCE:* 60. *IB:* 24. *BTEC Dip:* MP. *BTEC ExtDip:* PPP. Interview required.

U20 UNIVERSITY OF ULSTER
COLERAINE
CO. LONDONDERRY
NORTHERN IRELAND BT52 1SA
t: 028 7012 4221 f: 028 7012 4908
e: online@ulster.ac.uk
// www.ulster.ac.uk

H601 BEng Electronic Engineering
Duration: 4SW Hon
Entry Requirements: *GCE:* 280. *IB:* 24. Interview required. Admissions Test required.

GH56 BEng Electronics and Computer Systems
Duration: 4SW Hon
Entry Requirements: *GCE:* 280-300. *IB:* 24. Interview required. Admissions Test required.

H600 MEng Electronic Engineering
Duration: 5SW Hon
Entry Requirements: *GCE:* 300. *IB:* 25. Interview required. Admissions Test required.

H610 MEng Electronic Engineering (+German Master's degree)
Duration: 5SW Hon
Entry Requirements: *GCE:* 300. *IB:* 25. Interview required. Admissions Test required.

U40 UNIVERSITY OF THE WEST OF SCOTLAND
PAISLEY
RENFREWSHIRE
SCOTLAND PA1 2BE
t: 0141 848 3727 f: 0141 848 3623
e: admissions@uws.ac.uk
// www.uws.ac.uk

H601 BSc Computer Networking
Duration: 3FT/4FT Ord/Hon
Entry Requirements: *GCE:* CC. *SQAH:* BBC.

U80 UNIVERSITY COLLEGE LONDON (UNIVERSITY OF LONDON)
GOWER STREET
LONDON WC1E 6BT
t: 020 7679 3000 f: 020 7679 3001
// www.ucl.ac.uk

H600 BEng Electronic and Electrical Engineering
Duration: 3FT Hon
Entry Requirements: *GCE:* AAAe-ABBe. *SQAAH:* AAA-ABB. *BTEC ExtDip:* DDD. Interview required.

H613 MEng Electronic Engineering with Communications Engineering
Duration: 4FT Hon
Entry Requirements: *GCE:* AAAe-ABBe. *SQAAH:* AAA-ABB. *BTEC ExtDip:* DDD. Interview required.

H6G4 MEng Electronic Engineering with Computer Science
Duration: 4FT Hon
Entry Requirements: *GCE:* AAAe-ABBe. *SQAAH:* AAA-ABB. *BTEC ExtDip:* DDD. Interview required.

H615 MEng Electronic Engineering with Nanotechnology
Duration: 4FT Hon
Entry Requirements: *GCE:* AAAe-ABBe. *SQAAH:* AAA-ABB. *BTEC ExtDip:* DDD. Interview required.

H601 MEng Electronic and Electrical Engineering
Duration: 4FT Hon
Entry Requirements: *GCE:* AAAe-ABBe. *SQAAH:* AAA-ABB. *BTEC ExtDip:* DDD. Interview required.

H605 MEng Electronic and Electrical Engineering (International Programme)
Duration: 4FT Hon
Entry Requirements: *GCE:* AAAe-ABBe. *SQAAH:* AAA-ABB. *BTEC ExtDip:* DDD. Interview required.

U95 UXBRIDGE COLLEGE
PARK ROAD
UXBRIDGE
MIDDLESEX UB8 1NQ
t: 01895 853333 f: 01895 853377
e: enquiries@uxbridgecollege.ac.uk
// www.uxbridgecollege.ac.uk

006H HND Electrical & Electronic Engineering
Duration: 2FT HND
Entry Requirements: *OCR ND:* M2 *OCR NED:* M2 Interview required.

W05 THE UNIVERSITY OF WEST LONDON
ST MARY'S ROAD
EALING
LONDON W5 5RF
t: 0800 036 8888 f: 020 8566 1353
e: learning.advice@uwl.ac.uk
// www.uwl.ac.uk

JH9P BA Music Technology and Radio Broadcasting
Duration: 3FT Hon
Entry Requirements: *GCE:* 200. *IB:* 28. Interview required. Portfolio required.

H660 BEng Electrical & Electronic Engineering
Duration: 3FT Hon
Entry Requirements: *GCE:* 240. Interview required.

H613 BEng Electronics Engineering
Duration: 3FT Hon
Entry Requirements: *GCE:* 240. Interview required.

HH36 BSc Applied Sound Engineering
Duration: 3FT Hon
Entry Requirements: *GCE:* 240. Interview required.

W20 THE UNIVERSITY OF WARWICK
COVENTRY CV4 8UW
t: 024 7652 3723 f: 024 7652 4649
e: ugadmissions@warwick.ac.uk
// www.warwick.ac.uk

H610 BEng Electronic Engineering
Duration: 3FT Hon
Entry Requirements: *GCE:* AAB. *SQAAH:* AA-AB. *IB:* 36.

HH36 BEng Systems Engineering
Duration: 3FT Hon
Entry Requirements: *GCE:* AAB. *SQAAH:* AA-AB. *IB:* 36.

H612 MEng Electronic Engineering option - Business Management
Duration: 4FT Hon
Entry Requirements: *GCE:* BBB. *SQAAH:* AB-BB. *IB:* 34.

H612 MEng Electronic Engineering option - Communications
Duration: 4FT Hon
Entry Requirements: *GCE:* BBB. *SQAAH:* AB-BB. *IB:* 34.

H612 MEng Electronic Engineering
Duration: 4FT Hon
Entry Requirements: *GCE:* AAB. *SQAAH:* AA-AB. *IB:* 36.

H612 MEng Electronic Engineering option - Robotics
Duration: 4FT Hon
Entry Requirements: *GCE:* AAB. *SQAAH:* AB-BB. *IB:* 34.

HH63 MEng Systems Engineering
Duration: 4FT Hon
Entry Requirements: *GCE:* AAB. *SQAAH:* AA-AB. *IB:* 36.

HH63 MEng Systems Engineering option - Business Management
Duration: 4FT Hon
Entry Requirements: *GCE:* AAB-ABB. *SQAAH:* AA-AB. *IB:* 36.

HH63 MEng Systems Engineering option - Robotics
Duration: 4FT Hon
Entry Requirements: *GCE:* AAB-ABB. *SQAAH:* AA-AB. *IB:* 36.

HH63 MEng Systems Engineering option - Sustainability
Duration: 4FT Hon
Entry Requirements: *GCE:* AAB-ABB. *SQAAH:* AA-AB. *IB:* 36.

W25 WARWICKSHIRE COLLEGE
WARWICK NEW ROAD
LEAMINGTON SPA
WARWICKSHIRE CV32 5JE
t: 01926 884223 f: 01926 318 111
e: kgooch@warkscol.ac.uk
// www.warwickshire.ac.uk

006H HND Electrical/Electronic Engineering
Duration: 2FT HND
Entry Requirements: *GCE:* 120.

W50 UNIVERSITY OF WESTMINSTER
2ND FLOOR, CAVENDISH HOUSE
101 NEW CAVENDISH STREET,
LONDON W1W 6XH
t: 020 7915 5511
e: course-enquiries@westminster.ac.uk
// www.westminster.ac.uk

H650 BEng Computer Systems Engineering
Duration: 3FT/4SW Hon
Entry Requirements: *GCE:* BBB. *SQAH:* BBCC. *IB:* 32. Interview required.

H653 BEng Computer Systems Engineering with Foundation
Duration: 4FT Hon
Entry Requirements: *GCE:* CC-DDE. *IB:* 24. Interview required.

H610 BEng Electronic Engineering
Duration: 3FT/4SW Hon
Entry Requirements: *GCE:* BBB. *SQAH:* BBCC. *IB:* 32. Interview required.

H608 BEng Electronic Engineering with Foundation
Duration: 4FT Hon
Entry Requirements: *GCE:* CC-DDE. *IB:* 24. Interview required.

GHK6 BEng Mobile and Web Computing
Duration: 3FT/4SW Hon
Entry Requirements: *GCE:* BCC. *SQAH:* BBCC. *IB:* 30. Interview required.

GH4Q BEng Mobile and Web Computing with Foundation
Duration: 4FT Hon
Entry Requirements: *GCE:* CC-DDE. *IB:* 24. Interview required.

H657 BSc Computer Systems Engineering
Duration: 3FT/4SW Hon
Entry Requirements: *GCE:* AA-CCC. *SQAH:* BCCC-CCCCC. *IB:* 28. *OCR ND:* M1 *OCR NED:* M1 Interview required.

H656 BSc Computer Systems Engineering with Foundation
Duration: 4FT Hon
Entry Requirements: *GCE:* CC-DDE. *IB:* 24. Interview required.

H601 BSc Electronic Engineering
Duration: 3FT/4SW Hon
Entry Requirements: *GCE:* AA-CCC. *SQAH:* BCCC-CCCCC. *IB:* 28. Interview required.

H607 BSc Electronic Engineering with Foundation
Duration: 4FT Hon
Entry Requirements: *GCE:* CC-DDE. *IB:* 24. Interview required.

H655 MEng Computer Systems Engineering
Duration: 4FT/5SW Hon
Entry Requirements: *GCE:* BBB. *IB:* 32. Interview required.

H611 MEng Electronic Engineering
Duration: 4FT/5SW Hon
Entry Requirements: *IB:* 32. Interview required.

GH4P MEng Mobile and Web Computing
Duration: 4FT/5SW Hon
Entry Requirements: *GCE:* BBB. *IB:* 32. Interview required.

W67 WIGAN AND LEIGH COLLEGE
PO BOX 53
PARSON'S WALK
WIGAN
GREATER MANCHESTER WN1 1RS
t: 01942 761605 f: 01942 761164
e: applications@wigan-leigh.ac.uk
// www.wigan-leigh.ac.uk

006H HND Electrical and Electronic Engineering
Duration: 2FT HND
Entry Requirements: *GCE:* 60. Interview required.

W75 UNIVERSITY OF WOLVERHAMPTON
ADMISSIONS UNIT
MX207, CAMP STREET
WOLVERHAMPTON
WEST MIDLANDS WV1 1AD
t: 01902 321000 f: 01902 321896
e: admissions@wlv.ac.uk
// www.wlv.ac.uk

H691 BEng Electronics and Communications Engineering
Duration: 3FT/4SW Hon
Entry Requirements: *GCE:* 160-220.

H692 MEng Electronics and Communications Engineering
Duration: 4FT/5SW Hon
Entry Requirements: Contact the institution for details.

W81 WORCESTER COLLEGE OF TECHNOLOGY
DEANSWAY
WORCESTER WR1 2JF
t: 01905 725555 f: 01905 28906
// www.wortech.ac.uk

H620 FdSc Electrical Installation
Duration: 2FT Fdg
Entry Requirements: Contact the institution for details.

016H HND Engineering Electrical / Electronic
Duration: 2FT HND
Entry Requirements: Contact the institution for details.

026H HND Engineering Electrical / Electronic
Duration: 1.5SW HNC
Entry Requirements: Contact the institution for details.

Y50 THE UNIVERSITY OF YORK
STUDENT RECRUITMENT AND ADMISSIONS
UNIVERSITY OF YORK
HESLINGTON
YORK YO10 5DD
t: 01904 324000 f: 01904 323538
e: ug-admissions@york.ac.uk
// www.york.ac.uk

H642 BEng Digital Media Systems
Duration: 3FT/4SW Hon
Entry Requirements: *GCE:* BBB. *SQAH:* BBBBB. *SQAAH:* BB. *IB:* 32. *BTEC ExtDip:* DDM.

H610 BEng Electronic Engineering
Duration: 3FT/4SW Hon
Entry Requirements: *GCE:* BBB. *SQAH:* BBBBB. *SQAAH:* BB. *IB:* 32. *BTEC ExtDip:* DDM.

H6N2 BEng Electronic Engineering with Business Management
Duration: 3FT/4SW Hon
Entry Requirements: *GCE:* BBB. *SQAH:* BBBBB. *SQAAH:* BB. *IB:* 32. *BTEC ExtDip:* DDM.

H645 BEng Electronic Engineering with Digital Media Systems
Duration: 3FT/4SW Hon
Entry Requirements: *GCE:* BBB. *SQAH:* BBBBB. *SQAAH:* BB. *IB:* 32. *BTEC ExtDip:* DDM.

H667 BEng Electronic Engineering with Music Technology Systems
Duration: 3FT/4SW Hon
Entry Requirements: *GCE:* BBB. *SQAH:* BBBBB. *SQAAH:* BB. *IB:* 32. *BTEC ExtDip:* DDM.

H6F3 BEng Electronic Engineering with Nanotechnology
Duration: 3FT/4SW Hon
Entry Requirements: *GCE:* BBB. *SQAH:* BBBBB. *SQAAH:* BB. *IB:* 32. *BTEC ExtDip:* DDM.

H604 BEng Electronic Engineering with foundation year (4 years)
Duration: 4FT Hon
Entry Requirements: Contact the institution for details.

H621 BEng Electronic and Communication Engineering
Duration: 3FT/4SW Hon
Entry Requirements: *GCE:* BBB. *SQAH:* BBBBB. *SQAAH:* BB. *IB:* 32. *BTEC ExtDip:* DDM.

H634 BEng Electronic and Computer Engineering
Duration: 3FT/4SW Hon
Entry Requirements: *GCE:* BBB. *SQAH:* BBBBB. *SQAAH:* BB. *IB:* 32. *BTEC ExtDip:* DDM.

H663 BEng Music Technology Systems
Duration: 3FT/4SW Hon
Entry Requirements: *GCE:* BBB. *SQAH:* BBBBB. *SQAAH:* BB. *IB:* 32. *BTEC ExtDip:* DDM.

HJ69 BSc Music Technology
Duration: 3FT Hon
Entry Requirements: *GCE:* BBB. *SQAH:* BBBBB. *SQAAH:* BB. *IB:* 32. *BTEC ExtDip:* DDD.

H649 MEng Avionics
Duration: 4FT/5SW Hon
Entry Requirements: *GCE:* AAB. *SQAH:* AAAAB. *SQAAH:* AB. *IB:* 35. *BTEC ExtDip:* DDD.

H682 MEng Digital Media Systems
Duration: 4FT/5SW Hon
Entry Requirements: *GCE:* AAB. *SQAH:* AAAAB. *SQAAH:* AB. *IB:* 35. *BTEC ExtDip:* DDD.

H609 MEng Electronic Engineering
Duration: 4FT/5SW Hon
Entry Requirements: *GCE:* AAB. *SQAH:* AAAAB. *SQAAH:* AB. *IB:*
35. *BTEC ExtDip:* DDD.

H6NG MEng Electronic Engineering with Business Management
Duration: 4FT/5SW Hon
Entry Requirements: *GCE:* AAB. *SQAH:* AAAAB. *SQAAH:* AB. *IB:*
35. *BTEC ExtDip:* DDD.

H681 MEng Electronic Engineering with Digital Media Systems
Duration: 4FT/5SW Hon
Entry Requirements: *GCE:* AAB. *SQAH:* AAAAB. *SQAAH:* AB. *IB:*
35. *BTEC ExtDip:* DDD.

H669 MEng Electronic Engineering with Music Technology Systems
Duration: 4FT/5SW Hon
Entry Requirements: *GCE:* AAB. *SQAH:* AAAAB. *SQAAH:* AB. *IB:*
35. *BTEC ExtDip:* DDD.

H6FH MEng Electronic Engineering with Nanotechnology
Duration: 4FT/5SW Hon
Entry Requirements: *GCE:* AAB. *SQAH:* AAAAB. *SQAAH:* AB. *IB:*
35. *BTEC ExtDip:* DDD.

H629 MEng Electronic and Communication Engineering
Duration: 4FT/5SW Hon
Entry Requirements: *GCE:* AAB. *SQAH:* AAAAB. *SQAAH:* AB. *IB:*
35. *BTEC ExtDip:* DDD.

H639 MEng Electronic and Computer Engineering
Duration: 4FT/5SW Hon
Entry Requirements: *GCE:* AAB. *SQAH:* AAAAB. *SQAAH:* AB. *IB:*
35. *BTEC ExtDip:* DDD.

H666 MEng Music Technology Systems
Duration: 4FT/5SW Hon
Entry Requirements: *GCE:* AAB. *SQAH:* AAAAB. *SQAAH:* AB. *IB:*
34. *BTEC ExtDip:* DDD.

Y70 YORK COLLEGE
SIM BALK LANE
YORK YO23 2BB
t: 01904 770448 f: 01904 770499
e: admissions.team@yorkcollege.ac.uk
// www.yorkcollege.ac.uk

H600 FdSc Electrical Electronic Engineering
Duration: 2FT/3SW Fdg
Entry Requirements: *GCE:* CC. Interview required.

MECHANICAL ENGINEERING

A20 THE UNIVERSITY OF ABERDEEN
UNIVERSITY OFFICE
KING'S COLLEGE
ABERDEEN AB24 3FX
t: +44 (0) 1224 273504 f: +44 (0) 1224 272034
e: sras@abdn.ac.uk
// www.abdn.ac.uk/sras

H302 BEng Engineering (Mechanical with European Studies)
Duration: 4FT Hon
Entry Requirements: *GCE:* BBB. *SQAH:* BBBC. *IB:* 28.

H300 BEng Engineering (Mechanical)
Duration: 4FT Hon
Entry Requirements: *GCE:* BBB. *SQAH:* BBBC. *IB:* 28.

H301 BScEng Engineering (Mechanical)
Duration: 3FT/4FT Ord
Entry Requirements: Contact the institution for details.

H305 MEng Mechanical Engineering
Duration: 5FT Hon
Entry Requirements: *GCE:* BBB. *SQAH:* BBBB. *IB:* 30.

H306 MEng Mechanical Engineering with European Studies
Duration: 5FT Hon
Entry Requirements: *GCE:* BBB. *SQAH:* BBBB. *IB:* 30.

H3N2 MEng Mechanical Engineering with Management
Duration: 5FT Hon
Entry Requirements: Contact the institution for details.

A60 ANGLIA RUSKIN UNIVERSITY
BISHOP HALL LANE
CHELMSFORD
ESSEX CM1 1SQ
t: 0845 271 3333 f: 01245 251789
e: answers@anglia.ac.uk
// www.anglia.ac.uk

H300 BEng Mechanical Engineering
Duration: 3FT Hon
Entry Requirements: *GCE:* 150.

A80 ASTON UNIVERSITY, BIRMINGHAM
ASTON TRIANGLE
BIRMINGHAM B4 7ET
t: 0121 204 4444 f: 0121 204 3696
e: admissions@aston.ac.uk (automatic response)
// www.aston.ac.uk/prospective-students/ug

H300 BEng Mechanical Engineering
Duration: 3FT/4SW Hon
Entry Requirements: *GCE:* 300-320. *IB:* 32. *OCR NED:* D1

H301 MEng Mechanical Engineering
Duration: 4FT/5SW Hon
Entry Requirements: *GCE:* 340-360. *IB:* 34.

B11 BARKING AND DAGENHAM COLLEGE
DAGENHAM ROAD
ROMFORD
ESSEX RM7 0XU
t: 020 8090 3020 f: 020 8090 3021
e: engagement.services@barkingdagenhamcollege.ac.uk
// www.barkingdagenhamcollege.ac.uk

033H HND Automotive Engineering
Duration: 2FT HND
Entry Requirements: Contact the institution for details.

B15 BASINGSTOKE COLLEGE OF TECHNOLOGY
WORTING ROAD
BASINGSTOKE RG21 8TN
t: (Main) 01256 354141 f: 01256 306444
e: admissions@bcot.ac.uk
// www.bcot.ac.uk

HH37 FdSc Mechanical and Manufacturing Engineering
Duration: 2FT Fdg   CRB Check: Required
Entry Requirements: Contact the institution for details.

B16 UNIVERSITY OF BATH
CLAVERTON DOWN
BATH BA2 7AY
t: 01225 383019 f: 01225 386366
e: admissions@bath.ac.uk
// www.bath.ac.uk

H334 FdSc Motorsport Engineering
Duration: 2FT Fdg
Entry Requirements: *SQAAH:* AAA-AAB.

H330 MEng Automotive Engineering
Duration: 4FT Hon
Entry Requirements: *GCE:* A*AA. *SQAAH:* AAA. *IB:* 36.

H343 MEng Automotive Engineering (Sandwich)
Duration: 5SW Hon
Entry Requirements: *GCE:* A*AA. *SQAAH:* AAA. *IB:* 36.

H306 MEng Mechanical Engineering
Duration: 4FT Hon
Entry Requirements: *GCE:* A*AA. *SQAAH:* AAA. *IB:* 36.

H309 MEng Mechanical Engineering (Sandwich)
Duration: 5SW Hon
Entry Requirements: *GCE:* A*AA. *SQAAH:* AAA. *IB:* 36.

H762 MEng Mechanical Engineering with Advanced Design & Innovation (with Placement)
Duration: 5SW Hon
Entry Requirements: *GCE:* A*AA. *SQAAH:* AAA. *IB:* 36.

H761 MEng Mechanical Engineering with Advanced Design and Innovation
Duration: 4FT Hon
Entry Requirements: *GCE:* A*AA. *SQAAH:* AAA. *IB:* 36.

B23 BEDFORD COLLEGE
CAULDWELL STREET
BEDFORD MK42 9AH
t: 01234 291000 f: 01234 342674
e: info@bedford.ac.uk
// www.bedford.ac.uk

003H HNC Mechanical Engineering
Duration: 1FT HNC
Entry Requirements: Contact the institution for details.

003I HND Mechanical Engineering
Duration: 1FT HND
Entry Requirements: Contact the institution for details.

37HH HND Mechanical/Manufacturing Engineering
Duration: 2FT HND
Entry Requirements: *GCE:* 120-160. Interview required.

B25 BIRMINGHAM CITY UNIVERSITY
PERRY BARR
BIRMINGHAM B42 2SU
t: 0121 331 5595 f: 0121 331 7994
// www.bcu.ac.uk

H330 BEng Automotive Engineering
Duration: 3FT/4SW Hon
Entry Requirements: *GCE:* 300. *IB:* 30.

H338 BEng Automotive Engineering with Foundation Year
Duration: 4FT/5SW Hon
Entry Requirements: *GCE:* 200. *IB:* 24.

H300 BEng Mechanical Engineering
Duration: 3FT/4SW Hon
Entry Requirements: *GCE:* 300. *IB:* 30.

H308 BEng Mechanical Engineering with Foundation Year
Duration: 4FT/5SW Hon
Entry Requirements: *GCE:* 200. *IB:* 24.

H334 BSc Motorsports Technology
Duration: 3FT/4SW Hon
Entry Requirements: *GCE:* 300. *IB:* 29.

B32 THE UNIVERSITY OF BIRMINGHAM
EDGBASTON
BIRMINGHAM B15 2TT
t: 0121 415 8900 f: 0121 414 7159
e: admissions@bham.ac.uk
// www.birmingham.ac.uk

H302 BEng Mechanical Engineering (Automotive)
Duration: 3FT Hon
Entry Requirements: *GCE:* AAB. *SQAH:* AAABB-AABBB. *SQAAH:* AA.

H300 BEng/MEng Mechanical Engineering
Duration: 3FT Hon
Entry Requirements: *GCE:* AAB. *SQAH:* AAABB-AABBB. *SQAAH:* AA.

H391 BEng/MEng Mechanical Engineering with Foundation Year
Duration: 4FT Hon
Entry Requirements: Contact the institution for details.

HJ35 BEng/MEng Mechanical and Materials Engineering
Duration: 3FT Hon
Entry Requirements: *GCE:* AAB. *SQAH:* AAABB-AABBB. *SQAAH:* AA.

H301 MEng Mechanical Engineering
Duration: 4FT Hon
Entry Requirements: *GCE:* AAA. *SQAH:* AAAAB-AAABB. *SQAAH:* AA.

H330 MEng Mechanical Engineering (Automotive)
Duration: 4FT Hon
Entry Requirements: *GCE:* AAA. *SQAH:* AAAAB-AAABB. *SQAAH:* AA.

H303 MEng Mechanical Engineering with Industrial Year
Duration: 5FT Hon
Entry Requirements: Contact the institution for details.

HJ53 MEng Mechanical and Materials Engineering
Duration: 4FT Hon
Entry Requirements: *GCE:* AAA. *SQAH:* AAAAB-AAABB. *SQAAH:* AA.

B40 BLACKBURN COLLEGE
FEILDEN STREET
BLACKBURN BB2 1LH
t: 01254 292594 f: 01254 679647
e: he-admissions@blackburn.ac.uk
// www.blackburn.ac.uk

H302 BEng Mechanical Engineering
Duration: 3FT Hon
Entry Requirements: *GCE:* 160.

H301 BEng Mechanical Engineering (Top-Up)
Duration: 1FT/2FT Ord/Hon
Entry Requirements: Contact the institution for details.

003H HND Mechanical Engineering
Duration: 2FT HND
Entry Requirements: *GCE:* 120.

B41 BLACKPOOL AND THE FYLDE COLLEGE AN ASSOCIATE COLLEGE OF LANCASTER UNIVERSITY
ASHFIELD ROAD
BISPHAM
BLACKPOOL
LANCS FY2 0HB
t: 01253 504346 f: 01253 504198
e: admissions@blackpool.ac.uk
// www.blackpool.ac.uk

H334 BEng Automotive Engineering and Technology (Top-Up)
Duration: 1FT Hon
Entry Requirements: Contact the institution for details.

H131 FdEng Automotive Engineering and Technology
Duration: 2FT Fdg
Entry Requirements: *GCE:* 120-360. *IB:* 24. *OCR ND:* P *OCR NED:* P

HH31 FdEng Automotive Engineering and Technology (including Year 0)
Duration: 3FT Fdg
Entry Requirements: *GCE:* 100-360.

H331 FdEng Autosport Engineering and Technology (including Year 0)
Duration: 3FT Fdg
Entry Requirements: Contact the institution for details.

003H HND Mechanical Engineering
Duration: 2FT HND
Entry Requirements: *GCE:* 120-360. *IB:* 24.

B44 UNIVERSITY OF BOLTON
DEANE ROAD
BOLTON BL3 5AB
t: 01204 903903 f: 01204 399074
e: enquiries@bolton.ac.uk
// www.bolton.ac.uk

H330 BEng Automobile Engineering
Duration: 3FT Hon
Entry Requirements: *GCE:* 240. Interview required.

H336 BEng Automobile Engineering with foundation year
Duration: 4FT Hon
Entry Requirements: *GCE:* 80. Interview required.

H300 BEng Mechanical Engineering
Duration: 3FT Hon
Entry Requirements: *GCE:* 240. Interview required.

H301 BEng Mechanical Engineering with foundation year
Duration: 4FT Hon
Entry Requirements: *GCE:* 80. Interview required.

H340 BSc Sound Engineering & Design
Duration: 3FT Hon
Entry Requirements: *GCE:* 260. Interview required.

H344 BSc Sound Engineering & Design
Duration: 1FT Hon
Entry Requirements: Interview required.

H335 MEng Automobile Engineering
Duration: 4FT Hon
Entry Requirements: *GCE:* 300. Interview required.

H302 MEng Mechanical Engineering
Duration: 4FT Hon
Entry Requirements: *GCE:* 300. Interview required.

B50 BOURNEMOUTH UNIVERSITY
TALBOT CAMPUS
FERN BARROW
POOLE
DORSET BH12 5BB
t: 01202 524111
// www.bournemouth.ac.uk

H300 FdSc Engineering (Mechanical Design)
Duration: 2FT Fdg
Entry Requirements: Contact the institution for details.

B56 THE UNIVERSITY OF BRADFORD
RICHMOND ROAD
BRADFORD
WEST YORKSHIRE BD7 1DP
t: 0800 073 1225 f: 01274 235585
e: course-enquiries@bradford.ac.uk
// www.bradford.ac.uk

H300 BEng Mechanical Engineering
Duration: 3FT Hon
Entry Requirements: *GCE:* 240. *IB:* 24.

H301 BEng Mechanical Engineering (4 years)
Duration: 4SW Hon
Entry Requirements: *GCE:* 240. *IB:* 24.

H330 BEng Mechanical and Automotive Engineering
Duration: 3FT Hon
Entry Requirements: *GCE:* 240. *IB:* 24.

H331 BEng Mechanical and Automotive Engineering (4 years)
Duration: 4SW Hon
Entry Requirements: *GCE:* 240. *IB:* 24.

H390 BSc Automotive Design Technology
Duration: 3FT Hon
Entry Requirements: *GCE:* 240. *IB:* 24. Interview required.

H391 BSc Automotive Design Technology (4 years)
Duration: 4SW Hon
Entry Requirements: *GCE:* 240. *IB:* 24. Interview required.

H306 MEng Mechanical Engineering
Duration: 5SW Hon
Entry Requirements: *GCE:* 300. *IB:* 26.

H305 MEng Mechanical Engineering (4 years)
Duration: 4FT Hon
Entry Requirements: *GCE:* 300. *IB:* 26.

H392 MEng Mechanical and Automotive Engineering
Duration: 4FT Hon
Entry Requirements: *GCE:* 300. *IB:* 26.

H393 MEng Mechanical and Automotive Engineering
Duration: 5SW Hon
Entry Requirements: *GCE:* 300. *IB:* 26.

B60 BRADFORD COLLEGE: AN ASSOCIATE COLLEGE OF LEEDS METROPOLITAN UNIVERSITY
GREAT HORTON ROAD
BRADFORD
WEST YORKSHIRE BD7 1AY
t: 01274 433008 f: 01274 431652
e: heregistry@bradfordcollege.ac.uk
// www.bradfordcollege.ac.uk/
university-centre

011H HND Mechanical Engineering
Duration: 2FT HND
Entry Requirements: *GCE:* 100. Interview required. Admissions Test required.

B72 UNIVERSITY OF BRIGHTON
MITHRAS HOUSE 211
LEWES ROAD
BRIGHTON BN2 4AT
t: 01273 644644 f: 01273 642607
e: admissions@brighton.ac.uk
// www.brighton.ac.uk

H330 BEng Automotive Engineering (BEng)
Duration: 3FT/4SW Hon
Entry Requirements: *GCE:* BBB. *IB:* 32.

H300 BEng Mechanical Engineering
Duration: 3FT/4SW Hon
Entry Requirements: *GCE:* BBB. *IB:* 32.

H301 BEng Mechanical Engineering (with integrated Foundation Year)
Duration: 4FT Hon
Entry Requirements: *GCE:* BBC. *IB:* 30.

H331 BEng(Hons) Automotive Engineering (with Integrated Foundation Year)
Duration: 4FT Hon
Entry Requirements: Contact the institution for details.

H336 BSc Automotive Engineering (Top-Up)
Duration: 1FT Hon
Entry Requirements: HND required.

HH37 BSc Mechanical and Manufacturing Engineering (Top-Up)
Duration: 1FT Hon
Entry Requirements: HND required.

HH73 FdEng Mechanical and Manufacturing Engineering
Duration: 2FT Fdg
Entry Requirements: *GCE:* 120. *IB:* 24.

H335 MEng Automotive Engineering (MEng)
Duration: 4FT/5SW Hon
Entry Requirements: *GCE:* ABB. *IB:* 34.

H302 MEng Mechanical Engineering
Duration: 4FT/5SW Hon
Entry Requirements: *GCE:* BBB. *IB:* 32.

B77 BRISTOL, CITY OF BRISTOL COLLEGE
SOUTH BRISTOL SKILLS ACADEMY
CITY OF BRISTOL COLLEGE
PO BOX 2887 BS2 2BB
t: 0117 312 5000
e: HEAdmissions@cityofbristol.ac.uk
// www.cityofbristol.ac.uk

003H FdSc Engineering (Mechanical)
Duration: 2FT Fdg
Entry Requirements: *GCE:* 140. Interview required.

B78 UNIVERSITY OF BRISTOL
UNDERGRADUATE ADMISSIONS OFFICE
SENATE HOUSE
TYNDALL AVENUE
BRISTOL BS8 1TH
t: 0117 928 9000 f: 0117 331 7391
e: ug-admissions@bristol.ac.uk
// www.bristol.ac.uk

H305 BEng Mechanical Engineering
Duration: 3FT Hon
Entry Requirements: *GCE:* A*AA-AAB. *SQAH:* AAAAA-AAABB. *SQAAH:* AA-AB.

H300 MEng Mechanical Engineering
Duration: 4FT Hon
Entry Requirements: *GCE:* A*AA-AAB. *SQAH:* AAAAA-AAABB. *SQAAH:* AA-AB.

H301 MEng Mechanical Engineering with Study in Continental Europe
Duration: 4FT Hon
Entry Requirements: *GCE:* A*AA-AAB. *SQAH:* AAAAA-AAABB. *SQAAH:* AA-AB.

B80 UNIVERSITY OF THE WEST OF ENGLAND, BRISTOL
FRENCHAY CAMPUS
COLDHARBOUR LANE
BRISTOL BS16 1QY
t: +44 (0)117 32 83333 f: +44 (0)117 32 82810
e: admissions@uwe.ac.uk
// www.uwe.ac.uk

H300 BEng Mechanical Engineering
Duration: 3FT/4SW Hon
Entry Requirements: *GCE:* 280.

H330 BEng Motorsport Engineering
Duration: 3FT/4SW Hon
Entry Requirements: *GCE:* 280.

H301 MEng Mechanical Engineering
Duration: 4FT/5SW Hon
Entry Requirements: *GCE:* 300.

H334 MEng Motorsport Engineering
Duration: 4FT/5SW Hon
Entry Requirements: **GCE:** 300.

B84 BRUNEL UNIVERSITY
UXBRIDGE
MIDDLESEX UB8 3PH
t: 01895 265265 f: 01895 269790
e: admissions@brunel.ac.uk
// www.brunel.ac.uk

H303 BEng Mechanical Engineering
Duration: 3FT Hon
Entry Requirements: **GCE:** ABB. **SQAAH:** ABB. **IB:** 33. **BTEC SubDip:** D*. **BTEC Dip:** D*D. **BTEC ExtDip:** D*DD. **OCR ND:** D

H304 BEng Mechanical Engineering (4 year Thick SW)
Duration: 4SW Hon
Entry Requirements: **GCE:** ABB. **SQAAH:** ABB. **IB:** 33. **BTEC SubDip:** D*. **BTEC Dip:** D*D. **BTEC ExtDip:** D*DD. **OCR ND:** D

H330 BEng Mechanical Engineering with Automotive Design
Duration: 3FT Hon
Entry Requirements: **GCE:** ABB. **SQAAH:** ABB. **IB:** 33. **BTEC SubDip:** D*. **BTEC Dip:** D*D. **BTEC ExtDip:** D*DD. **OCR ND:** D

H342 BEng Mechanical Engineering with Automotive Design (4 year Thick SW)
Duration: 4SW Hon
Entry Requirements: **GCE:** ABB. **SQAAH:** ABB. **IB:** 33. **BTEC SubDip:** D*. **BTEC Dip:** D*D. **BTEC ExtDip:** D*DD. **OCR ND:** D

H3KF BEng Mechanical Engineering with Building Services
Duration: 3FT Hon
Entry Requirements: **GCE:** ABB. **SQAAH:** ABB. **IB:** 33. **BTEC SubDip:** D*. **BTEC Dip:** D*D. **BTEC ExtDip:** D*DD. **OCR ND:** D

H3K2 BEng Mechanical Engineering with Building Services (4 year Thick SW)
Duration: 4SW Hon
Entry Requirements: **GCE:** ABB. **SQAAH:** ABB. **IB:** 33. **BTEC SubDip:** D*. **BTEC Dip:** D*D. **BTEC ExtDip:** D*DD. **OCR ND:** D

H336 BEng Motorsport Engineering
Duration: 3FT Hon
Entry Requirements: **GCE:** ABB. **SQAAH:** ABB. **IB:** 33. **BTEC SubDip:** D*. **BTEC Dip:** D*D. **BTEC ExtDip:** D*DD. **OCR ND:** D

H335 BEng Motorsport Engineering (4 year Thick SW)
Duration: 4SW Hon
Entry Requirements: **GCE:** ABB. **SQAAH:** ABB. **IB:** 33. **BTEC SubDip:** D*. **BTEC Dip:** D*D. **BTEC ExtDip:** D*DD. **OCR ND:** D

H301 MEng Mechanical Engineering (4 years)
Duration: 4FT Hon
Entry Requirements: **GCE:** AAA-AAB. **SQAAH:** AAA-AAB. **IB:** 37. **BTEC ExtDip:** D*D*D*.

H302 MEng Mechanical Engineering (5 year Thick SW)
Duration: 5SW Hon
Entry Requirements: **GCE:** AAA-AAB. **SQAAH:** AAA-AAB. **IB:** 37. **BTEC ExtDip:** D*D*D*.

H320 MEng Mechanical Engineering with Automotive Design (4 years)
Duration: 4FT Hon
Entry Requirements: **GCE:** AAA-AAB. **SQAAH:** AAA-AAB. **IB:** 37. **BTEC ExtDip:** D*D*D*.

H321 MEng Mechanical Engineering with Automotive Design (5 year Thick SW)
Duration: 5SW Hon
Entry Requirements: **GCE:** AAA-AAB. **SQAAH:** AAA-AAB. **IB:** 37. **BTEC ExtDip:** D*D*D*.

H331 MEng Motorsport Engineering (4 years)
Duration: 4FT Hon
Entry Requirements: **GCE:** AAA-AAB. **SQAAH:** AAA-AAB. **IB:** 37. **BTEC ExtDip:** D*D*D*.

H334 MEng Motorsport Engineering (5 year Thick SW)
Duration: 5SW Hon
Entry Requirements: **GCE:** AAA-AAB. **SQAAH:** AAA-AAB. **IB:** 37. **BTEC ExtDip:** D*D*D*.

B94 BUCKINGHAMSHIRE NEW UNIVERSITY
QUEEN ALEXANDRA ROAD
HIGH WYCOMBE
BUCKINGHAMSHIRE HP11 2JZ
t: 0800 0565 660 f: 01494 605 023
e: admissions@bucks.ac.uk
// bucks.ac.uk

HH31 BEng Mechanical Engineering Design
Duration: 3FT Hon **CRB Check:** Required
Entry Requirements: Contact the institution for details.

C15 CARDIFF UNIVERSITY
PO BOX 927
30-36 NEWPORT ROAD
CARDIFF CF24 0DE
t: 029 2087 9999 f: 029 2087 6138
e: admissions@cardiff.ac.uk
// www.cardiff.ac.uk

H300 BEng Mechanical Engineering
Duration: 3FT Hon
Entry Requirements: **GCE:** AAB. **IB:** 32. Interview required. Admissions Test required.

H301 BEng Mechanical Engineering (Year in Industry)
Duration: 4SW Hon
Entry Requirements: **GCE:** AAB. **IB:** 32. Interview required. Admissions Test required.

H302 MEng Mechanical Engineering
Duration: 4FT Hon
Entry Requirements: *GCE:* AAB. *IB:* 32. Interview required.
Admissions Test required.

H307 MEng Mechanical Engineering (Year in Industry)
Duration: 5SW Hon
Entry Requirements: *GCE:* AAB. *IB:* 32. Interview required.
Admissions Test required.

H303 MEng Mechanical Engineering with Year in Europe (Germany)
Duration: 5SW Hon
Entry Requirements: *GCE:* AAB. *IB:* 32. Interview required.
Admissions Test required.

H305 MEng Mechanical Engineering with Year in Europe (Spain)
Duration: 5SW Hon
Entry Requirements: *GCE:* AAB. *IB:* 32. Interview required.
Admissions Test required.

H308 MEng Mechanical Engineering with a Year in Europe (France)
Duration: 5SW Hon
Entry Requirements: *GCE:* AAB. *IB:* 32. Interview required.
Admissions Test required.

C30 UNIVERSITY OF CENTRAL LANCASHIRE
PRESTON
LANCS PR1 2HE
t: 01772 201201 f: 01772 894954
e: uadmissions@uclan.ac.uk
// www.uclan.ac.uk

H391 BEng Mechanical Maintenance Engineering (Top-Up)
Duration: 1FT Hon
Entry Requirements: HND required.

H331 BEng Motor Sports Engineering
Duration: 3FT/4SW Hon
Entry Requirements: *GCE:* 240-280. *IB:* 24.

H330 BSc Motor Sport
Duration: 3FT/4SW Hon
Entry Requirements: *GCE:* 220. *IB:* 24.

H336 BSc Motor Sports (Foundation entry)
Duration: 4FT Hon
Entry Requirements: *GCE:* 100. *IB:* 24. *OCR ND:* P2 *OCR NED:* P3

H334 MEng Motor Sports Engineering
Duration: 4FT/5SW Hon
Entry Requirements: *GCE:* 280-320. *IB:* 25.

C60 CITY UNIVERSITY
NORTHAMPTON SQUARE
LONDON EC1V 0HB
t: 020 7040 5060 f: 020 7040 8995
e: ugadmissions@city.ac.uk
// www.city.ac.uk

H335 BEng Automotive and Motorsport Engineering (4 year SW) (c)
Duration: 4SW Hon
Entry Requirements: *GCE:* 340. *IB:* 30.

H331 BEng Automotive and Motorsport Engineering (c)
Duration: 3FT Hon
Entry Requirements: *GCE:* 340. *IB:* 30.

H301 BEng Mechanical Engineering (4 year SW) (i)
Duration: 4SW Hon
Entry Requirements: *GCE:* 340. *IB:* 30.

H302 BEng Mechanical Engineering (4 years including Foundation Year) (i)
Duration: 4FT Hon
Entry Requirements: *GCE:* 130. *SQAH:* BC.

H300 BEng Mechanical Engineering (i)
Duration: 3FT Hon
Entry Requirements: *GCE:* 340. *IB:* 30.

H330 MEng Automotive and Motorsport Engineering (4 years) (c)
Duration: 4FT Hon
Entry Requirements: *GCE:* 360. *IB:* 32.

H334 MEng Automotive and Motorsport Engineering (5 year SW) (c)
Duration: 5SW Hon
Entry Requirements: *GCE:* 360. *IB:* 32.

H304 MEng Mechanical Engineering (4 years) (i)
Duration: 4FT Hon
Entry Requirements: *GCE:* 360. *IB:* 32.

H305 MEng Mechanical Engineering (5 year SW) (i)
Duration: 5SW Hon
Entry Requirements: *GCE:* 360. *IB:* 32.

C75 COLCHESTER INSTITUTE
SHEEPEN ROAD
COLCHESTER
ESSEX CO3 3LL
t: 01206 712777 f: 01206 712800
e: info@colchester.ac.uk
// www.colchester.ac.uk

H300 HNC Engineering (Mechanical)
Duration: 1FT HNC
Entry Requirements: Contact the institution for details.

003H HND Engineering (Mechanical)
Duration: 2FT HND
Entry Requirements: Contact the institution for details.

C85 COVENTRY UNIVERSITY
THE STUDENT CENTRE
COVENTRY UNIVERSITY
1 GULSON RD
COVENTRY CV1 2JH
t: 024 7615 2222 f: 024 7615 2223
e: studentenquiries@coventry.ac.uk
// www.coventry.ac.uk

WHG3 BA Automotive Design
Duration: 3FT/4SW Hon
Entry Requirements: *Foundation:* Merit. *GCE:* BCC. *SQAH:* BCCCC. *IB:* 27. *BTEC ExtDip:* MMM. *OCR NED:* M3 Interview required. Portfolio required.

H335 BEng Motorsport Engineering
Duration: 3FT/4SW Hon
Entry Requirements: *GCE:* BBC. *SQAH:* BBCCC. *IB:* 29. *BTEC ExtDip:* DMM. *OCR NED:* M2

H343 BEng/MEng Automotive Engineering
Duration: 3FT/4FT/4SW/5SW Hon
Entry Requirements: *GCE:* BBC. *SQAH:* BBCCC. *IB:* 29. *BTEC ExtDip:* DMM. *OCR NED:* M2

H300 BEng/MEng Mechanical Engineering
Duration: 3FT/4FT/4SW/5SW Hon
Entry Requirements: *GCE:* BBC. *SQAH:* BBCCC. *IB:* 29. *BTEC ExtDip:* DMM. *OCR NED:* M2

D26 DE MONTFORT UNIVERSITY
THE GATEWAY
LEICESTER LE1 9BH
t: 0116 255 1551 f: 0116 250 6204
e: enquiries@dmu.ac.uk
// www.dmu.ac.uk

H301 BEng Mechanical Engineering
Duration: 3FT/4SW Hon
Entry Requirements: *GCE:* 300. *IB:* 28. *BTEC ExtDip:* DDM. Interview required.

D39 UNIVERSITY OF DERBY
KEDLESTON ROAD
DERBY DE22 1GB
t: 01332 591167 f: 01332 597724
e: askadmissions@derby.ac.uk
// www.derby.ac.uk

H300 BEng Mechanical Engineering
Duration: 3FT Hon
Entry Requirements: *GCE:* 260. *IB:* 28. *BTEC Dip:* D*D*. *BTEC ExtDip:* DMM. *OCR ND:* D *OCR NED:* M3

H335 BEng Motorcycle Engineering
Duration: 3FT Hon
Entry Requirements: *GCE:* 260. *IB:* 28. *BTEC Dip:* D*D*. *BTEC ExtDip:* DMM. *OCR ND:* D *OCR NED:* M3

H336 BEng Motorsport Engineering
Duration: 3FT Hon
Entry Requirements: *GCE:* 260. *IB:* 28. *BTEC Dip:* D*D*. *BTEC ExtDip:* DMM. *OCR ND:* D *OCR NED:* M3

HJ39 BSc Sound, Light and Live Event Technology
Duration: 3FT Hon
Entry Requirements: *GCE:* 260. *IB:* 28. *BTEC Dip:* D*D*. *BTEC ExtDip:* DMM. *OCR NED:* M2

H301 FYr Mechanical Engineering Foundation
Duration: 1FT FYr
Entry Requirements: *Foundation:* Pass. *GCE:* 160. *IB:* 24. *BTEC Dip:* D*D*. *BTEC ExtDip:* DMM. *OCR ND:* M2 *OCR NED:* P2

H332 FYr Motorcycle Engineering Foundation
Duration: 1FT FYr
Entry Requirements: *Foundation:* Pass. *GCE:* 160. *IB:* 24. *BTEC Dip:* D*D*. *BTEC ExtDip:* DMM. *OCR ND:* M2 *OCR NED:* P2

H333 FYr Motorsport Engineering Foundation
Duration: 1FT FYr
Entry Requirements: *Foundation:* Pass. *GCE:* 160. *IB:* 24. *BTEC Dip:* D*D*. *BTEC ExtDip:* DMM. *OCR ND:* M2 *OCR NED:* P2

HJ3X FYr Sound, Light & Live Event Technology Foundation
Duration: 1FT FYr
Entry Requirements: *Foundation:* Pass. *GCE:* 160. *IB:* 24. *BTEC Dip:* D*D*. *BTEC ExtDip:* DMM. *OCR ND:* M2 *OCR NED:* P2

H331 FdSc Motorcycle Engineering
Duration: 2FT Fdg
Entry Requirements: *GCE:* 160. *IB:* 26. *BTEC Dip:* D*D*. *BTEC ExtDip:* DMM. *OCR ND:* P1 *OCR NED:* P2 Interview required.

H330 FdSc Motorsport Engineering
Duration: 2FT Fdg
Entry Requirements: *GCE:* 160. *IB:* 26. *BTEC Dip:* D*D*. *BTEC ExtDip:* DMM. *OCR ND:* P1 *OCR NED:* P2 Interview required.

D52 DONCASTER COLLEGE
THE HUB
CHAPPELL DRIVE
SOUTH YORKSHIRE DN1 2RF
t: 01302 553610
e: he@don.ac.uk
// www.don.ac.uk

003H HND Mechanical Engineering and Production
Duration: 2FT HND
Entry Requirements: *GCE:* 40.

D65 UNIVERSITY OF DUNDEE
NETHERGATE
DUNDEE DD1 4HN
t: 01382 383838 f: 01382 388150
e: contactus@dundee.ac.uk
// www.dundee.ac.uk/admissions/undergraduate/

H300 BEng Mechanical Engineering
Duration: 4FT Hon
Entry Requirements: *GCE:* BCC. *SQAH:* ABBB. *IB:* 30.

D86 DURHAM UNIVERSITY
DURHAM UNIVERSITY
UNIVERSITY OFFICE
DURHAM DH1 3HP
t: 0191 334 2000 f: 0191 334 6055
e: admissions@durham.ac.uk
// www.durham.ac.uk

H300 MEng Mechanical Engineering
Duration: 4FT Hon
Entry Requirements: *GCE:* AAA. *SQAH:* AAAAB. *SQAAH:* AAA. *IB:* 37.

E56 THE UNIVERSITY OF EDINBURGH
STUDENT RECRUITMENT & ADMISSIONS
57 GEORGE SQUARE
EDINBURGH EH8 9JU
t: 0131 650 4360 f: 0131 651 1236
e: sra.enquiries@ed.ac.uk
// www.ed.ac.uk/studying/undergraduate/

H300 BEng Mechanical Engineering
Duration: 4FT Hon
Entry Requirements: *GCE:* AAA-ABB. *SQAH:* AAAA-ABBB.

H3N2 BEng Mechanical Engineering with Management
Duration: 4FT Hon
Entry Requirements: *GCE:* AAA-ABB. *SQAH:* AAAA-ABBB.

H3F8 BEng Mechanical Engineering with Renewable Energy
Duration: 4FT Hon
Entry Requirements: *GCE:* AAA-ABB. *SQAH:* AAAA-ABBB.

H303 MEng Mechanical Engineering
Duration: 5FT Hon
Entry Requirements: *GCE:* AAA-ABB. *SQAH:* AAAA-ABBB.

H3NF MEng Mechanical Engineering with Management
Duration: 5FT Hon
Entry Requirements: *GCE:* AAA-ABB. *SQAH:* AAAA-ABBB.

H3FV MEng Mechanical Engineering with Renewable Energy
Duration: 5FT Hon
Entry Requirements: *GCE:* AAA-ABB. *SQAH:* AAAA-ABBB.

E59 EDINBURGH NAPIER UNIVERSITY
CRAIGLOCKHART CAMPUS
EDINBURGH EH14 1DJ
t: +44 (0)8452 60 60 40 f: 0131 455 6464
e: info@napier.ac.uk
// www.napier.ac.uk

H300 BEng Mechanical Engineering
Duration: 3FT/4FT Ord/Hon
Entry Requirements: *GCE:* 245.

H301 MEng Mechanical Engineering
Duration: 5FT Hon
Entry Requirements: *GCE:* 260.

E81 EXETER COLLEGE
HELE ROAD
EXETER
DEVON EX4 4JS
t: 0845 111 6000
e: info@exe-coll.ac.uk
// www.exe-coll.ac.uk/he

H300 FdSc Mechanical Engineering
Duration: 2FT Fdg
Entry Requirements: *GCE:* 160.

E84 UNIVERSITY OF EXETER
LAVER BUILDING
NORTH PARK ROAD
EXETER
DEVON EX4 4QE
t: 01392 723044 f: 01392 722479
e: admissions@exeter.ac.uk
// www.exeter.ac.uk

H300 BEng Mechanical Engineering
Duration: 3FT Hon
Entry Requirements: *GCE:* AAB-ABB. *SQAH:* AAABB-AABBB. *SQAAH:* ABB-BBB.

H301 BEng Mechanical Engineering with Industrial Experience
Duration: 3FT Hon
Entry Requirements: *GCE:* AAB-ABB. *SQAH:* AAABB-AABBB. *SQAAH:* ABB-BBB.

H308 BEng Mechanical Engineering with International Study
Duration: 3FT Hon
Entry Requirements: *GCE:* AAB-ABB. *SQAH:* AAABB-AABBB. *SQAAH:* ABB-BBB.

H302 MEng Mechanical Engineering
Duration: 4FT Hon
Entry Requirements: *GCE:* AAA-AAB. *SQAH:* AAAAB-AAABB. *SQAAH:* AAB-ABB. *BTEC ExtDip:* DDM.

H303 MEng Mechanical Engineering with Industrial Experience
Duration: 4FT Hon
Entry Requirements: *GCE:* AAA-AAB. *SQAH:* AAAAB-AAABB. *SQAAH:* AAB-ABB. *BTEC ExtDip:* DDM.

H309 MEng Mechanical Engineering with International Study (4 Years)
Duration: 4FT Hon
Entry Requirements: *GCE:* AAA-AAB. *SQAH:* AAAAB-AAABB. *SQAAH:* AAB-ABB. *BTEC ExtDip:* DDM.

G14 UNIVERSITY OF GLAMORGAN, CARDIFF AND PONTYPRIDD
ENQUIRIES AND ADMISSIONS UNIT
PONTYPRIDD CF37 1DL
t: 08456 434030 f: 01443 654050
e: enquiries@glam.ac.uk
// www.glam.ac.uk

H300 BEng Mechanical Engineering
Duration: 3FT Hon
Entry Requirements: *GCE:* BBC. *IB:* 25. *BTEC SubDip:* M. *BTEC Dip:* D*D*. *BTEC ExtDip:* DMM.

H303 BEng Mechanical Engineering
Duration: 4SW Hon
Entry Requirements: *GCE:* BBC. *IB:* 25. *BTEC SubDip:* M. *BTEC Dip:* D*D*. *BTEC ExtDip:* DMM.

H301 FYr Mechanical Engineering Foundation Year
Duration: 1FT FYr
Entry Requirements: *GCE:* 40. *BTEC SubDip:* M. *BTEC Dip:* PP. *BTEC ExtDip:* PPP. Interview required.

73HH HND Mechanical Engineering
Duration: 2FT/3SW HND
Entry Requirements: *GCE:* DD. *IB:* 24. *BTEC SubDip:* D. *BTEC Dip:* MP. *BTEC ExtDip:* PPP. *OCR ND:* M2

G28 UNIVERSITY OF GLASGOW
71 SOUTHPARK AVENUE
UNIVERSITY OF GLASGOW
GLASGOW G12 8QQ
t: 0141 330 6062 f: 0141 330 2961
e: student.recruitment@glasgow.ac.uk
// www.glasgow.ac.uk

HH37 BEng Mechanical Design Engineering
Duration: 4FT Hon
Entry Requirements: *GCE:* ABB. *SQAH:* AAAB-BBB. *IB:* 32.

H300 BEng Mechanical Engineering
Duration: 4FT Hon
Entry Requirements: *GCE:* ABB. *SQAH:* AAAB-BBB. *IB:* 32.

H3R9 BEng Mechanical Engineering (European Curriculum)
Duration: 4FT Hon
Entry Requirements: *GCE:* ABB. *SQAH:* AAAB-BBB. *IB:* 32.

H3W2 BEng Product Design Engineering
Duration: 4FT Hon
Entry Requirements: *GCE:* ABB. *SQAH:* AAAB-BBB. *IB:* 32.

HHJ7 MEng Mechanical Design Engineering
Duration: 5FT Hon
Entry Requirements: *GCE:* AAB. *SQAH:* AAAA-AAABB. *IB:* 34.

H303 MEng Mechanical Design Engineering (Faster Route)
Duration: 4FT Hon
Entry Requirements: *GCE:* AAA. *SQAH:* AB. *SQAAH:* AA. *IB:* 38.

H302 MEng Mechanical Engineering
Duration: 5FT Hon
Entry Requirements: *GCE:* AAB. *SQAH:* AAAA-AAABB. *IB:* 34.

H3RX MEng Mechanical Engineering (European Curriculum)
Duration: 5FT Hon
Entry Requirements: *GCE:* AAB. *SQAH:* AAAA-AAABB. *IB:* 34.

H304 MEng Mechanical Engineering (Faster Route)
Duration: 4FT Hon
Entry Requirements: *GCE:* AAA. *SQAH:* AB. *SQAAH:* AA. *IB:* 38.

H305 MEng Mechanical Engineering - European Curriculum (Faster Route)
Duration: 4FT Hon
Entry Requirements: *GCE:* AAA. *SQAH:* AB. *SQAAH:* AA. *IB:* 38.

H3WG MEng Product Design Engineering
Duration: 5FT Hon
Entry Requirements: *GCE:* AAB. *SQAH:* AAAA-AAABB. *IB:* 34.

G42 GLASGOW CALEDONIAN UNIVERSITY
STUDENT RECRUITMENT & ADMISSIONS SERVICE
CITY CAMPUS
COWCADDENS ROAD
GLASGOW G4 0BA
t: 0141 331 3000 f: 0141 331 8676
e: undergraduate@gcu.ac.uk
// www.gcu.ac.uk

H360 BEng Mechanical Electronic Systems Engineering
Duration: 4FT/5SW Hon
Entry Requirements: Contact the institution for details.

H361 MEng Mechanical Electronic Systems Engineering
Duration: 5FT/6SW Hon
Entry Requirements: Contact the institution for details.

G70 UNIVERSITY OF GREENWICH
GREENWICH CAMPUS
OLD ROYAL NAVAL COLLEGE
PARK ROW
LONDON SE10 9LS
t: 020 8331 9000 f: 020 8331 8145
e: courseinfo@gre.ac.uk
// www.gre.ac.uk

H350 BEng Marine Engineering Technology
Duration: 3FT/4SW Hon
Entry Requirements: GCE: 200-220.

H300 BEng Mechanical Engineering
Duration: 3FT Hon
Entry Requirements: GCE: 260-280. IB: 24.

H308 BEng Mechanical Engineering (incl Foundation)
Duration: 4FT Hon
Entry Requirements: GCE: 160. IB: 24.

H301 BEng Mechanical Engineering Technology
Duration: 3FT Hon
Entry Requirements: GCE: 200-220. IB: 24.

H303 FdEng Mechanical Engineering
Duration: 2FT Fdg
Entry Requirements: IB: 24.

H304 MEng Mechanical Engineering
Duration: 4FT Hon
Entry Requirements: GCE: 32-360.

G80 GRIMSBY INSTITUTE OF FURTHER AND HIGHER EDUCATION
NUNS CORNER
GRIMSBY
NE LINCOLNSHIRE DN34 5BQ
t: 0800 328 3631
e: headmissions@grimsby.ac.uk
// www.grimsby.ac.uk

H313 BSc Refrigeration and Air Conditioning (Top-Up)
Duration: 1FT Hon
Entry Requirements: Contact the institution for details.

H311 FdSc Refrigeration & Air Conditioning Engineering
Duration: 2FT Fdg
Entry Requirements: Contact the institution for details.

H301 HNC Engineering (Mechanical)
Duration: 1FT HNC
Entry Requirements: Contact the institution for details.

H302 HND Engineering (Mechanical)
Duration: 2FT HND
Entry Requirements: Contact the institution for details.

H12 HARPER ADAMS UNIVERSITY COLLEGE
NEWPORT
SHROPSHIRE TF10 8NB
t: 01952 820280 f: 01952 813210
e: admissions@harper-adams.ac.uk
// www.harper-adams.ac.uk

H330 BEng Agricultural Engineering
Duration: 3FT/4SW Hon
Entry Requirements: GCE: 240-280. SQAH: ABBB. Interview required.

H336 BEng Off-Road Vehicle Design
Duration: 3FT/4SW Hon
Entry Requirements: GCE: 240-280. SQAH: ABBB. Interview required.

H333 BSc Agricultural Engineering
Duration: 3FT/4SW Hon
Entry Requirements: GCE: 180-220. SQAH: BBBC. Interview required.

H332 BSc Agricultural Engineering (top-up: ordinary)
Duration: 1FT Ord
Entry Requirements: Interview required. HND required.

H3N2 BSc Agricultural Engineering with Marketing & Management
Duration: 3FT/4SW Hon
Entry Requirements: GCE: 180-220. SQAH: BBBC. Interview required.

H3N5 BSc Off Road Vehicle Design with Marketing & Management
Duration: 4SW Hon
Entry Requirements: *GCE:* 180-220. *SQAH:* BBBC. Interview required.

H339 BSc Off-Road Vehicle Design
Duration: 3FT/4SW Hon
Entry Requirements: *GCE:* 180-220. *SQAH:* BBBC. Interview required.

23WH BSc Off-Road Vehicle Design (top-up)
Duration: 1.5FT/1FT Hon/Ord
Entry Requirements: Interview required. HND required.

H338 FdSc Agricultural Engineering
Duration: 2FT/3SW Fdg
Entry Requirements: *GCE:* 120-160. *SQAH:* CCC. Interview required.

H390 FdSc Agricultural Engineering (with year 0)
Duration: 4SW Fdg
Entry Requirements: Interview required.

HW32 FdSc Off-Road Vehicle Design
Duration: 3SW Fdg
Entry Requirements: *GCE:* 120-160. *SQAH:* CCC. Interview required.

H335 MEng Agricultural Engineering
Duration: 5SW Hon
Entry Requirements: *GCE:* 300-340. *SQAH:* AAAB. Interview required.

H337 MEng Off-Road Vehicle Design
Duration: 5SW Hon
Entry Requirements: *GCE:* 300-340. *SQAH:* AAAB. Interview required.

H14 HAVERING COLLEGE OF FURTHER AND HIGHER EDUCATION
ARDLEIGH GREEN ROAD
HORNCHURCH
ESSEX RM11 2LL
t: 01708 462793 f: 01708 462736
e: HE@havering-college.ac.uk
// www.havering-college.ac.uk

H330 FdEng Motorsport Engineering
Duration: 2FT Fdg
Entry Requirements: *GCE:* 120. Interview required.

H24 HERIOT-WATT UNIVERSITY, EDINBURGH
EDINBURGH CAMPUS
EDINBURGH EH14 4AS
t: 0131 449 5111 f: 0131 451 3630
e: ugadmissions@hw.ac.uk
// www.hw.ac.uk

H300 BEng Mechanical Engineering
Duration: 4FT Hon
Entry Requirements: *GCE:* BBC. *SQAH:* AABB-BBBBC. *SQAAH:* BB. *IB:* 29.

H302 MEng Industrial Engineering (Mechanical)
Duration: 5FT Hon
Entry Requirements: *GCE:* BBC. *SQAH:* AABB. *SQAAH:* AB. *IB:* 34.

H301 MEng Mechanical Engineering
Duration: 5FT Hon
Entry Requirements: *GCE:* BBC. *SQAH:* AABB. *SQAAH:* AB. *IB:* 34.

H36 UNIVERSITY OF HERTFORDSHIRE
UNIVERSITY ADMISSIONS SERVICE
COLLEGE LANE
HATFIELD
HERTS AL10 9AB
t: 01707 284800
// www.herts.ac.uk

H330 BEng Automotive Engineering
Duration: 3FT/4SW Hon
Entry Requirements: *GCE:* 260.

H348 BEng Automotive Engineering (Extended)
Duration: 4FT/5SW Hon
Entry Requirements: *GCE:* 80.

H335 BEng Automotive Engineering with Motorsport
Duration: 3FT/4SW Hon
Entry Requirements: *GCE:* 260.

H334 BEng Automotive Engineering with Motorsport (Extended)
Duration: 4FT/5SW Hon
Entry Requirements: Contact the institution for details.

H300 BEng Mechanical Engineering
Duration: 3FT/4SW Hon
Entry Requirements: *GCE:* 260.

H308 BEng Mechanical Engineering (Extended)
Duration: 4FT/5SW Ord/Hon
Entry Requirements: *GCE:* 80.

H342 BSc Automotive Technology with Management
Duration: 3FT/4SW Hon
Entry Requirements: *GCE:* 240.

H3N2 BSc Automotive Technology with Management (Extended)
Duration: 4FT/5SW Hon
Entry Requirements: *GCE:* 80.

H331 BSc Motorsport Technology
Duration: 3FT/4SW Hon
Entry Requirements: *GCE:* 240.

H337 BSc Motorsport Technology (Extended)
Duration: 4FT/5SW Hon
Entry Requirements: *GCE:* 80.

H341 MEng Automotive Engineering
Duration: 4FT Hon
Entry Requirements: *GCE:* 320. *IB:* 30.

H336 MEng Automotive Engineering with Motorsport
Duration: 4FT/5SW Hon
Entry Requirements: *GCE:* 320.

H301 MEng Mechanical Engineering
Duration: 4FT/5SW Hon
Entry Requirements: *GCE:* 320.

H49 UNIVERSITY OF THE HIGHLANDS AND ISLANDS
UHI EXECUTIVE OFFICE
NESS WALK
INVERNESS
SCOTLAND IV3 5SQ
t: 01463 279000 f: 01463 279001
e: info@uhi.ac.uk
// www.uhi.ac.uk

H300 BSc Mechanical Engineering
Duration: 1FT Ord
Entry Requirements: HND required.

H60 THE UNIVERSITY OF HUDDERSFIELD
QUEENSGATE
HUDDERSFIELD HD1 3DH
t: 01484 473969 f: 01484 472765
e: admissionsandrecords@hud.ac.uk
// www.hud.ac.uk

H333 BEng Automotive and Motorsport Engineering
Duration: 3FT/4SW Hon
Entry Requirements: *GCE:* 300.

H300 BEng Mechanical Engineering
Duration: 4SW Hon
Entry Requirements: *GCE:* 300.

H337 BSc Automotive and Motorsport Technology
Duration: 3FT/4SW Hon
Entry Requirements: *GCE:* 280.

H390 BSc Engineering and Technology Management
Duration: 3FT/4SW Hon
Entry Requirements: *GCE:* 280.

H301 BSc Mechanical Technology
Duration: 3FT/4SW Hon
Entry Requirements: *GCE:* 280.

H332 MEng Automotive and Motorsport Engineering
Duration: 5SW Hon
Entry Requirements: *GCE:* 340.

H303 MEng Mechanical Engineering
Duration: 5SW Hon
Entry Requirements: *GCE:* 340.

H72 THE UNIVERSITY OF HULL
THE UNIVERSITY OF HULL
COTTINGHAM ROAD
HULL HU6 7RX
t: 01482 466100 f: 01482 442290
e: admissions@hull.ac.uk
// www.hull.ac.uk

H300 BEng Mechanical Engineering
Duration: 3FT Hon
Entry Requirements: *GCE:* 280. *IB:* 27. *BTEC ExtDip:* DMM.

H302 BEng Mechanical Engineering (with foundation year)
Duration: 4FT Hon
Entry Requirements: Contact the institution for details.

H301 MEng Mechanical Engineering
Duration: 4FT Hon
Entry Requirements: *GCE:* 320. *IB:* 30. *BTEC ExtDip:* DDD.

I50 IMPERIAL COLLEGE LONDON
REGISTRY
SOUTH KENSINGTON CAMPUS
IMPERIAL COLLEGE LONDON
LONDON SW7 2AZ
t: 020 7589 5111 f: 020 7594 8004
// www.imperial.ac.uk

H301 MEng Mechanical Engineering
Duration: 4FT Hon
Entry Requirements: *GCE:* A*AA. *SQAAH:* AAA. *IB:* 40.

H304 MEng Mechanical Engineering with a Year Abroad
Duration: 4FT Hon
Entry Requirements: *GCE:* A*AA. *SQAAH:* AAA. *IB:* 40.

K24 THE UNIVERSITY OF KENT
RECRUITMENT & ADMISSIONS OFFICE
REGISTRY
UNIVERSITY OF KENT
CANTERBURY, KENT CT2 7NZ
t: 01227 827272 f: 01227 827077
e: information@kent.ac.uk
// www.kent.ac.uk

H300 FdEng Engineering (Mechanical Engineering)
Duration: 2FT Fdg
Entry Requirements: *OCR NED:* M2

K84 KINGSTON UNIVERSITY
STUDENT INFORMATION & ADVICE CENTRE
COOPER HOUSE
40-46 SURBITON ROAD
KINGSTON UPON THAMES KT1 2HX
t: 0844 8552177 f: 020 8547 7080
e: aps@kingston.ac.uk
// www.kingston.ac.uk

H300 BEng Mechanical Engineering
Duration: 3FT Hon
Entry Requirements: *GCE:* 240. *IB:* 26.

H301 BEng Mechanical Engineering (4-year SW)
Duration: 4SW Hon
Entry Requirements: *GCE:* 240. *IB:* 26.

H308 BEng Mechanical Engineering (Foundation)
Duration: 4FT/5SW Hon
Entry Requirements: *GCE:* 120. *IB:* 22.

H330 BSc Automotive Engineering
Duration: 3FT Hon
Entry Requirements: *GCE:* 160. *IB:* 24.

H394 BSc Automotive Engineering (4-year SW)
Duration: 4SW Hon
Entry Requirements: *GCE:* 160. *IB:* 24.

H302 BSc Mechanical Engineering
Duration: 3FT Hon
Entry Requirements: *GCE:* 160. *IB:* 24.

H305 BSc Mechanical Engineering (4-year SW)
Duration: 4SW Hon
Entry Requirements: *GCE:* 160. *IB:* 24.

H337 BSc Motorsport Engineering
Duration: 3FT Hon
Entry Requirements: *GCE:* 160. *IB:* 24.

H338 BSc Motorsport Engineering (4-year SW)
Duration: 4SW Hon
Entry Requirements: *GCE:* 160. *IB:* 24.

H303 MEng Mechanical Engineering
Duration: 4FT Hon
Entry Requirements: *GCE:* 300. *IB:* 30.

H304 MEng Mechanical Engineering
Duration: 5SW Hon
Entry Requirements: *GCE:* 300. *IB:* 30.

L14 LANCASTER UNIVERSITY
THE UNIVERSITY
LANCASTER
LANCASHIRE LA1 4YW
t: 01524 592029 f: 01524 846243
e: ugadmissions@lancaster.ac.uk
// www.lancs.ac.uk

H300 BEng Engineering (Mechanical)
Duration: 3FT Hon
Entry Requirements: *GCE:* AAB. *SQAH:* ABBBB. *SQAAH:* AAB. *IB:* 35.

H303 MEng Engineering (Mechanical)
Duration: 4FT Hon
Entry Requirements: *GCE:* AAA. *SQAH:* AAABB. *SQAAH:* AAA. *IB:* 36.

L23 UNIVERSITY OF LEEDS
THE UNIVERSITY OF LEEDS
WOODHOUSE LANE
LEEDS LS2 9JT
t: 0113 343 3999
e: admissions@leeds.ac.uk
// www.leeds.ac.uk

H330 MEng/BEng Automotive Engineering
Duration: 3FT/4FT Hon
Entry Requirements: *GCE:* AAA. *SQAAH:* AAA. *IB:* 38.

H300 MEng/BEng Mechanical Engineering
Duration: 3FT/4FT Hon
Entry Requirements: *GCE:* AAA. *SQAAH:* AAA. *IB:* 38.

L34 UNIVERSITY OF LEICESTER
UNIVERSITY ROAD
LEICESTER LE1 7RH
t: 0116 252 5281 f: 0116 252 2447
e: admissions@le.ac.uk
// www.le.ac.uk

H300 BEng Mechanical Engineering
Duration: 3FT Hon
Entry Requirements: *GCE:* BBB-BBC. *SQAH:* BBBBB-BBBCC. *SQAAH:* BBB-BBC.

H302 BEng Mechanical Engineering (with Year in Industry)
Duration: 4SW Hon
Entry Requirements: *GCE:* BBB-BBC. *SQAH:* BBBBB-BBBCC. *SQAAH:* BBB-BBC.

H301 BEng Mechanical Engineering (with a Year Abroad)
Duration: 3FT Hon
Entry Requirements: *GCE:* BBB-BBC. *SQAH:* BBBBB-BBBCC. *SQAAH:* BBB-BBC.

H305 MEng Mechanical Engineering
Duration: 4FT Hon
Entry Requirements: *GCE:* AAB-ABB. *SQAH:* AAABB-AABBB. *SQAAH:* AAB-ABB.

H307 MEng Mechanical Engineering (With a Year Abroad in USA)
Duration: 4FT Hon
Entry Requirements: *GCE:* AAB-ABB. *SQAH:* AAABB-AABBB. *SQAAH:* AAB-ABB.

H306 MEng Mechanical Engineering (with Year in Industry)
Duration: 5SW Hon
Entry Requirements: *GCE:* AAB-ABB. *SQAH:* AAABB-AABBB. *SQAAH:* AAB-ABB.

HJ35 BEng Mechanical and Materials Engineering
Duration: 3FT Hon
Entry Requirements: *GCE:* ABB. *SQAAH:* ABB. *IB:* 33. Interview required.

H301 MEng Mechanical Engineering (4 years)
Duration: 4FT Hon
Entry Requirements: *GCE:* AAB. *SQAAH:* AAB. *IB:* 35. Interview required.

H3NF MEng Mechanical Engineering with Business (4 years)
Duration: 4FT Hon
Entry Requirements: *GCE:* AAB. *SQAAH:* AAB. *IB:* 35. Interview required.

HJ3M MEng Mechanical and Materials Engineering
Duration: 4FT Hon
Entry Requirements: *GCE:* AAB. *SQAAH:* AAB. *IB:* 35. Interview required.

L39 UNIVERSITY OF LINCOLN
ADMISSIONS
BRAYFORD POOL
LINCOLN LN6 7TS
t: 01522 886097 f: 01522 886146
e: admissions@lincoln.ac.uk
// www.lincoln.ac.uk

H100 BEng Mechanical Engineering
Duration: 3FT Hon
Entry Requirements: *GCE:* 260. *IB:* 24. Interview required.

H300 MEng Mechanical Engineering
Duration: 4FT Hon
Entry Requirements: Contact the institution for details.

L41 THE UNIVERSITY OF LIVERPOOL
THE FOUNDATION BUILDING
BROWNLOW HILL
LIVERPOOL L69 7ZX
t: 0151 794 2000 f: 0151 708 6502
e: ugrecruitment@liv.ac.uk
// www.liv.ac.uk

H300 BEng Mechanical Engineering
Duration: 3FT Hon
Entry Requirements: *GCE:* ABB. *SQAAH:* ABB. *IB:* 33. Interview required.

H3N2 BEng Mechanical Engineering with Business
Duration: 3FT Hon
Entry Requirements: *GCE:* ABB. *SQAAH:* ABB. *IB:* 33. Interview required.

L42 LINCOLN COLLEGE
MONKS ROAD
LINCOLN LN2 5HQ
t: 01522 876000 f: 01522 876200
e: enquiries@lincolncollege.ac.uk
// www.lincolncollege.ac.uk

H300 HND Mechanical Engineering
Duration: 2FT HND
Entry Requirements: Contact the institution for details.

L51 LIVERPOOL JOHN MOORES UNIVERSITY
KINGSWAY HOUSE
HATTON GARDEN
LIVERPOOL L3 2AJ
t: 0151 231 5090 f: 0151 904 6368
e: courses@ljmu.ac.uk
// www.ljmu.ac.uk

H330 BEng Automotive Engineering
Duration: 3FT/4SW Hon
Entry Requirements: *GCE:* 260. Interview required. Admissions Test required.

H300 BEng Mechanical Engineering
Duration: 3FT/4SW Hon
Entry Requirements: *GCE:* 260. Interview required. Admissions Test required.

H350 BEng Mechanical and Marine Engineering
Duration: 3FT/4SW Hon
Entry Requirements: *GCE:* 260. Interview required. Admissions Test required.

H335 MEng Automotive Engineering
Duration: 4FT/5SW Hon
Entry Requirements: *GCE:* 280. Interview required. Admissions Test required.

H301 MEng Mechanical Engineering
Duration: 4FT/5SW Hon
Entry Requirements: *GCE:* 280. Interview required. Admissions Test required.

H390 MEng Mechanical and Marine Engineering
Duration: 4FT/5SW Hon
Entry Requirements: *GCE:* 280. Interview required. Admissions Test required.

L75 LONDON SOUTH BANK UNIVERSITY
ADMISSIONS AND RECRUITMENT CENTRE
90 LONDON ROAD
LONDON SE1 6LN
t: 0800 923 8888 f: 020 7815 8273
e: course.enquiry@lsbu.ac.uk
// www.lsbu.ac.uk

HJ39 BA Music and Sonic Media
Duration: 3FT Hon
Entry Requirements: *GCE:* 240. *IB:* 24.

H300 BEng Mechanical Engineering
Duration: 3FT/4SW Hon
Entry Requirements: *GCE:* 240. *IB:* 24.

H301 BSc Mechanical Engineering Design
Duration: 3FT Hon
Entry Requirements: *GCE:* 200. *IB:* 24.

L77 LOUGHBOROUGH COLLEGE
RADMOOR ROAD
LOUGHBOROUGH LE11 3BT
t: 0845 166 2950 f: 0845 833 2840
e: info@loucoll.ac.uk
// www.loucoll.ac.uk

H301 BEng Mechanical Engineeering (Top-Up)
Duration: 1FT Hon
Entry Requirements: Contact the institution for details.

H300 FdEng Mechanical Engineering
Duration: 2FT Fdg
Entry Requirements: *GCE:* 80. Interview required.

003H HND Engineering (Mechanical)
Duration: 2FT HND
Entry Requirements: *GCE:* 80. Interview required.

L79 LOUGHBOROUGH UNIVERSITY
LOUGHBOROUGH
LEICESTERSHIRE LE11 3TU
t: 01509 223522 f: 01509 223905
e: admissions@lboro.ac.uk
// www.lboro.ac.uk

H330 BEng Automotive Engineering
Duration: 3FT Hon
Entry Requirements: *GCE:* ABB. *SQAH:* BB. *SQAAH:* AB. *IB:* 32.

H341 BEng Automotive Engineering
Duration: 4SW Hon
Entry Requirements: *GCE:* ABB. *SQAH:* BB. *SQAAH:* AB. *IB:* 32.

H300 BEng Mechanical Engineering
Duration: 3FT Hon
Entry Requirements: *GCE:* ABB. *SQAH:* BBBBB. *SQAAH:* AB. *IB:* 33.

H301 BEng Mechanical Engineering
Duration: 4SW Hon
Entry Requirements: *GCE:* ABB. *SQAH:* BBBBB. *SQAAH:* AB. *IB:* 33.

H304 BEng Mechanical Engineering with a Foundation Year
Duration: 4FT Hon
Entry Requirements: *GCE:* ABC-BBB.

H342 MEng Automotive Engineering
Duration: 5SW Hon
Entry Requirements: *GCE:* AAA. *SQAH:* AA. *SQAAH:* AA. *IB:* 36.

H343 MEng Automotive Engineering
Duration: 4FT Hon
Entry Requirements: *GCE:* AAA. *SQAH:* AA. *SQAAH:* AA. *IB:* 36.

H302 MEng Mechanical Engineering
Duration: 5SW Hon
Entry Requirements: *GCE:* A*AA. *SQAH:* AAAAB. *SQAAH:* AA. *IB:* 34.

H303 MEng Mechanical Engineering
Duration: 4FT Hon
Entry Requirements: *GCE:* A*AA. *SQAH:* AAAAB. *SQAAH:* AA. *IB:* 35.

M20 THE UNIVERSITY OF MANCHESTER
RUTHERFORD BUILDING
OXFORD ROAD
MANCHESTER M13 9PL
t: 0161 275 2077 f: 0161 275 2106
e: ug-admissions@manchester.ac.uk
// www.manchester.ac.uk

H300 BEng Mechanical Engineering
Duration: 3FT Hon
Entry Requirements: *GCE:* AAB. *SQAAH:* AAB. *IB:* 35. Interview required.

H3N1 BEng Mechanical Engineering with Management
Duration: 3FT Hon
Entry Requirements: *GCE:* AAB. *SQAAH:* AAB. *IB:* 35. Interview required.

H303 MEng Mechanical Engineering
Duration: 4FT Hon
Entry Requirements: *GCE:* AAA. *SQAAH:* AAA. *IB:* 37. Interview required.

H301 MEng Mechanical Engineering with Industrial Experience (5 years)
Duration: 5FT Hon
Entry Requirements: *GCE:* AAA. *SQAAH:* AAA. *IB:* 37. Interview required.

H3ND MEng Mechanical Engineering with Management
Duration: 4FT Hon
Entry Requirements: *GCE:* AAA. *SQAAH:* AAA. *IB:* 37. Interview required.

M40 THE MANCHESTER METROPOLITAN UNIVERSITY
ADMISSIONS OFFICE
ALL SAINTS (GMS)
ALL SAINTS
MANCHESTER M15 6BH
t: 0161 247 2000
// www.mmu.ac.uk

H330 BEng Automotive Engineering
Duration: 3FT/4SW Hon
Entry Requirements: *GCE:* 280. *IB:* 27.

H334 BEng Automotive Engineering (Foundation)
Duration: 4FT/5SW Hon
Entry Requirements: *GCE:* 160. *IB:* 24. *BTEC Dip:* MM. *BTEC ExtDip:* MPP.

H300 BEng Mechanical Engineering
Duration: 3FT/4SW Hon
Entry Requirements: *GCE:* 280. *IB:* 27.

H308 BEng Mechanical Engineering (Foundation)
Duration: 4FT/5SW Hon
Entry Requirements: *GCE:* 160. *IB:* 24. *BTEC Dip:* MM. *BTEC ExtDip:* MPP.

HJ3X BSc Design Engineering
Duration: 3FT/4SW Hon
Entry Requirements: *GCE:* 280. *IB:* 27. *OCR NED:* M2

HJ39 BSc Design Engineering (Foundation)
Duration: 4FT/5SW Hon
Entry Requirements: *GCE:* 160. *IB:* 24. *BTEC Dip:* MM. *BTEC ExtDip:* MPP.

M99 MYERSCOUGH COLLEGE
MYERSCOUGH HALL
BILSBORROW
PRESTON PR3 0RY
t: 01995 642222 f: 01995 642333
e: enquiries@myerscough.ac.uk
// www.myerscough.ac.uk

HN3F BSc Machinery Management and Logistics (Top-up)
Duration: 1FT Hon
Entry Requirements: Interview required.

HN32 FdSc Machinery Management and Logistics
Duration: 2FT Fdg
Entry Requirements: *GCE:* A-C. *SQAH:* AA-CC. *SQAAH:* A-C. *IB:* 24. Interview required.

H334 FdSc Motorsport Management and Logistics
Duration: 2FT Fdg
Entry Requirements: *GCE:* A-C. *SQAH:* AA-CC. *SQAAH:* A-C. *IB:* 24. Interview required.

N21 NEWCASTLE UNIVERSITY
KING'S GATE
NEWCASTLE UPON TYNE NE1 7RU
t: 01912083333
// www.ncl.ac.uk

H355 BEng Marine Technology with Offshore Engineering
Duration: 3FT Hon
Entry Requirements: *GCE:* AAB-ABB. *SQAAH:* AAB-ABB. *BTEC ExtDip:* DDD.

HH73 BEng Mechanical Design and Manufacturing Engineering
Duration: 3FT Hon
Entry Requirements: *GCE:* AAB-ABB. *SQAAH:* AAB-ABB. *IB:* 35. Interview required.

H300 BEng Mechanical Engineering
Duration: 3FT Hon
Entry Requirements: *GCE:* AAB-ABB. *SQAAH:* AAB-ABB. *IB:* 35. Interview required.

H304 BEng Mechanical Engineering (4 years)
Duration: 4FT Hon
Entry Requirements: *GCE:* AAA-ABB. *SQAAH:* AAA-ABB. *IB:* 35.

H356 MEng Marine Technology with Offshore Engineering
Duration: 4FT Hon
Entry Requirements: *GCE:* AAB. *SQAAH:* AAB. *IB:* 37.

HH37 MEng Mechanical Design and Manufacturing Engineering
Duration: 4FT Hon
Entry Requirements: *GCE:* AAA-AAB. *SQAAH:* AAA-AAB. *IB:* 37.
Interview required.

H301 MEng Mechanical Engineering
Duration: 4FT Hon
Entry Requirements: *GCE:* AAA-AAB. *SQAAH:* AAA-AAB. *IB:* 37.
Interview required.

H305 MEng Mechanical Engineering (5 years)
Duration: 5FT Hon
Entry Requirements: *GCE:* AAA-AAB. *SQAAH:* AA-AB. *IB:* 37.

H3H6 MEng Mechanical Engineering with Mechatronics
Duration: 4FT Hon
Entry Requirements: *GCE:* AAA-AAB. *SQAAH:* AAA-AAB. *IB:* 37.
Interview required.

H3H9 MEng Mechanical Engineering with Microsystems
Duration: 4FT Hon
Entry Requirements: *GCE:* AAA-AAB. *SQAAH:* AAA-AAB. *IB:* 37.
Interview required.

H390 MEng Mechanical and Low Carbon Transport Engineering
Duration: 4FT Hon
Entry Requirements: *GCE:* AAA-AAB. *SQAAH:* AAA-AAB. *IB:* 37.
Interview required.

N23 NEWCASTLE COLLEGE
STUDENT SERVICES
RYE HILL CAMPUS
SCOTSWOOD ROAD
NEWCASTLE UPON TYNE NE4 7SA
t: 0191 200 4110 f: 0191 200 4349
e: enquiries@ncl-coll.ac.uk
// www.newcastlecollege.co.uk

HH3R BSc Mechanical Manufacturing Engineering Technologies [Top-up]
Duration: 1FT Hon
Entry Requirements: Contact the institution for details.

HH37 FdSc Mechanical/Manufacturing Engineering
Duration: 2FT Fdg
Entry Requirements: *GCE:* 160-200. *OCR ND:* P2 *OCR NED:* P3
Interview required.

N30 NEW COLLEGE NOTTINGHAM
ADAMS BUILDING
STONEY STREET
THE LACE MARKET
NOTTINGHAM NG1 1NG
t: 0115 910 0100 f: 0115 953 4349
e: he.team@ncn.ac.uk
// www.ncn.ac.uk

003H HNC Construction and the Built Environment (Building Services Engineering)
Duration: 1FT HNC
Entry Requirements: Contact the institution for details.

N37 UNIVERSITY OF WALES, NEWPORT
ADMISSIONS
LODGE ROAD
CAERLEON
NEWPORT NP18 3QT
t: 01633 432030 f: 01633 432850
e: admissions@newport.ac.uk
// www.newport.ac.uk

HH37 BEng Mechanical and Manufacturing Engineering
Duration: 3FT Hon
Entry Requirements: *GCE:* 240. *IB:* 24.

N41 NORTHBROOK COLLEGE SUSSEX
LITTLEHAMPTON ROAD
WORTHING
WEST SUSSEX BN12 6NU
t: 0845 155 6060 f: 01903 606073
e: enquiries@nbcol.ac.uk
// www.northbrook.ac.uk

H331 BSc Motorsport Technology (Top-Up)
Duration: 1FT Hon
Entry Requirements: Interview required.

H330 FdEng Motorsport Engineering
Duration: 2FT Fdg
Entry Requirements: *GCE:* 160. Interview required.

N64 NORTH LINDSEY COLLEGE
KINGSWAY
SCUNTHORPE
NORTH LINCS DN17 1AJ
t: 01724 294125 f: 01724 295378
e: he@northlindsey.ac.uk
// www.northlindsey.ac.uk

003H HND Mechanical Engineering
Duration: 2FT HND
Entry Requirements: Contact the institution for details.

N77 NORTHUMBRIA UNIVERSITY
TRINITY BUILDING
NORTHUMBERLAND ROAD
NEWCASTLE UPON TYNE NE1 8ST
t: 0191 243 7420 f: 0191 227 4561
e: er.admissions@northumbria.ac.uk
// www.northumbria.ac.uk

H303 BEng Mechanical Design Engineering
Duration: 1FT Hon
Entry Requirements: HND required.

H300 BEng Mechanical Engineering
Duration: 3FT/4SW Hon
Entry Requirements: *GCE:* 300. *SQAH:* BBBBC. *SQAAH:* BBC. *IB:* 26.

H308 BEng Mechanical Engineering
Duration: 4FT/5SW Hon
Entry Requirements: *GCE:* 200. *SQAH:* CCCC. *IB:* 24. *BTEC Dip:* DM. *OCR ND:* M1 *OCR NED:* P1

H304 MEng Mechanical Engineering
Duration: 4FT/5SW Hon
Entry Requirements: Contact the institution for details.

N84 THE UNIVERSITY OF NOTTINGHAM
THE ADMISSIONS OFFICE
THE UNIVERSITY OF NOTTINGHAM
UNIVERSITY PARK
NOTTINGHAM NG7 2RD
t: 0115 951 5151 f: 0115 951 4668
// www.nottingham.ac.uk

H302 BEng Mechanical Engineering
Duration: 3FT Hon
Entry Requirements: *GCE:* AAB. *SQAAH:* ABB-BBB. *IB:* 32.

H300 MEng Mechanical Engineering
Duration: 4FT Hon
Entry Requirements: *GCE:* AAA. *SQAAH:* AAA-AAB. *IB:* 36.

O33 OXFORD UNIVERSITY
UNDERGRADUATE ADMISSIONS OFFICE
UNIVERSITY OF OXFORD
WELLINGTON SQUARE
OXFORD OX1 2JD
t: 01865 288000 f: 01865 270212
e: undergraduate.admissions@admin.ox.ac.uk
// www.admissions.ox.ac.uk

H300 MEng Mechanical Engineering (4 years)
Duration: 4FT Hon
Entry Requirements: *GCE:* A*AA. *SQAH:* AAAAA-AAAAB. *SQAAH:* AAB. Interview required. Admissions Test required.

O66 OXFORD BROOKES UNIVERSITY
ADMISSIONS OFFICE
HEADINGTON CAMPUS
GIPSY LANE
OXFORD OX3 0BP
t: 01865 483040 f: 01865 483983
e: admissions@brookes.ac.uk
// www.brookes.ac.uk

H330 BEng Automotive Engineering
Duration: 3FT Hon
Entry Requirements: *GCE:* BBC. *IB:* 30.

H300 BEng Mechanical Engineering
Duration: 3FT Hon
Entry Requirements: *GCE:* BBC. *IB:* 30.

H334 BEng Motorsport Engineering
Duration: 3FT Hon
Entry Requirements: *GCE:* BBC. *IB:* 30.

HH13 BSc Computer Aided Mechanical Engineering
Duration: 3FT Hon
Entry Requirements: *GCE:* BBC. *IB:* 30. Interview required.

H331 BSc Motorsport Technology
Duration: 3FT/4SW Hon
Entry Requirements: *GCE:* BBC. *IB:* 30. Interview required.

H301 FdSc Mechanical Engineering (Abingdon and Witney)
Duration: 2FT Fdg
Entry Requirements: Contact the institution for details.

H33C FdSc Motorsport Engineering (Bridgwater College)
Duration: 2FT Fdg
Entry Requirements: *GCE:* DD.

H339 FdSc Motorsport Engineering (Brooklands)
Duration: 2FT Fdg
Entry Requirements: *GCE:* C.

H338 FdSc Motorsports- Performance and Automotive Technology(Oxf/Cherwell Valley College)
Duration: 2FT Fdg
Entry Requirements: *GCE:* C.

H341 MEng Automotive Engineering
Duration: 4FT Hon
Entry Requirements: *GCE:* ABB. *IB:* 30.

H302 MEng Mechanical Engineering
Duration: 4FT Hon
Entry Requirements: *GCE:* ABB. *IB:* 30.

H337 MEng Motorsport Engineering
Duration: 4FT Hon
Entry Requirements: *GCE:* ABB. *IB:* 30.

P60 PLYMOUTH UNIVERSITY
DRAKE CIRCUS
PLYMOUTH PL4 8AA
t: 01752 585858 f: 01752 588055
e: admissions@plymouth.ac.uk
// www.plymouth.ac.uk

H300 BEng Mechanical Engineering
Duration: 3FT/4SW Hon
Entry Requirements: *GCE:* 280. *IB:* 28.

H302 BEng Mechanical Engineering with Composites
Duration: 3FT/4SW Hon
Entry Requirements: *GCE:* 280. *IB:* 28.

H305 BEng Mechanical Engineering with Foundation Year
Duration: 5SW Hon
Entry Requirements: *GCE:* 180. *IB:* 24.

HH37 BSc Mechanical Design and Manufacture
Duration: 3FT Hon
Entry Requirements: *GCE:* 220. *IB:* 26.

H711 FdSc Mechanical Design and Manufacture
Duration: 2FT Fdg
Entry Requirements: *GCE:* 120-180. *IB:* 24.

H304 MEng Mechanical Engineering
Duration: 5SW Hon
Entry Requirements: *GCE:* 320. *IB:* 30.

H306 MEng Mechanical Engineering with Composites
Duration: 4FT/5SW Hon
Entry Requirements: *GCE:* 320. *IB:* 32.

P80 UNIVERSITY OF PORTSMOUTH
ACADEMIC REGISTRY
UNIVERSITY HOUSE
WINSTON CHURCHILL AVENUE
PORTSMOUTH PO1 2UP
t: 023 9284 8484 f: 023 9284 3082
e: admissions@port.ac.uk
// www.port.ac.uk

H300 BEng Mechanical Engineering
Duration: 3FT/4SW Hon
Entry Requirements: *GCE:* 240-280. *IB:* 26. *BTEC SubDip:* P. *BTEC Dip:* PP. *BTEC ExtDip:* DMM.

HH37 BEng Mechanical and Manufacturing Engineering
Duration: 3FT/4SW Hon
Entry Requirements: *GCE:* 200-240. *IB:* 26. *BTEC SubDip:* P. *BTEC Dip:* PP. *BTEC ExtDip:* MMM.

H304 MEng Mechanical Engineering
Duration: 4FT/5SW Hon
Entry Requirements: *GCE:* 300-360. *IB:* 27. *BTEC SubDip:* M. *BTEC Dip:* MM. *BTEC ExtDip:* DDD.

Q50 QUEEN MARY, UNIVERSITY OF LONDON
QUEEN MARY, UNIVERSITY OF LONDON
MILE END ROAD
LONDON E1 4NS
t: 020 7882 5555 f: 020 7882 5500
e: admissions@qmul.ac.uk
// www.qmul.ac.uk

H300 BEng Mechanical Engineering
Duration: 3FT Hon
Entry Requirements: *GCE:* 300. *IB:* 32.

H304 BEng Mechanical Engineering with Industrial Experience
Duration: 4FT Hon
Entry Requirements: *GCE:* 300. *IB:* 32.

H301 MEng Mechanical Engineering
Duration: 4FT Hon
Entry Requirements: *GCE:* 360. *IB:* 36.

H302 MEng Mechanical Engineering with Industrial Experience
Duration: 5FT Hon
Entry Requirements: *GCE:* 360. *IB:* 36.

Q75 QUEEN'S UNIVERSITY BELFAST
UNIVERSITY ROAD
BELFAST BT7 1NN
t: 028 9097 3838 f: 028 9097 5151
e: admissions@qub.ac.uk
// www.qub.ac.uk

H300 BEng Mechanical Engineering
Duration: 3FT Hon
Entry Requirements: *GCE:* BBC-BCC. *SQAH:* BBBBC-BBBCC. *SQAAH:* BBC-BCC.

H304 BEng Mechanical Engineering (with a Year in Industry)
Duration: 4SW Hon
Entry Requirements: *GCE:* BBC-BCC. *SQAH:* BBBBC-BBBCC. *SQAAH:* BBC-BCC.

H302 FdEng Mechanical Engineering
Duration: 2FT Fdg
Entry Requirements: Contact the institution for details.

HH37 MEng Mechanical and Manufacturing Engineering
Duration: 4FT Hon
Entry Requirements: *GCE:* ABB-BBB. *SQAH:* ABBBB-BBBBB. *SQAAH:* ABB-BBB.

HHH7 MEng Mechanical and Manufacturing Engineering (with a Year in Industry)
Duration: 5SW Hon
Entry Requirements: *GCE:* ABB-BBB. *SQAH:* ABBBB-BBBBB. *SQAAH:* ABB-BBB.

R36 ROBERT GORDON UNIVERSITY
ROBERT GORDON UNIVERSITY
SCHOOLHILL
ABERDEEN
SCOTLAND AB10 1FR
t: 01224 26 27 28 f: 01224 26 21 47
e: UGOffice@rgu.ac.uk
// www.rgu.ac.uk

H301 BEng Mechanical Engineering
Duration: 4FT Hon
Entry Requirements: *GCE:* BCC. *SQAH:* BBBC. *SQAAH:* BCC. *IB:* 27.

H350 BEng Mechanical and Offshore Engineering
Duration: 4FT Hon
Entry Requirements: *GCE:* BCC. *SQAH:* BBBC. *SQAAH:* BCC. *IB:* 27.

H304 MEng Mechanical Engineering
Duration: 4.5FT Hon
Entry Requirements: *GCE:* BBC. *SQAH:* ABBB-ABBCC. *SQAAH:* BBB. *IB:* 28.

H300 MEng Mechanical and Electrical Engineering
Duration: 4.5FT Hon
Entry Requirements: *GCE:* BBC. *SQAH:* ABBB-ABBCC. *SQAAH:* BBB. *IB:* 28.

H351 MEng Mechanical and Offshore Engineering
Duration: 4.5FT Hon
Entry Requirements: *GCE:* BBC. *SQAH:* ABBB-ABBCC. *SQAAH:* BBB. *IB:* 28.

S03 THE UNIVERSITY OF SALFORD
SALFORD M5 4WT
t: 0161 295 4545 f: 0161 295 4646
e: ug-admissions@salford.ac.uk
// www.salford.ac.uk

H304 BEng Mechanical Engineering
Duration: 3FT Hon
Entry Requirements: *GCE:* 260. *IB:* 30.

H302 BEng Mechanical Engineering with a Foundation Year
Duration: 4FT Hon
Entry Requirements: *GCE:* 160. *IB:* 26.

H301 MEng Mechanical Engineering
Duration: 4FT Hon
Entry Requirements: *GCE:* 300. *IB:* 35.

S18 THE UNIVERSITY OF SHEFFIELD
THE UNIVERSITY OF SHEFFIELD
LEVEL 2, ARTS TOWER
WESTERN BANK
SHEFFIELD S10 2TN
t: 0114 222 8030 f: 0114 222 8032
// www.sheffield.ac.uk

H302 BEng Mechanical Engineering (3 years)
Duration: 3FT Hon
Entry Requirements: *GCE:* AAB. *SQAH:* AAABB. *SQAAH:* AB. *IB:* 35. *BTEC ExtDip:* DDD. Interview required.

H305 BEng Mechanical Engineering with a Year in Industry
Duration: 4FT Hon
Entry Requirements: *GCE:* AAB. *SQAH:* AAABB. *SQAAH:* AB. *IB:* 35. *BTEC ExtDip:* DDD. Interview required.

H361 BEng Mechatronic and Robotic Engineering
Duration: 3FT Hon
Entry Requirements: *GCE:* ABB. *SQAH:* AABBB. *SQAAH:* AB. *IB:* 33. *BTEC ExtDip:* DDM.

H300 MEng Mechanical Engineering (4 years)
Duration: 4FT Hon
Entry Requirements: *GCE:* AAA. *SQAH:* AAAAB. *SQAAH:* AA. *IB:* 37. *BTEC ExtDip:* DDD. Interview required.

H3R1 MEng Mechanical Engineering with French
Duration: 4FT Hon
Entry Requirements: *GCE:* AAA. *SQAH:* AAAAB. *SQAAH:* AA. *IB:* 37. *BTEC ExtDip:* DDD. Interview required.

H3R2 MEng Mechanical Engineering with German
Duration: 4FT Hon
Entry Requirements: *GCE:* AAA. *SQAH:* AAAAB. *SQAAH:* AA. *IB:* 37. *BTEC ExtDip:* DDD. Interview required.

H3N2 MEng Mechanical Engineering with Industrial Management
Duration: 4FT Hon
Entry Requirements: *GCE:* AAA. *SQAH:* AAAAB. *SQAAH:* AA. *IB:* 37. *BTEC ExtDip:* DDD. Interview required.

H3R3 MEng Mechanical Engineering with Italian
Duration: 4FT Hon
Entry Requirements: *GCE:* AAA. *SQAH:* AAAAB. *SQAAH:* AA. *IB:* 37. *BTEC ExtDip:* DDD. Interview required.

H3R4 MEng Mechanical Engineering with Spanish
Duration: 4FT Hon
Entry Requirements: *GCE:* AAA. *SQAH:* AAAAB. *SQAAH:* AA. *IB:* 37. *BTEC ExtDip:* DDD. Interview required.

H301 MEng Mechanical Engineering with a Foundation Year (5 years)
Duration: 5FT Hon
Entry Requirements: *GCE:* ABB. *SQAH:* AABBB. *SQAAH:* AB. *IB:* 33. *BTEC ExtDip:* DDD. Interview required.

H304 MEng Mechanical Engineering with a Year in Industry
Duration: 5FT Hon
Entry Requirements: *GCE:* AAA. *SQAH:* AAAAB. *SQAAH:* AA. *IB:* 37. *BTEC ExtDip:* DDD. Interview required.

H3T7 MEng Mechanical Engineering with a Year in North America
Duration: 4FT Hon
Entry Requirements: *GCE:* AAA. *SQAH:* AAAAB. *SQAAH:* AA. *IB:* 37. *BTEC ExtDip:* DDD. Interview required.

H360 MEng Mechatronic and Robotic Engineeering
Duration: 4FT Hon
Entry Requirements: *GCE:* AAB. *SQAH:* AAABB. *SQAAH:* AB. *IB:* 35. *BTEC ExtDip:* DDD.

S21 SHEFFIELD HALLAM UNIVERSITY
CITY CAMPUS
HOWARD STREET
SHEFFIELD S1 1WB
t: 0114 225 5555 f: 0114 225 2167
e: admissions@shu.ac.uk
// www.shu.ac.uk

H330 BEng Automotive Engineering
Duration: 3FT/4SW Hon
Entry Requirements: *GCE:* 220.

H303 BEng Engineering (Mechanical)
Duration: 3FT/4SW Hon
Entry Requirements: *GCE:* 220.

H300 BEng Mechanical Engineering
Duration: 3FT/4SW Hon
Entry Requirements: *GCE:* 240.

H302 BEng Mechanical and Automotive Engineering
Duration: 3FT/4SW Hon
Entry Requirements: *GCE:* 220.

HH13 BSc Automotive Design Technology
Duration: 3FT/4SW Hon
Entry Requirements: *GCE:* 240.

H301 MEng Mechanical Engineering
Duration: 4FT/5SW Hon
Entry Requirements: *GCE:* 300.

S27 UNIVERSITY OF SOUTHAMPTON
HIGHFIELD
SOUTHAMPTON SO17 1BJ
t: 023 8059 4732 f: 023 8059 3037
e: admissions@soton.ac.uk
// www.southampton.ac.uk

H300 BEng Mechanical Engineering
Duration: 3FT Hon
Entry Requirements: *GCE:* AAA. *SQAH:* AAA. *IB:* 34.

H301 MEng Mechanical Engineering (4 years)
Duration: 4FT Hon
Entry Requirements: *GCE:* AAA. *SQAH:* AAA. *IB:* 34.

HJ35 MEng Mechanical Engineering/Advanced Materials
Duration: 4FT Hon
Entry Requirements: *GCE:* AAA. *SQAH:* AAA. *IB:* 34.

H390 MEng Mechanical Engineering/Automotive
Duration: 4FT Hon
Entry Requirements: *GCE:* AAA. *SQAH:* AAA. *IB:* 34.

HN32 MEng Mechanical Engineering/Engineering Management
Duration: 4FT Hon
Entry Requirements: *GCE:* AAA. *SQAAH:* AAA. *IB:* 34.

HH37 MEng Mechanical Engineering/Mechatronics
Duration: 4FT Hon
Entry Requirements: *GCE:* AAA. *SQAAH:* AAA. *IB:* 34.

HH35 MEng Mechanical Engineering/Naval Engineering
Duration: 4FT Hon
Entry Requirements: *GCE:* AAA. *SQAAH:* AAA. *IB:* 34.

S28 SOMERSET COLLEGE OF ARTS AND TECHNOLOGY
WELLINGTON ROAD
TAUNTON
SOMERSET TA1 5AX
t: 01823 366331 f: 01823 366418
e: enquiries@somerset.ac.uk
// www.somerset.ac.uk/student-area/considering-a-degree.html

H330 FdEng Engineering - Automotive
Duration: 2FT Fdg
Entry Requirements: *IB:* 24.

www.ucas.com

at the heart of connecting people to higher education

S30 SOUTHAMPTON SOLENT UNIVERSITY
EAST PARK TERRACE
SOUTHAMPTON
HAMPSHIRE SO14 0RT
t: +44 (0) 23 8031 9039 f: + 44 (0)23 8022 2259
e: admissions@solent.ac.uk
// www.solent.ac.uk/

HH73 BEng Mechanical Design
Duration: 3FT Hon
Entry Requirements: *GCE:* 120.

HH37 BEng Mechanical Design (with foundation)
Duration: 4FT Hon
Entry Requirements: *GCE:* 40.

H300 BEng Mechanical Design with IFY (Intl only, Sept)
Duration: 4FT Hon
Entry Requirements: Contact the institution for details.

H301 BEng Mechanical Engineering with IFY (International Only - Jan)
Duration: 4FT Hon
Entry Requirements: Contact the institution for details.

HH7H BSc Manufacturing & Mechanical Engineering
Duration: 3FT Hon
Entry Requirements: *GCE:* 180.

HH7J BSc Manufacturing & Mechanical Engineering (with foundation)
Duration: 4FT Hon
Entry Requirements: *GCE:* 40.

HH7I BSc Manufacturing & Mechanical Engineering with IFY (International Only - Jan)
Duration: 4FT Hon
Entry Requirements: Contact the institution for details.

HH3T BSc Manufacturing and Mechanical Engineering with IFY (Intl only, Sept)
Duration: 4FT Hon
Entry Requirements: Contact the institution for details.

H341 BSc Sound Engineering
Duration: 3FT Hon
Entry Requirements: *GCE:* 160.

H343 BSc Sound Engineering (with Foundation)
Duration: 4FT Hon
Entry Requirements: *GCE:* 40.

S32 SOUTH DEVON COLLEGE
LONG ROAD
PAIGNTON
DEVON TQ4 7EJ
t: 08000 213181 f: 01803 540541
e: university@southdevon.ac.uk
// www.southdevon.ac.uk/
welcome-to-university-level

H390 FdSc Engineering Technologies
Duration: 2FT Fdg
Entry Requirements: Contact the institution for details.

S41 SOUTH CHESHIRE COLLEGE
DANE BANK AVENUE
CREWE CW2 8AB
t: 01270 654654 f: 01270 651515
e: admissions@s-cheshire.ac.uk
// www.s-cheshire.ac.uk

H300 FdEng Mechanical Engineering
Duration: 2FT Fdg
Entry Requirements: Contact the institution for details.

S69 STEPHENSON COLLEGE COALVILLE
THORNBOROUGH ROAD
COALVILLE
LEICESTERSHIRE LE67 3TN
t: 01530 836136 f: 01530 814253
e: highereducation@stephensoncoll.ac.uk
// www.stephensoncoll.ac.uk

003H HND Mechanical Engineering
Duration: 2FT HND
Entry Requirements: Interview required.

S72 STAFFORDSHIRE UNIVERSITY
COLLEGE ROAD
STOKE ON TRENT ST4 2DE
t: 01782 292753 f: 01782 292740
e: admissions@staffs.ac.uk
// www.staffs.ac.uk

H330 BEng Automotive Engineering
Duration: 3FT/4SW Hon
Entry Requirements: *GCE:* 200-240. *IB:* 24.

H300 BEng Mechanical Engineering
Duration: 3FT/4SW Hon
Entry Requirements: *GCE:* 200-240. *IB:* 24.

H335 BSc Automotive Technology
Duration: 3FT Hon
Entry Requirements: *GCE:* 200-240. *IB:* 24.

H393 BSc Motorsport (Top-Up)
Duration: 1FT Hon
Entry Requirements: Contact the institution for details.

H391 BSc Motorsport Technology
Duration: 3FT Hon
Entry Requirements: *GCE:* 200-240. *IB:* 24.

H392 BSc Motorsport Technology (Top-Up)
Duration: 1.5FT Hon
Entry Requirements: Contact the institution for details.

H302 BSc (Hons) Mechanical Technology (Top-Up)
Duration: 1FT Hon
Entry Requirements: Contact the institution for details.

H336 FdSc Motorsport Technology
Duration: 2FT Fdg
Entry Requirements: *GCE:* 100. *IB:* 24.

S76 STOCKPORT COLLEGE
WELLINGTON ROAD SOUTH
STOCKPORT SK1 3UQ
t: 0161 958 3143 f: 0161 958 3663
e: susan.kelly@stockport.ac.uk
// www.stockport.ac.uk

003H HND Mechanical Engineering
Duration: 2FT HND
Entry Requirements: *GCE:* 80. Interview required. Admissions Test required.

S78 THE UNIVERSITY OF STRATHCLYDE
GLASGOW G1 1XQ
t: 0141 552 4400 f: 0141 552 0775
// www.strath.ac.uk

H300 BEng Mechanical Engineering
Duration: 4FT Hon
Entry Requirements: *GCE:* A*AA-AAB. *SQAH:* AAAAB-AAAB. *IB:* 32. Interview required.

H303 BEng Mechanical Engineering with International Study
Duration: 4FT Hon
Entry Requirements: *GCE:* A*AA-AAB. *SQAH:* AAAAB-AAAB. *IB:* 32. Interview required.

H302 MEng Mechanical Engineering
Duration: 5FT Hon
Entry Requirements: *GCE:* A*A*A-AAA. *SQAH:* AAAAAB-AAAAB. *IB:* 36. Interview required.

H3N3 MEng Mechanical Engineering with Financial Management (d)
Duration: 5FT Hon
Entry Requirements: *GCE:* A*A*A-AAA. *SQAH:* AAAAAB-AAAAB. *IB:* 36. Interview required.

H304 MEng Mechanical Engineering with International Study
Duration: 5FT Hon
Entry Requirements: *GCE:* A*A*A-AAA. *SQAH:* AAAAAB-AAAAB. *IB:* 36. Interview required.

H3J2 MEng Mechanical Engineering with Materials Engineering (d)
Duration: 5FT Hon
Entry Requirements: *GCE:* AAA. *SQAH:* AAAABB-AAAAB. *SQAAH:* AAA. *IB:* 36. Interview required.

S82 UNIVERSITY CAMPUS SUFFOLK (UCS)
WATERFRONT BUILDING
NEPTUNE QUAY
IPSWICH
SUFFOLK IP4 1QJ
t: 01473 338833 f: 01473 339900
e: info@ucs.ac.uk
// www.ucs.ac.uk

H300 FdSc Mechanical Engineering
Duration: 2FT Fdg
Entry Requirements: Contact the institution for details.

S84 UNIVERSITY OF SUNDERLAND
STUDENT HELPLINE
THE STUDENT GATEWAY
CHESTER ROAD
SUNDERLAND SR1 3SD
t: 0191 515 3000 f: 0191 515 3805
e: student.helpline@sunderland.ac.uk
// www.sunderland.ac.uk

H3WF BEng Automotive Engineering
Duration: 3FT/4SW Hon
Entry Requirements: *GCE:* 260. *IB:* 24. *OCR ND:* D *OCR NED:* M3

H3W2 BEng Mechanical Engineering
Duration: 3FT/4SW Hon
Entry Requirements: *GCE:* 260. *IB:* 24. *OCR ND:* D *OCR NED:* M3

S85 UNIVERSITY OF SURREY
STAG HILL
GUILDFORD
SURREY GU2 7XH
t: +44(0)1483 689305 f: +44(0)1483 689388
e: ugteam@surrey.ac.uk
// www.surrey.ac.uk

H300 BEng Mechanical Engineering (3 years)
Duration: 3FT Hon
Entry Requirements: *GCE:* ABB. *SQAH:* BBBB. Interview required.

H301 BEng Mechanical Engineering (4 years)
Duration: 4SW Hon
Entry Requirements: *GCE:* ABB. *SQAH:* BBBB. *IB:* 32. Interview required.

H309 MEng Mechanical Engineering (4 years)
Duration: 4FT Hon
Entry Requirements: *GCE:* AAA. Interview required.

H303 MEng Mechanical Engineering (5 years)
Duration: 5SW Hon
Entry Requirements: *GCE:* AAA. Interview required.

S90 UNIVERSITY OF SUSSEX
UNDERGRADUATE ADMISSIONS
SUSSEX HOUSE
UNIVERSITY OF SUSSEX
BRIGHTON BN1 9RH
t: 01273 678416 f: 01273 678545
e: ug.applicants@sussex.ac.uk
// www.sussex.ac.uk

H331 BEng Automotive Engineering
Duration: 3FT Hon
Entry Requirements: *GCE:* ABB. *SQAH:* AABBB. *SQAAH:* ABB. *IB:*
34. *BTEC SubDip:* D. *BTEC Dip:* DD. *BTEC ExtDip:* DDD. *OCR*
ND: D *OCR NED:* D2

H300 BEng Mechanical Engineering
Duration: 3FT Hon
Entry Requirements: *GCE:* ABB. *SQAH:* AABBB. *SQAAH:* ABB. *IB:*
34. *BTEC SubDip:* D. *BTEC Dip:* DD. *BTEC ExtDip:* DDD. *OCR*
ND: D *OCR NED:* D2

H330 MEng Automotive Engineering
Duration: 4FT Hon
Entry Requirements: *GCE:* AAB. *SQAH:* AAABB. *SQAAH:* AAB. *IB:*
35. *BTEC SubDip:* D. *BTEC Dip:* DD. *BTEC ExtDip:* DDD. *OCR*
ND: D *OCR NED:* D1

H301 MEng Mechanical Engineering
Duration: 4FT Hon
Entry Requirements: *GCE:* AAB. *SQAH:* AAABB. *SQAAH:* AAB. *IB:*
35. *BTEC SubDip:* D. *BTEC Dip:* DD. *BTEC ExtDip:* DDD. *OCR*
ND: D *OCR NED:* D1

S93 SWANSEA UNIVERSITY
SINGLETON PARK
SWANSEA SA2 8PP
t: 01792 295111 f: 01792 295110
e: admissions@swansea.ac.uk
// www.swansea.ac.uk

H300 BEng Mechanical Engineering
Duration: 3FT Hon
Entry Requirements: *GCE:* BBB. *IB:* 32.

H302 BEng Mechanical Engineering (with a Year in Europe)
Duration: 4FT Hon
Entry Requirements: *GCE:* ABB. *IB:* 33.

H305 BEng Mechanical Engineering (with a Year in Industry)
Duration: 4FT Hon
Entry Requirements: *GCE:* ABB. *IB:* 33.

H303 BEng Mechanical Engineering (with a Year in North America)
Duration: 4FT Hon
Entry Requirements: *GCE:* ABB. *IB:* 33.

HH13 BEng Product Design Technology
Duration: 3FT Hon
Entry Requirements: *GCE:* BBB. *IB:* 32.

HH1J BEng Product Design Technology (with a Year in Europe)
Duration: 4FT Hon
Entry Requirements: *GCE:* ABB. *IB:* 33.

HHD3 BEng Product Design Technology (with a Year in Industry)
Duration: 4FT Hon
Entry Requirements: *GCE:* ABB. *IB:* 33.

HH1H BEng Product Design Technology (with a Year in North America)
Duration: 4FT Hon
Entry Requirements: *GCE:* ABB. *IB:* 33.

H304 MEng Mechanical Engineering
Duration: 4FT Hon
Entry Requirements: *GCE:* AAB. *IB:* 34.

H306 MEng Mechanical Engineering (with a Year in Industry)
Duration: 5FT Hon
Entry Requirements: *GCE:* AAA. *IB:* 34.

S96 SWANSEA METROPOLITAN UNIVERSITY
MOUNT PLEASANT CAMPUS
SWANSEA SA1 6ED
t: 01792 481000 f: 01792 481061
e: gemma.green@smu.ac.uk
// www.smu.ac.uk

H330 BEng Automotive Engineering
Duration: 3FT Hon
Entry Requirements: *GCE:* 240-360. *IB:* 24. Interview required.

H348 BEng Automotive Engineering (4-year programme)
Duration: 4FT Hon
Entry Requirements: *GCE:* 80-360. *IB:* 24. Interview required.

HH37 BEng Mechanical and Manufacturing Engineering
Duration: 3FT Hon
Entry Requirements: *GCE:* 160-360. *IB:* 24. Interview required.

HH3R BEng Mechanical and Manufacturing Engineering (4 year programme)
Duration: 4FT Hon
Entry Requirements: *GCE:* 160-360. *IB:* 24. Interview required.

H331 BEng Motorcycle Engineering
Duration: 3FT Hon
Entry Requirements: *GCE:* 240-360. *IB:* 24. Interview required.

H390 BEng Motorcycle Engineering (4-year programme)
Duration: 4FT Hon
Entry Requirements: *GCE:* 80-360. *IB:* 24. Interview required.

H336 BEng Motorsport Engineering and Design
Duration: 3FT Hon
Entry Requirements: *GCE:* 240-360. *IB:* 24. Interview required.

H337 BEng Motorsport Engineering and Design (4 year programme)
Duration: 4FT Hon
Entry Requirements: *GCE:* 80-360. *IB:* 24. Interview required.

H332 BSc Automotive Engineering
Duration: 3FT Hon
Entry Requirements: *GCE:* 200-360. *IB:* 24. Interview required.

H33L BSc Motorcycle Engineering
Duration: 3FT Hon
Entry Requirements: *GCE:* 200-360. *IB:* 24. Interview required.

H333 BSc Motorsport Engineering
Duration: 3FT Hon
Entry Requirements: *GCE:* 200-360. *IB:* 24. Interview required.

H3N2 BSc Motorsport Management
Duration: 3FT Hon
Entry Requirements: *GCE:* 160-360. *IB:* 24. Interview required.

043H HND Automotive Engineering
Duration: 2FT HND
Entry Requirements: *GCE:* 200-360. *IB:* 24. Interview required.

H339 HND Motorcycle Engineering
Duration: 2FT HND
Entry Requirements: *GCE:* 200-360. *IB:* 24. Interview required.

033H HND Motorsport Engineering
Duration: 2FT HND
Entry Requirements: *GCE:* 200-360. *IB:* 24. Interview required.

2N3H HND Motorsport Management
Duration: 2FT HND
Entry Requirements: *GCE:* 80-360. *IB:* 24. Interview required.

T10 TAMESIDE COLLEGE
ASHTON CENTRE
BEAUFORT ROAD
ASHTON-UNDER-LYNE
LANCS OL6 6NX
t: 0161 908 6789 f: 0161 908 6611
e: info@tameside.ac.uk
// www.tameside.ac.uk

003H HND Mechanical Engineering
Duration: 2FT HND
Entry Requirements: *GCE:* 80-100. *IB:* 24.

T20 TEESSIDE UNIVERSITY
MIDDLESBROUGH TS1 3BA
t: 01642 218121 f: 01642 384201
e: registry@tees.ac.uk
// www.tees.ac.uk

H300 BEng Mechanical Engineering
Duration: 3FT/4SW Hon
Entry Requirements: *GCE:* 280. *IB:* 30. *BTEC SubDip:* M. *BTEC Dip:* D*D*. *BTEC ExtDip:* DDM. *OCR ND:* M2 *OCR NED:* M2 Interview required.

H310 BEng Mechanical Engineering (Extended)
Duration: 4FT/5SW Hon
Entry Requirements: *GCE:* 120-200. *BTEC SubDip:* D. *BTEC Dip:* MP. *BTEC ExtDip:* PPP. *OCR ND:* P2 *OCR NED:* P3 Interview required.

H331 BEng Tech Automotive Engineering
Duration: 1FT Hon
Entry Requirements: HND required.

H303 BEng Tech Mechanical Engineering
Duration: 1FT Hon
Entry Requirements: HND required.

H301 MEng Mechanical Engineering
Duration: 4FT/5SW Hon
Entry Requirements: *GCE:* 300-320. *IB:* 30. *BTEC SubDip:* M. *BTEC Dip:* MM. *BTEC ExtDip:* DDM. *OCR ND:* M2 *OCR NED:* D2 Interview required.

U20 UNIVERSITY OF ULSTER
COLERAINE
CO. LONDONDERRY
NORTHERN IRELAND BT52 1SA
t: 028 7012 4221 f: 028 7012 4908
e: online@ulster.ac.uk
// www.ulster.ac.uk

H300 BEng Mechanical Engineering
Duration: 4SW Hon
Entry Requirements: *GCE:* 280. *IB:* 24. Interview required.
Admissions Test required.

H302 MEng Mechanical Engineering
Duration: 5SW Hon
Entry Requirements: *GCE:* 300. *IB:* 25. Interview required.
Admissions Test required.

U40 UNIVERSITY OF THE WEST OF SCOTLAND
PAISLEY
RENFREWSHIRE
SCOTLAND PA1 2BE
t: 0141 848 3727 f: 0141 848 3623
e: admissions@uws.ac.uk
// www.uws.ac.uk

H300 BEng Mechanical Engineering
Duration: 3FT/4FT/5SW Ord/Hon
Entry Requirements: *GCE:* CC. *SQAH:* BBB.

H330 BEng Motorsport Design Engineering
Duration: 3FT/4FT Ord/Hon
Entry Requirements: *GCE:* CC. *SQAH:* BBC.

U80 UNIVERSITY COLLEGE LONDON (UNIVERSITY OF LONDON)
GOWER STREET
LONDON WC1E 6BT
t: 020 7679 3000 f: 020 7679 3001
// www.ucl.ac.uk

H300 BEng Mechanical Engineering
Duration: 3FT Hon
Entry Requirements: *GCE:* AABe. *SQAAH:* AAB. *IB:* 36. *BTEC ExtDip:* DDD. Interview required.

H301 MEng Mechanical Engineering
Duration: 4FT Hon
Entry Requirements: *GCE:* AAAe-AABe. *SQAAH:* AAA-AAB. Interview required.

W20 THE UNIVERSITY OF WARWICK
COVENTRY CV4 8UW
t: 024 7652 3723 f: 024 7652 4649
e: ugadmissions@warwick.ac.uk
// www.warwick.ac.uk

H330 BEng Automotive Engineering
Duration: 3FT Hon
Entry Requirements: *GCE:* AAB. *SQAAH:* AA-AB. *IB:* 36.

HH73 BEng Manufacturing and Mechanical Engineering
Duration: 3FT Hon
Entry Requirements: *GCE:* AAB. *SQAAH:* AA-AB. *IB:* 36.

H300 BEng Mechanical Engineering
Duration: 3FT Hon
Entry Requirements: *GCE:* AAB. *SQAAH:* AA-AB. *IB:* 36.

H335 MEng Automotive Engineering
Duration: 4FT Hon
Entry Requirements: *GCE:* AAB. *SQAAH:* AA-AB. *IB:* 36.

HH37 MEng Manufacturing and Mechanical Engineering
Duration: 4FT Hon
Entry Requirements: *GCE:* AAB. *SQAAH:* AA-AB. *IB:* 36.

HH37 MEng Manufacturing and Mechanical Engineering option - Business Management
Duration: 4FT Hon
Entry Requirements: *GCE:* AAB-ABB. *SQAAH:* AA-AB. *IB:* 36.

HH37 MEng Manufacturing and Mechanical Engineering option - Robotics
Duration: 4FT Hon
Entry Requirements: *GCE:* AAB-ABB. *SQAAH:* AA-AB. *IB:* 36.

HH37 MEng Manufacturing and Mechanical Engineering option - Sustainability
Duration: 4FT Hon
Entry Requirements: *GCE:* AAB-ABB. *SQAAH:* AA-AB. *IB:* 36.

H302 MEng Mechanical Engineering
Duration: 4FT Hon
Entry Requirements: *GCE:* AAB. *SQAAH:* AA-AB. *IB:* 36.

H302 MEng Mechanical Engineering option - Business Management
Duration: 4FT Hon
Entry Requirements: *GCE:* AAB-ABB. *SQAAH:* AA-AB. *IB:* 36.

H302 MEng Mechanical Engineering option - Sustainability
Duration: 4FT Hon
Entry Requirements: *GCE:* BBB. *SQAAH:* AB-BB. *IB:* 34.

H302 MEng Mechanical Engineering option - Fluid Dynamics
Duration: 4FT Hon
Entry Requirements: *GCE:* AAB-ABB. *SQAAH:* AA-AB. *IB:* 36.

W25 WARWICKSHIRE COLLEGE
WARWICK NEW ROAD
LEAMINGTON SPA
WARWICKSHIRE CV32 5JE
t: 01926 884223 f: 01926 318 111
e: kgooch@warkscol.ac.uk
// www.warwickshire.ac.uk

H331 FdEng Automotive Engineering
Duration: 2FT Fdg CRB Check: Required
Entry Requirements: Contact the institution for details.

H300 FdEng Mechanical Engineering
Duration: 2FT Fdg
Entry Requirements: Contact the institution for details.

H330 FdEng Motorsport Engineering
Duration: 2FT Fdg
Entry Requirements: *GCE:* 80.

W35 COLLEGE OF WEST ANGLIA
MAIN CAMPUS
TENNYSON AVENUE
KING'S LYNN
NORFOLK PE30 2QW
t: 01553 761144 f: 01553 770115
e: enquiries@col-westanglia.ac.uk
// www.col-westanglia.ac.uk

H330 FdSc Motorsport Engineering
Duration: 2FT Fdg
Entry Requirements: Contact the institution for details.

W67 WIGAN AND LEIGH COLLEGE
PO BOX 53
PARSON'S WALK
WIGAN
GREATER MANCHESTER WN1 1RS
t: 01942 761605 f: 01942 761164
e: applications@wigan-leigh.ac.uk
// www.wigan-leigh.ac.uk

37HH HND Mechanical Engineering
Duration: 2FT HND
Entry Requirements: *GCE:* 40-80. Interview required.

W75 UNIVERSITY OF WOLVERHAMPTON
ADMISSIONS UNIT
MX207, CAMP STREET
WOLVERHAMPTON
WEST MIDLANDS WV1 1AD
t: 01902 321000 f: 01902 321896
e: admissions@wlv.ac.uk
// www.wlv.ac.uk

H331 BEng Automotive Systems Engineering
Duration: 3FT/4SW Hon
Entry Requirements: *GCE:* 160-220. *IB:* 24.

H300 BEng Mechanical Engineering
Duration: 3FT/4SW Hon
Entry Requirements: *GCE:* 160-220. *IB:* 24.

H330 MEng Automotive Systems Engineering
Duration: 4FT/5SW Hon
Entry Requirements: Contact the institution for details.

H301 MEng Mechanical Engineering
Duration: 4FT/5SW Hon
Entry Requirements: Contact the institution for details.

W81 WORCESTER COLLEGE OF TECHNOLOGY
DEANSWAY
WORCESTER WR1 2JF
t: 01905 725555 f: 01905 28906
// www.wortech.ac.uk

003H HND Engineering Mechanical
Duration: 1.5FT/2FT HNC/HND
Entry Requirements: *GCE:* 120.

NAVAL ARCHITECTURE

N21 NEWCASTLE UNIVERSITY
KING'S GATE
NEWCASTLE UPON TYNE NE1 7RU
t: 01912083333
// www.ncl.ac.uk

H504 BEng Marine Technology with Marine Engineering
Duration: 3FT Hon
Entry Requirements: *GCE:* AAB-ABB. *SQAAH:* AAB-ABB. *BTEC ExtDip:* DDD.

H502 BEng Marine Technology with Naval Architecture
Duration: 3FT Hon
Entry Requirements: *GCE:* AAB-ABB. *SQAAH:* AAB-ABB. *BTEC ExtDip:* DDD.

H520 BEng Marine Technology with Small Craft Technology
Duration: 3FT Hon
Entry Requirements: *GCE:* AAB-ABB. *SQAAH:* AAB-ABB. *BTEC ExtDip:* DDD.

H501 MEng Marine Technology with Marine Engineering
Duration: 4FT Hon
Entry Requirements: *GCE:* AAB. *SQAAH:* AAB. *IB:* 37.

H503 MEng Marine Technology with Naval Architecture
Duration: 4FT Hon
Entry Requirements: *GCE:* AAB. *SQAAH:* AAB. *IB:* 37.

H524 MEng Marine Technology with Small Craft Technology
Duration: 4FT Hon
Entry Requirements: *GCE:* AAB. *SQAAH:* AAB. *IB:* 37.

S27 UNIVERSITY OF SOUTHAMPTON
HIGHFIELD
SOUTHAMPTON SO17 1BJ
t: 023 8059 4732 f: 023 8059 3037
e: admissions@soton.ac.uk
// www.southampton.ac.uk

H500 MEng Ship Science/Naval Engineering
Duration: 4FT Hon
Entry Requirements: *GCE:* AAB. *SQAAH:* AAB. *IB:* 34.

S30 SOUTHAMPTON SOLENT UNIVERSITY
EAST PARK TERRACE
SOUTHAMPTON
HAMPSHIRE SO14 0RT
t: +44 (0) 23 8031 9039 f: + 44 (0)23 8022 2259
e: admissions@solent.ac.uk
// www.solent.ac.uk/

H520 BEng Yacht and Powercraft Design
Duration: 3FT Hon
Entry Requirements: *GCE:* 180.

H528 BEng Yacht and Powercraft Design (with foundation)
Duration: 4FT Hon
Entry Requirements: *GCE:* 40.

H5Q3 BEng Yacht and Powercraft Design with IFY (Intl only, Sept)
Duration: 4FT Hon
Entry Requirements: Contact the institution for details.

H500 FdEng Marine Engineering
Duration: 3SW Fdg
Entry Requirements: *GCE:* 120.

S78 THE UNIVERSITY OF STRATHCLYDE
GLASGOW G1 1XQ
t: 0141 552 4400 f: 0141 552 0775
// www.strath.ac.uk

JH65 BEng Naval Architecture and Marine Engineering (g)
Duration: 4FT Hon
Entry Requirements: *GCE:* AAB-ABB. *SQAH:* AAAB-AABBB. *IB:* 32.
Interview required.

H512 BEng Naval Architecture with Ocean Engineering
Duration: 4FT Hon
Entry Requirements: *GCE:* AAB-ABB. *SQAH:* AAAB-AABBB. *IB:* 32.
Interview required.

H520 BEng Naval Architecture with Small Craft Engineering
Duration: 4FT Hon
Entry Requirements: *GCE:* AAB-ABB. *SQAH:* AAAB-AABBB. *IB:* 32.
Interview required.

HJ56 MEng Naval Architecture and Marine Engineering (g)
Duration: 5FT Hon
Entry Requirements: *GCE:* AAA-AAB. *SQAH:* AAAA-AAABB. *IB:* 36.
Interview required.

H513 MEng Naval Architecture with Ocean Engineering
Duration: 5FT Hon
Entry Requirements: *GCE:* AAA-AAB. *SQAH:* AAAA-AAABB. *IB:* 36.
Interview required.

H521 MEng Naval Architecture with Small Craft Engineering
Duration: 5FT Hon
Entry Requirements: *GCE:* AAA-AAB. *SQAH:* AAAA-AAABB. *IB:* 36.
Interview required.

H500 MEng Naval Architecture(g)
Duration: 5FT Ord
Entry Requirements: *GCE:* AAA-AAB. *SQAH:* AAAA-AAABB. *IB:* 36.
Interview required.

PRODUCTION AND MANUFACTURING ENGINEERING

B16 UNIVERSITY OF BATH
CLAVERTON DOWN
BATH BA2 7AY
t: 01225 383019 f: 01225 386366
e: admissions@bath.ac.uk
// www.bath.ac.uk

H716 MEng Mechanical Engineering with Manufacturing and Management
Duration: 4FT Hon
Entry Requirements: *GCE:* A*AA. *SQAAH:* AAA. *IB:* 36.

H713 MEng Mechanical Engineering with Manufacturing and Management (with Placement)
Duration: 5SW Hon
Entry Requirements: *GCE:* A*AA. *SQAAH:* AAA. *IB:* 36.

H714 MEng Mechanical Engineering with Manufacturing and Management with French
Duration: 5SW Hon
Entry Requirements: *GCE:* A*AA. *SQAAH:* AAA. *IB:* 36.

B40 BLACKBURN COLLEGE
FEILDEN STREET
BLACKBURN BB2 1LH
t: 01254 292594 f: 01254 679647
e: he-admissions@blackburn.ac.uk
// www.blackburn.ac.uk

H732 BEng Mechatronics
Duration: 3FT Hon
Entry Requirements: *GCE:* 160.

H731 BEng Mechatronics (Top-Up)
Duration: 1FT/2FT Ord/Hon
Entry Requirements: Contact the institution for details.

B41 BLACKPOOL AND THE FYLDE COLLEGE AN ASSOCIATE COLLEGE OF LANCASTER UNIVERSITY
ASHFIELD ROAD
BISPHAM
BLACKPOOL
LANCS FY2 0HB
t: 01253 504346 f: 01253 504198
e: admissions@blackpool.ac.uk
// www.blackpool.ac.uk

H730 BEng Mechatronics
Duration: 2FT Hon
Entry Requirements: HND required.

B50 BOURNEMOUTH UNIVERSITY
TALBOT CAMPUS
FERN BARROW
POOLE
DORSET BH12 5BB
t: 01202 524111
// www.bournemouth.ac.uk

H711 FdSc Engineering (Manufacturing Management)
Duration: 2FT Fdg
Entry Requirements: Contact the institution for details.

B56 THE UNIVERSITY OF BRADFORD
RICHMOND ROAD
BRADFORD
WEST YORKSHIRE BD7 1DP
t: 0800 073 1225 f: 01274 235585
e: course-enquiries@bradford.ac.uk
// www.bradford.ac.uk

H753 BEng Industrial Engineering
Duration: 3FT Hon
Entry Requirements: *GCE:* 240. *IB:* 24.

H750 BEng Industrial Engineering (4 years)
Duration: 4SW Hon
Entry Requirements: *GCE:* 240. *IB:* 26.

HW72 BSc Product Design
Duration: 3FT Hon
Entry Requirements: *GCE:* 240. *IB:* 24. Interview required.

HWR2 BSc Product Design (4 years)
Duration: 4SW Hon
Entry Requirements: *GCE:* 240. *IB:* 24. Interview required.

B84 BRUNEL UNIVERSITY
UXBRIDGE
MIDDLESEX UB8 3PH
t: 01895 265265 f: 01895 269790
e: admissions@brunel.ac.uk
// www.brunel.ac.uk

HW72 BA Industrial Design and Technology
Duration: 3FT Hon
Entry Requirements: *GCE:* ABB. *SQAAH:* ABB. *IB:* 33. *BTEC ExtDip:* D*DD. Interview required.

HWR2 BA Industrial Design and Technology (4 year Thick SW)
Duration: 4SW Hon
Entry Requirements: *GCE:* ABB. *SQAAH:* ABB. *IB:* 33. *BTEC ExtDip:* D*DD. Interview required.

H772 BSc Product Design
Duration: 3FT Hon
Entry Requirements: *GCE:* ABB. *SQAAH:* ABB. *IB:* 33. *BTEC ExtDip:* D*DD. Interview required.

H776 BSc Product Design (4 year Thick SW)
Duration: 4SW Hon
Entry Requirements: *GCE:* ABB. *SQAAH:* ABB. *IB:* 33. *BTEC ExtDip:* D*DD. Interview required.

WH27 BSc Product Design Engineering
Duration: 3FT Hon
Entry Requirements: *GCE:* ABB. *SQAAH:* ABB. *IB:* 33. *BTEC ExtDip:* D*DD. Interview required.

WHF7 BSc Product Design Engineering (4 year Thick SW)
Duration: 4SW Hon
Entry Requirements: *GCE:* ABB. *SQAAH:* ABB. *IB:* 33. *BTEC ExtDip:* D*DD. Interview required.

B94 BUCKINGHAMSHIRE NEW UNIVERSITY
QUEEN ALEXANDRA ROAD
HIGH WYCOMBE
BUCKINGHAMSHIRE HP11 2JZ
t: 0800 0565 660 f: 01494 605 023
e: admissions@bucks.ac.uk
// bucks.ac.uk

HW72 BSc Product Design
Duration: 3FT Hon
Entry Requirements: *GCE:* 200-240. *IB:* 24. *OCR ND:* M1 *OCR NED:* M3 Interview required.

C85 COVENTRY UNIVERSITY
THE STUDENT CENTRE
COVENTRY UNIVERSITY
1 GULSON RD
COVENTRY CV1 2JH
t: 024 7615 2222 f: 024 7615 2223
e: studentenquiries@coventry.ac.uk
// www.coventry.ac.uk

WH27 MDes Transport Design
Duration: 4FT Hon
Entry Requirements: *Foundation:* Merit. *GCE:* BCC. *SQAH:*
BCCCC. *IB:* 27. *BTEC ExtDip:* MMM. *OCR NED:* M3 Interview
required. Portfolio required.

D39 UNIVERSITY OF DERBY
KEDLESTON ROAD
DERBY DE22 1GB
t: 01332 591167 f: 01332 597724
e: askadmissions@derby.ac.uk
// www.derby.ac.uk

H702 BEng Manufacturing and Production Engineering
Duration: 3FT Hon
Entry Requirements: *GCE:* 260. *IB:* 28. *BTEC Dip:* D*D*. *BTEC ExtDip:* DMM. *OCR ND:* D *OCR NED:* M3

H703 FYr Manufacturing and Production Engineering Foundation
Duration: 1FT FYr
Entry Requirements: *Foundation:* Pass. *GCE:* 160. *IB:* 24. *BTEC Dip:* D*D*. *BTEC ExtDip:* DMM. *OCR ND:* M2 *OCR NED:* P2

D58 DUDLEY COLLEGE OF TECHNOLOGY
THE BROADWAY
DUDLEY DY1 4AS
t: 01384 363277/6 f: 01384 363311
e: admissions@dudleycol.ac.uk
// www.dudleycol.ac.uk

007H HND Engineering (Mechanical/Manufacture)
Duration: 2FT HND
Entry Requirements: *GCE:* 40-80.

E28 UNIVERSITY OF EAST LONDON
DOCKLANDS CAMPUS
UNIVERSITY WAY
LONDON E16 2RD
t: 020 8223 3333 f: 020 8223 2978
e: study@uel.ac.uk
// www.uel.ac.uk

H764 BSc Product Design
Duration: 3FT/4SW Hon
Entry Requirements: *GCE:* 240. *IB:* 24. Interview required.
Portfolio required.

E59 EDINBURGH NAPIER UNIVERSITY
CRAIGLOCKHART CAMPUS
EDINBURGH EH14 1DJ
t: +44 (0)8452 60 60 40 f: 0131 455 6464
e: info@napier.ac.uk
// www.napier.ac.uk

H711 BSc Product Design Engineering
Duration: 3FT/4FT Ord/Hon
Entry Requirements: *GCE:* 245.

E84 UNIVERSITY OF EXETER
LAVER BUILDING
NORTH PARK ROAD
EXETER
DEVON EX4 4QE
t: 01392 723044 f: 01392 722479
e: admissions@exeter.ac.uk
// www.exeter.ac.uk

H704 MEng Engineering and Management
Duration: 4FT Hon
Entry Requirements: *GCE:* AAA-AAB. *SQAH:* AAAAB-AAABB.
SQAAH: AAB-ABB. *BTEC ExtDip:* DDM.

F66 FARNBOROUGH COLLEGE OF TECHNOLOGY
BOUNDARY ROAD
FARNBOROUGH
HAMPSHIRE GU14 6SB
t: 01252 407028 f: 01252 407041
e: admissions@farn-ct.ac.uk
// www.farn-ct.ac.uk

H730 FdEng Mechatronics
Duration: 2FT Fdg
Entry Requirements: Contact the institution for details.

G14 UNIVERSITY OF GLAMORGAN, CARDIFF AND PONTYPRIDD
ENQUIRIES AND ADMISSIONS UNIT
PONTYPRIDD CF37 1DL
t: 08456 434030 f: 01443 654050
e: enquiries@glam.ac.uk
// www.glam.ac.uk

H730 BSc Mechatronic Engineering (Top-Up)
Duration: 1FT Ord
Entry Requirements: HND required.

G28 UNIVERSITY OF GLASGOW
71 SOUTHPARK AVENUE
UNIVERSITY OF GLASGOW
GLASGOW G12 8QQ
t: 0141 330 6062 f: 0141 330 2961
e: student.recruitment@glasgow.ac.uk
// www.glasgow.ac.uk

H730 BEng Mechatronics
Duration: 4FT Hon
Entry Requirements: *GCE:* ABB. *SQAH:* AAAB-BBB. *IB:* 32.

H731 MEng Mechatronics
Duration: 5FT Hon
Entry Requirements: *GCE:* AAB. *SQAH:* AAAA-AAABB. *IB:* 34.

G43 THE GLASGOW SCHOOL OF ART
167 RENFREW STREET
GLASGOW G3 6RQ
t: 0141 353 4434/4514 f: 0141 353 4408
e: admissions@gsa.ac.uk
// www.gsa.ac.uk

HW72 BDes Product Design
Duration: 4FT Hon
Entry Requirements: *GCE:* ABB. *SQAH:* AABB-ABBB. *IB:* 30.
Interview required. Portfolio required.

G70 UNIVERSITY OF GREENWICH
GREENWICH CAMPUS
OLD ROYAL NAVAL COLLEGE
PARK ROW
LONDON SE10 9LS
t: 020 8331 9000 f: 020 8331 8145
e: courseinfo@gre.ac.uk
// www.gre.ac.uk

H715 BEng Manufacturing Systems Engineering
Duration: 3FT Hon
Entry Requirements: *GCE:* 240. *IB:* 24.

H718 BEng Manufacturing Systems Engineering (incl Foundation)
Duration: 4FT Hon
Entry Requirements: *GCE:* 80. *IB:* 24.

H49 UNIVERSITY OF THE HIGHLANDS AND ISLANDS
UHI EXECUTIVE OFFICE
NESS WALK
INVERNESS
SCOTLAND IV3 5SQ
t: 01463 279000 f: 01463 279001
e: info@uhi.ac.uk
// www.uhi.ac.uk

107H HNC Fabrication, Welding and Inspection
Duration: 1FT HNC
Entry Requirements: *GCE:* D. *SQAH:* C.

H60 THE UNIVERSITY OF HUDDERSFIELD
QUEENSGATE
HUDDERSFIELD HD1 3DH
t: 01484 473969 f: 01484 472765
e: admissionsandrecords@hud.ac.uk
// www.hud.ac.uk

N9H7 BSc Logistics and Supply Chain Management
Duration: 3FT/4SW Hon
Entry Requirements: *GCE:* 260. *SQAH:* BBB. *IB:* 26.

H72 THE UNIVERSITY OF HULL
THE UNIVERSITY OF HULL
COTTINGHAM ROAD
HULL HU6 7RX
t: 01482 466100 f: 01482 442290
e: admissions@hull.ac.uk
// www.hull.ac.uk

H790 BSc Product Innovation
Duration: 3FT Hon
Entry Requirements: *GCE:* 260. *IB:* 26. *BTEC ExtDip:* MMM.

K24 THE UNIVERSITY OF KENT
RECRUITMENT & ADMISSIONS OFFICE
REGISTRY
UNIVERSITY OF KENT
CANTERBURY, KENT CT2 7NZ
t: 01227 827272 f: 01227 827077
e: information@kent.ac.uk
// www.kent.ac.uk

H700 FdEng Engineering (Manufacturing Engineering)
Duration: 2FT Fdg
Entry Requirements: *OCR NED:* M2

H790 FdEng Engineering (Plant and Process)
Duration: 2FT Hon
Entry Requirements: *OCR NED:* M2

L23 UNIVERSITY OF LEEDS
THE UNIVERSITY OF LEEDS
WOODHOUSE LANE
LEEDS LS2 9JT
t: 0113 343 3999
e: admissions@leeds.ac.uk
// www.leeds.ac.uk

H790 MDes Product Design
Duration: 3FT/4FT Hon
Entry Requirements: *GCE:* AAA. *SQAAH:* AAA. *IB:* 38.

L42 LINCOLN COLLEGE
MONKS ROAD
LINCOLN LN2 5HQ
t: 01522 876000 f: 01522 876200
e: enquiries@lincolncollege.ac.uk
// www.lincolncollege.ac.uk

H710 HND Manufacturing Engineering
Duration: 2FT HND
Entry Requirements: Contact the institution for details.

L51 LIVERPOOL JOHN MOORES UNIVERSITY
KINGSWAY HOUSE
HATTON GARDEN
LIVERPOOL L3 2AJ
t: 0151 231 5090 f: 0151 904 6368
e: courses@ljmu.ac.uk
// www.ljmu.ac.uk

H772 BSc Computer Aided Design
Duration: 3FT/4SW Hon
Entry Requirements: *GCE:* 280. *OCR ND:* M2 *OCR NED:* M2
Interview required.

H7N1 BSc Manufacturing Engineering and Management
Duration: 3FT/4SW Hon
Entry Requirements: Contact the institution for details.

L75 LONDON SOUTH BANK UNIVERSITY
ADMISSIONS AND RECRUITMENT CENTRE
90 LONDON ROAD
LONDON SE1 6LN
t: 0800 923 8888 f: 020 7815 8273
e: course.enquiry@lsbu.ac.uk
// www.lsbu.ac.uk

H770 BSc Engineering Product Design
Duration: 3FT/4SW Hon
Entry Requirements: *GCE:* 200. *IB:* 24. Portfolio required.

H711 BSc Product Design
Duration: 3FT/4SW Hon
Entry Requirements: *GCE:* 200. *IB:* 24. Portfolio required.

L79 LOUGHBOROUGH UNIVERSITY
LOUGHBOROUGH
LEICESTERSHIRE LE11 3TU
t: 01509 223522 f: 01509 223905
e: admissions@lboro.ac.uk
// www.lboro.ac.uk

H775 BA Industrial Design and Technology
Duration: 3FT Hon
Entry Requirements: *GCE:* 300. *SQAH:* BBBBB. *SQAAH:* BB. *IB:* 32. Interview required. Portfolio required.

H776 BA Industrial Design and Technology
Duration: 4SW Hon
Entry Requirements: *GCE:* 300. *SQAH:* BBBBB. *SQAAH:* BB. *IB:* 32. Interview required. Portfolio required.

H710 BEng Manufacturing Engineering
Duration: 3FT Hon
Entry Requirements: *GCE:* BBB. *SQAH:* BBBBB. *SQAAH:* BB. *IB:* 32.

HH1T BEng Manufacturing Engineering
Duration: 4SW Hon
Entry Requirements: *GCE:* BBB. *SQAAH:* BB. *IB:* 32.

H700 BEng Manufacturing Engineering with a Foundation Year
Duration: 4FT Hon
Entry Requirements: *GCE:* ABC-BBB.

H715 BEng Product Design Engineering
Duration: 4SW Hon
Entry Requirements: *GCE:* BBB. *SQAH:* BBBBB. *SQAAH:* BB. *IB:* 32.

HH1R BEng Product Design Engineering
Duration: 3FT Hon
Entry Requirements: *GCE:* BBB. *SQAH:* BBBBB. *SQAAH:* BB. *IB:* 32.

HH17 BEng Product Design Engineering with a Foundation Year
Duration: 4FT Hon
Entry Requirements: *GCE:* ABC-BBB.

HJ79 BSc Product Design and Technology
Duration: 4SW Hon
Entry Requirements: *GCE:* 300. *SQAH:* BBBBB. *SQAAH:* BB. *IB:* 32. Interview required. Portfolio required.

HJ7X BSc Product Design and Technology
Duration: 3FT Hon
Entry Requirements: *GCE:* 300. *SQAH:* BBBCC. *SQAAH:* BB. *IB:* 32. Interview required. Portfolio required.

CH67 BSc Sports Technology
Duration: 3FT Hon
Entry Requirements: *GCE:* ABB. *SQAH:* AB. *IB:* 33.

HC76 BSc Sports Technology
Duration: 4SW Hon
Entry Requirements: *GCE:* ABB. *SQAAH:* AB. *IB:* 33.

H790 MEng Innovative Manufacturing Engineering
Duration: 4FT Hon
Entry Requirements: *GCE:* AAA. *SQAH:* AAABB. *SQAAH:* AA. *IB:* 34.

HHC7 MEng Product Design Engineering
Duration: 4FT Hon
Entry Requirements: *GCE:* AAB. *SQAAH:* AB. *IB:* 34.

HHD7 MEng Product Design Engineering
Duration: 5SW Hon
Entry Requirements: *GCE:* AAB. *SQAAH:* AB. *IB:* 34.

M80 MIDDLESEX UNIVERSITY
MIDDLESEX UNIVERSITY
THE BURROUGHS
LONDON NW4 4BT
t: 020 8411 5555 f: 020 8411 5649
e: enquiries@mdx.ac.uk
// www.mdx.ac.uk

H730 BEng Design Engineering: Mechatronics
Duration: 3FT/4SW Hon
Entry Requirements: Contact the institution for details.

N84 THE UNIVERSITY OF NOTTINGHAM
THE ADMISSIONS OFFICE
THE UNIVERSITY OF NOTTINGHAM
UNIVERSITY PARK
NOTTINGHAM NG7 2RD
t: 0115 951 5151 f: 0115 951 4668
// www.nottingham.ac.uk

HN72 BEng Manufacturing Engineering and Management
Duration: 3FT Hon
Entry Requirements: *GCE:* AAB. *SQAAH:* ABB-BBB. *IB:* 32.

H700 BEng Product Design and Manufacture
Duration: 3FT Hon
Entry Requirements: *GCE:* BBC. *SQAAH:* BBC. *IB:* 30. Interview required.

H716 MEng Manufacturing Engineering & Management
Duration: 4FT Hon
Entry Requirements: *GCE:* AAA. *SQAAH:* AAA-AAB. *IB:* 36.

H715 MEng Product Design and Manufacture
Duration: 4FT Hon
Entry Requirements: *GCE:* ABB. *SQAAH:* ABB. *IB:* 34. Interview required.

N91 NOTTINGHAM TRENT UNIVERSITY
DRYDEN BUILDING
BURTON STREET
NOTTINGHAM NG1 4BU
t: +44 (0) 115 848 4200 f: +44 (0) 115 848 8869
e: applications@ntu.ac.uk
// www.ntu.ac.uk

H715 BSc Product Design
Duration: 3FT/4SW Hon
Entry Requirements: *GCE:* 280. *BTEC Dip:* D*D*. *BTEC ExtDip:* DMM.

P80 UNIVERSITY OF PORTSMOUTH
ACADEMIC REGISTRY
UNIVERSITY HOUSE
WINSTON CHURCHILL AVENUE
PORTSMOUTH PO1 2UP
t: 023 9284 8484 f: 023 9284 3082
e: admissions@port.ac.uk
// www.port.ac.uk

H7G4 BSc Computer Aided Product Design
Duration: 3FT/4SW Hon
Entry Requirements: *GCE:* 240-280. *IB:* 26. *BTEC SubDip:* P. *BTEC Dip:* PP. *BTEC ExtDip:* DMM.

H771 BSc Product Design and Innovation
Duration: 3FT/4SW Hon
Entry Requirements: *GCE:* 240-280. *IB:* 26. *BTEC SubDip:* P. *BTEC Dip:* PP. *BTEC ExtDip:* DMM.

Q75 QUEEN'S UNIVERSITY BELFAST
UNIVERSITY ROAD
BELFAST BT7 1NN
t: 028 9097 3838 f: 028 9097 5151
e: admissions@qub.ac.uk
// www.qub.ac.uk

H780 BEng Manufacturing Engineering
Duration: 3FT Hon
Entry Requirements: *GCE:* BBC-BCC. *SQAH:* BBBBC-BBBCC. *SQAAH:* BBC-BCC.

H784 BEng Manufacturing Engineering (with a Year in Industry)
Duration: 4SW Hon
Entry Requirements: *GCE:* BBC-BCC. *SQAH:* BBBBC-BBBCC. *SQAAH:* BBC-BCC.

S21 SHEFFIELD HALLAM UNIVERSITY
CITY CAMPUS
HOWARD STREET
SHEFFIELD S1 1WB
t: 0114 225 5555 f: 0114 225 2167
e: admissions@shu.ac.uk
// www.shu.ac.uk

H790 BEng Manufacturing Engineering
Duration: 3FT/4SW Hon
Entry Requirements: *GCE:* 220.

H770 BSc Product Design
Duration: 3FT/4SW Hon
Entry Requirements: *GCE:* 280.

S27 UNIVERSITY OF SOUTHAMPTON
HIGHFIELD
SOUTHAMPTON SO17 1BJ
t: 023 8059 4732 f: 023 8059 3037
e: admissions@soton.ac.uk
// www.southampton.ac.uk

H722 BEng/MEng Acoustical Engineering
Duration: 3FT/4FT Hon
Entry Requirements: *GCE:* ABB. *SQAAH:* AAA-ABB. *IB:* 34.
Interview required.

HW73 BSc Acoustics and Music
Duration: 3FT Hon
Entry Requirements: *GCE:* AAA-BBB. *IB:* 35. Interview required.

S28 SOMERSET COLLEGE OF ARTS AND TECHNOLOGY
WELLINGTON ROAD
TAUNTON
SOMERSET TA1 5AX
t: 01823 366331 f: 01823 366418
e: enquiries@somerset.ac.uk
// www.somerset.ac.uk/student-area/considering-a-degree.html

HH17 FdSc Engineering (Design & Manufacture)
Duration: 2FT Fdg
Entry Requirements: *GCE:* 120. *IB:* 24.

S46 SOUTH NOTTINGHAM COLLEGE
WEST BRIDGFORD CENTRE
GREYTHORN DRIVE
WEST BRIDGFORD
NOTTINGHAM NG2 7GA
t: 0115 914 6400 f: 0115 914 6444
e: enquiries@snc.ac.uk
// www.snc.ac.uk

097H HND Manufacturing Engineering
Duration: 2FT HND
Entry Requirements: Contact the institution for details.

S72 STAFFORDSHIRE UNIVERSITY
COLLEGE ROAD
STOKE ON TRENT ST4 2DE
t: 01782 292753 f: 01782 292740
e: admissions@staffs.ac.uk
// www.staffs.ac.uk

H771 BSc Product Design Technology
Duration: 3FT/4SW Hon
Entry Requirements: *GCE:* 200-240. *IB:* 24.

H710 BSc (Hons) Manufacturing Technology (Top-Up)
Duration: 1FT Hon
Entry Requirements: Contact the institution for details.

S78 THE UNIVERSITY OF STRATHCLYDE
GLASGOW G1 1XQ
t: 0141 552 4400 f: 0141 552 0775
// www.strath.ac.uk

H771 BEng Product Design Engineering
Duration: 4FT Hon
Entry Requirements: *GCE:* A*AA-ABB. *SQAH:* AAABBB-AAAB. *IB:* 34. Interview required.

HN72 BEng Production Engineering and Management
Duration: 4FT Hon
Entry Requirements: *GCE:* A*AA-ABB. *SQAH:* AAABBB-AAAB. *IB:* 34. Interview required.

H770 MEng Product Design Engineering
Duration: 5FT Hon
Entry Requirements: *GCE:* A*AA-AAB. *SQAH:* AAAABB-AAAA. *IB:* 36. Interview required.

HN7F MEng Production Engineering and Management
Duration: 5FT Hon
Entry Requirements: *GCE:* A*AA-AAB. *SQAH:* AAAABB-AAAA. *IB:* 36. Interview required.

S84 UNIVERSITY OF SUNDERLAND
STUDENT HELPLINE
THE STUDENT GATEWAY
CHESTER ROAD
SUNDERLAND SR1 3SD
t: 0191 515 3000 f: 0191 515 3805
e: student.helpline@sunderland.ac.uk
// www.sunderland.ac.uk

H700 BEng Manufacturing Engineering (Top-up)
Duration: 1FT Hon
Entry Requirements: HND required.

U20 UNIVERSITY OF ULSTER
COLERAINE
CO. LONDONDERRY
NORTHERN IRELAND BT52 1SA
t: 028 7012 4221 f: 028 7012 4908
e: online@ulster.ac.uk
// www.ulster.ac.uk

H710 BEng Engineering Management
Duration: 4SW Hon
Entry Requirements: GCE: 280. IB: 24. Interview required. Admissions Test required.

H730 BEng Mechatronic Engineering
Duration: 4SW Hon
Entry Requirements: GCE: 280. IB: 24. Interview required. Admissions Test required.

H712 MEng Engineering Management with DPP
Duration: 5SW Hon
Entry Requirements: GCE: 300. IB: 25. Interview required. Admissions Test required.

H731 MEng Mechatronic Engineering (+German Masters Degree)
Duration: 5FT Hon
Entry Requirements: GCE: 300. IB: 25. Interview required. Admissions Test required.

H733 MEng Mechatronic Engineering with DPP
Duration: 5FT Hon
Entry Requirements: GCE: 300. IB: 25. Interview required. Admissions Test required.

U40 UNIVERSITY OF THE WEST OF SCOTLAND
PAISLEY
RENFREWSHIRE
SCOTLAND PA1 2BE
t: 0141 848 3727 f: 0141 848 3623
e: admissions@uws.ac.uk
// www.uws.ac.uk

H703 BEng Engineering Management
Duration: 3FT/4FT Ord/Hon
Entry Requirements: GCE: CC. SQAH: BBC.

H730 BEng Mechatronics
Duration: 1FT Deg
Entry Requirements: Contact the institution for details.

H700 BEng Product Design & Development
Duration: 3FT/4FT/5SW Ord/Hon
Entry Requirements: GCE: CD. SQAH: BBC.

W25 WARWICKSHIRE COLLEGE
WARWICK NEW ROAD
LEAMINGTON SPA
WARWICKSHIRE CV32 5JE
t: 01926 884223 f: 01926 318 111
e: kgooch@warkscol.ac.uk
// www.warwickshire.ac.uk

H710 FdEng Maintenance and Manufacturing Engineering
Duration: 2FT Fdg
Entry Requirements: Contact the institution for details.

W75 UNIVERSITY OF WOLVERHAMPTON
ADMISSIONS UNIT
MX207, CAMP STREET
WOLVERHAMPTON
WEST MIDLANDS WV1 1AD
t: 01902 321000 f: 01902 321896
e: admissions@wlv.ac.uk
// www.wlv.ac.uk

H730 BEng Mechatronics
Duration: 3FT/4SW Hon
Entry Requirements: GCE: 160-220. IB: 24.

H731 MEng Mechatronics
Duration: 4FT/5SW Hon
Entry Requirements: Contact the institution for details.

W81 WORCESTER COLLEGE OF TECHNOLOGY
DEANSWAY
WORCESTER WR1 2JF
t: 01905 725555 f: 01905 28906
// www.wortech.ac.uk

007H HND Manufacturing Engineering
Duration: 1.5FT HNC
Entry Requirements: *GCE:* 120.

Y70 YORK COLLEGE
SIM BALK LANE
YORK YO23 2BB
t: 01904 770448 f: 01904 770499
e: admissions.team@yorkcollege.ac.uk
// www.yorkcollege.ac.uk

H710 FdSc Manufacturing Engineering
Duration: 2FT/3SW Fdg
Entry Requirements: *GCE:* CC.

GENERAL ENGINEERING

A20 THE UNIVERSITY OF ABERDEEN
UNIVERSITY OFFICE
KING'S COLLEGE
ABERDEEN AB24 3FX
t: +44 (0) 1224 273504 f: +44 (0) 1224 272034
e: sras@abdn.ac.uk
// www.abdn.ac.uk/sras

H100 BEng Engineering
Duration: 4FT Hon
Entry Requirements: *GCE:* BBB. *SQAH:* BBBC. *IB:* 28.

H101 BEng Engineering (International Foundation)
Duration: 4FT Hon
Entry Requirements: Contact the institution for details.

H102 BScEng Engineering (General)
Duration: 3FT/4FT Ord
Entry Requirements: Contact the institution for details.

H104 MEng Engineering
Duration: 5FT Hon
Entry Requirements: *GCE:* BBB. *SQAH:* BBBB. *IB:* 30.

A80 ASTON UNIVERSITY, BIRMINGHAM
ASTON TRIANGLE
BIRMINGHAM B4 7ET
t: 0121 204 4444 f: 0121 204 3696
e: admissions@aston.ac.uk (automatic response)
// www.aston.ac.uk/prospective-students/ug

H150 BEng Design Engineering
Duration: 3FT/4SW Hon
Entry Requirements: *GCE:* 300-320. *IB:* 32.

H102 BEng Engineering (Foundation)
Duration: 4FT/5SW Hon
Entry Requirements: *GCE:* 240-260. *IB:* 29.

B16 UNIVERSITY OF BATH
CLAVERTON DOWN
BATH BA2 7AY
t: 01225 383019 f: 01225 386366
e: admissions@bath.ac.uk
// www.bath.ac.uk

HH37 FdSc Engineering Systems
Duration: 2FT Fdg
Entry Requirements: Contact the institution for details.

B32 THE UNIVERSITY OF BIRMINGHAM
EDGBASTON
BIRMINGHAM B15 2TT
t: 0121 415 8900 f: 0121 414 7159
e: admissions@bham.ac.uk
// www.birmingham.ac.uk

H1NC BEng Computer Systems Engineering with Business Management
Duration: 3FT Hon
Entry Requirements: *GCE:* AAB. *SQAH:* AAABB-AABBB. *SQAAH:* AA.

H100 BEng/MEng Engineering with Foundation Year
Duration: 4FT Hon
Entry Requirements: *GCE:* BBC.

B41 BLACKPOOL AND THE FYLDE COLLEGE AN ASSOCIATE COLLEGE OF LANCASTER UNIVERSITY
ASHFIELD ROAD
BISPHAM
BLACKPOOL
LANCS FY2 0HB
t: 01253 504346 f: 01253 504198
e: admissions@blackpool.ac.uk
// www.blackpool.ac.uk

H140 BEng Mechanical and Production Engineering
Duration: 2FT Hon
Entry Requirements: Contact the institution for details.

001H HND General Engineering
Duration: 2FT HND
Entry Requirements: *GCE:* 120-360. *IB:* 24.

B50 BOURNEMOUTH UNIVERSITY
TALBOT CAMPUS
FERN BARROW
POOLE
DORSET BH12 5BB
t: 01202 524111
// www.bournemouth.ac.uk

H100 BSc Design Engineering
Duration: 4SW Hon
Entry Requirements: *GCE:* 300. *IB:* 31. *BTEC SubDip:* D. *BTEC Dip:* DD. *BTEC ExtDip:* DDM. Interview required.

H150 BSc Design Engineering Top-Up
Duration: 1FT Hon
Entry Requirements: HND required.

H101 BSc Product Design
Duration: 4SW Hon
Entry Requirements: *GCE:* 320. *IB:* 32. *BTEC SubDip:* D. *BTEC Dip:* DD. *BTEC ExtDip:* DDM. Interview required. Portfolio required.

H105 MEng Engineering
Duration: 4FT Hon
Entry Requirements: *GCE:* 280. *IB:* 30. *BTEC SubDip:* D. *BTEC Dip:* DM. *BTEC ExtDip:* DMM.

B56 THE UNIVERSITY OF BRADFORD
RICHMOND ROAD
BRADFORD
WEST YORKSHIRE BD7 1DP
t: 0800 073 1225 f: 01274 235585
e: course-enquiries@bradford.ac.uk
// www.bradford.ac.uk

HN1F BEng Engineering and Management
Duration: 4SW Hon
Entry Requirements: *GCE:* 240. *IB:* 26.

HND2 BEng Engineering and Management
Duration: 3FT Hon
Entry Requirements: *GCE:* 240. *IB:* 26.

H101 BEng Engineering with foundation year
Duration: 4FT Hon
Entry Requirements: *GCE:* 160.

H102 BEng Engineering with foundation year (International)
Duration: 4FT Hon
Entry Requirements: *GCE:* 160.

H123 BSc Healthcare Science (Clinical Engineering)
Duration: 3FT Hon
Entry Requirements: *GCE:* 220. *IB:* 24.

B60 BRADFORD COLLEGE: AN ASSOCIATE COLLEGE OF LEEDS METROPOLITAN UNIVERSITY
GREAT HORTON ROAD
BRADFORD
WEST YORKSHIRE BD7 1AY
t: 01274 433008 f: 01274 431652
e: heregistry@bradfordcollege.ac.uk
// www.bradfordcollege.ac.uk/university-centre

H100 BEng Engineering
Duration: 1FT Hon
Entry Requirements: Contact the institution for details.

B78 UNIVERSITY OF BRISTOL
UNDERGRADUATE ADMISSIONS OFFICE
SENATE HOUSE
TYNDALL AVENUE
BRISTOL BS8 1TH
t: 0117 928 9000 f: 0117 331 7391
e: ug-admissions@bristol.ac.uk
// www.bristol.ac.uk

H150 MEng Engineering Design with Study in Industry
Duration: 5FT Hon
Entry Requirements: *GCE:* A*AA-AAB. *SQAH:* AAAAA-AAABB. *SQAAH:* AA-AB.

B80 UNIVERSITY OF THE WEST OF ENGLAND, BRISTOL
FRENCHAY CAMPUS
COLDHARBOUR LANE
BRISTOL BS16 1QY
t: +44 (0)117 32 83333 f: +44 (0)117 32 82810
e: admissions@uwe.ac.uk
// www.uwe.ac.uk

H131 BSc Creative Product Design
Duration: 3FT/4SW Hon
Entry Requirements: *GCE:* 300. Interview required.

H110 BSc Engineering
Duration: 1FT Hon
Entry Requirements: Contact the institution for details.

H100 FYr Engineering Foundation (Year 0)
Duration: 1FT FYr
Entry Requirements: *GCE:* 180.

B84 BRUNEL UNIVERSITY
UXBRIDGE
MIDDLESEX UB8 3PH
t: 01895 265265 f: 01895 269790
e: admissions@brunel.ac.uk
// www.brunel.ac.uk

H100 BEng Engineering with an Integrated Foundation Year
Duration: 4FT Hon
Entry Requirements: *GCE:* AAB-CCD. *SQAAH:* BCC-CCD. *BTEC ExtDip:* DMM.

C05 UNIVERSITY OF CAMBRIDGE
CAMBRIDGE ADMISSIONS OFFICE
FITZWILLIAM HOUSE
32 TRUMPINGTON STREET
CAMBRIDGE CB2 1QY
t: 01223 333 308 f: 01223 746 868
e: admissions@cam.ac.uk
// www.study.cam.ac.uk/undergraduate/

H100 MEng Engineering (4 years)
Duration: 4FT Hon
Entry Requirements: *GCE:* A*AA. *SQAAH:* AAA-AAB. Interview required.

H100 MEng Engineering (4 years) option - Manufacturing Engineering
Duration: 4FT Hon
Entry Requirements: *GCE:* A*AA. *SQAAH:* AAA-AAB. Interview required.

H100 MEng Engineering (4 years) option - Management Studies
Duration: 4FT Hon
Entry Requirements: *GCE:* A*AA. *SQAAH:* AAA-AAB. Interview required.

H100 MEng Engineering (4 years) option - Aerospace and Aerothermal Engineering
Duration: 4FT Hon
Entry Requirements: *GCE:* A*AA. *SQAAH:* AAA-AAB. Interview required.

H100 MEng Engineering (4 years) option - Electrical and Electronic Engineering
Duration: 4FT Hon
Entry Requirements: *GCE:* A*AA. *SQAAH:* AAA-AAB. Interview required.

H100 MEng Engineering (4 years) option - Mechanical Engineering
Duration: 4FT Hon
Entry Requirements: *GCE:* A*AA. *SQAAH:* AAA-AAB. Interview required.

H100 MEng Engineering (4 years) option - Energy and the Environment
Duration: 4FT Hon
Entry Requirements: *GCE:* A*AA. *SQAAH:* AAA-AAB. Interview required.

H100 MEng Engineering (4 years) option - Electrical and Information Sciences
Duration: 4FT Hon
Entry Requirements: *GCE:* A*AA. *SQAAH:* AAA-AAB. Interview required.

H100 MEng Engineering (4 years) option - Information and Computer Engineering
Duration: 4FT Hon
Entry Requirements: *GCE:* A*AA. *SQAAH:* AAA-AAB. Interview required.

H100 MEng Engineering (4 years) option - Instrumentation and Control
Duration: 4FT Hon
Entry Requirements: *GCE:* A*AA. *SQAAH:* AAA-AAB. Interview required.

C10 CANTERBURY CHRIST CHURCH UNIVERSITY
NORTH HOLMES ROAD
CANTERBURY
KENT CT1 1QU
t: 01227 782900 f: 01227 782888
e: admissions@canterbury.ac.uk
// www.canterbury.ac.uk

001H HNC General Engineering
Duration: 1FT HNC
Entry Requirements: Contact the institution for details.

C15 CARDIFF UNIVERSITY
PO BOX 927
30-36 NEWPORT ROAD
CARDIFF CF24 0DE
t: 029 2087 9999 f: 029 2087 6138
e: admissions@cardiff.ac.uk
// www.cardiff.ac.uk

H101 BEng Engineering Foundation Year
Duration: 4FT Hon
Entry Requirements: *GCE:* ABB. *IB:* 30.

H110 BEng Integrated Engineering
Duration: 3FT Hon
Entry Requirements: *GCE:* ABB. *IB:* 32.

H111 BEng Integrated Engineering (with a year in industry)
Duration: 4SW Hon
Entry Requirements: *GCE:* ABB. *IB:* 32.

H113 MEng Integrated Engineering
Duration: 4FT Hon
Entry Requirements: *GCE:* ABB. *IB:* 32.

H114 MEng Integrated Engineering (with a year in industry)
Duration: 5SW Hon
Entry Requirements: *GCE:* ABB. *IB:* 32.

H115 MEng Integrated Engineering with Year in Europe(France)
Duration: 5SW Hon
Entry Requirements: *GCE:* ABB. *IB:* 32.

H116 MEng Integrated Engineering with a Year in Europe(Germany)
Duration: 5SW Hon
Entry Requirements: *GCE:* ABB. *IB:* 32.

H117 MEng Integrated Engineering with a year in Europe (Spain)
Duration: 5SW Hon
Entry Requirements: *GCE:* ABB. *IB:* 32.

C30 UNIVERSITY OF CENTRAL LANCASHIRE
PRESTON
LANCS PR1 2HE
t: 01772 201201 f: 01772 894954
e: uadmissions@uclan.ac.uk
// www.uclan.ac.uk

H132 BEng Computer Aided Engineering
Duration: 3FT Hon
Entry Requirements: *GCE:* 240-280. *IB:* 24.

H101 BEng Engineering Development
Duration: 3FT/4SW Hon
Entry Requirements: Contact the institution for details.

H102 BEng Engineering Development (Foundation Entry)
Duration: 4FT/5SW Hon
Entry Requirements: Contact the institution for details.

H130 FdEng Computer Aided Engineering
Duration: 2FT Fdg
Entry Requirements: *GCE:* 80.

H121 FdSc Fire Safety Engineering
Duration: 2FT Fdg
Entry Requirements: *GCE:* 160. *IB:* 24. *OCR ND:* M2 *OCR NED:* P2

H133 MEng Computer Aided Engineering
Duration: 4FT Hon
Entry Requirements: *GCE:* 280-320. *IB:* 25.

H134 MEng Computer Aided Engineering (Sandwich)
Duration: 5SW Hon
Entry Requirements: *GCE:* 280-320. *IB:* 25.

H103 MEng Engineering Development
Duration: 4FT/5SW Hon
Entry Requirements: Contact the institution for details.

H12C MEng Fire Engineering
Duration: 4FT Hon
Entry Requirements: Contact the institution for details.

C60 CITY UNIVERSITY
NORTHAMPTON SQUARE
LONDON EC1V 0HB
t: 020 7040 5060 f: 020 7040 8995
e: ugadmissions@city.ac.uk
// www.city.ac.uk

H1N2 BEng Engineering with Management and Entrepreneurship
Duration: 3FT Hon
Entry Requirements: *GCE:* 340. *IB:* 30.

H100 Cert International Foundation (Engineering)
Duration: 1FT FYr
Entry Requirements: Contact the institution for details.

C78 CORNWALL COLLEGE
POOL
REDRUTH
CORNWALL TR15 3RD
t: 01209 616161 f: 01209 611612
e: he.admissions@cornwall.ac.uk
// www.cornwall.ac.uk

H100 FdSc Engineering
Duration: 2FT Fdg   CRB Check: Required
Entry Requirements: *GCE:* 80-120. Interview required.

001H HNC General Engineering (Electrical Pathway Available)
Duration: 1FT HNC
Entry Requirements: Contact the institution for details.

00CH HND General Engineering (Electrical Pathway Available)
Duration: 2FT HND
Entry Requirements: Contact the institution for details.

C85 COVENTRY UNIVERSITY
THE STUDENT CENTRE
COVENTRY UNIVERSITY
1 GULSON RD
COVENTRY CV1 2JH
t: 024 7615 2222 f: 024 7615 2223
e: studentenquiries@coventry.ac.uk
// www.coventry.ac.uk

H1T9 BEng Engineering Studies
Duration: 1FT Hon
Entry Requirements: Contact the institution for details.

H1K1 BEng Structural Engineering with Architecture
Duration: 3FT/4SW Hon
Entry Requirements: *GCE:* BCC. *SQAH:* BCCCC. *IB:* 28. *BTEC ExtDip:* DMM. *OCR NED:* M2

HN1C BSc Engineering Business Management
Duration: 1FT Hon
Entry Requirements: Contact the institution for details.

H673 BSc Rehabilitation Engineering
Duration: 4FT Hon   CRB Check: Required
Entry Requirements: *GCE:* BCC. *SQAH:* BCCCC. *IB:* 28. *BTEC ExtDip:* DMM. *OCR NED:* M2 Interview required.

H100 FYr Engineering (Foundation)
Duration: 1FT FYr
Entry Requirements: *GCE:* 100. *IB:* 24. *BTEC Dip:* MP. *BTEC ExtDip:* PPP. *OCR ND:* P2 *OCR NED:* P3

C99 UNIVERSITY OF CUMBRIA
FUSEHILL STREET
CARLISLE
CUMBRIA CA1 2HH
t: 01228 616234 f: 01228 616235
// www.cumbria.ac.uk

H100 FdEng Engineering
Duration: 2FT Fdg
Entry Requirements: *GCE:* 120.

D26 DE MONTFORT UNIVERSITY
THE GATEWAY
LEICESTER LE1 9BH
t: 0116 255 1551 f: 0116 250 6204
e: enquiries@dmu.ac.uk
// www.dmu.ac.uk

H108 BEng Engineering (Foundation) (Electronic, Mechanical and Mechatronic)
Duration: 4FT/5SW Hon
Entry Requirements: *GCE:* 120. *IB:* 24. *OCR NED:* P2

WH21 MDes Design Products
Duration: 4FT Hon
Entry Requirements: *Foundation:* Pass. *GCE:* 280. *IB:* 30. *BTEC Dip:* D*D*. *BTEC ExtDip:* DMM. Interview required. Portfolio required.

D86 DURHAM UNIVERSITY
DURHAM UNIVERSITY
UNIVERSITY OFFICE
DURHAM DH1 3HP
t: 0191 334 2000 f: 0191 334 6055
e: admissions@durham.ac.uk
// www.durham.ac.uk

H103 BEng General Engineering
Duration: 3FT Hon
Entry Requirements: *GCE:* AAB. *SQAH:* AAABB. *SQAAH:* AAB. *IB:* 36.

H104 BEng General Engineering with Foundation
Duration: 4FT Hon
Entry Requirements: Interview required.

H150 MEng Design and Operations Engineering
Duration: 4FT Hon
Entry Requirements: *GCE:* AAA. *SQAH:* AAAAB. *SQAAH:* AAA. *IB:* 37.

H100 MEng General Engineering
Duration: 4FT Hon
Entry Requirements: *GCE:* AAA. *SQAH:* AAAAB. *SQAAH:* AAA. *IB:* 37.

E56 THE UNIVERSITY OF EDINBURGH
STUDENT RECRUITMENT & ADMISSIONS
57 GEORGE SQUARE
EDINBURGH EH8 9JU
t: 0131 650 4360 f: 0131 651 1236
e: sra.enquiries@ed.ac.uk
// www.ed.ac.uk/studying/undergraduate/

H100 BEng Engineering
Duration: 4FT Hon
Entry Requirements: *GCE:* AAA-ABB. *SQAH:* AAAA-ABBB.

CH91 BEng Integrated Foundation Programme (Engineering)
Duration: 4FT Hon
Entry Requirements: Contact the institution for details.

E59 EDINBURGH NAPIER UNIVERSITY
CRAIGLOCKHART CAMPUS
EDINBURGH EH14 1DJ
t: +44 (0)8452 60 60 40 f: 0131 455 6464
e: info@napier.ac.uk
// www.napier.ac.uk

H1N2 BEng Engineering with Management
Duration: 3FT/4FT Ord/Hon
Entry Requirements: *GCE:* 245.

E81 EXETER COLLEGE
HELE ROAD
EXETER
DEVON EX4 4JS
t: 0845 111 6000
e: info@exe-coll.ac.uk
// www.exe-coll.ac.uk/he

H000 FdSc Engineering
Duration: 2FT Fdg
Entry Requirements: *GCE:* 160.

E84 UNIVERSITY OF EXETER
LAVER BUILDING
NORTH PARK ROAD
EXETER
DEVON EX4 4QE
t: 01392 723044 f: 01392 722479
e: admissions@exeter.ac.uk
// www.exeter.ac.uk

H101 BEng Engineering
Duration: 3FT Hon
Entry Requirements: *GCE:* AAB-ABB. *SQAH:* AAABB-AABBB. *SQAAH:* ABB-BBB.

HN12 BEng Engineering and Management
Duration: 3FT Hon
Entry Requirements: *GCE:* AAB-ABB. *SQAH:* AAABB-AABBB. *SQAAH:* ABB-BBB.

HN21 BEng Engineering and Management with Industrial Experience
Duration: 3FT Hon
Entry Requirements: *GCE:* AAB-ABB. *SQAH:* AAABB-AABBB. *SQAAH:* ABB-BBB.

NH21 BEng Engineering and Management with International Study
Duration: 3FT Hon
Entry Requirements: *GCE:* AAB-ABB. *SQAH:* AAABB-AABBB. *SQAAH:* ABB-BBB.

H190 BEng Materials Engineering
Duration: 3FT Hon
Entry Requirements: *GCE:* AAB-ABB. *SQAH:* AAABB-AABBB. *SQAAH:* ABB-BBB.

H195 BEng Materials Engineering with Industrial Experience
Duration: 3FT Hon
Entry Requirements: *GCE:* AAB-ABB. *SQAH:* AAABB-AABBB. *SQAAH:* ABB-BBB.

H197 BEng Materials Engineering with International Study
Duration: 3FT Hon
Entry Requirements: *GCE:* AAB-ABB. *SQAH:* AAABB-AABBB. *SQAAH:* ABB-BBB.

GH11 BSc Mathematics and Engineering
Duration: 3FT Hon
Entry Requirements: *GCE:* A*AA-AAB. *SQAH:* AAAAA-AABBB. *SQAAH:* AAA-ABB.

H104 MEng Engineering
Duration: 4FT Hon
Entry Requirements: *GCE:* AAA-AAB. *SQAH:* AAAAB-AAABB. *SQAAH:* AAB-ABB. *BTEC ExtDip:* DDM.

HN1F MEng Engineering and Management with International Study (4 years)
Duration: 4FT Hon
Entry Requirements: *GCE:* AAA-AAB. *SQAH:* AAAAB-AAABB. *SQAAH:* AAB-ABB. *BTEC ExtDip:* DDM.

H191 MEng Materials Engineering
Duration: 4FT Hon
Entry Requirements: *GCE:* AAA-AAB. *SQAH:* AAAAB-AAABB. *SQAAH:* AAB-ABB. *BTEC ExtDip:* DDM.

H196 MEng Materials Engineering with Industrial Experience (4 years)
Duration: 4FT Hon
Entry Requirements: *GCE:* AAA-AAB. *SQAH:* AAAAB-AAABB. *SQAAH:* AAB-ABB. *BTEC ExtDip:* DDM.

H198 MEng Materials Engineering with International Study (4 years)
Duration: 4FT Hon
Entry Requirements: *GCE:* AAA-AAB. *SQAH:* AAAAB-AAABB. *SQAAH:* AAB-ABB. *BTEC ExtDip:* DDM.

G28 UNIVERSITY OF GLASGOW
71 SOUTHPARK AVENUE
UNIVERSITY OF GLASGOW
GLASGOW G12 8QQ
t: 0141 330 6062 f: 0141 330 2961
e: student.recruitment@glasgow.ac.uk
// www.glasgow.ac.uk

H111 BTechEd Technological Education
Duration: 4FT Hon
Entry Requirements: *GCE:* ABB. *SQAH:* AAAB-BBB. *IB:* 32. Interview required.

H150 MEng Product Design Engineering (Faster Route)
Duration: 4FT Hon
Entry Requirements: *GCE:* AAA. *SQAH:* AB. *SQAAH:* AA. *IB:* 38.

G42 GLASGOW CALEDONIAN UNIVERSITY
STUDENT RECRUITMENT & ADMISSIONS SERVICE
CITY CAMPUS
COWCADDENS ROAD
GLASGOW G4 0BA
t: 0141 331 3000 f: 0141 331 8676
e: undergraduate@gcu.ac.uk
// www.gcu.ac.uk

HN12 BA International Design Management (Entry to year 3 only)
Duration: 2FT Hon
Entry Requirements: Contact the institution for details.

H131 BEng Computer-Aided Mechanical Engineering
Duration: 4FT/5SW Hon
Entry Requirements: Contact the institution for details.

H121 BSc Fire Risk Engineering
Duration: 4FT Hon
Entry Requirements: *GCE:* 270.

H132 MEng Computer Aided Mechanical Engineering
Duration: 5FT/6SW Hon
Entry Requirements: Contact the institution for details.

G70 UNIVERSITY OF GREENWICH
GREENWICH CAMPUS
OLD ROYAL NAVAL COLLEGE
PARK ROW
LONDON SE10 9LS
t: 020 8331 9000 f: 020 8331 8145
e: courseinfo@gre.ac.uk
// www.gre.ac.uk

HN1F BEng Engineering Business Management
Duration: 3FT Hon
Entry Requirements: *GCE:* 260-280. *IB:* 24.

HNC2 BSc Engineering Business Management (including Foundation year)
Duration: 4FT Hon
Entry Requirements: *GCE:* 160.

G80 GRIMSBY INSTITUTE OF FURTHER AND HIGHER EDUCATION
NUNS CORNER
GRIMSBY
NE LINCOLNSHIRE DN34 5BQ
t: 0800 328 3631
e: headmissions@grimsby.ac.uk
// www.grimsby.ac.uk

H102 BSc Engineering Management Top-up
Duration: 1FT Hon
Entry Requirements: Contact the institution for details.

H151 FdSc Engineering Management
Duration: 2FT Fdg
Entry Requirements: Contact the institution for details.

H14 HAVERING COLLEGE OF FURTHER AND HIGHER EDUCATION
ARDLEIGH GREEN ROAD
HORNCHURCH
ESSEX RM11 2LL
t: 01708 462793 f: 01708 462736
e: HE@havering-college.ac.uk
// www.havering-college.ac.uk

H101 BEng Engineering
Duration: 1FT Hon
Entry Requirements: Interview required.

H24 HERIOT-WATT UNIVERSITY, EDINBURGH
EDINBURGH CAMPUS
EDINBURGH EH14 4AS
t: 0131 449 5111 f: 0131 451 3630
e: ugadmissions@hw.ac.uk
// www.hw.ac.uk

H100 BEng Engineering
Duration: 4FT Hon
Entry Requirements: *GCE:* BBB. *SQAH:* AABB-BBBBC. *IB:* 29.

H36 UNIVERSITY OF HERTFORDSHIRE
UNIVERSITY ADMISSIONS SERVICE
COLLEGE LANE
HATFIELD
HERTS AL10 9AB
t: 01707 284800
// www.herts.ac.uk

H131 BSc Engineering Product Design
Duration: 3FT/4SW Hon
Entry Requirements: Contact the institution for details.

H49 UNIVERSITY OF THE HIGHLANDS AND ISLANDS
UHI EXECUTIVE OFFICE
NESS WALK
INVERNESS
SCOTLAND IV3 5SQ
t: 01463 279000 f: 01463 279001
e: info@uhi.ac.uk
// www.uhi.ac.uk

161H HNC Computer Aided Draughting & Design
Duration: 1FT HNC
Entry Requirements: *GCE:* D. *SQAH:* C.

H60 THE UNIVERSITY OF HUDDERSFIELD
QUEENSGATE
HUDDERSFIELD HD1 3DH
t: 01484 473969 f: 01484 472765
e: admissionsandrecords@hud.ac.uk
// www.hud.ac.uk

H108 BEng Engineering Foundation (General)
Duration: 5SW Hon
Entry Requirements: *GCE:* 100.

H100 BEng Engineering with Technology Management (Mechanical and Manufacturing)
Duration: 1FT/2SW Hon/Ord
Entry Requirements: HND required.

H101 BEng Engineering with Technology Mgmt (Industrial Measurement & Control) (Top-Up)
Duration: 2SW/1FT Hon
Entry Requirements: HND required.

H72 THE UNIVERSITY OF HULL
THE UNIVERSITY OF HULL
COTTINGHAM ROAD
HULL HU6 7RX
t: 01482 466100 f: 01482 442290
e: admissions@hull.ac.uk
// www.hull.ac.uk

H130 BEng Computer Aided Engineering
Duration: 3FT Hon
Entry Requirements: *GCE:* 280. *IB:* 27. *BTEC ExtDip:* DMM.

H131 BEng Computer Aided Engineering (with foundation year)
Duration: 4FT Hon
Entry Requirements: Contact the institution for details.

HW12 BSc Electronic Product Design
Duration: 3FT Hon
Entry Requirements: *GCE:* 260. *IB:* 26. *BTEC ExtDip:* MMM.

H73 HULL COLLEGE
QUEEN'S GARDENS
HULL HU1 3DG
t: 01482 329943 f: 01482 598733
e: info@hull-college.ac.uk
// www.hull-college.ac.uk/higher-education

H100 FdSc Engineering Technology
Duration: 2FT Fdg
Entry Requirements: Interview required.

K84 KINGSTON UNIVERSITY
STUDENT INFORMATION & ADVICE CENTRE
COOPER HOUSE
40-46 SURBITON ROAD
KINGSTON UPON THAMES KT1 2HX
t: 0844 8552177 f: 020 8547 7080
e: aps@kingston.ac.uk
// www.kingston.ac.uk

WH21 BSc Product Design
Duration: 3FT Hon
Entry Requirements: *GCE:* 240. Interview required. Portfolio required.

011H HND Engineering (pathways in Aerospace, Automotive, Mechanical Eng)
Duration: 2FT HND
Entry Requirements: *GCE:* 80. *IB:* 22.

L14 LANCASTER UNIVERSITY
THE UNIVERSITY
LANCASTER
LANCASHIRE LA1 4YW
t: 01524 592029 f: 01524 846243
e: ugadmissions@lancaster.ac.uk
// www.lancs.ac.uk

H100 BEng Engineering
Duration: 3FT Hon
Entry Requirements: *GCE:* AAB. *SQAH:* ABBBB. *SQAAH:* AAB. *IB:* 35.

H101 BEng Engineering (Study Abroad)
Duration: 3FT Hon
Entry Requirements: *GCE:* AAB. *SQAH:* ABBBB. *SQAAH:* AAB. *IB:* 35.

H104 MEng Engineering (Study Abroad)
Duration: 4FT Hon
Entry Requirements: *GCE:* AAA. *SQAH:* AAABB. *SQAAH:* AAA. *IB:* 36.

L34 UNIVERSITY OF LEICESTER
UNIVERSITY ROAD
LEICESTER LE1 7RH
t: 0116 252 5281 f: 0116 252 2447
e: admissions@le.ac.uk
// www.le.ac.uk

H100 BEng General Engineering
Duration: 3FT Hon
Entry Requirements: *GCE:* BBB-BBC. *SQAH:* BBBBB-BBBCC. *SQAAH:* BBB-BBC.

H102 BEng General Engineering (with Year in Industry)
Duration: 4SW Hon
Entry Requirements: *GCE:* BBB-BBC. *SQAH:* BBBBB-BBBCC. *SQAAH:* BBB-BBC.

H103 BEng General Engineering (with a year abroad)
Duration: 3FT Hon
Entry Requirements: *GCE:* BBB-BBC. *SQAH:* BBBBB-BBBCC. *SQAAH:* BBB-BBC.

H105 MEng General Engineering
Duration: 4FT Hon
Entry Requirements: *GCE:* AAB-ABB. *SQAH:* AAABB-AABBB. *SQAAH:* AAB-ABB.

H107 MEng General Engineering (with Year in Industry)
Duration: 5SW Hon
Entry Requirements: *GCE:* AAB-ABB. *SQAH:* AAABB-AABBB. *SQAAH:* AAB-ABB.

H104 MEng General Engineering (with a year abroad)
Duration: 4FT Hon
Entry Requirements: *GCE:* AAB-ABB. *SQAH:* AAABB-AABBB. *SQAAH:* AAB-ABB.

L36 LEICESTER COLLEGE
FREEMEN'S PARK CAMPUS
AYLESTONE ROAD
LEICESTER LE2 7LW
t: 0116 224 2240 f: 0116 224 2041
e: info@leicestercollege.ac.uk
// www.leicestercollege.ac.uk

001H HND Engineering
Duration: 2FT HND
Entry Requirements: Contact the institution for details.

L41 THE UNIVERSITY OF LIVERPOOL
THE FOUNDATION BUILDING
BROWNLOW HILL
LIVERPOOL L69 7ZX
t: 0151 794 2000 f: 0151 708 6502
e: ugrecruitment@liv.ac.uk
// www.liv.ac.uk

H100 BEng Engineering
Duration: 3FT Hon
Entry Requirements: *GCE:* ABB. *SQAAH:* ABB. *IB:* 33. Interview required.

H109 BEng Engineering Foundation
Duration: 4FT Hon
Entry Requirements: Contact the institution for details.

H1WF BEng Engineering with Product Design
Duration: 3FT Hon
Entry Requirements: *GCE:* ABB. *SQAAH:* ABB. *IB:* 33. Interview required.

H101 MEng Engineering (4 years)
Duration: 4FT Hon
Entry Requirements: *GCE:* AAB. *SQAAH:* AAB. *IB:* 35. Interview required.

H1WG MEng Engineering with Product Design (4 years)
Duration: 4FT Hon
Entry Requirements: *GCE:* AAB. *SQAAH:* AAB. *IB:* 35. Interview required.

L43 LIVERPOOL COMMUNITY COLLEGE
LIVERPOOL COMMUNITY COLLEGE
CLARENCE STREET
LIVERPOOL L3 5TP
t: 0151 252 3352 f: 0151 252 3351
e: enquiry@liv-coll.ac.uk
// www.liv-coll.ac.uk

H100 HNC General Engineering
Duration: 1FT HNC
Entry Requirements: Contact the institution for details.

L51 LIVERPOOL JOHN MOORES UNIVERSITY
KINGSWAY HOUSE
HATTON GARDEN
LIVERPOOL L3 2AJ
t: 0151 231 5090 f: 0151 904 6368
e: courses@ljmu.ac.uk
// www.ljmu.ac.uk

H108 BEng Engineering and Technology (with Foundation Year)
Duration: 5SW Hon
Entry Requirements: *GCE:* 160. *OCR ND:* M2 *OCR NED:* P2

L62 THE LONDON COLLEGE, UCK
VICTORIA GARDENS
NOTTING HILL GATE
LONDON W11 3PE
t: 020 7243 4000 f: 020 7243 1484
e: admissions@lcuck.ac.uk
// www.lcuck.ac.uk

001H Dip Engineering Science
Duration: 1FT Oth
Entry Requirements: Contact the institution for details.

L75 LONDON SOUTH BANK UNIVERSITY
ADMISSIONS AND RECRUITMENT CENTRE
90 LONDON ROAD
LONDON SE1 6LN
t: 0800 923 8888 f: 020 7815 8273
e: course.enquiry@lsbu.ac.uk
// www.lsbu.ac.uk

H101 FYr Engineering Foundation
Duration: 1FT FYr
Entry Requirements: *GCE:* 40. *IB:* 24.

HF13 FdSc Clinical Technology
Duration: 2FT Fdg
Entry Requirements: Contact the institution for details.

061H HND Computer Aided Engineering
Duration: 2FT HND
Entry Requirements: *GCE:* 200. *IB:* 24.

L77 LOUGHBOROUGH COLLEGE
RADMOOR ROAD
LOUGHBOROUGH LE11 3BT
t: 0845 166 2950 f: 0845 833 2840
e: info@loucoll.ac.uk
// www.loucoll.ac.uk

H100 FYR Engineering (Year 0)
Duration: 1FT FYr
Entry Requirements: Contact the institution for details.

L79 LOUGHBOROUGH UNIVERSITY
LOUGHBOROUGH
LEICESTERSHIRE LE11 3TU
t: 01509 223522 f: 01509 223905
e: admissions@lboro.ac.uk
// www.lboro.ac.uk

HJ15 BEng Design with Engineering Materials
Duration: 3FT Hon
Entry Requirements: *GCE:* ABC-BBB. *SQAH:* BBBB. *SQAAH:* BB.
IB: 30. *BTEC ExtDip:* DDM.

HJ1M BEng Design with Engineering Materials
Duration: 4SW Hon
Entry Requirements: *SQAH:* BB. *SQAAH:* BB. *IB:* 32.

HF19 BSc Science and Engineering Foundation Studies
Duration: 4FT Hon
Entry Requirements: Contact the institution for details.

H1J5 MEng Design with Engineering Materials
Duration: 4FT Hon
Entry Requirements: *GCE:* AAB. *SQAH:* BBB. *SQAAH:* AB. *BTEC ExtDip:* DDD.

H1JM MEng Design with Engineering Materials
Duration: 5SW Hon
Entry Requirements: *GCE:* AAB. *SQAAH:* AB. *BTEC ExtDip:* DDD.

M20 THE UNIVERSITY OF MANCHESTER
RUTHERFORD BUILDING
OXFORD ROAD
MANCHESTER M13 9PL
t: 0161 275 2077 f: 0161 275 2106
e: ug-admissions@manchester.ac.uk
// www.manchester.ac.uk

H108 BEng Engineering with an Integrated Foundation Year
Duration: 4FT/5FT Hon
Entry Requirements: Contact the institution for details.

M40 THE MANCHESTER METROPOLITAN UNIVERSITY
ADMISSIONS OFFICE
ALL SAINTS (GMS)
ALL SAINTS
MANCHESTER M15 6BH
t: 0161 247 2000
// www.mmu.ac.uk

H110 BEng Engineering
Duration: 3FT/4SW Hon
Entry Requirements: *GCE:* 280. *IB:* 27.

H108 BEng Engineering (Foundation)
Duration: 4FT/5SW Hon
Entry Requirements: *GCE:* 160. *IB:* 24. *BTEC Dip:* MM. *BTEC ExtDip:* MPP.

M80 MIDDLESEX UNIVERSITY
MIDDLESEX UNIVERSITY
THE BURROUGHS
LONDON NW4 4BT
t: 020 8411 5555 f: 020 8411 5649
e: enquiries@mdx.ac.uk
// www.mdx.ac.uk

H150 BEng Design Engineering
Duration: 3FT Hon
Entry Requirements: Contact the institution for details.

N21 NEWCASTLE UNIVERSITY
KING'S GATE
NEWCASTLE UPON TYNE NE1 7RU
t: 01912083333
// www.ncl.ac.uk

H101 FYr Engineering Foundation year
Duration: 1FT FYr
Entry Requirements: *GCE:* AAB-BBB. *SQAAH:* AB-BB. *IB:* 35.

H103 FYr Engineering Foundation year
Duration: 1FT FYr
Entry Requirements: *GCE:* AAB. *SQAAH:* AA-AB. *IB:* 37. *BTEC ExtDip:* DDD.

N23 NEWCASTLE COLLEGE
STUDENT SERVICES
RYE HILL CAMPUS
SCOTSWOOD ROAD
NEWCASTLE UPON TYNE NE4 7SA
t: 0191 200 4110 f: 0191 200 4349
e: enquiries@ncl-coll.ac.uk
// www.newcastlecollege.co.uk

H190 BSc Management of Engineering Technologies [Top-up]
Duration: 1FT Hon
Entry Requirements: Contact the institution for details.

H100 FdSc Multi-Skill Engineering
Duration: 2FT Fdg
Entry Requirements: *GCE:* 160-200. *OCR ND:* P2 *OCR NED:* P3
Interview required.

N37 UNIVERSITY OF WALES, NEWPORT
ADMISSIONS
LODGE ROAD
CAERLEON
NEWPORT NP18 3QT
t: 01633 432030 f: 01633 432850
e: admissions@newport.ac.uk
// www.newport.ac.uk

H121 BSc Fire Safety Engineering
Duration: 3FT Hon
Entry Requirements: *GCE:* 240. *IB:* 24.

H101 FdEng Engineering
Duration: 2FT Fdg
Entry Requirements: *GCE:* 80. *IB:* 24.

001H HND Engineering
Duration: 2FT HND
Entry Requirements: *GCE:* 80. *IB:* 24.

121H HND Fire Safety Engineering
Duration: 2FT HND
Entry Requirements: *GCE:* 80. *IB:* 24.

N38 UNIVERSITY OF NORTHAMPTON
PARK CAMPUS
BOUGHTON GREEN ROAD
NORTHAMPTON NN2 7AL
t: 0800 358 2232 f: 01604 722083
e: admissions@northampton.ac.uk
// www.northampton.ac.uk

H101 BEng/MEng Engineering
Duration: 3FT/4FT Hon
Entry Requirements: *GCE:* 260-280. *SQAH:* AAA-BBBB. *IB:* 24.
BTEC Dip: DD. *BTEC ExtDip:* DMM. *OCR ND:* D *OCR NED:* M2

H10A BSc Engineering (Top-Up)
Duration: 1FT Hon
Entry Requirements: HND required.

001H HND Engineering
Duration: 2FT HND
Entry Requirements: *GCE:* 140-160. *SQAH:* BC-CCC. *IB:* 24.
BTEC Dip: MP. *BTEC ExtDip:* MPP. *OCR ND:* P1 *OCR NED:* P2

N84 THE UNIVERSITY OF NOTTINGHAM
THE ADMISSIONS OFFICE
THE UNIVERSITY OF NOTTINGHAM
UNIVERSITY PARK
NOTTINGHAM NG7 2RD
t: 0115 951 5151 f: 0115 951 4668
// www.nottingham.ac.uk

H151 BEng Design Engineering
Duration: 3FT Hon
Entry Requirements: *GCE:* AAB. *SQAAH:* ABB-BBB. *IB:* 32.

G1HD BEng Mathematics with Engineering
Duration: 3FT Hon
Entry Requirements: *GCE:* AAA-A*AB. *SQAAH:* AAA. *IB:* 38.

H100 BEng/MEng Engineering with Foundation Year
Duration: 4FT/5FT Hon
Entry Requirements: *GCE:* BBB. *SQAAH:* BBB. *IB:* 32.

H150 MEng Design Engineering
Duration: 4FT Hon
Entry Requirements: *GCE:* AAA. *SQAAH:* AAA-AAB. *IB:* 36.

H102 MEng Engineering with Foundation Year
Duration: 3FT/4FT Hon
Entry Requirements: *GCE:* BBB. *SQAAH:* BBB. *IB:* 32.

G1H1 MMath Mathematics with Engineering
Duration: 4FT Hon
Entry Requirements: *GCE:* AAA-A*AB. *SQAAH:* AAA. *IB:* 38.

O33 OXFORD UNIVERSITY
UNDERGRADUATE ADMISSIONS OFFICE
UNIVERSITY OF OXFORD
WELLINGTON SQUARE
OXFORD OX1 2JD
t: 01865 288000 f: 01865 270212
e: undergraduate.admissions@admin.ox.ac.uk
// www.admissions.ox.ac.uk

H100 MEng Engineering (4 years)
Duration: 4FT Hon
Entry Requirements: *GCE:* A*AA. *SQAH:* AAAAA-AAAAB. *SQAAH:* AAB. Interview required. Admissions Test required.

HLN0 MEng Engineering, Economics and Management (4 years)
Duration: 4FT Hon
Entry Requirements: *GCE:* A*AA. *SQAH:* AAAAA-AAAAB. *SQAAH:* AAB. Interview required. Admissions Test required.

O66 OXFORD BROOKES UNIVERSITY
ADMISSIONS OFFICE
HEADINGTON CAMPUS
GIPSY LANE
OXFORD OX3 0BP
t: 01865 483040 f: 01865 483983
e: admissions@brookes.ac.uk
// www.brookes.ac.uk

H108 BEng Engineering Foundation
Duration: 4FT Hon
Entry Requirements: *GCE:* DD.

H131 BSc Multimedia Production
Duration: 3FT Hon
Entry Requirements: *GCE:* BBC. *IB:* 30. Interview required.

P56 UNIVERSITY CENTRE PETERBOROUGH
PARK CRESCENT
PETERBOROUGH PE1 4DZ
t: 0845 1965750 f: 01733 767986
e: UCPenquiries@anglia.ac.uk
// www.anglia.ac.uk/ucp

H110 BEng Integrated Engineering
Duration: 3FT Hon
Entry Requirements: Contact the institution for details.

H100 FdSc Engineering
Duration: 2FT Fdg
Entry Requirements: *GCE:* 200.

P60 PLYMOUTH UNIVERSITY
DRAKE CIRCUS
PLYMOUTH PL4 8AA
t: 01752 585858 f: 01752 588055
e: admissions@plymouth.ac.uk
// www.plymouth.ac.uk

H108 FYr Foundation Pathways in Technology
Duration: 1FT FYr
Entry Requirements: *GCE:* 120. *IB:* 24.

P80 UNIVERSITY OF PORTSMOUTH
ACADEMIC REGISTRY
UNIVERSITY HOUSE
WINSTON CHURCHILL AVENUE
PORTSMOUTH PO1 2UP
t: 023 9284 8484 f: 023 9284 3082
e: admissions@port.ac.uk
// www.port.ac.uk

H108 BEng Engineering and Technology with Foundation Year
Duration: 4FT/5SW Hon
Entry Requirements: *GCE:* 80-120. *IB:* 24. *BTEC SubDip:* P.
BTEC Dip: PP. *BTEC ExtDip:* PPP.

Q50 QUEEN MARY, UNIVERSITY OF LONDON
QUEEN MARY, UNIVERSITY OF LONDON
MILE END ROAD
LONDON E1 4NS
t: 020 7882 5555 f: 020 7882 5500
e: admissions@qmul.ac.uk
// www.qmul.ac.uk

WH21 BEng Design & Innovation
Duration: 3FT Hon
Entry Requirements: *GCE:* 300. *IB:* 32. Interview required.
Portfolio required.

HHX1 BEng Science & Engineering Foundation Programme (Engineering 4 Year)
Duration: 4FT Hon
Entry Requirements: *GCE:* 240-300.

HHY1 MEng Science & Engineering Foundation Programme (Engineering 5 Year)
Duration: 5FT Hon
Entry Requirements: *GCE:* 240-300.

Q75 QUEEN'S UNIVERSITY BELFAST
UNIVERSITY ROAD
BELFAST BT7 1NN
t: 028 9097 3838 f: 028 9097 5151
e: admissions@qub.ac.uk
// www.qub.ac.uk

H150 BEng Product Design and Development
Duration: 3FT Hon
Entry Requirements: *GCE:* BCC-CCCb. *SQAH:* BBBCC. *SQAAH:* BCC. *IB:* 29.

H153 FdEng Product Design and Development
Duration: 2FT Fdg
Entry Requirements: Contact the institution for details.

H152 MEng Product Design and Development
Duration: 4FT Hon
Entry Requirements: *GCE:* BBB-BBCb. *SQAAH:* BBB. *IB:* 32.

R36 ROBERT GORDON UNIVERSITY
ROBERT GORDON UNIVERSITY
SCHOOLHILL
ABERDEEN
SCOTLAND AB10 1FR
t: 01224 26 27 28 f: 01224 26 21 47
e: UGOffice@rgu.ac.uk
// www.rgu.ac.uk

H100 MEng/BEng Engineering
Duration: 4FT Hon
Entry Requirements: *GCE:* BCC. *SQAH:* BBBC. *SQAAH:* BCC. *IB:* 27.

S18 THE UNIVERSITY OF SHEFFIELD
THE UNIVERSITY OF SHEFFIELD
LEVEL 2, ARTS TOWER
WESTERN BANK
SHEFFIELD S10 2TN
t: 0114 222 8030 f: 0114 222 8032
// www.sheffield.ac.uk

H673 BEng Bioengineering
Duration: 3FT Hon
Entry Requirements: *GCE:* ABB. *SQAH:* AABBB. *SQAAH:* AB. *IB:* 33. *BTEC ExtDip:* DDM.

H67H BEng Bioengineering with a Year in Industry
Duration: 4FT Hon
Entry Requirements: *GCE:* ABB. *SQAH:* AABBB. *SQAAH:* AB. *IB:* 33. *BTEC ExtDip:* DDM.

H130 BEng Computer Systems Engineering (3 years)
Duration: 3FT Hon
Entry Requirements: *GCE:* ABB. *SQAH:* AABBB. *SQAAH:* AB. *IB:* 33. *BTEC ExtDip:* DDM.

JH56 BEng Material Science and Engineering (Biomaterials)
Duration: 3FT Hon
Entry Requirements: *GCE:* ABC-BBB. *SQAH:* BBBBB. *SQAAH:* BB. *IB:* 32. *BTEC Dip:* DD. *BTEC ExtDip:* DDM. Interview required.

JH51 BEng Materials Science and Engineering (3 years)
Duration: 3FT Hon
Entry Requirements: *GCE:* ABC-BBB. *SQAH:* BBBBB. *SQAAH:* BB. *IB:* 32. *BTEC Dip:* DD. *BTEC ExtDip:* DDM. Interview required.

FHF1 BEng Materials Science and Engineering (Industrial Management)
Duration: 3FT Hon
Entry Requirements: *GCE:* ABC-BBB. *SQAH:* BBBBB. *SQAAH:* BB. *IB:* 32. *BTEC Dip:* DD. *BTEC ExtDip:* DDM. Interview required.

JH5D BEng Materials Science and Engineering with a Year in Japan (4 years)
Duration: 4FT Hon
Entry Requirements: *GCE:* ABC-BBB. *SQAH:* BBBBB. *SQAAH:* BB. *IB:* 32. *BTEC ExtDip:* DDM. Interview required.

H675 MEng Bioengineering
Duration: 4FT Hon
Entry Requirements: *GCE:* AAB. *SQAH:* AAABB. *SQAAH:* AB. *IB:* 35. *BTEC ExtDip:* DDD.

H160 MEng Bioengineering with a Foundation Year
Duration: 5FT Hon
Entry Requirements: *GCE:* AAB. *SQAH:* AAABB. *SQAAH:* AB. *IB:* 35. *BTEC ExtDip:* DDD. Interview required.

H67I MEng Bioengineering with a Year in Industry
Duration: 5FT Hon
Entry Requirements: *GCE:* ABB. *SQAH:* AAABB. *SQAAH:* AB. *IB:* 35. *BTEC ExtDip:* DDD.

JH5P MEng Material Science and Engineering (Biomaterials)
Duration: 4FT Deg
Entry Requirements: *GCE:* AAB. *SQAH:* AAABB. *SQAAH:* AB. *IB:* 35. *BTEC Dip:* DD. *BTEC ExtDip:* DDD. Interview required.

FH21 MEng Materials Science and Engineering (Industrial Management)
Duration: 4FT Hon
Entry Requirements: *GCE:* AAB. *SQAH:* AAABB. *SQAAH:* AB. *IB:* 35. *BTEC Dip:* DD. *BTEC ExtDip:* DDD. Interview required.

JH5C MEng Materials Science and Engineering with a Year in Japan
Duration: 5FT Hon
Entry Requirements: *GCE:* AAB. *SQAH:* AAABB. *SQAAH:* AB. *IB:* 35. *BTEC ExtDip:* DDD. Interview required.

S21 SHEFFIELD HALLAM UNIVERSITY
CITY CAMPUS
HOWARD STREET
SHEFFIELD S1 1WB
t: 0114 225 5555 f: 0114 225 2167
e: admissions@shu.ac.uk
// www.shu.ac.uk

H199 BEng Forensic Engineering
Duration: 3FT/4SW Hon
Entry Requirements: *GCE:* 220.

HW12 BSc Computer-Aided Design Technology
Duration: 3FT/4SW Hon
Entry Requirements: *GCE:* 240.

WH21 BSc Design Technology
Duration: 3FT/4SW Hon
Entry Requirements: *GCE:* 240.

HG11 Fyr Engineering and Mathematics (Year 0)
Duration: 1FT FYr
Entry Requirements: Contact the institution for details.

S27 UNIVERSITY OF SOUTHAMPTON
HIGHFIELD
SOUTHAMPTON SO17 1BJ
t: 023 8059 4732 f: 023 8059 3037
e: admissions@soton.ac.uk
// www.southampton.ac.uk

H008 BEng/MEng Engineering with Foundation Year
Duration: 4FT/5FT Hon
Entry Requirements: *GCE:* BBB. *SQAH:* BBBBB. *IB:* 30.

S30 SOUTHAMPTON SOLENT UNIVERSITY
EAST PARK TERRACE
SOUTHAMPTON
HAMPSHIRE SO14 0RT
t: +44 (0) 23 8031 9039 f: + 44 (0)23 8022 2259
e: admissions@solent.ac.uk
// www.solent.ac.uk/

H1N1 BEng Engineering with Business
Duration: 3FT Hon
Entry Requirements: *GCE:* 120.

H1N2 BEng Engineering with Business (with foundation)
Duration: 4FT Hon
Entry Requirements: *GCE:* 40.

H1NC BEng Engineering with Business with IFY (Intl only, Sept)
Duration: 4FT Hon
Entry Requirements: Contact the institution for details.

H100 BSc Engineering (International Only)
Duration: 1FT Hon
Entry Requirements: Contact the institution for details.

001H HND Manufacturing and Mechanical Engineering
Duration: 2FT HND
Entry Requirements: *GCE:* 40.

S35 SOUTHPORT COLLEGE
MORNINGTON ROAD
SOUTHPORT
MERSEYSIDE PR9 0TT
t: 08450066236 f: 01704 392610
e: guidance@southport-college.ac.uk
// www.southport-college.ac.uk

H100 HND Engineering
Duration: 2FT HND
Entry Requirements: Contact the institution for details.

S36 UNIVERSITY OF ST ANDREWS
ST KATHARINE'S WEST
16 THE SCORES
ST ANDREWS
FIFE KY16 9AX
t: 01334 462150 f: 01334 463330
e: admissions@st-andrews.ac.uk
// www.st-andrews.ac.uk

FH31 BSc Gateway to Physics and Engineering
Duration: 4FT Hon
Entry Requirements: Contact the institution for details.

FH3C MPhys Gateway to Physics and Engineering
Duration: 5FT Hon
Entry Requirements: Contact the institution for details.

S43 SOUTH ESSEX COLLEGE OF FURTHER & HIGHER EDUCATION
LUKER ROAD
SOUTHEND-ON-SEA
ESSEX SS1 1ND
t: 0845 52 12345 f: 01702 432320
e: Admissions@southessex.ac.uk
// www.southessex.ac.uk

H100 FdSc Engineering
Duration: 2FT Fdg
Entry Requirements: *GCE:* 120. Interview required.

S72 STAFFORDSHIRE UNIVERSITY
COLLEGE ROAD
STOKE ON TRENT ST4 2DE
t: 01782 292753 f: 01782 292740
e: admissions@staffs.ac.uk
// www.staffs.ac.uk

H132 BSc Computer Games Design
Duration: 3FT/4SW Hon
Entry Requirements: *GCE:* 240-280. *IB:* 24.

H133 BSc Computer Games Design (Top-Up)
Duration: 2FT Hon
Entry Requirements: Contact the institution for details.

H130 MEng Computer Games Design
Duration: 4FT/5SW Hon
Entry Requirements: *GCE:* 240-280. *IB:* 24.

www.ucas.com

at the heart of connecting people to higher education

S78 THE UNIVERSITY OF STRATHCLYDE
GLASGOW G1 1XQ
t: 0141 552 4400 f: 0141 552 0775
// www.strath.ac.uk

CH61 BEng Sports Engineering
Duration: 4FT Hon
Entry Requirements: *GCE:* A*AA-ABB. *SQAH:* AAAA-AAABBB. *IB:* 34. Interview required.

HC16 MEng Sports Engineering
Duration: 5FT Hon
Entry Requirements: *GCE:* A*AA-AAB. *SQAH:* AAAABB-AAAA. *IB:* 36. Interview required.

S82 UNIVERSITY CAMPUS SUFFOLK (UCS)
WATERFRONT BUILDING
NEPTUNE QUAY
IPSWICH
SUFFOLK IP4 1QJ
t: 01473 338833 f: 01473 339900
e: info@ucs.ac.uk
// www.ucs.ac.uk

H191 BEng Operations Engineering (Level 3 Entry Only)
Duration: 1FT Hon
Entry Requirements: Contact the institution for details.

H190 FdSc Operations Engineering
Duration: 2FT Fdg
Entry Requirements: *GCE:* 200. *IB:* 28. *BTEC ExtDip:* DMM.

S90 UNIVERSITY OF SUSSEX
UNDERGRADUATE ADMISSIONS
SUSSEX HOUSE
UNIVERSITY OF SUSSEX
BRIGHTON BN1 9RH
t: 01273 678416 f: 01273 678545
e: ug.applicants@sussex.ac.uk
// www.sussex.ac.uk

H100 BEng Engineering (with a foundation year)
Duration: 4FT Hon
Entry Requirements: *GCE:* BCC-CCC. *SQAH:* BCCCC-CCCCC. *IB:* 28. *BTEC SubDip:* D. *BTEC Dip:* DD. *BTEC ExtDip:* DDD.

HW12 BSc Product Design
Duration: 3FT Hon
Entry Requirements: *GCE:* ABB-BBB. *SQAH:* AABBB-ABBBB. *IB:* 32. *BTEC SubDip:* D. *BTEC Dip:* DD. *BTEC ExtDip:* DDD. *OCR ND:* D *OCR NED:* D2

HW1F BSc Product Design (with a professional placement year)
Duration: 4SW Hon
Entry Requirements: *GCE:* ABB-BBB. *SQAH:* AABBB-ABBBB. *IB:* 32. *BTEC SubDip:* D. *BTEC Dip:* DD. *BTEC ExtDip:* DDD. *OCR ND:* D *OCR NED:* D2

S93 SWANSEA UNIVERSITY
SINGLETON PARK
SWANSEA SA2 8PP
t: 01792 295111 f: 01792 295110
e: admissions@swansea.ac.uk
// www.swansea.ac.uk

H101 BEng Engineering with deferred choice of specialism (including Foundation Year)
Duration: 4FT Hon
Entry Requirements: *GCE:* 240.

H150 BEng Product Design Engineering
Duration: 3FT Hon
Entry Requirements: *GCE:* AAB. *IB:* 32.

H152 BEng Product Design Engineering (with a Year in Europe)
Duration: 4FT Hon
Entry Requirements: *GCE:* ABB. *IB:* 33.

H154 BEng Product Design Engineering (with a Year in Industry)
Duration: 4FT Hon
Entry Requirements: *GCE:* ABB. *IB:* 33.

H153 BEng Product Design Engineering (with a Year in North America)
Duration: 4FT Hon
Entry Requirements: *GCE:* ABB. *IB:* 33.

CH61 BEng Sports Science and Engineering
Duration: 3FT Hon
Entry Requirements: *GCE:* BBB. *IB:* 32.

H155 MEng Product Design Engineering
Duration: 4FT Deg
Entry Requirements: *GCE:* AAA. *IB:* 34.

H156 MEng Product Design Engineering (with a Year in Industry)
Duration: 5FT Hon
Entry Requirements: *GCE:* AAA. *IB:* 36.

CH6C MEng Sports Science and Engineering
Duration: 4FT Hon
Entry Requirements: *GCE:* AAB. *IB:* 34.

T20 TEESSIDE UNIVERSITY
MIDDLESBROUGH TS1 3BA
t: 01642 218121 f: 01642 384201
e: registry@tees.ac.uk
// www.tees.ac.uk

H631 BEng Tech Renewable Energy Engineering
Duration: 1FT Hon
Entry Requirements: HND required.

U20 UNIVERSITY OF ULSTER
COLERAINE
CO. LONDONDERRY
NORTHERN IRELAND BT52 1SA
t: 028 7012 4221 f: 028 7012 4908
e: online@ulster.ac.uk
// www.ulster.ac.uk

H1W2 BSc Technology with Design
Duration: 4SW Hon
Entry Requirements: *GCE:* 280. *IB:* 24. Interview required.
Admissions Test required.

U40 UNIVERSITY OF THE WEST OF SCOTLAND
PAISLEY
RENFREWSHIRE
SCOTLAND PA1 2BE
t: 0141 848 3727 f: 0141 848 3623
e: admissions@uws.ac.uk
// www.uws.ac.uk

H130 BSc Computer-Aided Design
Duration: 1FT/2FT Ord/Hon
Entry Requirements: HND required.

U80 UNIVERSITY COLLEGE LONDON (UNIVERSITY OF LONDON)
GOWER STREET
LONDON WC1E 6BT
t: 020 7679 3000 f: 020 7679 3001
// www.ucl.ac.uk

H1N3 BEng Engineering with Business Finance
Duration: 3FT Hon
Entry Requirements: *GCE:* AAAe-AABe. *SQAAH:* AAA-AAB. Interview required.

H1NH MEng Engineering with Business Finance
Duration: 4FT Hon
Entry Requirements: *GCE:* A*AAe-AAAe. *SQAAH:* AAA. Interview required.

W05 THE UNIVERSITY OF WEST LONDON
ST MARY'S ROAD
EALING
LONDON W5 5RF
t: 0800 036 8888 f: 020 8566 1353
e: learning.advice@uwl.ac.uk
// www.uwl.ac.uk

H100 BEng Engineering (Top-Up)
Duration: 1FT Hon
Entry Requirements: HND required.

W17 WARRINGTON COLLEGIATE
WINWICK ROAD CAMPUS
WINWICK ROAD
WARRINGTON
CHESHIRE WA2 8QA
t: 01925 494494 f: 01925 418328
e: admissions@warrington.ac.uk
// www.warrington.ac.uk

H100 HND Engineering
Duration: 2FT HND
Entry Requirements: Contact the institution for details.

W20 THE UNIVERSITY OF WARWICK
COVENTRY CV4 8UW
t: 024 7652 3723 f: 024 7652 4649
e: ugadmissions@warwick.ac.uk
// www.warwick.ac.uk

H100 BEng Engineering
Duration: 3FT Hon
Entry Requirements: *GCE:* AAB. *SQAAH:* AA-AB. *IB:* 36.

HN12 BEng Engineering Business Management
Duration: 3FT Hon
Entry Requirements: *GCE:* AAB. *SQAAH:* AA-AB. *IB:* 36.

H1N1 BSc Engineering and Business Studies
Duration: 3FT Hon
Entry Requirements: *GCE:* AAB. *SQAAH:* AA-AB. *IB:* 36.

H102 MEng Engineering option - Business Management
Duration: 4FT Hon
Entry Requirements: *GCE:* AAB-ABB. *SQAAH:* AA-AB. *IB:* 36.

H102 MEng Engineering option - Communications
Duration: 4FT Hon
Entry Requirements: *GCE:* AAB-ABB. *SQAAH:* AA-AB. *IB:* 36.

H102 MEng Engineering option - Robotics
Duration: 4FT Hon
Entry Requirements: *GCE:* AAB-ABB. *SQAAH:* AA-AB. *IB:* 36.

H102 MEng Engineering
Duration: 4FT Hon
Entry Requirements: *GCE:* AAB. *SQAAH:* AA-AB. *IB:* 36.

H102 MEng Engineering option - Fluid Dynamics
Duration: 4FT Hon
Entry Requirements: *GCE:* AAB-ABB. *SQAAH:* AA-AB. *IB:* 36.

H102 MEng Engineering option - Sustainability
Duration: 4FT Hon
Entry Requirements: *GCE:* BBB. *SQAAH:* AB-BB. *IB:* 34.

W25 WARWICKSHIRE COLLEGE
WARWICK NEW ROAD
LEAMINGTON SPA
WARWICKSHIRE CV32 5JE
t: 01926 884223 f: 01926 318 111
e: kgooch@warkscol.ac.uk
// www.warwickshire.ac.uk

H100 FdEng Engineering
Duration: 2FT Fdg
Entry Requirements: *GCE:* 120.

007H HND Engineering
Duration: 1FT/2FT HNC/HND
Entry Requirements: *GCE:* 120.

W75 UNIVERSITY OF WOLVERHAMPTON
ADMISSIONS UNIT
MX207, CAMP STREET
WOLVERHAMPTON
WEST MIDLANDS WV1 1AD
t: 01902 321000 f: 01902 321896
e: admissions@wlv.ac.uk
// www.wlv.ac.uk

H151 BEng Engineering Design Management
Duration: 3FT/4SW Hon
Entry Requirements: *GCE:* 240.

HN12 BSc Fire and Rescue
Duration: 3FT Hon   CRB Check: Required
Entry Requirements: Contact the institution for details.

H102 FdSc Engineering
Duration: 2FT Fdg
Entry Requirements: Contact the institution for details.

H150 MEng Engineering Design Management
Duration: 4FT/5SW Hon
Entry Requirements: Contact the institution for details.

OTHERS IN ENGINEERING

B41 BLACKPOOL AND THE FYLDE COLLEGE AN ASSOCIATE COLLEGE OF LANCASTER UNIVERSITY
ASHFIELD ROAD
BISPHAM
BLACKPOOL
LANCS FY2 0HB
t: 01253 504346 f: 01253 504198
e: admissions@blackpool.ac.uk
// www.blackpool.ac.uk

H991 BEng Engineering Illustration (Top-Up)
Duration: 1FT Hon
Entry Requirements: Contact the institution for details.

H901 BEng Sustainable Energy Technology (Top-Up)
Duration: 1FT Hon
Entry Requirements: Contact the institution for details.

H990 FdEng Engineering Illustration
Duration: 2FT Fdg
Entry Requirements: *GCE:* 120-360. *IB:* 24.

B56 THE UNIVERSITY OF BRADFORD
RICHMOND ROAD
BRADFORD
WEST YORKSHIRE BD7 1DP
t: 0800 073 1225 f: 01274 235585
e: course-enquiries@bradford.ac.uk
// www.bradford.ac.uk

H900 BSc Clinical Technology
Duration: 3FT Hon
Entry Requirements: *GCE:* 200. *IB:* 24.

H901 BSc Clinical Technology (4 years)
Duration: 4SW Hon
Entry Requirements: *GCE:* 200. *IB:* 24.

C15 CARDIFF UNIVERSITY
PO BOX 927
30-36 NEWPORT ROAD
CARDIFF CF24 0DE
t: 029 2087 9999 f: 029 2087 6138
e: admissions@cardiff.ac.uk
// www.cardiff.ac.uk

H992 MEng Architectural Engineering with Year in Europe (Germany)
Duration: 5SW Hon
Entry Requirements: *GCE:* AAB. *SQAAH:* AAB. Interview required. Admissions Test required.

H990 MEng Architectural Engineering with Year in Europe (Spain)
Duration: 5SW Hon
Entry Requirements: *GCE:* AAB. *SQAAH:* AAB. Interview required. Admissions Test required.

W75 UNIVERSITY OF WOLVERHAMPTON
ADMISSIONS UNIT
MX207, CAMP STREET
WOLVERHAMPTON
WEST MIDLANDS WV1 1AD
t: 01902 321000 f: 01902 321896
e: admissions@wlv.ac.uk
// www.wlv.ac.uk

LH29 BSc Armed Forces and Combat Engineering
Duration: 3FT Hon   CRB Check: Required
Entry Requirements: Contact the institution for details.

MATHEMATICS

A20 THE UNIVERSITY OF ABERDEEN
UNIVERSITY OFFICE
KING'S COLLEGE
ABERDEEN AB24 3FX
t: +44 (0) 1224 273504 f: +44 (0) 1224 272034
e: sras@abdn.ac.uk
// www.abdn.ac.uk/sras

G100 BSc Mathematics
Duration: 4FT Hon
Entry Requirements: *GCE:* 240. *SQAH:* BBBB. *SQAAH:* BCC. *IB:* 28.

G101 BSc Mathematics (International Foundation)
Duration: 4FT Hon
Entry Requirements: Contact the institution for details.

G102 MA Mathematics
Duration: 4FT Hon
Entry Requirements: *GCE:* BBB. *SQAH:* BBBB. *IB:* 30.

A40 ABERYSTWYTH UNIVERSITY
ABERYSTWYTH UNIVERSITY, WELCOME CENTRE
PENGLAIS CAMPUS
ABERYSTWYTH
CEREDIGION SY23 3FB
t: 01970 622021 f: 01970 627410
e: ug-admissions@aber.ac.uk
// www.aber.ac.uk

G100 BSc Mathematics
Duration: 3FT Hon
Entry Requirements: *GCE:* 320.

G102 BSc Mathematics (Ordinary)
Duration: 3FT Ord
Entry Requirements: *GCE:* 120.

G103 MMath Mathematics (4 years)
Duration: 4FT Hon
Entry Requirements: *GCE:* 340. *IB:* 34.

A80 ASTON UNIVERSITY, BIRMINGHAM
ASTON TRIANGLE
BIRMINGHAM B4 7ET
t: 0121 204 4444 f: 0121 204 3696
e: admissions@aston.ac.uk (automatic response)
// www.aston.ac.uk/prospective-students/ug

G100 BSc Mathematics
Duration: 3FT/4SW Hon
Entry Requirements: *GCE:* 320-340. *IB:* 32.

B16 UNIVERSITY OF BATH
CLAVERTON DOWN
BATH BA2 7AY
t: 01225 383019 f: 01225 386366
e: admissions@bath.ac.uk
// www.bath.ac.uk

G140 BSc Mathematical Sciences
Duration: 3FT Hon
Entry Requirements: *GCE:* A*AA-A*AB. *SQAAH:* AAA. *IB:* 38.

G100 BSc Mathematics
Duration: 3FT Hon
Entry Requirements: *GCE:* A*AA-A*AB. *SQAAH:* AAA. *IB:* 38.

G101 BSc Mathematics (Sandwich)
Duration: 4SW Hon
Entry Requirements: *GCE:* A*AA-A*AB. *SQAAH:* AAA. *IB:* 38.

G103 MMath Mathematics
Duration: 4FT Hon
Entry Requirements: *GCE:* A*AA-A*AB. *SQAAH:* AAA. *IB:* 38.

G104 MMath Mathematics (with a Year Abroad)
Duration: 4FT Hon
Entry Requirements: *GCE:* A*AA-A*AB. *SQAAH:* AAA. *IB:* 38.

B32 THE UNIVERSITY OF BIRMINGHAM
EDGBASTON
BIRMINGHAM B15 2TT
t: 0121 415 8900 f: 0121 414 7159
e: admissions@bham.ac.uk
// www.birmingham.ac.uk

G100 BSc Mathematics
Duration: 3FT Hon
Entry Requirements: *GCE:* AAA-AAB. *SQAH:* AAAAB-AAABB. *SQAAH:* AA.

G101 BSc Mathematics Foundation Year
Duration: 4FT Hon
Entry Requirements: Contact the institution for details.

G141 BSc Mathematics with Study in Continental Europe (4 years)
Duration: 4FT Hon
Entry Requirements: *GCE:* A*AA. *SQAH:* AAAAA. *SQAAH:* AA.

G103 MSci Mathematics
Duration: 4FT Hon
Entry Requirements: *GCE:* A*AA. *SQAH:* AAAAA. *SQAAH:* AA.

B44 UNIVERSITY OF BOLTON
DEANE ROAD
BOLTON BL3 5AB
t: 01204 903903 f: 01204 399074
e: enquiries@bolton.ac.uk
// www.bolton.ac.uk

G100 BSc Mathematics
Duration: 3FT Hon
Entry Requirements: *GCE:* 260. Interview required.

B72 UNIVERSITY OF BRIGHTON
MITHRAS HOUSE 211
LEWES ROAD
BRIGHTON BN2 4AT
t: 01273 644644 f: 01273 642607
e: admissions@brighton.ac.uk
// www.brighton.ac.uk

G100 BSc Mathematics
Duration: 3FT/4SW Hon
Entry Requirements: *GCE:* BBB. *IB:* 30.

B78 UNIVERSITY OF BRISTOL
UNDERGRADUATE ADMISSIONS OFFICE
SENATE HOUSE
TYNDALL AVENUE
BRISTOL BS8 1TH
t: 0117 928 9000 f: 0117 331 7391
e: ug-admissions@bristol.ac.uk
// www.bristol.ac.uk

G100 BSc Mathematics
Duration: 3FT Hon
Entry Requirements: *GCE:* A*AA. *SQAH:* AAAAA. *SQAAH:* AA.

G101 BSc Mathematics with Study in Continental Europe (4 years)
Duration: 4FT Hon
Entry Requirements: *GCE:* A*AA. *SQAH:* AAAAA. *SQAAH:* AA.

G103 MSci Mathematics
Duration: 4FT Hon
Entry Requirements: *GCE:* A*AA. *SQAH:* AAAAA. *SQAAH:* AA.

G104 MSci Mathematics with Study in Continental Europe
Duration: 4FT Hon
Entry Requirements: *GCE:* A*AA. *SQAH:* AAAAA. *SQAAH:* AA.

B80 UNIVERSITY OF THE WEST OF ENGLAND, BRISTOL
FRENCHAY CAMPUS
COLDHARBOUR LANE
BRISTOL BS16 1QY
t: +44 (0)117 32 83333 f: +44 (0)117 32 82810
e: admissions@uwe.ac.uk
// www.uwe.ac.uk

G101 BSc Mathematics
Duration: 3FT/4SW Hon
Entry Requirements: *GCE:* 300.

G100 FYr Mathematics Foundation (Year 0)
Duration: 1FT FYr
Entry Requirements: *GCE:* 180.

B84 BRUNEL UNIVERSITY
UXBRIDGE
MIDDLESEX UB8 3PH
t: 01895 265265 f: 01895 269790
e: admissions@brunel.ac.uk
// www.brunel.ac.uk

G103 BSc Mathematics
Duration: 3FT Hon
Entry Requirements: *GCE:* ABB. *SQAAH:* ABB. *IB:* 33. *BTEC ExtDip:* D*DD.

G104 BSc Mathematics (4 year Thick SW)
Duration: 4SW Hon
Entry Requirements: *GCE:* ABB. *SQAAH:* ABB. *IB:* 33. *BTEC ExtDip:* D*DD.

G100 MMath Mathematics (4 years)
Duration: 4FT Hon
Entry Requirements: *GCE:* AAA. *SQAAH:* AAA. *IB:* 37.

G101 MMath Mathematics (5 year Thick SW)
Duration: 5FT Hon
Entry Requirements: *GCE:* AAA. *SQAAH:* AAA. *IB:* 37.

C05 UNIVERSITY OF CAMBRIDGE
CAMBRIDGE ADMISSIONS OFFICE
FITZWILLIAM HOUSE
32 TRUMPINGTON STREET
CAMBRIDGE CB2 1QY
t: 01223 333 308 f: 01223 746 868
e: admissions@cam.ac.uk
// www.study.cam.ac.uk/undergraduate/

G100 BA/MMath Mathematics
Duration: 3FT/4FT Hon
Entry Requirements: *GCE:* A*AA. *SQAAH:* AAA-AAB. Interview required.

G100 BA/MMath Mathematics option - Mathematics with Physics
Duration: 3FT/4FT Hon
Entry Requirements: *GCE:* A*AA. *SQAAH:* AAA-AAB. Interview required.

C15 CARDIFF UNIVERSITY
PO BOX 927
30-36 NEWPORT ROAD
CARDIFF CF24 0DE
t: 029 2087 9999 f: 029 2087 6138
e: admissions@cardiff.ac.uk
// www.cardiff.ac.uk

G100 BSc Mathematics
Duration: 3FT Hon
Entry Requirements: *GCE:* AAB. *SQAH:* AABBB. *SQAAH:* AABBB.
IB: 34. *OCR ND:* D *OCR NED:* M2 Interview required.

G101 MMath Mathematics
Duration: 4FT Hon
Entry Requirements: *GCE:* A*AB-AAA. *SQAH:* AAABB. *SQAAH:*
AAABB. *IB:* 35. *OCR ND:* D *OCR NED:* M1 Interview required.

C30 UNIVERSITY OF CENTRAL LANCASHIRE
PRESTON
LANCS PR1 2HE
t: 01772 201201 f: 01772 894954
e: uadmissions@uclan.ac.uk
// www.uclan.ac.uk

G100 BSc Mathematics
Duration: 3FT Hon
Entry Requirements: *GCE:* 280. *IB:* 26. *OCR ND:* D

C55 UNIVERSITY OF CHESTER
PARKGATE ROAD
CHESTER CH1 4BJ
t: 01244 511000 f: 01244 511300
e: enquiries@chester.ac.uk
// www.chester.ac.uk

G100 BSc Mathematics
Duration: 3FT Hon
Entry Requirements: *GCE:* 240-280. *SQAH:* BBBB. *IB:* 26.

C60 CITY UNIVERSITY
NORTHAMPTON SQUARE
LONDON EC1V 0HB
t: 020 7040 5060 f: 020 7040 8995
e: ugadmissions@city.ac.uk
// www.city.ac.uk

G100 BSc Mathematical Science (3 years or 4 year SW)
Duration: 3FT Hon
Entry Requirements: *GCE:* 360. *IB:* 32.

G101 Cert International Foundation (Mathematics)
Duration: 1FT FYr
Entry Requirements: Contact the institution for details.

C85 COVENTRY UNIVERSITY
THE STUDENT CENTRE
COVENTRY UNIVERSITY
1 GULSON RD
COVENTRY CV1 2JH
t: 024 7615 2222 f: 024 7615 2223
e: studentenquiries@coventry.ac.uk
// www.coventry.ac.uk

G100 BSc Mathematics
Duration: 3FT/4SW Hon
Entry Requirements: *GCE:* BBC. *SQAH:* BCCCC. *IB:* 29.

D65 UNIVERSITY OF DUNDEE
NETHERGATE
DUNDEE DD1 4HN
t: 01382 383838 f: 01382 388150
e: contactus@dundee.ac.uk
// www.dundee.ac.uk/admissions/
undergraduate/

G100 BSc Mathematics
Duration: 4FT Hon
Entry Requirements: *GCE:* BCC. *SQAH:* ABBB. *IB:* 30.

D86 DURHAM UNIVERSITY
DURHAM UNIVERSITY
UNIVERSITY OFFICE
DURHAM DH1 3HP
t: 0191 334 2000 f: 0191 334 6055
e: admissions@durham.ac.uk
// www.durham.ac.uk

G100 BSc Mathematics (3 years)
Duration: 3FT Hon
Entry Requirements: *GCE:* A*AA-AAA. *SQAAH:* AAA. *IB:* 38.

G104 BSc Mathematics (European Studies) (4 years)
Duration: 4FT Hon
Entry Requirements: *GCE:* A*AA-AAA. *SQAAH:* AAA. *IB:* 38.

G107 BSc Mathematics with Foundation
Duration: 4FT Hon
Entry Requirements: Contact the institution for details.

G103 MMath Mathematics (4 years)
Duration: 4FT Hon
Entry Requirements: *GCE:* A*AA-AAA. *SQAAH:* AAA. *IB:* 38.

G101 MMath Mathematics (European Studies)
Duration: 4FT Hon
Entry Requirements: *GCE:* A*AA-AAA. *SQAAH:* AAA. *IB:* 38.

E14 UNIVERSITY OF EAST ANGLIA
NORWICH NR4 7TJ
t: 01603 591515 f: 01603 591523
e: admissions@uea.ac.uk
// www.uea.ac.uk

G100 BSc Mathematics
Duration: 3FT Hon   CRB Check: Required
Entry Requirements: *GCE:* AAB. *SQAH:* AAABB. *SQAAH:* AAB. *IB:* 33.

G103 MMath Mathematics (4 years)
Duration: 4FT Hon
Entry Requirements: *GCE:* A*AB-A*BB. *IB:* 34. *BTEC ExtDip:* D*DD.

G106 MMath Mathematics with a year in Australia
Duration: 4FT Hon   CRB Check: Required
Entry Requirements: *GCE:* A*AA-A*AB. *IB:* 35. *BTEC ExtDip:* D*DD.

G102 MMath Mathematics with a year in North America (4 years)
Duration: 4FT Hon   CRB Check: Required
Entry Requirements: *GCE:* A*AA-A*AB. *SQAH:* AAAA. *SQAAH:* AAA. *IB:* 35. *BTEC ExtDip:* D*DD.

E56 THE UNIVERSITY OF EDINBURGH
STUDENT RECRUITMENT & ADMISSIONS
57 GEORGE SQUARE
EDINBURGH EH8 9JU
t: 0131 650 4360 f: 0131 651 1236
e: sra.enquiries@ed.ac.uk
// www.ed.ac.uk/studying/undergraduate/

G103 BSc Integrated Foundation Programme (Mathematics)
Duration: 4FT Hon
Entry Requirements: Contact the institution for details.

G100 BSc Mathematics
Duration: 4FT Hon
Entry Requirements: *GCE:* AAA-ABB. *SQAH:* AAAA-ABBB.

G102 MA Mathematics
Duration: 4FT Hon
Entry Requirements: *GCE:* AAA-ABB. *SQAH:* AAAA-ABBB.

G101 MMath Mathematics
Duration: 5FT Hon
Entry Requirements: *GCE:* AAA-ABB. *SQAH:* AAAA-ABBB.

E70 THE UNIVERSITY OF ESSEX
WIVENHOE PARK
COLCHESTER
ESSEX CO4 3SQ
t: 01206 873666 f: 01206 874477
e: admit@essex.ac.uk
// www.essex.ac.uk

G100 BSc Mathematics
Duration: 3FT Hon
Entry Requirements: *GCE:* ABB-BBB. *SQAH:* AAAB-AABB. *BTEC ExtDip:* DDM.

G102 BSc Mathematics (Including Year Abroad)
Duration: 4FT Hon
Entry Requirements: *GCE:* ABB-BBB. *SQAH:* AAAB-AABB. *BTEC ExtDip:* DDM.

E84 UNIVERSITY OF EXETER
LAVER BUILDING
NORTH PARK ROAD
EXETER
DEVON EX4 4QE
t: 01392 723044 f: 01392 722479
e: admissions@exeter.ac.uk
// www.exeter.ac.uk

G100 BSc Mathematics
Duration: 3FT Hon
Entry Requirements: *GCE:* A*AA-AAB. *SQAH:* AAAAA-AABBB. *SQAAH:* AAA-ABB.

G102 MMath Mathematics
Duration: 4FT Hon
Entry Requirements: *GCE:* A*AA-AAB. *SQAH:* AAAAA-AABBB. *SQAAH:* AAA-ABB.

G103 MSci Mathematics (4years)
Duration: 4FT Hon
Entry Requirements: *GCE:* A*AA-AAB. *SQAH:* AAAAA-AABBB. *SQAAH:* AAA-ABB.

G14 UNIVERSITY OF GLAMORGAN, CARDIFF AND PONTYPRIDD
ENQUIRIES AND ADMISSIONS UNIT
PONTYPRIDD CF37 1DL
t: 08456 434030 f: 01443 654050
e: enquiries@glam.ac.uk
// www.glam.ac.uk

G100 BSc Mathematics
Duration: 3FT/4SW Hon
Entry Requirements: *GCE:* BBB. *IB:* 26. *BTEC SubDip:* M. *BTEC Dip:* MM. *BTEC ExtDip:* DDM. Interview required.

G108 FYr Mathematics Foundation Year
Duration: 1FT FYr
Entry Requirements: *GCE:* BBB. *IB:* 26. *BTEC SubDip:* M. *BTEC Dip:* PP. *BTEC ExtDip:* PPP. Interview required.

G28 UNIVERSITY OF GLASGOW
71 SOUTHPARK AVENUE
UNIVERSITY OF GLASGOW
GLASGOW G12 8QQ
t: 0141 330 6062 f: 0141 330 2961
e: student.recruitment@glasgow.ac.uk
// www.glasgow.ac.uk

G100 BSc Mathematics
Duration: 4FT Hon
Entry Requirements: *GCE:* ABB. *SQAH:* AAAB-BBBB. *IB:* 32.

G105 BSc Mathematics (Faster Route)
Duration: 3FT Hon
Entry Requirements: *GCE:* AAA. *SQAAH:* AAA. *IB:* 38.

G102 MA Mathematics
Duration: 4FT Hon
Entry Requirements: *GCE:* ABB. *SQAH:* AAAB-ABBB. *IB:* 36.

G101 MSci Mathematics
Duration: 5FT Hon
Entry Requirements: *GCE:* ABB. *SQAH:* AAAB-BBBB. *IB:* 32.

G103 MSci Mathematics (Faster Route)
Duration: 4FT Hon
Entry Requirements: *GCE:* AAA. *SQAAH:* AAA. *IB:* 38.

G70 UNIVERSITY OF GREENWICH
GREENWICH CAMPUS
OLD ROYAL NAVAL COLLEGE
PARK ROW
LONDON SE10 9LS
t: 020 8331 9000 f: 020 8331 8145
e: courseinfo@gre.ac.uk
// www.gre.ac.uk

G140 BSc Mathematics
Duration: 3FT Hon
Entry Requirements: *GCE:* 260.

H24 HERIOT-WATT UNIVERSITY, EDINBURGH
EDINBURGH CAMPUS
EDINBURGH EH14 4AS
t: 0131 449 5111 f: 0131 451 3630
e: ugadmissions@hw.ac.uk
// www.hw.ac.uk

G100 BSc Mathematics
Duration: 3FT/4FT Hon
Entry Requirements: *GCE:* BBB. *SQAH:* ABBBC. *SQAAH:* BBB. *IB:* 26.

G101 MMath Mathematics
Duration: 4FT/5FT Hon
Entry Requirements: *GCE:* BBB. *SQAH:* ABBBC. *SQAAH:* BBB. *IB:* 26.

H36 UNIVERSITY OF HERTFORDSHIRE
UNIVERSITY ADMISSIONS SERVICE
COLLEGE LANE
HATFIELD
HERTS AL10 9AB
t: 01707 284800
// www.herts.ac.uk

G100 BSc Mathematics
Duration: 3FT/4SW Hon
Entry Requirements: *GCE:* 260.

I50 IMPERIAL COLLEGE LONDON
REGISTRY
SOUTH KENSINGTON CAMPUS
IMPERIAL COLLEGE LONDON
LONDON SW7 2AZ
t: 020 7589 5111 f: 020 7594 8004
// www.imperial.ac.uk

G100 BSc Mathematics
Duration: 3FT Hon
Entry Requirements: *GCE:* A*A*A. *SQAAH:* AAA. *IB:* 39.

G102 BSc Mathematics with Mathematical Computation
Duration: 3FT Hon
Entry Requirements: *GCE:* A*A*A. *SQAAH:* AAA. *IB:* 39.

G101 BSc Mathematics with a Year in Europe
Duration: 4FT Hon
Entry Requirements: *GCE:* A*A*A. *SQAAH:* AAA. *IB:* 39.

G103 MSci Mathematics
Duration: 4FT Hon
Entry Requirements: *GCE:* A*A*A. *SQAAH:* AAA. *IB:* 39.

G104 MSci Mathematics with a Year in Europe
Duration: 4FT Hon
Entry Requirements: *GCE:* A*A*A. *SQAAH:* AAA. *IB:* 39.

K12 KEELE UNIVERSITY
KEELE UNIVERSITY
STAFFORDSHIRE ST5 5BG
t: 01782 734005 f: 01782 632343
e: undergraduate@keele.ac.uk
// www.keele.ac.uk

G100 BSc Mathematics
Duration: 3FT Hon
Entry Requirements: *GCE:* ABC.

G105 BSc Mathematics (Major with 2nd subject)
Duration: 3FT Hon
Entry Requirements: *GCE:* ABC.

G101 BSc Mathematics with Science Foundation Year
Duration: 4FT Hon
Entry Requirements: *GCE:* CC.

K24 THE UNIVERSITY OF KENT
RECRUITMENT & ADMISSIONS OFFICE
REGISTRY
UNIVERSITY OF KENT
CANTERBURY, KENT CT2 7NZ
t: 01227 827272 f: 01227 827077
e: information@kent.ac.uk
// www.kent.ac.uk

G100 BSc Mathematics (3 or 4 years)
Duration: 3FT/4SW Hon
Entry Requirements: *GCE:* 300. *IB:* 33. *OCR ND:* D *OCR NED:* M2

G108 BSc Mathematics with a foundation year (4 years)
Duration: 4FT Hon
Entry Requirements: *GCE:* 240. *IB:* 33. *OCR ND:* M2 *OCR NED:* M3

K60 KING'S COLLEGE LONDON (UNIVERSITY OF LONDON)
STRAND
LONDON WC2R 2LS
t: 020 7836 5454 f: 020 7848 7171
e: prospective@kcl.ac.uk
// www.kcl.ac.uk/prospectus

G100 BSc Mathematics
Duration: 3FT Hon
Entry Requirements: *GCE:* A*AAa-AAAc. *SQAH:* AAB. *SQAAH:* AA. *IB:* 38.

G103 MSci Mathematics
Duration: 4FT Hon
Entry Requirements: *GCE:* A*AAa-AAAc. *SQAH:* AAB. *SQAAH:* AA. *IB:* 38.

K84 KINGSTON UNIVERSITY
STUDENT INFORMATION & ADVICE CENTRE
COOPER HOUSE
40-46 SURBITON ROAD
KINGSTON UPON THAMES KT1 2HX
t: 0844 8552177 f: 020 8547 7080
e: aps@kingston.ac.uk
// www.kingston.ac.uk

G100 BSc Mathematical Sciences
Duration: 3FT Hon
Entry Requirements: *GCE:* 280.

G102 BSc Mathematical Sciences
Duration: 4SW Hon
Entry Requirements: *GCE:* 280.

G108 BSc Mathematical Sciences (Foundation)
Duration: 4FT Hon
Entry Requirements: *GCE:* 80.

L14 LANCASTER UNIVERSITY
THE UNIVERSITY
LANCASTER
LANCASHIRE LA1 4YW
t: 01524 592029 f: 01524 846243
e: ugadmissions@lancaster.ac.uk
// www.lancs.ac.uk

G100 BSc/MSci Mathematics
Duration: 3FT Hon
Entry Requirements: *GCE:* AAA. *SQAH:* AAABB. *SQAAH:* AAA. *IB:* 36.

G103 MSci Mathematics (Study Abroad)
Duration: 4FT Hon
Entry Requirements: *GCE:* AAA. *SQAH:* AAABB. *SQAAH:* AAA. *IB:* 36.

L23 UNIVERSITY OF LEEDS
THE UNIVERSITY OF LEEDS
WOODHOUSE LANE
LEEDS LS2 9JT
t: 0113 343 3999
e: admissions@leeds.ac.uk
// www.leeds.ac.uk

G100 BSc Mathematics
Duration: 3FT Hon
Entry Requirements: *GCE:* AAB. *SQAAH:* AAB. *IB:* 34.

G101 MMath Mathematics
Duration: 4FT Hon
Entry Requirements: *GCE:* AAB. *SQAAH:* AAB. *IB:* 34.

L34 UNIVERSITY OF LEICESTER
UNIVERSITY ROAD
LEICESTER LE1 7RH
t: 0116 252 5281 f: 0116 252 2447
e: admissions@le.ac.uk
// www.le.ac.uk

G102 BA Mathematics
Duration: 3FT Hon
Entry Requirements: *GCE:* AAB. *SQAH:* AAAAB-AAABB. *SQAAH:* AAB. *IB:* 34.

G100 BSc Mathematics
Duration: 3FT Hon
Entry Requirements: *GCE:* AAB. *SQAH:* AAAAB-AAABB. *SQAAH:* AAB. *IB:* 34.

G101 BSc Mathematics (with a year abroad)
Duration: 4FT Hon
Entry Requirements: *GCE:* AAB. *SQAH:* AAAAB-AAABB. *SQAAH:* AAB. *IB:* 34.

G105 MMath Mathematics
Duration: 4FT Hon
Entry Requirements: *GCE:* AAB. *SQAH:* AAAAB-AAABB. *SQAAH:* AAB. *IB:* 34.

G107 MMath Mathematics (with a year abroad)
Duration: 4FT Hon
Entry Requirements: *GCE:* AAB. *SQAH:* AAAAB-AAABB. *SQAAH:* AAB. *IB:* 34.

L41 THE UNIVERSITY OF LIVERPOOL
THE FOUNDATION BUILDING
BROWNLOW HILL
LIVERPOOL L69 7ZX
t: 0151 794 2000 f: 0151 708 6502
e: ugrecruitment@liv.ac.uk
// www.liv.ac.uk

G108 BSc Mathematical Sciences (Foundation) (1+3)
Duration: 4FT Hon
Entry Requirements: Contact the institution for details.

G100 BSc Mathematics
Duration: 3FT Hon
Entry Requirements: *GCE:* ABB. *SQAAH:* ABB. *IB:* 33. Interview required.

G101 MMath Mathematics
Duration: 4FT Hon
Entry Requirements: *GCE:* ABB. *SQAAH:* ABB. *IB:* 33. Interview required.

L68 LONDON METROPOLITAN UNIVERSITY
166-220 HOLLOWAY ROAD
LONDON N7 8DB
t: 020 7133 4200
e: admissions@londonmet.ac.uk
// www.londonmet.ac.uk

G101 BSc Mathematical Sciences
Duration: 3FT Hon
Entry Requirements: *GCE:* 200. *IB:* 28.

G100 BSc Mathematics
Duration: 3FT Hon
Entry Requirements: *GCE:* 200. *IB:* 28.

L79 LOUGHBOROUGH UNIVERSITY
LOUGHBOROUGH
LEICESTERSHIRE LE11 3TU
t: 01509 223522 f: 01509 223905
e: admissions@lboro.ac.uk
// www.lboro.ac.uk

G100 BSc Mathematics
Duration: 3FT Hon
Entry Requirements: *GCE:* AAA-AAB. *SQAH:* ABB. *SQAAH:* AA. *IB:* 36.

G101 BSc Mathematics
Duration: 4SW Hon
Entry Requirements: *GCE:* AAA-AAB. *SQAH:* ABB. *SQAAH:* AA. *IB:* 36.

G103 MMath Mathematics
Duration: 4FT Hon
Entry Requirements: *GCE:* AAA-AAB. *SQAH:* ABB. *SQAAH:* AA. *IB:* 36.

G104 MMath Mathematics
Duration: 5SW Hon
Entry Requirements: *GCE:* AAA-AAB. *SQAH:* ABB. *SQAAH:* AA. *IB:* 36.

M20 THE UNIVERSITY OF MANCHESTER
RUTHERFORD BUILDING
OXFORD ROAD
MANCHESTER M13 9PL
t: 0161 275 2077 f: 0161 275 2106
e: ug-admissions@manchester.ac.uk
// www.manchester.ac.uk

G100 BSc Mathematics
Duration: 3FT Hon
Entry Requirements: *GCE:* A*AB-AAB. *SQAH:* AAAAB. *SQAAH:* AAB. *IB:* 36. Interview required.

F800 MGeog Geography (Integrated Masters)
Duration: 4FT Hon
Entry Requirements: *GCE:* AAA. *SQAH:* AAAAA-AAAAB. *SQAAH:* AAA. *IB:* 36.

G104 MMath Mathematics
Duration: 4FT Hon
Entry Requirements: *GCE:* A*AB-AAB. *SQAH:* AAAAB. *SQAAH:* AAB. *IB:* 36. Interview required.

M40 THE MANCHESTER METROPOLITAN UNIVERSITY
ADMISSIONS OFFICE
ALL SAINTS (GMS)
ALL SAINTS
MANCHESTER M15 6BH
t: 0161 247 2000
// www.mmu.ac.uk

G100 BSc Mathematics
Duration: 3FT Hon
Entry Requirements: *GCE:* 240-280.

G109 BSc Mathematics (Foundation)
Duration: 4FT Hon
Entry Requirements: *GCE:* 160. *IB:* 24. *BTEC Dip:* MM. *BTEC ExtDip:* MPP.

N21 NEWCASTLE UNIVERSITY
KING'S GATE
NEWCASTLE UPON TYNE NE1 7RU
t: 01912083333
// www.ncl.ac.uk

G100 BSc Mathematics
Duration: 3FT Hon
Entry Requirements: *GCE:* AAB. *SQAAH:* AB.

G101 FYr Mathematics Foundation year
Duration: 1FT FYr
Entry Requirements: Contact the institution for details.

G103 MMath Mathematics (4 years)
Duration: 4FT Hon
Entry Requirements: *GCE:* AAB. *SQAAH:* AB.

N77 NORTHUMBRIA UNIVERSITY
TRINITY BUILDING
NORTHUMBERLAND ROAD
NEWCASTLE UPON TYNE NE1 8ST
t: 0191 243 7420 f: 0191 227 4561
e: er.admissions@northumbria.ac.uk
// www.northumbria.ac.uk

G100 BSc Mathematics
Duration: 3FT/4SW Hon
Entry Requirements: *GCE:* 320. *SQAH:* BBBBB. *SQAAH:* BBB. *IB:* 27.

G101 MMath Mathematics
Duration: 4FT/5SW Hon
Entry Requirements: *GCE:* 340. *SQAH:* ABBBB. *SQAAH:* ABC. *IB:* 28.

N84 THE UNIVERSITY OF NOTTINGHAM
THE ADMISSIONS OFFICE
THE UNIVERSITY OF NOTTINGHAM
UNIVERSITY PARK
NOTTINGHAM NG7 2RD
t: 0115 951 5151 f: 0115 951 4668
// www.nottingham.ac.uk

G100 BSc Mathematics
Duration: 3FT Hon
Entry Requirements: *GCE:* AAA-A*AB. *SQAAH:* AAA. *IB:* 38.

G104 BSc Mathematics (International Study)
Duration: 4FT Hon
Entry Requirements: *GCE:* AAA-A*AB. *SQAAH:* AAA. *IB:* 38.

G103 MMath Mathematics (4 years)
Duration: 4FT Hon
Entry Requirements: *GCE:* AAA-A*AB. *SQAAH:* AAA. *IB:* 38.

N91 NOTTINGHAM TRENT UNIVERSITY
DRYDEN BUILDING
BURTON STREET
NOTTINGHAM NG1 4BU
t: +44 (0) 115 848 4200 f: +44 (0) 115 848 8869
e: applications@ntu.ac.uk
// www.ntu.ac.uk

G100 BSc Mathematics
Duration: 3FT Hon
Entry Requirements: *GCE:* 300. *BTEC ExtDip:* DDM. *OCR NED:* D2

O33 OXFORD UNIVERSITY
UNDERGRADUATE ADMISSIONS OFFICE
UNIVERSITY OF OXFORD
WELLINGTON SQUARE
OXFORD OX1 2JD
t: 01865 288000 f: 01865 270212
e: undergraduate.admissions@admin.ox.ac.uk
// www.admissions.ox.ac.uk

G100 BA Mathematics (3 or 4 years)
Duration: 3FT/4FT Hon
Entry Requirements: *GCE:* A*A*A. *SQAH:* AAAAA-AAAAB. *SQAAH:* AAB. Interview required. Admissions Test required.

O66 OXFORD BROOKES UNIVERSITY
ADMISSIONS OFFICE
HEADINGTON CAMPUS
GIPSY LANE
OXFORD OX3 0BP
t: 01865 483040 f: 01865 483983
e: admissions@brookes.ac.uk
// www.brookes.ac.uk

G100 BSc Mathematics
Duration: 3FT Hon
Entry Requirements: *GCE:* BBC.

P60 PLYMOUTH UNIVERSITY
DRAKE CIRCUS
PLYMOUTH PL4 8AA
t: 01752 585858 f: 01752 588055
e: admissions@plymouth.ac.uk
// www.plymouth.ac.uk

G100 BSc Mathematics
Duration: 3FT/4FT Hon
Entry Requirements: *GCE:* 320. *IB:* 30.

P80 UNIVERSITY OF PORTSMOUTH
ACADEMIC REGISTRY
UNIVERSITY HOUSE
WINSTON CHURCHILL AVENUE
PORTSMOUTH PO1 2UP
t: 023 9284 8484 f: 023 9284 3082
e: admissions@port.ac.uk
// www.port.ac.uk

G100 BSc Mathematics
Duration: 3FT/4SW Hon
Entry Requirements: *GCE:* 260-300. *IB:* 26. *BTEC SubDip:* P. *BTEC Dip:* PP. *BTEC ExtDip:* DMM.

Q50 QUEEN MARY, UNIVERSITY OF LONDON
QUEEN MARY, UNIVERSITY OF LONDON
MILE END ROAD
LONDON E1 4NS
t: 020 7882 5555 f: 020 7882 5500
e: admissions@qmul.ac.uk
// www.qmul.ac.uk

G100 BSc Mathematics
Duration: 3FT Hon
Entry Requirements: *GCE:* 340. *IB:* 36.

G102 MSci Mathematics
Duration: 4FT Hon
Entry Requirements: *GCE:* 360. *IB:* 36.

Q75 QUEEN'S UNIVERSITY BELFAST
UNIVERSITY ROAD
BELFAST BT7 1NN
t: 028 9097 3838 f: 028 9097 5151
e: admissions@qub.ac.uk
// www.qub.ac.uk

G100 BSc Mathematics
Duration: 3FT Hon
Entry Requirements: *GCE:* ABC-ACCb. *IB:* 32.

G104 BSc Mathematics with Extended Studies in Europe
Duration: 4FT Hon
Entry Requirements: *GCE:* ABC-ACCb. *IB:* 32.

G103 MSci Mathematics
Duration: 4FT Hon
Entry Requirements: *GCE:* AAB-ABBa. *IB:* 34.

R12 THE UNIVERSITY OF READING
THE UNIVERSITY OF READING
PO BOX 217
READING RG6 6AH
t: 0118 378 8619 f: 0118 378 8924
e: student.recruitment@reading.ac.uk
// www.reading.ac.uk

G100 BSc Mathematics
Duration: 3FT Hon
Entry Requirements: *GCE:* 320-340.

G103 MMath Mathematics (MMath) (4 years)
Duration: 4FT Hon
Entry Requirements: *GCE:* 340. *SQAH:* AABBB. *SQAAH:* AAB. *BTEC Dip:* DD. *BTEC ExtDip:* DDD. *OCR ND:* D *OCR NED:* M3

R72 ROYAL HOLLOWAY, UNIVERSITY OF LONDON
ROYAL HOLLOWAY, UNIVERSITY OF LONDON
EGHAM
SURREY TW20 0EX
t: 01784 414944 f: 01784 473662
e: Admissions@rhul.ac.uk
// www.rhul.ac.uk

G100 BSc Mathematics
Duration: 3FT Hon
Entry Requirements: *IB:* 35.

G108 BSc Science Foundation - Option: Mathematics
Duration: 4FT Hon
Entry Requirements: Contact the institution for details.

G103 MSci Mathematics
Duration: 4FT Hon
Entry Requirements: *IB:* 35.

S03 THE UNIVERSITY OF SALFORD
SALFORD M5 4WT
t: 0161 295 4545 f: 0161 295 4646
e: ug-admissions@salford.ac.uk
// www.salford.ac.uk

G100 BSc Mathematics
Duration: 3FT Hon
Entry Requirements: *GCE:* 300. *IB:* 35.

S18 THE UNIVERSITY OF SHEFFIELD
THE UNIVERSITY OF SHEFFIELD
LEVEL 2, ARTS TOWER
WESTERN BANK
SHEFFIELD S10 2TN
t: 0114 222 8030 f: 0114 222 8032
// www.sheffield.ac.uk

G100 BSc Mathematics (3 years)
Duration: 3FT Hon
Entry Requirements: *GCE:* AAB. *SQAH:* AAABB. *SQAAH:* AB. *IB:* 35. *BTEC ExtDip:* DDD.

G103 MMath Mathematics
Duration: 4FT Hon
Entry Requirements: *GCE:* AAA. *SQAH:* AAAAB. *SQAAH:* AA. *IB:* 37. *BTEC ExtDip:* DDD.

G109 MMath Mathematics Foundation Year (4 or 5 years)
Duration: 4FT Hon
Entry Requirements: *GCE:* ABB. *SQAH:* BBBBB. *SQAAH:* BB. *IB:* 33.

G106 MMath Mathematics with Study Abroad
Duration: 4FT Hon
Entry Requirements: *GCE:* AAA. *SQAH:* AAAAB. *SQAAH:* AA. *IB:* 37. *BTEC ExtDip:* DDD.

G102 MMath Mathematics with Study in Europe (4 years)
Duration: 4FT Hon
Entry Requirements: *GCE:* AAB. *SQAH:* AAABB. *SQAAH:* AB. *IB:* 35. *BTEC ExtDip:* DDD.

S21 SHEFFIELD HALLAM UNIVERSITY
CITY CAMPUS
HOWARD STREET
SHEFFIELD S1 1WB
t: 0114 225 5555 f: 0114 225 2167
e: admissions@shu.ac.uk
// www.shu.ac.uk

G100 BSc Mathematics
Duration: 3FT Hon
Entry Requirements: *GCE:* 280.

S27 UNIVERSITY OF SOUTHAMPTON
HIGHFIELD
SOUTHAMPTON SO17 1BJ
t: 023 8059 4732 f: 023 8059 3037
e: admissions@soton.ac.uk
// www.southampton.ac.uk

G100 BSc Mathematics
Duration: 3FT Hon
Entry Requirements: *GCE:* AAA-AAB. *SQAH:* AAAAA. *SQAAH:* AA. *IB:* 36.

G103 MMath Mathematics (4 years)
Duration: 4FT Hon
Entry Requirements: *GCE:* AAA-AAB. *SQAH:* AAAAA. *SQAAH:* AA. *IB:* 36.

S36 UNIVERSITY OF ST ANDREWS
ST KATHARINE'S WEST
16 THE SCORES
ST ANDREWS
FIFE KY16 9AX
t: 01334 462150 f: 01334 463330
e: admissions@st-andrews.ac.uk
// www.st-andrews.ac.uk

G101 BSc Mathematics
Duration: 4FT Hon
Entry Requirements: *GCE:* AAA. *SQAH:* AAAB. *IB:* 36.

G102 MA Mathematics
Duration: 4FT Hon
Entry Requirements: *GCE:* AAA. *SQAH:* AAAB. *IB:* 36.

G100 MMath Mathematics
Duration: 4FT Hon
Entry Requirements: *GCE:* AAA. *SQAH:* AAAB. *SQAAH:* BB. *IB:* 36.

S75 THE UNIVERSITY OF STIRLING
STUDENT RECRUITMENT & ADMISSIONS SERVICE
UNIVERSITY OF STIRLING
STIRLING
SCOTLAND FK9 4LA
t: 01786 467044 f: 01786 466800
e: admissions@stir.ac.uk
// www.stir.ac.uk

G100 BSc Mathematics (3-year degree only)
Duration: 3FT Deg
Entry Requirements: *GCE:* BBC. *SQAH:* BBBB. *SQAAH:* AAA-CCC. *IB:* 32. *BTEC ExtDip:* DMM.

S78 THE UNIVERSITY OF STRATHCLYDE
GLASGOW G1 1XQ
t: 0141 552 4400 f: 0141 552 0775
// www.strath.ac.uk

G100 BSc Mathematics (a)
Duration: 4FT Hon
Entry Requirements: *GCE:* AAB-BBB. *SQAH:* ABBBC-ABBB. *IB:* 32.

G101 MMath Mathematics(a)
Duration: 5FT Hon
Entry Requirements: *GCE:* AAA-ABB. *SQAH:* AAABBB-AAAB. *IB:* 36.

S85 UNIVERSITY OF SURREY
STAG HILL
GUILDFORD
SURREY GU2 7XH
t: +44(0)1483 689305 f: +44(0)1483 689388
e: ugteam@surrey.ac.uk
// www.surrey.ac.uk

G101 BSc Mathematics (3 years)
Duration: 3FT Hon
Entry Requirements: *GCE:* 340. Interview required.

G102 BSc Mathematics (4 years)
Duration: 4SW Hon
Entry Requirements: *GCE:* 340. Interview required.

G100 MMath Mathematics (MMath) (4 years)
Duration: 4SW Hon
Entry Requirements: *GCE:* 360. Interview required.

G104 MMath Mathematics (MMath) (4 years)
Duration: 4FT Hon
Entry Requirements: *GCE:* 360. Interview required.

G103 MMath Mathematics (MMath) (5 years)
Duration: 5SW Hon
Entry Requirements: *GCE:* 360.

S90 UNIVERSITY OF SUSSEX
UNDERGRADUATE ADMISSIONS
SUSSEX HOUSE
UNIVERSITY OF SUSSEX
BRIGHTON BN1 9RH
t: 01273 678416 f: 01273 678545
e: ug.applicants@sussex.ac.uk
// www.sussex.ac.uk

G100 BSc Mathematics
Duration: 3FT Hon
Entry Requirements: *GCE:* AAA-AAB. *SQAH:* AAAAA-AAABB.
SQAAH: AAB. *IB:* 35. *BTEC SubDip:* D. *BTEC Dip:* DD. *BTEC ExtDip:* DDD. *OCR ND:* D *OCR NED:* D1

G103 MMath Mathematics
Duration: 4FT Hon
Entry Requirements: *GCE:* AAA. *SQAH:* AAAAA. *SQAAH:* AAA. *IB:* 35. *BTEC SubDip:* D. *BTEC Dip:* DD. *BTEC ExtDip:* DDD. *OCR ND:* D *OCR NED:* D1

S93 SWANSEA UNIVERSITY
SINGLETON PARK
SWANSEA SA2 8PP
t: 01792 295111 f: 01792 295110
e: admissions@swansea.ac.uk
// www.swansea.ac.uk

G100 BSc Mathematics
Duration: 3FT Hon
Entry Requirements: *GCE:* ABB. *IB:* 33.

GR12 BSc Mathematics and German
Duration: 4FT Hon
Entry Requirements: *GCE:* ABB. *IB:* 33.

G103 MMath Mathematics
Duration: 4FT Hon
Entry Requirements: *GCE:* AAB. *IB:* 34.

U80 UNIVERSITY COLLEGE LONDON (UNIVERSITY OF LONDON)
GOWER STREET
LONDON WC1E 6BT
t: 020 7679 3000 f: 020 7679 3001
// www.ucl.ac.uk

G100 BSc Mathematics
Duration: 3FT Hon
Entry Requirements: *GCE:* A*A*Ae-A*AAe. *SQAAH:* AAA. Interview required. Admissions Test required.

G107 MSci Mathematics
Duration: 4FT Hon
Entry Requirements: *GCE:* A*A*Ae-A*AAe. *SQAAH:* AAA. Interview required. Admissions Test required.

W20 THE UNIVERSITY OF WARWICK
COVENTRY CV4 8UW
t: 024 7652 3723 f: 024 7652 4649
e: ugadmissions@warwick.ac.uk
// www.warwick.ac.uk

G100 BSc Mathematics
Duration: 3FT Hon
Entry Requirements: *GCE:* A*A*Aa-A*AA. *SQAH:* AAABB. *SQAAH:* AA. *IB:* 39.

G103 MMath Mathematics
Duration: 4FT Hon
Entry Requirements: *GCE:* A*A*Aa-A*AA. *SQAH:* AAABB. *SQAAH:* AA. *IB:* 39.

W75 UNIVERSITY OF WOLVERHAMPTON
ADMISSIONS UNIT
MX207, CAMP STREET
WOLVERHAMPTON
WEST MIDLANDS WV1 1AD
t: 01902 321000 f: 01902 321896
e: admissions@wlv.ac.uk
// www.wlv.ac.uk

G100 BSc Mathematics
Duration: 3FT/4SW Hon
Entry Requirements: *GCE:* 160-220.

Y50 THE UNIVERSITY OF YORK
STUDENT RECRUITMENT AND ADMISSIONS
UNIVERSITY OF YORK
HESLINGTON
YORK YO10 5DD
t: 01904 324000 f: 01904 323538
e: ug-admissions@york.ac.uk
// www.york.ac.uk

G100 BA/BSc Mathematics
Duration: 3FT Hon
Entry Requirements: *GCE:* AAA-AAB. *SQAH:* AAAAA-AAAAB. *SQAAH:* AA-AB. *IB:* 36.

G101 BA/BSc Mathematics with a year in Europe (4 years)
Duration: 4FT Hon
Entry Requirements: *GCE:* AAA-AAB. *SQAH:* AAAAA. *SQAAH:* AA. *IB:* 36.

G102 MMath Mathematics (4 years)
Duration: 4FT Hon
Entry Requirements: *GCE:* AAA-AAB. *SQAH:* AAAAA-AAAAB. *SQAAH:* AA-AB. *IB:* 36. *BTEC ExtDip:* DDD.

PURE MATHEMATICS

A40 ABERYSTWYTH UNIVERSITY
ABERYSTWYTH UNIVERSITY, WELCOME CENTRE
PENGLAIS CAMPUS
ABERYSTWYTH
CEREDIGION SY23 3FB
t: 01970 622021 f: 01970 627410
e: ug-admissions@aber.ac.uk
// www.aber.ac.uk

G130 BSc Applied Mathematics/Pure Mathematics
Duration: 3FT Hon
Entry Requirements: *GCE:* 320. *IB:* 27.

GGC3 BSc Pure Mathematics/Statistics
Duration: 3FT Hon
Entry Requirements: *GCE:* 320. *IB:* 27.

B32 THE UNIVERSITY OF BIRMINGHAM
EDGBASTON
BIRMINGHAM B15 2TT
t: 0121 415 8900 f: 0121 414 7159
e: admissions@bham.ac.uk
// www.birmingham.ac.uk

GG1L BSc Pure Mathematics and Computer Science (with an Industrial Year)
Duration: 4FT Hon
Entry Requirements: Contact the institution for details.

GI1C MSci Pure Mathematics and Computer Science
Duration: 4FT Hon
Entry Requirements: *GCE:* A*AA. *SQAH:* AAAAA. *SQAAH:* AA.

GGL1 MSci Pure Mathematics and Computer Science (with an Industrial Year)
Duration: 5FT Hon
Entry Requirements: Contact the institution for details.

C15 CARDIFF UNIVERSITY
PO BOX 927
30-36 NEWPORT ROAD
CARDIFF CF24 0DE
t: 029 2087 9999 f: 029 2087 6138
e: admissions@cardiff.ac.uk
// www.cardiff.ac.uk

G111 BSc Mathematics and its Applications with Professional Placement
Duration: 4SW Hon
Entry Requirements: *GCE:* AAB. *SQAH:* AABBB. *SQAAH:* AABBB. *IB:* 34. *OCR ND:* D *OCR NED:* M2 Interview required.

G28 UNIVERSITY OF GLASGOW
71 SOUTHPARK AVENUE
UNIVERSITY OF GLASGOW
GLASGOW G12 8QQ
t: 0141 330 6062 f: 0141 330 2961
e: student.recruitment@glasgow.ac.uk
// www.glasgow.ac.uk

NG4D BSc Accounting and Pure Mathematics
Duration: 4FT Hon
Entry Requirements: *GCE:* AAB. *SQAH:* AAAABB-AAABB. *IB:* 34.

NG31 BSc Finance and Pure Mathematics
Duration: 4FT Hon
Entry Requirements: *GCE:* AAB. *SQAH:* AAAABB-AAABB. *IB:* 34.

G111 BSc Pure Mathematics
Duration: 4FT Hon
Entry Requirements: *GCE:* ABB. *SQAH:* AAAB-BBBB. *IB:* 32.

G113 BSc Pure Mathematics (Faster Route)
Duration: 3FT Hon
Entry Requirements: *GCE:* AAA. *SQAAH:* AAA. *IB:* 38.

GGCJ BSc Pure Mathematics and Statistics
Duration: 4FT Hon
Entry Requirements: *GCE:* ABB. *SQAH:* AAAB-BBBB. *IB:* 32.

GGDJ BSc Pure Mathematics and Statistics (Faster Route)
Duration: 3FT Hon
Entry Requirements: *GCE:* AAA. *SQAAH:* AAA. *IB:* 38.

G110 MSci Pure Mathematics
Duration: 5FT Hon
Entry Requirements: *GCE:* ABB. *SQAH:* AAAB-BBBB. *IB:* 32.

G112 MSci Pure Mathematics (Faster Route)
Duration: 4FT Hon
Entry Requirements: *GCE:* AAA. *SQAAH:* AAA. *IB:* 38.

GGDH MSci Pure Mathematics and Statistics
Duration: 5FT Hon
Entry Requirements: *GCE:* ABB. *SQAH:* AAAB-BBBB. *IB:* 32.

GG3C MSci Pure Mathematics and Statistics (Faster Route)
Duration: 4FT Hon
Entry Requirements: *GCE:* AAA. *SQAAH:* AAA. *IB:* 38.

I50 IMPERIAL COLLEGE LONDON
REGISTRY
SOUTH KENSINGTON CAMPUS
IMPERIAL COLLEGE LONDON
LONDON SW7 2AZ
t: 020 7589 5111 f: 020 7594 8004
// www.imperial.ac.uk

G125 BSc Mathematics (Pure Mathematics)
Duration: 3FT Hon
Entry Requirements: *GCE:* A*A*A. *SQAAH:* AAA. *IB:* 39.

IG11 MEng Mathematics and Computer Science (Pure Maths and Computational Logic)
Duration: 4FT Hon
Entry Requirements: Contact the institution for details.

L41 THE UNIVERSITY OF LIVERPOOL
THE FOUNDATION BUILDING
BROWNLOW HILL
LIVERPOOL L69 7ZX
t: 0151 794 2000 f: 0151 708 6502
e: ugrecruitment@liv.ac.uk
// www.liv.ac.uk

G110 BSc Pure Mathematics
Duration: 3FT Hon
Entry Requirements: *GCE:* ABB. *SQAAH:* ABB. *IB:* 33. Interview required.

O11 THE OPEN UNIVERSITY
PO BOX 197
MILTON KEYNES MK7 6BJ
t: +44 (0) 845 300 6090 f: +44 (0) 1908 654914
e: general-enquiries@open.ac.uk
// www8.open.ac.uk/choose/ou/ucas-ou

GBGI CertHE Mathematical Sciences
Duration: 2FT Cer
Entry Requirements: Contact the institution for details.

GAFH DipHE Mathematical Sciences
Duration: 4FT Dip
Entry Requirements: Contact the institution for details.

Q50 QUEEN MARY, UNIVERSITY OF LONDON
QUEEN MARY, UNIVERSITY OF LONDON
MILE END ROAD
LONDON E1 4NS
t: 020 7882 5555 f: 020 7882 5500
e: admissions@qmul.ac.uk
// www.qmul.ac.uk

G110 BSc Pure Mathematics
Duration: 3FT Hon
Entry Requirements: *GCE:* 340. *IB:* 36.

S36 UNIVERSITY OF ST ANDREWS
ST KATHARINE'S WEST
16 THE SCORES
ST ANDREWS
FIFE KY16 9AX
t: 01334 462150 f: 01334 463330
e: admissions@st-andrews.ac.uk
// www.st-andrews.ac.uk

G110 MMath Pure Mathematics
Duration: 4FT Hon
Entry Requirements: *GCE:* AAA. *SQAH:* AAAB. *SQAAH:* BB. *IB:* 36.

S93 SWANSEA UNIVERSITY
SINGLETON PARK
SWANSEA SA2 8PP
t: 01792 295111 f: 01792 295110
e: admissions@swansea.ac.uk
// www.swansea.ac.uk

G110 BSc Pure Mathematics
Duration: 3FT Hon
Entry Requirements: *GCE:* ABB. *IB:* 33.

APPLIED MATHEMATICS

A20 THE UNIVERSITY OF ABERDEEN
UNIVERSITY OFFICE
KING'S COLLEGE
ABERDEEN AB24 3FX
t: +44 (0) 1224 273504 f: +44 (0) 1224 272034
e: sras@abdn.ac.uk
// www.abdn.ac.uk/sras

G120 BSc Applied Mathematics
Duration: 4FT Hon
Entry Requirements: *GCE:* BBB. *SQAH:* BBBB. *SQAAH:* BCC. *IB:* 28.

G122 MA Applied Mathematics
Duration: 4FT/3FT Hon/Ord
Entry Requirements: Contact the institution for details.

A40 ABERYSTWYTH UNIVERSITY
ABERYSTWYTH UNIVERSITY, WELCOME CENTRE
PENGLAIS CAMPUS
ABERYSTWYTH
CEREDIGION SY23 3FB
t: 01970 622021 f: 01970 627410
e: ug-admissions@aber.ac.uk
// www.aber.ac.uk

GG13 BSc Applied Mathematics/Statistics
Duration: 3FT Hon
Entry Requirements: *GCE:* 320. *IB:* 27.

B32 THE UNIVERSITY OF BIRMINGHAM
EDGBASTON
BIRMINGHAM B15 2TT
t: 0121 415 8900 f: 0121 414 7159
e: admissions@bham.ac.uk
// www.birmingham.ac.uk

F3DG MSci Theoretical Physics and Applied Mathematics
Duration: 4FT Hon
Entry Requirements: *GCE:* A*AA. *SQAH:* AAAAA. *SQAAH:* AA.

C15 CARDIFF UNIVERSITY
PO BOX 927
30-36 NEWPORT ROAD
CARDIFF CF24 0DE
t: 029 2087 9999 f: 029 2087 6138
e: admissions@cardiff.ac.uk
// www.cardiff.ac.uk

G120 BSc Mathematics and its Applications
Duration: 3FT Hon
Entry Requirements: *GCE:* AAB. *SQAH:* AABBB. *SQAAH:* AABBB.
IB: 34. *OCR ND:* D *OCR NED:* M2 Interview required.

C85 COVENTRY UNIVERSITY
THE STUDENT CENTRE
COVENTRY UNIVERSITY
1 GULSON RD
COVENTRY CV1 2JH
t: 024 7615 2222 f: 024 7615 2223
e: studentenquiries@coventry.ac.uk
// www.coventry.ac.uk

G120 BSc Applied Mathematics and Theoretical Physics
Duration: 3FT/4SW Hon
Entry Requirements: *GCE:* BCC. *SQAH:* BCCCC. *IB:* 28.

D39 UNIVERSITY OF DERBY
KEDLESTON ROAD
DERBY DE22 1GB
t: 01332 591167 f: 01332 597724
e: askadmissions@derby.ac.uk
// www.derby.ac.uk

G120 BSc Mathematics
Duration: 3FT Hon
Entry Requirements: *GCE:* 280. *IB:* 28. *BTEC Dip:* D*D*. *BTEC ExtDip:* DMM. *OCR NED:* M2

E56 THE UNIVERSITY OF EDINBURGH
STUDENT RECRUITMENT & ADMISSIONS
57 GEORGE SQUARE
EDINBURGH EH8 9JU
t: 0131 650 4360 f: 0131 651 1236
e: sra.enquiries@ed.ac.uk
// www.ed.ac.uk/studying/undergraduate/

G120 BSc Applied Mathematics
Duration: 4FT Hon
Entry Requirements: *GCE:* AAA-ABB. *SQAH:* AAAA-ABBB.

G14 UNIVERSITY OF GLAMORGAN, CARDIFF AND PONTYPRIDD
ENQUIRIES AND ADMISSIONS UNIT
PONTYPRIDD CF37 1DL
t: 08456 434030 f: 01443 654050
e: enquiries@glam.ac.uk
// www.glam.ac.uk

CFG0 FYr Science Foundation Year
Duration: 1FT FYr
Entry Requirements: *GCE:* 40. *IB:* 24. *BTEC Dip:* MM. *BTEC ExtDip:* MPP. Interview required.

G28 UNIVERSITY OF GLASGOW
71 SOUTHPARK AVENUE
UNIVERSITY OF GLASGOW
GLASGOW G12 8QQ
t: 0141 330 6062 f: 0141 330 2961
e: student.recruitment@glasgow.ac.uk
// www.glasgow.ac.uk

NG41 BSc Accounting and Applied Mathematics
Duration: 4FT Hon
Entry Requirements: *GCE:* AAB. *SQAH:* AAAABB-AAABB. *IB:* 34.

G122 BSc Applied Mathematics
Duration: 4FT Hon
Entry Requirements: *GCE:* ABB. *SQAH:* AAAB-BBBB. *IB:* 32.

G123 BSc Applied Mathematics (Faster Route)
Duration: 3FT Hon
Entry Requirements: *GCE:* AAA. *SQAAH:* AAA. *IB:* 38.

GN12 BSc Applied Mathematics and Business & Management
Duration: 4FT Hon
Entry Requirements: *GCE:* ABB. *SQAH:* AAAB-BBBB. *IB:* 32.

GF1C BSc Applied Mathematics and Chemistry
Duration: 4FT Hon
Entry Requirements: *GCE:* ABB. *SQAH:* AAAB-BBBB. *IB:* 32.

GG41 BSc Applied Mathematics and Computing Science
Duration: 4FT Hon
Entry Requirements: *GCE:* ABB. *SQAH:* AAAB-BBBB. *IB:* 32.

GF18 BSc Applied Mathematics and Geography
Duration: 4FT Hon
Entry Requirements: *GCE:* ABB. *SQAH:* AAAB-BBBB. *IB:* 32.

GVC5 BSc Applied Mathematics and Philosophy
Duration: 4FT Hon
Entry Requirements: *GCE:* ABB. *SQAH:* AAAB-BBBB. *IB:* 32.

GC18 BSc Applied Mathematics and Psychology
Duration: 4FT Hon
Entry Requirements: *GCE:* ABB. *SQAH:* AAAA-AABB. *IB:* 36.

GG1J BSc Applied Mathematics and Statistics (Faster Route)
Duration: 3FT Hon
Entry Requirements: *GCE:* AAA. *SQAAH:* AAA. *IB:* 38.

GN13 BSc Finance and Applied Mathematics
Duration: 4FT Hon
Entry Requirements: *GCE:* AAB. *SQAH:* AAAABB-AAABB. *IB:* 34.

G120 MSci Applied Mathematics
Duration: 5FT Hon
Entry Requirements: *GCE:* ABB. *SQAH:* AAAB-BBBB. *IB:* 32.

G124 MSci Applied Mathematics (Faster Route)
Duration: 4FT Hon
Entry Requirements: *GCE:* AAA. *SQAAH:* AAA. *IB:* 38.

FGN1 MSci Applied Mathematics and Astronomy
Duration: 5FT Hon
Entry Requirements: *GCE:* ABB. *SQAH:* AAAB-BBBB. *IB:* 32.

GF1D MSci Applied Mathematics and Chemistry
Duration: 5FT Hon
Entry Requirements: *GCE:* ABB. *SQAH:* AAAB-BBBB. *IB:* 32.

GG14 MSci Applied Mathematics and Computing Science
Duration: 5FT Hon
Entry Requirements: *GCE:* ABB. *SQAH:* AAAB-BBBB. *IB:* 32.

GFC3 MSci Applied Mathematics and Physics
Duration: 5FT Hon
Entry Requirements: *GCE:* ABB. *SQAH:* AAAB-BBBB. *IB:* 32.

GGD3 MSci Applied Mathematics and Statistics
Duration: 5FT Hon
Entry Requirements: *GCE:* ABB. *SQAH:* AAAB-BBBB. *IB:* 32.

GGCH MSci Applied Mathematics and Statistics (Faster Route)
Duration: 4FT Hon
Entry Requirements: *GCE:* AAA. *SQAAH:* AAA. *IB:* 38.

L75 LONDON SOUTH BANK UNIVERSITY
ADMISSIONS AND RECRUITMENT CENTRE
90 LONDON ROAD
LONDON SE1 6LN
t: 0800 923 8888 f: 020 7815 8273
e: course.enquiry@lsbu.ac.uk
// www.lsbu.ac.uk

CFG0 BSc Applied Science
Duration: 3FT/4SW Hon
Entry Requirements: *GCE:* 200. *IB:* 24.

N84 THE UNIVERSITY OF NOTTINGHAM
THE ADMISSIONS OFFICE
THE UNIVERSITY OF NOTTINGHAM
UNIVERSITY PARK
NOTTINGHAM NG7 2RD
t: 0115 951 5151 f: 0115 951 4668
// www.nottingham.ac.uk

G120 BSc Financial Mathematics
Duration: 3FT Hon
Entry Requirements: *GCE:* AAA-A*AB. *SQAAH:* AAA. *IB:* 38.

S27 UNIVERSITY OF SOUTHAMPTON
HIGHFIELD
SOUTHAMPTON SO17 1BJ
t: 023 8059 4732 f: 023 8059 3037
e: admissions@soton.ac.uk
// www.southampton.ac.uk

G120 BSc Mathematical Studies
Duration: 3FT Hon
Entry Requirements: *GCE:* AAA-AAB. *SQAH:* AAAAA. *SQAAH:* AA. *IB:* 36.

S36 UNIVERSITY OF ST ANDREWS
ST KATHARINE'S WEST
16 THE SCORES
ST ANDREWS
FIFE KY16 9AX
t: 01334 462150 f: 01334 463330
e: admissions@st-andrews.ac.uk
// www.st-andrews.ac.uk

G120 MMath Applied Mathematics
Duration: 4FT Hon
Entry Requirements: *GCE:* AAA. *SQAH:* AAAB. *SQAAH:* BB. *IB:* 36.

S75 THE UNIVERSITY OF STIRLING
STUDENT RECRUITMENT & ADMISSIONS SERVICE
UNIVERSITY OF STIRLING
STIRLING
SCOTLAND FK9 4LA
t: 01786 467044 f: 01786 466800
e: admissions@stir.ac.uk
// www.stir.ac.uk

G120 BSc Mathematics and its Applications
Duration: 4FT Hon
Entry Requirements: *GCE:* BBC. *SQAH:* BBBB. *SQAAH:* AAA-CCC.
IB: 32. *BTEC ExtDip:* DMM.

S93 SWANSEA UNIVERSITY
SINGLETON PARK
SWANSEA SA2 8PP
t: 01792 295111 f: 01792 295110
e: admissions@swansea.ac.uk
// www.swansea.ac.uk

G120 BSc Applied Mathematics
Duration: 3FT Hon
Entry Requirements: *GCE:* ABB. *IB:* 33.

NUMERICAL ANALYSIS

B16 UNIVERSITY OF BATH
CLAVERTON DOWN
BATH BA2 7AY
t: 01225 383019 f: 01225 386366
e: admissions@bath.ac.uk
// www.bath.ac.uk

G141 BSc Mathematical Sciences (Sandwich)
Duration: 4SW Hon
Entry Requirements: *GCE:* A*AA-A*AB. *SQAAH:* AAA. *IB:* 38.

O66 OXFORD BROOKES UNIVERSITY
ADMISSIONS OFFICE
HEADINGTON CAMPUS
GIPSY LANE
OXFORD OX3 0BP
t: 01865 483040 f: 01865 483983
e: admissions@brookes.ac.uk
// www.brookes.ac.uk

G140 BSc Mathematical Sciences
Duration: 3FT Hon
Entry Requirements: *GCE:* BCC. *IB:* 30.

S90 UNIVERSITY OF SUSSEX
UNDERGRADUATE ADMISSIONS
SUSSEX HOUSE
UNIVERSITY OF SUSSEX
BRIGHTON BN1 9RH
t: 01273 678416 f: 01273 678545
e: ug.applicants@sussex.ac.uk
// www.sussex.ac.uk

G140 BSc Mathematics (with a foundation year)
Duration: 4FT Hon
Entry Requirements: *GCE:* CD. *SQAH:* CCCDD. *IB:* 28.

MATHEMATICAL MODELLING

L23 UNIVERSITY OF LEEDS
THE UNIVERSITY OF LEEDS
WOODHOUSE LANE
LEEDS LS2 9JT
t: 0113 343 3999
e: admissions@leeds.ac.uk
// www.leeds.ac.uk

G150 BSc Mathematical Studies
Duration: 3FT Hon
Entry Requirements: *GCE:* AAB. *SQAAH:* AAB. *IB:* 34.

N21 NEWCASTLE UNIVERSITY
KING'S GATE
NEWCASTLE UPON TYNE NE1 7RU
t: 01912083333
// www.ncl.ac.uk

GN13 BSc Financial Mathematics
Duration: 3FT Hon
Entry Requirements: *GCE:* AAB. *SQAAH:* AB.

G1NF BSc Financial Mathematics with Management
Duration: 3FT Hon
Entry Requirements: *GCE:* AAB. *SQAAH:* AB.

ENGINEERING/INDUSTRIAL MATHEMATICS

A20 THE UNIVERSITY OF ABERDEEN
UNIVERSITY OFFICE
KING'S COLLEGE
ABERDEEN AB24 3FX
t: +44 (0) 1224 273504 f: +44 (0) 1224 272034
e: sras@abdn.ac.uk
// www.abdn.ac.uk/sras

G190 BSc Mathematics and Engineering Mathematics
Duration: 4FT Hon
Entry Requirements: *GCE:* 240. *SQAH:* BBBB. *SQAAH:* BCC. *IB:* 28.

B78 UNIVERSITY OF BRISTOL
UNDERGRADUATE ADMISSIONS OFFICE
SENATE HOUSE
TYNDALL AVENUE
BRISTOL BS8 1TH
t: 0117 928 9000 f: 0117 331 7391
e: ug-admissions@bristol.ac.uk
// www.bristol.ac.uk

G162 BEng Engineering Mathematics
Duration: 3FT Hon
Entry Requirements: Contact the institution for details.

G161 MEng Engineering Mathematics
Duration: 4FT Hon
Entry Requirements: *GCE:* A*AB-AAA. *SQAH:* AAAAA. *SQAAH:* AA.

G160 MEng Engineering Mathematics with Study Abroad
Duration: 4FT Hon
Entry Requirements: *GCE:* A*AB-AAA. *SQAH:* AAAAA. *SQAAH:* AA.

P80 UNIVERSITY OF PORTSMOUTH
ACADEMIC REGISTRY
UNIVERSITY HOUSE
WINSTON CHURCHILL AVENUE
PORTSMOUTH PO1 2UP
t: 023 9284 8484 f: 023 9284 3082
e: admissions@port.ac.uk
// www.port.ac.uk

G161 BSc Mathematics for Finance and Management
Duration: 3FT/4SW Hon
Entry Requirements: *GCE:* 260-300. *IB:* 26. *BTEC SubDip:* P. *BTEC Dip:* PP. *BTEC ExtDip:* DMM.

OPERATIONAL RESEARCH

A20 THE UNIVERSITY OF ABERDEEN
UNIVERSITY OFFICE
KING'S COLLEGE
ABERDEEN AB24 3FX
t: +44 (0) 1224 273504 f: +44 (0) 1224 272034
e: sras@abdn.ac.uk
// www.abdn.ac.uk/sras

F390 MPhys Physics with Complex Systems Modelling
Duration: 5FT Hon
Entry Requirements: *GCE:* ABB. *SQAH:* AABB. *IB:* 32.

C15 CARDIFF UNIVERSITY
PO BOX 927
30-36 NEWPORT ROAD
CARDIFF CF24 0DE
t: 029 2087 9999 f: 029 2087 6138
e: admissions@cardiff.ac.uk
// www.cardiff.ac.uk

G991 BSc Mathematics, Operational Research and Statistics
Duration: 3FT Hon
Entry Requirements: *GCE:* AAB. *SQAH:* AABBB. *SQAAH:* AABBB. *IB:* 34. *OCR ND:* D *OCR NED:* M2 Interview required.

G990 BSc Mathematics,Operational Research & Statistics with Professional Placement
Duration: 4SW Hon
Entry Requirements: *GCE:* AAB. *SQAH:* AABBB. *SQAAH:* AABBB. *IB:* 34. *OCR ND:* D *OCR NED:* M2 Interview required.

G14 UNIVERSITY OF GLAMORGAN, CARDIFF AND PONTYPRIDD
ENQUIRIES AND ADMISSIONS UNIT
PONTYPRIDD CF37 1DL
t: 08456 434030 f: 01443 654050
e: enquiries@glam.ac.uk
// www.glam.ac.uk

G201 BSc Computing Mathematics
Duration: 3FT Hon
Entry Requirements: *GCE:* BBC. *IB:* 26. *BTEC SubDip:* M. *BTEC Dip:* DD. *BTEC ExtDip:* DMM. Interview required.

G70 UNIVERSITY OF GREENWICH
GREENWICH CAMPUS
OLD ROYAL NAVAL COLLEGE
PARK ROW
LONDON SE10 9LS
t: 020 8331 9000 f: 020 8331 8145
e: courseinfo@gre.ac.uk
// www.gre.ac.uk

G200 BSc Mathematics for Decision Science
Duration: 3FT/4SW Hon
Entry Requirements: *GCE:* 260. *IB:* 24.

K24 THE UNIVERSITY OF KENT
RECRUITMENT & ADMISSIONS OFFICE
REGISTRY
UNIVERSITY OF KENT
CANTERBURY, KENT CT2 7NZ
t: 01227 827272 f: 01227 827077
e: information@kent.ac.uk
// www.kent.ac.uk

NG1F BSc Business Information Technology with a year in Industry
Duration: 4SW Hon
Entry Requirements: *GCE:* 280. *IB:* 33. *OCR ND:* D *OCR NED:* M2

S27 UNIVERSITY OF SOUTHAMPTON
HIGHFIELD
SOUTHAMPTON SO17 1BJ
t: 023 8059 4732 f: 023 8059 3037
e: admissions@soton.ac.uk
// www.southampton.ac.uk

GL12 BSc Mathematics, Operational Research, Statistics and Economics
Duration: 3FT Hon
Entry Requirements: *GCE:* AAA-AAB. *SQAH:* AAAAA. *SQAAH:* AA. *IB:* 36.

S78 THE UNIVERSITY OF STRATHCLYDE
GLASGOW G1 1XQ
t: 0141 552 4400 f: 0141 552 0775
// www.strath.ac.uk

NG42 BA Accounting and Business Technology
Duration: 4FT Hon
Entry Requirements: *GCE:* AAA. *SQAH:* AAAAAB-AAAA. *IB:* 36.

GN24 BA Accounting and Management Science
Duration: 4FT Hon
Entry Requirements: *GCE:* AAA. *SQAH:* AAAAAB-AAAA. *IB:* 36.

NG12 BA Business Enterprise and Business Technology
Duration: 4FT Hon
Entry Requirements: *GCE:* AAB. *SQAH:* AAAABB-AAAB. *IB:* 36.

G290 BA Business Technology
Duration: 4FT Hon
Entry Requirements: *GCE:* AAB. *SQAH:* AAAABB-AAAB. *IB:* 36.

GL21 BA Business Technology and Economics
Duration: 4FT Hon
Entry Requirements: *GCE:* AAB. *SQAH:* AAAABB-AAAB. *IB:* 36.

GN23 BA Business Technology and Finance
Duration: 4FT Hon
Entry Requirements: *GCE:* AAB. *SQAH:* AAAABB-AAAB. *IB:* 36.

GN26 BA Business Technology and Human Resource Management
Duration: 4FT Hon
Entry Requirements: *GCE:* AAB. *SQAH:* AAAABB-AAAB. *IB:* 36.

GN22 BA Business Technology and Management
Duration: 4FT Hon
Entry Requirements: *GCE:* AAB. *SQAH:* AAAABB-AAAB. *IB:* 36.

G291 BA Business Technology and Management Science
Duration: 4FT Hon
Entry Requirements: *GCE:* AAB. *SQAH:* AAAABB-AAAB. *IB:* 36.

GN25 BA Business Technology and Marketing
Duration: 4FT Hon
Entry Requirements: *GCE:* AAB. *SQAH:* AAAABB-AAAB. *IB:* 36.

LG12 BA Economics and Management Science
Duration: 4FT Hon
Entry Requirements: *GCE:* AAB. *SQAH:* AAAABB-AAAB. *IB:* 36.

NG32 BA Finance and Management Science
Duration: 4FT Hon
Entry Requirements: *GCE:* AAB. *SQAH:* AAAABB-AAAB. *IB:* 36.

NG62 BA Human Resource Management and Management Science
Duration: 4FT Hon
Entry Requirements: *GCE:* AAB. *SQAH:* AAAABB-AAAB. *IB:* 36.

G200 BA Management Science
Duration: 4FT Hon
Entry Requirements: *GCE:* AAB. *SQAH:* AAAABB-AAAB. *IB:* 36.

GM22 BA Management Science and Business Law
Duration: 4FT Hon
Entry Requirements: *GCE:* AAB. *SQAH:* AAAABB-AAAB. *IB:* 36.

NG52 BA Management Science and Marketing
Duration: 4FT Hon
Entry Requirements: *GCE:* AAB. *SQAH:* AAAABB-AAAB. *IB:* 36.

NG22 BA Management and Management Science
Duration: 4FT Hon
Entry Requirements: *GCE:* AAB. *SQAH:* AAAABB-AAAB. *IB:* 36.

U40 UNIVERSITY OF THE WEST OF SCOTLAND
PAISLEY
RENFREWSHIRE
SCOTLAND PA1 2BE
t: 0141 848 3727 f: 0141 848 3623
e: admissions@uws.ac.uk
// www.uws.ac.uk

G290 BSc Business Technology
Duration: 3FT/4FT/5SW Ord/Hon
Entry Requirements: *GCE:* CD. *SQAH:* BCC.

STATISTICS

A40 ABERYSTWYTH UNIVERSITY
ABERYSTWYTH UNIVERSITY, WELCOME CENTRE
PENGLAIS CAMPUS
ABERYSTWYTH
CEREDIGION SY23 3FB
t: 01970 622021 f: 01970 627410
e: ug-admissions@aber.ac.uk
// www.aber.ac.uk

F8G3 BSc Geography with Statistics
Duration: 3FT Hon
Entry Requirements: *GCE:* 300. *IB:* 28.

N4G3 BScEcon Accounting & Finance with Statistics
Duration: 3FT Hon
Entry Requirements: *GCE:* 300. *IB:* 27.

B16 UNIVERSITY OF BATH
CLAVERTON DOWN
BATH BA2 7AY
t: 01225 383019 f: 01225 386366
e: admissions@bath.ac.uk
// www.bath.ac.uk

GG13 BSc Mathematics and Statistics
Duration: 3FT Hon
Entry Requirements: *GCE:* A*AA-A*AB. *SQAAH:* AAA. *IB:* 38.

GG31 BSc Mathematics and Statistics (Sandwich)
Duration: 4SW Hon
Entry Requirements: *GCE:* A*AA-A*AB. *SQAAH:* AAA. *IB:* 38.

G300 BSc Statistics
Duration: 3FT Hon
Entry Requirements: *GCE:* A*AA-A*AB. *SQAAH:* AAA. *IB:* 38.

G301 BSc Statistics (Sandwich)
Duration: 4SW Hon
Entry Requirements: *GCE:* A*AA-A*AB. *SQAAH:* AAA. *IB:* 38.

B32 THE UNIVERSITY OF BIRMINGHAM
EDGBASTON
BIRMINGHAM B15 2TT
t: 0121 415 8900 f: 0121 414 7159
e: admissions@bham.ac.uk
// www.birmingham.ac.uk

LG13 BSc Mathematical Economics and Statistics
Duration: 3FT Hon
Entry Requirements: *GCE:* AAA. *SQAH:* AAABB. *SQAAH:* AA.

B78 UNIVERSITY OF BRISTOL
UNDERGRADUATE ADMISSIONS OFFICE
SENATE HOUSE
TYNDALL AVENUE
BRISTOL BS8 1TH
t: 0117 928 9000 f: 0117 331 7391
e: ug-admissions@bristol.ac.uk
// www.bristol.ac.uk

G1G3 BSc Mathematics with Statistics
Duration: 3FT Hon
Entry Requirements: *GCE:* A*AA. *SQAH:* AAAAA. *SQAAH:* AA.

G1GH MSci Mathematics with Statistics
Duration: 4FT Hon
Entry Requirements: *GCE:* A*AA. *SQAH:* AAAAA. *SQAAH:* AA.

B80 UNIVERSITY OF THE WEST OF ENGLAND, BRISTOL
FRENCHAY CAMPUS
COLDHARBOUR LANE
BRISTOL BS16 1QY
t: +44 (0)117 32 83333 f: +44 (0)117 32 82810
e: admissions@uwe.ac.uk
// www.uwe.ac.uk

G300 BSc Statistics
Duration: 3FT/4SW Hon
Entry Requirements: *GCE:* 300.

C60 CITY UNIVERSITY
NORTHAMPTON SQUARE
LONDON EC1V 0HB
t: 020 7040 5060 f: 020 7040 8995
e: ugadmissions@city.ac.uk
// www.city.ac.uk

G322 BSc Actuarial Science (3 years)
Duration: 3FT Hon
Entry Requirements: *GCE:* A*AA. *SQAH:* AAABB. *IB:* 35.

G320 BSc Actuarial Science (Foundation)
Duration: 4FT Hon
Entry Requirements: *GCE:* BBB. *IB:* 24.

G1G3 BSc Mathematical Science with Statistics (3 years or 4 year SW)
Duration: 3FT Hon
Entry Requirements: *GCE:* 360. *IB:* 32.

C85 COVENTRY UNIVERSITY
THE STUDENT CENTRE
COVENTRY UNIVERSITY
1 GULSON RD
COVENTRY CV1 2JH
t: 024 7615 2222 f: 024 7615 2223
e: studentenquiries@coventry.ac.uk
// www.coventry.ac.uk

GG13 BSc Mathematics and Statistics
Duration: 3FT/4SW Hon
Entry Requirements: *GCE:* CCC. *SQAH:* CCCCC. *IB:* 27.

E14 UNIVERSITY OF EAST ANGLIA
NORWICH NR4 7TJ
t: 01603 591515 f: 01603 591523
e: admissions@uea.ac.uk
// www.uea.ac.uk

G390 BSc Business Statistics
Duration: 3FT Hon   CRB Check: Required
Entry Requirements: *GCE:* AAB. *SQAH:* AAABB. *SQAAH:* AAB. *IB:* 33. *BTEC ExtDip:* DDD. Interview required.

E56 THE UNIVERSITY OF EDINBURGH
STUDENT RECRUITMENT & ADMISSIONS
57 GEORGE SQUARE
EDINBURGH EH8 9JU
t: 0131 650 4360 f: 0131 651 1236
e: sra.enquiries@ed.ac.uk
// www.ed.ac.uk/studying/undergraduate/

GG13 BSc Mathematics and Statistics
Duration: 4FT Hon
Entry Requirements: *GCE:* AAA-ABB. *SQAH:* AAAA-ABBB.

LG13 MA Economics and Statistics
Duration: 4FT Hon
Entry Requirements: *GCE:* AAA-ABC. *SQAH:* AAAA-ABBC. *IB:* 34.

G28 UNIVERSITY OF GLASGOW
71 SOUTHPARK AVENUE
UNIVERSITY OF GLASGOW
GLASGOW G12 8QQ
t: 0141 330 6062 f: 0141 330 2961
e: student.recruitment@glasgow.ac.uk
// www.glasgow.ac.uk

GN34 BSc Accounting and Statistics
Duration: 4FT Hon
Entry Requirements: *GCE:* AAB. *SQAH:* AAAABB-AAABB. *IB:* 34.

GG31 BSc Applied Mathematics and Statistics
Duration: 4FT Hon
Entry Requirements: *GCE:* ABB. *SQAH:* AAAB-BBBB. *IB:* 32.

GG34 BSc Computing Science/Statistics
Duration: 4FT Hon
Entry Requirements: *GCE:* ABB. *SQAH:* AAAB-BBBB. *IB:* 32.

GN33 BSc Finance and Statistics
Duration: 4FT Hon
Entry Requirements: *GCE:* AAB. *SQAH:* AAAABB-AAABB. *IB:* 34.

FG83 BSc Geography and Statistics
Duration: 4FT Hon
Entry Requirements: *GCE:* ABB. *SQAH:* AAAB-BBBB. *IB:* 32.

GG3D BSc Mathematical and Statistical Studies
Duration: 3FT Ord
Entry Requirements: *GCE:* ABB. *SQAH:* AAAB-BBBB. *IB:* 32.

GGC3 BSc Mathematics and Statistics
Duration: 4FT Hon
Entry Requirements: *GCE:* ABB. *SQAH:* AAAB-BBBB. *IB:* 32.

GG13 BSc Mathematics and Statistics (Faster Route)
Duration: 3FT Hon
Entry Requirements: *GCE:* AAA. *SQAAH:* AAA. *IB:* 38.

CG83 BSc Psychology/Statistics
Duration: 4FT Hon
Entry Requirements: *GCE:* ABB. *SQAH:* AAAA-AABB. *IB:* 36.

G300 BSc Statistics
Duration: 4FT Hon
Entry Requirements: *GCE:* ABB. *SQAH:* AAAB-BBBB. *IB:* 32.

G304 BSc Statistics (Faster Route)
Duration: 3FT Hon
Entry Requirements: *GCE:* AAA. *SQAAH:* AAA. *IB:* 38.

NG23 BSc Statistics and Business & Management
Duration: 4FT Hon
Entry Requirements: *GCE:* ABB. *SQAH:* AAAB-BBBB. *IB:* 32.

GL31 BSc Statistics and Economics
Duration: 4FT Hon
Entry Requirements: *GCE:* ABB. *SQAH:* AAAB-BBBB. *IB:* 32.

G301 MA Statistics
Duration: 4FT Hon
Entry Requirements: *GCE:* ABB. *SQAH:* AAAB-ABBB. *IB:* 36.

G305 MSc Statistics with Work Placement
Duration: 5FT Hon
Entry Requirements: Contact the institution for details.

GGH1 MSci Mathematics and Statistics
Duration: 5FT Hon
Entry Requirements: *GCE:* ABB. *SQAH:* AAAB-BBBB. *IB:* 32.

GG1H MSci Mathematics and Statistics (Faster Route)
Duration: 4FT Hon
Entry Requirements: *GCE:* AAA. *SQAAH:* AAA. *IB:* 38.

G302 MSci Statistics
Duration: 5FT Hon
Entry Requirements: *GCE:* ABB. *SQAH:* AAAB-BBBB. *IB:* 32.

G303 MSci Statistics (Faster Route)
Duration: 4FT Hon
Entry Requirements: *GCE:* AAA. *SQAAH:* AAA. *IB:* 38.

G70 UNIVERSITY OF GREENWICH
GREENWICH CAMPUS
OLD ROYAL NAVAL COLLEGE
PARK ROW
LONDON SE10 9LS
t: 020 8331 9000 f: 020 8331 8145
e: courseinfo@gre.ac.uk
// www.gre.ac.uk

G900 BSc Mathematics, Statistics and Computing
Duration: 3FT Hon
Entry Requirements: *GCE:* 260. *IB:* 24.

G311 BSc Statistics
Duration: 3FT Hon
Entry Requirements: *GCE:* 260. *IB:* 24.

H24 HERIOT-WATT UNIVERSITY, EDINBURGH
EDINBURGH CAMPUS
EDINBURGH EH14 4AS
t: 0131 449 5111 f: 0131 451 3630
e: ugadmissions@hw.ac.uk
// www.hw.ac.uk

GG13 BSc Actuarial Science
Duration: 3FT/4FT Hon
Entry Requirements: *GCE:* ABB. *SQAH:* AAAB. *SQAAH:* ABB. *IB:* 27.

GGC3 BSc Financial Mathematics
Duration: 4FT Hon
Entry Requirements: *GCE:* ABB. *SQAH:* AAAB. *SQAAH:* ABB. *IB:* 27.

GGD3 BSc Mathematical, Statistical and Actuarial Sciences
Duration: 3FT/4FT Hon
Entry Requirements: *GCE:* BBB. *SQAH:* ABBBC. *SQAAH:* BBB. *IB:* 28.

G1G3 BSc Mathematics with Statistics
Duration: 3FT/4FT Hon
Entry Requirements: *GCE:* BBB. *SQAH:* ABBBC. *SQAAH:* BBB. *IB:* 26.

G300 BSc Statistical Modelling
Duration: 4FT Hon
Entry Requirements: *GCE:* ABB. *SQAH:* AAAB. *SQAAH:* ABB. *IB:* 27.

I50 IMPERIAL COLLEGE LONDON
REGISTRY
SOUTH KENSINGTON CAMPUS
IMPERIAL COLLEGE LONDON
LONDON SW7 2AZ
t: 020 7589 5111 f: 020 7594 8004
// www.imperial.ac.uk

G1G3 BSc Mathematics with Statistics
Duration: 3FT Hon
Entry Requirements: *GCE:* A*A*A. *SQAAH:* AAA. *IB:* 39.

G1GH BSc Mathematics with Statistics for Finance
Duration: 3FT Hon
Entry Requirements: *GCE:* A*A*A. *SQAAH:* AAA. *IB:* 39.

GG31 BSc Mathematics, Optimisation and Statistics
Duration: 3FT Hon
Entry Requirements: *GCE:* A*A*A. *SQAAH:* AAA. *IB:* 39.

GI43 MEng Mathematics and Computer Science (Computational Statistics)
Duration: 4FT Hon
Entry Requirements: Contact the institution for details.

K24 THE UNIVERSITY OF KENT
RECRUITMENT & ADMISSIONS OFFICE
REGISTRY
UNIVERSITY OF KENT
CANTERBURY, KENT CT2 7NZ
t: 01227 827272 f: 01227 827077
e: information@kent.ac.uk
// www.kent.ac.uk

GG13 BSc Mathematics and Statistics (3 or 4 years)
Duration: 3FT/4SW Hon
Entry Requirements: *GCE:* 300. *IB:* 33. *OCR ND:* D *OCR NED:* M2

K84 KINGSTON UNIVERSITY
STUDENT INFORMATION & ADVICE CENTRE
COOPER HOUSE
40-46 SURBITON ROAD
KINGSTON UPON THAMES KT1 2HX
t: 0844 8552177 f: 020 8547 7080
e: aps@kingston.ac.uk
// www.kingston.ac.uk

GGCH BSc Actuarial Mathematics and Statistics (including year 0)
Duration: 4FT Hon
Entry Requirements: *GCE:* 80.

G6G3 BSc Games Technology with Statistics (including year 0)
Duration: 4FT Hon
Entry Requirements: *GCE:* 80.

G3N2 BSc Statistics with Business
Duration: 3FT Hon
Entry Requirements: *GCE:* 280.

G3NF BSc Statistics with Business
Duration: 4SW Hon
Entry Requirements: *GCE:* 280.

G3NG BSc Statistics with Business (Foundation)
Duration: 4FT Hon
Entry Requirements: *GCE:* 80.

L14 LANCASTER UNIVERSITY
THE UNIVERSITY
LANCASTER
LANCASHIRE LA1 4YW
t: 01524 592029 f: 01524 846243
e: ugadmissions@lancaster.ac.uk
// www.lancs.ac.uk

CG83 BSc Psychology and Statistics
Duration: 3FT Hon
Entry Requirements: *GCE:* AAB. *SQAH:* ABBBB. *SQAAH:* ABB. *IB:* 35.

G1G3 BSc/MSci Mathematics with Statistics
Duration: 3FT Hon
Entry Requirements: *GCE:* AAA. *SQAH:* AAABB. *SQAAH:* AAA. *IB:* 36.

G300 BSc/MSci Statistics
Duration: 3FT Hon
Entry Requirements: *GCE:* AAA. *SQAH:* AAABB. *SQAAH:* AAA. *IB:* 36.

G1GH MSci Mathematics with Statistics (Study Abroad)
Duration: 4FT Hon
Entry Requirements: *GCE:* AAA. *SQAH:* AAABB. *SQAAH:* AAA. *IB:* 36.

G301 MSci Statistics (Study Abroad)
Duration: 4FT Hon
Entry Requirements: *GCE:* AAA. *SQAH:* AAABB. *SQAAH:* AAA. *IB:* 36.

L23 UNIVERSITY OF LEEDS
THE UNIVERSITY OF LEEDS
WOODHOUSE LANE
LEEDS LS2 9JT
t: 0113 343 3999
e: admissions@leeds.ac.uk
// www.leeds.ac.uk

GG13 BSc Mathematics and Statistics
Duration: 3FT Hon
Entry Requirements: *GCE:* AAB. *SQAAH:* AAB. *IB:* 34.

GG1H MMath Mathematics and Statistics
Duration: 4FT Hon
Entry Requirements: Contact the institution for details.

L41 THE UNIVERSITY OF LIVERPOOL
THE FOUNDATION BUILDING
BROWNLOW HILL
LIVERPOOL L69 7ZX
t: 0151 794 2000 f: 0151 708 6502
e: ugrecruitment@liv.ac.uk
// www.liv.ac.uk

GG13 BSc Mathematics and Statistics
Duration: 3FT Hon
Entry Requirements: *GCE:* ABB. *SQAAH:* ABB. *IB:* 33. Interview required.

L68 LONDON METROPOLITAN UNIVERSITY
166-220 HOLLOWAY ROAD
LONDON N7 8DB
t: 020 7133 4200
e: admissions@londonmet.ac.uk
// www.londonmet.ac.uk

GG13 BSc Mathematics and Statistics
Duration: 3FT Hon
Entry Requirements: *GCE:* 200. *IB:* 28.

L72 LONDON SCHOOL OF ECONOMICS AND POLITICAL SCIENCE (UNIVERSITY OF LONDON)
HOUGHTON STREET
LONDON WC2A 2AE
t: 020 7955 7125 f: 020 7955 6001
e: ug.admissions@lse.ac.uk
// www.lse.ac.uk

G0N0 BSc Business Mathematics & Statistics
Duration: 3FT Hon
Entry Requirements: *GCE:* AAA. *SQAH:* AAAAA. *SQAAH:* AAA. *IB:* 38.

G3N3 BSc Statistics with Finance
Duration: 3FT Hon
Entry Requirements: *GCE:* AAA. *SQAH:* AAAAA. *SQAAH:* AAA. *IB:* 38.

L79 LOUGHBOROUGH UNIVERSITY
LOUGHBOROUGH
LEICESTERSHIRE LE11 3TU
t: 01509 223522 f: 01509 223905
e: admissions@lboro.ac.uk
// www.lboro.ac.uk

GG13 BSc Mathematics with Statistics
Duration: 3FT Hon
Entry Requirements: *GCE:* AAA-AAB. *SQAH:* BBBB. *SQAAH:* AAB. *IB:* 36.

GG1H BSc Mathematics with Statistics
Duration: 4SW Hon
Entry Requirements: *GCE:* AAA-AAB. *SQAH:* BBBB. *SQAAH:* AAB. *IB:* 36.

M20 THE UNIVERSITY OF MANCHESTER
RUTHERFORD BUILDING
OXFORD ROAD
MANCHESTER M13 9PL
t: 0161 275 2077 f: 0161 275 2106
e: ug-admissions@manchester.ac.uk
// www.manchester.ac.uk

GGC3 BSc Mathematics and Statistics
Duration: 3FT Hon
Entry Requirements: *GCE:* A*AB-AAB. *SQAH:* AAAAB. *SQAAH:* AAB. *IB:* 36. Interview required.

GG13 MMath Mathematics and Statistics
Duration: 4FT Hon
Entry Requirements: *GCE:* A*AB-AAB. *SQAH:* AAAAB. *SQAAH:* AAB. *IB:* 36. Interview required.

N21 NEWCASTLE UNIVERSITY
KING'S GATE
NEWCASTLE UPON TYNE NE1 7RU
t: 01912083333
// www.ncl.ac.uk

GG13 BSc Mathematics and Statistics
Duration: 3FT Hon
Entry Requirements: *GCE:* AAB. *SQAAH:* AB.

G300 BSc Statistics
Duration: 3FT Hon
Entry Requirements: *GCE:* AAB. *SQAAH:* AB.

GGC3 MMathStat Mathematics and Statistics (4 years)
Duration: 4FT Hon
Entry Requirements: *GCE:* AAB. *SQAAH:* AB.

O33 OXFORD UNIVERSITY
UNDERGRADUATE ADMISSIONS OFFICE
UNIVERSITY OF OXFORD
WELLINGTON SQUARE
OXFORD OX1 2JD
t: 01865 288000 f: 01865 270212
e: undergraduate.admissions@admin.ox.ac.uk
// www.admissions.ox.ac.uk

GG13 BA Mathematics and Statistics (3 or 4 years)
Duration: 3FT/4FT Hon
Entry Requirements: *GCE:* A*A*A. *SQAH:* AAAAA-AAAAB. *SQAAH:* AAB. Interview required. Admissions Test required.

O66 OXFORD BROOKES UNIVERSITY
ADMISSIONS OFFICE
HEADINGTON CAMPUS
GIPSY LANE
OXFORD OX3 0BP
t: 01865 483040 f: 01865 483983
e: admissions@brookes.ac.uk
// www.brookes.ac.uk

NG2H BA/BSc Business Management/Statistics
Duration: 3FT Hon
Entry Requirements: *GCE:* BCC.

BG13 BA/BSc Human Biosciences/Statistics
Duration: 3FT Hon
Entry Requirements: *GCE:* BCC.

GG13 BA/BSc Mathematics/Statistics
Duration: 3FT Hon
Entry Requirements: *GCE:* BBC. *IB:* 30.

GG4H BSc Computer Science/Statistics
Duration: 3FT Hon
Entry Requirements: *GCE:* BBC. *IB:* 30.

P60 PLYMOUTH UNIVERSITY
DRAKE CIRCUS
PLYMOUTH PL4 8AA
t: 01752 585858 f: 01752 588055
e: admissions@plymouth.ac.uk
// www.plymouth.ac.uk

G3N2 BSc Applied Statistics with Management
Duration: 1FT Hon
Entry Requirements: Contact the institution for details.

GG13 BSc Mathematics and Statistics
Duration: 3FT Hon
Entry Requirements: *GCE:* 320. *IB:* 30.

GGC3 BSc Mathematics and Statistics with Foundation Year
Duration: 4FT Hon
Entry Requirements: *GCE:* 180. *IB:* 24.

P80 UNIVERSITY OF PORTSMOUTH
ACADEMIC REGISTRY
UNIVERSITY HOUSE
WINSTON CHURCHILL AVENUE
PORTSMOUTH PO1 2UP
t: 023 9284 8484 f: 023 9284 3082
e: admissions@port.ac.uk
// www.port.ac.uk

GG13 BSc Mathematics with Statistics
Duration: 3FT/4SW Hon
Entry Requirements: *GCE:* 260-300. *IB:* 26. *BTEC SubDip:* P.
BTEC Dip: PP. *BTEC ExtDip:* DMM.

Q50 QUEEN MARY, UNIVERSITY OF LONDON
QUEEN MARY, UNIVERSITY OF LONDON
MILE END ROAD
LONDON E1 4NS
t: 020 7882 5555 f: 020 7882 5500
e: admissions@qmul.ac.uk
// www.qmul.ac.uk

GG31 BSc Mathematics and Statistics
Duration: 3FT Hon
Entry Requirements: *GCE:* 340. *IB:* 36.

G1G3 MSci Mathematics with Statistics
Duration: 4FT Hon
Entry Requirements: *GCE:* 360. *IB:* 36.

Q75 QUEEN'S UNIVERSITY BELFAST
UNIVERSITY ROAD
BELFAST BT7 1NN
t: 028 9097 3838 f: 028 9097 5151
e: admissions@qub.ac.uk
// www.qub.ac.uk

GG13 BSc Mathematics and Statistics & Operational Research
Duration: 3FT Hon
Entry Requirements: *GCE:* ABC-ACCb. *IB:* 32.

GGC3 MSci Mathematics and Statistics & Operational Research
Duration: 4FT Hon
Entry Requirements: *GCE:* AAB-ABBa. *IB:* 34.

R12 THE UNIVERSITY OF READING
THE UNIVERSITY OF READING
PO BOX 217
READING RG6 6AH
t: 0118 378 8619 f: 0118 378 8924
e: student.recruitment@reading.ac.uk
// www.reading.ac.uk

G301 BSc Applied Statistics
Duration: 4SW Hon
Entry Requirements: *GCE:* 320.

GN35 BSc Business Statistics and Marketing
Duration: 3FT Hon
Entry Requirements: *GCE:* 320.

GGC3 BSc Mathematics and Applied Statistics
Duration: 4SW Hon
Entry Requirements: *GCE:* 320-340.

GG13 BSc Mathematics and Statistics
Duration: 3FT Hon
Entry Requirements: *GCE:* 320-340.

G300 BSc Statistics
Duration: 3FT Hon
Entry Requirements: *GCE:* 320.

R72 ROYAL HOLLOWAY, UNIVERSITY OF LONDON
ROYAL HOLLOWAY, UNIVERSITY OF LONDON
EGHAM
SURREY TW20 0EX
t: 01784 414944 f: 01784 473662
e: Admissions@rhul.ac.uk
// www.rhul.ac.uk

G1G3 BSc Mathematics with Statistics
Duration: 3FT Hon
Entry Requirements: *IB:* 35.

S27 UNIVERSITY OF SOUTHAMPTON
HIGHFIELD
SOUTHAMPTON SO17 1BJ
t: 023 8059 4732 f: 023 8059 3037
e: admissions@soton.ac.uk
// www.southampton.ac.uk

G1G3 BSc Mathematics with Statistics
Duration: 3FT Hon
Entry Requirements: *GCE:* AAA-AAB. *SQAH:* AAAAA. *SQAAH:* AA.
IB: 36.

S36 UNIVERSITY OF ST ANDREWS
ST KATHARINE'S WEST
16 THE SCORES
ST ANDREWS
FIFE KY16 9AX
t: 01334 462150 f: 01334 463330
e: admissions@st-andrews.ac.uk
// www.st-andrews.ac.uk

CG13 BSc Biology and Statistics
Duration: 4FT Hon
Entry Requirements: *GCE:* AAA. *SQAH:* AAAB. *IB:* 36.

GG34 BSc Computer Science and Statistics
Duration: 4FT Hon
Entry Requirements: *GCE:* AAA. *SQAH:* AAAB. *IB:* 36.

GL31 BSc Economics and Statistics
Duration: 4FT Hon
Entry Requirements: *GCE:* AAA. *SQAH:* AAAB. *IB:* 38.

FG83 BSc Geography and Statistics
Duration: 4FT Hon
Entry Requirements: *GCE:* AAA. *SQAH:* AAAB. *IB:* 36.

GG3K BSc Internet Computer Science-Statistics
Duration: 4FT Hon
Entry Requirements: *GCE:* AAA. *SQAH:* AAAB. *IB:* 36.

GVH5 BSc Logic & Philosophy of Science and Statistics
Duration: 4FT Hon
Entry Requirements: *GCE:* AAA. *SQAH:* AAAB. *IB:* 36.

GN32 BSc Management Science and Statistics
Duration: 4FT Hon
Entry Requirements: *GCE:* AAA. *SQAH:* AAAA. *IB:* 38.

G301 BSc Statistics
Duration: 4FT Hon
Entry Requirements: *GCE:* AAA. *SQAH:* AAAB. *IB:* 36.

GLH1 MA Economics and Statistics
Duration: 4FT Hon
Entry Requirements: *GCE:* AAA. *SQAH:* AAAB. *IB:* 38.

GV35 MA Philosophy and Statistics
Duration: 4FT Hon
Entry Requirements: *GCE:* AAA. *SQAH:* AAAB. *IB:* 36.

G302 MA Statistics
Duration: 4FT Hon
Entry Requirements: *GCE:* AAA. *SQAH:* AAAB. *IB:* 36.

G300 MMath Statistics
Duration: 4FT Hon
Entry Requirements: *GCE:* AAA. *SQAH:* AAAB. *SQAAH:* BB. *IB:* 36.

S72 STAFFORDSHIRE UNIVERSITY
COLLEGE ROAD
STOKE ON TRENT ST4 2DE
t: 01782 292753 f: 01782 292740
e: admissions@staffs.ac.uk
// www.staffs.ac.uk

GG13 BSc Mathematics & Applied Statistics
Duration: 3FT/4SW Hon
Entry Requirements: *GCE:* 240-280. *IB:* 24.

S78 THE UNIVERSITY OF STRATHCLYDE
GLASGOW G1 1XQ
t: 0141 552 4400 f: 0141 552 0775
// www.strath.ac.uk

LG1C BA Economics, Mathematics and Statistics
Duration: 4FT Hon
Entry Requirements: *GCE:* AAB. *SQAH:* AAAABB-AAAB. *IB:* 36.

NG33 BA Finance, Mathematics and Statistics
Duration: 4FT Hon
Entry Requirements: *GCE:* AAB. *SQAH:* AAAABB-AAAB. *IB:* 36.

G000 BA Management Science, Mathematics and Statistics
Duration: 4FT Hon
Entry Requirements: *GCE:* AAB. *SQAH:* AAAABB-AAAB. *IB:* 36.

GN34 BSc Mathematics, Statistics and Accounting
Duration: 4FT Hon
Entry Requirements: *GCE:* AAB. *SQAH:* AAAABB-AAAA. *IB:* 36.

GN33 BSc Mathematics, Statistics and Finance
Duration: 4FT Hon
Entry Requirements: *GCE:* AAB-BBB. *SQAH:* ABBBC-ABBB. *IB:* 32.

S85 UNIVERSITY OF SURREY
STAG HILL
GUILDFORD
SURREY GU2 7XH
t: +44(0)1483 689305 f: +44(0)1483 689388
e: ugteam@surrey.ac.uk
// www.surrey.ac.uk

G1G3 BSc Mathematics with Statistics (3 years)
Duration: 3FT Hon
Entry Requirements: *GCE:* 340. Interview required.

G1GH BSc Mathematics with Statistics (4 years)
Duration: 4SW Hon
Entry Requirements: *GCE:* 340. Interview required.

www.ucas.com

at the heart of connecting people to higher education

S93 SWANSEA UNIVERSITY
SINGLETON PARK
SWANSEA SA2 8PP
t: 01792 295111 f: 01792 295110
e: admissions@swansea.ac.uk
// www.swansea.ac.uk

G3N3 BSc Actuarial Studies
Duration: 3FT Hon
Entry Requirements: *GCE:* ABB. *IB:* 33.

G3NH BSc Actuarial Studies (with a year abroad) (4 years)
Duration: 4FT Hon
Entry Requirements: *GCE:* ABB. *IB:* 33.

G3NK BSc Actuarial Studies with Accounting
Duration: 3FT Hon
Entry Requirements: *GCE:* ABB. *IB:* 33.

G3N4 BSc Actuarial Studies with Accounting with a year abroad
Duration: 4FT Hon
Entry Requirements: *GCE:* ABB. *IB:* 33.

U80 UNIVERSITY COLLEGE LONDON (UNIVERSITY OF LONDON)
GOWER STREET
LONDON WC1E 6BT
t: 020 7679 3000 f: 020 7679 3001
// www.ucl.ac.uk

GG13 BSc Mathematics and Statistical Science
Duration: 3FT Hon
Entry Requirements: *GCE:* A*A*Ae-A*AAe. *SQAAH:* AAA. Interview required. Admissions Test required.

G300 BSc Statistics
Duration: 3FT Hon
Entry Requirements: *GCE:* A*AAe-AAAe. *SQAAH:* AAA. Interview required.

GN32 BSc Statistics and Management for Business
Duration: 3FT Hon
Entry Requirements: *GCE:* A*AAe-AAAe. *SQAAH:* AAA. Interview required.

GLN0 BSc Statistics, Economics and Finance
Duration: 3FT Hon
Entry Requirements: *GCE:* A*AAe-AAAe. *SQAAH:* AAA. Interview required.

GLR0 BSc Statistics, Economics and a Language
Duration: 3FT Hon
Entry Requirements: *GCE:* A*AAe-AAAe. *SQAAH:* AAA. Interview required.

LG13 BScEcon Economics and Statistics
Duration: 3FT Hon
Entry Requirements: *GCE:* A*AAe-AAAe. *SQAAH:* AAA. Interview required.

GGC3 MSci Mathematics and Statistical Science
Duration: 4FT Hon
Entry Requirements: *GCE:* A*A*Ae-A*AAe. *SQAAH:* AAA. Interview required. Admissions Test required.

G305 MSci Statistical Science (International Programme)
Duration: 4FT Hon
Entry Requirements: *GCE:* A*AAe-AAAe. *SQAAH:* AAA. Interview required.

W20 THE UNIVERSITY OF WARWICK
COVENTRY CV4 8UW
t: 024 7652 3723 f: 024 7652 4649
e: ugadmissions@warwick.ac.uk
// www.warwick.ac.uk

GG13 BSc Mathematics and Statistics
Duration: 3FT Hon
Entry Requirements: *SQAAH:* AA. Interview required.

GLN0 BSc Mathematics, Operational Research, Statistics, Economics
Duration: 3FT Hon
Entry Requirements: *SQAAH:* AA. Interview required.

G0L0 BSc.MMORSE Mathematics, Operational Research, Statistics and Economics
Duration: 4FT Hon
Entry Requirements: *SQAAH:* AA. Interview required.

GGC3 MMathStat Mathematics and Statistics
Duration: 4FT Hon
Entry Requirements: *SQAAH:* AA. Interview required.

Y50 THE UNIVERSITY OF YORK
STUDENT RECRUITMENT AND ADMISSIONS
UNIVERSITY OF YORK
HESLINGTON
YORK YO10 5DD
t: 01904 324000 f: 01904 323538
e: ug-admissions@york.ac.uk
// www.york.ac.uk

GG13 BA/BSc Mathematics and Statistics (Equal)
Duration: 3FT Hon
Entry Requirements: *GCE:* AAB. *SQAH:* AAAAB. *SQAAH:* AB. *IB:* 35.

MATHEMATICS COMBINATIONS

A20 THE UNIVERSITY OF ABERDEEN
UNIVERSITY OFFICE
KING'S COLLEGE
ABERDEEN AB24 3FX
t: +44 (0) 1224 273504 f: +44 (0) 1224 272034
e: sras@abdn.ac.uk
// www.abdn.ac.uk/sras

F1G1 BSc Chemistry with Mathematics
Duration: 4FT Hon
Entry Requirements: *GCE:* BBB. *SQAH:* BBBB. *IB:* 30.

GGK1 BSc Computing Science and Mathematics
Duration: 4FT Hon
Entry Requirements: *GCE:* 240. *SQAH:* BBBB. *SQAAH:* BCC. *IB:* 28.

FG31 BSc Mathematics and Physics
Duration: 4FT Hon
Entry Requirements: *GCE:* 240. *SQAH:* BBBB. *SQAAH:* BCC. *IB:* 28.

G1R1 BSc Mathematics with French
Duration: 4FT Hon
Entry Requirements: *GCE:* 240. *SQAH:* BBBB. *SQAAH:* BCC. *IB:* 28.

G1Q5 BSc Mathematics with Gaelic
Duration: 4FT Hon
Entry Requirements: *GCE:* 240. *SQAH:* BBBB. *SQAAH:* BCC. *IB:* 28.

G1R2 BSc Mathematics with German
Duration: 4FT Hon
Entry Requirements: *GCE:* 240. *SQAH:* BBBB. *SQAAH:* BCC. *IB:* 28.

G1R4 BSc Mathematics with Spanish
Duration: 4FT Hon
Entry Requirements: *GCE:* 240. *SQAH:* BBBB. *SQAAH:* BCC. *IB:* 28.

GG41 MA Computing and Mathematics
Duration: 4FT Hon
Entry Requirements: *GCE:* BBB. *SQAH:* BBBB. *IB:* 30.

LG11 MA Economics and Mathematics
Duration: 4FT Hon
Entry Requirements: *GCE:* BBB. *SQAH:* BBBB. *IB:* 30.

RG11 MA French and Mathematics
Duration: 5FT Hon
Entry Requirements: *GCE:* BBB. *SQAH:* BBBB. *IB:* 30.

RG21 MA German and Mathematics
Duration: 5FT Hon
Entry Requirements: *GCE:* BBB. *SQAH:* BBBB. *IB:* 30.

RG41 MA Hispanic Studies and Mathematics
Duration: 5FT Hon
Entry Requirements: *GCE:* BBB. *SQAH:* BBBB. *IB:* 30.

VG11 MA History and Mathematics
Duration: 4FT Hon
Entry Requirements: *GCE:* BBB. *SQAH:* BBBB. *IB:* 30.

GN12 MA Management Studies and Mathematics
Duration: 4FT Hon
Entry Requirements: *GCE:* BBB. *SQAH:* BBBB. *IB:* 30.

GV15 MA Mathematics and Philosophy
Duration: 4FT Hon
Entry Requirements: *GCE:* BBB. *SQAH:* BBBB. *IB:* 30.

GF13 MA Mathematics and Physics
Duration: 4FT Hon
Entry Requirements: *GCE:* BBB. *SQAH:* BBBB. *IB:* 30.

GL13 MA Mathematics and Sociology
Duration: 4FT Hon
Entry Requirements: *GCE:* BBB. *SQAH:* BBBB. *IB:* 30.

G1G4 MA Mathematics with Computing
Duration: 4FT Hon
Entry Requirements: Contact the institution for details.

G1Q8 MA Mathematics with Gaelic
Duration: 4FT Hon
Entry Requirements: *GCE:* BBB. *SQAH:* BBBB. *IB:* 30.

A40 ABERYSTWYTH UNIVERSITY
ABERYSTWYTH UNIVERSITY, WELCOME CENTRE
PENGLAIS CAMPUS
ABERYSTWYTH
CEREDIGION SY23 3FB
t: 01970 622021 f: 01970 627410
e: ug-admissions@aber.ac.uk
// www.aber.ac.uk

GQ15 BA Cymraeg/Mathematics
Duration: 3FT Hon
Entry Requirements: *GCE:* 320. *IB:* 27.

X3G1 BA Education with Mathematics
Duration: 3FT Hon
Entry Requirements: *GCE:* 280. *IB:* 28.

M1G1 BA Law with Mathematics
Duration: 3FT Hon
Entry Requirements: *GCE:* 340. *IB:* 28.

GW14 BA Mathematics/Drama & Theatre Studies
Duration: 3FT Hon
Entry Requirements: *GCE:* 320. *IB:* 27.

GW16 BA Mathematics/Film & Television Studies
Duration: 3FT Hon
Entry Requirements: *GCE:* 320. *IB:* 27.

GR11 BA Mathematics/French (4 years)
Duration: 4FT Hon
Entry Requirements: *GCE:* 320. *IB:* 27.

GR12 BA Mathematics/German (4 years)
Duration: 4FT Hon
Entry Requirements: *GCE:* 320. *IB:* 27.

GQC5 BA Mathematics/Gwyddeleg: Iaith a Lln
Duration: 4FT Hon
Entry Requirements: *GCE:* 320. *IB:* 27.

GV11 BA Mathematics/History
Duration: 3FT Hon
Entry Requirements: *GCE:* 320. *IB:* 27.

GQ1M BA Mathematics/Irish Language & Literature
Duration: 4SW Hon
Entry Requirements: *GCE:* 320. *IB:* 27.

GG14 BSc Computer Science/Mathematics
Duration: 3FT Hon
Entry Requirements: *GCE:* 320. *IB:* 27.

GX13 BSc Education/Mathematics
Duration: 3FT Hon
Entry Requirements: *GCE:* 320. *IB:* 27.

G1N3 BSc Financial Mathematics
Duration: 3FT Hon
Entry Requirements: *GCE:* 320. *IB:* 27.

G1N4 BSc Mathematics with Accounting & Finance
Duration: 3FT Hon
Entry Requirements: *GCE:* 320. *IB:* 27.

G1N1 BSc Mathematics with Business & Management
Duration: 3FT Hon
Entry Requirements: *GCE:* 320. *IB:* 27.

G1L1 BSc Mathematics with Economics
Duration: 3FT Hon
Entry Requirements: *GCE:* 320. *IB:* 27.

G1X3 BSc Mathematics with Education
Duration: 3FT Hon
Entry Requirements: *GCE:* 320. *IB:* 27.

G1F8 BSc Mathematics with Physical Geography
Duration: 3FT Hon
Entry Requirements: *GCE:* 320. *IB:* 28.

FG31 BSc Mathematics/Physics
Duration: 3FT Hon
Entry Requirements: *GCE:* 280. *IB:* 27.

F8G1 BSc Physical Geography with Mathematics
Duration: 3FT Hon
Entry Requirements: *GCE:* 300. *IB:* 28.

FG81 BSc Physical Geography/Mathematics
Duration: 3FT Hon
Entry Requirements: *GCE:* 320. *IB:* 28.

N4G1 BScEcon Accounting & Finance with Mathematics
Duration: 3FT Hon
Entry Requirements: *GCE:* 300. *IB:* 27.

N1G1 BScEcon Business & Management with Mathematics
Duration: 3FT Hon
Entry Requirements: *GCE:* 280. *IB:* 27.

L1G1 BScEcon Economics with Mathematics
Duration: 3FT Hon
Entry Requirements: *GCE:* 300. *IB:* 27.

A80 ASTON UNIVERSITY, BIRMINGHAM
ASTON TRIANGLE
BIRMINGHAM B4 7ET
t: 0121 204 4444 f: 0121 204 3696
e: admissions@aston.ac.uk (automatic response)
// www.aston.ac.uk/prospective-students/ug

GN11 BSc Mathematics and Business
Duration: 4SW Hon
Entry Requirements: *GCE:* 300-340. *SQAH:* ABBBB. *SQAAH:* ABB. *IB:* 32.

G190 BSc Mathematics with Computing
Duration: 3FT/4SW Hon
Entry Requirements: *GCE:* 320-340. *IB:* 32.

G1L1 BSc Mathematics with Economics
Duration: 4SW Hon
Entry Requirements: *GCE:* 320-340. *SQAH:* ABBBB. *SQAAH:* ABB. *IB:* 32.

B16 UNIVERSITY OF BATH
CLAVERTON DOWN
BATH BA2 7AY
t: 01225 383019 f: 01225 386366
e: admissions@bath.ac.uk
// www.bath.ac.uk

G4GD BSc Computer Science with Mathematics
Duration: 3FT Hon
Entry Requirements: *GCE:* AAA. *SQAAH:* AAB. *IB:* 36.

G4GA BSc Computer Science with Mathematics (Placement)
Duration: 4SW Hon
Entry Requirements: *GCE:* AAA. *SQAAH:* AAB. *IB:* 36.

I10B BSc Computer Science with Mathematics with Study Year Abroad
Duration: 4FT Hon
Entry Requirements: Contact the institution for details.

GF13 BSc Mathematics and Physics
Duration: 3FT Hon
Entry Requirements: *GCE:* AAA. *SQAAH:* AAB.

FG31 BSc Mathematics and Physics (Sandwich)
Duration: 4FT/4SW Hon
Entry Requirements: *GCE:* AAA. *SQAAH:* AAB.

G4GC MComp Computer Science and Mathematics with Study Year Abroad
Duration: 5FT Hon
Entry Requirements: Contact the institution for details.

G4G1 MComp Computer Science with Mathematics
Duration: 4FT Hon
Entry Requirements: Contact the institution for details.

GLG1 MComp Computer Science with Mathematics (Placement)
Duration: 5FT Hon
Entry Requirements: Contact the institution for details.

FG3C MSci Mathematics and Physics
Duration: 4FT Deg
Entry Requirements: *GCE:* AAA. *SQAAH:* AAB.

B22 UNIVERSITY OF BEDFORDSHIRE
PARK SQUARE
LUTON
BEDS LU1 3JU
t: 0844 8482234 f: 01582 489323
e: admissions@beds.ac.uk
// www.beds.ac.uk

G4G1 BSc Computing and Mathematics
Duration: 3FT Hon
Entry Requirements: *Foundation:* Pass. *GCE:* 200. *SQAH:* BCC.
SQAAH: BCC. *IB:* 24. *OCR ND:* M1 *OCR NED:* P1

B32 THE UNIVERSITY OF BIRMINGHAM
EDGBASTON
BIRMINGHAM B15 2TT
t: 0121 415 8900 f: 0121 414 7159
e: admissions@bham.ac.uk
// www.birmingham.ac.uk

GV14 BA Archaeology & Ancient History and Mathematics
Duration: 3FT Hon
Entry Requirements: *GCE:* ABB. *SQAH:* AAAAA-ABBBB. *SQAAH:* AB. *IB:* 34.

GR11 BA French Studies and Mathematics (4 years)
Duration: 4FT Hon
Entry Requirements: *GCE:* ABB. *SQAH:* ABBBB. *SQAAH:* AB. *IB:* 32.

GR12 BA German Studies and Mathematics (4 years)
Duration: 4FT Hon
Entry Requirements: *GCE:* ABB. *SQAH:* ABBBB. *SQAAH:* AB. *IB:* 32.

GR13 BA Italian Studies and Mathematics (4 years)
Duration: 4FT Hon
Entry Requirements: *GCE:* ABB. *SQAH:* AABBB. *SQAAH:* AB. *IB:* 34.

GW13 BA Mathematics and Music
Duration: 3FT Hon
Entry Requirements: *GCE:* AAB. *SQAH:* AAAAA-AABBB. *SQAAH:* AA-AB. *IB:* 34.

GV15 BA Mathematics and Philosophy
Duration: 3FT Hon
Entry Requirements: *GCE:* ABB. *SQAH:* AABBB. *SQAAH:* AB. *IB:* 34.

GR15 BA Mathematics and Portuguese (4 years)
Duration: 4FT Hon
Entry Requirements: *GCE:* ABB. *SQAH:* AABBB. *SQAAH:* AB.

R9G1 BA Modern Languages with Mathematics (4 years)
Duration: 4FT Hon
Entry Requirements: *GCE:* ABB. *SQAH:* AABBB. *SQAAH:* AB. *IB:* 32.

GG14 BSc Mathematics and Computer Science
Duration: 3FT Hon
Entry Requirements: *GCE:* AAA-AAB. *SQAH:* AAAAB-AAABB. *SQAAH:* AA.

GGD4 BSc Mathematics and Computer Science with an Industrial Year
Duration: 4FT Hon
Entry Requirements: Contact the institution for details.

GC17 BSc Mathematics and Sports Science
Duration: 3FT Hon
Entry Requirements: *GCE:* AAA-AAB. *SQAH:* AAAAB-AAABB. *SQAAH:* AA.

G1N2 BSc Mathematics with Business Management
Duration: 3FT Hon
Entry Requirements: *GCE:* AAA-AAB. *SQAH:* AAAAB-AAABB. *SQAAH:* AA.

G1V5 BSc Mathematics with Philosophy
Duration: 3FT Hon
Entry Requirements: *GCE:* AAA-AAB. *SQAH:* AAAAB-AAABB. *SQAAH:* AA.

CFG0 BSc Natural Sciences
Duration: 3FT Hon
Entry Requirements: *GCE:* A*AA. *SQAH:* AAAAA. *SQAAH:* AA. *IB:* 38.

FCG0 BSc Natural Sciences with Study in Continental Europe (4 years)
Duration: 4FT Hon
Entry Requirements: *GCE:* A*AA. *SQAH:* AAAAA. *SQAAH:* AA. *IB:* 38.

GGC4 BSc Pure Mathematics and Computer Science
Duration: 3FT Hon
Entry Requirements: *GCE:* AAA-AAB. *SQAH:* AAAAB-AAABB. *SQAAH:* AA.

FG31 BSc Theoretical Physics and Applied Mathematics
Duration: 3FT Hon
Entry Requirements: *GCE:* AAA. *SQAH:* AAAAB-AAABB. *SQAAH:* AA.

GI11 MSci Mathematics and Computer Science
Duration: 4FT Hon
Entry Requirements: *GCE:* A*AA. *SQAH:* AAAAA. *SQAAH:* AA.

GG41 MSci Mathematics and Computer Science (with an Industrial Year)
Duration: 5FT Hon
Entry Requirements: Contact the institution for details.

G1NF MSci Mathematics with Business Management
Duration: 4FT Hon
Entry Requirements: *GCE:* A*AA. *SQAH:* AAAAA. *SQAAH:* AA.

B38 BISHOP GROSSETESTE UNIVERSITY COLLEGE LINCOLN
BISHOP GROSSETESTE UNIVERSITY COLLEGE
LINCOLN LN1 3DY
t: 01522 583658 f: 01522 530243
e: admissions@bishopg.ac.uk
// www.bishopg.ac.uk/courses

X3G1 BA Early Childhood Studies with Mathematics
Duration: 3FT Hon   CRB Check: Required
Entry Requirements: *GCE:* 220. *IB:* 24.

X3GA BA Education Studies with Mathematics
Duration: 3FT Hon   CRB Check: Required
Entry Requirements: Contact the institution for details.

QG31 BA English and Mathematics
Duration: 3FT Hon   CRB Check: Required
Entry Requirements: Contact the institution for details.

Q3G1 BA English with Mathematics
Duration: 3FT Hon   CRB Check: Required
Entry Requirements: Contact the institution for details.

XG31 BSc Early Childhood Studies and Mathematics
Duration: 3FT Hon   CRB Check: Required
Entry Requirements: *GCE:* 220. *IB:* 24.

X1G1 BSc Education Studies and Mathematics
Duration: 3FT Hon   CRB Check: Required
Entry Requirements: *GCE:* 220.

GC10 BSc Mathematics and Science
Duration: 3FT Hon
Entry Requirements: *GCE:* 220.

XG3C BSc Special Educational Needs & Inclusion and Mathematics
Duration: 3FT Hon   CRB Check: Required
Entry Requirements: Contact the institution for details.

CG6C BSc Sport and Mathematics
Duration: 3FT Hon   CRB Check: Required
Entry Requirements: Contact the institution for details.

B56 THE UNIVERSITY OF BRADFORD
RICHMOND ROAD
BRADFORD
WEST YORKSHIRE BD7 1DP
t: 0800 073 1225 f: 01274 235585
e: course-enquiries@bradford.ac.uk
// www.bradford.ac.uk

GG14 BSc Computational Mathematics
Duration: 3FT Hon
Entry Requirements: *GCE:* 240. *IB:* 24.

GG1K BSc Computational Mathematics
Duration: 4SW Hon
Entry Requirements: *GCE:* 240. *IB:* 24.

B72 UNIVERSITY OF BRIGHTON
MITHRAS HOUSE 211
LEWES ROAD
BRIGHTON BN2 4AT
t: 01273 644644 f: 01273 642607
e: admissions@brighton.ac.uk
// www.brighton.ac.uk

XG1C BA Key Stage 2/Key Stage 3 Mathematics Education with QTS
Duration: 3FT/4FT Hon
Entry Requirements: *GCE:* BBC. *IB:* 28. Interview required.

XG11 BA Mathematics Education with QTS (Secondary) (2 years)
Duration: 2FT Hon
Entry Requirements: Interview required.

GN11 BSc Mathematics and Business
Duration: 3FT Hon
Entry Requirements: *GCE:* BBB. *IB:* 28. Interview required.

GG10 BSc Mathematics and Computing
Duration: 3FT Hon
Entry Requirements: *GCE:* BBB. *IB:* 28. Interview required.

GX13 BSc Mathematics and Education
Duration: 3FT Hon
Entry Requirements: *GCE:* BBB. *IB:* 28. Interview required.

G1N1 BSc Mathematics with Business
Duration: 3FT/4SW Hon
Entry Requirements: *GCE:* BBB. *IB:* 30.

G1N3 BSc Mathematics with Finance
Duration: 3FT/4SW Hon
Entry Requirements: *GCE:* BBB. *IB:* 30.

B78 UNIVERSITY OF BRISTOL
UNDERGRADUATE ADMISSIONS OFFICE
SENATE HOUSE
TYNDALL AVENUE
BRISTOL BS8 1TH
t: 0117 928 9000 f: 0117 331 7391
e: ug-admissions@bristol.ac.uk
// www.bristol.ac.uk

LG11 BSc Economics and Mathematics
Duration: 3FT Hon
Entry Requirements: *GCE:* A*AA-AAA. *SQAH:* AAAA. *SQAAH:* AA. *IB:* 38.

GG14 BSc Mathematics and Computer Science
Duration: 3FT Hon
Entry Requirements: *GCE:* A*AA-AAA. *SQAH:* AAAAA. *SQAAH:* AAA.

VG51 BSc Mathematics and Philosophy
Duration: 3FT Hon
Entry Requirements: *GCE:* A*AA. *SQAH:* AAAAA. *SQAAH:* AA.

GG1K MEng Mathematics and Computer Science
Duration: 4FT Hon
Entry Requirements: *GCE:* A*AA-AAA. *SQAH:* AAAAA. *SQAAH:* AAA.

GV15 MSci Mathematics and Philosophy
Duration: 4FT Hon
Entry Requirements: *GCE:* A*AA. *SQAH:* AAAAA. *SQAAH:* AA.

GFC3 MSci Mathematics and Physics
Duration: 4FT Hon
Entry Requirements: *GCE:* A*AA. *SQAH:* AAAAA. *SQAAH:* AA.

B84 BRUNEL UNIVERSITY
UXBRIDGE
MIDDLESEX UB8 3PH
t: 01895 265265 f: 01895 269790
e: admissions@brunel.ac.uk
// www.brunel.ac.uk

GNC2 BSC Mathematical and Management Studies (4 year Thick SW)
Duration: 4SW Hon
Entry Requirements: *GCE:* ABB. *SQAAH:* ABB. *IB:* 33. *BTEC ExtDip:* D*DD.

GN13 BSc Financial Mathematics
Duration: 3FT Hon
Entry Requirements: *GCE:* ABB. *SQAAH:* ABB. *IB:* 33. *BTEC ExtDip:* D*DD.

GND3 BSc Financial Mathematics (4 year Thick SW)
Duration: 4SW Hon
Entry Requirements: *GCE:* ABB. *SQAAH:* ABB. *IB:* 33. *BTEC ExtDip:* D*DD.

GND2 BSc Mathematical and Management Studies
Duration: 3FT Hon
Entry Requirements: *GCE:* ABB. *SQAAH:* ABB. *IB:* 33. *BTEC ExtDip:* D*DD.

G1NG BSc Mathematics & Statistics with Management
Duration: 3FT Hon
Entry Requirements: *GCE:* ABB. *SQAAH:* ABB. *IB:* 33. *BTEC ExtDip:* D*DD.

G1NF BSc Mathematics & Statistics with Management (4 year Thick SW)
Duration: 4SW Hon
Entry Requirements: *GCE:* ABB. *SQAAH:* ABB. *IB:* 33. *BTEC ExtDip:* D*DD.

GGC4 BSc Mathematics and Computing
Duration: 3FT Hon
Entry Requirements: *GCE:* ABB. *SQAAH:* ABB. *IB:* 33. *BTEC ExtDip:* D*DD.

GG14 BSc Mathematics and Computing (4 year Thick SW)
Duration: 4SW Hon
Entry Requirements: *GCE:* ABB. *SQAAH:* ABB. *IB:* 33. *BTEC ExtDip:* D*DD.

G1GL BSc Mathematics with Computer Science
Duration: 3FT Hon
Entry Requirements: *GCE:* ABB. *SQAAH:* ABB. *IB:* 33. *BTEC ExtDip:* D*DD.

G1GK BSc Mathematics with Computer Science (4 year Thick SW)
Duration: 4SW Hon
Entry Requirements: *GCE:* ABB. *SQAAH:* ABB. *IB:* 33. *BTEC ExtDip:* D*DD.

GN1H MMath Financial Mathematics (4 years)
Duration: 4FT Hon
Entry Requirements: *GCE:* AAA. *SQAAH:* AAA. *IB:* 37.

GN1J MMath Financial Mathematics (5 year Thick SW)
Duration: 5FT Hon
Entry Requirements: *GCE:* AAA. *SQAAH:* AAA. *IB:* 37.

C10 CANTERBURY CHRIST CHURCH UNIVERSITY
NORTH HOLMES ROAD
CANTERBURY
KENT CT1 1QU
t: 01227 782900 f: 01227 782888
e: admissions@canterbury.ac.uk
// www.canterbury.ac.uk

GFC0 BSc Integrated Science 'International Only'
Duration: 4FT Hon
Entry Requirements: Interview required.

G1X1 BSc Mathematics with Secondary Education (QTS)
Duration: 3FT Hon **CRB Check:** Required
Entry Requirements: *GCE:* 280. *IB:* 24. Interview required.

C15 CARDIFF UNIVERSITY
PO BOX 927
30-36 NEWPORT ROAD
CARDIFF CF24 0DE
t: 029 2087 9999 f: 029 2087 6138
e: admissions@cardiff.ac.uk
// www.cardiff.ac.uk

GR11 BA French/Mathematics (4 years)
Duration: 4FT Hon
Entry Requirements: *GCE:* AAB. *SQAH:* AAABB. *SQAAH:* AAB. *IB:* 36.

GR12 BA German/Mathematics (4 years)
Duration: 4FT Hon
Entry Requirements: *GCE:* ABB. *SQAH:* AABBB-ABBBB. *SQAAH:* ABB. *IB:* 34.

GW13 BA Mathematics/Music
Duration: 3FT Hon
Entry Requirements: *GCE:* AAB. *SQAH:* AAABB. *SQAAH:* AAB. *IB:* 35.

GV15 BA Mathematics/Philosophy
Duration: 3FT Hon
Entry Requirements: *GCE:* AAB. *SQAAH:* AAB. *IB:* 35. *OCR NED:* D2 Interview required.

VG61 BA Mathematics/Religious Studies
Duration: 3FT Hon
Entry Requirements: *GCE:* AAB. *SQAH:* AABBB. *SQAAH:* AAB. *IB:* 34. *OCR ND:* D *OCR NED:* M2 Interview required.

QG51 BA Mathematics/Welsh
Duration: 3FT Hon
Entry Requirements: *GCE:* AAB. *IB:* 34. *OCR NED:* M3 Interview required.

GG14 BSc Computing and Mathematics
Duration: 3FT Hon
Entry Requirements: *GCE:* ABB. *SQAH:* AAABB. *SQAAH:* ABB. *IB:* 33. Interview required.

IG11 BSc Computing and Mathematics (Year in Industry)
Duration: 4FT Hon
Entry Requirements: *GCE:* ABB. *SQAH:* AAABB. *SQAAH:* ABB. *IB:* 33. Interview required.

FG31 BSc Physics and Mathematics
Duration: 3FT Hon
Entry Requirements: *GCE:* ABB. *IB:* 32. *OCR NED:* M2 Interview required.

C30 UNIVERSITY OF CENTRAL LANCASHIRE
PRESTON
LANCS PR1 2HE
t: 01772 201201 f: 01772 894954
e: uadmissions@uclan.ac.uk
// www.uclan.ac.uk

CFG0 BSc Science (Foundation entry)
Duration: 4FT Hon
Entry Requirements: *GCE:* 40.

C55 UNIVERSITY OF CHESTER
PARKGATE ROAD
CHESTER CH1 4BJ
t: 01244 511000 f: 01244 511300
e: enquiries@chester.ac.uk
// www.chester.ac.uk

XG31 BA Education Studies and Mathematics
Duration: 3FT Hon
Entry Requirements: *GCE:* 240-280. *SQAH:* BBBB. *IB:* 26.

QG31 BA English and Mathematics
Duration: 3FT Hon
Entry Requirements: *GCE:* 260-300. *SQAH:* BBBB. *IB:* 28.

GR11 BA Mathematics and French
Duration: 4FT Hon
Entry Requirements: *GCE:* 240-280. *SQAH:* BBBB. *IB:* 26.

GR12 BA Mathematics and German
Duration: 4FT Hon
Entry Requirements: *GCE:* 240-280. *SQAH:* BBBB. *IB:* 26.

GR14 BA Mathematics and Spanish
Duration: 4FT Hon
Entry Requirements: *GCE:* 240-280. *SQAH:* BBBB. *IB:* 26.

GC18 BSc Mathematics and Psychology
Duration: 3FT Hon
Entry Requirements: *GCE:* 260-300. *SQAH:* BBBB. *IB:* 28.

GC16 BSc Mathematics and Sport & Exercise Sciences
Duration: 3FT Hon
Entry Requirements: *GCE:* 260-300. *SQAH:* BBBB. *IB:* 28.

C58 UNIVERSITY OF CHICHESTER
BISHOP OTTER CAMPUS
COLLEGE LANE
CHICHESTER
WEST SUSSEX PO19 6PE
t: 01243 816002 f: 01243 816161
e: admissions@chi.ac.uk
// www.chiuni.ac.uk

G1X1 BA Mathematics and Teaching for Key Stages 2 & 3
Duration: 3FT Hon CRB Check: Required
Entry Requirements: *GCE:* BCC-CCC. *SQAAH:* BCC-CCC. *IB:* 28.
Interview required.

G1XC BA Primary Education (Mathematics) (ages 5-11)
Duration: 3FT Hon CRB Check: Required
Entry Requirements: *GCE:* BBB. *SQAH:* BBBB-BBBC. *SQAAH:* BBC.
IB: 30. Interview required.

XG31 BSc Mathematics and Learning
Duration: 3FT Hon CRB Check: Required
Entry Requirements: Interview required.

C60 CITY UNIVERSITY
NORTHAMPTON SQUARE
LONDON EC1V 0HB
t: 020 7040 5060 f: 020 7040 8995
e: ugadmissions@city.ac.uk
// www.city.ac.uk

G1G4 BSc Mathematical Science with Computer Science (3 years or 4 year SW)
Duration: 3FT Hon
Entry Requirements: *GCE:* 360. *IB:* 32.

G1L1 BSc Mathematical Science with Finance & Economics (3 years or 4 year SW)
Duration: 3FT Hon
Entry Requirements: *GCE:* 360. *IB:* 32.

GN13 BSc Mathematics and Finance (3 years or 4 year SW)
Duration: 3FT Hon
Entry Requirements: *GCE:* 360. *IB:* 32.

C99 UNIVERSITY OF CUMBRIA
FUSEHILL STREET
CARLISLE
CUMBRIA CA1 2HH
t: 01228 616234 f: 01228 616235
// www.cumbria.ac.uk

FCG0 BSc Applied Science (Top-Up)
Duration: 1FT Hon
Entry Requirements: HND required.

D39 UNIVERSITY OF DERBY
KEDLESTON ROAD
DERBY DE22 1GB
t: 01332 591167 f: 01332 597724
e: askadmissions@derby.ac.uk
// www.derby.ac.uk

TG71 BA/BSc American Studies and Mathematics
Duration: 3FT Hon
Entry Requirements: *Foundation:* Distinction. *GCE:* 260-300. *IB:* 28. *BTEC Dip:* D*D*. *BTEC ExtDip:* DMM. *OCR NED:* M2

MG21 BA/BSc Applied Criminology and Mathematics
Duration: 3FT Hon
Entry Requirements: *Foundation:* Distinction. *GCE:* 260-300. *IB:* 28. *BTEC Dip:* D*D*. *BTEC ExtDip:* DMM. *OCR NED:* M2

WG81 BA/BSc Creative Writing and Mathematics
Duration: 3FT Hon
Entry Requirements: *Foundation:* Distinction. *GCE:* 260-300. *IB:* 28. *BTEC Dip:* D*D*. *BTEC ExtDip:* DMM. *OCR NED:* M2

WG51 BA/BSc Dance & Movement Studies and Mathematics
Duration: 3FT Hon
Entry Requirements: *Foundation:* Distinction. *GCE:* 260-300. *IB:* 28. *BTEC Dip:* D*D*. *BTEC ExtDip:* DMM. *OCR NED:* M2

LG51 BA/BSc Early Childhood Studies and Mathematics
Duration: 3FT Hon
Entry Requirements: *Foundation:* Distinction. *GCE:* 260-300. *IB:* 28. *BTEC Dip:* D*D*. *BTEC ExtDip:* DMM. *OCR NED:* M2

VG11 BA/BSc History and Mathematics
Duration: 3FT Hon
Entry Requirements: *Foundation:* Distinction. *GCE:* 260-300. *IB:* 28. *BTEC Dip:* D*D*. *BTEC ExtDip:* DMM. *OCR NED:* M2

MG11 BA/BSc Law and Mathematics
Duration: 3FT Hon
Entry Requirements: *Foundation:* Distinction. *GCE:* 260-300. *IB:* 28. *BTEC Dip:* D*D*. *BTEC ExtDip:* DMM. *OCR NED:* M2

GW18 BA/BSc Mathematics and Professional Writing
Duration: 3FT Hon
Entry Requirements: *Foundation:* Distinction. *GCE:* 260-300. *IB:* 28. *BTEC Dip:* D*D*. *BTEC ExtDip:* DMM. *OCR NED:* M2

GK12 BA/BSc Mathematics and Property Development
Duration: 3FT Hon
Entry Requirements: *Foundation:* Distinction. *GCE:* 260-300. *IB:* 28. *BTEC Dip:* D*D*. *BTEC ExtDip:* DMM. *OCR NED:* M2

GN14 BSc Accounting and Mathematics
Duration: 3FT Hon
Entry Requirements: *Foundation:* Distinction. *GCE:* 260-300. *IB:* 28. *BTEC Dip:* D*D*. *BTEC ExtDip:* DMM. *OCR NED:* M2

FG61 BSc Geology and Mathematics
Duration: 3FT Hon
Entry Requirements: *Foundation:* Distinction. *GCE:* 260-300. *IB:* 28. *BTEC Dip:* D*D*. *BTEC ExtDip:* DMM. *OCR NED:* M2

GK11 BSc Mathematics and Architectural Design
Duration: 3FT Hon
Entry Requirements: *Foundation:* Distinction. *GCE:* 260-300. *IB:* 28. *BTEC Dip:* D*D*. *BTEC ExtDip:* DMM. *OCR NED:* M2

CG11 BSc Mathematics and Biology
Duration: 3FT Hon
Entry Requirements: *Foundation:* Distinction. *GCE:* 260-300. *IB:* 28. *BTEC Dip:* D*D*. *BTEC ExtDip:* DMM. *OCR NED:* M2

GN12 BSc Mathematics and Business Management
Duration: 3FT Hon
Entry Requirements: *Foundation:* Distinction. *GCE:* 260-300. *IB:* 28. *BTEC Dip:* D*D*. *BTEC ExtDip:* DMM. *OCR NED:* M2

GG41 BSc Mathematics and Computer Science
Duration: 4SW Hon
Entry Requirements: *GCE:* 300. *IB:* 28. *BTEC Dip:* D*D*. *BTEC ExtDip:* DMM. *OCR NED:* D2

GQ13 BSc Mathematics and English
Duration: 3FT Hon
Entry Requirements: *Foundation:* Distinction. *GCE:* 260-300. *IB:* 28. *BTEC Dip:* D*D*. *BTEC ExtDip:* DMM. *OCR NED:* M2

GF17 BSc Mathematics and Environmental Hazards
Duration: 3FT Hon
Entry Requirements: *Foundation:* Distinction. *GCE:* 260-300. *IB:* 28. *BTEC Dip:* D*D*. *BTEC ExtDip:* DMM. *OCR NED:* M2

GN16 BSc Mathematics and Human Resource Management
Duration: 3FT Hon
Entry Requirements: *Foundation:* Distinction. *GCE:* 260-300. *IB:* 28. *BTEC Dip:* D*D*. *BTEC ExtDip:* DMM. *OCR NED:* M2

GL12 BSc Mathematics and International Relations & Global Development
Duration: 3FT Hon
Entry Requirements: *Foundation:* Distinction. *GCE:* 260-300. *IB:* 28. *BTEC Dip:* D*D*. *BTEC ExtDip:* DMM. *OCR NED:* M2

GL13 BSc Mathematics and Sociology
Duration: 3FT Hon
Entry Requirements: *Foundation:* Distinction. *GCE:* 260-300. *IB:* 28. *BTEC Dip:* D*D*. *BTEC ExtDip:* DMM. *OCR NED:* M2

GW14 BSc Mathematics and Theatre Studies
Duration: 3FT Hon
Entry Requirements: *Foundation:* Distinction. *GCE:* 260-300. *IB:* 28. *BTEC Dip:* D*D*. *BTEC ExtDip:* DMM. *OCR NED:* M2

GL19 BSc Mathematics and Third World Development
Duration: 3FT Hon
Entry Requirements: *Foundation:* Distinction. *GCE:* 260-300. *IB:* 28. *BTEC Dip:* D*D*. *BTEC ExtDip:* DMM. *OCR NED:* M2

GC13 BSc Mathematics and Zoology
Duration: 3FT Hon
Entry Requirements: *Foundation:* Distinction. *GCE:* 260-300. *IB:* 28. *BTEC Dip:* D*D*. *BTEC ExtDip:* DMM. *OCR NED:* M2

G1X3 BSc Mathematics with Education
Duration: 3FT Hon
Entry Requirements: *GCE:* 280. *IB:* 28. *BTEC Dip:* D*D*. *BTEC ExtDip:* DMM. *OCR NED:* M2

CG61 BSc Sport & Exercise Studies and Mathematics
Duration: 3FT Hon
Entry Requirements: *Foundation:* Distinction. *GCE:* 260-300. *IB:* 28. *BTEC Dip:* D*D*. *BTEC ExtDip:* DMM. *OCR NED:* M2

D65 UNIVERSITY OF DUNDEE
NETHERGATE
DUNDEE DD1 4HN
t: 01382 383838 f: 01382 388150
e: contactus@dundee.ac.uk
// www.dundee.ac.uk/admissions/undergraduate/

GN14 BSc Accountancy and Mathematics
Duration: 4FT Hon
Entry Requirements: *GCE:* BCC. *SQAH:* ABBB. *IB:* 30.

CG11 BSc Mathematical Biology
Duration: 4FT Hon
Entry Requirements: *GCE:* BCC. *SQAH:* ABBB. *IB:* 30.

GG14 BSc Mathematics and Applied Computing
Duration: 4FT Hon
Entry Requirements: *GCE:* BCC. *SQAH:* ABBB. *IB:* 30.

GL11 BSc Mathematics and Economics
Duration: 4FT Hon
Entry Requirements: *GCE:* BCC. *SQAH:* ABBB. *IB:* 30.

GLD1 BSc Mathematics and Financial Economics
Duration: 4FT Hon
Entry Requirements: *GCE:* BCC. *SQAH:* ABBB. *IB:* 30.

FG31 BSc Mathematics and Physics
Duration: 4FT Hon
Entry Requirements: *GCE:* BCC. *SQAH:* ABBB. *IB:* 30.

CG81 BSc Mathematics and Psychology
Duration: 4FT Hon
Entry Requirements: *GCE:* BCC. *SQAH:* ABBB. *IB:* 30.

LNG0 MA Business Economics with Marketing and Mathematics
Duration: 4FT Hon
Entry Requirements: *GCE:* BCC. *SQAH:* ABBB. *IB:* 30.

GQ13 MA English and Mathematics
Duration: 4FT Hon
Entry Requirements: *GCE:* BCC. *SQAH:* ABBB. *IB:* 30.

D86 DURHAM UNIVERSITY
DURHAM UNIVERSITY
UNIVERSITY OFFICE
DURHAM DH1 3HP
t: 0191 334 2000 f: 0191 334 6055
e: admissions@durham.ac.uk
// www.durham.ac.uk

X1G1 BA Education Studies (Mathematics)
Duration: 3FT Hon
Entry Requirements: *GCE:* AAB. *SQAH:* AAABB. *SQAAH:* AAB. *IB:* 36.

CFG0 BSc Natural Sciences
Duration: 3FT Hon
Entry Requirements: *GCE:* A*AA. *SQAH:* AAAAA. *SQAAH:* AAA. *IB:* 38.

FGC0 MSci Natural Sciences
Duration: 4FT Hon
Entry Requirements: *GCE:* A*AA. *SQAH:* AAAAA. *SQAAH:* AAA. *IB:* 38.

E14 UNIVERSITY OF EAST ANGLIA
NORWICH NR4 7TJ
t: 01603 591515 f: 01603 591523
e: admissions@uea.ac.uk
// www.uea.ac.uk

G1N1 BSc Mathematics with Business
Duration: 3FT Hon CRB Check: Required
Entry Requirements: *GCE:* AAB. *SQAH:* AAABB. *SQAAH:* AAB. *IB:* 33. *BTEC ExtDip:* DDD.

CFG0 BSc Natural Sciences
Duration: 3FT Hon CRB Check: Required
Entry Requirements: *GCE:* AAA. *SQAH:* AAAAA. *SQAAH:* AAA. *IB:* 34. *BTEC ExtDip:* DDD. Interview required.

CFGA BSc Natural Sciences with a Year Abroad
Duration: 4FT Hon CRB Check: Required
Entry Requirements: *GCE:* A*AA. *SQAH:* AAAAA. *SQAAH:* AAA. *IB:* 35. *BTEC ExtDip:* D*DD. Interview required.

GCF0 BSc Natural Sciences with a Year in Industry
Duration: 4SW Hon CRB Check: Required
Entry Requirements: *GCE:* A*AA. *SQAH:* AAAAA. *SQAAH:* AAA. *IB:* 35. *BTEC ExtDip:* D*DD. Interview required.

CGF0 MNatSci Natural Sciences
Duration: 4FT Hon CRB Check: Required
Entry Requirements: *GCE:* A*AA. *SQAH:* AAAAA. *SQAAH:* AAA. *IB:* 35. *BTEC ExtDip:* D*DD. Interview required.

E28 UNIVERSITY OF EAST LONDON
DOCKLANDS CAMPUS
UNIVERSITY WAY
LONDON E16 2RD
t: 020 8223 3333 f: 020 8223 2978
e: study@uel.ac.uk
// www.uel.ac.uk

L1G1 BA Business Economics with Mathematics
Duration: 3FT Hon
Entry Requirements: *GCE:* 240. *IB:* 24. *OCR ND:* M1 *OCR NED:* P1 Interview required.

N2G1 BA Business Management with Mathematics
Duration: 3FT Hon
Entry Requirements: *GCE:* 240. *IB:* 24. *OCR ND:* M1 *OCR NED:* P1 Interview required.

X3G1 BA Education Studies with Mathematics
Duration: 3FT Hon
Entry Requirements: *GCE:* 240.

C7G1 BSc Biochemistry with Mathematics
Duration: 3FT Hon
Entry Requirements: *GCE:* 240. *IB:* 24.

G5G1 BSc Business Information Systems with Mathematics
Duration: 3FT Hon
Entry Requirements: *GCE:* 240. *IB:* 24. *OCR ND:* M1 *OCR NED:* P1 Interview required.

G4G1 BSc Computer Networks with Mathematics
Duration: 3FT Hon
Entry Requirements: *GCE:* 240. *IB:* 24. *OCR ND:* M1 *OCR NED:* P1 Interview required.

G4GC BSc Computing with Mathematics
Duration: 3FT Hon
Entry Requirements: *GCE:* 240.

G6G1 BSc Software Engineering with Mathematics
Duration: 3FT Hon
Entry Requirements: *GCE:* 240.

E42 EDGE HILL UNIVERSITY
ORMSKIRK
LANCASHIRE L39 4QP
t: 01695 657000 f: 01695 584355
e: study@edgehill.ac.uk
// www.edgehill.ac.uk

X1G1 BSc Secondary Mathematics Education with QTS
Duration: 2FT Hon   CRB Check: Required
Entry Requirements: Interview required. HND required.

X1GC BSc Secondary Mathematics Education with QTS
Duration: 3FT Hon   CRB Check: Required
Entry Requirements: *GCE:* 280. *IB:* 26. *OCR ND:* D *OCR NED:* M2
Interview required.

E56 THE UNIVERSITY OF EDINBURGH
STUDENT RECRUITMENT & ADMISSIONS
57 GEORGE SQUARE
EDINBURGH EH8 9JU
t: 0131 650 4360 f: 0131 651 1236
e: sra.enquiries@ed.ac.uk
// www.ed.ac.uk/studying/undergraduate/

GG17 BSc Artificial Intelligence and Mathematics
Duration: 4FT Hon
Entry Requirements: *GCE:* AAA-ABB. *SQAH:* AAAA-ABBB.

GG14 BSc Computer Science and Mathematics
Duration: 4FT Hon
Entry Requirements: *GCE:* AAA-ABB. *SQAH:* AAAA-ABBB.

GN11 BSc Mathematics and Business Studies
Duration: 4FT Hon
Entry Requirements: *GCE:* AAA-ABB. *SQAH:* AAAA-ABBB.

GW13 BSc Mathematics and Music
Duration: 4FT Hon
Entry Requirements: *GCE:* AAA-ABB. *SQAH:* AAAA-ABBB.

GF13 BSc Mathematics and Physics
Duration: 4FT Hon
Entry Requirements: *GCE:* AAA-ABB. *SQAH:* AAAA-ABBB.

G1N2 BSc Mathematics with Management
Duration: 4FT Hon
Entry Requirements: *GCE:* AAA-ABB. *SQAH:* AAAA-ABBB.

LG11 MA Economics and Mathematics
Duration: 4FT Hon
Entry Requirements: *GCE:* AAA-ABC. *SQAH:* AAAA-ABBC. *IB:* 34.

VG51 MA Philosophy and Mathematics
Duration: 4FT Hon
Entry Requirements: *GCE:* AAA-ABC. *SQAH:* AAAA-ABBC. *IB:* 34.

E70 THE UNIVERSITY OF ESSEX
WIVENHOE PARK
COLCHESTER
ESSEX CO4 3SQ
t: 01206 873666 f: 01206 874477
e: admit@essex.ac.uk
// www.essex.ac.uk

GN14 BSc Accounting and Mathematics
Duration: 3FT Hon
Entry Requirements: *GCE:* ABB-BBB. *SQAH:* AAAB-AABB. *BTEC ExtDip:* DDM.

GN1K BSc Accounting and Mathematics (Including Year Abroad)
Duration: 4FT Hon
Entry Requirements: *GCE:* ABB-BBB. *SQAH:* AAAB-AABB. *BTEC ExtDip:* DDM.

GG14 BSc Computing and Mathematics
Duration: 3FT Hon
Entry Requirements: *GCE:* ABB-BBB. *SQAH:* AAAB-AABB. *BTEC ExtDip:* DDM.

GG1L BSc Computing and Mathematics (Including Year Abroad)
Duration: 4FT Hon
Entry Requirements: *GCE:* ABB-BBB. *SQAH:* AAAB-AABB. *BTEC ExtDip:* DDM.

LG11 BSc Economics and Mathematics
Duration: 3FT Hon
Entry Requirements: *GCE:* ABB-BBB. *SQAH:* AAAB-AABB. *BTEC ExtDip:* DDM.

LG1C BSc Economics and Mathematics (Including Year Abroad)
Duration: 4FT Hon
Entry Requirements: *GCE:* ABB-BBB. *SQAH:* AAAB-AABB. *BTEC ExtDip:* DDM.

L1G1 BSc Economics with Mathematics
Duration: 3FT Hon
Entry Requirements: *GCE:* ABB. *SQAH:* AAAB. *IB:* 34.

GN13 BSc Finance and Mathematics
Duration: 3FT Hon
Entry Requirements: *GCE:* ABB-BBB. *SQAH:* AAAB-AABB. *BTEC ExtDip:* DDM.

GN1H BSc Finance and Mathematics (Including Year Abroad)
Duration: 4FT Hon
Entry Requirements: *GCE:* ABB-BBB. *SQAH:* AAAB-AABB. *BTEC ExtDip:* DDM.

NG21 BSc Management and Mathematics
Duration: 3FT Hon
Entry Requirements: *GCE:* ABB-BBB. *SQAH:* AAAB-AABB. *BTEC ExtDip:* DDM.

NG2C BSc Management and Mathematics (Including Year Abroad)
Duration: 4FT Hon
Entry Requirements: *GCE:* ABB-BBB. *SQAH:* AAAB-AABB. *BTEC ExtDip:* DDM.

N2G1 BSc Management with Mathematics
Duration: 3FT Hon
Entry Requirements: *GCE:* ABB-BBB. *SQAH:* AAAB-AABB. *BTEC ExtDip:* DDM.

N2GC BSc Management with Mathematics (Including Year Abroad)
Duration: 4FT Hon
Entry Requirements: *GCE:* ABB-BBB. *SQAH:* AAAB-AABB. *BTEC ExtDip:* DDM.

NGL0 BSc Management, Mathematics and Economics
Duration: 3FT Hon
Entry Requirements: *GCE:* ABB-BBB. *SQAH:* AAAB-AABB. *BTEC ExtDip:* DDM.

LGN0 BSc Management, Mathematics and Economics (Including Year Abroad)
Duration: 4FT Hon
Entry Requirements: *GCE:* ABB-BBB. *SQAH:* AAAB-AABB. *BTEC ExtDip:* DDM.

NGL1 BSc Management, Mathematics and Economics (including Foundation Year)
Duration: 4FT Hon
Entry Requirements: *GCE:* 180. *SQAH:* CCCD. *IB:* 24.

GV19 BSc Mathematics and Humanities
Duration: 3FT Hon
Entry Requirements: *GCE:* ABB-BBB. *SQAH:* AAAB-AABB. *BTEC ExtDip:* DDM.

GV1X BSc Mathematics and Humanities (Including Year Abroad)
Duration: 4FT Hon
Entry Requirements: *GCE:* ABB-BBB. *SQAH:* AAAB-AABB. *BTEC ExtDip:* DDM.

G190 BSc Mathematics for Secondary Teaching
Duration: 3FT/4FT Hon
Entry Requirements: *GCE:* ABB-BBB. *SQAH:* AAAB-AABB. *BTEC ExtDip:* DDM.

GX11 BSc Mathematics for Secondary Teaching (Including Year Abroad)
Duration: 4FT Hon
Entry Requirements: *GCE:* ABB-BBB. *SQAH:* AAAB-AABB. *BTEC ExtDip:* DDM.

G1GK BSc Mathematics with Computing
Duration: 3FT Hon
Entry Requirements: *GCE:* ABB-BBB. *SQAH:* AAAB-AABB. *BTEC ExtDip:* DDM.

G1G4 BSc Mathematics with Computing (Including Year Abroad)
Duration: 4FT Hon
Entry Requirements: *GCE:* ABB-BBB. *SQAH:* AAAB-AABB. *BTEC ExtDip:* DDM.

G1L1 BSc Mathematics with Economics
Duration: 3FT Hon
Entry Requirements: *GCE:* ABB-BBB. *SQAH:* AAAB-AABB. *BTEC ExtDip:* DDM.

G1LC BSc Mathematics with Economics (Including Year Abroad)
Duration: 4FT Hon
Entry Requirements: *GCE:* ABB-BBB. *SQAH:* AAAB-AABB. *BTEC ExtDip:* DDM.

G1R9 BSc Mathematics with a Modern Language
Duration: 3FT Hon
Entry Requirements: *GCE:* ABB-BBB. *SQAH:* AAAB-AABB. *BTEC ExtDip:* DDM.

GCR9 BSc Mathematics with a Modern Language (Including Year Abroad)
Duration: 4FT Hon
Entry Requirements: *GCE:* ABB-BBB. *SQAH:* AAAB-AABB. *BTEC ExtDip:* DDM.

GG1K BSc Mathematics, Cryptography and Network Security
Duration: 3FT Hon
Entry Requirements: *GCE:* ABB-BBB. *SQAH:* AAAB-AABB. *BTEC ExtDip:* DDM.

GGC4 BSc Mathematics, Cryptography and Network Security (Including Year Abroad)
Duration: 4FT Hon
Entry Requirements: *GCE:* ABB-BBB. *SQAH:* AAAB-AABB. *BTEC ExtDip:* DDM.

E84 UNIVERSITY OF EXETER
LAVER BUILDING
NORTH PARK ROAD
EXETER
DEVON EX4 4QE
t: 01392 723044 f: 01392 722479
e: admissions@exeter.ac.uk
// www.exeter.ac.uk

GG41 BSc Computer Science and Mathematics
Duration: 3FT Hon
Entry Requirements: *GCE:* A*AA-AAB. *SQAH:* AAAA-AABBB. *SQAAH:* AAA-ABB.

GG4C BSc Computer Science and Mathematics with Industrial Placement (4 years)
Duration: 4FT Hon
Entry Requirements: *GCE:* A*AA-AAB. *SQAH:* AAAAA-AABBB. *SQAAH:* AAA-ABB.

GG14 BSc Mathematics and Computer Science
Duration: 3FT Hon
Entry Requirements: *GCE:* A*AA-AAB. *SQAH:* AAAAA-AABBB. *SQAAH:* AAA-ABB.

FG31 BSc Mathematics and Physics
Duration: 3FT Hon
Entry Requirements: *GCE:* A*AA-AAB. *SQAH:* AAAAA-AAABB. *SQAAH:* AAA-ABB. Interview required.

GF19 BSc Mathematics and the Environment (Cornwall Campus)
Duration: 3FT Hon
Entry Requirements: *GCE:* A*AA-AAB. *SQAH:* AAAAA-AABBB. *SQAAH:* AAA-ABB.

G1N4 BSc Mathematics with Accounting
Duration: 3FT Hon
Entry Requirements: *GCE:* A*AA-AAB. *SQAH:* AAAAA-AABBB. *SQAAH:* AAA-ABB.

G1L1 BSc Mathematics with Economics
Duration: 3FT Hon
Entry Requirements: *GCE:* A*AA-AAB. *SQAH:* AAAAA-AABBB. *SQAAH:* AAA-ABB.

G1N3 BSc Mathematics with Finance
Duration: 3FT Hon
Entry Requirements: *GCE:* A*AA-AAB. *SQAH:* AAAAA-AABBB. *SQAAH:* AAA-ABB.

G1N2 BSc Mathematics with Management
Duration: 3FT Hon
Entry Requirements: *GCE:* A*AA-AAB. *SQAH:* AAAAA-AABBB. *SQAAH:* AAA-ABB.

GG4D MSci Computer Science and Mathematics (4 years)
Duration: 4FT Hon
Entry Requirements: *GCE:* A*AA-AAB. *SQAH:* AAAAA-AABBB. *SQAAH:* AAA-ABB.

G1N1 MSci Mathematics, Business and Finance (4 years)
Duration: 4FT Hon
Entry Requirements: *GCE:* A*AA-AAB. *SQAH:* AAAAA-AABBB. *SQAAH:* AAA-ABB.

G14 UNIVERSITY OF GLAMORGAN, CARDIFF AND PONTYPRIDD
ENQUIRIES AND ADMISSIONS UNIT
PONTYPRIDD CF37 1DL
t: 08456 434030 f: 01443 654050
e: enquiries@glam.ac.uk
// www.glam.ac.uk

G1N3 BSc Financial Mathematics
Duration: 3FT Hon
Entry Requirements: *GCE:* BBB. *IB:* 26. *BTEC SubDip:* M. *BTEC Dip:* MM. *BTEC ExtDip:* DDM. Interview required.

G191 BSc Mathematical Sciences
Duration: 3FT Hon
Entry Requirements: *GCE:* CCC. *IB:* 26. *BTEC SubDip:* M. *BTEC Dip:* DD. *BTEC ExtDip:* MMM. Interview required.

GN1K BSc Mathematics and Accounting
Duration: 3FT Hon
Entry Requirements: *GCE:* BBB. *IB:* 26. *BTEC SubDip:* M. *BTEC Dip:* DD. *BTEC ExtDip:* MMM. Interview required.

G1NK BSc Mathematics with Accounting
Duration: 3FT Hon
Entry Requirements: *GCE:* BBB. *IB:* 26. *BTEC SubDip:* M. *BTEC Dip:* MM. *BTEC ExtDip:* DDM. Interview required.

G1X9 BSc Mathematics with Education
Duration: 3FT Hon
Entry Requirements: *GCE:* BBB. *IB:* 26. *BTEC SubDip:* M. *BTEC Dip:* MM. *BTEC ExtDip:* DDM. Interview required.

G28 UNIVERSITY OF GLASGOW
71 SOUTHPARK AVENUE
UNIVERSITY OF GLASGOW
GLASGOW G12 8QQ
t: 0141 330 6062 f: 0141 330 2961
e: student.recruitment@glasgow.ac.uk
// www.glasgow.ac.uk

NG4C BSc Accounting and Mathematics
Duration: 4FT Hon
Entry Requirements: *GCE:* AAB. *SQAH:* AAAABB-AAABB. *IB:* 34.

GF15 BSc Applied Mathematics and Astronomy
Duration: 4FT Hon
Entry Requirements: *GCE:* ABB. *SQAH:* AAAB-BBBB. *IB:* 32.

LG1C BSc Applied Mathematics and Economics
Duration: 3FT/4FT Deg/Hon
Entry Requirements: *GCE:* ABB. *SQAH:* AAAB-BBBB. *IB:* 32.

GF13 BSc Applied Mathematics and Physics
Duration: 4FT Hon
Entry Requirements: *GCE:* ABB. *SQAH:* AAAB-BBBB. *IB:* 32.

FGM1 BSc Astronomy and Mathematics
Duration: 4FT Hon
Entry Requirements: *GCE:* ABB. *SQAH:* AAAB-BBBB. *IB:* 32.

GF11 BSc Chemistry and Mathematics
Duration: 4FT Hon
Entry Requirements: *GCE:* ABB. *SQAH:* AAAB-BBBB. *IB:* 32.

GGK1 BSc Computing Science/Mathematics
Duration: 4FT Hon
Entry Requirements: *GCE:* ABB. *SQAH:* AAAB-BBBB. *IB:* 32.

NG3C BSc Finance and Mathematics
Duration: 4FT Hon
Entry Requirements: *GCE:* AAB. *SQAH:* AAAABB-AAABB. *IB:* 34.

FG81 BSc Geography and Mathematics
Duration: 4FT Hon
Entry Requirements: *GCE:* ABB. *SQAH:* AAAB-BBBB. *IB:* 32.

CG81 BSc Mathematics and Psychology
Duration: 4FT Hon
Entry Requirements: *GCE:* ABB. *SQAH:* AAAA-AABB. *IB:* 36.

NG21 BSc Mathematics/Business & Management
Duration: 4FT Hon
Entry Requirements: *GCE:* ABB. *SQAH:* AAAB-BBBB. *IB:* 32.

LG1D BSc Mathematics/Economics
Duration: 4FT Hon
Entry Requirements: *GCE:* ABB. *SQAH:* AAAB-BBBB. *IB:* 32.

GVD5 BSc Mathematics/Philosophy
Duration: 4FT Hon
Entry Requirements: *GCE:* ABB. *SQAH:* AAAB-BBBB. *IB:* 32.

GF14 BSc Mathematics/Physics
Duration: 4FT Hon
Entry Requirements: *GCE:* ABB. *SQAH:* AAAB-BBBB. *IB:* 32.

GV14 MA Archaeology/Mathematics
Duration: 4FT Hon
Entry Requirements: *GCE:* ABB. *SQAH:* AAAB-ABBB. *IB:* 34.

GNC2 MA Business & Management/Mathematics
Duration: 4FT Hon
Entry Requirements: *GCE:* ABB. *SQAH:* AAAB-ABBB. *IB:* 34.

GND2 MA Business & Management/Mathematics
Duration: 4FT Hon
Entry Requirements: *GCE:* ABB. *SQAH:* AAAA-AABB. *IB:* 36.

LG11 MA Business Economics/Mathematics
Duration: 4FT Hon
Entry Requirements: *GCE:* ABB. *SQAH:* AAAA-AABB. *IB:* 36.

GQ15 MA Celtic Civilisation/Mathematics
Duration: 4FT Hon
Entry Requirements: *GCE:* ABB. *SQAH:* AAAB-ABBB. *IB:* 34.

GQC5 MA Celtic Studies/Mathematics
Duration: 4FT Hon
Entry Requirements: *GCE:* ABB. *SQAH:* AAAB-ABBB. *IB:* 34.

RG78 MA Central & East European Studies/Mathematics
Duration: 4FT Hon
Entry Requirements: Contact the institution for details.

GQ18 MA Classics/Mathematics
Duration: 4FT Hon
Entry Requirements: *GCE:* ABB. *SQAH:* AAAB-ABBB. *IB:* 34.

GGM1 MA Digital Media & Information Studies/Mathematics
Duration: 4FT Hon
Entry Requirements: *GCE:* ABB. *SQAH:* AAAB-ABBB. *IB:* 34.

GV13 MA Economic & Social History/Mathematics
Duration: 4FT Hon
Entry Requirements: *GCE:* ABB. *SQAH:* AAAB-ABBB. *IB:* 36.

VG31 MA Economic & Social History/Mathematics
Duration: 4FT Hon
Entry Requirements: *GCE:* ABB. *SQAH:* AAAA-AABB. *IB:* 36.

GL11 MA Economics/Mathematics
Duration: 4FT Hon
Entry Requirements: *GCE:* ABB. *SQAH:* AAAA-AABB. *IB:* 36.

GLC1 MA Economics/Mathematics
Duration: 4FT Hon
Entry Requirements: *GCE:* ABB. *SQAH:* AAAB-ABBB. *IB:* 36.

QG3D MA English Language/Mathematics
Duration: 4FT Hon
Entry Requirements: *GCE:* ABB. *SQAH:* AAAB-ABBB. *IB:* 36.

QG3C MA English Literature/Mathematics
Duration: 4FT Hon
Entry Requirements: *GCE:* ABB. *SQAH:* AAAB-ABBB. *IB:* 36.

GR11 MA French/Mathematics
Duration: 5FT Hon
Entry Requirements: *GCE:* ABB. *SQAH:* AAAB-ABBB. *IB:* 36.

QG51 MA Gaelic/Mathematics
Duration: 4FT Hon
Entry Requirements: *GCE:* ABB. *SQAH:* AAAB-ABBB. *IB:* 36.

GR12 MA German/Mathematics
Duration: 5FT Hon
Entry Requirements: *GCE:* ABB. *SQAH:* AAAB-ABBB. *IB:* 36.

GVC3 MA History of Art/Mathematics
Duration: 4FT Hon
Entry Requirements: *GCE:* ABB. *SQAH:* AAAB-ABBB. *IB:* 36.

GV11 MA History/Mathematics
Duration: 4FT Hon
Entry Requirements: *GCE:* ABB. *SQAH:* AAAB-ABBB. *IB:* 36.

GR13 MA Italian/Mathematics
Duration: 5FT Hon
Entry Requirements: *GCE:* ABB. *SQAH:* AAAB-ABBB. *IB:* 36.

GQ16 MA Latin/Mathematics
Duration: 4FT Hon
Entry Requirements: *GCE:* ABB. *SQAH:* AAAB-ABBB. *IB:* 36.

GW13 MA Mathematics/Music
Duration: 4FT Hon
Entry Requirements: *GCE:* ABB. *SQAH:* AAAB-ABBB. *IB:* 36.

GV15 MA Mathematics/Philosophy
Duration: 4FT Hon
Entry Requirements: *GCE:* ABB. *SQAH:* AAAB-ABBB. *IB:* 36.

VG51 MA Mathematics/Philosophy
Duration: 4FT Hon
Entry Requirements: *GCE:* ABB. *SQAH:* AAAA-AABB. *IB:* 36.

GL12 MA Mathematics/Politics
Duration: 4FT Hon
Entry Requirements: *GCE:* ABB. *SQAH:* AAAB-ABBB. *IB:* 36.

LG21 MA Mathematics/Politics
Duration: 4FT Hon
Entry Requirements: *GCE:* ABB. *SQAH:* AAAA-AABB. *IB:* 36.

GR17 MA Mathematics/Russian
Duration: 5FT Hon
Entry Requirements: *GCE:* ABB. *SQAH:* AAAB-ABBB. *IB:* 36.

GVC2 MA Mathematics/Scottish History
Duration: 4FT Hon
Entry Requirements: *GCE:* ABB. *SQAH:* AAAB-ABBB. *IB:* 36.

GQ12 MA Mathematics/Scottish Literature
Duration: 4FT Hon
Entry Requirements: *GCE:* ABB. *SQAH:* AAAB-ABBB. *IB:* 36.

GW14 MA Mathematics/Theatre Studies
Duration: 4FT Hon
Entry Requirements: *GCE:* ABB. *SQAH:* AAAB-ABBB. *IB:* 36.

GV16 MA Mathematics/Theology & Religious Studies
Duration: 4FT Hon
Entry Requirements: *GCE:* ABB. *SQAH:* AAAB-ABBB. *IB:* 36.

RG41 MA Spanish/Mathematics
Duration: 5FT Hon
Entry Requirements: *GCE:* ABB. *SQAH:* AAAB-ABBB. *IB:* 36.

FG5D MSci Astronomy and Mathematics
Duration: 5FT Hon
Entry Requirements: *GCE:* ABB. *SQAH:* AAAB-BBBB. *IB:* 32.

FG11 MSci Chemistry and Mathematics
Duration: 5FT Hon
Entry Requirements: *GCE:* ABB. *SQAH:* AAAB-BBBB. *IB:* 32.

GG4C MSci Computing Science/Mathematics
Duration: 5FT Hon
Entry Requirements: *GCE:* ABB. *SQAH:* AAAB-BBBB. *IB:* 32.

FGJ1 MSci Mathematics and Physics
Duration: 5FT Hon
Entry Requirements: *GCE:* ABB. *SQAH:* AAAB-BBBB. *IB:* 32.

G70 UNIVERSITY OF GREENWICH
GREENWICH CAMPUS
OLD ROYAL NAVAL COLLEGE
PARK ROW
LONDON SE10 9LS
t: 020 8331 9000 f: 020 8331 8145
e: courseinfo@gre.ac.uk
// www.gre.ac.uk

GG41 BSc Mathematics and Computing
Duration: 3FT Hon
Entry Requirements: *GCE:* 260. *IB:* 24.

LG11 BSc Mathematics and Economics
Duration: 3FT Hon
Entry Requirements: *GCE:* 260. *IB:* 24.

G1N2 BSc Mathematics with Business
Duration: 3FT Hon
Entry Requirements: *GCE:* 260. *IB:* 24.

G1L1 BSc Mathematics with Economics
Duration: 3FT Hon
Entry Requirements: *GCE:* 260. *IB:* 24.

CFG0 BSc Science (Extended)
Duration: 4FT Hon
Entry Requirements: *GCE:* 80. *IB:* 24.

G74 GREENWICH SCHOOL OF MANAGEMENT
MERIDIAN HOUSE
ROYAL HILL
GREENWICH
LONDON SE10 8RD
t: +44(0)20 8516 7800 f: +44(0)20 8516 7801
e: admissions@greenwich-college.ac.uk
// www.greenwich-college.ac.uk/
?utm_source=UCAS&utm_medium=Profil

NG11 BSc Business Management and Information Technology (with Foundation Year)
Duration: 4FT Hon
Entry Requirements: *OCR ND:* P3 Interview required.

GN41 BSc Computer Science with Business Informatics (Accelerated with Foundation Year)
Duration: 3FT Hon
Entry Requirements: *OCR ND:* P3 Interview required.

H24 HERIOT-WATT UNIVERSITY, EDINBURGH
EDINBURGH CAMPUS
EDINBURGH EH14 4AS
t: 0131 449 5111 f: 0131 451 3630
e: ugadmissions@hw.ac.uk
// www.hw.ac.uk

CFG0 BSc Combined Studies option - Accountancy and Finance
Duration: 4FT Hon
Entry Requirements: *GCE:* ABB. *SQAH:* AAAB-ABBBC. *IB:* 29.

CFG0 BSc Combined Studies
Duration: 4FT Hon
Entry Requirements: *GCE:* ABB. *SQAH:* AAAB-ABBBC. *IB:* 29.

GG14 BSc Mathematics and Computer Science
Duration: 3FT/4FT Hon
Entry Requirements: *GCE:* BBB. *SQAH:* ABBBC. *SQAAH:* BBB. *IB:* 28.

G1G4 BSc Mathematics with Computer Science
Duration: 3FT/4FT Hon
Entry Requirements: *GCE:* BBB. *SQAH:* ABBBC. *SQAAH:* BBB. *IB:* 28.

G1N3 BSc Mathematics with Finance
Duration: 3FT/4FT Hon
Entry Requirements: *GCE:* BBB. *SQAH:* ABBBC. *SQAAH:* BBB. *IB:* 26.

G1R1 BSc Mathematics with French
Duration: 3FT/4FT Hon
Entry Requirements: *GCE:* BBB. *SQAH:* ABBBC. *IB:* 26.

G1R2 BSc Mathematics with German
Duration: 4FT Hon
Entry Requirements: *GCE:* BBB. *SQAH:* ABBBC. *IB:* 26.

G1F3 BSc Mathematics with Physics
Duration: 4FT Hon
Entry Requirements: *GCE:* BBB. *SQAH:* ABBBC. *SQAAH:* AAC. *IB:* 26.

G1C8 BSc Mathematics with Psychology
Duration: 3FT/4FT Hon
Entry Requirements: *GCE:* BBB. *SQAH:* ABBBC. *SQAAH:* BBB. *IB:* 26.

G1R4 BSc Mathematics with Spanish
Duration: 4FT Hon
Entry Requirements: *GCE:* BBB. *SQAH:* ABBBC. *IB:* 26.

H36 UNIVERSITY OF HERTFORDSHIRE
UNIVERSITY ADMISSIONS SERVICE
COLLEGE LANE
HATFIELD
HERTS AL10 9AB
t: 01707 284800
// www.herts.ac.uk

X3G1 BA Education Studies with Mathematics
Duration: 3FT Hon
Entry Requirements: Contact the institution for details.

N1G1 BSc Business/Mathematics
Duration: 3FT/4SW Hon
Entry Requirements: *GCE:* 300.

G4G1 BSc Computing/Mathematics
Duration: 3FT/4SW Hon
Entry Requirements: *GCE:* 280.

L1G1 BSc Economics/Mathematics
Duration: 3FT/4SW Hon
Entry Requirements: *GCE:* 280.

F9G1 BSc Environmental Studies/Mathematics
Duration: 3FT/4SW Hon
Entry Requirements: *GCE:* 280.

RG8C BSc European Studies/Mathematics
Duration: 3FT/4SW Hon
Entry Requirements: *GCE:* 280.

GN13 BSc Financial Mathematics
Duration: 3FT/4SW Hon
Entry Requirements: *GCE:* 260.

B9G1 BSc Health Studies/Mathematics
Duration: 3FT/4SW Hon
Entry Requirements: *GCE:* 280.

B1G1 BSc Human Biology/Mathematics
Duration: 3FT/4SW Hon
Entry Requirements: *GCE:* 280.

L7G1 BSc Human Geography/Mathematics
Duration: 3FT/4SW Hon
Entry Requirements: *GCE:* 280.

P5G1 BSc Journalism & Media Cultures/Mathematics
Duration: 3FT/4SW Hon
Entry Requirements: *GCE:* 300.

G1N1 BSc Mathematics/Business
Duration: 3FT/4SW Hon
Entry Requirements: *GCE:* 300.

G1G4 BSc Mathematics/Computing
Duration: 3FT/4SW Hon
Entry Requirements: *GCE:* 280.

G1L1 BSc Mathematics/Economics
Duration: 3FT/4SW Hon
Entry Requirements: *GCE:* 280.

G1F9 BSc Mathematics/Environmental Studies
Duration: 3FT/4SW Hon
Entry Requirements: *GCE:* 280.

G1R8 BSc Mathematics/European Studies
Duration: 3FT/4SW Hon
Entry Requirements: *GCE:* 280.

G1R1 BSc Mathematics/French
Duration: 3FT/4SW Hon
Entry Requirements: *GCE:* 280.

G1B9 BSc Mathematics/Health Studies
Duration: 3FT/4SW Hon
Entry Requirements: *GCE:* 280.

G1B1 BSc Mathematics/Human Biology
Duration: 3FT/4SW Hon
Entry Requirements: *GCE:* 280.

G1L7 BSc Mathematics/Human Geography
Duration: 3FT/4SW Hon
Entry Requirements: *GCE:* 280.

G1P5 BSc Mathematics/Journalism & Media Cultures
Duration: 3FT/4SW Hon
Entry Requirements: *GCE:* 300.

G1V5 BSc Mathematics/Philosophy
Duration: 3FT/4SW Hon
Entry Requirements: *GCE:* 300.

G1C8 BSc Mathematics/Psychology
Duration: 3FT/4SW Hon
Entry Requirements: *GCE:* 320.

G1R4 BSc Mathematics/Spanish
Duration: 3FT/4SW Hon
Entry Requirements: *GCE:* 280.

V5G1 BSc Philosophy/Mathematics
Duration: 3FT/4SW Hon
Entry Requirements: *GCE:* 300.

C8G1 BSc Psychology/Mathematics
Duration: 3FT/4SW Hon
Entry Requirements: *GCE:* 320.

H72 THE UNIVERSITY OF HULL
THE UNIVERSITY OF HULL
COTTINGHAM ROAD
HULL HU6 7RX
t: 01482 466100 f: 01482 442290
e: admissions@hull.ac.uk
// www.hull.ac.uk

F1G2 BSc Physics with Mathematics
Duration: 3FT Hon
Entry Requirements: *GCE:* 280-300. *IB:* 28. *BTEC ExtDip:* DDM.

F3G1 MPhys Physics with Mathematics
Duration: 4FT Hon
Entry Requirements: *GCE:* 280-300. *IB:* 28. *BTEC ExtDip:* DDM.

I50 IMPERIAL COLLEGE LONDON
REGISTRY
SOUTH KENSINGTON CAMPUS
IMPERIAL COLLEGE LONDON
LONDON SW7 2AZ
t: 020 7589 5111 f: 020 7594 8004
// www.imperial.ac.uk

GG14 BEng Mathematics and Computer Science
Duration: 3FT Hon
Entry Requirements: *GCE:* A*A*A. *SQAAH:* AAA. *IB:* 39.

G1F3 BSc Mathematics with Applied Mathematics/Mathematical Physics
Duration: 3FT Hon
Entry Requirements: *GCE:* A*A*A. *SQAAH:* AAA. *IB:* 39.

GG41 MEng Mathematics and Computer Science
Duration: 4FT Hon
Entry Requirements: *GCE:* A*A*A. *SQAAH:* AAA. *IB:* 39.

K12 KEELE UNIVERSITY
KEELE UNIVERSITY
STAFFORDSHIRE ST5 5BG
t: 01782 734005 f: 01782 632343
e: undergraduate@keele.ac.uk
// www.keele.ac.uk

NG41 BSc Accounting and Mathematics
Duration: 3FT Hon
Entry Requirements: *GCE:* ABB.

GT17 BSc American Studies and Mathematics
Duration: 3FT Hon
Entry Requirements: *GCE:* BBB.

FG71 BSc Applied Environmental Science and Mathematics
Duration: 3FT Hon
Entry Requirements: *GCE:* BBC.

CG8C BSc Applied Psychology and Mathematics
Duration: 4FT Deg
Entry Requirements: *GCE:* BBC.

FG51 BSc Astrophysics and Mathematics
Duration: 3FT Hon
Entry Requirements: *GCE:* BBC.

CG11 BSc Biology and Mathematics
Duration: 3FT Hon
Entry Requirements: *GCE:* BBC.

GN19 BSc Business Management and Mathematics
Duration: 3FT Hon
Entry Requirements: *GCE:* ABB.

FG11 BSc Chemistry and Mathematics
Duration: 3FT Hon
Entry Requirements: *GCE:* BBC.

GG14 BSc Computer Science and Mathematics
Duration: 3FT Hon
Entry Requirements: *GCE:* BBC.

LG31 BSc Computer Science and Sociology
Duration: 3FT Hon
Entry Requirements: *GCE:* BBC.

GG41 BSc Creative Computing and Mathematics
Duration: 3FT Hon
Entry Requirements: *GCE:* BBC.

GL11 BSc Economics and Mathematics
Duration: 3FT Hon
Entry Requirements: *GCE:* ABB.

GX13 BSc Educational Studies and Mathematics
Duration: 3FT Hon
Entry Requirements: *GCE:* BBC.

PG3C BSc Film Studies and Mathematics
Duration: 3FT Hon
Entry Requirements: *GCE:* BBB.

GN13 BSc Finance and Mathematics
Duration: 3FT Hon
Entry Requirements: *GCE:* ABB.

FG41 BSc Forensic Science and Mathematics
Duration: 3FT Hon
Entry Requirements: *GCE:* BBC.

LG71 BSc Geography and Mathematics
Duration: 3FT Hon
Entry Requirements: *GCE:* BBC.

GV11 BSc History and Mathematics
Duration: 3FT Hon
Entry Requirements: *GCE:* BBB.

CG1C BSc Human Biology and Mathematics
Duration: 3FT Hon
Entry Requirements: *GCE:* BBC.

GL17 BSc Human Geography and Mathematics
Duration: 3FT Hon
Entry Requirements: *GCE:* BBC.

GG15 BSc Information Systems and Mathematics
Duration: 3FT Hon
Entry Requirements: *GCE:* BBC.

NG11 BSc International Business and Mathematics
Duration: 3FT Hon
Entry Requirements: *GCE:* ABB.

GL12 BSc International Relations and Mathematics
Duration: 3FT Hon
Entry Requirements: *GCE:* BBB.

GM11 BSc Law and Mathematics
Duration: 3FT Hon
Entry Requirements: *GCE:* ABB.

GN15 BSc Marketing and Mathematics
Duration: 3FT Hon
Entry Requirements: *GCE:* ABB.

PG31 BSc Mathematics and Media, Communications & Culture
Duration: 3FT Hon
Entry Requirements: *GCE:* BBC.

FGC1 BSc Mathematics and Medicinal Chemistry
Duration: 3FT Hon
Entry Requirements: *GCE:* BBC.

GW13 BSc Mathematics and Music
Duration: 3FT Hon
Entry Requirements: *GCE:* BBC.

BG11 BSc Mathematics and Neuroscience
Duration: 3FT Hon
Entry Requirements: *GCE:* BBC.

GV15 BSc Mathematics and Philosophy
Duration: 3FT Hon
Entry Requirements: *GCE:* BBB.

FG81 BSc Mathematics and Physical Geography
Duration: 3FT Hon
Entry Requirements: *GCE:* BBC.

FG31 BSc Mathematics and Physics
Duration: 3FT Hon
Entry Requirements: *GCE:* BBC.

CG81 BSc Mathematics and Psychology
Duration: 3FT Hon
Entry Requirements: *GCE:* BBC.

GL13 BSc Mathematics and Sociology
Duration: 3FT Hon
Entry Requirements: *GCE:* BBC.

GG71 BSc Smart Systems and Mathematics
Duration: 3FT Hon
Entry Requirements: *GCE:* BBC.

K24 THE UNIVERSITY OF KENT
RECRUITMENT & ADMISSIONS OFFICE
REGISTRY
UNIVERSITY OF KENT
CANTERBURY, KENT CT2 7NZ
t: 01227 827272 f: 01227 827077
e: information@kent.ac.uk
// www.kent.ac.uk

GN14 BA Mathematics and Accounting & Finance (3 or 4 years)
Duration: 3FT/4SW Hon
Entry Requirements: *GCE:* 300. *IB:* 33. *OCR ND:* D *OCR NED:* M2

GN13 BSc Financial Mathematics
Duration: 3FT/4SW Hon
Entry Requirements: *GCE:* 300. *IB:* 33. *OCR ND:* D *OCR NED:* M2

K60 KING'S COLLEGE LONDON (UNIVERSITY OF LONDON)
STRAND
LONDON WC2R 2LS
t: 020 7836 5454 f: 020 7848 7171
e: prospective@kcl.ac.uk
// www.kcl.ac.uk/prospectus

GV15 BA Mathematics and Philosophy
Duration: 3FT Hon
Entry Requirements: *GCE:* A*AAa-AAAc. *SQAH:* AAB. *SQAAH:* AA. *IB:* 38.

GG14 BSc Mathematics and Computer Science
Duration: 3FT Hon
Entry Requirements: *GCE:* A*AAa-AAAc. *SQAH:* AAB. *SQAAH:* AA. *IB:* 38.

FG31 BSc Mathematics and Physics
Duration: 3FT Hon
Entry Requirements: *GCE:* A*AAa-AAAc. *SQAH:* AAB. *SQAAH:* AA. *IB:* 38.

FGJ1 BSc Mathematics and Physics with Astrophysics
Duration: 3FT Hon
Entry Requirements: *GCE:* AAA. *SQAH:* AAB. *SQAAH:* AA. *IB:* 38.

G1N2 BSc Mathematics with Management & Finance
Duration: 3FT Hon
Entry Requirements: *GCE:* A*AAa-AAAc. *SQAH:* AAB. *SQAAH:* AA. *IB:* 38.

FGH1 MSci Mathematics and Physics
Duration: 4FT Hon
Entry Requirements: *GCE:* A*AAa-AAAc. *SQAH:* AAB. *SQAAH:* AA. *IB:* 38.

K84 KINGSTON UNIVERSITY
STUDENT INFORMATION & ADVICE CENTRE
COOPER HOUSE
40-46 SURBITON ROAD
KINGSTON UPON THAMES KT1 2HX
t: 0844 8552177 f: 020 8547 7080
e: aps@kingston.ac.uk
// www.kingston.ac.uk

XG11 BA Primary Teaching (Mathematics)
Duration: 3FT Hon
Entry Requirements: *GCE:* 240. Interview required.

GG14 BSc Mathematics and Computing
Duration: 3FT Hon
Entry Requirements: *GCE:* 280.

GGC4 BSc Mathematics and Computing
Duration: 4SW Hon
Entry Requirements: *GCE:* 280.

GG1K BSc Mathematics and Computing (including year 0)
Duration: 4FT Hon
Entry Requirements: *GCE:* 80.

G1N2 BSc Mathematics with Business
Duration: 3FT Hon
Entry Requirements: *GCE:* 280.

G1NF BSc Mathematics with Business
Duration: 4SW Hon
Entry Requirements: *GCE:* 280.

G1NG BSc Mathematics with Business (Foundation)
Duration: 4FT Hon
Entry Requirements: *GCE:* 80.

L14 LANCASTER UNIVERSITY
THE UNIVERSITY
LANCASTER
LANCASHIRE LA1 4YW
t: 01524 592029 f: 01524 846243
e: ugadmissions@lancaster.ac.uk
// www.lancs.ac.uk

GL11 BA Economics and Mathematics
Duration: 3FT Hon
Entry Requirements: *GCE:* AAB. *SQAH:* ABBBB. *SQAAH:* ABB. *IB:* 35.

GR11 BA French Studies and Mathematics
Duration: 4SW Hon
Entry Requirements: *GCE:* AAB. *SQAH:* BBBBB. *SQAAH:* ABB. *IB:* 35.

GR12 BA German Studies and Mathematics
Duration: 4SW Hon
Entry Requirements: *GCE:* AAB. *SQAH:* BBBBB. *SQAAH:* BBB. *IB:* 35.

GV15 BA Mathematics and Philosophy
Duration: 3FT Hon
Entry Requirements: *GCE:* AAB. *SQAH:* ABBBB. *SQAAH:* ABB. *IB:* 35.

GR14 BA Spanish Studies and Mathematics
Duration: 4SW Hon
Entry Requirements: *GCE:* AAB. *SQAH:* BBBBB. *SQAAH:* BBB. *IB:* 35.

NG41 BSc Accounting, Finance and Mathematics
Duration: 3FT Hon
Entry Requirements: *GCE:* AAA. *SQAH:* AAABB. *SQAAH:* AAA. *IB:* 36.

GG14 BSc Computer Science and Mathematics
Duration: 3FT Hon
Entry Requirements: *GCE:* AAB. *SQAH:* ABBBB. *SQAAH:* ABB. *IB:* 35.

GF19 BSc Environmental Mathematics
Duration: 3FT Hon
Entry Requirements: *GCE:* AAB. *SQAH:* ABBBB. *SQAAH:* AAB. *IB:* 35.

GN13 BSc Financial Mathematics
Duration: 3FT Hon
Entry Requirements: *GCE:* AAA. *SQAH:* AAABB. *SQAAH:* AAA. *IB:* 36.

NG21 BSc Management Mathematics
Duration: 3FT Hon
Entry Requirements: *GCE:* AAB. *SQAH:* ABBBB. *SQAAH:* ABB. *IB:* 35.

GFC0 BSc Natural Sciences
Duration: 3FT Hon
Entry Requirements: *GCE:* AAA. *SQAH:* AAABB. *SQAAH:* AAA. *IB:* 36.

CFG0 BSc Natural Sciences/North America
Duration: 3FT Hon
Entry Requirements: *GCE:* AAA. *SQAH:* AAABB. *SQAAH:* AAA. *IB:* 36.

F3GC BSc Theoretical Physics with Mathematics
Duration: 3FT Hon
Entry Requirements: *GCE:* AAA. *SQAH:* AAABB. *SQAAH:* AAA. *IB:* 36.

F3G1 MSci Theoretical Physics with Mathematics
Duration: 4FT Hon
Entry Requirements: *GCE:* A*AA. *IB:* 38.

F3G5 MSci Theoretical Physics with Mathematics (North America)
Duration: 4FT Hon
Entry Requirements: Contact the institution for details.

L23 UNIVERSITY OF LEEDS
THE UNIVERSITY OF LEEDS
WOODHOUSE LANE
LEEDS LS2 9JT
t: 0113 343 3999
e: admissions@leeds.ac.uk
// www.leeds.ac.uk

NG31 BSc Actuarial Mathematics
Duration: 3FT Hon
Entry Requirements: *GCE:* AAB. *SQAAH:* AAB. *IB:* 34.

CG11 BSc Biology and Mathematics
Duration: 3FT Hon
Entry Requirements: *GCE:* AAB. *SQAAH:* ABB.

FG11 BSc Chemistry and Mathematics
Duration: 3FT Hon
Entry Requirements: *GCE:* AAB. *SQAAH:* ABB. *IB:* 30.

G4G1 BSc Computer Science with Mathematics
Duration: 3FT Hon
Entry Requirements: *GCE:* AAA. *SQAAH:* AAA. *IB:* 38.

GL11 BSc Economics and Mathematics
Duration: 3FT Hon
Entry Requirements: *GCE:* AAB. *SQAAH:* AAB.

GR11 BSc French and Mathematics
Duration: 4FT Hon
Entry Requirements: *GCE:* AAB. *SQAAH:* AAB. *IB:* 36.

FG81 BSc Geography and Mathematics
Duration: 3FT Hon
Entry Requirements: *GCE:* AAB. *SQAAH:* AAB.

GR12 BSc German and Mathematics
Duration: 4FT Hon
Entry Requirements: *GCE:* AAB. *SQAAH:* ABB.

GN12 BSc Management and Mathematics
Duration: 3FT Hon
Entry Requirements: *GCE:* AAB. *SQAAH:* ABB.

GW13 BSc Mathematics and Music
Duration: 3FT Hon
Entry Requirements: *GCE:* AAB. *SQAAH:* AAB.

GVC5 BSc Mathematics and Philosophy
Duration: 3FT Hon
Entry Requirements: *GCE:* AAB. *SQAAH:* AAB. *IB:* 36.

G1N3 BSc Mathematics with Finance
Duration: 3FT Hon
Entry Requirements: *GCE:* AAB. *SQAAH:* AAB. *IB:* 34.

FG31 BSc Physics and Mathematics
Duration: 3FT Hon
Entry Requirements: *GCE:* AAB. *SQAAH:* AAB.

L34 UNIVERSITY OF LEICESTER
UNIVERSITY ROAD
LEICESTER LE1 7RH
t: 0116 252 5281 f: 0116 252 2447
e: admissions@le.ac.uk
// www.le.ac.uk

GN13 BSc Financial Mathematics
Duration: 3FT Hon
Entry Requirements: *GCE:* AAB. *SQAH:* AAAAB-AAABB. *SQAAH:* AAB. *IB:* 34.

G1L1 BSc Mathematics with Economics
Duration: 3FT Hon
Entry Requirements: *GCE:* AAB. *SQAH:* AAAAB-AAABB. *SQAAH:* AAB. *IB:* 34.

G1N1 BSc Mathematics with Management
Duration: 3FT Hon
Entry Requirements: *GCE:* AAB. *SQAH:* AAAAB-AAABB. *SQAAH:* AAB. *IB:* 34.

L41 THE UNIVERSITY OF LIVERPOOL
THE FOUNDATION BUILDING
BROWNLOW HILL
LIVERPOOL L69 7ZX
t: 0151 794 2000 f: 0151 708 6502
e: ugrecruitment@liv.ac.uk
// www.liv.ac.uk

GL11 BA Economics and Mathematics
Duration: 3FT Hon
Entry Requirements: *GCE:* ABB. *SQAAH:* ABB. *IB:* 33. Interview required.

GR11 BA French and Mathematics
Duration: 4FT Hon
Entry Requirements: *GCE:* ABB. *SQAAH:* ABB. *IB:* 33. Interview required.

GV15 BA Mathematics and Philosophy
Duration: 3FT Hon
Entry Requirements: *GCE:* AAB. *SQAH:* AAABB. *SQAAH:* AAB. *IB:* 35. Interview required.

G1R9 BSc Mathematical Sciences with a European Language (4 years)
Duration: 4FT Hon
Entry Requirements: *GCE:* ABB. *SQAAH:* ABB. *IB:* 33. Interview required.

GN11 BSc Mathematics and Business Studies
Duration: 3FT Hon
Entry Requirements: *GCE:* ABB. *SQAAH:* ABB. *IB:* 33. Interview required.

GG14 BSc Mathematics and Computer Science
Duration: 3FT Hon
Entry Requirements: *GCE:* ABB. *SQAAH:* ABB. *IB:* 33. Interview required.

G1X3 BSc Mathematics with Education
Duration: 3FT Hon
Entry Requirements: *GCE:* ABB. *SQAAH:* ABB. *IB:* 33. Interview required.

G1N3 BSc Mathematics with Finance
Duration: 3FT Hon
Entry Requirements: *GCE:* ABB. *SQAAH:* ABB. *IB:* 33. Interview required.

G1F7 BSc Mathematics with Ocean & Climate Studies
Duration: 3FT Hon
Entry Requirements: *GCE:* ABB. *SQAAH:* ABB. *IB:* 33. Interview required.

FG31 BSc Physics and Mathematics
Duration: 3FT Hon
Entry Requirements: *GCE:* ABB. *SQAAH:* ABB. *IB:* 33. Interview required.

FGH1 MMath Mathematical Physics
Duration: 4FT Hon
Entry Requirements: *GCE:* ABB. *SQAAH:* ABB. *IB:* 33. Interview required.

L46 LIVERPOOL HOPE UNIVERSITY
HOPE PARK
LIVERPOOL L16 9JD
t: 0151 291 3331 f: 0151 291 3434
e: administration@hope.ac.uk
// www.hope.ac.uk

X3G1 BA Education and Mathematics
Duration: 3FT Hon   CRB Check: Required
Entry Requirements: *GCE:* 300-320. *IB:* 25.

X1GD BA Primary Teaching with Mathematics
Duration: 4FT Hon   CRB Check: Required
Entry Requirements: *GCE:* 300-320. *IB:* 25. Interview required.
Admissions Test required.

NG41 BSc Accounting and Mathematics
Duration: 3FT Hon
Entry Requirements: *GCE:* 300-320. *IB:* 25.

GF18 BSc Geography and Mathematics
Duration: 3FT Hon
Entry Requirements: *GCE:* 300-320. *IB:* 25.

LG51 BSc Health and Mathematics
Duration: 3FT Hon
Entry Requirements: *GCE:* 300-320. *IB:* 25.

GC11 BSc Human Biology and Mathematics
Duration: 3FT Hon
Entry Requirements: *GCE:* 300-320. *IB:* 25.

GC18 BSc Mathematics and Psychology
Duration: 3FT Hon
Entry Requirements: *GCE:* 300-320. *IB:* 25.

L51 LIVERPOOL JOHN MOORES UNIVERSITY
KINGSWAY HOUSE
HATTON GARDEN
LIVERPOOL L3 2AJ
t: 0151 231 5090 f: 0151 904 6368
e: courses@ljmu.ac.uk
// www.ljmu.ac.uk

XG30 BA Mathematics and Education Studies
Duration: 3FT Hon
Entry Requirements: *GCE:* 260.

GN11 BSc Mathematics
Duration: 4SW Hon
Entry Requirements: *GCE:* 260. *IB:* 24.

L68 LONDON METROPOLITAN UNIVERSITY
166-220 HOLLOWAY ROAD
LONDON N7 8DB
t: 020 7133 4200
e: admissions@londonmet.ac.uk
// www.londonmet.ac.uk

NG31 BSc Financial Mathematics
Duration: 3FT Hon
Entry Requirements: *GCE:* 200. *IB:* 28.

GGC4 BSc Mathematics and Computer Science
Duration: 3FT Hon
Entry Requirements: *GCE:* 200. *IB:* 28.

L72 LONDON SCHOOL OF ECONOMICS AND POLITICAL SCIENCE (UNIVERSITY OF LONDON)
HOUGHTON STREET
LONDON WC2A 2AE
t: 020 7955 7125 f: 020 7955 6001
e: ug.admissions@lse.ac.uk
// www.lse.ac.uk

GL11 BSc Mathematics and Economics
Duration: 3FT Hon
Entry Requirements: *GCE:* A*AA. *SQAH:* AAAAA. *SQAAH:* AAA. *IB:* 38.

G1L1 BSc Mathematics with Economics
Duration: 3FT Hon
Entry Requirements: *GCE:* A*AA. *SQAH:* AAAAA. *SQAAH:* AAA. *IB:* 38.

L79 LOUGHBOROUGH UNIVERSITY
LOUGHBOROUGH
LEICESTERSHIRE LE11 3TU
t: 01509 223522 f: 01509 223905
e: admissions@lboro.ac.uk
// www.lboro.ac.uk

GG4C BSc Computer Science and Mathematics
Duration: 3FT Hon
Entry Requirements: *GCE:* AAB-ABB. *SQAH:* BBBBB. *SQAAH:* AB. *IB:* 32. *BTEC ExtDip:* DDD.

GG4D BSc Computer Science and Mathematics
Duration: 4SW Hon
Entry Requirements: *GCE:* AAB-ABB. *SQAH:* BBBBB. *SQAAH:* AB. *IB:* 32. *BTEC ExtDip:* DDD.

GN13 BSc Financial Mathematics
Duration: 3FT Hon
Entry Requirements: *GCE:* AAA-AAB. *SQAH:* ABB. *SQAAH:* AA. *IB:* 36.

GNC3 BSc Financial Mathematics
Duration: 4SW Hon
Entry Requirements: *GCE:* AAA-AAB. *SQAH:* ABB. *SQAAH:* AA. *IB:* 36.

G1N4 BSc Mathematics and Accounting and Financial Management
Duration: 3FT Hon
Entry Requirements: *GCE:* AAA-AAB. *SQAH:* ABB. *SQAAH:* AA. *IB:* 36.

G1NK BSc Mathematics and Accounting and Financial Management
Duration: 4SW Hon
Entry Requirements: *GCE:* AAA-AAB. *SQAH:* ABB. *SQAAH:* AA. *IB:* 36.

CG61 BSc Mathematics and Sports Science
Duration: 3FT Hon
Entry Requirements: *GCE:* AAA-AAB. *SQAH:* ABB. *SQAAH:* AA. *IB:* 36.

GC16 BSc Mathematics and Sports Science
Duration: 4SW Hon
Entry Requirements: *GCE:* AAA-AAB. *SQAH:* ABB. *SQAAH:* AA. *IB:* 36.

G1L1 BSc Mathematics with Economics
Duration: 3FT Hon
Entry Requirements: *GCE:* AAA-AAB. *SQAH:* ABB. *SQAAH:* AA. *IB:* 36.

G1LC BSc Mathematics with Economics
Duration: 4SW Hon
Entry Requirements: *GCE:* AAA-AAB. *SQAH:* ABB. *SQAAH:* AA. *IB:* 36.

G1N2 BSc Mathematics with Management
Duration: 3FT Hon
Entry Requirements: *GCE:* AAA-AAB. *SQAH:* ABB. *SQAAH:* AA. *IB:* 36.

G1NF BSc Mathematics with Management
Duration: 4SW Hon
Entry Requirements: *GCE:* AAA-AAB. *SQAH:* ABB. *SQAAH:* AA. *IB:* 36.

G1X3 BSc Mathematics with Mathematics Education
Duration: 3FT Hon
Entry Requirements: *GCE:* AAA-AAB. *SQAH:* ABB. *SQAAH:* AA. *IB:* 36.

G1XH BSc Mathematics with Mathematics Education
Duration: 4SW Hon
Entry Requirements: *GCE:* AAA-AAB. *SQAH:* ABB. *SQAAH:* AA. *IB:* 36.

FG31 BSc Physics and Mathematics
Duration: 3FT Hon
Entry Requirements: *GCE:* AAB-ABB. *SQAH:* AB. *SQAAH:* AB. *IB:* 34.

GF13 BSc Physics and Mathematics
Duration: 4SW Hon
Entry Requirements: *GCE:* AAB-ABB. *SQAH:* AB. *SQAAH:* AB. *IB:* 34.

FG3C MPhys Physics and Mathematics
Duration: 4FT Hon
Entry Requirements: *GCE:* AAA-AAB. *SQAH:* AA. *SQAAH:* AA. *IB:* 36.

FG3D MPhys Physics and Mathematics
Duration: 5SW Hon
Entry Requirements: *GCE:* AAA-AAB. *SQAH:* AA. *SQAAH:* AA. *IB:* 36.

GGK1 MSci Computer Science and Mathematics
Duration: 4FT Hon
Entry Requirements: *GCE:* AAA-AAB. *SQAH:* AAAAA. *SQAAH:* AB. *IB:* 34. *BTEC ExtDip:* DDD.

GGL1 MSci Computer Science and Mathematics
Duration: 5SW Hon
Entry Requirements: *GCE:* AAA-AAB. *SQAH:* AAAAA. *SQAAH:* AB. *IB:* 34. *BTEC ExtDip:* DDD.

M20 THE UNIVERSITY OF MANCHESTER
RUTHERFORD BUILDING
OXFORD ROAD
MANCHESTER M13 9PL
t: 0161 275 2077 f: 0161 275 2106
e: ug-admissions@manchester.ac.uk
// www.manchester.ac.uk

NG31 BSc Actuarial Science and Mathematics
Duration: 3FT Hon
Entry Requirements: *GCE:* A*AB-AAB. *SQAH:* AAAAB. *SQAAH:* AAB. *IB:* 36. Interview required.

GG14 BSc Computer Science and Mathematics
Duration: 3FT Hon
Entry Requirements: *GCE:* AAB. *SQAH:* AAAAB. *SQAAH:* AAB. *IB:* 35. Interview required.

GG41 BSc Computer Science and Mathematics with Industrial Experience (4 years)
Duration: 4FT Hon
Entry Requirements: *GCE:* AAB. *SQAH:* AAAAB. *SQAAH:* AAB. *IB:* 35. Interview required.

GV15 BSc Mathematics and Philosophy
Duration: 3FT Hon
Entry Requirements: *GCE:* A*AB-AAB. *SQAH:* AAAAB. *SQAAH:* AAB. *IB:* 36. Interview required.

FG31 BSc Mathematics and Physics
Duration: 3FT Hon
Entry Requirements: *GCE:* A*A*A-A*AA. *SQAAH:* AAA. Interview required.

G1N2 BSc Mathematics with Business & Management
Duration: 3FT Hon
Entry Requirements: *GCE:* A*AB-AAB. *SQAH:* AAAAB. *SQAAH:* AAB. *IB:* 36. Interview required.

G1N3 BSc Mathematics with Finance
Duration: 3FT Hon
Entry Requirements: *GCE:* A*AB-AAB. *SQAH:* AAAAB. *SQAAH:* AAB. *IB:* 36. Interview required.

G1NH BSc Mathematics with Financial Mathematics
Duration: 3FT Hon
Entry Requirements: *GCE:* A*AB-AAB. *SQAH:* AAAAB. *SQAAH:* AAB. *IB:* 36. Interview required.

G1R9 BSc Mathematics with a Modern Language (4 years)
Duration: 4FT Hon
Entry Requirements: *GCE:* A*AB-AAB. *SQAH:* AAAAB. *SQAAH:* AAB. *IB:* 36. Interview required.

G1NJ MMath Mathematics with Financial Mathematics
Duration: 4FT Hon
Entry Requirements: *GCE:* A*AB-AAB. *SQAH:* AAAAB. *SQAAH:* AAB. *IB:* 36. Interview required.

FG3C MMath&Phys Mathematics and Physics
Duration: 4FT Hon
Entry Requirements: *GCE:* A*A*A-A*AA. *SQAAH:* AAA. Interview required.

M40 THE MANCHESTER METROPOLITAN UNIVERSITY
ADMISSIONS OFFICE
ALL SAINTS (GMS)
ALL SAINTS
MANCHESTER M15 6BH
t: 0161 247 2000
// www.mmu.ac.uk

GL11 BA/BSc Economics/Mathematics
Duration: 3FT Hon
Entry Requirements: *GCE:* 240-280. *IB:* 29.

XG31 BA/BSc Education Studies/Mathematics
Duration: 3FT Hon **CRB Check:** Required
Entry Requirements: *GCE:* 240-280. *IB:* 29.

G190 BSc Financial Mathematics
Duration: 3FT Hon
Entry Requirements: *GCE:* 260.

N21 NEWCASTLE UNIVERSITY
KING'S GATE
NEWCASTLE UPON TYNE NE1 7RU
t: 01912083333
// www.ncl.ac.uk

NG41 BSc Accounting and Mathematics
Duration: 3FT Hon
Entry Requirements: *GCE:* AAB. *SQAH:* AAABB. *IB:* 35.

GL11 BSc Economics and Mathematics
Duration: 3FT Hon
Entry Requirements: *GCE:* AAB. *SQAH:* AAABB. *IB:* 35.

CG81 BSc Mathematics and Psychology
Duration: 3FT Hon
Entry Requirements: *GCE:* AAB. *SQAH:* AAABB. *IB:* 35.

G1C1 BSc Mathematics with Biology
Duration: 3FT Hon
Entry Requirements: *GCE:* AAB. *SQAAH:* AB.

G1N2 BSc Mathematics with Management
Duration: 3FT Hon
Entry Requirements: *GCE:* AAB. *SQAAH:* AB.

N37 UNIVERSITY OF WALES, NEWPORT
ADMISSIONS
LODGE ROAD
CAERLEON
NEWPORT NP18 3QT
t: 01633 432030 f: 01633 432850
e: admissions@newport.ac.uk
// www.newport.ac.uk

XG11 BSc Secondary Mathematics with ICT with QTS (2 years)
Duration: 2FT Ord **CRB Check:** Required
Entry Requirements: Interview required.

XG1C BSc Secondary Mathematics with Science with QTS (2 years)
Duration: 2FT Ord **CRB Check:** Required
Entry Requirements: Interview required.

XF1A BSc Secondary Science with Mathematics with QTS (2 years)
Duration: 2FT Ord **CRB Check:** Required
Entry Requirements: Interview required.

N77 NORTHUMBRIA UNIVERSITY
TRINITY BUILDING
NORTHUMBERLAND ROAD
NEWCASTLE UPON TYNE NE1 8ST
t: 0191 243 7420 f: 0191 227 4561
e: er.admissions@northumbria.ac.uk
// www.northumbria.ac.uk

G1N2 BSc Mathematics with Business
Duration: 3FT/4SW Hon
Entry Requirements: *GCE:* 320. *SQAH:* BBBBB. *SQAAH:* BBB. *IB:* 27.

G1N1 MMath Mathematics with Business
Duration: 4FT/5SW Hon
Entry Requirements: Contact the institution for details.

N84 THE UNIVERSITY OF NOTTINGHAM
THE ADMISSIONS OFFICE
THE UNIVERSITY OF NOTTINGHAM
UNIVERSITY PARK
NOTTINGHAM NG7 2RD
t: 0115 951 5151 f: 0115 951 4668
// www.nottingham.ac.uk

GG41 BSc Mathematics and Computer Science
Duration: 3FT Hon
Entry Requirements: *GCE:* AAA-AAB. *SQAAH:* AAA-AAB. *IB:* 38.

GL11 BSc Mathematics and Economics
Duration: 3FT Hon
Entry Requirements: *GCE:* AAA. *SQAAH:* AAA. *IB:* 38.

GN12 BSc Mathematics and Management Studies
Duration: 3FT Hon
Entry Requirements: *GCE:* AAA-AAB. *SQAAH:* AAA-AAB. *IB:* 38.

GV15 BSc Mathematics and Philosophy
Duration: 3FT Hon
Entry Requirements: *GCE:* AAA-AAB. *SQAAH:* AAA-AAB. *IB:* 38.

GG14 MSci Mathematics and Computer Science
Duration: 4FT Hon
Entry Requirements: *GCE:* AAA-AAB. *SQAAH:* AAA-AAB. *IB:* 38.

N91 NOTTINGHAM TRENT UNIVERSITY
DRYDEN BUILDING
BURTON STREET
NOTTINGHAM NG1 4BU
t: +44 (0) 115 848 4200 f: +44 (0) 115 848 8869
e: applications@ntu.ac.uk
// www.ntu.ac.uk

GG4C BSc Computer Science and Mathematics
Duration: 3FT/4SW Hon
Entry Requirements: *GCE:* 280.

GN13 BSc Financial Mathematics
Duration: 3FT/4SW Hon
Entry Requirements: *GCE:* 280. *BTEC Dip:* D*D*. *BTEC ExtDip:* DMM. *OCR NED:* M2

CG6C BSc Sport Science and Mathematics
Duration: 3FT Hon
Entry Requirements: *GCE:* 280.

O33 OXFORD UNIVERSITY
UNDERGRADUATE ADMISSIONS OFFICE
UNIVERSITY OF OXFORD
WELLINGTON SQUARE
OXFORD OX1 2JD
t: 01865 288000 f: 01865 270212
e: undergraduate.admissions@admin.ox.ac.uk
// www.admissions.ox.ac.uk

GG14 BA Mathematics and Computer Science (3 or 4 years)
Duration: 3FT/4FT Hon
Entry Requirements: *GCE:* A*AA. *SQAH:* AAAAA-AAAAB. *SQAAH:* AAB. Interview required. Admissions Test required.

GV15 BA Mathematics and Philosophy (4 years)
Duration: 4FT Hon
Entry Requirements: *GCE:* A*A*A. *SQAH:* AAAAA-AAAAB. *SQAAH:* AAB. Interview required. Admissions Test required.

O66 OXFORD BROOKES UNIVERSITY
ADMISSIONS OFFICE
HEADINGTON CAMPUS
GIPSY LANE
OXFORD OX3 0BP
t: 01865 483040 f: 01865 483983
e: admissions@brookes.ac.uk
// www.brookes.ac.uk

NG21 BA/BSc Business Management/Mathematics
Duration: 3FT Hon
Entry Requirements: *GCE:* BBC.

XG31 BA/BSc Education Studies/Mathematics
Duration: 3FT Hon
Entry Requirements: Contact the institution for details.

GW13 BA/BSc Mathematics/Music
Duration: 3FT Hon
Entry Requirements: *GCE:* BCC.

GV15 BA/BSc Mathematics/Philosophy
Duration: 3FT Hon
Entry Requirements: *GCE:* BBC-CCD.

GG41 BSc Computer Science/Mathematics
Duration: 3FT Hon
Entry Requirements: *GCE:* BBC. *IB:* 30.

BGC1 BSc Human Biosciences/Mathematics
Duration: 3FT Hon
Entry Requirements: Contact the institution for details.

P60 PLYMOUTH UNIVERSITY
DRAKE CIRCUS
PLYMOUTH PL4 8AA
t: 01752 585858 f: 01752 588055
e: admissions@plymouth.ac.uk
// www.plymouth.ac.uk

X1G1 BEd Primary (Mathematics)
Duration: 3FT Hon   CRB Check: Required
Entry Requirements: IB: 26. OCR ND: D Interview required.

G1X3 BSc Mathematics with Education
Duration: 3FT Hon
Entry Requirements: GCE: 320. IB: 30.

G1N3 BSc Mathematics with Finance
Duration: 3FT Hon
Entry Requirements: GCE: 320. IB: 30.

Q50 QUEEN MARY, UNIVERSITY OF LONDON
QUEEN MARY, UNIVERSITY OF LONDON
MILE END ROAD
LONDON E1 4NS
t: 020 7882 5555 f: 020 7882 5500
e: admissions@qmul.ac.uk
// www.qmul.ac.uk

GG41 BSc Computer Science and Mathematics
Duration: 3FT Hon
Entry Requirements: GCE: 340. IB: 32.

G1N1 BSc Mathematics with Business Management
Duration: 3FT Hon
Entry Requirements: GCE: 340. IB: 36.

G1N4 BSc Mathematics with Finance & Accounting
Duration: 3FT Hon
Entry Requirements: GCE: 340. IB: 36.

G1C8 BSc Mathematics with Psychology
Duration: 3FT Hon
Entry Requirements: GCE: 340. IB: 36.

GN13 BSc Mathematics, Business Management and Finance
Duration: 3FT Hon
Entry Requirements: GCE: 340. IB: 36.

GL11 BSc Mathematics, Statistics and Financial Economics
Duration: 3FT Hon
Entry Requirements: GCE: AAB. IB: 36.

GGX1 BSc Science & Engineering Foundation Programme (Mathematical Science 4 Year)
Duration: 4FT Hon
Entry Requirements: GCE: 280. IB: 26.

LG11 BScEcon Economics, Statistics and Mathematics
Duration: 3FT Hon
Entry Requirements: GCE: AAB. SQAAH: AAB. IB: 36.

GGY1 MSci Science & Engineering Foundation Programme (Mathematical Science 5 Year)
Duration: 5FT Hon
Entry Requirements: GCE: 280-300. IB: 28.

Q75 QUEEN'S UNIVERSITY BELFAST
UNIVERSITY ROAD
BELFAST BT7 1NN
t: 028 9097 3838 f: 028 9097 5151
e: admissions@qub.ac.uk
// www.qub.ac.uk

GF13 BSc Applied Mathematics and Physics
Duration: 3FT Hon
Entry Requirements: GCE: ABC-ABDb. IB: 32.

G1G4 BSc Computational Mathematics
Duration: 3FT/4FT Hon
Entry Requirements: GCE: ABC-ACCb. IB: 32.

GG41 BSc Mathematics and Computer Science
Duration: 3FT Hon
Entry Requirements: GCE: ABC-ACCb. IB: 32.

G1N3 BSc Mathematics with Finance
Duration: 3FT Hon
Entry Requirements: Contact the institution for details.

GFC3 MSci Applied Mathematics and Physics
Duration: 4FT Hon
Entry Requirements: GCE: AAB-ABBa. IB: 34.

GGK1 MSci Mathematics and Computer Science
Duration: 4FT Hon
Entry Requirements: GCE: AAB-ABBa. IB: 34.

R12 THE UNIVERSITY OF READING
THE UNIVERSITY OF READING
PO BOX 217
READING RG6 6AH
t: 0118 378 8619 f: 0118 378 8924
e: student.recruitment@reading.ac.uk
// www.reading.ac.uk

G1G4 BSc Computational Mathematics
Duration: 3FT Hon
Entry Requirements: GCE: 320-340.

GL11 BSc Mathematics and Economics
Duration: 3FT Hon
Entry Requirements: *GCE:* 320-340.

GF19 BSc Mathematics and Meteorology
Duration: 3FT Hon
Entry Requirements: *GCE:* 320-340.

GC18 BSc Mathematics and Psychology
Duration: 3FT Hon
Entry Requirements: *GCE:* AAB. *SQAH:* AABBB. *SQAAH:* AAB.
BTEC Dip: DD. *BTEC ExtDip:* DDD. *OCR ND:* D *OCR NED:* M3

G1N3 BSc Mathematics with Finance and Investment Banking
Duration: 3FT Hon
Entry Requirements: *GCE:* 360. *SQAH:* AAABB. *SQAAH:* AAB.
BTEC Dip: DD. *BTEC ExtDip:* DDD. *OCR ND:* D *OCR NED:* M3

GFC9 MMath Mathematics and Meteorology (MMath) (4 years)
Duration: 4FT Hon
Entry Requirements: *GCE:* 340. *SQAH:* AABBB. *SQAAH:* AAB.
BTEC Dip: DD. *BTEC ExtDip:* DDD. *OCR ND:* D *OCR NED:* M3

R48 ROEHAMPTON UNIVERSITY
ROEHAMPTON LANE
LONDON SW15 5PU
t: 020 8392 3232 f: 020 8392 3470
e: enquiries@roehampton.ac.uk
// www.roehampton.ac.uk

XGC1 BA Primary Education Foundation Stage & Key Stage 1 (Mathematic Education)
Duration: 3FT Hon   CRB Check: Required
Entry Requirements: *GCE:* 320. *IB:* 27. *BTEC ExtDip:* DDM. *OCR NED:* D2 Interview required.

XG1C BA Primary Education Key Stage 2 (Mathematics Education)
Duration: 3FT Hon   CRB Check: Required
Entry Requirements: *GCE:* 320. *IB:* 27. *BTEC ExtDip:* DDM. *OCR NED:* D2 Interview required.

R72 ROYAL HOLLOWAY, UNIVERSITY OF LONDON
ROYAL HOLLOWAY, UNIVERSITY OF LONDON
EGHAM
SURREY TW20 0EX
t: 01784 414944 f: 01784 473662
e: Admissions@rhul.ac.uk
// www.rhul.ac.uk

R1G1 BA French with Mathematics
Duration: 4FT Hon
Entry Requirements: *GCE:* ABB. *SQAH:* AABBB. *SQAAH:* ABB. *IB:* 34.

N2G1 BA Management with Mathematics
Duration: 3FT Hon
Entry Requirements: *GCE:* AAB. *SQAH:* AAAAB. *SQAAH:* AAB. *IB:* 35.

GW13 BA Mathematics and Music
Duration: 3FT Hon
Entry Requirements: *GCE:* 340. *SQAH:* AAAAB. *SQAAH:* A. *IB:* 35.

G1R1 BA Mathematics with French
Duration: 3FT Hon
Entry Requirements: *GCE:* 320. *SQAH:* AABBB. *SQAAH:* A. *IB:* 34.

G1R4 BA Mathematics with Spanish
Duration: 3FT Hon
Entry Requirements: *GCE:* 320. *SQAH:* AABBB. *SQAAH:* A. *IB:* 34.

GG41 BSc Computer Science and Mathematics
Duration: 3FT Hon
Entry Requirements: *GCE:* ABC. *IB:* 32.

LG11 BSc Economics and Mathematics
Duration: 3FT Hon
Entry Requirements: *GCE:* AAB. *IB:* 35.

NG31 BSc Finance and Mathematics
Duration: 3FT Hon
Entry Requirements: *GCE:* AAB. *IB:* 35.

GN12 BSc Mathematics and Management
Duration: 3FT Hon
Entry Requirements: *IB:* 35.

GF13 BSc Mathematics and Physics
Duration: 3FT Hon
Entry Requirements: *IB:* 35.

GC18 BSc Mathematics and Psychology
Duration: 3FT Hon
Entry Requirements: *IB:* 35.

G1R2 BSc Mathematics with German
Duration: 3FT Hon
Entry Requirements: *GCE:* 320. *SQAH:* AABBB. *SQAAH:* A. *IB:* 34.

G1R3 BSc Mathematics with Italian
Duration: 3FT Hon
Entry Requirements: *GCE:* 320. *SQAH:* AABBB. *SQAAH:* A. *IB:* 34.

G1N2 BSc Mathematics with Management
Duration: 3FT Hon
Entry Requirements: *IB:* 35.

G1V5 BSc Mathematics with Philosophy
Duration: 3FT Hon
Entry Requirements: *GCE:* 320. *IB:* 34.

GFC3 MSci Mathematics and Physics
Duration: 4FT Hon
Entry Requirements: *IB:* 35.

S18 THE UNIVERSITY OF SHEFFIELD
THE UNIVERSITY OF SHEFFIELD
LEVEL 2, ARTS TOWER
WESTERN BANK
SHEFFIELD S10 2TN
t: 0114 222 8030 f: 0114 222 8032
// www.sheffield.ac.uk

NG41 BA Accounting & Financial Management and Mathematics
Duration: 3FT Hon
Entry Requirements: *GCE:* AAB. *SQAH:* AAABB. *SQAAH:* AB. *IB:* 35. *BTEC ExtDip:* DDD.

NG21 BA Business Management and Mathematics
Duration: 3FT Hon
Entry Requirements: *GCE:* AAB. *SQAH:* AAABB. *SQAAH:* AB. *IB:* 35. *BTEC ExtDip:* DDD.

GG41 BSc Computer Science and Mathematics (3 years)
Duration: 3FT Hon
Entry Requirements: *GCE:* AAB. *SQAH:* AAABB. *SQAAH:* A. *IB:* 35. *BTEC Dip:* DD. *BTEC ExtDip:* DDD.

LG11 BSc Economics and Mathematics
Duration: 3FT Hon
Entry Requirements: *GCE:* AAB. *SQAH:* AAABB. *SQAAH:* AB. *IB:* 35. *BTEC Dip:* DD. *BTEC ExtDip:* DDD.

GN13 BSc Financial Mathematics
Duration: 3FT Hon
Entry Requirements: *GCE:* AAB. *SQAH:* AAABB. *SQAAH:* AB. *IB:* 35. *BTEC ExtDip:* DDD.

VG51 BSc Mathematics and Philosophy (3 years)
Duration: 3FT Hon
Entry Requirements: *GCE:* AAB. *SQAH:* AAABB. *SQAAH:* AB. *IB:* 35. *BTEC ExtDip:* DDD.

G4G1 MComp Computer Science with Mathematics (4 years)
Duration: 4FT Hon
Entry Requirements: *GCE:* AAB. *SQAH:* AAABB. *SQAAH:* A. *IB:* 35. *BTEC Dip:* DD. *BTEC ExtDip:* DDD.

G1R1 MMath Mathematics with French
Duration: 4FT Hon
Entry Requirements: *GCE:* AAB. *SQAH:* AAABB. *SQAAH:* AB. *IB:* 35. *BTEC ExtDip:* DDD.

G1R2 MMath Mathematics with German
Duration: 4FT Hon
Entry Requirements: *GCE:* AAB. *SQAH:* AAABB. *SQAAH:* AB. *IB:* 35. *BTEC ExtDip:* DDD.

G1R4 MMath Mathematics with Spanish
Duration: 4FT Hon
Entry Requirements: *GCE:* AAB. *SQAH:* AAABB. *SQAAH:* AB. *IB:* 35. *BTEC ExtDip:* DDD.

S21 SHEFFIELD HALLAM UNIVERSITY
CITY CAMPUS
HOWARD STREET
SHEFFIELD S1 1WB
t: 0114 225 5555 f: 0114 225 2167
e: admissions@shu.ac.uk
// www.shu.ac.uk

XG11 BSc Mathematics with Education and Qualified Teacher Status
Duration: 3FT Hon
Entry Requirements: *GCE:* 200-240.

S27 UNIVERSITY OF SOUTHAMPTON
HIGHFIELD
SOUTHAMPTON SO17 1BJ
t: 023 8059 4732 f: 023 8059 3037
e: admissions@soton.ac.uk
// www.southampton.ac.uk

VG51 BA Philosophy and Mathematics
Duration: 3FT Hon
Entry Requirements: *GCE:* AAB. *IB:* 34.

G1N3 BSc Mathematics with Actuarial Science
Duration: 3FT Hon
Entry Requirements: *GCE:* AAA-AAB. *SQAH:* AAAAA. *SQAAH:* AA. *IB:* 36.

G1F5 BSc Mathematics with Astronomy
Duration: 3FT Hon
Entry Requirements: *GCE:* AAA-AAB. *SQAH:* AAAAA. *SQAAH:* AA. *IB:* 36.

G1C1 BSc Mathematics with Biology
Duration: 3FT Hon
Entry Requirements: *GCE:* AAA-AAB. *SQAH:* AAAAA. *SQAAH:* AA. *IB:* 36.

G1G4 BSc Mathematics with Computer Science
Duration: 3FT Hon
Entry Requirements: *GCE:* AAA-AAB. *SQAH:* AAAAA. *SQAAH:* AA. *IB:* 36.

G1NH BSc Mathematics with Finance
Duration: 3FT Hon
Entry Requirements: *GCE:* AAA-AAB. *SQAH:* AAAAA. *SQAAH:* AA. *IB:* 36.

G1R1 BSc Mathematics with French
Duration: 4FT Hon
Entry Requirements: *GCE:* AAA-AAB. *SQAH:* AAAAA. *SQAAH:* AA. *IB:* 36.

G1R2 BSc Mathematics with German
Duration: 4FT Hon
Entry Requirements: *GCE:* AAA-AAB. *SQAH:* AAAAA. *SQAAH:* AA.
IB: 36.

G1W3 BSc Mathematics with Music
Duration: 3FT Hon
Entry Requirements: *GCE:* AAA-AAB. *SQAH:* AAAAA. *SQAAH:* AA.
IB: 36.

G1F3 BSc Mathematics with Physics
Duration: 3FT Hon
Entry Requirements: *GCE:* AAA-AAB. *SQAH:* AAAAA. *SQAAH:* AA.
IB: 36.

G1R4 BSc Mathematics with Spanish
Duration: 4FT Hon
Entry Requirements: *GCE:* AAA-AAB. *SQAH:* AAAAA. *SQAAH:* AA.
IB: 36.

F3G1 BSc Physics with Mathematics
Duration: 3FT Hon
Entry Requirements: *GCE:* 340. *IB:* 34.

F1GC MChem Chemistry with Mathematics
Duration: 4FT Hon
Entry Requirements: *GCE:* AAB-ABB. *SQAH:* AABBB. *SQAAH:* ABB.
IB: 34. Interview required.

F3GC MPhys Physics with Mathematics (4 years)
Duration: 4FT Hon
Entry Requirements: *GCE:* 340. *IB:* 34.

S36 UNIVERSITY OF ST ANDREWS
ST KATHARINE'S WEST
16 THE SCORES
ST ANDREWS
FIFE KY16 9AX
t: 01334 462150 f: 01334 463330
e: admissions@st-andrews.ac.uk
// www.st-andrews.ac.uk

CG11 BSc Biology and Mathematics
Duration: 4FT Hon
Entry Requirements: *GCE:* AAA. *SQAH:* AAAB. *IB:* 36.

FG11 BSc Chemistry and Mathematics
Duration: 4FT Hon
Entry Requirements: *GCE:* AAA. *SQAH:* AAAB. *IB:* 36.

GG14 BSc Computer Science and Mathematics
Duration: 4FT Hon
Entry Requirements: *GCE:* AAA. *SQAH:* AAAA. *IB:* 38.

GLC1 BSc Economics and Mathematics
Duration: 4FT Hon
Entry Requirements: *GCE:* AAA. *SQAH:* AAAB. *IB:* 38.

GF18 BSc Geography and Mathematics
Duration: 4FT Hon
Entry Requirements: *GCE:* AAA. *SQAH:* AAAB. *IB:* 36.

GG1K BSc Internet Computer Science-Mathematics
Duration: 4FT Hon
Entry Requirements: *GCE:* AAA. *SQAH:* AAAB. *IB:* 36.

GVC5 BSc Logic & Philosophy of Science and Mathematics
Duration: 4FT Hon
Entry Requirements: *GCE:* AAA. *SQAH:* AAAB. *IB:* 36.

GN12 BSc Management Science and Mathematics
Duration: 4FT Hon
Entry Requirements: *GCE:* AAA. *SQAH:* AAAA. *IB:* 38.

FG31 BSc Mathematics and Physics
Duration: 3FT/4FT Hon
Entry Requirements: *GCE:* AAA. *SQAH:* AAAA. *SQAAH:* AA. *IB:* 38.

GC18 BSc Mathematics and Psychology
Duration: 4FT Hon
Entry Requirements: *GCE:* AAA. *SQAH:* AAAB. *IB:* 36.

G1F8 BSc Mathematics with Geography
Duration: 4FT Hon
Entry Requirements: *GCE:* AAA. *SQAH:* AAAB. *IB:* 36.

GVC1 MA Ancient History and Mathematics
Duration: 4FT Hon
Entry Requirements: *GCE:* AAA. *SQAH:* AAAB. *IB:* 36.

GT16 MA Arabic and Mathematics
Duration: 4FT Hon
Entry Requirements: *GCE:* AAA. *SQAH:* AAAB. *IB:* 36.

TG61 MA Arabic and Mathematics (year abroad)
Duration: 5FT Hon
Entry Requirements: *GCE:* AAA. *SQAH:* AAAB. *IB:* 36.

GV13 MA Art History and Mathematics
Duration: 4FT Hon
Entry Requirements: *GCE:* AAA. *SQAH:* AAAB. *IB:* 36.

VG61 MA Biblical Studies and Mathematics
Duration: 4FT Hon
Entry Requirements: *GCE:* AAA. *SQAH:* AAAB. *IB:* 36.

QG81 MA Classical Studies and Mathematics
Duration: 4FT Hon
Entry Requirements: *GCE:* AAA. *SQAH:* AAAB. *IB:* 36.

GL11 MA Economics and Mathematics
Duration: 4FT Hon
Entry Requirements: *GCE:* AAA. *SQAH:* AAAB. *IB:* 38.

GQ14 MA Hebrew and Mathematics
Duration: 4FT Hon
Entry Requirements: *GCE:* AAA. *SQAH:* AAAB. *IB:* 36.

LG21 MA International Relations and Mathematics
Duration: 4FT Hon
Entry Requirements: *GCE:* AAA. *SQAH:* AAAA. *IB:* 38.

GR13 MA Italian and Mathematics
Duration: 4FT Hon
Entry Requirements: *GCE:* AAA. *SQAH:* AAAB. *IB:* 36.

GQ16 MA Latin and Mathematics
Duration: 4FT Hon
Entry Requirements: *GCE:* AAA. *SQAH:* AAAB. *IB:* 36.

GV11 MA Mathematics and Mediaeval History
Duration: 4FT Hon
Entry Requirements: *GCE:* AAA. *SQAH:* AAAB. *IB:* 36.

GVD1 MA Mathematics and Modern History
Duration: 4FT Hon
Entry Requirements: *GCE:* AAA. *SQAH:* AAAB. *IB:* 36.

GV15 MA Mathematics and Philosophy
Duration: 4FT Hon
Entry Requirements: *GCE:* AAA. *SQAH:* AAAB. *IB:* 36.

CG81 MA Mathematics and Psychology
Duration: 4FT Hon
Entry Requirements: *GCE:* AAA. *SQAH:* AAAB. *IB:* 36.

GR17 MA Mathematics and Russian
Duration: 4FT Hon
Entry Requirements: *GCE:* AAA. *SQAH:* AAAB. *IB:* 36.

RG71 MA Mathematics and Russian (year abroad)
Duration: 5FT Hon
Entry Requirements: *GCE:* AAA. *SQAH:* AAAB. *IB:* 36.

GV12 MA Mathematics and Scottish History
Duration: 4FT Hon
Entry Requirements: *GCE:* AAA. *SQAH:* AAAB. *IB:* 36.

GR14 MA Mathematics and Spanish
Duration: 4FT Hon
Entry Requirements: *GCE:* AAA. *SQAH:* AAAB. *IB:* 36.

GRC4 MA Mathematics and Spanish (year abroad)
Duration: 5FT Hon
Entry Requirements: *GCE:* AAA. *SQAH:* AAAB. *IB:* 36.

GV16 MA Mathematics and Theological Studies
Duration: 4FT Hon
Entry Requirements: *GCE:* AAA. *SQAH:* AAAB. *IB:* 36.

G1RT MA Mathematics with Russian
Duration: 4FT Hon
Entry Requirements: *GCE:* AAA. *SQAH:* AAAB. *IB:* 36.

G1R9 MA Mathematics with Russian (year abroad)
Duration: 5FT Hon
Entry Requirements: *GCE:* AAA. *SQAH:* AAAB. *IB:* 36.

G1RL MA Mathematics with Spanish
Duration: 4FT Hon
Entry Requirements: *GCE:* AAA. *SQAH:* AAAB. *IB:* 36.

G1RX MA Mathematics with Spanish (year abroad)
Duration: 5FT Hon
Entry Requirements: *GCE:* AAA. *SQAH:* AAAB. *IB:* 36.

R2G1 MA Hons German and Mathematics
Duration: 4FT Hon
Entry Requirements: Contact the institution for details.

GR21 MA Hons German and Mathematics (year abroad)
Duration: 5FT Hon
Entry Requirements: Contact the institution for details.

RG31 MA Hons Italian and Mathematics (year abroad)
Duration: 5FT Hon
Entry Requirements: *GCE:* AAA. *SQAH:* AAAB. *IB:* 36.

F1G1 MChem Chemistry with Mathematics
Duration: 5FT Hon
Entry Requirements: *GCE:* AAA. *SQAH:* AAAB. *IB:* 36.

FGH1 MPhys Mathematics and Theoretical Physics
Duration: 4FT/5FT Hon
Entry Requirements: *GCE:* AAA. *SQAH:* AAAA. *SQAAH:* AA. *IB:* 38.

S75 THE UNIVERSITY OF STIRLING
STUDENT RECRUITMENT & ADMISSIONS SERVICE
UNIVERSITY OF STIRLING
STIRLING
SCOTLAND FK9 4LA
t: 01786 467044 f: 01786 466800
e: admissions@stir.ac.uk
// www.stir.ac.uk

GL11 BA Economics and Mathematics
Duration: 4FT Hon
Entry Requirements: *GCE:* BBC. *SQAH:* BBBB. *SQAAH:* AAA-CCC.
IB: 32. *BTEC ExtDip:* DMM.

GN13 BA Finance and Mathematics
Duration: 4FT Hon
Entry Requirements: *GCE:* BBC. *SQAH:* BBBB. *SQAAH:* AAA-CCC.
IB: 32. *BTEC ExtDip:* DMM.

GR11 BA French and Mathematics
Duration: 4FT Hon
Entry Requirements: *GCE:* BBC. *SQAH:* BBBB. *SQAAH:* AAA-CCC.
IB: 32. *BTEC ExtDip:* DMM.

GN14 BAcc Accountancy and Mathematics
Duration: 4FT Hon
Entry Requirements: *GCE:* BBC. *SQAH:* BBBB. *SQAAH:* AAA-CCC.
IB: 32. *BTEC ExtDip:* DMM.

CG11 BSc Biology and Mathematics
Duration: 4FT Hon
Entry Requirements: *GCE:* BBC. *SQAH:* BBBB. *SQAAH:* AAA-CCC.
IB: 32. *BTEC ExtDip:* DMM.

G4G1 BSc Computing Science and Mathematics
Duration: 4FT Hon
Entry Requirements: *GCE:* BBC. *SQAH:* BBBB. *SQAAH:* AAA-CCC. *IB:* 32. *BTEC ExtDip:* DMM.

F9G1 BSc Environmental Science and Mathematics
Duration: 4FT Hon
Entry Requirements: *GCE:* BBC. *SQAH:* BBBB. *SQAAH:* AAA-CCC. *IB:* 32. *BTEC ExtDip:* DMM.

NG21 BSc Management Science and Mathematics
Duration: 4FT Hon
Entry Requirements: *GCE:* BBC. *SQAH:* BBBB. *SQAAH:* AAA-CCC. *IB:* 32. *BTEC ExtDip:* DMM.

GX11 BSc Mathematics and Professional Education
Duration: 4FT Hon   CRB Check: Required
Entry Requirements: *GCE:* BBC. *SQAH:* BBBB. *SQAAH:* AAA-CCC. *IB:* 32. *BTEC ExtDip:* DMM.

CG81 BSc Mathematics and Psychology
Duration: 4FT Hon
Entry Requirements: *GCE:* BBC. *SQAH:* BBBB. *SQAAH:* AAA-CCC. *IB:* 32. *BTEC ExtDip:* DMM.

S78 THE UNIVERSITY OF STRATHCLYDE
GLASGOW G1 1XQ
t: 0141 552 4400 f: 0141 552 0775
// www.strath.ac.uk

NG41 BA Accounting and Mathematics & Statistics
Duration: 4FT Hon
Entry Requirements: *GCE:* AAA. *SQAH:* AAAAAB-AAAA. *IB:* 36.

CG81 BA Psychology and Mathematics
Duration: 4FT Hon
Entry Requirements: *GCE:* ABB. *SQAH:* AAABB-AAAB. *IB:* 34.

GG14 BSc Mathematics and Computer Science
Duration: 4FT Hon
Entry Requirements: *GCE:* AAB-BBB. *SQAH:* ABBBC-ABBB. *IB:* 32.

GF13 BSc Mathematics and Physics
Duration: 4FT Hon
Entry Requirements: *GCE:* AAB-BBB. *SQAH:* ABBBC-ABBB. *IB:* 32.

G1XC BSc Mathematics with Teaching
Duration: 4FT Hon   CRB Check: Required
Entry Requirements: *GCE:* AAB-BBB. *SQAH:* ABBBC-ABBB. *IB:* 32.

G1L1 BSc Mathematics, Statistics and Economics
Duration: 4FT Hon
Entry Requirements: *GCE:* AAB-BBB. *SQAH:* ABBBC-ABBB. *IB:* 32.

GN12 BSc Mathematics, Statistics and Management Science
Duration: 4FT Hon
Entry Requirements: *GCE:* AAB-BBB. *SQAH:* ABBBC-ABBB. *IB:* 32.

S79 STRANMILLIS UNIVERSITY COLLEGE: A COLLEGE OF QUEEN'S UNIVERSITY BELFAST
STRANMILLIS ROAD
BELFAST BT9 5DY
t: 028 9038 1271 f: 028 9038 4444
e: Registry@stran.ac.uk
// www.stran.ac.uk

XG10 BEd Mathematics & Science with Education
Duration: 4FT Hon   CRB Check: Required
Entry Requirements: *GCE:* BCC. Interview required.

S84 UNIVERSITY OF SUNDERLAND
STUDENT HELPLINE
THE STUDENT GATEWAY
CHESTER ROAD
SUNDERLAND SR1 3SD
t: 0191 515 3000 f: 0191 515 3805
e: student.helpline@sunderland.ac.uk
// www.sunderland.ac.uk

XG11 BSc Mathematics Education (11-18 years)
Duration: 2FT Hon
Entry Requirements: *GCE:* 260-360. Interview required. HND required.

S85 UNIVERSITY OF SURREY
STAG HILL
GUILDFORD
SURREY GU2 7XH
t: +44(0)1483 689305 f: +44(0)1483 689388
e: ugteam@surrey.ac.uk
// www.surrey.ac.uk

GG1K BSc Mathematics and Computing Science (3 years)
Duration: 3FT Hon
Entry Requirements: *GCE:* 340. Interview required.

GG14 BSc Mathematics and Computing Science (4 years)
Duration: 4SW Hon
Entry Requirements: *GCE:* 340. Interview required.

GF1H BSc Mathematics and Physics
Duration: 3FT/4SW Hon
Entry Requirements: Contact the institution for details.

G1W3 BSc Mathematics with Music (3 years)
Duration: 3FT Hon
Entry Requirements: *GCE:* 340. Interview required.

G1WH BSc Mathematics with Music (4 years)
Duration: 4SW Hon
Entry Requirements: *GCE:* 340. Interview required.

GF13 MMath Mathematics and Physics
Duration: 4FT Hon
Entry Requirements: Contact the institution for details.

GF1I MPhys Mathematics and Physics
Duration: 4FT Hon
Entry Requirements: Contact the institution for details.

S90 UNIVERSITY OF SUSSEX
UNDERGRADUATE ADMISSIONS
SUSSEX HOUSE
UNIVERSITY OF SUSSEX
BRIGHTON BN1 9RH
t: 01273 678416 f: 01273 678545
e: ug.applicants@sussex.ac.uk
// www.sussex.ac.uk

G1G4 BSc Mathematics with Computer Science
Duration: 3FT Hon
Entry Requirements: *GCE:* AAA-AAB. *SQAH:* AAAAA-AAABB. *SQAAH:* AAB. *IB:* 35. *BTEC SubDip:* D. *BTEC Dip:* DD. *BTEC ExtDip:* DDD. *OCR ND:* D *OCR NED:* D1

G1L1 BSc Mathematics with Economics
Duration: 3FT Hon
Entry Requirements: *GCE:* AAA-AAB. *SQAH:* AAAAA-AAABB. *SQAAH:* AAB. *IB:* 35. *BTEC SubDip:* D. *BTEC Dip:* DD. *BTEC ExtDip:* DDD. *OCR ND:* D *OCR NED:* D1

GF13 BSc Mathematics with Physics
Duration: 3FT Hon
Entry Requirements: Contact the institution for details.

G1GK MMath Mathematics with Computer Science
Duration: 4FT Hon
Entry Requirements: *GCE:* AAA. *SQAH:* AAAAA. *SQAAH:* AAA. *IB:* 35. *BTEC SubDip:* D. *BTEC Dip:* DD. *BTEC ExtDip:* DDD. *OCR ND:* D *OCR NED:* D1

G1LC MMath Mathematics with Economics
Duration: 4FT Hon
Entry Requirements: *GCE:* AAA. *SQAH:* AAAAA. *SQAAH:* AAA. *IB:* 35. *BTEC SubDip:* D. *BTEC Dip:* DD. *BTEC ExtDip:* DDD. *OCR ND:* D *OCR NED:* D1

G1F3 MMath Mathematics with Physics
Duration: 4FT Hon
Entry Requirements: Contact the institution for details.

S93 SWANSEA UNIVERSITY
SINGLETON PARK
SWANSEA SA2 8PP
t: 01792 295111 f: 01792 295110
e: admissions@swansea.ac.uk
// www.swansea.ac.uk

GG41 BSc Computer Science and Pure Mathematics
Duration: 3FT Hon
Entry Requirements: *GCE:* ABB. *IB:* 33.

GL11 BSc Economics and Mathematics
Duration: 3FT Hon
Entry Requirements: *GCE:* ABB. *IB:* 33.

GN12 BSc Management Science and Mathematics
Duration: 3FT Hon
Entry Requirements: *GCE:* ABB. *IB:* 33.

GNC2 BSc Management Science and Mathematics (with a year abroad)
Duration: 4FT Hon
Entry Requirements: *GCE:* ABB. *IB:* 33.

G1R3 BSc Mathematics (with Italian) (4 years)
Duration: 4FT Hon
Entry Requirements: *GCE:* 240-300.

GR11 BSc Mathematics and French
Duration: 4FT Hon
Entry Requirements: *GCE:* ABB. *IB:* 33.

GF18 BSc Mathematics and Geo-Informatics
Duration: 3FT Hon
Entry Requirements: *GCE:* ABB. *IB:* 33.

FG31 BSc Mathematics and Physics
Duration: 3FT Hon
Entry Requirements: *GCE:* ABB. *IB:* 33.

GR14 BSc Mathematics and Spanish
Duration: 4FT Hon
Entry Requirements: *GCE:* ABB. *IB:* 33.

GC16 BSc Mathematics and Sport Science
Duration: 3FT Hon
Entry Requirements: *GCE:* ABB. *IB:* 33.

GQ15 BSc Mathematics and Welsh
Duration: 3FT/4FT Hon
Entry Requirements: *GCE:* ABB. *IB:* 33.

G4GC BSc Mathematics for Computer Science
Duration: 3FT Hon
Entry Requirements: *GCE:* ABB. *IB:* 33.

G190 BSc Mathematics for Finance
Duration: 3FT Hon
Entry Requirements: *GCE:* ABB. *IB:* 33.

G1G4 BSc Mathematics for Information and Communication Technology
Duration: 3FT Hon
Entry Requirements: *GCE:* ABB. *IB:* 33.

G410 BSc Computing Mathematics
Duration: 3FT/4SW Hon
Entry Requirements: *IB:* 30. *OCR ND:* D *OCR NED:* M2 Interview required.

F1G1 BSc Chemistry with Mathematics
Duration: 3FT Hon
Entry Requirements: *GCE:* AAAe-AABe. *SQAAH:* AAA-AAB. *BTEC ExtDip:* DDD. Interview required.

GF13 BSc Mathematics and Physics
Duration: 3FT Hon
Entry Requirements: *GCE:* A*A*Ae-A*AAe. *SQAAH:* AAA. Interview required. Admissions Test required.

G1L1 BSc Mathematics with Economics
Duration: 3FT Hon
Entry Requirements: *GCE:* A*A*Ae-A*AAe. *SQAAH:* AAA. Interview required. Admissions Test required.

G1N2 BSc Mathematics with Management Studies
Duration: 3FT Hon
Entry Requirements: *GCE:* A*A*Ae-A*AAe. *SQAAH:* AAA. Interview required. Admissions Test required.

G1F3 BSc Mathematics with Mathematical Physics
Duration: 3FT Hon
Entry Requirements: *GCE:* A*A*Ae-A*AAe. *SQAAH:* AAA. Interview required. Admissions Test required.

G1T9 BSc Mathematics with Modern Languages
Duration: 3FT Hon
Entry Requirements: *GCE:* A*A*Ae-A*AAe. *SQAAH:* AAA. Interview required. Admissions Test required.

F1GC MSci Chemistry with Mathematics
Duration: 4FT Hon
Entry Requirements: *GCE:* AAAe-AABe. *SQAAH:* AAA-AAB. *BTEC ExtDip:* DDD. Interview required.

GF1H MSci Mathematics and Physics
Duration: 4FT Hon
Entry Requirements: *GCE:* A*A*Ae-A*AAe. *SQAAH:* AAA. Interview required. Admissions Test required.

G1LC MSci Mathematics with Economics
Duration: 4FT Hon
Entry Requirements: *GCE:* A*A*Ae-A*AAe. *SQAAH:* AAA. Interview required. Admissions Test required.

G1NF MSci Mathematics with Management Studies
Duration: 4FT Hon
Entry Requirements: *GCE:* A*A*Ae-A*AAe. *SQAAH:* AAA. Interview required. Admissions Test required.

G1FH MSci Mathematics with Mathematical Physics
Duration: 4FT Hon
Entry Requirements: *GCE:* A*A*Ae-A*AAe. *SQAAH:* AAA. Interview required. Admissions Test required.

G1TX MSci Mathematics with Modern Languages
Duration: 4FT Hon
Entry Requirements: *GCE:* A*A*Ae-A*AAe. *SQAAH:* AAA. Interview required. Admissions Test required.

G190 BSc Discrete Mathematics
Duration: 3FT Hon
Entry Requirements: *GCE:* A*AA. *SQAAH:* AA. *IB:* 38.

G1NC BSc Mathematics and Business Studies
Duration: 3FT Hon
Entry Requirements: *GCE:* A*A*Aa-A*AA. *SQAH:* AAABB. *SQAAH:* AA. *IB:* 39.

GL11 BSc Mathematics and Economics
Duration: 3FT Hon
Entry Requirements: *GCE:* A*A*Aa-A*AA. *SQAH:* AAABB. *SQAAH:* AA. *IB:* 39.

GV15 BSc Mathematics and Philosophy
Duration: 3FT Hon
Entry Requirements: *GCE:* A*A*Aa-A*AA. *SQAH:* AAABB. *SQAAH:* AA. *IB:* 39.

GF13 BSc Mathematics and Physics
Duration: 3FT Hon
Entry Requirements: *GCE:* A*AA. *SQAAH:* AA. *IB:* 39.

FG31 MPhys Mathematics and Physics
Duration: 4FT Hon
Entry Requirements: *GCE:* A*AA. *SQAAH:* AA. *IB:* 39.

W76 UNIVERSITY OF WINCHESTER
WINCHESTER
HANTS SO22 4NR
t: 01962 827234 f: 01962 827288
e: course.enquiries@winchester.ac.uk
// www.winchester.ac.uk

XGC1 BA Mathematics: Primary (3 years QTS)
Duration: 3FT Hon
Entry Requirements: *GCE:* 280-300. Interview required.

Y50 THE UNIVERSITY OF YORK
STUDENT RECRUITMENT AND ADMISSIONS
UNIVERSITY OF YORK
HESLINGTON
YORK YO10 5DD
t: 01904 324000 f: 01904 323538
e: ug-admissions@york.ac.uk
// www.york.ac.uk

QG11 BA Linguistics/Mathematics (Equal)
Duration: 3FT Hon
Entry Requirements: *GCE:* AAB. *SQAH:* AAAAB. *SQAAH:* AB. *IB:* 35.

LG11 BA/BSc Economics/Mathematics (Equal)
Duration: 3FT Hon
Entry Requirements: *GCE:* AAA-AAB. *SQAH:* AAAAA-AAAAB. *SQAAH:* AA-AB. *IB:* 36.

GV15 BA/BSc Mathematics/Philosophy (Equal)
Duration: 3FT Hon
Entry Requirements: *GCE:* AAB. *SQAH:* AAAAB. *SQAAH:* AB. *IB:* 35.

GF13 BA/BSc Mathematics/Physics (Equal)
Duration: 3FT Hon
Entry Requirements: *GCE:* AAB. *SQAH:* AAAAB. *SQAAH:* AB. *IB:* 35.

GFD3 BA/BSc Mathematics/Physics (Equal) with a year in Europe
Duration: 4FT Hon
Entry Requirements: *GCE:* AAB. *SQAH:* AAAAB. *SQAAH:* AB. *IB:* 35.

GG41 BSc Computer Science/Mathematics (Equal)
Duration: 3FT Hon
Entry Requirements: *GCE:* AAB. *SQAH:* AAAAB. *SQAAH:* AB. *IB:* 35. *BTEC ExtDip:* DDD.

GGK1 BSc Computer Science/Mathematics (Equal) (Yr in Ind)
Duration: 4SW Hon
Entry Requirements: *GCE:* AAB. *SQAH:* AAAAB. *SQAAH:* AB. *IB:* 35. *BTEC ExtDip:* DDD.

GL11 BSc Mathematics / Finance (Equal)
Duration: 3FT Hon
Entry Requirements: *GCE:* AAB. *SQAH:* AAAAB. *SQAAH:* AB. *IB:* 35.

GG14 MMath Mathematics/Computer Science (Equal) (4 years)
Duration: 4FT Hon
Entry Requirements: *GCE:* AAB. *SQAH:* AAAAB. *SQAAH:* AB. *IB:* 35. *BTEC ExtDip:* DDD.

GG1K MMath Mathematics/Computer Science (Equal) (Yr in Ind)
Duration: 5SW Hon
Entry Requirements: *GCE:* AAB. *SQAH:* AAAAB. *SQAAH:* AB. *IB:* 35. *BTEC ExtDip:* DDD.

GFC3 MMath Mathematics/Physics (Equal) (4 years)
Duration: 4FT Hon
Entry Requirements: *GCE:* AAA. *SQAH:* AAAAA. *SQAAH:* AA. *IB:* 36.

OTHERS IN MATHEMATICS

C85 COVENTRY UNIVERSITY
THE STUDENT CENTRE
COVENTRY UNIVERSITY
1 GULSON RD
COVENTRY CV1 2JH
t: 024 7615 2222 f: 024 7615 2223
e: studentenquiries@coventry.ac.uk
// www.coventry.ac.uk

G900 BSc Informatics
Duration: 1FT Hon
Entry Requirements: Contact the institution for details.

D65 UNIVERSITY OF DUNDEE
NETHERGATE
DUNDEE DD1 4HN
t: 01382 383838 f: 01382 388150
e: contactus@dundee.ac.uk
// www.dundee.ac.uk/admissions/ undergraduate/

N1G9 BSc International Business with E-Commerce
Duration: 4FT Hon
Entry Requirements: *GCE:* BCC. *SQAH:* ABBB. *IB:* 30.

K84 KINGSTON UNIVERSITY
STUDENT INFORMATION & ADVICE CENTRE
COOPER HOUSE
40-46 SURBITON ROAD
KINGSTON UPON THAMES KT1 2HX
t: 0844 8552177 f: 020 8547 7080
e: aps@kingston.ac.uk
// www.kingston.ac.uk

G9N1 BSc Financial Mathematics with Business
Duration: 3FT Hon
Entry Requirements: *GCE:* 280.

G9NC BSc Financial Mathematics with Business
Duration: 4SW Hon
Entry Requirements: *GCE:* 280.

G9ND BSc Financial Mathematics with Business
Duration: 4FT Hon
Entry Requirements: *GCE:* 80.

Q50 QUEEN MARY, UNIVERSITY OF LONDON
QUEEN MARY, UNIVERSITY OF LONDON
MILE END ROAD
LONDON E1 4NS
t: 020 7882 5555 f: 020 7882 5500
e: admissions@qmul.ac.uk
// www.qmul.ac.uk

GGX4 BSc Science & Engineering Foundation Programme (Computer Science 4 Year)
Duration: 4FT Hon
Entry Requirements: *GCE:* 260.

GGY4 BSc/MSci Science & Engineering Foundation Programme (Computer Science 5 Year)
Duration: 5FT Hon
Entry Requirements: *GCE:* 260.

PS